G. Berger

YO-BZE-619

Austrian Economics
Volume III

Schools of Thought in Economics

Series Editor: Mark Blaug

Emeritus Professor of the Economics of Education, University of London and Consultant Professor of Economics, University of Buckingham

Austrian Economics
Volume III

Edited by

Stephen Littlechild

Professor of Commerce
University of Birmingham

EDWARD ELGAR

© Stephen Littlechild 1990

All rights reserved. No part of this publication may be reproduced, stored in a retrieval system, or transmitted in any form or by any means, electronic, mechanical, photocopying, recording, or otherwise without the prior permission of the publisher.

Published by
Edward Elgar Publishing Limited
Gower House
Croft Road
Aldershot
Hants GU11 3HR
England

Edward Elgar Publishing Company
Old Post Road
Brookfield
Vermont 05036
USA

British Library Cataloguing in Publication Data

Austrian economics. - (Schools of thought in
  economics).
  1. Economics. Theories of the Austrian school
  I. Littlechild, Stephen   II. Series
  330.15'7

Library of Congress Cataloging-in-Publication Data

Austrian economics / edited by Stephen Littlechild.
    p. cm. — (Schools of thought in economics; 10)
  Includes bibliographical references.
  Contents: v. 1. History and methodology — v. 2. Money and capital
  — v. 3. Market process.
  ISBN 1-85278-120-3 (set)
  1. Austrian school of economists. 2. Economics—Austria—History.
3. Economics—History. I. Littlechild, S.C. II. Series.
HB98.A96 1990   89-23731
330.15'7—dc20   CIP

ISBN 1 85278 352 4 (vol. III)
      1 85278 120 3 (3 vol. set)

Printed in Great Britain by Galliard (Printers) Ltd, Great Yarmouth

Contents

Acknowledgements

The editor and publishers wish to thank the following for permission to use copyright material.

American Economic Association for articles: F. A. Hayek (1945), 'The Use of Knowledge in Society', *American Economic Review*, **XXXV** (4), Sept., pp.519-30, reprinted as Chap. IV in his (1948) *Individualism and Economic Order*, University of Chicago Press, and (1972) Henry Regnery Co., pp.77-91; T. Cowan and R. Fink (1985), 'Inconsistant Equilibrium Constructs: The Evenly Rotating Economy of Mises and Rothbard', *American Economic Review*, **75** (4), Sept., pp.866-9.

Basil Blackwell Ltd. for articles: S. C. Littlechild (1981), 'Misleading Calculations of the Social Costs of Monopoly Power', *Economic Journal*, **91**, June, pp.348-63; F. A. Hayek (1940), 'Socialist Calculation III: The Competitive 'Solution', *Economica*, **II** (26), NS May, reprinted as Chap.IX in his (1948) *Individualism and Economic Order*, University of Chicago Press, and (1972) Henry Regnery Co., pp.181-208.

The Center for Libertarian Studies for articles: D. Lavoie (1981), 'A Critique of Standard Accounts of the Socialist Calculation Debate', *Journal of Libertarian Studies*, **V** (1), pp.41-87; G. P. O'Driscoll, Jr (1977), 'Spontaneous Order and the Co-ordination Economic Activities', *Journal of Libertarian Studies*, **I**, Spring, pp. 137-51, reprinted in Spadaro (ed) (1978), *New Directions in Austrian Economics*, pp.111-42.

Contemporary Books Inc. for extracts: L. von Mises (1949), 'The Scope and Method of Catallactics', Chap. XIV, pp.232-56 and 'The Limits of Property Rights and the Problems of External Costs and External Economies' in his *Human Action*. Copyright © 1949 by Ludwig von Mises.

Center for the Study of Market Processes for article: J. Wiseman (1985), 'Economics, Subjectivism, and Public Choice', *Market Process*, **3** (2), Fall, pp.14-15.

D. C. Heath and Co. for extracts: S. C. Littlechild (1982), 'Equilibrium and the Market Process', Chap.8, pp.85-100, and I. M. Kirzner (1982), 'Uncertainty, Discovery and Human Action: A Study of the Entrepreneurial Profile in the Misesian System', Chap.12 in I. M. Kirzner, ed., *Method, Process and Austrian Economics*, pp.139-59.

Institute for Humane Studies at George Mason University for extract: L. M. Lachmann (1976), 'On the Central Concept of Austrian Economics: Market Process' in E. G. Dolan, ed., *The Foundations of Modern Austrian Economics*, Sheed and Ward, pp.126-32.

Israel M. Kirzner for (1985) 'Prices, the Communication of Knowledge, and the Discovery Process' in K. R. Leube and A. H. Zlabinger, eds., *The Political Economy of Freedom: Essays in Honour of F. A. Hayek*, Philosophia Verlag, pp.193-206.

Ludwig von Mises Institute for article: H. H. Hoppe (1985), 'The Justice of Economic Efficiency' *Austrian Economics Newsletter*, **9** (2), Winter, pp.1-4.

Macmillan Publishers Ltd. and New York University Press for extract: U. Fehl (1987), 'Spontaneous Order and the Subjectivity of Expectations: A Contribution to the Lachmann-O'Driscoll Problem' in I. M. Kirzner, ed., *Subjectivism, Intelligibility and Economic Understanding*, pp.72-86.

Mario J. Rizzo for article: (1985) 'Rules versus Cost-Benefit Analysis in the Common Law' from the *Cato Journal*, **4** (3), Winter, pp.865-84.

Murray N. Rothbard for article: (1956) 'Toward a Reconstruction of Utility and Welfare Economics' from M. Sennholz, ed., *On Freedom and Free Enterprise*, Princeton : D. Van Nostrand, Ch.XVII, pp.224-62.

Routledge and Kegan Paul for extracts: L. von Mises (1920), 'Economic Calculation in a Socialist Community', [in the Socialist Commonwealth], trans. from German article in F. A. Hayek, ed. (1935), *Collectivist Economic Planning*, pp.87-130; and F. A. Hayek (1946), 'The Meaning of Competition', Stafford Little Lecture, Princeton University, May, repr. in his *Individualism and Economic Order*, 1948, Henry Regnery, 1972, pp.92-106.

G. L. S. Shackle for (1978), 'Professor Kirzner on Entrepreneurship', *Austrian Economics Newsletter*, **4** (1), Spring 1983, pp.7-8, originally presented as discussant's comments in a conference on 'Subjectivism and Industrial Organisation', Birmingham, June.

Tieto Ltd for article: F. A. Hayek (1937), 'Economics and Knowledge', *Economica*, **IV**, pp.33-54.

The University of Chicago Press for extracts and article: I. M. Kirzner (1973), 'Entrepreneurship and Equilibrating Process' in his *Competition and Entrepreneurship*, pp.69-75; F. A. Hayek (1978), 'Competition as a Discovery Procedure', Chap.12 in his *New Studies in Philosophy, Politics, Economics and the History of Ideas*, pp.179-90; M J. Rizzo (1980), 'Law Amid Flux: The Economics of Negligence and Strict Liability in Tort', *The Journal of Legal Studies*, **IX**, March, p.291 and pp.317-18.

Unwin Hyman Ltd and Harper and Row, Publishers, Inc. for extracts: J. A. Schumpeter (1950), 'The Process of Creative Destruction' and 'Monopolistic Practices', in his *Capitalism, Socialism and Democracy*, 3rd Edition, Chaps.VII and VIII plus extract from Preface, 1950. Copyright © 1942, 1947 by Joseph A. Schumpeter.

Western Economic Association International for articles: J. High (1984-5), 'Bork's Paradox: Static vs Dynamic Efficiency in Antitrust Analysis', *Contemporary Policy Issues*, **3** (2), Winter, pp.21-34; K.I. Vaughn (1980), 'Economic Calculation Under Socialism: The Austrian Contribution', *Economic Inquiry*, **XVIII**, Oct., pp.535-54.

Lawrence H. White for his article: (1976) 'Entrepreneurship, Imagination and the Question of Equilibration', unpublished paper.

Wincott Foundation for F. A. Hayek (1973), 'Economic Freedom and Representative Government', Fourth Wincott Memorial Lecture.

Every effort has been made to trace all the copyright holders, but if any have been inadvertently overlooked the publishers will be pleased to make the necessary arrangement at the first opportunity.

Preface

A volume of readings on the Austrian School of Economics is justified not only by the historical contributions of this School, but also by the remarkable resurgence of interest in its ideas over the last decade. Early reflections of this resurgence include the Conference on Austrian Economics held at South Royalton, Vermont, in June 1974 (see the *Proceedings* edited by Dolan, 1976); the award of the Nobel Prize to Professor Hayek later that year; the establishment of the Austrian Economics Seminar at New York University in 1975; and first publication of the *Austrian Economics Newsletter* in 1977. An extensive series of lectures, conferences, research fellowships and publications has been supported by the Institute for Humane Studies, the Liberty Fund, the Charles Koch Foundation and other charitable foundations. Major programmes in Austrian economics have been established at New York, George Mason and Auburn Universities. There is a Ludwig von Mises Institute at Auburn University, which now publishes the *Austrian Economics Newsletter* and the *Review of Austrian Economics*; and a Centre for the Study of Market Processes at George Mason University, which publishes the semi-annual *Market Process*. There are increasingly frequent references to Austrian ideas in economics journals, textbooks and the daily Press.

Public policy has also moved decisively in directions long advocated by Austrians. This is particularly true in Britain, but the same phenomenon is observable worldwide. Industrial policy, Keynesian demand management, central planning, nationalization, socialism, and most strikingly communism, are all on the retreat. Firm monetary policy, deregulation and privatization are the order of the day. The merits of the market mechanism are better appreciated, and there is a growing acknowledgement of the vital role of those institutional and constitutional arrangements, such as stable currency, low taxation, property rights, and the rule of law, upon which the creativity, responsiveness and efficiency of the market depend.

Somewhat paradoxically, these developments have made it even more important to consider precisely what is the appropriate role of government. What kinds of property rights, regulations and anti-trust policies will best promote competition, innovation and efficiency? How best can market forces be harnessed to deal with currencies, law enforcement and the environment? Austrians have written on all these issues, and their ideas are repeatedly surfacing in current debates.

This series of readings is intended to comprise 'key articles which have not previously been reprinted in book form'. The aim is to include important and relevant items which would not otherwise be easily available to scholars working alone or at libraries of limited depth. On the advice of the series editor, these guidelines exclude original books and collections of articles by a single author. However, exceptions can be made for particularly important items without which the collection would be seriously incomplete.

Within these constraints, and noting that the level of copyright fees precluded the inclusion of several worthwhile items, I have tried to give a broad picture of the ideas of the Austrian school, with particular emphasis on the topics of interest today. The contributions of the founders of the Austrian school, which are mainly in books and well documented in the mainstream literature, have largely been represented by biographical sketches. As far as possible, I have refrained from selecting articles by later members (Mises, Hayek, Kirzner and Lachmann) which have been reprinted in volumes of their collected papers. These decisions have enabled the inclusion of a wider variety of recent articles by younger scholars. I have also favoured publications from less accessible sources (notably the *Austrian Economics Newsletter* and *Market Process*), scholarly book reviews which give indications of further reading, and in a few cases brief excerpts from papers which give the flavour of the authors' arguments.

The readings have been divided into three volumes, each containing a brief introduction to the readings, together with some suggestions for further reading. The latter are taken mainly from the recent literature: I have not attempted to provide comprehensive bibliographies of the major works.

I am grateful to many people, especially Israel Kirzner, Ludwig Lachmann, Don Lavoie, Murray Rothbard, Larry White, the series editor Mark Blaug and the publisher Edward Elgar, for helpful discussions and suggestions concerning selection of readings. None of these is to be held responsible for the final choice of contents.

Introduction

The Competitive Market Process

Austrians have always emphasized that competition is a process taking place over time. Consequently, they have never attached the same importance to the concept of equilibrium as have neoclassical economists. They do not see the economy as generally in or near equilibrium. They see equilibrium as explaining the direction in which the economy is moving at any time, but it is the market process itself which is of prime importance. Mises and Hayek set out this perspective. As noted in the introduction to Volume I, they differ between themselves as to whether the revision of plans in the light of new information is considered to be an *a priori* or an empirical proposition. Littlechild argues that the mathematical models later developed by Arrow-Debreu and Hahn correspond quite closely to the equilibrium concepts of Mises and Hayek, respectively. See also Böehm (1986). Cowen and Fink criticize the role of equilibrium proposed by Mises: not surprisingly, this paper has proved controversial amongst most Austrians (e.g. Gunning 1989).

Kirzner has most thoroughly developed the concept of market process. Following Mises, he sees the act of choice as encompassing entrepreneurial alertness as well as Robbinsian economizing. He also emphasizes the equilibrating role of the entrepreneur in discovering and exploiting hitherto unnoticed opportunities for profit. For further exposition see Kirzner (1979 and 1985). This view stands in contrast to Schumpeter's vision of the entrepreneur as a disequilibrating force. Lachmann and White doubted the extent to which the market process is equilibrating. O'Driscoll highlights the difference between Kirzner and Lachmann and questions whether Lachmann's approach is consistent with the Austrian concept of 'spontaneous order' in a market economy. See also White (1979) and the resulting interchange with Lachmann, and more generally Lachmann (1986).

An even more radical questioning is associated with Shackle, who emphasizes the creative (and, by implication, disequilibrating) nature of choice, leading to a 'kaleidic economy', 'subject to sudden landslides of re-adjustment to a new, precarious and emphemeral, pseudo-equilibrium' (Shackle 1972, p.433). This distinction between the entrepreneur as discoverer and the entrepreneur as creator is neatly encapsulated in Shackle's memorable question: 'Were Dante, Michaelangelo, Shakespeare, Newton and Beethoven merely alert?' Littlechild (1979) sets out and contrasts the alternative viewpoints of Kirzner and Shackle.

Kirzner's second paper here is partly a response to his critics (notably High 1980, 1986). He emphasizes the need to appreciate what entrepreneurship and the resulting systematic market forces *do* in fact achieve, by 'the liberation of mankind from the chaos of complete mutual ignorance'. The paper is also an explanation of how entrepreneurial discovery is consistent with uncertainty. His latest volume of essays in fact describes market capitalism 'as an ongoing *process of creative discovery*'. (Kirzner 1985, p.ix, italics added.) Similarly, Fehl argues that it is possible to reconcile the radical subjectivism of Lachmann and Shackle with the traditional Austrian belief in spontaneous order. Boettke *et al.* (1986) discuss these issues. Langlois (1983) presents an evolutionary view of the market process.

The notion of competition as a dynamic process, rather than as an equilibrium state, is popularly associated with Joseph Schumpeter. Indeed, to the average economist, at least until recently, he is probably the best-known Austrian economist. This is somewhat ironic, in that Schumpeter's commitment to Walrasian general equilibrium renders him distinctly suspect to modern Austrians (Kirzner, 1979; Rothbard, 1987). Nevertheless, he was brought up in the Austrian school, a contemporary of Mises, and his metaphor of competition as 'a perennial gale of creative destruction' reflects a powerful Austrian theme. In this excerpt, Schumpeter argues that practices and public policies which appear to restrict competition in the short term may be necessary to promote innovation and efficiency over the long term. This point is increasingly accepted by economists, though there are differences about precisely what practices and policies are thereby appropriate. (See, for example, the compilation by Oakman (1986) of Austrian views on intellectual property rights.)

Hayek's paper on the meaning of competition, less well-known than it ought to be, is a pointed critique of the 1930s theories of perfect and monopolistic competition, and equally applicable today. In Chapter 14, Hayek sets out more explicitly the crucial role of the price mechanism in conveying knowledge in a market economy. (See also Böehm, 1989.) Developing this theme, Kirzner argues that the social function served by market prices is captured far more significantly by the concept of *discovery* of *new* knowledge, than by the concept of *communication* of *existing* knowledge. This leads Kirzner to draw attention to the distorting effects which government regulation may have on the discovery process.

Littlechild applies the Schumpeter–Hayek–Kirzner concept of competition as a process to argue that recent calculations of the social cost of monopoly are biased and misconceived because of their underlying assumption of equilibrium. High contrasts the static efficiency properties of neoclassical perfect competition with the dynamic efficiency properties of the Austrian competitive process, arguing that the former implies a more stringent anti-trust policy, while the latter does not provide grounds for anti-trust law at all. For further and more extensive treatments of competition policy, and of monopoly itself, where there is some difference between the positions taken by Rothbard and Kirzner, see Armentano (1978, 1982, 1986), Block (1977), Kirzner (1973, 1985), Mises (1966, Ch.XVI), O'Driscoll (1982, 1986), O'Driscoll and Rizzo (1985, ch.7) and Rothbard (1962). Pasour (1987) and DiLorenzo (1987) discuss rent-seeking and public choice.

Central Planning

Part IV opens with the pioneering contributions of Mises and Hayek to the great debate on central planning. Mises had claimed that rational economic planning was impossible without private ownership: 'where there is no free market, there is no economic calculation'. The 'market socialists' denied this. Hayek reviewed the ensuing debate and concluded that the alternative of 'market socialism' proposed to meet Mises' objections was equally vulnerable to the same line of criticism. In a later paper, Hayek sets out more explicitly the crucial role of the price mechanism in conveying knowledge in a market economy.

It was widely believed, however, that the critics had won the debate, and that 'market socialism' had refuted Mises. Vaughn suggests that the Mises–Hayek critique was not fully appreciated at the time, because it was based not on the conventional neoclassical theory of equilibrium, but on an underlying but then unfamiliar theory of market process. Similarly, Lavoie argues that the 'standard account' of the socialist calculation debate is riddled with errors. Kirzner (1987) suggests that the socialist economic planning debate was an important catalyst in the process by which Austrians gradually developed their understanding of the market as a competitive entrepreneurial process of discovery. For further discussion, see Rothbard (1976) and Lavoie (1985, 1986a). Other variants of national planning are criticized by Hayek (1976) and Lavoie (1986b).

Public Policy

For much of the last half-century, mainstream economics has adopted the framework of welfare economics for analysing public policy. The Chicago and Austrian schools have been notable sceptics. Rothbard presents a thorough critique of welfare economics, and proposes a reconstruction based on the rule of unanimity and the concept of 'demonstrated preference'. He concludes that the free market always increases social utility and that no act of government can ever do so. See also Rothbard (1962, 1970) and Lavoie (1982). Austrians have generally been associated with a free-market position, although Streissler (in Part I, Vol.I) shows that this has by no means always been the case (see also Böehm, 1986), and not all Austrians today would go as far as Rothbard.

Most Austrians have stressed that economic theory or praxeology is 'value free': it can be used to assess whether a given policy is likely to achieve a specified end, but cannot itself determine which ends ought to be sought (Kirzner 1976). However, some Austrians, notably Rothbard and Hoppe, have argued that the choice of ends should not be merely arbitrary, and that a 'rational ethics' is possible. Economists should therefore refrain from any policy pronouncements unless the assumed goals of policy can be supported by a coherent and defencible ethical system (Rothbard 1976 and above). Hoppe argues that private property is not merely an *efficient* means of achieving wealth, it is also a *just* institution, and indeed any deviation from it is not only economically inefficient but unethical as well. These ideas, which lead into the realms of ethics and political philosophy, are developed further in Hoppe (1989). For an alternative discussion, see the last three chapters in Kirzner (1979).

What do Austrian economists have to say about law and economics? An influential body of legal opinion, led by Richard Posner, argues that the common law ought to aim at maximizing economic efficiency. Rizzo claims that this would be possible only in a static world of general equilibrium but would then be unnecessary. In a dynamic world, efficiency is an impossible goal, and the certainty and simplicity of a static law is therefore required. Specifically, a system of strict liability is to be preferred to one of negligence. See also Rizzo (1979a). In a second paper, Rizzo further argues that 'the judiciary can promote economic and other forms of liberty by returning to the classic common law adherence to abstract rules and eschewing the now-fashionable balancing of economic or social interests'.

Austrians have devoted considerable thought to the legal and constitutional framework within which the market economy operates. In line with the analyses of Knight, Coase and many modern economists, Mises points out that, although the presence of 'externalities' causes producers to ignore certain social disadvantages of their actions, this is not the result of 'market failure' but of an inadequacy in the existing system of private property rights. Thus Block (1979, 1980) argues that the problems of road congestion could be remedied by private ownership of roads.

Mises also notes that property rights are frequently modified in order to benefit particular interest groups at the expense of others. Wiseman argues that, in order to be policy-relevant, both Austrian and mainstream neoclassical economics need to embrace – indeed, be absorbed by – the newly developing concept of public choice. (See also Wiseman 1985, 1988.) Finally, Hayek explains why certain changes in democratic constitutions are necessary in order to reestablish the market economy on a firmer and more durable basis.

References and Further Reading

Armentano, Dominick T. (1978), 'A Critique of Neoclassical and Austrian Monopoly Theory', in Spadaro (1978), pp.94-110.

Armentano, Dominick T. (1982), *Antitrust and Monopoly: Anatomy of a Policy Failure*, New York: John Wiley & Sons.

Armentano, Dominick T. (1986), *Antitrust Policy: the Case for Repeal*, Washington D.C.: The Cato Institute.

Block, Walter (1977), 'Austrian Monopoly Theory: A Critique', *Journal of Libertarian Studies*, **1**(4), Autumn, pp.271-80.

Block, Walter (1979), 'Free Market Transportation: Denationalizing the Roads', *Journal of Libertarian Studies*, **III**(2), Summer, pp.209-38.

Block, Walter (1980), 'Congestion and Road Pricing', *Journal of Libertarian Studies*, **IV**(3), Summer, pp.299-332.

~ Böehm, Stephen (1986), 'Time and Equilibrium: Hayek's Notion of Intertemporral Equilibrium Reconsidered', in Kirzner (1986), Ch.2 pp.16-29.

~ Böehm, Stephen (1989), 'Hayek on Knowledge Equilibrium and Prices', *Wirtschafts Politische Blatter*, 2, pp.210-13.

~ Boettke, Pete, Steven Horwitz and David L. Prychitko (1986), 'Beyond Equilibrium Economics', *Market Process*, **4**(2), Autumn, pp.6-9, 20-25.

Dilorenzo, Thomas J. (1987), 'Competition and Political Entrepreneurship: Austrian Insights into Public Choice Theory', *Review of Austrian Economics*, 2, pp.59-71.

Gunning, J. Patrick (1989), 'Mises on the Evenly Rotating Economy', *The Review of Austrian Economics*, 3, pp.123-35.

Hayek, Friedrich A. (1948), 'Socialist Calculation I-II', repr. in his *Individualism and Economic Order*, Chicago: University of Chicago Press, Chs VII-IX.

Hayek, Friedrich A. (1976), 'The New Confusion about "Planning"', *The Morgan Guarantee Survey*, January, repr. as Laissez Faire Quarter Pamphlet no.2, Laissez Faire Books, New York, repr. in Hayek (1978), *New Studies*.

Hayek, Friedrich A. (1978), *New Studies in Philosophy, Politics, Economics and the History of Ideas*, Chicago: University of Chicago Press.

~ High, Jack (1980), Review article on Kirzner, *Perception, Opportunity and Profit* in *Austrian Economics Newsletter*, **2**(3), Spring, pp.1, 12-14.

~ High, Jack (1986), 'Equilibration and Disequilibration in the Market Process', in Kirzner (1986), Ch.9, pp.111-21.

Hoppe, Hans Hermann (1989), *A Theory of Socialism and Capitalis*, Mises Institute, Auburn University.

Kirzner, Israel M. (1973), *Competition and Entrepreneurship*, Chicago: University of Chicago Press.

Kirzner, Israel M. (1976), 'The Theory of Capital', in Dolan, Edwin G. (ed.), *The Foundations of Modern Austrian Economics*, Kansas City: Sheed & Ward Inc.

Kirzner, Israel M. (1979), *Perception, Opportunity and Profit*, Chicago: University of Chicago Press.

Kirzner, Israel M. (ed.) (1982), *Method, Process and Austrian Economics*, Lexington, Mass. and Toronto: D.C. Heath & Co., Lexington Books.

Kirzner, Israel M. (1984), 'Economic Planning and the Knowledge Problem', *Cato Journal*, **4**(2), Autumn, pp.407-18.

Kirzner, Israel M. (1985), *Discovery and the Capitalist Process*, Chicago and London: University of Chicago Press.

Kirzner, Israel M. (ed.) (1986), *Subjectivism, Intelligibility and Economic Understanding*, Basingstoke and London: Macmillan.

– Kirzner, Israel M. (1987), 'The Economic Calculation Debate: Lessons for Austrians', *Review of Austrian Economics*, **2**, pp.1-18.

Lachmann, Ludwig M. (1986), *The Market as an Economic Process*, Oxford and New York: Basil Blackwell.

– Langlois, Richard N. (1983), 'The Market Process: An Evolutionary View', *Market Process*, **1**(2), Summer, pp.2, 12-15.

Lavoie, Donald C. (1982), 'The Development of the Misesian Theory of Interventionism', in Kirzner (1982), Ch.14, pp.169-84.

Lavoie, Donald C. (1985), *Rivalry and Central Planning: The Calculation Debate Reconsidered*, Cambridge, Cambridge University Press.

– Lavoie, Donald C. (1986a), 'The Market as a Procedure for Discovery and Conveyance of Inarticulate Knowledge', *Comparative Economic Studies*, **XXVIII**(1), Spring, pp.1-19.

Lavoie, Donald C. (1986b), *National Economic Planning: What is Left?*, Fairfax Va.: Institute for Humane Studies, George Mason University.

Littlechild, Stephen C. (1978), *The Fallacy of the Mixed Economy*, Hobart Paper No.80, London: Institute of Economic Affairs, June; 2nd edn, 1986.

Littlechild, Stephen C. (1979), 'Radical Subjectivism or Radical Suberversion?' [comment on Shackle (1979)] in Rizzo (1979b), pp.32-50.

Mises, Ludwig von (1966), *Human Action*, Yale University Press 1949, 3rd edn Henry Regnery Co.

– Oakman, Bruce (1986), 'Patents: An Austrian Perspective', *Economic Papers*, (The Economic Society of Australia), **5**(1), March.

O'Driscoll, Gerald P. Jr (1982), 'Monopoly in Theory and Practice', in Kirzner (1982), Ch.16, pp.189-214.

O'Driscoll, Gerald P. Jr (1986), 'Competition as a Process: A Law and Economics perspective', in Richard N. Langlois (ed.) *Economics as a Process*, Cambridge: Cambridge University Press, Ch.7, pp.153-69.

O'Driscoll, Gerald P. and Mario J. Rizzo (1985), *The Economics of Time and Ignorance*, Oxford and New York: Basil Blackwell.

Pasour, E.C. Jr (1987), 'Rent Seeking: Some Conceptual Problems and Implications', *Review of Austrian Economics*, **1**, pp.123-43.

Rizzo, Mario J. (1979a), 'Uncertainty, Subjectivity and the Economic Analysis of Law', in Rizzo (1979b) Ch.4, pp.71-89.

Rizzo, Mario J. (ed.) (1979b), *Time, Uncertainty and Disequilibrium*, Lexington Mass. and Toronto: D. C. Heath & Co., Lexington Books.

Rothbard, Murray N. (1962), *Man, Economy and State*, 2 vols, Van Nostrand Inc.

Rothbard, Murray N. (1970), *Power and Market: Government and the Economy*, Menlo Park, Ca.: Institute for Humane Studies, Inc.

Rothbard, Murray N. (1976), 'Ludwig von Mises and Economic Calculation under Socialism', in Laurence S. Moss (ed.), *The Economics of Ludwig von Mises*, Kansas City: Sheed & Ward, pp.67-77.

Rothbard, Murray N. (1987), 'Breaking out of the Walrasian Box: The Cases of Schumpeter and Hansen', *Journal of Austrian Economics*, **1**, pp.97-108.

Shackle, George L. S. (1972), *Epistemics and Economics*, Cambridge: Cambridge University Press.

Shackle, George L. S. (1979), 'Imagination, Formalism and Choice' in Rizzo (1979b), Ch.2, pp.19-31.

Spadaro, Louis M. (1978), *New Directions in Austrian Economics*, Kansas City: Sheed Andrews and McMeel, Inc.

White, Lawrence H. (1979), 'The Austrian School and Spontaneous Order: Comment on O'Driscoll', *Austrian Economic Newsletter*, **2**(1), Spring, pp.6-7 (plus exchange of letters between White and L. M. Lachmann (1979), in *Austrian Economics Newsletter*, **2**(2), Autumn, pp.6-7).

Wiseman, Jack (1985), 'Economic Efficiency and Efficient Public Policy', in Horst Hanusch *et al.* (eds), *Public Sector and Political Economy Today*, Stuttgart: Gustav Fischer Verlag.

Wiseman, Jack (1989), *Cost, Choice and Political Economy*, Aldershot: Edward Elgar.

Part I
The Competitive Market
Process:
Equilibrium

[1]

Part Four

Catallactics or Economics of the Market Society

XIV. THE SCOPE AND METHOD OF CATALLACTICS

1. The Delimitation of Catallactic Problems

THERE have never been any doubts and uncertainties about the scope of economic science. Ever since people have been eager for a systematic study of economics or political economy, all have agreed that it is the task of this branch of knowledge to investigate the market phenomena, that is, the determination of the mutual exchange ratios of the goods and services negotiated on markets, their origin in human action and their effects upon later action. The intricacy of a precise definition of the scope of economics does not stem from uncertainty with regard to the orbit of the phenomena to be investigated. It is due to the fact that the attempts to elucidate the phenomena concerned must go beyond the range of the market and of market transactions. In order to conceive the market fully one is forced to study the action of hypothetical isolated individuals on one hand and to contrast the market system with an imaginary socialist commonwealth on the other hand. In studying interpersonal exchange one cannot avoid dealing with autistic exchange. But then it is no longer possible to define neatly the boundaries between the kind of action which is the proper field of economic science in the narrower sense, and other action. Economics widens its horizon and turns into a general science of all and every human action, into praxeology. The question emerges of how to distinguish precisely, within the broader field of general praxeology, a narrower orbit of specifically economic problems.

The abortive attempts to solve this problem of a precise delimitation of the scope of catallactics have chosen as a criterion either the motives causing action or the goals which action aims at. But the variety and manifoldness of the motives instigating a man's action is without relevance for a comprehensive study of acting. Every action is motivated by the urge to remove a felt uneasiness. It does not matter for the science of action how people qualify this uneasiness from a physiological, psychological, or ethical point of view. It is the task of economics to deal with all commodity prices as they are really asked and paid in market transactions. It must not restrict its investigations to the study of those prices which result or are likely to result from a conduct displaying attitudes to which psychology, ethics, or any other way of looking at human behavior would attach a definite label. The classification of actions according to their various motives may be momentous for psychology and may provide a yardstick for a moral evaluation; for economics it is inconsequential. Essentially the same is valid with regard to the endeavors to restrict the scope of economics to those actions which aim at supplying people with tangible material things of the external universe. Strictly speaking, people do not long for tangible goods as such, but for the services which these goods are fitted to render them. They want to attain the increment in well-being which these services are able to convey. But if this is so, it is not permissible to except from the orbit of "economic" action those actions which remove uneasiness directly without the interposition of any tangible and visible things. The advice of a doctor, the instruction of a teacher, the recital of an artist, and other personal services are no less an object of economic studies than the architect's plans for the construction of a building, the scientist's formula for the production of a chemical compound, and the author's contribution to the publishing of a book.

The subject matter of catallactics is all market phenomena with all their roots, ramifications, and consequences. It is a fact that people in dealing on the market are motivated not only by the desire to get food, shelter, and sexual enjoyment, but also by manifold "ideal" urges. Acting man is always concerned both with "material" and "ideal" things. He chooses between various alternatives, no matter whether they are to be classified as material or ideal. In the actual scales of value material and ideal things are jumbled together. Even if it were feasible to draw a sharp line between material and ideal concerns, one must realize that every concrete action either aims at the realization both of material and ideal ends or is the outcome of a choice between something material and something ideal.

Whether it is possible to separate neatly those actions which aim at the satisfaction of needs exclusively conditioned by man's physiological constitution from other "higher" needs can be left undecided. But we must not overlook the fact that in reality no food is valued solely for its nutritive power and no garment or house solely for the protection it affords against cold weather and rain. It cannot be denied that the demand for goods is widely influenced by metaphysical, religious, and ethical considerations, by aesthetic value judgments, by customs, habits, prejudices, tradition, changing fashions, and many other things. To an economist who would try to restrict his investi-

The Scope and Method of Catallactics 235

gations to "material" aspects only, the subject matter of inquiry vanishes as soon he wants to catch it.

All that can be contended is this: Economics is mainly concerned with the analysis of the determination of money prices of goods and services exchanged on the market. In order to accomplish this task it must start from a comprehensive theory of human action. Moreover, it must study not only the market phenomena, but no less the hypothetical conduct of an isolated man and of a socialist community. Finally, it must not restrict its investigations to those modes of action which in mundane speech are called "economic" actions, but must deal also with actions which are in a loose manner of speech called "uneconomic."

The scope of praxeology, the general theory of human action, can be precisely defined and circumscribed. The specifically economic problems, the problems of economic action in the narrower sense, can only by and large be disengaged from the comprehensive body of praxeological theory. Accidental facts of the history of science and conventions play a role in all attempts to provide a definition of the scope of "genuine" economics.

Not logical or epistemological rigor, but considerations of expediency and traditional convention make us declare that the field of catallactics or of economics in the narrower sense is the analysis of the market phenomena. This is tantamount to the statement: Catallactics is the analysis of those actions which are conducted on the basis of monetary calculation. Market exchange and monetary calculation are inseparably linked together. A market in which there is direct exchange only is merely an imaginary construction. On the other hand, money and monetary calculation are conditioned by the existence of the market.

It is certainly one of the tasks of economics to analyze the working of an imaginary socialist system of production. But access to this study too is possible only through the study of catallactics, the elucidation of a system in which there are money prices and economic calculation.

The Denial of Economics

There are doctrines flatly denying that there can be a science of economics. What is taught nowadays at most of the universities under the label of economics is practically a denial of it.

He who contests the existence of economics virtually denies that man's well-being is disturbed by any scarcity of external factors. Everybody, he implies, could enjoy the perfect satisfaction of all his wishes, provided a reform succeeds in overcoming certain obstacles brought about by inap-

propriate man-made institutions. Nature is open-handed, it lavishly loads
mankind with presents. Conditions could be paradisiac for an indefinite
number of people. Scarcity is an artificial product of established practices.
The abolition of such practices would result in abundance.

In the doctrine of Karl Marx and his followers scarcity is a historical
category only. It is the feature of the primeval history of mankind which
will be forever liquidated by the abolition of private property. Once mankind has effected the leap from the realm of necessity into the realm of
freedom [1] and thereby reached "the higher phase of communist society"
there will be abundance and consequently it will be feasible to give "to
each according to his needs." [2] There is in the vast flood of Marxian writings not the slightest allusion to the possibility that a communist society in
its "higher phase" might have to face a scarcity of natural factors of production. The fact of the disutility of labor is spirited away by the assertion
that to work, under communism of course, will no longer be pain but
pleasure, "the primary necessity of life." [3] The unpleasant experiences of
the Russian "experiment" are interpreted as caused by the capitalists'
hostility, by the fact that socialism in one country only is not yet perfect
and therefore has not yet been able to bring about the "higher phase," and,
more recently, by the war.

Then there are the radical inflationists as represented, for example, by
Proudhon, Ernest Solvay, and, in present-day America, by the doctrine of
"functional finance." In their opinion scarcity is created by the artificial
checks upon credit expansion and other methods of increasing the quantity
of money in circulation, enjoined upon the gullible public by the selfish
class interests of bankers and other exploiters. They recommend unlimited
public spending as the panacea.

The foremost American champion of the substitution of an economy of
abundance for the allegedly artificial economy of scarcity is the former
Vice-President of the United States, Henry A. Wallace. Mr. Wallace will
be remembered in history as the originator of the vastest scheme ever
carried out to restrict by government decree the supply of essential food-
stuffs and raw materials. However, this record in no way impairs the popularity of his teachings.

Such is the myth of potential plenty and abundance. Economics may
leave it to the historians and psychologists to explain the popularity of this
kind of wishful thinking and indulgence in daydreams. All that economics
has to say about such idle talk is that economics deals with the problems
man has to face on account of the fact that his life is conditioned by natural
factors. It deals with action, i.e., with the conscious endeavors to remove
as far as possible felt uneasiness. It has nothing to assert with regard to the

1. Cf. Engels, *Herrn Eugen Dührings Umwälzung der Wissenschaft* (7th ed.
Stuttgart, 1910), p. 306.
2. Cf. Karl Marx, *Zur Kritik des sozialdemokratischen Parteiprogramms von
Gotha*, ed. Kreibich (Reichenberg, 1920), p. 17.
3. Cf. *ibid.*

The Scope and Method of Catallactics   237

state of affairs in an unrealizable and for human reason even inconceivable universe of unlimited opportunities. In such a world, it may be admitted, there will be no law of value, no scarcity, and no economic problems. These things will be absent because there will be no choices to be made, no action, and no tasks to be solved by reason. Beings which would have thrived in such a world would never have developed reasoning and thinking. If ever such a world were to be given to the descendants of the human race, these blessed beings would see their power to think wither away and would cease to be human. For the primary task of reason is to cope consciously with the limitations imposed upon man by nature, to fight against scarcity. Acting and thinking man is the product of a universe of scarcity in which whatever well-being can be attained is the prize of toil and trouble, of conduct popularly called economic.

2. The Method of Imaginary Constructions

The specific method of economics is the method of imaginary constructions.

This method is the method of praxeology. That it has been carefully elaborated and perfected in the field of economic studies in the narrower sense is due to the fact that economics, at least until now, has been the best-developed part of praxeology. Everyone who wants to express an opinion about the problems commonly called economic takes recourse to this method. The employment of these imaginary constructions is, to be sure, not a procedure peculiar to the scientific analysis of these problems. The layman in dealing with them resorts to the same method. But while the layman's constructions are more or less confused and muddled, economics is intent upon elaborating them with the utmost care, scrupulousness, and precision, and upon examining their conditions and assumptions critically.

An imaginary construction is a conceptual image of a sequence of events logically evolved from the elements of action employed in its formation. It is a product of deduction, ultimately derived from the fundamental category of action, the act of preferring and setting aside. In designing such an imaginary construction the economist is not concerned with the question of whether or not it depicts the conditions of reality which he wants to analyze. Nor does he bother about the question of whether or not such a system as his imaginary construction posits could be conceived as really existent and in operation. Even imaginary constructions which are inconceivable, self-contradictory, or unrealizable can render useful, even indispensable services in the comprehension of reality, provided the economist knows how to use them properly.

The method of imaginary constructions is justified by its success. Praxeology cannot, like the natural sciences, base its teachings upon laboratory experiments and sensory perception of external objects. It had to develop methods entirely different from those of physics and biology. It would be a serious blunder to look for analogies to the imaginary constructions in the field of the natural sciences. The imaginary constructions of praxeology can never be confronted with any experience of things external and can never be appraised from the point of view of such experience. Their function is to serve man in a scrutiny which cannot rely upon his senses. In confronting the imaginary constructions with reality we cannot raise the question of whether they correspond to experience and depict adequately the empirical data. We must ask whether the assumptions of our construction are identical with the conditions of those actions which we want to conceive.

The main formula for designing of imaginary constructions is to abstract from the operation of some conditions present in actual action. Then we are in a position to grasp the hypothetical consequences of the absence of these conditions and to conceive the effects of their existence. Thus we conceive the category of action by constructing the image of a state in which there is no action, either because the individual is fully contented and does not feel any uneasiness or because he does not know any procedure from which an improvement in his well-being (state of satisfaction) could be expected. Thus we conceive the notion of originary interest from an imaginary construction in which no distinction is made between satisfactions in periods of time equal in length but unequal with regard to their distance from the instant of action.

The method of imaginary constructions is indispensable for praxeology; it is the only method of praxeological and economic inquiry. It is, to be sure, a method very difficult to handle because it can easily result in fallacious syllogisms. It leads along a sharp edge; on both sides yawns the chasm of absurdity and nonsense. Only merciless self-criticism can prevent a man from falling headlong into these abysmal depths.

3. The Pure Market Economy

The imaginary construction of a pure or unhampered market economy assumes that there is division of labor and private ownership (control) of the means of production and that consequently there is market exchange of goods and services. It assumes that the

The Scope and Method of Catallactics   239

operation of the market is not obstructed by institutional factors. It assumes that the government, the social apparatus of compulsion and coercion, is intent upon preserving the operation of the market system, abstains from hindering its functioning, and protects it against encroachments on the part of other people. The market is free; there is no interference of factors, foreign to the market, with prices, wage rates, and interest rates. Starting from these assumptions economics tries to elucidate the operation of a pure market economy. Only at a later stage, having exhausted everything which can be learned from the study of this imaginary construction, does it turn to the study of the various problems raised by interference with the market on the part of governments and other agencies employing coercion and compulsion.

It is amazing that this logically incontestable procedure, the only one that is fitted to solve the problems involved, has been passionately attacked. People have branded it as a prepossession in favor of a liberal economic policy, which they stigmatize as reactionary, economic royalism, Manchesterism, negativism, and so on. They deny that anything can be gained for the knowledge of reality from occupation with this imaginary construction. However, these turbulent critics contradict themselves as they take recourse to the same method in advancing their own assertions. In asking for minimum wage rates they depict the alleged unsatisfactory conditions of a free labor market and in asking for tariffs they describe the alleged disasters brought about by free trade. There is, of course, no other way available for the elucidation of a measure limiting the free play of the factors operating on an unhampered market than to study first the state of affairs prevailing under economic freedom.

It is true that economists have drawn from their investigations the conclusion that the goals which most people, practically even all people, are intent on attaining by toiling and working and by economic policy, can best be realized where the free market system is not impeded by government decrees. But this is not a preconceived judgment stemming from an insufficient occupation with the operation of government interference with business. It is, on the contrary, the result of a careful, unbiased scrutiny of all aspects of interventionism.

It is also true that the classical economists and their epigones used to call the system of unhampered market economy "natural" and government meddling with market phenomena "artificial" and "disturbing." But this terminology also was the product of their careful scrutiny of the problems of interventionism. They were in con-

formity with the semantic practice of their age in calling an undesirable state of social affairs "contrary to nature."

Theism and Deism of the Age of Enlightenment viewed the regularity of natural phenomena as an emanation of the decrees of Provi-
dence. When the philosophers of the Enlightenment discovered that
there prevails a regularity of phenomena also in human action and in
social evolution, they were prepared to interpret it likewise as evidence of the paternal care of the Creator of the universe. This was
the true meaning of the doctrine of the predetermined harmony as
expounded by some economists.[4] The social philosophy of paternal
despotism laid stress upon the divine mission of kings and autocrats
predestined to rule the peoples. The liberals retorted that the operation
of an unhampered market, on which the consumer—i.e., every citizen
—is sovereign, brings about more satisfactory results than the decrees
of anointed rulers. Observe the functioning of the market system,
they said, and you will discover in it the finger of God.

Along with the imaginary construction of a pure market economy
the classical economists elaborated its logical counterpart, the imaginary construction of a socialist commonwealth. In the heuristic
process which finally led to the discovery of the operation of a
market economy this image of a socialist order even had logical
priority. The question which preoccupied the economists was whether
a tailor could be supplied with bread and shoes if there was no government decree compelling the baker and the shoemaker to provide
for his needs. The first thought was that authoritarian interference is
required to make every specialist serve his fellow citizens. The
economists were taken aback when they discovered that no such
compulsion is needed. In contrasting productivity and profitability,
self-interest and public welfare, selfishness and altruism, the economists implicitly referred to the image of a socialist system. Their
astonishment at the "automatic," as it were, steering of the market
system was precisely due to the fact that they realized that an "anarchic" state of production results in supplying people better than
the orders of a centralized omnipotent government. The idea of
socialism—a system of the division of labor entirely controlled and
managed by a planning authority—did not originate in the heads of
utopian reformers. These utopians.aimed rather at the autarkic coexistence of small self-sufficient bodies; take, for instance, Fourier's
phalange. The radicalism of the reformers turned toward socialism

4. The doctrine of the predetermined harmony in the operation of an unhampered market system must not be confused with the theorem of the harmony
of the rightly understood interests within a market system, although there is a
certain congeniality between them. Cf. below, pp. 669–678.

The Scope and Method of Catallactics   241

when they took the image of an economy managed by a national government or a world authority, implied in the theories of the economists, as a model for their new order.

The Maximization of Profits

It is generally believed that economists, in dealing with the problems of a market economy, are quite unrealistic in assuming that all men are always eager to gain the highest attainable advantage. They construct, it is said, the image of a perfectly selfish and rationalistic being for whom nothing counts but profit. Such a homo oeconomicus may be a likeness of stock jobbers and speculators. But the immense majority are very different. Nothing for the cognition of reality can be learned from the study of the conduct of this delusive image.

It is not necessary to enter again into a refutation of all the confusion, error, and distortion inherent in this contention. The first two parts of this book have unmasked the fallacies implied. At this point it is enough to deal with the problem of the maximization of profits.

Praxeology in general and economics in its special field assume with regard to the springs of human action nothing other than that acting man wants to remove uneasiness. Under the particular conditions of dealing on the market, action means buying and selling. Everything that economics asserts about demand and supply refers to every instance of demand and supply and not only to demand and supply brought about by some special circumstances requiring a particular description or definition. To assert that a man, faced with the alternative of getting more or less for a commodity he wants to sell, *ceteris paribus* chooses the high price, does not require any further assumption. A higher price means for the seller a better satisfaction of his wants. The same applies mutatis mutandis to the buyer. The amount saved in buying the commodity concerned enables him to spend more for the satisfaction of other needs. To buy in the cheapest market and to sell in the dearest market is, other things being equal, not conduct which would presuppose any special assumptions concerning the actor's motives and morality. It is merely the necessary offshoot of any action under the conditions of market exchange.

In his capacity as a businessman a man is a servant of the consumers, bound to comply with their wishes. He cannot indulge in his own whims and fancies. But his customers' whims and fancies are for him ultimate law, provided these customers are ready to pay for them. He is under the necessity of adjusting his conduct to the demand of the consumers. If the consumers, without a taste for the beautiful, prefer things ugly and vulgar, he must, contrary to his own convictions, supply them with such things.[5] If consumers do not want to pay a higher price for domestic products than

5. A painter is a businessman if he is intent upon making paintings which could be sold at the highest price. A painter who does not compromise with the taste of the buying public and, disdaining all unpleasant consequences, lets himself be guided solely by his own ideals is an artist, a creative genius. Cf. above, pp. 138–140.

for those produced abroad, he must buy the foreign product, provided it
is cheaper. An employer cannot grant favors at the expense of his customers. He cannot pay wage rates higher than those determined by the
market if the buyers are not ready to pay proportionately higher prices
for commodities produced in plants in which wage rates are higher than
in other plants.

It is different with man in his capacity as spender of his income. He is
free to do what he likes best. He can bestow alms. He can, motivated by
various doctrines and prejudices, discriminate against goods of a certain
origin or source and prefer the worse or more expensive product to the
—technologically—better and cheaper one. As a rule people in buying do
not make gifts to the seller. But nonetheless that happens. The boundaries
between buying goods and services needed and giving alms are sometimes
difficult to discern. He who buys at a charity sale usually combines a purchase with a donation for a charitable purpose. He who gives a dime to a
blind street musician certainly does not pay for the questionable performance; he simply gives alms.

Man in acting is a unity. The businessman who owns the whole firm
may sometimes efface the boundaries between business and charity. If he
wants to relieve a distressed friend, delicacy of feeling may prompt him
to resort to a procedure which spares the latter the embarrassment of living
on alms. He gives the friend a job in his office although he does not need
his help or could hire an equivalent helper at a lower salary. Then the
salary granted appears formally as a part of business outlays. In fact it is
the spending of a fraction of the businessman's income. It is, from a correct
point of view, consumption and not an expenditure designed to increase
the firm's profits.[6]

Awkward mistakes are due to the tendency to look only upon things
tangible, visible, and measurable, and to neglect everything else. What the
consumer buys is not simply food or calories. He does not want to feed like
a wolf, he wants to eat like a man. Food satisfies the appetite of many
people the better, the more appetizingly and tastefully it is prepared, the
finer the table is set, and the more agreeable the environment is in which
the food is consumed. Such things are regarded as of no consequence by
a consideration exclusively occupied with the chemical aspects of the
process of digestion.[7] But the fact that they play an important role in the
determination of food prices is perfectly compatible with the assertion
that people prefer, ceteris paribus, to buy in the cheapest market. Whenever a buyer, in choosing between two things which chemists and tech-

6. Such overlapping of the boundaries between business outlays and consump-
tive spending is often encouraged by institutional conditions. An expenditure
debited to the account of trading expenses reduces net profits and thereby the
amount of taxes due. If taxes absorb 50 per cent of profits, the charitable businessman spends only 50 per cent of the gift out of his own pocket. The rest burdens
the Department of Internal Revenue.

7. To be sure, a consideration from the point of view of the physiology of
nutrition will not regard such things as negligible.

The Scope and Method of Catallactics   243

nologists deem perfectly equal, prefers the more expensive, he has a reason. If he does not err, he pays for services which chemistry and technology cannot comprehend with their specific methods of investigation. If a man prefers an expensive place to a cheaper one because he likes to sip his cocktails in the neighborhood of a duke or of café society, we may remark on his ridiculous vanity. But we must not say that the man's conduct does not aim at an improvement of his own state of satisfaction.

What a man does is always aimed at an improvement of his own state of satisfaction. In this sense—and in no other—we are free to use the term selfishness and to emphasize that action is necessarily always selfish. Even an action directly aiming at the improvement of other people's conditions is selfish. The actor considers it as more satisfactory for himself to make other people eat than to eat himself. His uneasiness is caused by the awareness of the fact that other people are in want.

It is a fact that many people behave in another way and prefer to fill their own stomach and not that of their fellow citizens. But this has nothing to do with economics; it is a datum of historical experience. At any rate, economics refers to every kind of action, no matter whether motivated by the urge of a man to eat or to make other people eat.

If maximizing profits means that a man in all market transactions aims at increasing to the utmost the advantage derived, it is a pleonastic and periphrastic circumlocution. It only asserts what is implied in the very category of action. If it means anything else, it is the expression of an erroneous idea.

Some economists believe that it is the task of economics to establish how in the whole of society the greatest possible satisfaction of all people or of the greatest number could be attained. They do not realize that there is no method which would allow us to measure the state of satisfaction attained by various individuals. They misconstrue the character of judgments which are based on the comparison between various people's happiness. While expressing arbitrary value judgments, they believe themselves to be establishing facts. One may call it just to rob the rich in order to make presents to the poor. However, to call something fair or unfair is always a subjective value judgment and as such purely personal and not liable to any verification or falsification. Economics is not intent upon pronouncing value judgments. It aims at a cognition of the consequences of certain modes of acting.

It has been asserted that the physiological needs of all men are of the same kind and that this equality provides a standard for the measurement of the degree of their objective satisfaction. In expressing such opinions and in recommending the use of such criteria to guide the government's policy, one proposes to deal with men as the breeder deals with his cattle. But the reformers fail to realize that there is no universal principle of alimentation valid for all men. Which one of the various principles one chooses depends entirely on the aims one wants to attain. The cattle breeder does not feed his cows in order to make them happy, but in order to attain the ends which he has assigned to them in his own plans. He may prefer more milk or more meat or something else. What type of man do the man breeders want to rear—athletes or mathematicians? Warriors or factory hands? He who would make man the material of a purposeful system of breeding and feeding would arrogate to himself despotic powers and would use his fellow citizens as means for the attainment of his own ends, which differ from those they themselves are aiming at.

The value judgments of an individual differentiate between what makes him more satisfied and what less. The value judgments a man pronounces about another man's satisfaction do not assert anything about this other man's satisfaction. They only assert what condition of this other man better satisfies the man who pronounces the judgment. The reformers searching for the maximum of general satisfaction have told us merely what state of other people's affairs would best suit themselves.

4. The Autistic Economy

No other imaginary construction has caused more offense than that of an isolated economic actor entirely dependent on himself. However, economics cannot do without it. In order to study interpersonal exchange it must compare it with conditions under which it is absent. It constructs two varieties of the image of an autistic economy in which there is only autistic exchange: the economy of an isolated individual and the economy of a socialist society. In employing this imaginary construction the economists do not bother about the problem of whether or not such a system could really work.[8] They are fully aware of the fact that their imaginary construction is fictitious. Robinson Crusoe, who, for all that, may have existed, and the general manager of a perfectly isolated socialist commonwealth that never existed, would not have been in a position to plan and to act as people can only when taking recourse to economic calculation. However, in the frame of our imaginary construction we are free to pretend that they could calculate whenever such a fiction may be useful for the discussion of the specific problem to be dealt with.

The imaginary construction of an autistic economy is at the bottom of the popular distinction between productivity and profitability as it developed as a yardstick of value judgments. Those resorting to this distinction consider the autistic economy, especially that of the socialist type, the most desirable and most perfect system of economic management. Every phenomenon of the market economy is judged with regard to whether or not it could be justified from the

8. We are dealing here with problems of theory, not of history. We can therefore abstain from refuting the objections raised against the concept of an isolated actor by referring to the historical role of the self-sufficient household economy.

The Scope and Method of Catallactics 245

viewpoint of a socialist system. Only to acting that would be purposeful in the plans of such a system's manager are positive value and
the epithet *productive* attached. All other activities performed in the
market economy are called unproductive in spite of the fact that they
may be profitable to those who perform them. Thus, for example,
sales promotion, advertising, and banking are considered as activities
profitable but nonproductive.

Economics, of course, has nothing to say about such arbitrary value
judgments.

5. The State of Rest and the Evenly Rotating Economy

The only method of dealing with the problem of action is to
conceive that action ultimately aims at bringing about a state of
affairs in which there is no longer any action, whether because all
uneasiness has been removed or because any further removal of felt
uneasiness is out of the question. Action thus tends toward a state
of rest, absence of action.

The theory of prices accordingly analyzes interpersonal exchange
from this aspect. People keep on exchanging on the market until no
further exchange is possible because no party expects any further improvement of its own conditions from a new act of exchange. The
potential buyers consider the prices asked by the potential sellers
unsatisfactory, and vice versa. No more transactions take place. A
state of rest emerges. This state of rest, which we may call the *plain
state of rest*, is not merely an imaginary construction. It comes to
pass again and again. When the stock market closes, the brokers have
carried out all orders which could be executed at the market price.
Only those potential sellers and buyers who consider the market
price too low or too high respectively have not sold or bought.[9] The
same is valid with regard to all transactions. The whole market economy is a big exchange or market place, as it were. At any instant
all those transactions take place which the parties are ready to enter
into at the realizable price. New sales can only be effected when the
valuations of the parties have changed.

It has been asserted that the notion of the plain state of rest is
unsatisfactory. It refers, people have said, only to the determination
of prices of goods of which a definite supply is already available, and
does not say anything about the effects brought about by these prices

9. For the sake of simplicity we disregard the price fluctuations in the course
of the business day.

upon production. The objection is unfounded. The theorems implied in the notion of the plain state of rest are valid with regard to all transactions without exception. It is true, the buyers of factors of production will immediately embark upon producing and very soon reenter the market in order to sell their products and to buy what they want for their own consumption and for continuing production processes. But this does not invalidate the scheme. This scheme, to be sure, does not contend that the state of rest will last. The lull will certainly disappear as soon as the momentary conditions which brought it about change.

The notion of the plain state of rest is not an imaginary construction but the adequate description of what happens again and again on every market. In this regard it differs radically from the imaginary construction of the final state of rest.

In dealing with the plain state of rest we look only at what is going on right now. We restrict our attention to what has happened momentarily and disregard what will happen later, in the next instant or tomorrow or later. We are dealing only with prices really paid in sales, i.e., with the prices of the immediate past. We do not ask whether or not future prices will equal these prices.

But now we go a step further. We pay attention to factors which are bound to bring about a tendency toward price changes. We try to find out to what goal this tendency must lead before all its driving force is exhausted and a new state of rest emerges. The price corresponding to this future state of rest was called the *natural price* by older economists; nowadays the term *static price* is often used. In order to avoid misleading associations it is more expedient to call it the *final price* and accordingly to speak of the *final state of rest*. This final state of rest is an imaginary construction, not a description of reality. For the final state of rest will never be attained. New disturbing factors will emerge before it will be realized. What makes it necessary to take recourse to this imaginary construction is the fact that the market at every instant is moving toward a final state of rest. Every later new instant can create new facts altering this final state of rest. But the market is always disquieted by a striving after a definite final state of rest.

The market price is a real phenomenon; it is the exchange ratio which was actual in business transacted. The final price is a hypothetical price. The market prices are historical facts and we are therefore in a position to note them with numerical exactitude in dollars and cents. The final price can only be defined by defining the conditions required for its emergence. No definite numerical value in

The Scope and Method of Catallactics 247

monetary terms or in quantities of other goods can be attributed to it. It will never appear on the market. The market price can never coincide with the final price coordinated to the instant in which this market structure is actual. But catallactics would fail lamentably in its task of analyzing the problems of price determination if it were to neglect dealing with the final price. For in the market situation from which the market price emerges there are already latent forces operating which will go on bringing about price changes until, provided no new data appear, the final price and the final state of rest are established. We would unduly restrict our study of price determination if we were to look only upon the momentary market prices and the plain state of rest and to disregard the fact that the market is already agitated by factors which must result in further price changes and a tendency toward a different state of rest.

The phenomenon with which we have to cope is the fact that changes in the factors which determine the formation of prices do not produce all their effects at once. A span of time must elapse before all their effects are exhausted. Between the appearance of a new datum and the perfect adjustment of the market to it some time must pass. (And, of course, while this period of time elapses, other new data appear.) In dealing with the effects of any change in the factors operating on the market, we must never forget that we are dealing with events taking place in succession, with a series of effects succeeding one another. We are not in a position to know in advance how much time will have to elapse. But we know for certain that some time must elapse, although this period may sometimes be so small that it hardly plays any role in practical life.

Economists often erred in neglecting the element of time. Take for instance the controversy concerning the effects of changes in the quantity of money. Some people were only concerned with its long-run effects, i.e., with the final prices and the final state of rest. Others saw only the short-run effects, i.e., the prices of the instant following the change in the data. Both were mistaken and their conclusions were consequently vitiated. Many more examples of the same blunder could be cited.

The imaginary construction of the final state of rest is marked by paying full regard to change in the temporal succession of events. In this respect it differs from the imaginary construction of the *evenly rotating economy* which is characterized by the elimination of change in the data and of the time element. (It is inexpedient and misleading to call this imaginary construction, as is usual, the static economy or the static equilibrium, and it is a bad mistake to confuse it with the

imaginary construction of a stationary economy.[10]) The evenly
rotating economy is a fictitious system in which the market prices
of all goods and services coincide with the final prices. There are
in its frame no price changes whatever; there is perfect price stability. The same market transactions are repeated again and again. The
goods of the higher orders pass in the same quantities through the
same stages of processing until ultimately the produced consumers'
goods come into the hands of the consumers and are consumed. No
changes in the market data occur. Today does not differ from yesterday and tomorrow will not differ from today. The system is in
perpetual flux, but it remains always at the same spot. It revolves
evenly round a fixed center, it rotates evenly. The plain state of rest
is disarranged again and again, but it is instantly reestablished at the
previous level. All factors, including those bringing about the recurring disarrangement of the plain state of rest, are constant. Therefore prices—commonly called static or equilibrium prices—remain
constant too.

The essence of this imaginary construction is the elimination of
the lapse of time and of the perpetual change in the market phenomena.
The notion of any change with regard to supply and demand is incompatible with this construction. Only such changes as do not
affect the configuration of the price-determining factors can be
considered in its frame. It is not necessary to people the imaginary
world of the evenly rotating economy with immortal, non-aging and
nonproliferating men. We are free to assume that infants are born,
grow old, and finally die, provided that total population figures and
the number of people in every age group remain equal. Then the
demand for commodities whose consumption is limited to certain
age groups does not alter, although the individuals from whom it
originates are not the same.

In reality there is never such a thing as an evenly rotating economic system. However, in order to analyze the problems of change
in the data and of unevenly and irregularly varying movement, we
must confront them with a fictitious state in which both are hypothetically eliminated. It is therefore preposterous to maintain that the
construction of an evenly rotating economy does not elucidate conditions within a changing universe and to require the economists to
substitute a study of "dynamics" for their alleged exclusive occupation with "statics." This so-called static method is precisely the proper
mental tool for the examination of change. There is no means of
studying the complex phenomena of action other than first to ab-

10. See below, pp. 251–252.

The Scope and Method of Catallactics 249

stract from change altogether, then to introduce an isolated factor provoking change, and ultimately to analyze its effects under the assumption that other things remain equal. It is furthermore absurd to believe that the services rendered by the construction of an evenly rotating economy are the more valuable the more the object of our studies, the realm of real action, corresponds to this construction in respect to absence of change. The static method, the employment of the imaginary construction of an evenly rotating economy, is the only adequate method of analyzing the changes concerned without regard to whether they are great or small, sudden or slow.

The objections hitherto raised against the use of the imaginary construction of an evenly rotating economy missed the mark entirely. Their authors did not grasp in what respect this construction is problematic and why it can easily engender error and confusion.

Action is change, and change is in the temporal sequence. But in the evenly rotating economy change and succession of events are eliminated. Action is to make choices and to cope with an uncertain future. But in the evenly rotating economy there is no choosing and the future is not uncertain as it does not differ from the present known state. Such a rigid system is not peopled with living men making choices and liable to error; it is a world of soulless unthinking automatons; it is not a human society, it is an ant hill.

These insoluble contradictions, however, do not affect the service which this imaginary construction renders for the only problem for whose treatment it is both appropriate and indispensable: the problem of the relation between the prices of products and those of the factors required for their production, and the implied problems of entrepreneurship and of profit and loss. In order to grasp the function of entrepreneurship and the meaning of profit and loss, we construct a system from which they are absent. This image is merely a tool for our thinking. It is not the description of a possible and realizable state of affairs. It is even out of the question to carry the imaginary construction of an evenly rotating system to its ultimate logical consequences. For it is impossible to eliminate the entrepreneur from the picture of a market economy. The various complementary factors of production cannot come together spontaneously. They need to be combined by the purposive efforts of men aiming at certain ends and motivated by the urge to improve their state of satisfaction. In eliminating the entrepreneur one eliminates the driving force of the whole market system.

Then there is a second deficiency. In the imaginary construction of an evenly rotating economy, indirect exchange and the use of money are tacitly implied. But what kind of money can that be? In a system without change in which there is no uncertainty whatever about the future, nobody needs to hold cash. Every individual knows precisely what amount of money he will need at any future date. He is therefore in a position to lend all the funds he receives in such a way that the loans fall due on the date he will need them. Let us assume that there is only gold money and only one central bank. With the successive progress toward the state of an evenly rotating economy all individuals and firms restrict step by step their holding of cash and the quantities of gold thus released flow into nonmonetary—industrial—employment. When the equilibrium of the evenly rotating economy is finally reached, there are no more cash holdings; no more gold is used for monetary purposes. The individuals and firms own claims against the central bank, the maturity of each part of which precisely corresponds to the amount they will need on the respective dates for the settlement of their obligations. The central bank does not need any reserves as the total sum of the daily payments of its customers exactly equals the total sum of withdrawals. All transactions can in fact be effected through transfer in the bank's books without any recourse to cash. Thus the "money" of this system is not a medium of exchange; it is not money at all; it is merely a *numéraire*, an ethereal and undetermined unit of accounting of that vague and indefinable character which the fancy of some economists and the errors of many laymen mistakenly have attributed to money. The interposition of these numerical expressions between seller and buyer does not affect the essence of the sales; it is neutral with regard to the people's economic activities. But the notion of a neutral money is unrealizable and inconceivable in itself.[11] If we were to use the inexpedient terminology employed in many contemporary economic writings, we would have to say: Money is necessarily a "dynamic factor"; there is no room left for money in a "static" system. But the very notion of a market economy without money is self-contradictory.

The imaginary construction of an evenly rotating system is a limiting notion. In its frame there is in fact no longer any action. Automatic reaction is substituted for the conscious striving of thinking man after the removal of uneasiness. We can employ this problematic imaginary construction only if we never forget what purposes it is designed to serve. We want first of all to analyze the tendency, prevailing in every action, toward the establishment of an evenly rotating economy; in doing so, we must always take into account that this

11. Cf. below, pp. 413–416.

The Scope and Method of Catallactics 251

tendency can never attain its goal in a universe not perfectly rigid and immutable, that is, in a universe which is living and not dead. Secondly we need to comprehend in what respects the conditions of a living world in which there is action differ from those of a rigid world. This we can discover only by the *argumentum a contrario* provided by the image of a rigid economy. Thus we are led to the insight that dealing with the uncertain conditions of the unknown future—that is, speculation—is inherent in every action, and that profit and loss are necessary features of acting which cannot be conjured away by any wishful thinking. The procedures adopted by those economists who are fully aware of these fundamental cognitions may be called the *logical method* of economics as contrasted with the technique of the *mathematical method*.

The mathematical economists disregard dealing with the actions which, under the imaginary and unrealizable assumption that no further new data will emerge, are supposed to bring about the evenly rotating economy. They do not notice the individual speculator who aims not at the establishment of the evenly rotating economy but at profiting from an action which adjusts the conduct of affairs better to the attainment of the ends sought by acting, the best possible removal of uneasiness. They stress exclusively the imaginary state of equilibrium which the whole complex of all such actions would attain in the absence of any further change in the data. They describe this imaginary equilibrium by sets of simultaneous differential equations. They fail to recognize that the state of affairs they are dealing with is a state in which there is no longer any action but only a succession of events provoked by a mystical prime mover. They devote all their efforts to describing, in mathematical symbols, various "equilibria," that is, states of rest and the absence of action. They deal with equilibrium as if it were a real entity and not a limiting notion, a mere mental tool. What they are doing is vain playing with mathematical symbols, a pastime not suited to convey any knowledge.[12]

6. The Stationary Economy

The imaginary construction of a stationary economy has sometimes been confused with that of an evenly rotating economy. But in fact these two constructions differ.

The stationary economy is an economy in which the wealth and income of the individuals remain unchanged. With this image

12. For a further critical examination of mathematical economics see below, pp. 347–354.

changes are compatible which would be incompatible with the construction of the evenly rotating economy. Population figures may rise or drop provided that they are accompanied by a corresponding rise or drop in the sum of wealth and income. The demand for some commodities may change; but these changes must occur so slowly that the transfer of capital from those branches of production which are to be restricted in accordance with them into those to be expanded can be effected by not replacing equipment used up in the shrinking branches and instead investing in the expanding ones.

The imaginary construction of a stationary economy leads to two further imaginary constructions: the progressing (expanding) economy and the retrogressing (shrinking) economy. In the former the per capita quota of wealth and income of the individuals and the population figure tend toward a higher numerical value, in the latter toward a lower numerical value.

In the stationary economy the total sum of all profits and of all losses is zero. In the progressing economy the total amount of profits exceeds the total amount of losses. In the retrogressing economy the total amount of profits is smaller than the total amount of losses.

The precariousness of these three imaginary constructions is to be seen in the fact that they imply the possibility of the measurement of wealth and income. As such measurements cannot be made and are not even conceivable, it is out of the question to apply them for a rigorous classification of the conditions of reality. Whenever economic history ventures to classify economic evolution within a certain period according to the scheme stationary, progressing, or retrogressing, it resorts in fact to historical understanding and does not "measure."

7. The Integration of Catallactic Functions

When men in dealing with the problems of their own actions, and when economic history, descriptive economics, and economic statistics in reporting other people's actions, employ the terms entrepreneur, capitalist, landowner, worker, and consumer, they speak of ideal types. When economics employs the same terms it speaks of catallactic categories. The entrepreneurs, capitalists, landowners, workers, and consumers of economic theory are not living men as one meets them in the reality of life and history. They are the embodiment of distinct functions in the market operations. The fact that both acting men and historical sciences apply in their reasoning the results of economics and that they construct their ideal types on the basis of

The Scope and Method of Catallactics 253

and with reference to the categories of praxeological theory, does not modify the radical logical distinction between ideal type and economic category. The economic categories we are concerned with refer to purely integrated functions, the ideal types refer to historical events. Living and acting man by necessity combines various functions. He is never merely a consumer. He is in addition either an entrepreneur, landowner, capitalist, or worker, or a person supported by the intake earned by such people. Moreover, the functions of the entrepreneur, the landowner, the capitalist, and the worker are very often combined by the same persons. History is intent upon classifying men according to the ends they aim at and the means they employ for the attainment of these ends. Economics, exploring the structure of acting in the market society without any regard to the ends people aim at and the means they employ, is intent upon discerning categories and functions. These are two different tasks. The difference can best be demonstrated in discussing the catallactic concept of the entrepreneur.

In the imaginary construction of the evenly rotating economy there is no room left for entrepreneurial activity, because this construction eliminates any change of data that could affect prices. As soon as one abandons this assumption of rigidity of data, one finds that action must needs be affected by every change in the data. As action necessarily is directed toward influencing a future state of affairs, even if sometimes only the immediate future of the next instant, it is affected by every incorrectly anticipated change in the data occurring in the period of time between its beginning and the end of the period for which it aimed to provide (period of provision [13]). Thus the outcome of action is always uncertain. Action is always speculation. This is valid not only with regard to a market economy but no less for Robinson Crusoe, the imaginary isolated actor, and for the conditions of a socialist economy. In the imaginary construction of an evenly rotating system nobody is an entrepreneur and speculator. In any real and living economy every actor is always an entrepreneur and speculator; the people taken care of by the actors—the minor family members in the market society and the masses of a socialist society—are, although themselves not actors and therefore not speculators, affected by the outcome of the actors' speculations.

Economics, in speaking of entrepreneurs, has in view not men, but a definite function. This function is not the particular feature of a special group or class of men; it is inherent in every action and burdens every actor. In embodying this function in an imaginary figure,

13. Cf. below, p. 478.

we resort to a methodological makeshift. The term entrepreneur as used by catallactic theory means: acting man exclusively seen from the aspect of the uncertainty inherent in every action. In using this term one must never forget that every action is embedded in the flux of time and therefore involves a speculation. The capitalists, the landowners, and the laborers are by necessity speculators. So is the consumer in providing for anticipated future needs. There's many a slip 'twixt cup and lip.

Let us try to think the imaginary construction of a pure entrepreneur to its ultimate logical consequences. This entrepreneur does not own any capital. The capital required for his entrepreneurial activities is lent to him by the capitalists in the form of money loans. The law, it is true, considers him the proprietor of the various means of production purchased by expending the sums borrowed. Nevertheless he remains propertyless for the amount of his assets is balanced by his liabilities. If he succeeds, the net profit is his. If he fails, the loss must fall upon the capitalists who have lent him the funds. Such an entrepreneur would, in fact, be an employee of the capitalists who speculates on their account and takes a 100 per cent share in the net profits without being concerned about the losses. But even if the entrepreneur is in a position to provide himself a part of the capital required and borrows only the rest, things are essentially not different. To the extent that the losses incurred cannot be borne out of the entrepreneur's own funds, they fall upon the lending capitalists, whatever the terms of the contract may be. A capitalist is always also virtually an entrepreneur and speculator. He always runs the chance of losing his funds. There is no such thing as a perfectly safe investment.

The self-sufficient landowner who tills his estate only to supply his own household is affected by all changes influencing the fertility of his farm or the object of his needs. Within a market economy the result of a farmer's activities is affected by all changes regarding the importance of his piece of land for supplying the market. The farmer is clearly, even from the point of view of mundane terminology, an entrepreneur. No proprietor of any means of production, whether they are represented in tangible goods or in money, remains untouched by the uncertainty of the future. The employment of any tangible goods or money for production, i.e., the provision for later days, is in itself an entrepreneurial activity.

Things are essentially the same for the laborer. He is born the proprietor of certain abilities; his innate faculties are a means of production which is better fitted for some kinds of work, less fitted

The Scope and Method of Catallactics 255

for others, and not at all fitted for still others.[14] If he has acquired the skill needed for the performance of certain kinds of labor, he is, with regard to the time and the material outlays absorbed by this training, in the position of an investor. He has made an input in the expectation of being compensated by an adequate output. The laborer is an entrepreneur in so far as his wages are determined by the price the market allows for the kind of work he can perform. This price varies according to the change in conditions in the same way in which the price of every other factor of production varies.

In the context of economic theory the meaning of the terms concerned is this: Entrepreneur means acting man in regard to the changes occurring in the data of the market. Capitalist and landowner mean acting man in regard to the changes in value and price which, even with all the market data remaining equal, are brought about by the mere passing of time as a consequence of the different valuation of present goods and of future goods. Worker means man in regard to the employment of the factor of production human labor. Thus every function is nicely integrated: the entrepreneur earns profit or suffers loss; the owners of means of production (capital goods or land) earn originary interest; the workers earn wages. In this sense we elaborate the imaginary construction of *functional distribution* as different from the actual historical distribution.[15]

Economics, however, always did and still does use the term "entrepreneur" in a sense other than that attached to it in the imaginary construction of functional distribution. It also calls entrepreneurs those who are especially eager to profit from adjusting production to the expected changes in conditions, those who have more initiative, more venturesomeness, and a quicker eye than the crowd, the pushing and promoting pioneers of economic improvement. This notion is nar-

14. In what sense labor is to be seen as a nonspecific factor of production see above, pp. 133–135.

15. Let us emphasize again that everybody, laymen included, in dealing with the problems of income determination always takes recourse to this imaginary construction. The economists did not invent it; they only purged it of the deficiencies peculiar to the popular notion. For an epistemological treatment of functional distribution cf. John Bates Clark, *The Distribution of Wealth* (New York, 1908), p. 5, and Eugen von Böhm-Bawerk, *Gesammelte Schriften*, ed. F. X. Weiss (Vienna, 1924), p. 299. The term "distribution" must not deceive anybody; its employment in this context is to be explained by the role played in the history of economic thought by the imaginary construction of a socialist state (cf. above, p. 240). There is in the operation of a market economy nothing which could properly be called distribution. Goods are not first produced and then distributed, as would be the case in a socialist state. The word "distribution" as applied in the term "functional distribution" complies with the meaning attached to "distribution" 150 years ago. In present-day English usage "distribution" signifies dispersal of goods among consumers as effected by commerce.

rower than the concept of an entrepreneur as used in the construction of functional distribution; it does not include many instances which the latter includes. It is awkward that the same term should be used to signify two different notions. It would have been more expedient to employ another term for this second notion—for instance, the term "promoter."

It is to be admitted that the notion of the entrepreneur-promoter cannot be defined with praxeological rigor. (In this it is like the notion of money which also defies—different from the notion of a medium of exchange—a rigid praxeological definition.[16]) However, economics cannot do without the promoter concept. For it refers to a datum that is a general characteristic of human nature, that is present in all market transactions and marks them profoundly. This is the fact that various individuals do not react to a change in conditions with the same quickness and in the same way. The inequality of men, which is due to differences both in their inborn qualities and in the vicissitudes of their lives, manifests itself in this way too. There are in the market pacemakers and others who only imitate the procedures of their more agile fellow citizens. The phenomenon of leadership is no less real on the market than in any other branch of human activities. The driving force of the market, the element tending toward unceasing innovation and improvement, is provided by the restlessness of the promoter and his eagerness to make profits as large as possible.

There is, however, no danger that the equivocal use of this term may result in any ambiguity in the exposition of the catallactic system. Wherever any doubts are likely to appear, they can be dispelled by the employment of the term promoter instead of entrepreneur.

The Entrepreneurial Function in the Stationary Economy

The futures market can relieve an entrepreneur of a part of his entrepreneurial function. As far as an entrepreneur has "insured" himself through suitable forward transactions against losses he may possibly suffer, he ceases to be an entrepreneur and the entrepreneurial function devolves on the other party to the contract. The cotton spinner who when buying raw cotton for his mill sells the same quantity forward has abandoned a part of his entrepreneurial function. He will neither profit nor lose from changes in the cotton price occurring in the period concerned. Of course, he does not entirely cease to serve in the entrepreneurial function. Those changes in the price of yarn in general or in the price of the special counts and kinds he produces which are not brought about by a change in the price of raw cotton affect him nonetheless. Even if he spins only as

16. Cf. below, p. 395.

The Scope and Method of Catallactics 257

a contractor for a remuneration agreed upon, he is still in an entrepreneurial function with regard to the funds invested in his outfit.

We may construct the image of an economy in which the conditions required for the establishment of futures markets are realized for all kinds of goods and services. In such an imaginary construction the entrepreneurial function is fully separated from all other functions. There emerges a class of pure entrepreneurs. The prices determined on the futures markets direct the whole apparatus of production. The dealers in futures alone make profits and suffer losses. All other people are insured, as it were, against the possible adverse effects of the uncertainty of the future. They enjoy security in this regard. The heads of the various business units are employees, as it were, with a fixed income.

If we further assume that this economy is a stationary economy and that all futures transactions are concentrated in one corporation, it is obvious that the total amount of losses precisely equals the total amount of profits. We need only to nationalize this corporation in order to bring about a socialist state without profits and losses, a state of undisturbed security and stability. But this is so only because our definition of a stationary economy implies equality of the total sum of losses and that of profits. In a changing economy an excess either of profits or of losses must emerge.

It would be a waste of time to dwell longer upon such oversophisticated images which do not further the analysis of economic problems. The only reason for mentioning them is that they reflect ideas which are at the bottom of some criticisms made against the economic system of capitalism and of some delusive plans suggested for a socialist control of business. Now, it is true that a socialist scheme is logically compatible with the unrealizable imaginary constructions of an evenly rotating economy and of a stationary economy. The predilection with which mathematical economists almost exclusively deal with the conditions of these imaginary constructions and with the state of "equilibrium" implied in them, has made people oblivious of the fact that these are unreal, self-contradictory and imaginary expedients of thought and nothing else. They are certainly not suitable models for the construction of a living society of acting men.

[2]

Economics and Knowledge[1]

By F. A. von Hayek

I

THE ambiguity of the title of this paper is not accidental.
Its main subject is, of course, the rôle which assumptions
and propositions about the knowledge possessed by the
different members of society play in economic analysis. But
this is by no means unconnected with the other question
which might be discussed under the same title, the question
to what extent formal economic analysis conveys any knowledge about what happens in the real world. Indeed my
main contention will be that the tautologies, of which formal
equilibrium analysis in economics essentially consists, can
be turned into propositions which tell us anything about
causation in the real world only in so far as we are able to
fill those formal propositions with definite statements about
how knowledge is acquired and communicated. In short
I shall contend that the empirical element in economic
theory—the only part which is concerned, not merely with
implications but with causes and effects, and which leads
therefore to conclusions which, at any rate in principle,
are capable of verification[2]—consists of propositions about
the acquisition of knowledge.

Perhaps I should begin by reminding you of the interesting
fact that in quite a number of the more recent attempts
made in different fields to push theoretical investigation
beyond the limits of traditional equilibrium analysis, the
answer has soon proved to turn on one question which, if
not identical with mine, is at least part of it, namely the
question of foresight. I think the field where, as one would
expect, the discussion of the assumptions concerning foresight first attracted wider attention was the theory of
risk.[3] The stimulus which was exercised in this connection

[1] Presidential Address to the London Economic Club, November 10th, 1936.
[2] Or rather falsification. Cf. K. Popper, *Logik der Forschung*, Vienna, 1935, *passim*.
[3] A more complete survey of the process by which the significance of anticipations was
gradually introduced into economic analysis would probably have to begin with Professor
Irving Fisher's *Appreciation and Interest* (1896).

by the work of Professor F. H. Knight may yet prove to have
a profound influence far beyond its special field. Not much
later the assumptions to be made concerning foresight proved
to be of fundamental importance for the solution of the
puzzles of the theory of imperfect competition, the questions
of duopoly and oligopoly. And since then it has become
more and more obvious that in the treatment of the more
" dynamic " questions of money and industrial fluctuations
the assumptions to be made about foresight and " anticipations " play an equally central rôle, and that in particular
the concepts which were taken over into these fields from
pure equilibrium analysis, like those of an equilibrium rate
of interest, could be properly defined only in terms of
assumptions concerning foresight. The situation seems
here to be that before we can explain why people commit
mistakes, we must first explain why they should ever be
right.

In general it seems that we have come to a point where
we all realise that the concept of equilibrium itself can be
made definite and clear only in terms of assumptions concerning foresight, although we may not yet all agree what
exactly these essential assumptions are. This question will
occupy me later in this paper. At the moment I am only
concerned to show that at the present juncture, whether
we want to define the boundaries of economic statics or
whether we want to go beyond it, we cannot escape the
vexed problem of the exact position which assumptions
about foresight are to have in our reasoning. Can this be
merely an accident ?

As I have already suggested, the reason for this seems
to me to be that we have to deal here only with a special
aspect of a much wider question which we ought to have
faced at a much earlier point. Questions essentially similar
to those mentioned arise in fact as soon as we try to apply
the system of tautologies—those series of propositions which
are necessarily true because they are merely transformations
of the assumptions from which we start, and which constitute the main content of equilibrium analysis[1]—to the

---

[1] I should like to make it clear from the outset that I use the term " equilibrium analysis "
throughout this paper in the narrower sense in which it is equivalent to what Professor Hans
Mayer has christened the " functional " (as distinguished from the " causal- genetic ") approach,
and to what used to be loosely described as the " mathematical school ". It is true round this
approach that most of the theoretical discussions of the past ten or fifteen years have taken
place. It is true that Professor Mayer has held out before us the prospect of another, " causal-
genetic " approach, but it can hardly be denied that this is still largely a promise. It should,

situation of a society consisting of several independent persons. I have long felt that the concept of equilibrium itself and the methods which we employ in pure analysis, have a clear meaning only when confined to the analysis of the action of a single person, and that we are really passing into a different sphere and silently introducing a new element of altogether different character when we apply it to the explanation of the interactions of a number of different individuals.

I am certain there are many who regard with impatience and distrust the whole tendency, which is inherent in all modern equilibrium analysis, to turn economics into a branch of pure logic, a set of self-evident propositions which, like mathematics or geometry, are subject to no other test but internal consistency. But it seems that if only this process is carried far enough it carries its own remedy with it. In distilling from our reasoning about the facts of economic life those parts which are truly *a priori*, we not only isolate one element of our reasoning as a sort of Pure Logic of Choice in all its purity, but we also isolate, and emphasise the importance of, another element which has been too much neglected. My criticism of the recent tendencies to make economic theory more and more formal is not that they have gone too far, but that they have not yet been carried far enough to complete the isolation of this branch of logic and to restore to its rightful place the investigation of causal processes, using formal economic theory as a tool in the same way as mathematics.

II

But before I can prove my contention that the tautological propositions of pure equilibrium analysis as such are not directly applicable to the explanation of social relations, I must first show that the concept of equilibrium *has* a clear meaning if applied to the actions of a single individual, and what this meaning is. Against my contention it might be argued that it is precisely here that the concept of equilibrium is of no significance, because, if one

however, be mentioned here that some of the most stimulating suggestions on problems closely related to those treated here have come from his circle. Cf., H. Mayer, "Der Erkenntniswert der funktionellen Preistheorien," *Die Wirtschaftstheorie der Gegenwart*, Vol. II, 1931; P. N. Rosenstein-Rodan, " Das Zeitmoment in der mathematischen Theorie des wirtschaftlichen Gleichgewichts," *Zeitschrift für Nationalökonomie*, Vol. I, No. 1, and " The Rôle of Time in Economic Theory," ECONOMICA (N.S.), Vol. I (1), 1934.

wanted to apply it, all one could say would be that an isolated person was always in equilibrium. But this last statement, although a truism, shows nothing but the way in which the concept of equilibrium is typically misused. What is relevant is not whether a person as such is or is not in equilibrium, but which of his actions stand in equilibrium relationships to each other. All propositions of equilibrium analysis, such as the proposition that relative values will correspond to relative costs, or that a person will equalise the marginal returns of any one factor in its different uses, are propositions about the relations between actions. Actions of a person can be said to be in equilibrium in so far as they can be understood as part of one plan. Only if this is the case, only if all these actions have been decided upon at one and the same moment, and in consideration of the same set of circumstances, have our statements about their interconnections, which we deduce from our assumptions about the knowledge and the preferences of the person, any application. It is important to remember that the so-called " data ", from which we set out in this sort of analysis, are (apart from his tastes) all facts given to the person in question, the things as they are known to (or believed by) him to exist, and not in any sense objective facts. It is only because of this that the propositions we deduce are necessarily *a priori* valid, and that we preserve the consistency of the argument.[1]

The two main conclusions from these considerations are, *firstly*, that since equilibrium relations exist between the successive actions of a person only in so far as they are part of the execution of the same plan, any change in the relevant knowledge of the person, that is, any change which leads him to alter his plan, disrupts the equilibrium relation between his actions taken before and those taken after the change in his knowledge. In other words, the equilibrium relationship comprises only his actions during the period during which his anticipations prove correct. *Secondly*, that since equilibrium is a relationship between actions, and since the actions of one person must necessarily take place successively in time, it is obvious that the passage of time is essential to give the concept of equilibrium any meaning. This deserves mention since many economists

[1] Cf., on this point particularly L. Mises, *Grundprobleme der Nationalökonomie*, Jena, 1933, pp. 22 *et seq.*, 160 *et seq.*

appear to have been unable to find a place for time in equilibrium analysis and consequently have suggested that equilibrium must be conceived as timeless. This seems to me to be a meaningless statement.

III

Now, in spite of what I have said before about the doubtful meaning of equilibrium analysis in this sense if applied to the conditions of a competitive society, I do not of course want to deny that the concept was originally introduced precisely to describe the idea of some sort of balance between the actions of different individuals. All I have argued so far is that the sense in which we use the concept of equilibrium to describe the interdependence of the different actions of one person does not immediately admit of application to the relations between actions of different people. The question really is what use we make of it when we speak of equilibrium with reference to a competitive system.

The first answer which would seem to follow from our approach is that equilibrium in this connection exists if the actions of all members of the society over a period are all executions of their respective individual plans on which each decided at the beginning of the period. But when we inquire further what exactly this implies, it appears that this answer raises more difficulties than it solves. There is no special difficulty about the concept of an isolated person (or a group of persons directed by one of them) acting over a period according to a preconceived plan. In this case, the execution of the plan need not satisfy any special criteria in order to be conceivable. It may of course be based on wrong assumptions concerning the external facts and on this account may have to be changed. But there will always be a conceivable set of external events which would make it possible for the plan to be executed as originally conceived.

The situation is, however, different with the plans determined upon simultaneously but independently by a number of persons. In the first instance, in order that all these plans can be carried out, it is necessary for them to be based on the expectation of the same set of external events, since, if different people were to base their plans on conflicting expectations, no set of external events could make the execution of all these plans possible. And, secondly, in a society based on exchange their plans will to a considerable extent refer to actions which require corresponding actions on the part of other individuals. This means that the plans of different individuals must in a special sense be compatible if it is to be even conceivable that they will be able to carry all of them out.[1] Or, to put the same thing in different words, since some of the " data " on which any one person will base his plans will be the expectation that other people will act in a particular way, it is essential for the compatibility of the different plans that the plans of the one contain exactly those actions which form the data for the plans of the other.

In the traditional treatment of equilibrium analysis part of this difficulty is apparently avoided by the assumption that the data, in the form of demand schedules representing individual tastes and technical facts, will be equally given to all individuals and that their acting on the same premises will somehow lead to their plans becoming adapted to each other. That this does not really overcome the difficulty created by the fact that one person's decisions are the other person's data, and that it involves to some degree circular reasoning, has often been pointed out. What, however, seems so far to have escaped notice is that this whole procedure involves a confusion of a much more general character, of which the point just mentioned is just a special instance, and which is due to an equivocation of the term " datum ". The data which now are supposed to be objective facts and the same for all people are evidently no longer the same thing as the data which formed the starting point for the tautological transformations of the Pure Logic of Choice. There " data " meant all facts, and only the facts, which were present in the mind of the acting person, and only this subjective interpretation of the term datum made those propositions necessary truths. " Datum " meant given,

---

[1] It has long been a subject of wonder to me why there should, to my knowledge, have been no systematic attempts in sociology to analyse social relations in terms of correspondence and non-correspondence, or compatibility and non-compatibility, of individual aims and desires. It seems that the mathematical technique of *analysis situs* (topology) and particularly such concepts developed by it as that of *homeomorphism* might prove very useful in this connection, although it may appear doubtful whether even this technique, at any rate in the present state of its development, is adequate to the complexity of the structures with which we have to deal. A first attempt made recently in this direction by an eminent mathematician (Karl Menger, *Moral, Wille und Weltgestaltung*, Vienna, 1934) has so far not yet led to very illuminating results. But we may look forward with interest to the treatise on exact sociological theory which Professor Menger has promised for the near future. (Cf.," Einige neuere Fortschritte in der exakten Behandlung sozialwissenschaftlicher Probleme," in *Neuere Fortschritte in den exakten Wissenschaften*, Vienna, 1936, p. 132.)

known, to the person under consideration. But in the
transition from the analysis of the action of an individual
to the analysis of the situation in a society the concept has
undergone an insidious change of meaning.

IV

The confusion about the concept of a datum is at the
bottom of so many of our difficulties in this field that it is
necessary to consider it in somewhat more detail. Datum
means of course something given, but the question which
is left open, and which in the social sciences is capable of
two different answers, is to whom the facts are supposed
to be given. Economists appear subconsciously always to
have been somewhat uneasy about this point, and to have
reassured themselves against the feeling that they did not
quite know to whom the facts were given by underlining
the fact that they *were* given — even by using such
pleonastic expressions as " given data ". But this does
not solve the question whether the facts referred to are
supposed to be given to the observing economist, or to the
persons whose actions he wants to explain, and if to the
latter, whether it is assumed that the same facts are known
to all the different persons in the system, or whether the
" data " for the different persons may be different.

There seems to be no possible doubt that these two concepts of " data ", on the one hand in the sense of the objective
real facts, as the observing economist is supposed to know
them, and on the other in the subjective sense, as things
known to the persons whose behaviour we try to explain,
are really fundamentally different and ought to be kept
carefully apart. And, as we shall see, the question why the
data in the subjective sense of the term should ever come
to correspond to the objective data is one of the main problems
we have to answer.

The usefulness of the distinction becomes immediately
apparent when we apply it to the question of what we can
mean by the concept of a society being at any one moment
in a state of equilibrium. There are evidently two senses
in which it can be said that the subjective data, given to
the different persons, and the individual plans, which
necessarily follow from them, are in agreement. We may
merely mean that these plans are mutually compatible and
that there is consequently a conceivable set of external

events which will allow all people to carry out their plans and not cause any disappointments. If this mutual compatibility of intentions were not given, and if in consequence no set of external events could satisfy all expectations, we could clearly say that this is not a state of equilibrium. We have a situation where a revision of the plans on the part of at least some people is inevitable, or, to use a phrase which in the past has had a rather vague meaning, but which seems to fit this case perfectly, where endogenous disturbances are inevitable.

There is, however, still the other question of whether the individual subjective sets of data correspond to the objective data, and whether in consequence the expectations on which plans were based are borne out by the facts. If correspondence between data in this sense were required for equilibrium it would never be possible to decide otherwise than *ex post*, at the end of the period for which people have planned, whether at the beginning the society has been in equilibrium. It seems to be more in conformity with established usage to say in such a case that the equilibrium, as defined in the first sense, may be disturbed by an unforeseen development of the (objective) data, and to describe this as an exogenous disturbance. In fact it seems hardly possible to attach any definite meaning to the much used concept of a change in the (objective) data unless we distinguish between external developments in conformity with, and those different from, general expectations, and define as a " change " any divergence of the actual from the expected development, irrespective of whether it means a " change " in some absolute sense. Surely if the alternations of the seasons suddenly ceased and the weather remained constant from a certain day onward, this would represent a change of data in our sense, that is a change relative to expectations, although in an absolute sense it would not represent a change but rather an absence of change. But all this means that we can speak of a change in data only if equilibrium in the first sense exists, that is, if expectations coincide. If they conflicted, any development of the external facts might bear out somebody's expectations and disappoint those of others, and there would be no possibility of deciding what was a change in the objective data.[1]

[1] Cf. " The Maintenance of Capital," ECONOMICA (N.S.), Vol. II, 1935, p. 265.

V

For a society then we *can* speak of a *state* of equilibrium at a point of time—but it means only that compatibility exists between the different plans which the individuals composing it have made for action in time. And equilibrium will continue, once it exists, so long as the external data correspond to the common expectations of all the members of the society. The continuance of a state of equilibrium in this sense is then not dependent on the objective data being constant in an absolute sense, and is not necessarily confined to a stationary process. Equilibrium analysis becomes in principle applicable to a progressive society and to those inter-temporal price relationships which have given us so much trouble in recent times.[1]

These considerations seem to throw considerable light on the relationship between equilibrium and foresight, which has been somewhat hotly debated in recent times.[2] It appears that the concept of equilibrium merely means that the foresight of the different members of the society is in a special sense correct. It must be correct in the sense that every person's plan is based on the expectation of just those actions of other people which those other people intend to perform, and that all these plans are based on the expectation of the same set of external facts, so that under certain conditions nobody will have any reason to change his plans. Correct foresight is then not, as it has sometimes been understood, a precondition which must exist in order that equilibrium may be arrived at. It is rather

[1] This separation of the concept of equilibrium from that of a stationary state seems to me to be no more than the necessary outcome of a process which has been going on for a fairly long time. That this association of the two concepts is not essential but only due to historical reasons is to-day probably generally felt. If complete separation has not yet been effected, it is apparently only because no alternative definition of a state of equilibrium had yet been suggested which has made it possible to state in a general form those propositions of equilibrium analysis which are essentially independent of the concept of a stationary state. Yet it is evident that most of the propositions of equilibrium analysis are not supposed to be applicable only in that stationary state which will probably never be reached. The process of separation seems to have begun with Marshall and his distinction between long and short run equilibria. (Cf., statements like this : " For the nature of equilibrium itself, and that of the causes by which it is determined, depend on the length of the period over which the market is taken to extend." *Principles*, Vol. I, 6, 7th ed., p. 330.) The idea of a state of equilibrium which was not a stationary state was already inherent in my " Das intertemporale Gleichgewichtssystem der Preise und die Bewegungen des Geldwertes " (*Weltwirtschaftliches Archiv*, Vol. XXVIII, June, 1928) and is, of course, essential if we want to use the equilibrium apparatus for the explanation of any of the phenomena connected with " investment ". On the whole matter much historical information will be found in E. Schams, Komparative Statistik, *Zeitschrift für Nationalökonomie* II/1, 1930.

[2] Cf. particularly O. Morgenstern, " Vollkommene Voraussicht und Wirtschaftliches Gleichgewicht," *Zeitschrift für Nationalökonomie*, Vol. VI, p. 3.

the defining characteristic of a state of equilibrium. Nor need foresight for this purpose be perfect in the sense that it need extend into the indefinite future, or that everybody must foresee everything correctly. We should rather say that equilibrium will last so long as the anticipations prove correct, and that they need to be correct only on those points which are relevant for the decisions of the individuals. But on this question of what is relevant foresight or knowledge, more later.

Before I proceed further I should probably stop for a moment to illustrate by a concrete example what I have just said about the meaning of a state of equilibrium and how it can be disturbed. Consider the preparations which will be going on at any moment for the production of houses. Brickmakers, plumbers and others will all be producing materials which in each case will correspond to a certain quantity of houses for which just this quantity of the particular material will be required. Similarly we may conceive of prospective buyers as accumulating savings which will enable them at certain dates to buy definite quantities of houses. If all these activities represent preparations for the production (and acquisition) of the same amount of houses we can say that there is equilibrium between them in the sense that all the people engaged in them may find that they can carry out their plans.[1] This need not be so, because other circumstances which are not part of their plan of action may turn out to be different from what they expected. Part of the materials may be destroyed by an accident, weather conditions may make building impossible, or an invention may alter the proportions in which the different factors are wanted. This is what we call a change in the (objective) data, which disturbs the equilibrium which has existed. But if the different plans were from

---

[1] Another example of more general importance would, of course, be the correspondence between "investment" and "saving" in the sense of the proportion (in terms of relative cost) in which entrepreneurs provide producers' goods and consumers' goods for a particular date, and the proportion in which consumers in general will at this date distribute their resources between producers' goods and consumers' goods. (Cf. my "Preiserwartungen, monetäre Störungen und Fehlinvestitionen," *Ekonomisk Tidskrift*, Vol. 34, 1935 (French translation : "Prévisions de Prix, Perturbations Monétaires et Faux Investissements," *Revue des Sciences Economiques*, October, 1935) and "The Maintenance of Capital," ECONOMICA (N.S.), Vol. II, 1935, pp. 268–273.) It may be of interest in this connection to mention that in the course of investigations of the same field, which led the present author to these speculations, the theory of crises, the great French sociologist G. Tarde stressed the "contradiction de croyances" or "contradiction de jugements" or "contradictions des espérances" as the main cause of these phenomena (*Psychologie Economique*, Paris, 1902, Vol. II, pp. 128–9 ; Cf. also N. Pinkus, *Das Problem des Normalen in der Nationalökonomie*, Leipzig, 1906, pp. 252 and 275).

the beginning incompatible, it is inevitable that somebody's plans will be upset and have to be altered, and that in consequence the whole complex of actions over the period will not show those characteristics which apply if all the actions of each individual can be understood as part of a single individual plan he has made at the beginning.[1]

VI

When in all this I emphasise the distinction between mere inter-compatibility of the individual plans[2] and the correspondence between them and the actual external facts or objective data, I do not of course mean to suggest that the subjective inter-agreement is not in some way brought about by the external facts. There would of course be no reason why the subjective data of different people should ever correspond unless they were due to the experience of the same objective facts. But the point is that pure equilibrium analysis is not concerned with the way in which this correspondence is brought about. In the description of an existing state of equilibrium which it provides, it is simply assumed that the subjective data coincide with the objective facts. The equilibrium relationships cannot be deduced merely from the objective facts, since the analysis of what people will do can only start from what is known to them. Nor can equilibrium analysis start merely from a given set of subjective data, since the subjective data of different people would be either compatible or incompatible, that is, they would already determine whether equilibrium did or did not exist.

We shall not get much further here unless we ask for the reasons for our concern with the admittedly fictitious state of equilibrium. Whatever may occasionally have been said by over-pure economists, there seems to be no possible

---

[1] It is an interesting question, but one which I cannot discuss here, whether in order that we can speak of equilibrium, every single individual must be right, or whether it would not be sufficient if, in consequence of a compensation of errors in different directions, quantities of the different commodities coming on the market were the same as if every individual had been right. It seems to me as if equilibrium in the strict sense would require the first condition to be satisfied, but I can conceive that a wider concept, requiring only the second condition, might occasionally be useful. A fuller discussion of this problem would have to consider the whole question of the significance which some economists (including Pareto) attach to the law of great numbers in this connection. On the general point see P. N. Rosenstein-Rodan, " The Coordination of the General Theories of Money and Price," ECONOMICA, August, 1936.

[2] Or, since in view of the tautological character of the Pure Logic of Choice, " individual plans " and " subjective data " can be used interchangeably, between the agreement between the subjective data of the different individuals.

doubt that the only justification for this is the supposed existence of a tendency towards equilibrium. It is only with this assertion that economics ceases to be an exercise in pure logic and becomes an empirical science ; and it is to economics as an empirical science that we must now turn.

In the light of our analysis of the meaning of a state of equilibrium it should be easy to say what is the real content of the assertion that a tendency towards equilibrium exists. It can hardly mean anything but that under certain conditions the knowledge and intentions of the different members of society are supposed to come more and more into agreement, or, to put the same thing in less general and less exact but more concrete terms, that the expectations of the people and particularly of the entrepreneurs will become more and more correct. In this form the assertion of the existence of a tendency towards equilibrium is clearly an empirical proposition, that is, an assertion about what happens in the real world which ought, at least in principle, to be capable of verification. And it gives our somewhat abstract statement a rather plausible common-sense meaning. The only trouble is that we are still pretty much in the dark about (*a*) the *conditions* under which this tendency is supposed to exist, and (*b*) the nature of the *process* by which individual knowledge is changed.

VII

In the usual presentations of equilibrium analysis it is generally made to appear as if these questions of how the equilibrium comes about were solved. But if we look closer it soon becomes evident that these apparent demonstrations amount to no more than the apparent proof of what is already assumed.[1] The device generally adopted for this purpose is the assumption of a perfect market where every event becomes known instantaneously to every member. It is necessary to remember here that the perfect market which is required to satisfy the assumptions of equilibrium analysis must not be confined to the markets of all the individual commodities ; the whole economic system must be assumed

---

[1] This seems to be implicitly admitted, although hardly consciously recognised, when in recent times it is frequently stressed that equilibrium analysis only describes the conditions of equilibrium without attempting to derive the position of equilibrium from the data. Equilibrium analysis in this sense would, of course, be pure logic and contain no assertions about the real world.

ECONOMICS AND KNOWLEDGE

to be one perfect market in which everybody knows everything. The assumption of a perfect market then means nothing less than that all the members of the community, even if they are not supposed to be strictly omniscient, are at least supposed to know automatically all that is relevant for their decisions. It seems that that skeleton in our cupboard, the " economic man ", whom we have exorcised with prayer and fasting, has returned through the back door in the form of a quasi-omniscient individual.

The statement that, if people know everything, they are in equilibrium is true simply because that is how we define equilibrium. The assumption of a perfect market in this sense is just another way of saying that equilibrium exists, but does not get us any nearer an explanation of when and how such a state will come about. It is clear that if we want to make the assertion that under certain conditions people will approach that state we must explain by what process they will acquire the necessary knowledge. Of course any assumption about the actual acquisition of knowledge in the course of this process will also be of a hypothetical character. But this does not mean that all such assumptions are equally justified. We have to deal here with assumptions about causation, so that what we assume must not only be regarded as possible (which is certainly not the case if we just regard people as omniscient) but must also be regarded as likely to be true, and it must be possible, at least in principle, to demonstrate that it is true in particular cases.

The essential point. here is that it is these apparently subsidiary hypotheses or assumptions that people do learn from experience, and about how they acquire knowledge, which constitute the empirical content of our propositions about what happens in the real world. They usually appear disguised and incomplete as a description of the type of market to which our proposition refers ; but this is only one, though perhaps the most important, aspect of the more general problem of how knowledge is acquired and communicated. The important thing of which economists frequently do not seem to be aware is that the nature of these hypotheses is in many respects rather different from the more general assumptions from which the Pure Logic of Choice starts. The main differences seem to me to be two :

Firstly, the assumptions from which the Pure Logic of Choice starts are facts which we know to be common to all human thought. They may be regarded as axioms which define or delimit the field within which we are able to understand or mentally to reconstruct the processes of thought of other people. They are therefore universally applicable to the field in which we are interested—although of course where *in concreto* the limits of this field are is an empirical question. They refer to a type of human action (what we commonly call rational, or even merely conscious, as distinguished from instinctive action) rather than to the particular conditions under which this action is undertaken. But the assumptions or hypotheses, which we have to introduce when we want to explain the social processes, concern the relation of the thought of an individual to the outside world, the question to what extent and how his knowledge corresponds to the external facts. And the hypotheses must necessarily run in terms of assertions about causal connections, about how experience creates knowledge.

Secondly, while in the field of the Pure Logic of Choice our analysis can be made exhaustive, that is, while we can here develop a formal apparatus which covers all conceivable situations, the supplementary hypotheses must of necessity be selective, that is, we must select from the infinite variety of possible situations such ideal types as for some reason we regard as specially relevant to conditions in the real world.[1] Of course we could also develop a separate science, the subject matter of which was *per definitionem* confined to a " perfect market " or some similarly defined object, just as the Logic of Choice applies only to persons who have to allot limited means among a variety of ends. And for the field so defined our propositions would again become *a priori* true. But for such a procedure we should lack the justification which consists in the assumption that the situation in the real world is similar to what we assume it to be.

---

[1] The distinction drawn here may help to solve the old difference between economists and sociologists about the rôle which " ideal types " play in the reasoning of economic theory. The sociologists used to emphasise that the usual procedure of economic theory involved the assumption of particular ideal types, while the economic theorist pointed out that his reasoning was of such generality that he need not make use of any " ideal types ". The truth seems to be that within the field of the Pure Logic of Choice, in which the economist was largely interested, he was right in his assertion, but that as soon as he wanted to use it for the explanation of a social process he had to use " ideal types " of one sort or another.

VIII

I must now turn to the question of what the concrete hypotheses are concerning the conditions under which people are supposed to acquire the relevant knowledge and the process by which they are supposed to acquire it. If it were at all clear what the hypotheses usually employed in this respect were, we should have to scrutinise them in two respects : we should have to investigate whether they were necessary and sufficient to explain a movement towards equilibrium, and we should have to show to what extent they were borne out by reality. But I am afraid I am now getting to a stage where it becomes exceedingly difficult to say what exactly are the assumptions on the basis of which we assert that there will be a tendency towards equilibrium, and to claim that our analysis has an application to the real world. I cannot pretend that I have as yet got much further on this point. Consequently all I can do is to ask a number of questions to which we shall have to find an answer if we want to be clear about the significance of our argument.

The only condition, about the necessity of which for the establishment of an equilibrium economists seem to be fairly agreed, is the " constancy of the data ". But after what we have seen about the vagueness of the concept of " datum " we shall suspect, and rightly, that this does not get us much farther. Even if we assume—as we probably must—that here the term is used in its objective sense (which includes, it will be remembered, the preferences of the different individuals) it is by no means clear that this is either required or sufficient in order that people shall actually acquire the necessary knowledge, or that it was meant as a statement of the conditions under which they will do so. It is rather significant that at any rate some authors[1] feel it necessary to add " perfect knowledge " as an additional and separate condition. And indeed we shall see that constancy of the objective data is neither a necessary nor a sufficient condition. That it cannot be a necessary condition follows from the facts, firstly, that nobody would want to interpret it in the absolute sense that nothing must ever happen in the world, and, secondly, that, as we have seen, as soon as we want to include changes which occur periodically or

---

[1] *Vide* N. Kaldor, " A Classificatory Note on the Determinateness of Equilibrium," *Review of Economic Studies*, Vol. I, No. 2, 1934, p. 123.

perhaps even changes which proceed at a constant rate, the only way in which we can define constancy is with reference to expectations. All that this condition amounts to then is that there must be some discernible regularity in the world which makes it possible to predict events correctly. But while this is clearly not sufficient to prove that people will learn to foresee events correctly, the same is true to a hardly less degree even about constancy of data in an absolute sense. For any one individual, constancy of the data does in no way mean constancy of all the facts independent of himself, since, of course, only the tastes and not the actions of the other people can in this sense be assumed to be constant. And as all those other people will change their decisions as they gain experience about the external facts and other people's action, there is no reason why these processes of successive changes should ever come to an end. These difficulties are well known[1] and I only mention them here to remind you how little we actually know about the conditions under which an equilibrium will ever be reached. But I do not propose to follow this line of approach further, though not because this question of the empirical probability that people will learn (that is, that their subjective data will come to correspond with each other and with the objective facts) is lacking in unsolved and highly interesting problems. The reason is rather that there seems to me to be another and more fruitful way of approach to the central problem.

IX

The questions I have just discussed concerning the conditions under which people are likely to acquire the necessary knowledge, and the process by which they will acquire it, has at least received some attention in past discussions. But there is a further question which seems to me to be at least equally important, but which appears to have received no attention at all, and that is how much knowledge and what sort of knowledge the different individuals must possess in order that we may be able to speak of equilibrium. It is clear that if the concept is to have any empirical significance it cannot presuppose that everybody knows everything. I have already had to use the undefined term " relevant

---

[1] On all this cf. N. Kaldor, loc. cit., *passim.*

knowledge ", that is, the knowledge which is relevant to a particular person. But what is this relevant knowledge ? It can hardly mean simply the knowledge which actually influenced his actions, because his decisions might have been different not only if, for instance, the knowledge he possessed had been correct instead of incorrect, but also if he had possessed knowledge about altogether different fields.

Clearly there is here a problem of the *Division of Knowledge* which is quite analogous to, and at least as important as, the problem of the division of labour. But while the latter has been one of the main subjects of investigation ever since the beginning of our science, the former has been as completely neglected, although it seems to me to be the really central problem of economics as a social science.[1] The problem which we pretend to solve is how the spontaneous interaction of a number of people, each possessing only bits of knowledge, brings about a state of affairs in which prices correspond to costs, *etc.*, and which could be brought about by deliberate direction only by somebody who possessed the combined knowledge of all those individuals. And experience shows us that something of this sort does happen, since the empirical observation that prices do tend to correspond to costs was the beginning of our science. But in our analysis, instead of showing what bits of information the different persons must possess in order to bring about that result, we fall in effect back on the assumption that everybody knows everything and so evade any real solution of the problem.

Before, however, we can proceed further, to consider this division of knowledge among different persons, it is necessary to become more specific about the sort of knowledge which is relevant in this connection. It has become customary among economists to stress only the need of knowledge of prices, apparently because—as a consequence of the confusions between objective and subjective data— the complete knowledge of the objective facts was taken for granted. In recent times even the knowledge of current prices has been taken so much for granted that the only connection in which the question of knowledge has been regarded as problematic has been the anticipation of future

[1] I am not certain, but I hope, that the distinction between the Pure Logic of Choice and economics as a social science is essentially the same distinction as that which Professor A. Ammon has in mind when he stresses again and again that a " *Theorie des Wirtschaftens* " is not yet a " *Theorie der Volkswirtschaft* ".

prices. But, as I have already indicated at the beginning, price expectations and even the knowledge of current prices are only a very small section of the problem of knowledge as I see it. The wider aspect of the problem of knowledge with which I am concerned is the knowledge of the basic fact of how the different commodities can be obtained and used,[1] and under what conditions they are actually obtained and used, that is, the general question of why the subjective data to the different persons correspond to the objective facts. Our problem of knowledge here is just the existence of this correspondence which in much of current equilibrium analysis is simply assumed to exist, but which we have to explain if we want to show why the propositions, which are necessarily true about the attitude of a person towards things which he believes to have certain properties, should come to be true of the actions of society with regard to things which either do possess these properties, or which, for some reason we shall have to explain, are commonly believed by the members of society to possess these properties.[2]

But to revert to the special problem I have been discussing, the amount of knowledge different individuals must possess in order that equilibrium may prevail (or the " relevant " knowledge they must possess), we shall get nearer to an answer if we remember how it can become apparent either that equilibrium did not exist or that it is being disturbed. We have seen that the equilibrium connections will be severed if any person changes his plans, either because his

---

[1] Knowledge in this sense is more than what is usually described as skill, and the division of knowledge of which we here speak more than is meant by the division of labour. To put it shortly, " skill " refers only to the knowledge of which a person makes use in his trade, while the further knowledge about which we must know something in order to be able to say anything about the processes in society, is the knowledge of alternative possibilities of action of which he makes no direct use. It may be added here that knowledge, in the sense in which the term is here used, is identical with foresight only in the sense in which all knowledge is capacity to predict.

[2] That all propositions of economic theory refer to things which are defined in terms of human attitudes towards them, that is, that for instance the " sugar " about which economic theory may occasionally speak, is not defined by its " objective " qualities, but by the fact that people believe that it will serve certain needs of theirs in a certain way, is the source of all sorts of difficulties and confusions, particularly in connection with the problem of " verification ". It is, of course, also in this connection that the contrast between the *verstehende* social science and the behaviourist approach becomes so glaring. I am not certain that the behaviourists in the social sciences are quite aware of *how* much of the traditional approach they would have to abandon if they wanted to be consistent, or that they would want to adhere to it consistently if they were aware of this. It would, for instance, imply that propositions of the theory of money would have to refer exclusively to, say, " round discs of metal, bearing a certain stamp," or some similarly defined physical object or group of objects.

tastes change (which does not concern us here) or because new facts become known to him. But there are evidently two different ways in which he may learn of new facts which make him change his plans, which for our purposes are of altogether different significance. He may learn of the new facts as it were by accident, that is in a way which is not a necessary consequence of his attempt to execute his original plan, or it may be inevitable that in the course of his attempt he will find that the facts are different from what he expected. It is obvious that, in order that he may proceed according to plan, his knowledge needs to be correct only on the points on which it will necessarily be confirmed or corrected in the course of the execution of the plan. But he may have no knowledge of things which, if he possessed it, would certainly affect his plan.

The conclusion then which we must draw is that the relevant knowledge which he must possess in order that equilibrium may prevail is the knowledge which he is bound to acquire in view of the position in which he originally is, and the plans which he then makes. It is certainly not all the knowledge which, if he acquired it by accident, would be useful to him, and lead to a change in his plan. And we may therefore very well have a position of equilibrium only because some people have no chance of learning about facts which, if they knew them, would induce them to alter their plans. Or, in other words, it is only relative to the knowledge which a person is bound to acquire in the course of the carrying out of his original plan and its successive alterations that an equilibrium is likely to be reached.

While such a position represents in one sense a position of equilibrium, it is however clear that it is not an equilibrium in the special sense in which equilibrium is regarded as a sort of optimum position. In order that the results of the combination of individual bits of knowledge should be comparable to the results of direction by an omniscient dictator, further conditions must apparently be introduced.[1] And while it seems quite clear that it is possible to define the amount of knowledge which individuals must possess in order that this result should be obtained, I know of no real attempt in this direction. One condition would

---

[1] These conditions are usually described as absence of " frictions ". In a recently published article (" Quantity of Capital and the Rate of Interest," *Journal of Political Economy*, Vol. XLIV/5, 1936, p. 638) Professor F. H. Knight rightly points out that " ' error ' is the usual meaning of friction in economic discussion ".

probably be that each of the alternative uses of any sort of resources is known to the owner of some such resources actually used for another purpose and that in this way all the different uses of these resources are connected, either directly or indirectly.[1] But I mention this condition only as an instance of how it will in most cases be sufficient that in each field there is a certain margin of people who possess among them all the relevant knowledge. To elaborate this further would be an interesting and a very important task, but a task that would far exceed the limits of this paper.

But although what I have said on this point has been largely in the form of a criticism, I do not want to appear unduly despondent about what we have already achieved in this field. Even if we have jumped over an essential link in our argument, I still believe that by what is implicit in its reasoning, economics has come nearer than any other social science to an answer to that central question of all social sciences, how the combination of fragments of knowledge existing in different minds can bring about results which, if they were to be brought about deliberately, would require a knowledge on the part of the directing mind which no single person can possess. To show that in this sense the spontaneous actions of individuals will under conditions which we can define bring about a distribution of resources which can be understood as if it were made according to a single plan, although nobody has planned it, seems to me indeed an answer to the problem which has sometimes been metaphorically described as that of the " social mind ". But we must not be surprised that such claims on our part have usually been rejected by sociologists, since we have not based them on the right grounds.

There is only one more point in this connection which

---

[1] This would be one, but probably not yet a sufficient, condition to ensure that, with a given state of demand, the marginal productivity of the different factors of production in their different uses should be equalised and that in this sense an equilibrium of production should be brought about. That it is not necessary, as one might think, that every possible alternative use of any kind of resources should be known to at least one among the owners of each group of such resources which are used for one particular purpose is due to the fact that the alternatives known to the owners of the resources in a particular use are reflected in the prices of these resources. In this way it may be a sufficient distribution of knowledge of the alternative uses, $m, n, o, \ldots y, z$, of a commodity, if A, who uses the quantity of these resources in his possession for m, knows of n, and B, who uses his for n, knows of m, while C who uses his for o, knows of n, etc., etc., until we get to L, who uses his for z, but only knows of y. I am not clear to what extent in addition to this a particular distribution of the knowledge of the different proportions is required in which different factors can be combined in the production of any one commodity. For complete equilibrium additional assumptions will be required about the knowledge which consumers possess about the serviceability of the commodities for the satisfaction of their wants.

I should like to mention. This is that if the tendency towards equilibrium, which we have reason to believe to exist on empirical grounds, is only towards an equilibrium relative to that knowledge which people will acquire in the course of their economic activity, and if any other change of knowledge must be regarded as a " change in the data " in the usual sense of the term, which falls outside the sphere of equilibrium analysis, this would mean that equilibrium analysis can really tell us nothing about the significance of such changes in knowledge, and would go far to account for the fact that pure analysis seems to have so extraordinarily little to say about institutions, such as the press, the purpose of which is to communicate knowledge. And it might even explain why the preoccupation with pure analysis should so frequently create a peculiar blindness to the rôle played in real life by such institutions as advertising.

X

With these rather desultory remarks on topics which would deserve much more careful examination I must conclude my survey of these problems. There are only one or two further remarks which I want to add.

One is that, in stressing the nature of the empirical propositions of which we must make use if the formal apparatus of equilibrium analysis is to serve for an explanation of the real world, and in emphasising that the propositions about how people will learn, which are relevant in this connection, are of a fundamentally different nature from those of formal analysis, I do not mean to suggest that there opens here and now a wide field for empirical research. I very much doubt whether such investigation would teach us anything new. The important point is rather that we should become clear about what the questions of fact are on which the applicability of our argument to the real world depends, or, to put the same thing in other words, at what point our argument, when it is applied to phenomena of the real world, becomes subject to verification.

The second point is that I do not want of course to suggest that the sort of problems I have been discussing were foreign to the arguments of the economists of the older generations. The only objection that can be made against them is that they have so mixed up the two sorts of propositions, the *a priori* and the empirical, of which every realistic economist makes constant use, that it is frequently quite impossible to see what sort of validity they claimed for a particular statement. More recent work has been freer from this fault—but only at the price of leaving more and more obscure what sort of relevance their arguments had to the phenomena of the real world. All I have tried to do has been to find the way back to the common-sense meaning of our analysis, of which, I am afraid, we are apt to lose sight as our analysis becomes more elaborate. You may even feel that most of what I have said has been commonplace. But from time to time it is probably necessary to detach oneself from the technicalities of the argument and to ask quite naïvely what it is all about. If I have only shown that in some respects the answer to this question is not only not obvious, but that occasionally we do not even quite know what it is, I have succeeded in my purpose.

[3]

8

Equilibrium and the Market Process

S.C. Littlechild

Introduction

For many years, the concept of the market process made little headway against the prevailing concept of equilibrium. However, during the last decade or so, there has been increasing dissatisfaction with the straight-jacket of equilibrium and an increasing willingness to explore ideas of process. Uncertainty, expectations, learning, and revision of plans are phrases nowadays in common use.

Ironically, the leaders in this movement include mathematical economists, those whom Ludwig von Mises derided for "vain playing with mathematical symbols, a pastime not suited to convey any knowledge" (Mises 1966, p. 250). It seems appropriate therefore, to explore how far the latest ideas and models of mathematical economists are consistent with Austrian concepts of equilibrium and the market process and, specifically, with the views of the two major figures in the modern Austrian school: Ludwig von Mises and F.A. Hayek.

For this purpose, we shall examine the stimulating and provocative inaugural lecture given by F.H. Hahn (1973b) at the University of Cambridge, entitled "On the notion of equilibrium in economics."[1] This lecture is of interest and importance for several reasons. It contains a nontechnical guide to the rapidly growing mathematical literature going beyond the Arrow-Debreu model of general equilibrium, written by one who has been actively involved in those developments. It represents a major position statement on methodology by a sometime president of the Econometric Society. Finally, it constitutes a call for economists to take into consideration the sequential process by which actual economies evolve, a topic that until then had largely been neglected by mainstream economic theories.

We begin with an outline and comparison of the views of Mises and Hayek and then attempt to relate Hahn's ideas to this context. In the final sections we appraise Hahn's suggestion for the direction of future research in this area.

I should like to acknowledge helpful comments by F.H. Hahn, L.M. Lachmann, and G.J. Stigler on some early notes for this chapter and valuable discussion with I.M. Kirzner and L.H. White at the New York conference. Hahn and Lachmann have also commented on the revised version (see postscript).

86   Method, Process, and Austrian Economics

It is perhaps unnecessary to emphasize that a great number of economists, of very diverse backgrounds, have made useful and often potentially
important contributions to the understanding of the market process.[2] Limitations of time and space prevent a comprehensive survey, valuable though
that could be. In the confines of this chapter it seems most fruitful to concentrate on a detailed comparison of the ideas of three leading figures.

Mises's Views on Equilibrium and Market Process

For Mises, the market is a process. The state of the market is continually
changing. The market process is characterized by profits and losses as the
judgments made by entrepreneurs turn out to be correct or incorrect. A system in which there is no uncertainty about the future, and hence no profits
and losses, is not a possible state of affairs. However, an important role in
Mises's scheme of thought is played by the equilibrium concept of an
"evenly rotating economy," which is characterized by the elimination of
change and stability of prices. How can this be?

Mises certainly acknowledges—indeed emphasizes—that the perfect
foresight implied by such an economy is not characteristic of the real world,
but to analyse the problems of change one has to confront them with a fictitious state in which change is absent.

> Such a rigid system is not peopled with living men making choices and
> liable to error, it is a world of soulless unthinking automatons; it is not a
> human society it is an ant-hill.

> These insoluble contradictions, however, do not affect the service which
> this imaginary construction renders for the only problems for whose treat-
> ment it is both appropriate and indispensable: the problem of the relation
> between the prices of products and those of the factors required for their
> production, and the implied problems of entrepreneurship and of profit
> and loss (Mises 1966, p. 248).

The concept of evenly rotating economy is useful, in Mises's view, precisely because of "the tendency, prevailing in every action, toward the
establishment of an evenly rotating economy" (1966, p. 250). He explains
that the logical (nonmathematical) economist shows how

> the activities of enterprising men, the promoters and speculators, eager to
> profit from discrepancies in the price structure, tend toward eradicating
> such discrepancies and thereby also toward blotting out the sources of
> entrepreneurial profit and loss. He shows how this process would finally
> result in the establishment of the evenly rotating economy (1966, pp.
> 355–356).

The use of the concept of the evenly rotating economy reflects Mises's view that "the method of economics is the method of imaginary constructions" (Mises 1966, p. 236). This involves "abstract[ing] from the operation of some conditions present in actual action. Then we are in a position to grasp the hypothetical consequences of the absence of these conditions and to conceive the effects of their existence" (p. 237). Parenthetically, we may question whether "the method of imaginary constructions is justified by its success" (p. 236). Do we really need the concept of the evenly rotating economy "to grasp the function of enterpreneurship and the meaning of profit and loss" (p. 248), or to obtain "the insight that dealing with the uncertain conditions of the unknown future—that is, speculation—is inherent in every action, and that profit and loss are necessary features of acting which cannot be conjured away by any wishful thinking" (p. 250)?

Finally, we may emphasize once again that Mises does not claim that equilibrium is—at least in certain places, at certain times, and for certain purposes—a reasonably close approximation to the real world. Unlike (most) neoclassical economists, Mises explicitly rejects such a claim:

> It is furthermore absurd to believe that the services rendered by the construction of an evenly rotating economy are the more valuable the more the object of our studies, the realm of real action, corresponds to this construction in respect to absence of change. The static method, the employment of the imaginary construction of an evenly rotating economy, is the only adequate method of analyzing the changes concerned without regard to whether they are great or small, sudden or slow (1966, p. 248).

Similarly, part of Mises's criticism of mathematical economists is that "they deal with equilibrium as if it were a real entity and not a limiting notion, a mere mental tool" (p. 250).

Hayek on Economics and Knowledge

Hayek has championed the cause of process versus equilibrium just as vigorously as Mises. "The Meaning of Competition" is devoted to the thesis that "competition is by its nature a dynamic process whose essential characteristics are assumed away by the assumptions underlying static analysis" (Hayek 1946, p. 94). This general coincidence of views is not surprising, given that Hayek was a pupil of Mises and educated in the same Austrian school of thought. Nevertheless, the direction and extent of influence are by no means clear. Hayek's seminal paper on "Economics and Knowledge" was delivered in London in 1936, and he refers to a related idea inherent in an article published in German in 1928. In contrast, the first edition of *Human Action* was not published until 1949, although it is based to some extent on a treatise written in German in 1940, and it has been suggested that Mises probably conceived the idea of the market process around 1910 (Lachmann 1971, p. 193).

"Economics and Knowledge" contains the most explicit statement of Hayek's views on equilibrium. He defines the actions of a person as in equilibrium insofar as they can be understood as part of a single plan. Since equilibrium is a relationship between actions, which must necessarily take place successively in time, "it is obvious that the passage of time is essential to give the concept of equilibrium any meaning" (Hayek 1937, p. 37). Following this line of approach, a society can be said to be in equilibrium at a point in time, but only in the sense that the different plans of the individuals comprising it are mutually compatible. Such an equilibrium, once it exists, will continue only so long as the external data correspond to the common expectations of the members of the society.

Equilibrium is thus defined, not in terms of prices and quantities, but in terms of expectations and plans. As a result, the concept of equilibrium is clearly separated from the concept of a stationary state. Hayek's role in the origination of this idea has recently been affirmed (Milgate 1979). [Surprisingly he makes no reference to Hayek's own view that "this is no more than the necessary outcome of a process which has been going on for a fairly long time" (Hayek 1937, p. 41, n. 6); this was the idea already inherent in the paper written in 1928.]

In the present context, it is appropriate to point out that, although the concept of the evenly rotating economy assumes no change in the underlying data, nonetheless Mises emphasized that it was misleading to call it a static equilibrium and a bad mistake to confuse it with a stationary economy. Mises's approach is less advanced than Hayek's in this respect, but in retrospect we can see that it is in the same spirit, and arguably the Hayekian equilibrium concept can be used for the same purposes as Mises used the evenly rotating economy.

Hayek then enquires into "the reasons for our concern with the admittedly fictitious state of equilibrium:

> the only justification for this is the supposed existence of a tendency toward equilibrium. It is only by the assertion that such a tendency exists that economics ceases to be an exercise in pure logic and becomes an empirical science. . . . [This] assertion can hardly mean anything but that, under certain conditions, the knowledge and intentions of the different members of society are supposed to come more and more into agreement. . . . [This] is clearly an empirical proposition (1946, pp. 44–45).

Commentators in the Austrian literature have emphasized and discussed the contrast between Hayek's view that the tendency to equilibrium is an empirical matter and Mises's view that it follows logically from the "activities of enterprising men."[3] This is not our present concern. We emphasize instead the agreement between Mises and Hayek that (1) equilibrium is a "fictitious," not a realistic, state of the economy; (2) an equilibrium concept is important only because of the *tendency* to equilibrium; and (3) this tendency relies on an aspect of human nature—call it entrepreneurial alertness or learning—which (as Israel Kirzner has repeatedly emphasized) is not encompassed by Robbinsian economising or choice in the face of given data.

Hayek goes on to confess that "we are still pretty much in the dark about (a) the conditions under which this tendency is supposed to exist and (b) the nature of the process by which individual knowledge is changed" (1937, p. 45). The first question involves the investigation of whether particular hypotheses about learning are necessary and sufficient to explain a movement to equilibrium in particular circumstances; the second involves the investigation of how people actually do learn. In effect, Hayek is sketching out a program of research that might involve the use of formal mathematical models to tackle the first question and applied psychology to tackle the second.

Such a program of research would not, of course, commend itself to Mises, chiefly because from his point of view it would be unnecessary and outside the scope of economics. Somewhat more surprisingly, Hayek does not pursue this line of research either; nor does he encourage others to do so. Admittedly he is not a mathematician, but in his Nobel lecture he was at pains "to avoid giving the impression that I generally reject the mathematical method in economics," and emphasized the qualitative insights that mathematics could provide: "We could scarcely have achieved that comprehensive picture of the mutual interdependencies of the different events in a market without this algebraic technique" (Hayek 1974, p. 252). Nor is Hayek a psychologist, but he is one of the very few economists to have published a book embodying original research in psychology.

The reason Hayek gives for abandoning this line of enquiry is that "there seems to me to be another and more fruitful way of approach to the central problem," namely, to pose the further question "how much knowledge and what sort of knowledge the different individuals must possess in order that we may be able to speak of equilibrium" (1937, p. 50). For Hayek, this "problem of the division of knowledge" is "the really central problem of economics as a social science." He points out that the (minimum) relevant knowledge that each person must possess for equilibrium to exist is certainly not all the knowledge that might be useful to him. Consequently, an equilibrium is not necessarily "a sort of optimum position" (1937, p. 53). This raises the further question of what conditions are necessary and sufficient "in order that the results of the combination of individual bits of knowledge should be comparable to the results of directions by

90   Method, Process, and Austrian Economics

an omniscient dictator.'' In effect, Hayek is enquiring into the conditions
for the existence and (as we would now say) Pareto efficiency of equilibrium.

To summarize, in the first part of his paper, Hayek introduces the concept of equilibrium as mutual compatibility of plans over time, which is in
principle distinct from the concept of stationarity. This aspect of his work is
beginning to receive general notice. In the middle part of the paper he
argues (contra Mises) that the existence of a tendency to equilibrium is an
empirical matter. This is the part that most Austrian commentators have
emphasized. In the last part of the paper he in effect sketches out two alternative programs of research that follow from the earlier insights. The first
program focuses on the nature of the market process and the conditions for
it to converge to equilibrium; the second focuses on the conditions for the
existence and efficiency of equilibrium. For our present purposes, it is this
last part of the paper that is of most interest. And what is of greatest significance is that Hayek opts for the second research program rather than the
first—that is, for the study of equilibrium rather than process.

Hahn on Equilibrium in Economics

The central argument of Hahn's lecture may be summarized quite briefly.
Equilibrium is a central organizing idea in economics. The various different
concepts of equilibrium have in common the notion of mutual consistency
of plans. The Arrow-Debreu model of equilibrium has the advantage of
clarity and is of great use for many purposes, but it also presents three specific difficulties: (1) it is possible to define equilibrium states (the core) that
in general are not equal to the Arrow-Debreu equilibrium; (2) when there
are increasing returns there may be no equilibrium; and (3) the Arrow-
Debreu model is inadequate to handle uncertainty (since it might necessitate
contingent futures markets that might not exist). What is required is an
equilibrium notion that reflects ''the sequential character of actual economies'' in an ''essential'' way. It will need explicitly to incorporate concepts
of information, expectations, and uncertainty. Hahn proposes a formal
model that can be used to analyze these problems and then discusses the
nature, existence, and efficiency of equilibrium in this model. The last part
of his lecture is devoted to refuting certain objections to his approach and
exploring some of its implications.

For Hahn, the Arrow-Debreu model has the advantage of being ''precise, complete and unambiguous'' (1973b, p. 3). With the aid of it, ''it is
often possible to say something about the direction in which some variables
will move next,''—for example, when the economy is in a state of disequilibrium (1973b, p. 9).[4] It is not claimed that the Arrow-Debreu model is a

Equilibrium and the Market Process   91

realistic description of the actual world: Hahn elsewhere explicitly rejects that claim.[5] In fact, the model makes "a significant contribution to the understanding of Keynesian economics just by describing so precisely what would have to be the case if there were to be no Keynesian problems" (1973b, p. 34).[6] "This negative role of Arrow-Debreu equilibrium I consider almost to be sufficient justification for it" (1973b, p. 14).

To summarize, the Arrow-Debreu general equilibrium model has the advantage of clarity, may be used to indicate directions of change, is not claimed to be a realistic description, and may (arguably) be used in the method of "imaginary constructions." But as shown, these are precisely the same claims that Mises makes for his model of the evenly rotating economy. Thus the first point to make is that Hahn and Mises share a similar view of the role of general equilibrium (in its timeless sense).

Despite its usefulness, Hahn does not believe that the Arrow-Debreu concept of equilibrium is the most useful one. What is required is an equilibrium notion that reflects "the sequential character of actual economies" in an essential way, that is, it should not be possible to reformulate the model in a nonsequential way (1973b, p. 16). "This in turn requires that information processes and costs, transactions and tranactions costs and also expectations and uncertainty be explicitly and essentially included in the equilibrium notion. This is what the Arrow-Debreu construction does not do" (1973b, p. 16).

These concepts that Hahn emphasizes, such as ignorance and uncertainty, theories and perception, information and expectations, learning and plan revision, all lie at the heart of the subjectivist approach. The term "sequential character" of actual economies surely refers to the market process, and indeed Hahn remarks that "we should like to be able to describe and predict the course of economic processes in great detail" (1973b, p. 10). His concluding remarks not merely acknowledge the importance of perceptions and expectations but urge further work in this direction as a matter of first priority.

> . . . the main progress to be made now is to recognize quite explicitly the sequential structure of the economies which we study and to wrestle with some of the very serious conceptual problems which this raises. In particular *the distinction between the perceived environment and the environment* and the consequential importance of the theories which are held by agents seems to be bound to become increasingly important in analysis (Hahn 1973b, p. 40). (Emphasis added.)

Thus, the second point to make about Hahn's lecture is that, compared to most previous work in mathematical economics, it represents an important step forward in the direction of subjectivism.

To analyze these problems, Hahn proposes the following model (1973b, pp. 18–20, 25–26). At any time, an economic agent holds a *theory* that comprises, roughly speaking, his conditional predictions about the way in which the economy will develop and about the consequences of his own actions. He is said to be learning if his theory changes over time. (Here, learning does not refer to the mere updating of a conditional forecast in the light of more recent information, nor does the absence of learning mean that the forecast must be constant. Rather, learning means a change in the *method* of making forecasts.) The agent is assumed to abandon his theory when it is sufficiently and systematically falsified. The agent also has a *policy*, which specifies his actions conditional on any pattern of development in the economy.

The agent is said to be in equilibrium if his policy does not change over time. This in turn requires (1) that he is not learning and (2) that his objectives do not change. The economy is said to be in equilibrium when it develops in such a way that it does not cause agents to change the theories that they hold or the policies that they pursue. This requires, roughly speaking, that the actions of agents not be systematically and persistently inconsistent and that the agents hold subjective probability distributions that converge to observed frequencies.

We are now in a position to make a third point of comparison. The concepts of individual and general equilibrium that Hahn defines are in principle the same as those proposed by Hayek. To be sure, they are defined more rigorously, using more sophisticated mathematical and statistical techniques. But for both authors (1) an individual is in equilibrium as long as his actions form part of a single plan, uninterrupted by learning; (2) an economy is in equilibrium when the plans of its members are mutually compatible; and (3) the concept of equilibrium is quite distinct from that of the stationary state. In effect, Hahn's equilibrium is a stochastic version of Hayekian equilibrium.

Once Hahn has set up his model and defined his concept of equilibrium, his instinct is to look immediately for an existence theorem. "But I must note an important and interesting open question of a technical kind before I justify the approach. In order that any kind of equilibrium, even in simple cases, can be shown to exist, I must show that there are theories which, if agents held them, would in that economy not be falsified" (1973b, p. 27). He recognizes that this will be a difficult task in the complex model he has constructed, but it is not merely a technical mathematical question that is at issue: there is a real problem that lies behind it. "For what one is asking in the last resort is whether it is possible to have a decentralized economy in which agents have adapted themselves to their economic environment and where their expectations in the widest sense are in the proper meaning not falsified" (1973b, p. 28). Almost immediately thereafter, on discussing the problems raised by increasing returns, Hahn takes up the question of whether one can any longer speak of the efficient allocation of resources, and he notes the kind of global problems that decentralization may pose.

Once again, this is reminiscent of Hayek who, recall, identified two directions for further research: analysis of the market process leading to equilibrium and analysis of the conditions for the existence and efficiency of equilibrium. Hayek recommended the second approach to explain how a decentralized economy is not only possible but efficient, and this is precisely the line that Hahn has taken.

To summarize, in examining Hahn's lecture we have been led to four conclusions. First, the Arrow-Debreu equilibrium concept plays substantially the same role for Hahn as the evenly rotating economy does for Mises. Second, Hahn's paper represents a significant step for mathematical economics in the direction of subjectivism. Third, the revised concept of equilibrium that Hahn proposes as a means of analyzing the sequential character of actual economies is essentially a stochastic version of Hayekian equilibrium, both being couched in terms of compatibility of plans over time and both quite distinct from the concept of a stationary state. Finally, as a means of understanding the properties of a decentralized economy, both Hayek and Hahn consider it fruitful to concentrate on studying the conditions for the existence and efficiency of equilibrium.

We are thus led to a very striking overall conclusion. Recent developments in mathematical economics, as expounded and encouraged by Hahn, have returned economic theory precisely to the path that Hayek sketched out in 1937. The techniques of analysis are of course more sophisticated, and in that sense a useful advance has been made, but the underlying philosophies are the same.[7] With respect to this branch of economic theory, as Lachmann has observed in a private communication, Austrians can hardly complain that their ideas have been overlooked: the mathematical economists, albeit unwittingly, have done precisely what Hayek asked of them!

Equilibrium versus Market Process?

In recommending the study of equilibrium, it is fairly clear that Hayek is not counseling that the study of market processes should be abandoned. He notes that "this question of the empirical probability that people will learn" is not "lacking in unsolved and highly interesting questions" (1937, pp. 49–50). But these questions "have at least received some attention in past discussions," whereas the problem of the knowledge required for equilibrium is "at least equally important but one which appears to have received no attention at all." We may safely take it, from Hayek's other writings if not from this paper, that the study of equilibrium is advocated to obtain additional insights and not to preclude the futher formal study of the market process. Only a few years later, for example, he is arguing strongly that competition is properly to be viewed as a process of discovery, and not as an equilibrium state (Hayek 1946).

This is not the view that Hahn takes. Remarks scattered throughout his lecture give the impression that he favors the study of equilibrium to the *exclusion* of the study of process. He gives three quite different reasons: first, that equilibrium (in his modified sense) is a realistic description of the world; second, that it would be impossible to construct a theory of process anyway, so that equilibrium represents the limit of what economists have to say; and third, that it is the particular duty of economists to study equilibrium. We shall examine these arguments in turn and contrast them with the Austrian position.

Hahn's first argument is that equilibrium (in the extended Hayek-Hahn sense) is useful in practice because it is a realistic description of the world. ". . . it is precisely the empirical claim for the usefulness of the equilibrium notion that the theories and motives of agents are sufficiently stable and we are not allowed to invoke changing theories or motives to help us out of falsified predictions" (Hahn 1973b, p. 23). Now it is not entirely clear that this argument is valid. To make and test predictions it is necessary that the observer be able to specify the theories and motives of the agents, and these may or may not be stable. For example, one might test the hypothesis that during times of inflation people have changing theories of price expectations against the null hypothesis that they have stable theories. Hahn also seems to be in error in claiming that if a "higher-level" theory of the learning process were available the concept of equilibrium would be otiose. "If a definite behaviour pattern can be established for all situations then nothing would be gained by labelling any particular behaviour as equilibrium behaviour" (Hahn 1973b, p. 11). It would certainly be true that the omniscient observer could explain or predict an agent's behaviour over any period of time, regardless of whether the agent was in equilibrium over the whole of that period. *But the agent himself would not know this "higher-level" theory.* (If he did, this knowledge would become part of his own theory, and he would no longer be learning.) As Hayek himself emphasized, the point is not whether any particular behavior is equilibrium behaviour but whether particular actions are in an equilibrium relationship with other actions (1948, p. 36). It is useful to be able to describe certain actions as part of one plan, and other (subsequent) actions as part of a different plan adopted as a result of learning.

However, the main point to make here is that the view that the economy is or can be in a state of equilibrium (for any significant period of time) is diametrically opposed to the Austrian position. We have already noted the views of Mises and Hayek on the "fictitious" nature of equilibrium; Lachmann has made the point quite explicitly. ". . . we must assume that Profes-

Equilibrium and the Market Process   95

sor Hahn envisages some time sequences in which nothing is learned by a participant and others in which something is learned. Needless to say, the former variety cannot exist. Time and knowledge belong together. As soon as we permit time to elapse, we must permit knowledge to change. The pattern of knowledge never stands still'' (1976, p. 36).

For the Austrians, the concept of equilibrium is used to characterize not the *state* of the economy but the direction of *changes* in the state. To use Kenneth Boulding's analogy of the dog chasing the cat, equilibrium for the dog is where the cat is—but the dog might never catch the cat! The concept is nevertheless useful because it explains the direction in which the dog is running. To assume the existence of equilibrium in empirical work can thus provide so-called insights that are positively misleading, and quite inappropriate suggestions for policy may be derived (Littlechild 1981).

Hahn's second argument is that a model involving learning would necessitate a "higher-level" theory of the learning process. "Such a theory is not available at present. . . . In our present state of knowledge however it is routine behaviour and not behaviour which we can hope to describe. Indeed one of the reasons why an equilibrium notion is useful is that it serves to make precise the limits of economic analysis'' (1973b, p. 21). That we do not have a theory of the learning process is not disputed. Some would argue with L.M. Lachmann that we *cannot* have one: "Expectations, it is true, are largely a response to events experienced in the past, but the modus operandi of the response is not the same in all cases even of the same experience. This experience, before being transformed into expectations, has, so to speak, to pass through a 'filter' in the human mind, and the undefinable character of this process makes the outcome of it unpredictable'' (Lachmann 1943).

We should realize, nevertheless, that all applications of economic theory—even the application of insights from the Arrow-Debreu model—involve implicit assumptions about learning. For example, in the illustration given by Hahn, an excess of intended investment over intended savings will begin to take effect only when, and as fast as, frustrated borrowers and alert lenders recognize the true nature of the situation and react accordingly.

The most appropriate avenue for research, as Lachmann suggests, is probably to explore the effects of different assumptions about learning:[*]

> Under these circumstances, what can the economist do but construct various hypothetical types of expectations conceived as responses to various hypothetical situations, and then leave the process of selection to empirical verification in the light of economic history? Several such "ideal types" either of expectations, like Lord Keynes' "long-term" and "short-term" expectations, or of the holders of expectations, like Professor Schumpeter's "static producer" and "dynamic entrepreneur" or Professor

96   Method, Process, and Austrian Economics

Hicks' "sensitive" and "insensitive" traders, have already been evolved
and served to elucidate important dynamic problems (Lachmann 1943).

This approach would seem to worry Hahn, who earlier remarked "Of
course, one of the reasons why so much of our effort is devoted to the study
of equilibria is that they are singularly well suited to study. We all know the
endless variety of adjustment models, not uncongenial to commonsense,
one is capable of constructing. No unifying principle, such as maximization, seems available" (Hahn 1970, p. 1). (The discussant questioned
whether *any* of the adjustment models so far developed are congenial to
commonsense!) Lachmann's argument is that variety is not a defect: "we
need not deplore unduly the indeterminateness of expectations, for it is
intelligibility and not determinateness that social science should strive to
achieve" (1943).

At this point we may acknowledge a related objection raised by Mises,
namely, that market processes are incapable of being modelled mathemati-
cally:

> The problems of process analysis, i.e., the only economic problems that
> matter, defy any mathematical approach. The introduction of time para-
> meters into the equations is no solution. It does not even indicate the essen-
> tial short-comings of the mathematical method. The statements that every
> change involves time and that change is always in the temporal sequence are
> merely a way of expressing the fact that as far as there is rigidity and
> unchangeability there is not time. The main deficiency of mathematical
> economics is not the fact that it ignores the temporal sequence, but that it
> ignores the operation of the market process.

> The mathematical method is at a loss to show how from a state of nonequil-
> ibrium those actions spring up which tend toward the establishment of
> equilibrium. It is, of course, possible to indicate the mathematical opera-
> tions required for the transformation of the mathematical description of a
> definite state of nonequilibrium into the mathematical description of the
> state of equilibrium. But these mathematical operations by no means
> describe the market process actuated by the discrepancies in the price struc-
> ture (Mises 1966, p. 356).

The objection has validity, but is it perhaps overstated? Consider the case of
arbitrage. One possibility is to model entrepreneurial alertness by a positive
probability of discovering hitherto-unknown arbitrage opportunities. (Littlechild 1979; Littlechild and Owen 1980) Perhaps, in a similar way, one
could model the "creation" of longer-term investment opportunities, or the
adoption by an agent of a new theory (in the sense of Hahn).

Discussion of these problems would take us too far afield, however. I
simply wish to establish here that the lack of an accepted theory of learning
does not preclude the development of formal economic models of market

processes and that the concept of equilibrium certainly does not represent "the limit of economic analysis."

Hahn's final argument is that economists are better engaged studying equilibrium than the laws of motion of a capitalist society: "I am certain that in such an ambitious intellectual programme the expertise of the economist will only be a very small part of what is required. In the meantime there are many important problems in all societies which if they are not understood by economists will not be understood by anyone and it is here that our main obligation must lie" (1973b, pp. 39–40).

An opposite view may also be advanced. The study of economic processes can be done usefully on a scale less grand than the aforesaid "laws of motion." Particularly important, for example, is the study of how markets generate, disseminate, and respond to information. Insofar as only very general propositions about learning are involved, and ideal types are used for illustration, the study of economic processes does not require significant inputs from disciplines other than economics. (More precisely, the economic theory of such processes requires no more noneconomic inputs than the economic theory of equilibrium. Applied studies may require further inputs in either case.) It follows that the study of economic processes is just as much the proper domain of the economist as is the study of equilibrium; indeed for Mises, as for all Austrian economists, the "imaginary constructions such as equilibrium . . . are only tools of reasoning. The sole task of economics is analysis of the actions of men, is the analysis of processes" (1966, p. 357). Moreover, no one else will study economic processes if the economist does not.

This is not the place to appraise the relative merits of process and equilibrium per se. However, since the study of economic processes has been almost entirely neglected during the past half-century (in contrast to the half-century preceding Hayek's paper), it seems more likely that, in the immediate future, a higher return is to be obtained from studying processes rather than from further refining the equilibrium concept.[9]

Conclusions

We set out to discover how far the recent developments in mathematical economics, as exemplified by Hahn's inaugural lecture, are consistent with the ideas of Austrian economists, notably Mises and Hayek. We found that (1) Hahn's view of the nature and role of Arrow-Debreu equilibrium is substantially the same as Mises's view of the evenly rotating economy; (2) Hahn's emphasis on "the distinction between the perceived environment and the environment" reflects a central tenet of the subjectivist approach; (3) Hahn's redefinition of equilibrium as mutual compatibility of plans over

98   Method, Process, and Austrian Economics

time is a stochastic version of Hayekian equilibrium; and (4) Hahn's focus on the existence and properties of equilibrium, rather than on the nature of the market process, parallels the earlier argument of Hayek. However, we argued that Hayek, unlike Hahn, did not mean to exclude the study of process; that Hahn's view that the (modified) equilibrium is a useful concept precisely because it realistically describes the world is not shared by Austrians; that Austrians would agree with Hahn that there cannot be a definitive higher-level theory of the learning process but that, nevertheless, models can be built to analyze plausible types of learning process; and that, contra Hahn, there is likely to be a higher payoff in the immediate future from studying processes rather than equilibrium.

Hahn has provided us with a clear and colorful map of largely unfamiliar territory. He has described the country we know and the reports currently coming in from the advance scouts and has sketched out his own view of the terrain ahead. Furthermore, in advising on our route, he has drawn attention to the beauty of some familiar features and warned against the impenetrable forests elsewhere. We must be grateful to him for the map, but perhaps the forests are not so impenetrable as they seem, and the glimpses we have already had through them suggest that the less familiar routes will provide better access to more exciting vistas beyond.

Notes

1. Hahn's lecture has elsewhere been appraised by Coddington (1975), Loasby (1976), and Hutchison (1977, chap. 4).

2. Notably L.M. Lachmann, I.M. Kirzner, and G.L.S. Shackle from the Austrian/subjectivist camp, and R. Radner and J.M. Grandmont among mathematical economists.

3. Compare Lachmann (1943; 1971; 1974; 1976), Kirzner (1974; 1979; chaps. 2, 9), White (1976).

4. "In an economy with unemployed resources an excess of intended investment over intended savings is used to predict that incomes will not persist at their present level and indeed are very likely to rise." (p. 9) Compare Hayek (1974, p. 251) "We have indeed good reason to believe that unemployment indicates that the structure of relative prices and wages has been distorted . . . and that to restore equality between the demand and supply of labour in all sectors changes of relative prices and some transfer of labour will be necessary." Both Hayek and Hahn immediately make the point that one may not be able to specify in quantitative, as opposed to qualitative, terms what the final point of equilibrium will be.

5. "It was, I believe, always understood that the equilibrium of Arrow-Debreu is not a description of an actual economy" (Hahn 1973a, p. 329). See also p. 323.

Equilibrium and the Market Process   99

6. This last argument is by no means convincing. Even if the Arrow-Debreu model is conceded to demonstrate that under certain assumptions there will be no Keynesian problems, this does not imply that the converse is true. A similar difficulty arises with Hahn's assertion that the Arrow-Debreu model may be used to dispose of a false claim about natural resources. See Coddington (1975, pp. 552–556), Loasby (1976, p. 47), Hutchison (1977, pp. 86–87), and Lachmann (1976, pp. 36–37) for vigorous criticism.

7. A fuller account of these developments would of course need to consider the important contributions of Hicks, who in turn remarks in his preface to *Value and Capital* that "they were not by any means entirely my own ideas; they came into being as a sort of social process which went on among the people who were working there [at LSE], at that time, under the leadership of Professor Robbins" (1939).

8. L.M. Lachmann, "The Role of Expectations in Economics as a Social Science," *Economica* 10 (February 1943). All quotes reprinted with permission.

9. As Hutchison points out, Hahn himself once questioned the marginal utility of further elaboration of general equilibrium analysis (1977, pp. 82–83). "It cannot be denied that there is something scandalous in the spectacle of so many people refining the analysis of economic states which they give no reason to suppose will ever, or have ever, come about" (Hahn 1970, p. 1). Presumably this reservation referred only to the Arrow-Debreu equilibrium concept.

References

Coddington, A. December 1975. The rationale of general equilibrium theory. *Economic Inquiry* 13:539–558.

Dolan, E.G., ed. 1976. *The foundations of modern Austrian economics.* Kansas City: Sheed & Ward.

Hahn, F.H. 1970. Some adjustment problems. *Econometrica* 38:1–17.

———. 1973a. The winter of our discontent. *Economica* 40:322–330.

———. 1973b. On the notion of equilibrium in economics. Inaugural lecture. Cambridge: Cambridge University Press.

Hayek, F.A. 1937. Economics and knowledge. *Economica* 4:33–54. Page references to reprint in Hayek (1948).

———. 1946. The meaning of competition. Stafford Little Lecture, Princeton University, May 1946. Page references to reprint in Hayek (1948).

———. 1948. *Individualism and economic order.* Chicago: University of Chicago.

———. 1974. The pretence of knowledge. Nobel Memorial Lecture.

Hicks, J.R. 1939. *Value and Capital.* London: Oxford University Press.

100 Method, Process, and Austrian Economics

Hutchison, T.W. 1977. *Knowledge and ignorance in economics.* Oxford: Basil Blackwell.

Kirzner, I.M. 1974. On the method of Austrian economics. Lecture given at Austrian Economics Conference, South Royalton, Vermont, June 1974. Reprinted in Dolan (1976, pp. 40-51).

———. 1979. *Perception, opportunity and profit.* Chicago: University of Chicago.

Lachmann, L.M. 1943. The role of expectations in economics as a social science. *Economica* 10:12-23. Reprinted in Lachmann (1977, pp. 65-80).

———. 1971. Ludwig von Mises and the market process. In *Toward Liberty: Essays in Honor of Ludwig von Mises,* ed. F.A. Hayek. 2 vols. Menlo Park, Calif: Institute of Humane Studies, 2:38-52. Reprinted in Lachmann (1977, pp. 181-193).

———. 1974. On the central concept of Austrian economics: market process. Lecture given at Austrian Economics Conference, South Royalton, Vermont, June 1974. Reprinted in Dolan (1976, pp. 126-132).

———. 1976. From Mises to Shackle: an essay. *Journal of Economic Literature* 14:54-62.

———. 1977. *Capital, expectations and the market process.* Kansas City: Sheed, Andrews & McMeel.

Littlechild, S.C. 1979. An entrepreneurial theory of games. *Metroeconomica* 31:145-165.

———. 1981. Misleading calculations of the social costs of monopoly power. *The Economic Journal* 91:348-363.

Littlechild, S.C., and Owen, G. 1980. An Austrian model of the entrepreneurial market process. *Journal of Economic Theory* 23:361-379.

Loasby, B.J. 1976. *Choice, complexity and ignorance.* Cambridge: Cambridge University.

Milgate, M. 1979. On the origin of the notion of "intertemporal equilibrium. *Economica* 46:1-10.

Mises, Ludwig von. 1966. *Human Action.* 3d ed. Chicago: Henry Regnery.

White, L.H. 1976. Entrepreneurship, imagination and the question of equilibrium. Unpublished paper.

[4]

Inconsistent Equilibrium Constructs: The Evenly Rotating Economy of Mises and Rothbard

By Tyler Cowen and Richard Fink*

The growing disillusionment with the Arrow-Hahn-Debreu model of general equilibrium has led to an examination of alternative constructions. Among the alternatives that have recently been studied are temporary equilibria, rational expectations equilibria, and the evenly rotating economy (ERE).[1] This note will focus on the ERE. We will argue that, whatever problems equilibrium constructs may have in general, these problems are compounded by serious inconsistencies in both the nature of the ERE and its suggested uses.

We focus on four particular features of the ERE. First, it is the result of a convergence process initiated by a freeze of tastes, technology, and resources (Murray Rothbard, 1962, p. 273; Mises does not specify the conditions required for convergence); second, the events of a single market "day" continually repeat themselves (Ludwig Mises, 1949, p. 247; Rothbard, p. 273); third, the ERE does not contain the Arrow-Hahn-Debreu restrictions of perfect futures markets and approximate convexities; fourth, the ERE contains money and money prices (Mises, pp. 416-17, 538; Rothbard, passim).

*Departments of Economics, George Mason University, Fairfax, VA 22030, and Harvard University, Cambridge, MA 02138, respectively. We thank the Center for the Study of Market Processes for support on this project.

[1] Not only is the ERE frequently used in modern "Austrian" literature (see Roger Garrison, 1978, for an example) but is also gaining numerous other adherents. In a recent talk at Harvard University ("Principles of Monetary and Fiscal Policy," 1984) Robert Lucas expressed his admiration for Mises' ERE and noted its close similarity with much of his own work with overlapping generations models. However, since Mises and Rothbard contain the primary statement and defense of the ERE, we shall focus our attention on their writings. Despite our critical tone, we wish to note our appreciation of the elements of market process and order analysis in Rothbard and Mises.

Both Mises and Rothbard propose the following uses of the ERE:

1) *The ERE can be used to explain or "predict" the direction of change* (Mises, pp. 244-45; Rothbard, pp. 275-76). Since the market economy is supposedly always moving towards the ERE, a clear notion of the relevant end-state will tell us what state of affairs the market is tending to establish (but will never actually reach).[2]

2) *The ERE is an analytical building block or stepping stone towards analyzing complex phenomena in a world of change* (Rothbard, p. 276).

3) *The ERE is a starting point for an analysis of the effects of particular changes.* If we wish to analyze the effects of an exogenous shock upon the economic system, we start with a state where there is no change and then allow the new change to work its way through the system until the economy settles into equilibrium once again. Thus, we can isolate the effects of this change (Mises, p. 248).

4) *The ERE is used as a foil.* Since the ERE is *so* unrealistic, it is supposed to shed light upon the real world by method of contrast. For instance, examining a world in which there is no uncertainty and, hence, no entrepreneurship, may help shed light on the nature of entrepreneurship in the real world (Mises, p. 248).

I. The ERE: A Critique

Using the ERE to explain the direction of change in a market rests upon the notion that there is a "tendency" for a market economy to approach equilibrium. "If our *data* —values, technology, and resources—remained constant, the economy would move

[2] Mises attaches the label "final state of rest" (p. 245) to this use of the ERE.

toward the final equilibrium position and remain there" (Rothbard, p. 275). Although Rothbard later claims that verbal analysis is capable of explaining the convergence path (p. 278), no such explanation is forthcoming. In fact, there is no reason to believe that the economic system will settle into an equilibrium state, for as the analysis of Gerard Debreu (1959) implies, sequential transactions are *not* consistent with the notion of an intertemporal general equilibrium.[3] Instead, all transactions across time must already be perfectly coordinated on the first day of trading. Any attempt to do away with this stipulation is bound to encounter all of the problems that have plagued mathematical general equilibrium convergence theory in the past. Unless the equilibrium of the system is preordained (as it is in Debreu), it is nearly impossible for the learning processes of actors to be so highly proficient and adaptable as to allow for an actual convergence to equilibrium.[4]

Among the specific problems preventing perfect plan coordination are income effects, disequilibrium production and consumption, nonconvexities, strategic behavior (resulting from externalities), and the potentially false price signals generated by the process of convergence. Mathematical general equilibrium theory usually places serious (and unrealistic) restrictions on these problems in order to generate a process of convergence. Even then, it is still often impossible to demonstrate convergence (see Franklin Fisher, 1976). How can the *ERE* explain convergence without such restrictions?[5]

However, even if we ignore the above problems, all that the Rothbard-Mises analysis implies is that there is a tendency towards equilibrium *in a world with frozen data*. Of course, this implies little or nothing about whether there is a tendency towards equilibrium in a world where the data are not frozen. All that *ERE* theorists are saying is that, if we freeze the disequilibrating forces, then the equilibrating forces will prevail. But on this basis we may likewise assert a tendency towards *disequilibrium*. By allowing the data to change just as it does in the real world, and "freezing" all individual learning, we can demonstrate that the economy would degenerate into a series of successively less-coordinated states of disequilibrium. However, this would clearly be an illegitimate proof of a real world tendency towards disequilibrium, just as the Rothbard-Mises analysis does not succeed in establishing a real world tendency towards equilibrium.

The second function of the *ERE*—a starting point for analyzing the determination of market price (or other phenomena)—is also open to question. While it is desirable to analyze price determination in a simpler setting before examining the real world, it is doubtful whether the *ERE* is the proper initial setting, because *there are no prices in the ERE*. Prices are institutions that have evolved over time in order to help coordinate the plans of market participants. In a world in which all plans are already coordinated and actors possess all relevant information, prices would not serve any function.[6] The only prices that would exist in the *ERE* are the *ex post* barter ratios resulting from realized transactions, such as "ten apples for one horse." However, the notion of price as an *ex ante* disequilibrium institution which communicates knowledge (see Friedrich Hayek, 1945) has no place in the *ERE*.

Rothbard and Mises simply assume that prices exist in the *ERE* and then explain their determination. Interestingly, the contradictions involved with this assumption are

---

[3]Also see Frank Hahn (1972).

[4]Roman Frydman (1982) and George Richardson (1960) argue that learning processes will never converge upon an equilibrium. Existing "Austrian" models demonstrate convergence only for single markets under highly restrictive assumptions. See Jack High (1980, pp. 148–76); S. C. Littlechild and G. Owen (1980).

[5]Because the *ERE* does not stipulate a convex consumption set, people may have tastes for new and unique events or technologies where the "newness" or "uniqueness" is valued per se, thus making the initial "tastes freeze" self-contradictory. Likewise, the notion of freezing resources or resource patterns makes sense only in a world with no disequilibrium production or consumption to disturb the ability of physical processes to reproduce themselves.

[6]See John Hicks (1967, p. 3) who argues that numeraire prices are not even used for accounting purposes by *GE* (and presumably, *ERE*) market participants.

not denied; Rothbard and Mises emphasize the contradictory nature of the *ERE*, but still stress its usefulness. However, by forcing prices into a framework (the *ERE*) where they cannot logically exist, we must inevitably distract attention from the disequilibrium features of prices that characterize the real world. Even the static allocative function of prices is misrepresented by the *ERE*, since the allocative efficiency of the system is achieved by actors' knowledge of the external data (the "real factors") rather than by their observations of prices. How can an imaginary construct illuminate an institution that performs absolutely no function within that construct?

The *ERE* is also used as a starting point for analyzing the effects of an exogenous shock upon the economic system. Much of the analysis of the preceding section is applicable to our critique of this use of the *ERE* as well. The most important question for the economist studying the effects of an exogenous shock is how market institutions (prices, interest rates, firms, etc.) will deal with this change and how, in turn, this change will affect these institutions. However, a model with no institutions (or "make believe" institutions that serve no real function) is unsuitable for this task.

Depending upon the nature of the problem, introducing a change into an equilibrium setting may either understate or overstate the coordination problems that a market economy faces. Since all other activities are already coordinated, the disruptive nature of the change may be understated since the actors trying to deal with this change need not worry about transactions costs or plan conflicts among themselves. Furthermore, since the bonds that link individual plans in a disequilibrium world (such as *ex ante* prices) do not exist in the *ERE*, then the disruptive effects of the change upon these bonds will be either ignored or misrepresented.

The other possibility has equally serious analytical consequences. In equilibrium, many of the institutions that help coordinate behavior in a world of uncertainty are absent. Thus, we are giving the market economy an unfair test. We are throwing a new change into a system that, because it has anticipated all of the old changes, has no means for coping with the new change. In addition, many of the exogenous shocks introduced into the *ERE* also contradict the initial equilibrium conditions. For instance, using the *ERE* as a starting point for an analysis of monetary intervention (for example, Rothbard and Mises' business cycle theory) involves the contradiction of superimposing an increase in the money supply upon an essentially moneyless world.

The fourth proposed use of the *ERE*, as a "foil," seems to command the broadest support among *ERE* theorists. However, using the *ERE* as a foil contradicts the first three suggested uses of the *ERE*. If it is possible to look at the *ERE* in order to see what a price *is not*, what an interest rate *is not*, then this should be the *only* possible use for the *ERE*. If, as Mises claims (p. 348), the *ERE* has no human action, then we cannot claim there is a tendency towards equilibrium, since this would imply the nonsensical conclusion that there is a tendency for human action (and human institutions) to disappear. Nor could it be desirable to analyze price determination in the *ERE* as an "initial step" since our *ERE* foil tells us that there is neither price nor action in equilibrium. Finally, if the *ERE* reflects everything that the real world is not, introducing a change into the *ERE* and letting it work its way through the system cannot be a promising endeavor. At best, all such a procedure could be used for is to tell us how the real world does *not* react to change. Yet, when proponents of the *ERE* use the construct to analyze change, it is no longer viewed as a foil; instead it is looked upon as the initial "state of rest" that change acts upon. This is a clear inconsistency—the *ERE* either can be an initial state for an economy that is about to experience change, or it can be a foil, but it cannot be both. The very arguments made by Mises for using the *ERE* as a foil explain why it is of little value for serving any other purposes:

> ...[I]n the evenly rotating economy there is no choosing and the future is not uncertain as it does not differ from the present known state. Such a rigid

system is not peopled with living men making choices and liable to error; it is a world of soulless unthinking automatons; it is not a human society, it is an ant hill. [p. 248]

However, the *ERE* is a poor foil because it is neither completely unrealistic nor internally consistent.[7] If one desires to use equilibrium as a foil, Debreu's model is superior to the *ERE*. The Debreu model is completely and consistently unrealistic: it has no money, no sequential transactions, perfect futures markets, and all of the other extreme assumptions necessary to accurately illustrate the other worldliness of the equilibrium concept. Nevertheless, regardless of one's opinion of the usefulness of the Debreu foil, the *ERE* is neither a useful substitute for, nor complement to, the standard *GE* model.

---

[7] The most important inconsistencies in the *ERE* are the existence of money and money prices and the absence of perfect futures markets. The first inconsistency tends to generate "neutrality of money" results, while the second leads to an underestimation of the difficulty of reasonably tight interpersonal coordination.

REFERENCES

Debreu, Gerald, *Theory of Value,* New Haven: Yale University Press, 1959.

Fisher, Franklin, "The Stability of General Equilibrium: Results and Problems," in M. Artis and A. Nobay, eds., *Essays in Economic Analysis,* New York: Cambridge University Press, 1976.

Frydman, Roman, "Toward an Understanding of Market Processes: Individual Expectations, Learning, and Convergence to Rational Expectations Equilibrium," *American Economic Review,* September 1982, *72,* 652–82.

Garrison, Roger, "Austrian Macroeconomics," in Louis Spadaro, ed., *New Directions in Austrian Economics,* Kansas City: Sheed, Andrews, and McMeel, 1978.

Hahn, Frank, "On the Foundations of Monetary Theory," in M. Artis and A. Nobay, eds., *Essays in Modern Economics,* New York: Barnes and Noble, 1972.

_____, *On the Notion of Equilibrium in Economics,* New York: Cambridge University Press, 1973.

Hayek, Friedrich, "The Use of Knowledge in Society," in *Individualism and Economic Order,* Chicago: University of Chicago Press, 1945.

Hicks, John, *Critical Essays in Monetary Theory,* New York: Oxford University Press, 1967.

High, Jack, "Maximizing, Action, and Market Adjustment," unpublished doctoral dissertation, UCLA, 1980.

Littlechild, S. C, and Owen, G., "An Austrian Model of the Entrepreneurial Market Process," *Journal of Economic Theory,* December 1980, *23,* 361–79.

Mises, Ludwig, *Human Action,* New Haven: Yale University Press, 1949.

Richardson, George B., *Information and Investment,* New York: Oxford University Press, 1960.

Rothbard, Murray, *Man, Economy, and State,* Los Angeles: Nash Publishing, 1962.

White, Larry, "The Austrian School and Spontaneous Order: Comment on O'Driscoll," *Austrian Economics Newsletter,* Spring 1979.

_____, "Mises, Hayek, Hahn, and the Market Process: Comment on Littlechild," in Israel Kirzner, ed., *Method, Process, and Austrian Economics,* New York: Lexington Books, 1982.

Part II
The Competitive Market Process:
Market Process

[5]

ENTREPRENEURSHIP AND THE EQUILIBRATING PROCESS

It was stated in the first chapter that our emphasis on the market *process*, rather than on the more usually emphasized market equilibrium, stems from an awareness of the role of entrepreneurship, which is largely ignored by contemporary expositions of the theory of price. It is for this reason that I have given priority to the notion of entrepreneurship. I am now in a position to anticipate the discussions of later chapters and indicate briefly how the entrepreneurial role as I have developed it is in fact the crucial element in the market process.

A state of market disequilibrium is characterized by widespread ignorance. Market participants are unaware of the real opportunities for beneficial exchange which are available to them in the market. The result of this state of ignorance is that countless opportunities are passed up. For each product, as well as for each resource, opportunities for mutually beneficial exchange among potential buyers and sellers are missed. The potential sellers are unaware that sufficiently

24. Cf. the following statements by F. H. Knight in *Risk, Uncertainty and Profit* (Boston: Houghton and Mifflin, 1921): "What we call 'control' consists mainly of selecting some one else to do the 'controlling'" (p. 291); "The responsible decision is not the concrete ordering of policy, but ordering an orderer as a 'laborer' to order it" (p. 297). Cf. also Triffin, *Monopolistic Competition*, p. 184 and n. 39.

69

The Entrepreneur

eager buyers are waiting, who might make it worth their while to sell. Potential buyers are unaware that sufficiently eager sellers are waiting, who might make it attractive for them to buy. Resources are being used to produce products which consumers value less urgently, because producers (and potential producers) are not aware that these resources can produce more urgently needed products. Products are being produced with resources badly needed for other products because producers are not aware that alternative, less critically needed resources can be used to achieve the same results.

The task of a theory of the market is to provide insight into the course of events set in motion by the state of market disequilibrium. The crucial question concerns the nature of the forces that bring about changes in the buying, selling, producing, and consuming decisions that make up the market. And it is here that the entrepreneurial notion is indispensable. So long as we perceive all decision-makers as exclusively Robbinsian, each "mechanically" selecting the best course out of the alternatives believed to be available, our theory completely lacks a way of explaining how yesterday's plans are replaced today by new plans. So long as our decision-makers continue to believe that the alternative courses of action made available to them by the market are what they believed them to be yesterday, we are powerless (without resorting to exogenous changes in tastes or in resource availability) to account for any plan made today being different from that made yesterday. With the ends and means believed to be given today exactly as they were believed to be given yesterday, decision-makers will "automatically" arrive at the same optimum positions yielded by the data yesterday. For any price to change, or for any change in method of production or in the choice of product to occur, we must presume that some decision-makers are no longer attempting to carry out the plans they sought to carry out yesterday. There is nothing in the picture of a market of purely Robbinsian decision-

Entrepreneurship and the Equilibrating Process

makers, even with the injection of liberal doses of ignorance concerning the ends and means believed to be relevant, which can explain how yesterday's market experiences can account for changes in plans that might generate alterations in prices, in outputs, or in the use of inputs.

For this is it necessary to introduce the insight that men *learn* from their experiences in the market. It is necessary to postulate that out of the mistakes which led market participants to choose less-than-optimal courses of action yesterday, there can be expected to develop systematic *changes in expectations* concerning ends and means that can generate corresponding *alterations in plans*. Men entered the market yesterday attempting to carry out plans based on their beliefs concerning the ends worth pursuing and the means available. These beliefs reflected expectations, concerning the decisions other men would be making. The prices a market participant expected to receive for the resources or the products he would sell and the prices he expected to have to pay for the resources or products he would buy all went to determine the optimum course of market action for him. The discovery, during the course of yesterday's market experiences, that the other market participants were *not* making these expected decisions can be seen as generating changes in the corresponding price expectations with which market participants enter the market today.

For such a process of discovery of changing ends-means frameworks it is necessary to introduce something from outside the Robbinsian economizing terms of reference. For the purposes of the economist it is not necessary to explore the *psychology* of the learning process, which is the result of market experiences in which plans were found to be unworkable (or in which it has been found that alternative, preferable courses of action were in fact available).[25] But it is neces-

25. See F. A. Hayek, "Economics and Knowledge," in his *Individualism*

The Entrepreneur

sary to build formally into our theory the insight that such a learning process can be relied upon. For this, the recognition of the entrepreneurial element in individual action is completely adequate. As soon as we broaden our theoretical vision of the individual decision-maker from a "mechanical" Robbinsian economizer to Mises's *homo agens*, with the universally human entrepreneurial elements of alertness in his makeup, we can cope with the task of explaining the changes which market forces systematically generate.

And the analytical device of concentrating *all* entrepreneurship into the role of the hypothetical pure entrepreneurs enables us to achieve the same kind of explanation. We may in this way continue to envisage a market in which consumers and resource owners are strictly Robbinsian economizers, exclusively price-takers, and shift the entire burden of price changes and changes in methods of production and of output quality and quantity upon the pure entrepreneurs. As we have seen earlier, this becomes all the easier once we perceive the near-inevitability of an entrepreneurial role's being filled by the producer.

All this leads me to express a certain dissatisfaction with the role assigned to the entrepreneur in the Schumpeterian system. We will return a little later in this chapter to Schumpeter's vision of the entrepreneur, as well as the views of the other leading writers on this topic. Here it is enough to observe that Schumpeter's entrepreneur and the one developed here can in many ways be recognized — and, let me add, reassuringly recognized — as the same individual. But there is one important respect — if only in emphasis — in which Schumpeter's treatment differs from my own. Schumpeter's enterpreneur acts to *disturb* an existing equilibrium situation. Entrepreneurial activity *disrupts* the continuing circular flow. The entrepreneur is pictured as *initiating* change and as gen-

and Economic Order (London: Routledge and Kegan Paul), 1949), p. 46; I. M. Kirzner, "Methodological Individualism," p. 795.

Entrepreneurship and the Equilibrating Process

crating *new* opportunities. Although each burst of entrepreneurial innovation leads eventually to a new equilibrium situation, the entrepreneur is presented as a *disequilibrating*, rather than an equilibrating, force. Economic development, which Schumpeter of course makes utterly dependent upon entrepreneurship, is "entirely foreign to what may be observed in . . . the tendency towards equilibrium."[26]

By contrast my own treatment of the entrepreneur emphasizes the equilibrating aspects of his role. I see the situation upon which the entrepreneurial role impinges as one of inherent disequilibrium rather than of equilibrium — as one churning with opportunities for desirable changes rather than as one of placid evenness. Although for me, too, it is only through the entrepreneur that changes can arise, I see these changes as *equilibrating changes*. For me the changes the entrepreneur initiates are always toward the hypothetical state of equilibrium; they are changes brought about *in response to* the existing pattern of mistaken decisions, a pattern characterized by missed opportunities. The entrepreneur, in my view, *brings into mutual adjustment* those discordant elements which resulted from prior market ignorance.

My emphasis on this difference between Schumpeter's discussion and my own underscores the crucial importance of entrepreneurship for the *market process*. A treatment such as Schumpeter's, which invokes entrepreneurship as an exogenous force lifting the economy from one state of equilibrium (to eventually attain another such state as a result of "imitators"), is likely to convey the impression that for the *attainment* of equilibrium no entrepreneurial role is, in principle, required at all. Such a treatment is, in other words, likely to generate the utterly mistaken view that the state of equilibrium can establish itself without any social device to deploy and

26. J. A. Schumpeter, *The Theory of Economic Development* (Cambridge: Harvard University Press, 1934), p. 64.

The Entrepreneur

marshal the scattered pieces of information which are the only source of such a state.[27]

It is to stress my contrary view, that it is only entrepreneurship which might (at least in theory, if exogenous changes are barred) eventually lead to equilibrium, that I feel it necessary to draw attention to entrepreneurship as a *responding* agency. I view the entrepreneur not as a source of innovative ideas ex nihilo, but as being *alert* to the opportunities that exist *already* and are waiting to be noticed. In economic development, too, the entrepreneur is to be seen as responding to opportunities rather than creating them; as capturing profit opportunities rather than generating them. When profitable capital-using methods of production are technologically available, where the flow of savings is sufficient to provide the necessary capital, entrepreneurship is required to ensure that this innovation will in fact be introduced.[28] Without entrepreneurship, without alertness to the new possibility, the long-term benefits may remain untapped. It is highly desirable to maintain a framework of analysis which shows the market process at work in essentially the same way both for a simple economy in which multiperiod plans are not made and for the complex economy in which such plans, involving the use of capital, are made. For this process it is utterly essential to invoke entrepreneurship. That most contemporary treatments of price theory fail to perceive this is perhaps the principal cause for my dissatisfaction with them. Schumpeter's unfortunate emphasis upon the entrepreneur as pushing the economy *away* from equilibrium helps promote the quite erroneous belief that entrepreneurship is somehow unnecessary to un-

27. See F. A. Hayek, "The Use of Knowledge in Society," *American Economic Review* 35 (September 1945): 529–30 (reprinted in *Individualism and Economic Order*, pp. 90–91), for the charge that Schumpeter himself in fact fell prey to this mistaken view.

28. See M. N. Rothbard, *Man, Economy and State* (Princeton, N.J., Van Nostrand, 1962), 2:493–94.

Entrepreneurship in the Literature

derstanding the way the market tends toward the equilibrium position.[29]

ENTREPRENEURSHIP IN THE LITERATURE

As was remarked earlier, one of our complaints concerning contemporary theories of price arises from their virtual elimination of entrepreneurship. What is required, I have argued, is a reformulation of price theory to readmit the entrepreneurial role to its rightful position as crucial to the very operation of the market. Despite my criticisms in this respect, however, it is by no means my contention that the entrepreneurial role has not received careful attention in the literature. There exists, of course, a well-developed line of contributions to the theory of entrepreneurship and entrepreneurial profit. Moreover, these discussions have involved several of the best-known names in modern economic thought. And from time to time articles still appear in the journals, dealing with one or another aspect of the problem. My complaint is not directed primarily at the shortcomings in this literature; rather I regret that the entrepreneurial role is not recognized as crucial to the market determination of the course of price movements. It seems desirable at this point to refer very briefly to the literature on entrepreneurial profit and to indicate the matters on which my approach diverges from the various strands of thought that are to be distinguished within that literature.[30]

As a general preliminary remark, it is worth noting that the primary concern of many of the contributors to this literature

29. For further discussion of the points raised in this section see I. M. Kirzner, "Entrepreneurship and the Market Approach to Development," in *Toward Liberty* (Menlo Park, Calif.: Institute for Humane Studies, 1971).

30. For general surveys of the literature see F. H. Knight, "Profit," in *Encyclopedia of the Social Sciences* (New York: Macmillan, 1934), reprinted in W. Fellner and B. Haley, eds., *Readings in the Theory of Income Distribution* (New York: Blakiston, 1949); J. F. Weston, "The Profit Concept and Theory: A Restatement," *Journal of Political Economy* 62 (April 1954): 152–70.

[6]

On the Central Concept of Austrian Economics: Market Process

Ludwig M. Lachmann

In setting up the market process as the central concept of Austrian economics, as opposed to the general-equilibrium approach of the neoclassical school, Austrian economists have a choice of strategies: They might, on the one hand, attempt to show the absurdity of the notion of general equilibrium, the arid formalism of the style of thought that gave rise to it, and its "irrelevance" to many urgent problems. They might, without denying the significance of equilibrating forces, stress the time aspect and show that the equilibrating forces can never do their work in time, that long before general equilibrium is established some change will supervene to render the data obsolete. They would, however, face the objection that the notion of market process requires equilibrating forces to make it work, an objection that, because it is a half-truth, might be hard to refute without drawing a distinction between "equilibrium of the individual" and "equilibrium of the economic system."

In my view, however, Austrian economists should present their case for the market process by offering a fairly comprehensive account of the human forces governing it rather than by engaging in piecemeal discussions of its various interconnected aspects, which must, in the absence of the total picture, remain obscure. The defects of the neoclassical style become obvious if the Austrian economists simply point to facts the neoclassical conceptual tools are unable to explain.

What keeps the market process in perpetual motion? Why does it never end, denoting the final state of equilibrium of our system? If Austrian economists answered by saying, "Something unexpected always happens," they would be accused of vagueness and reminded that only perpetual "changes in data" could have this effect. An attempt to show that continuous autonomous changes in demand or supply do account for the permanent character of the market process would involve a drawn-out discussion of the effects of ever-changing patterns of knowledge on the conduct of consumers and producers, a discussion in which Austrian economists would be at a serious disadvantage without prior elucidation of the term *knowledge*.

The market process is the outward manifestation of an unending stream of knowledge. This insight is fundamental to Austrian economics. The pattern of knowledge is continuously changing in society, a process hard to describe. Knowledge defies all attempts to treat it as a "datum" or an object identifiable in time and space.

Knowledge may be acquired at a cost, but is not always, as when we witness an accident or "learn by doing" for other than cognitive reasons. Sometimes, knowledge is jealously and expensively guarded; sometimes, it may be broadcast to reach a maximum number of listeners, as in advertising. Now knowledge, whether costly or free, may prove valuable to one and useless to another, owing to the complementarity of new and old knowledge and the diversity of human interests. Hence it is impossible to gauge the range of application of some bit of knowledge until it is obsolete. But we can never be certain that knowledge is obsolete since the future is unknown. All useful knowledge probably tends to be diffused, but in being applied for various purposes it also may change character, hence the difficulty of *identifying* it.

Knowledge then is an elusive concept wholly refractory to neoclassical methods. It cannot be quantified, has no location in space, and defies insertion into any complex of functional relationships. Though it varies in time, it is no variable, either dependent or independent. *As soon as we permit time to elapse, we must permit knowledge to change, and knowledge cannot be regarded as a function of anything else.* The state of knowledge of a society cannot be the same at two successive points of time, and time cannot elapse without demand and supply shifting. The stream of knowledge produces ever new disequilibrium situations, and entrepreneurs continually manage to find new price-cost differences to exploit. When one is eliminated by strenuous competition, the stream of knowledge throws up another. Profit is a permanent income from ever-changing sources.

Certain consequences of what has been said seem to concern the modus operandi of the market, but one appears to be significant for the methodology of all social sciences.

In the first place, how do we determine the true origin of any particular bit of knowledge? When and how do ill-founded surmises and half-baked ideas acquire the status of respectable knowledge? We can neither answer nor ignore these questions. Two things we may assert with reasonable confidence. As Karl Popper showed, we cannot have future knowledge in the present.[1] Also, men sometimes act on the basis of what cannot really be called knowledge. Here we encounter the problem of expectations.

Although old knowledge is continually being superseded by new knowledge, though nobody knows which piece will be obsolete tomorrow, men have to act with regard to the future and make plans based on expectations. Experience teaches us that in an uncertain world different men hold different expectations about the same future event. This fact has certain implications for growth theory — in my view important implications — with which I deal in my paper "Toward a Critique of Macroeconomics" (included in this volume). Here we are concerned with the fact that divergent expectations entail incoherent plans. At another place I argued that "what keeps this process in continuous motion is the occurrence of unexpected change as well as the inconsistency of human plans. Both are necessary conditions."[2] Are we entitled, then, to be confident that the market process will in the end eliminate incoherence of plans which would thus prove to be only transient? What is being asked

On the Central Concept: "Market Process"   129

here is a fairly fundamental question about the nature of the market process.

The subject of expectations, a subjective element in human action, is eminently "Austrian." Expectations must be regarded as autonomous, as autonomous as human preferences are. To be sure, they are modified by experience, but we are unable to postulate any particular mode of change. To say that the market gradually produces a consistency among plans is to say that the divergence of expectations, on which the initial incoherence of plans rests, will gradually be turned into convergence. But to reach this conclusion we must deny the autonomous character of expectations. We have to make the (diminishing) degree of divergence of expectations a function of the time sequence of the stages of the market process. If the stream of knowledge is not a function of anything, how can the degree of divergence of expectations, which are but rudimentary forms of incomplete knowledge, be made a function of time?

Unsuccessful plans have to be revised. No doubt planners learn from experience. But what they learn is not known; also different men learn different lessons. We might say that unsuccessful planners make capital losses and thus gradually lose their control over resources and their ability to engage in new enterprises; the successful are able to plan with more confidence and on a much larger scale. Mises used such an argument. But how can we be sure? History shows many examples of men who were "ahead of their times," whose expectations were vindicated when it was too late, who had to give up the struggle for lack of resources when a few more would have brought them triumph instead of defeat. There is no reason why a man who fails three times should not succeed the fourth. Expectations are autonomous. We cannot predict their mode of change as prompted by failure or success.

What we have here is a difference of opinion on the nature of the market process. For one view the market process is propelled by a mechanism of given and known forces of demand and supply. The outcome of the interaction of these forces, namely, equilibrium, is in principle predictable. But outside forces in the

form of autonomous changes in demand and supply continually
impinge on the system and prevent equilibrium from being
reached. The system is ever moving in the direction of *an*
equilibrium, but it never gets there. The competitive action of
entrepreneurs tending to wipe out price-cost differences is regarded as "equilibrating"; for in equilibrium no such differences
could exist.

The other view, which I happen to hold, regards the distinction between external forces and the internal market mechanism
as essentially misleading. Successive stages in the flow of knowledge must be manifest in both. Market action is not independent
of expectations, and every expectation is an attempt "to catch a
glimpse of future knowledge now." To say that each market
moves toward a price that "clears" it has little meaning where
speculators are busy piling up and unloading stocks. The relationship between different markets in disequilibrium is infinitely
complex. I shall say nothing more about it here, though I deal
with some aspects of this complex problem in "Toward a
Critique of Macroeconomics" (included in this volume).

Having set out to replace the paradigm of general equilibrium
by that of the market process, why should we concentrate on the
equilibrating nature of the latter — on showing that but for the
perennial impact of external forces general equilibrium would
be reached after all? It might be held, however, that every
process must have a *direction*, and unless we are able to show that
every stage of the market process "points" in the direction of
equilibrium, no satisfactory theory of the market process is
possible.

But this is not a convincing view. In the first place, though a
process may have a direction at each point of time, it may change
direction over time. The direction the process follows need not
be the same throughout. Second and more important, two kinds
of process have to be distinguished here. The first is a limited
process, in the course of which we witness the successive modes
of interaction of a set of forces, given initially and limited in
number. Such a process may terminate or go on forever; whatever happens depends entirely on the nature of the (given) set of

forces. The system may be subjected to random shocks from external sources, which it may take some time to absorb, such absorption interfering with the interaction of the forces. The second variety of process is the very opposite of the first. No initial set of forces delimits the boundaries of events. Any force from anywhere may at any time affect our process, and forces that impinged on it yesterday may suddenly vanish from the scene. There is no end or final point of rest in sight. Need I assert that history is a process of the second, not of the first, variety?

While our market process is not of the first kind, it is not completely unlimited. Two things may be said about it. The notion of general equilibrium is to be abandoned, but that of *individual equilibrium* is ·to be retained at all costs. It is simply tantamount to *rational action*. Without it we should lose our "sense of direction." The market process consists of a sequence of individual interactions, each denoting the encounter (and sometimes collision) of a number of plans, which, while coherent individually and reflecting the individual equilibrium of the actor, are incoherent as a group. The process would not go on otherwise.

Walrasians, in using the same notion of equilibrium on the three levels of analysis — the individual, the market, and the entire system — succumbed to the fallacy of ·unwarranted generalization: they erroneously believed that the key that unlocks one door will also unlock a number of others. Action controlled by one mind is, as Mises showed, necessarily consistent. The actions of a number of minds in the same market lack such consistency, as the simultaneous presence of bulls and bears shows. Consistency of actions in a number of markets within a system constitutes an even greater presumption.

Finally, the divergence of expectations, apart from being an obstacle to equilibrium, has an important positive function in a market economy. *It is an anticipatory device.* The more extended the range of expectations, the greater the likelihood that somebody will catch a glimpse of things to come and be "right." Those who take their orientation from the future rather than the present, the "speculators," permit the future to make its impact on the market process earlier than otherwise. They contrive to inject a glimpse of future knowledge into the emergent market pattern. Of course they may make mistakes for which they will pay. Without divergent expectations and incoherent plans, however, it could not happen at all.

NOTES

1.   Karl R. Popper, *The Poverty of Historicism* (London: Routledge & Kegan Paul, 1957).
2.   Ludwig M. Lachmann, "Methodological Individualism and the Market Economy," in *Roads to Freedom: Essays in Honour of Friedrich A. von Hayek,* ed. Erich Streissler et al. (London: Routledge & Kegan Paul, 1969), p.91.

[7]

Entrepreneurship, Imagination,

and the Question of Equilibration

For economists of the present-day Austrian School, an understanding of the market process hinges on the concept of entrepreneurship. It is the entrepreneur who generates the market process.
Motivated by the possibility of pure profit, he is continually
working to adjust production to meet what he anticipates will be
the most urgent demands of buyers. He makes and revises his plans
on the basis of past experience, current knowledge, and expectations
regarding the future. Though agitative, entrepreneurship is an
attempt at greater coordination.

Various authors within and about the Austrian tradition have
emphasized one face or the other--agitation or coordination--of
the Janus of entrepreneurship. Schumpeter depicted the entrepreneur as innovative and disruptive, unleashing a "gale of creative
destruction".[1] Professor Israel Kirzner's recent <u>Competition and
Entrepreneurship</u> takes the opposite tack, viewing entrepreneurial
activity as responsive and unambiguously equilibrating. "For me,"
Kirzner notes, "the changes the entrepreneur initiates are always
toward the hypothetical state of equilibrium."[2] The book accordingly
identifies <u>alertness</u> to market discrepancies as the defining characteristic of entrepreneurship. Professor D. T. Armentano has
recently offered an insightful Schumpeterian critique of Kirzner's
emphasis on equilibration.[3]

The present paper approaches the question somewhat differently, emphasizing the uncertainty and expectation which underlie entrepreneurship. It will argue that the pervasive uncertainty faced by entrepreneurs, stressed by Mises but deliberately downplayed by Kirzner, suggests speculation or _imagination_ more than alertness to be characteristic of entrepreneurship. A focus on the imaginative aspect of entrepreneurial activity will, in addition, permit some reconciliation of the Schumpeterian and Kirznerian perspectives. Finally, the question of equilibration is appraised with respect to Hayekian dynamic equilibrium. If dynamic equilibrium (there is no room for entrepreneurship in static theories) can be defined only with respect to the expectations of market participants, as Professor Hayek argued some forty years ago[4], and expectations diverge, as Professor Lachmann is always pointing out, then entrepreneurial activity cannot be so unambiguously equilibrating as Kirzner suggests.

Kirzner's account of the entrepreneur in the market centers on his discussion of the "pure entrepreneur". This hypothetical figure is described as "a decision-maker whose entire role arises out of his alertness to hitherto unnoticed opportunities."[5] The pure entrepreneur "proceeds by his alertness to discover and exploit situations in which he is able to sell for high prices that which he can buy for low prices."[6] The producer, in his role as pure entrepreneur, "is seen displaying nothing but alertness to the existence of price differences between inputs and outputs."[7] The fact that productive processes which turn low-priced inputs into higher-priced outputs consume time does not for Kirzner alter the nature of entrepreneurial activity, "except by introducing the uncertainties involved in an unknown future"--an alteration which in fact introduces the essence of entrepreneurship.

Though elsewhere he recognizes "the relatively precarious character of all perceived profit opportunities"[8], Kirzner deliberately abstracts from such considerations in his discussion of pure entrepreneurship. There is no sense of the uncertainty facing every entrepreneurial project, of the fact that it may engender loss instead of profit. Opportunities for profit, in these passages, are accorded an objective existence. Once the alert entrepreneur has discovered such an opportunity, it is as though he has discovered a "free ten-dollar bill" to be resting in his hand, "available for the grasping".[9]

As an _ex post_ view of _successful_ entrepreneurship Professor Kirzner's discussion is commendable, and it offers a valuable contrast to attempts to cast entrepreneurship in the Robbinsian mold of mere economization. As a portrait of entrepreneurship in general, however, it slights an important feature: the uncertainty bred by time. The omission, to be sure, is deliberate. Kirzner's express intention is to emphasize "that the entrepreneur's decision-- despite its unavoidably speculative character--represents his judgement that an opportunity for profit _does_ exist."[10] This formulation, recognizing that the existence of an opportunity for profit is a matter of the entrepreneur's _judgement_ and not (necessarily) fact, is more careful and illuminating than earlier formulations which make no such distinction.

3

An "opportunity for profit" which requires the passage of time for its exploitation certainly cannot be said (ex ante at least) to exist in any objective sense. Entrepreneurial profit can be realized, if at all, only in the future. It is noteworthy that Kirzner refers to his as an "arbitrage" theory of profit, suggesting essential likeness to those transactions which instantaneously exploit interlocal price discrepancies in commodity or currency markets. Indeed, he never distinguishes between arbitrageurship and entrepreneurship.[11]

The crucial difference is time. The arbitrageur, dealing in contemporaneous markets, displays alertness to price discrepancies which do in fact exist. His opportunities for arbitrage profit are "there", and it seems of little use to distinguish between ex ante and ex post views of the situation. For the entrepreneur things are different. While successful entrepreneurship (by necessity viewed ex post) exhibits important and essential similarities to arbitrageurship--features Kirzner has valuably developed--to equate the two seems to beg the entire question.

The producer as pure entrepreneur faces the ineluctable fact that time must elapse between the committing of resources to production and sale of the end product. The configuration of buyer demand which will prevail in the future, though past patterns and trends may provide some guidance, can never be precisely known. As Professor G. L. S. Shackle rightly insists, "at that point in time when the decision is taken to commit some resources to a particular line of production, it is the nature of things impossible for anyone to know precisely and for certain what will be the

4

market exchange value of the end-product at that future date when
it will be ready." Thus, "In all production, because it takes
time, there is an ineradicable uncertainty."[12]

"Uncertainty", like numerous other terms in economics, can
be understood in two senses, one "subjective" and the other "objective". The first designates an attitude or state of mind on the
part of the decision-maker, while the second signifies the indeterminateness or unpredictability of future states of human affairs.
The attitude reflects experience with the nature of things, of
course, and the nature of things is of interest for its impact on
human plans.

The attitudes of decision-makers and the specific psychological
process of decision-making, one elaborate account of which has been
offered by Shackle[13], are largely beside the point here. Discussion
of uncertainty need not contest or obscure the Kirznerian insight
that "when an entrepreneur does enter into an admittedly risky
venture he does so because he believes that on balance, it offers
an attractive opportunity."[14] What must be drawn out, however,
is the strictly subjective status to be accorded to the existence
of an opportunity at the time of decision-making. Entrepreneurial
decision-making, in an uncertain world, must rely upon qualified
beliefs or expectations.

Entrepreneurial expectations are beliefs concerning the relevant future data of the market: the demand for the product, relative costs and prices, the actions of potential competitors, and
the like.[15] They are, in Lachmann's words, "working hypotheses"
whose formation "is incidental to the endeavor to diagnose the

5

situation in which action must be taken, in the face of an uncertain future".[16] Though expectations embody an imperfect knowledge
of the present, and are necessitated by imperfect foresight, it
would be misleading to view them, as Lachmann apparently does, as
imperfect knowledge of the future. No real knowledge is possible
of an indeterminate and not-yet-existent state of affairs, a future
which is in principle unpredictable and which the expecting entrepreneur's actions will help bring about. The impossibility of
predicting the economic future follows from the impossibility of
predicting human decisions, in this case of consumers and other
entrepreneurs.[17]

A statement by Shackle is particularly relevant here:

> The orthodox class of approach to the problem of
> how men can cope with uncertainty is to look upon them
> as suffering from the slight defectiveness and incom-
> pleteness of their knowledge of a future objectively
> given. My approach is to view them as liberated by the
> non-existence of any objective future to invent it in
> an image chosen by them from a range of possibilities
> constrained only by the orderliness of nature and the
> facts of their own present circumstances. Uncertainty
> is freedom, freedom for the imagination, freedom to
> hope. We therefore must largely discard, in my view,
> the apparatus of thought which assumes that we can know
> the future, if only we take the trouble. We are not
> like people who have a badly printed railway timetable,
> with misprints and some pages smudged or torn out. We
> are like people who have got to run the trains themselves.[18]

Rather than a display of alertness to objectively existing
opportunities (though again this may turn out to be a proper characterization in particular cases) or even to subjectively existing
opportunities (since alertness to one's own beliefs makes little
sense), entrepreneurship characteristically requires a display of
imagination. Rather than upon a discovery of actual input-output
price discrepancies (since future output prices are not yet a

reality), the entrepreneur must act upon his envisionment or
<u>expectation</u> of price conditions becoming or remaining such in the
future that profit will emerge. The "deliberate search for profit
opportunities" which as Kirzner notes is "the essence of the entrepreneurial role"[19] is not so much a search as an exercise in
constrained imagination. Entrepreneurial projects are not waiting
to be sought out so much as to be thought up. The entrepreneur's
plans must be based on expectations, and these must be created by
him: an image of future markets is available not throught sight
but through insight. As the future is not given, Shackle explains,
expectation is "the act of the <u>invention</u> of possibilities and of
their capacity to come true (as a sequel to appropriate policies)"
and entrepreneurship "an <u>originative and imaginative art</u>".[20] The
mental processes of the entrepreneur must be both active and creative.[21]

Needless to say, entrepreneurship is not to be regarded as
fanciful or divorced from reality. On the contrary, entrepreneurial
imagination is considerably constrained by knowledge of current
market signals and trends and the desire to anticipate contingent
future market data as correctly as possible for the sake of success.
Information regarding some (though not the totality) of the events
to take place in the future is available and is sought by the
entrepreneur. He must interpret this information, and more importantly must supplement it with assumptions created and chosen by
means of imagination. This combination of imagination and limited
foreknowledge is known as <u>foresight</u>, its contents as expectations.[22]

That success is not always forthcoming is unsurprising on this
view of entrepreneurship. Failure of plans is generally due to
a failure of expectations to conform to or encompass all actual
market developments.[23] Kirzner's attention to the arbitrageurial
aspects of pure entrepreneurship unfortunately leads him, except
in his excellent opening sketch of the market process, to emphasize
profit to the virtual exclusion of loss.

Kirzner's insightful and suggestive treatment of entrepreneurial innovation is also more awkward than need be. Contrasting his
own description of the entrepreneurial role with Schumpeter's,
he writes:

> For me the important feature of entrepreneurship is
> not so much the ability to break away from routine as
> the ability to perceive new opportunities which others
> have not yet noticed. Entrepreneurship for me is not
> so much the introduction of new products or of new
> techniques of production as the ability to see where
> new products have become unsuspectedly valuable to
> consumers and where new methods of production have,
> unknown to others, become feasible.[24]

These distictions are, from a subjectivist viewpoint, unneccessary.
If opportunities for pure profit require imagination, and exist
ex ante only in the expectations or mind of the imaginative entrepreneur, then clearly new opportunities cannot be said to exist
until they are conceived of or "noticed" by an entrepreneur willing
to "break away from routine". It is certainly awkward to speak
of the situation as one in which hypothetical new products "have
become unsuspectedly valuable to consumers". In fact consumers
are not yet aware of these products, and can hardly be said to have
changed their valuations of them without elaborate assumptions
about latent demand schedules covering non-existent commodities.

Even then the relevant change occurs not in the valuations of the consumers but in the outlook of the entrepreneur. He cannot see their demand schedules; he can only imagine them.

J. W. N. Watkins has noted that "innovations in the supply of economic goods and services must be based on a hypothesis about the latent demand for them, a hypothesis which can usually be tested only after the innovation has been made."[25] The very same is true for what may be termed "imitations"--entreprencurial projects which do not involve the introduction of a new-and-different product or service (technological innovations are not of concern here). The "imitative" entrepreneur also faces uncertainty in his decision, also adjusts production to meet an anticipated constellation of demand, and may also reap pure profit. The objective physical characteristics of the product (its similarity or dissimilarity to currently availiable products) are irrelevent to the question of entrepreneurship. The Schumpeterian innovator may be admitted to the broader ranks of entrepreneurship without his being denatured when the role of imagination is recognized. An arbitrageurial account of entrepreneurship is ill-equipped to deal with innovation, for the notion of discovering price discrepancies is severely strained in a situation where no prices of any kind (let alone future prices) exist for the new-and-different commodity under consideration.

Every entrepreneur must imagine (try to anticipate) the market conditions and future demand which would greet the arrival of his product or service. Of course, perfect foresight is unavailable. His expectations are likely to be falsified to some degree, and

9

his plans sooner or later will probably fail to be completely
realized. As expectations in an exchange economy primarily concern
the actions of other market participants (consumers and other
entrepreneurs), failure reveals that the entrepreneur's plans were
<u>inconsistent</u> with the plans of others (assuming internal coherence
of his plans). It is of considerable theoretical interest to consider the logical conditions for the perfect success of all plans,
a state of dynamic equilibrium, but even more intriguing with
respect to entrepreneurship is the question of whether any tendency
exists to move toward this state--the question of equilibration.

F. A. Hayek's classic essay "Economics and Knowledge" (1936)
brilliantly examines the notion of equilibrium and its relevence
to the real world. "All propositions of equilibrium analysis,"
Hayek argues, " . . . are propositions about the relations between
actions." The actions of a single individual can be said to be
in equilibrium "in so far as they can be understood as part of
one plan"; that is, for as long as he considers his plan the most
conducive to success and does not feel compelled to alter it.
This will be the case (it would seem) only while his expectations
are fulfilled. For the actions (and interactions) of a number of
individuals, these conditions are generalized. Equilibrium for
a market society exists "if all the actions of all members of the
society over a period are all executions of their respective individual plans on which each decided at the beginning of the period."[26]

In order that all the plans of various individuals may be
carried out they must be mutually consistent in the special sense
that each person's plans must contain exactly those actions which

10

others expect of him (as part of their plans). Were this "mutual
compatibility of intentions" not given, failure and revision of
the plans of some people as the result of endogenous disturbances
would be inevitable. Equilibrium may also be upset by exogenous
disturbances, unforeseen developments in the objective data (though
these may be unambiguo̊sly regarded as such only if expectations
coincide and thus they are unanimously unforeseen).[27]

The defining characteristic of a state of equilibrium, then,
is correct foresight on the part of market participants.. Foresight
"must be correct in the sense that every person's plan is based
on the expectation of just those actions of other people which
those other people intend to perform and that all these plans are
based on the expectation of the same set of external facts, so
that under certain conditions nobody will have any reason to change
his plans."[28]

In the light of this analysis the real content of the assertion
that a tendency toward equilibrium exists becomes clear: "It can
hardly mean anything but that, under certain conditions, the knowledge and intentions of the different members of society are supposed to come more and more into agreement or, to put the same
thing in less general and less exact but more concrete terms, that
the expectations of the people and particularly of the entrepreneurs will become more and more correct."[29] The question of equilibration is thus one of the conditions under which and the process
by which entrepreneurship can be supposed to foster an improvement
in foresight.

11

Equilibrium in this sense, as Hayek points out, carries no
promise of optimality. More efficient uses for resources may be
available and yet equilibrium be maintained, so long as such possibilities do not occur to entrepreneurs. Kirzner's description
of equilibrium, on the other hand, does specify Pareto optimality:
"When the decisions of all market participants dovetail completely,
so that each plan correctly assumes the corresponding plans of
the other participants and no possibility exists for any altered
plans that would be simultaneously preferred by the relevant participants, there is nothing left for the entrepreneur to do. He
will be unable to discover possibilities /for profit7."[30] The
optimality consideration, though consistent with Kirzner's emphasis
on the objective existence of profitable opportunities, seems
entirely subsidiary to the consideration of correct expectations
or foresight. What is important is not the existence or nonexist-
ence of optimality from the viewpoint of an omniscient observer,
but from the viewpoint of the entrepreneur in the market. (Would
he resign himself to zero entrepreneurial profits were equalization
of rates of return in all pursuits to obtain during some period?)
An assumption of perfect knowledge on the part of all market participants would eliminate any difference between the two viewpoints,
but Hayek has shown such an assumption to be unecessary for equilibrium conditions to prevail. The relevant knowledge which each
market participant must possess is only that knowledge "which he
is bound to acquire in view of the position in which he originally
is, and the plans which he then makes. It is certainly not all
the knowledge which, if he acquired it by accident, would be

12

useful to him and lead to a change in plan."[31]   It seems difficult
to demonstrate, and question-begging to suppose, prior to consideration of the equilibrating process, that entrepreneurs are <u>bound</u>
to acquire knowledge of intertemporal opportunities which will in
fact yield profit.   It is, as suggested before, logically nonsensical to speak of the adoption of an entrepreneurial plan as depending on its actual, <u>ex post</u> outcome.[32]

Actual outcomes, profit and loss, do play important roles in
the market <u>learning process</u>, a process which may well provide
equilibration.   Current expectations, founded on the revision of
earlier expectations in the light of experience, are themselves
revised later on as further experience is gained.[33]   Entrepreneurial
experience comes from the testing of plans (based on expectations)
in the market, with profit and loss the chief indicators of the
success or failure of expectations to conform to actual market
developments.   The information they provide, however, must be
interpreted.[34]

The task of interpretation seems considerably more difficult
in the event of losses than the event of profits.   Profits clearly
signal the actual existence of an opportunity for pure gain, though
it may happen that the opportunity has vanished or has been thoroughly exploited by the time response is forthcoming on the part
of some entrepreneurs.   Losses, on the other hand, signal only the
inconsistency of the entrepreneur's previous plan with the plans
of others in the market.   Losses point out a need for the revision
of plans, but provide little more in the way of positive guidance.
The failure of some plans is inevitable given the coexistence of

                                           same
divergent plans concerning the/means, and it cannot be assumed

that the resulting revisions will produce the consistency of plans

necessary for stability. Entrepreneurs can and do learn from

experience, but they cannot be expected always to learn the best

lesson. That the real world, moreover, is one of "continuous

unexpected change" means, Lachmann explains, that "even while men

are gaining additional knowledge by learning from earlier mistakes,

at the very same time some their existing knowledge is becoming

obsolete."[35]

        Profit and loss serve another function, that of determining

in part the resources available for future planning. The relation-

ship of the pure entrepreneur to the capitalist (both are roles and

need not--some would argue ought not--be assigned to separate players)

is a complex issue which cannot be examined here, but it is clear

enough that the market process will tend to eliminate those whose

foresight is seldom correct and to reward those whose foresight

proves more correct. While this weeding out and fertilizing process

is undoubtedly responsible for that level of foresight among entre-

preneurs to which material progress and coordination in economic

life bear witness[36], it is not clear that its speed can always

sufficiently exceed that with which new entrepreneurs crop up, so

as to increase the level of foresight.

        The issue of equilibration, it appears, is no longer so easily

resolved when attention is freed from pre-occupation with entre-

preneurial success. The Kirznerian perspective on entrepreneur-

ship is extremely important, and goes a long way toward explaining

the coordination of tastes, technologies, and resources.[37] The

coordination of entrepreneurial intentions and expectations, however, requires further consideration. The entrepreneur acting on
"alertness to <u>hitherto unnoticed</u> opportunities" is bound to upset
the expectations of other entrepreneurs (since they have not foreseen the opportunity), concerning his actions at the very least.
In adjusting production to meet anticipated demand, in coordinating
a market over time as he imagines it, the entrepreneur will upset
the plans of others whose expectations concerning that market
diverge. As this experience will lead each of them to revise his
expectations and presumably his plan of action (each in accordance
with his own interpretation of events), there seems no reason why
this series of successive changes should ever conclude.[38]

Complete equilibration of entrepreneurial plans would require
reconciliation not only of various plans currently being made, but
also of plans currently being made with plans to be made in the
future.[39] The formidability (indeed impossibility) of this task--
the realization that the entrepreneurial process could never complete it and is unlikely to even make much headway after a point--
suggests again the questionability of (unqualifiedly) characterizing
entrepreneurship as equilibrating. It is at least clear that
this question merits further investigation.

Notes

1   Joseph A. Schumpeter, "The Process of Creative Destruction" in
     Capitalism, Socialism, and Democracy; reprinted in Yale Brozen,
     ed., The Competitive Economy (Morristown, NJ: General Learning
     Press, 1975).

2   Israel M. Kirzner, Competition and Entrepreneurship (Chicago:
     The University of Chicago Press, 1973), p. 73.

3   D. T. Armentano, "Competition and Monopoly Theory: Some
     Austrian Perspectives", unpublished manuscript prepared for
     the Symposium on Austrian Economics, June 1975.

4   Freidrich A. Hayek, "Economics and Knowledge", reprinted in
     Individualism and Economic Order (Chicago: Henry Regnery
     Company, 1972).

5   Kirzner, op. cit., p. 39. Emphasis added.

6   ibid., p. 48.

7   ibid., p. 46.

8   ibid., p. 78.

9   ibid., p. 47.

10   ibid., p. 86. Emphasis in the original.

11   I am indebted to Professor Lachmann for this observation.

12   G. L. S. Shackle, "The Economist's View of Profit", reprinted
     in Uncertainty in Economics (Cambridge: Cambridge University
     Press, 1955), p. 81.

13   In too many books and articles to enumerate, but a useful
     introduction to which may be found in Time in Economics
     (Amsterdam: North Holland Publishing Company, 1967), p. 46f.

14   Kirzner, op. cit., pp. 82-83. Emphasis added.

15   B. S. Keirstead, An Essay in the Theory of Profits and Income
     Distribution (Oxford: Basil Blackwell, 1953), p. 23. Though
     flawed in many respects, this book gives an interesting account
     of entrepreneurship and makes a serious attempt to deal with
     the role of expectations.

16   Ludwig M. Lachmann, Capital and its Structure (London: G. Bell
     and Sons, 1956), p. 23.

16

17   Compare Lachmann's Law: "The impossibility of prediction in
      economics follows from the facts that economic change is linked
      to change in knowledge, and future knowledge cannot be gained
      before its time," which, if concerned not with technological
      discoveries but the knowledge to be gleaned from the testing
      of current plans, seems either to be circular or to point out
      a matter of practical and not principled impossibility.
      Lachmann, "Professor Shackle on the Economic Significance of
      Time", Metroeconomica, vol. XI, fasc. I-II (Aprile-Agosto,
      1959), p. 71.

18   Shackle, review of R. A. D. Egerton's Investment Decisions
      Under Uncertainty, The Economic Journal, vol. LXXIV, no. 293
      (March, 1964), p. 172. Emphasis in the original.

19   Kirzner, op. cit., p. 83. Ex post and ex ante views of profit
      both have their place and neither need exclude the other as
      Kirzner fears. See Shackle, "The Nature and Role of Profit",
      reprinted in Uncertainty in Economics, op. cit.

20   Shackle, Epistemics and Economics (Cambridge: Cambridge
      University Press, 1972), p. 364. Emphasis in the first phrase
      added.

21   See Alan Coddington, "Creaking Semaphore and Beyond", The
      British Journal for the Philosophy of Science, vol. 26, no. 2
      (June, 1975), p. 152. Professor Kirzner has stressed only
      the active nature of entrepreneurial thought. Professor
      Armentano (op. cit., p. 10) has noted the creativity of
      entrepreneurial action but not thought.

22   This conception is implicit in Shackle, "The Nature and Role
      of Profit", loc. cit., p. 100.

23   Other possible reasons for failure include internal inconsis-
      tency of plans and misjudgement of the resources at hand.
      Lachmann, "The Role of Expectations in Economics as a Social
      Science", Economica, vol. X, no. 37 (February, 1943), p. 15.

24   Kirzner, op. cit., p. 81.

25   J. W. N. Watkins, "Decision and Uncertainty", The British
      Journal for the Philosophy of Science, vol. VI, no. 21
      (May 1955), p. 66.

26   Hayek, "Economics and Knowledge", loc. cit., pp. 36-38.

27   ibid., pp. 40-41.

28   ibid., p. 42.

29   ibid., p. 45.

30   Kirzner, op. cit., p. 26. Emphasis added.

31   Hayek, op. cit., p. 53.

32   Shackle, "The Nature and Role of Profit", loc. cit., p. 99. The "heady scent of profits" to which Kirzner refers (op. cit., p. 222) is entirely in the nose of the beholder.

33   Lachmann, Capital and its Structure, op. cit., p. 23.

34   Lachmann, "The Science of Human Action", Economica, (new series) vol. XVIII, no. 72 (November, 1951), pp. 419-20.

35   Lachmann, The Legacy of Max Weber (Berkeley: The Glendessary Press, 1971), p. 46.

36   Cf. Hayek, "The Maintainance of Capital", Economica, (new series) vol. II, no. 7 (August, 1935), pp. 265-66.

37   See especially Kirzner, op. cit., p. 219f.

38   Cf. Hayek, "Economics and Knowledge", loc. cit., p. 49. Cf. also Shackle, General Thought Schemes and the Economist, the Woolwich Economic Paper no. 2 (London: The Department of Economics and Management, Woolwich Polytechnic, 1964), pp. 14-15.

39   Kirzner, An Essay on Capital (New York: Augustus M. Kelly, 1966), p. 30.

[8]

Journal of Libertarian Studies, Vol. 1, No. 2, pp. 137-151. Pergamon Press 1977. Printed in Great Britain.

SPONTANEOUS ORDER AND THE COORDINATION OF ECONOMIC ACTIVITIES*

GERALD P. O'DRISCOLL, JR.

Department of Economics, Iowa State University

This paper is an essay on the coordination of economic activities. It is exploratory and speculative, connecting arguments that I have made in several other places. The essay is an attempt to give a coherent picture of some of the theoretical and practical problems facing economists, as well as society in general. As this paper is being written for a conference on Austrian economics, I propose to deal with questions specifically from the viewpoint of Austrian economics. It is not that I propose to defend the proposition that economists of this school possess a uniquely correct perspective of the issues, but merely that they have much to say on the particular questions with which I will deal. I trust that my references to economists not normally considered to be members of the Austrian School will demonstrate the universality of the problems discussed here.

Those economists who view a system of free exchange — Adam Smith's "obvious and simple system of natural liberty[1]" — as the solution of the coordination problem in economics face intellectual challenges from at least four sources: first, the continuing challenge of the Keynesian legacy; second, the challenge from what James Buchanan has termed the "modern Ricardians"; third, the challenge from the new movement for national planning; and finally, the challenge from certain economists in the Austrian school.

In previous papers, I have dealt with the Austrian Analysis of monetary theory (or macroeconomics) as it is concerned with the coordination of economic activities. Accordingly, I will begin with this general problem.

*The original version of this paper was presented at a conference on Austrian economics at Windsor Castle, August 1976, and will be published in the "Studies in Economic Theory" series of Sheed, Andrews and McMeel, Inc.

THE KEYNESIAN LEGACY

It has become clear in recent years that Keynes' *General Theory* is a very confused work, so much that it is virtually an ink-blot test for economists: an economist's perception of its contents tells more about the beliefs of the reader than the contents of that book.[2] Indeed, Keynes' sympathetic critics are compelled to point out these confusions in their attempts to argue that he made a significant contribution to our understanding of the economic system. The best example of this is Axel Leijonhufvud's *On Keynesian Economics and the Economics of Keynes*.[3] We are told there that Keynes had important insights into coordination failures in market systems. Specifically, Leijonhufvud's Keynes argued that banking and financial systems can operate so as to impede rather than to facilitate the adjustment to a change in the equilibrium rate of interest. Securities markets are incapable of moving from a higher to a lower equilibrium rate of interest, without attendant fluctuations in income and employment. This is true whether the assumed disturbance consists of a downward shift in the marginal efficiency of investment (Keynes' marginal efficiency of capital), or an increase in the savings schedule (a decreased marginal propensity to consume out of current income). The existence of bearish speculators in securities markets impedes smooth adjustment of those markets. Keynes' bears do this by speculating against any rise in the prices of long-lived assets, real or financial.[4] Keynesian bears speculate on the basis of the historical perception that they possess of a "normal" long run rate of interest. If this normal long-rate could be taken as summarizing the real forces determining the equilibrium rate of interest, then it is quite reasonable, from a profit-maximizing viewpoint, for speculators to treat deviations from the rate as temporary fluctuations.[5] Indeed, Keynes' speculators behave precisely the way textbook examples suggest, in that they act so as to hasten the return to the *perceived* equilibrium position (though this effect is not part of their intention, of course). But in this instance, speculative activity, following a guide that normally proves reliable, proves to be disequilibrating in its effects. Speculators are misled into identifying as but a transitory fluctuation what in fact is the consequence of a shift in parameters.

In microtheory it is customary to point out that speculators who misidentify an equilibrium position will suffer capital losses, and that, in any case, market forces will restore equilibrium. But Keynes raised an important issue: bearish speculators, in exhibiting liquidity preference, can initiate deflationary pressures.[6] Unless we assume that wage and price changes occur *infinitely* fast, then price deflation will be accompanied by quantity-adjustments.[7] In effect, the resulting speculative losses become socialized. To put a Keynesian proposition in Hayekian terms, the unintended consequences of a speculative search for liquidity generates falling income and general illiquidity. If one adopts the position — as do most Austrians — that the market *process* is a continuing search for opportunities, one cannot dismiss out of hand the possibility that speculation of the Keynesian variety could inhibit the equilibrating market forces. And unless one adopts the view that prices are always correct, which no Austrian would do, then one must confront this Keynesian information problem.

Several points need to be made here. I have been talking of "Leijonhufvud's Keynes", because of the problematical nature of *The General Theory*. Yet my paraphrase of Leijonhufvud's interpretation is a fairly straight-forward argument about discoordinating market processes. The obvious question that comes to mind in this context is why Keynes didn't say all this explicitly and simply if this is what he meant? The thesis, as I have presented it, can obviously be put very succinctly. What makes Leijonhufvud's presentation of it so difficult is the web of confusion sown by

Keynes.

In order to show that his interpretation has captured the authentic Keynes, Leijonhufvud not only must do battle with conflicting interpretations, but must deal with Keynes' own imprecision and confusion. The clearest example of these problems occurs in Leijonhufvud's discussion of Keynes' views on capital. Before examining this discussion, however, one must consider the intellectual background to the treatment of capital questions in *The General Theory*.

Hayek was quite critical of Keynes' earlier book, the *Treatise on Money*, when he reviewed that work. The general tenor of this criticism is that Keynes, at the time he wrote that book, was largely ignorant of capital theory. Hayek recognized that Keynes was presenting a neo-Wicksellian theory, but without the necessary theoretical foundations.[8] And he observed that:

> It is *a priori* unlikely that an attempt to utilise the conclusions drawn from a certain theory without accepting that theory itself should be successful. But, in the case of an author of Mr. Heynes' intellectual calibre, the attempt produces results which are truly remarkable.[9]

In an amazing piece of candor, Keynes all but admitted the legitimacy of Hayek's criticism; after defending himself by observing that there was no "satisfactory theory" of capital in "completed form", Keynes stated:

> Nevertheless, substantially I concede Dr. Hayek's point. I agree with him that a clear account of the factors determining the natural rate of interest ought to have a place in a completed *Treatise on Money*, and that it is lacking in mine: and I can only plead that I had much to say for which such a theory is not required and that my own ideas about it were still too much in embryo to deserve publication. Later on, I will endeavor to make good this deficiency.[10]

Did Keynes ever "make good this deficiency"? I do not believe so, and offer the following observations in support of this judgment. Much of the confusion surrounding the nature of Keynes' message can be accounted for if one accepts the thesis that Keynes remained largely ignorant of capital theory. He had difficulty, then, in presenting his message because he did not possess the requisite technical knowledge. Of course, one could also infer that Keynes was not sure of the message that he wished to present. There is evidence for this interpretation in the recent observation of one of his close associates at Cambridge, Joan Robinson, who noted that certain of Keynes' putative followers "sometimes had some trouble in getting Maynard to see what the point of his revolution really was".[11]

But I would offer as a final judgment of Keynes the observation of his recent interpreter, Axel Leijonhufvud. By far the most difficult chapter of the latter's book is the fourth, "The General Theory of Liquidity Preference", in which both the state of capital theory in the thirties and Keynes' own views on the subject are presented. Of this complexity, Leijonhufvud remarks: "This chapter will be a lengthy affair, partly because of the intrinsic difficulty of capital theory, partly because Keynes did not work out his ideas on the subject in much detail so that we are left with only what amounts to an unfinished sketch".[12] In short, Keynes never made up the self-admitted deficiency of the *Treatise*. But it is only by having thus demonstrated Keynes' lack of knowledge and clarity that Leijonhufvud can make it at all plausible that Keynes had a comparatively simple point to make (i.e., stickiness of interest rates), though this point is not the one commonly attributed to him (i.e., stickiness of money wage rates).

There are several approaches that one can take to Keynes' challenge. Conceptual errors abound in *The General Theory*; and I have suggested that in the area of capital theory, Keynes is quite confused. One can fairly easily engage in piecemeal criticism of Keynes' ideas. I do not believe that the Keynesian system can stand up to such a criticism. But I am not sure that this is a fruitful approach, though I myself have adopted it on previous occasions.[13] The reasons are several-fold. First, no one, I believe, can get beyond the exegetical problem — I refer the reader again to my ink-blot analogy. No matter which Keynes one criticizes, a new Keynes is proffered in its stead. More to the point, one must consider the possibility that the most interesting recent interpretation bears scant resemblance to Keynes' ideas. Yeager has argued, for instance, that Leijonhufvud and Clower both seem prepared to credit Keynes with their own,

original contribution.[14] Perhaps, then, Keynes is the wrong target of any criticism.

Nonetheless, the Keynesian *debate* does raise important theoretical issues that Austrians must confront, regardless of who is adjudged the author of particular views. And I believe that there is one unifying theme running through most, if not all versions of Keynesian economics: the self-correcting forces of the market economy cannot be relied upon to maintain full-employment and reasonable price stability. In its most extreme version, this criticism might even deny the existence of self-correcting market forces. It is to the issue of the strength of these market forces that Austrians should address themselves, for it is now becoming increasingly accepted that macro-economics is in fact concerned with the coordination of economic activities. Leijonhufvud has stated the problem as follows:

> ...The central issue in macroeconomic theory is — once again — the extent to which the economy, or at least its market sectors, may properly be regarded as a self-regulating system...How well or badly, do its "automatic" mechanisms perform?[15]

Before continuing, it would be well to consider this latter issue in detail.

THE PRINCIPLE OF SPONTANEOUS ORDER

The principle of spontaneous order — or of "undesigned order", as it might more properly be called — can be viewed as the first principle of economics. Indeed, James Buchanan has recently gone so far as to suggest that it is the *only* principle of economics. The principle is, in any case, a cornerstone of modern economics, whether we trace modern (i.e., post-mercantilist) economics back to Adam Smith and the other Scottish moral philosophers, or to the Physiocrats. With this principle, scholars for the first time could see economic phenomena as interdependent events. Indeed, this principle made it possible to reason systematically and coherently about economic phenomena. Much of nineteenth century economics can be seen as consisting of developments of this principle (along with minority criticisms of the principle and the systems of thought deduced therefrom).

On the other hand, most of twentieth century

economics has consisted of reactions against systems in which this principle plays a central role. In this, Keynesian economics is but one among a family of theories that deny the existence of a spontaneous or undesigned market order in which plans are coordinated. The reaction has been so complete, that what was taken by earlier economists to be an empirical law — the existence of a spontaneous market order — is now frequently viewed as the product of ideological bias or prejudice. If anything, modern economic discussions presuppose the absence of the very order whose existence was the cornerstone of much of nineteenth century economics.[16]

It is apparent now that the principle was not firmly enough established in economics to withstand the criticisms that were levied against it. Yet the question of the existence of a spontaneously-generated order remains the central question of economics — and of social theory in general — even though it is seldom recognized as such. Theories of the instability of investment, and of saving, and of aggregate demand, are all variants of the general proposition that the economy lacks strong forces leading to an undesigned order. These are not simply disputes of technical economics, narrowly defined, though they too long have been treated as such. The question of the necessary amount of governmental stabilization policy will not be decided by running yet another money-demand equation through a computer. Nonetheless, it is imperative that the question be addressed directly once again.[17]

As intellectual descendants of Carl Menger, most Austrian economists have defended the proposition that spontaneous market forces are capable of producing an overall order in society. Hayek, for one, is well-known for his emphasis on the role of the nonpurposive social organizations in this process.[18] Indeed, the persistence of members of this school in their views in the face of the contrary opinion of much of the profession has contributed to their isolation from the rest of the profession. In this sense, and alone among the neoclassical schools, the Austrians can today lay claim to being the inheritors of the Smithian system. In this, the bicentenary of the publication of *The Wealth*

of Nations, it would be well for Austrian economists to seize the opportunity to re-establish the importance of the principle of spontaneous order — an order that, though designed by no one, emerges from the individual and independent planning of market transactors.

THE NEW RICARDIANS[19]

There is yet another tradition in the history of economics, distinct from both the Austrian and Smithian traditions, and from those that are overtly hostile to these traditions. It is a tradition epitomized by David Ricardo's general approach to economic questions. In the Ricardian tradition, attention is focused on the long run, in which full adjustment to all disturbances has occurred. Periods of transition are abstracted from.[20] It would be anachronistic to credit Ricardo with a theory of perfect information, but he wrote as though the labourers, capitalists and rentiers of his system had full access to future events. The difference between the Smithian and Ricardian traditions is a subtle, though important one; and it separates theorists even today.

In Smith's world, changes are constantly occurring, and adaptations to these changes are never complete. These changes may be of comparatively simple variety, such as variations in the corn harvest from year to year (with attendant effects on real wage rates).[21] More importantly, Smith was concerned with the continuous process of market adaptation to invention and further extensions of the division of labor. Changes in institutions and the legal structure are of prime concern.[22] It is not, of course, that Smith had nothing to say about the long run. His value theory is a long run theory, though I find it one of the least developed parts of his system.[23] Nonetheless, the emphasis in *The Wealth of Nations* is on change. Moreover, Smith's actors suffer various illusions and misunderstandings about future events, and, indeed, their own self-interest. None of this would make sense in a Ricardian world.

Whether it is a question of monetary economics, or of fiscal policy, Ricardo generally treats all disturbances as though they were fully and completely anticipated.[24] In the

Ricardian world, then, the problem of coordination disappears. It is not that Ricardo denied the principle of spontaneous order. Rather he did not treat the emergence of coordinated behaviour on the market as a problem. He in effect *assumed* that economic behavior will be coordinated. Most importantly, and unlike Smith, Ricardo generally ignored the question of what institutional arrangements are necessary for the emergence of that order upon which the soundness of his arguments depends.

The institutional setting and the allocation mechanism matter in economics precisely because behavior in a changing world is not automatically coordinated. Laws and institutions have a significant impact on human behavior precisely because some facilitate and some inhibit the flow of information that is necessary for adaptation in a changing world. This realization is certainly contained in *The Wealth of Nations* — Smith's emphasis on the importance of these matters suffuses that work. Not so with Ricardo's *Principles*.

Professor Lachmann has recently reminded us that the problem of economic coordination is intimately involved with the twin problems of acquisition and diffusion of knowledge among transactors. In dealing with the characteristic assumption that the state of knowledge is among the data of the system, he queries:

> Do we assume that all market actors know all the tastes and resources in all markets in which they, actually or potentially, do or might operate? But if so, equilibrium should at once be attained in all markets. If we were to make this assumption there could be no disequilibrium, no dealings at "false prices". Walras' auctioneer would become superfluous. If, on the other hand, we do not make it, how do we delimit the extent of each actor's knowledge at each point of time, and how do we deal with the flow of knowledge between actors over time?[25]

All this talk about the importance of information may seem prosaic to economists at this point. But the radical implications of imperfect knowledge have simply not been generally absorbed in economic theory. For, *inter alia*, imperfection of knowledge means that prices do not necessarily coordinate economic behavior, as those prices are influenced by the inconsistent expectations on the basis of "false" price signals. To justify one's faith in the coordinating function of markets, one cannot simply assume that prices are coordinating, or at their (*ex ante*) equilibrium level. Rather, one must be concerned with the institutional environment of economic systems, and the appropriateness of these institutions for the emergence of a spontaneous market order. One must be concerned, then, with specifying the situations in which prices will coordinate, and those situations in which prices will not coordinate economic activity. By his attention to the long run, in which, *ex hypothesi,* all such problems disappear because full adjustment to all changes has occurred, Ricardo (and his followers) ignored these difficulties.

The problem of economic coordination is a theoretical and practical issue not merely because decision-making is decentralized, though this is an important aspect of the problem. Of even more importance is the fact that we live in a world of constant change. Were there decentralized decision-making, but an unchanging environment, it might be reasonable to suppose that economic activity could be coordinated under a wide variety of institutional and allocational arrangements. Learning would occur due to the repetition of events, with adjustments made as past errors were revealed.[26] A price system and appropriate market institutions are of practical significance precisely because of the need to register the effects of continuous changes in the data, changes which are given to no one in their entirety. On the other hand, it is doubtful whether money, prices or the market system would exist in the stationary state. Those who ignore this aspect of imperfect information are caught in the dilemma of dealing with phenomena, most of which would not exist in the world as they assume that world to exist — a world of perfectly coordinated plans.[27]

Ricardo and his epigones thus obscured the basic questions of social order that Smith had raised. They shifted the emphasis away from these questions to the theorems and lemmas of value theory. Their legacy is still with us today. Walras and Lausanne School introduced the concept of *general* equilibrium into economics. But in other respects the Walrasian system is quite similar to the Ricardian: both are perfectly coordinated systems. By the sheer logic of these systems, neither is obviously concerned with the coordination of economic activities — this coordination is implicitly assumed to take place. In such systems laws and institutions cannot matter. Monetary disturbances can have no significant effects — for the transition periods in which money clearly matters are de-emphasized or ignored in the Ricardian system.[28] In such systems, the market would not be viewed as a process in which continual adjustment to continual change occurs, but a state of affairs in which this process was at an end.

The Chicago School can be fairly described as the modern Ricardians. In Kirzner's terminology, the transactors in the Chicago world are nothing but Robbinsian maximizers.[29] Chicago economists are Ricardian in their approach to questions of tax and expenditure policy and monetary policy, to cite two examples previously mentioned for Ricardo. The Ricardian bent of the Chicago School is important to the Austrian School for at least two reasons.

First, the time has passed when members of the Chicago School were articulate, but minority members of the profession. Increasingly, economic discussions and debates are influenced by their approach. Second, on issues involving coordination questions, their Ricardian leanings *re-enforce* the Walrasian approach of the dominant mathematical, general equilibrium theorists. This is an important point because economists are beginning to recognize the distinctiveness of the Marshallian approach (*vis à vis* the Walrasian approach) of Chicago School economists. And the differences between Chicago School economists and the rest of the profession are important for a wide variety of issues, such as the role of empirical research, partial vs. general equilibrium analysis, etc. But as regards the coordination of economic activities, the new Ricardians and the neo-Walrasians are more of one mind. They tend to take for granted that markets coordinate economic activities. By doing so, they ignore the complex questions of economic coordination, upon the solution of which depends the degree of economic coordination.

This approach is objectionable because of the conclusions it engenders when markets demonstrably are not coordinating economic activity. The "market failure"' mentality is an effect of this approach.[30] "The market system" is adjudged a failure in such cases, with scant recognition that " the market" is a metaphor for a complex of interrelationships and institutions, any one of which may be the source of the problem. That members of the Chicago School are generally more sanguine about the efficacy of this system hardly mitigates against the methodological point being made here.

Austrian economists and other adherents to the principle of spontaneous order will receive little support, and should generally expect overt hostility from the Chicago School on a wide range of economic questions.[31] Austrian economists tend to view most economic questions as issues involving the principle of spontaneous order. Accordingly, they take characteristic positions on these questions. Two of the areas where disagreement between the two schools is particularly intense are monetary and capital theory. Quite apart from their differences over the determination of the *equilibrium* values of interest rates, the two schools are sharply divided over the approach to questions of capital and interest theory, as well as those of monetary theory. Being Ricardians, members of the Chicago School naturally keep questions of monetary theory and capital theory quite distinct, since these are distinct problems in long run equilibrium analysis. As did Ricardo, they treat deviations from the equilibrium rate of interest as temporary fluctuations. The transitional periods in which monetary disturbances influence the accumulation of capital and the level of rate of interest are typically ignored or at least de-emphasized.

On the other hand, many of the twentieth century members of the Austrian School have dealt with the interface between monetary and capital theory. Mises and Hayek were most persistent in their analysis of the interrelation between monetary and capital questions, precisely because of their interest in adjustment problems. Hayek, for instance, has been consistent in treating economic fluctuations as manifestations of economic discoordination, brought on by monetary disturbances.[32] For Hayek, monetary disturbances change entrepreneurial expectations, and lead to capital accumulation that, *ex post,* is revealed to have been malinvestment. These malinvestments cause real scarcities, whose existence become manifest in subsequent price changes. The price changes compel entrepreneurs — because of the capital losses that they are then incurring — to revise their investment plans. It is in this sense that modern Austrians view cyclical expansions brought about by monetary and credit inflation as self-reversing and inherently unstable.[33]

Hayek and Mises thus deal with phenomena virtually ignored by monetary theorists of the Chicago School — the transition period between a monetary disturbance and complete adjustment to its effects.[34] To the extent that Professor Friedman, for instance, deals with the transition period, it is only in terms of one, comparatively narrow problem — anticipation of future price levels.[35] As a practical matter, monetarists generally view inflation as synchronized inflation, with all prices rising *pari passu.* For Hayek and Mises, synchronized inflation is a fantasy, so long as monetary disturbances impinge at specific points.[36] And full adjustment to inflation would be all but inconceivable, as it would involve each actor's anticipating correctly the precise changes in each relative price that will occur in each future period, due to the assumed monetary disturbance.[37]

Once again, the Ricardian approach to monetary questions blinds its users to the issues considered paramount by the Austrians. In so doing, this approach inhibits an understanding of important issues confronting market economists. For the Ricardian — quantity theory approach is one in which prices continue their coordinating function even in an inflation. Yet, the point at issue is whether spontaneous market forces operate as usual in an inflation. If monetary disturbances not only generate pure price inflation, but also interfere with the coordinating mechanisms in an economy, then the quantity theory approach ignores an important research programme in economics — the study of the monetary

framework necessary for prices to fulfill their coordinating function.[38] In the words of one expositor of Hayek's ideas:

> [Hayek] regarded prices...as empirical reflectors of specific circumstances and price changes as an *inter-related* series of changes in these "signals", which produced a gradual adaptation in the entire price structure (and hence in the outputs of different commodities and services) to the constant, unpredictable changes in the real world. Pricing, in short, is seen as a continuous information-collecting and disseminating process, but it is the institutional framework that determines both the extent to which and the degree of success with which, prices are enabled to perform this potential signalling or allocative function.[39]

PLANNING[40]

That nonpurposive social organizations will naturally evolve, and that an undesigned order can be the product of self-regarding acts are radical ideas in Western thought. These ideas run counter to the dominant approach to social questions, and were in ascendancy for only a brief period in Western intellectual history. It is not, then, entirely surprising that in economics these ideas have not gained complete acceptance; and that among the general public, even the so-called educated public, they are scarcely understood at all. But there is danger that because of essentially reactionary developments in social thought, the insights that were the product of the Enlightenment will be all but lost in practice. Adam Smith has aptly characterized the far older conception of social order:

> The man of system...seems to imagine that he can arrange the different members of a great society with as much ease as the hand arranges the different pieces upon the chessboard; he does not consider that the pieces upon the chessboard have no other principle of motion besides that which the hand impresses upon them; but that, in the great chessboard of human society, every single piece has a principle of motion of its own, altogether different from that which the legislature might choose to impress upon it. If those two principles coincide and act in the same direction, the game of human society will go on easily and harmoniously, and is very likely to be happy and successful. If they are opposite or different, the game will go on miserably, and the society must be at all times in the highest degree of disorder.[41]

The liberal conception of society of **Adam Smith** and the classical economists stands in sharp contrast with this older view. Yet once again in the United States, we see evidence of this older conception's becoming prominent, under the guise of national economic planning.

Proposals for planning are embodiments of the chess-game conception of social affairs, adapted to the problem of economic allocation. These proposals implicitly or explicitly deny that market forces guide decision making, so as to produce an overall, yet undesigned order; and they virtually ignore the function and role of nonpurposive economic organizations.

It is not that the arguments for national (i.e., central) economic planning constitute a direct *intellectual* challenge to opponents of such planning. As Professor Hayek has recently demonstrated in a devastating rebuttal of these proposals, modern exponents of "planning" possess as naïve and ill-thought out an approach to the problem as did the Bolsheviks and European socialists in the immediate post-World War I period. As he notes:

> The conception [collectivist economic planning], originally developed by some of the organizers of the German war economy during World War I, was thoroughly discussed by economists in the 1920's and 1930's; and all those familiar with that discussion will agree that it greatly contributed to the clarification of concepts and that one ought today to be entitled to assume that no competent economist who lived through that discussion would ever again talk about the issues in terms of the vague and confused concepts initially bandied about.[42]

Indeed, if this debate were being carried out in the scholarly arena, I doubt that the proposals put forth by those in favor of central planning would survive Hayek's recent criticisms. Unfortunately, the debate is not being carried forth in learned journals, or, generally, by learned men; rather, the proposals are being developed in the pages of the *New York Times,* and are being presented by politicians, businessmen and labor union leaders. This is an instance where those who accept the Smithian insights have won the intellectual battle, but are in danger of seeing their arguments lose out in practice. This situation surely represents a dilemma for economists. Economists generally disdain polemics, but they now face a situation in which influencing important political questions depends on their ability to present economic ideas in a polemical fashion. Certainly those economists who have chosen, for whatever reasons,[43] to ally themselves with the misleading arguments of the "planners" have not eschewed polemics.[44]

Hayek has done an admirable job of marshalling the chief arguments against central planning in his recent article. I do not intend to repeat these arguments here. But it is worth reminding ourselves of the central confusion of the early advocates of central planning, as it is the central confusion of the current advocates. The confusion concerns the very concept, "planning". If nothing else developed from the earlier debates over the question, it was the realization that a market economy is characterized by *continual* planning and plan-revision, albeit on a decentralized level.[45] As Hayek put it over thirty years ago, and recently repeated:

> The dispute between the modern planners and their opponents, is, therefore, *not* a dispute on whether we ought to choose intelligently between the various possible organizations of society; it is not a dispute on whether we ought to employ foresight and systematic thinking in planning our common affairs. It is a dispute about what is the best way of so doing. The question is whether for this purpose it is better that the holder of coercive power should confine himself in general to creating conditions under which the knowledge and initiative of individuals are given the best scope so that *they* can plan most successfully; or whether a rational utilization of our resources requires *central* direction and organization of all our activities according to some consciously constructed "blueprint". The socialists of all parties have appropriated the term "planning" for planning of the latter type, and it is now generally accepted in this sense. But though this is meant to suggest that this is the only rational way of handling our affairs, it does not, of course, prove this. It remains the point on which the planners and the liberals disagree.[46]

The challenge of "planning" confronts liberal economists with both the necessity and the opportunity of once again entering the popular debate over the trend of society that we will shape for the future. For it must be remembered that in constructing economics upon the principle of spontaneous order, earlier economists were ultimately interested in the problem of social and poltical organization. In part, then, I am proposing a return to an earlier conception of our task as engaging in political economy, though we now recognize a specifically scientific part of this field, *viz.,* economics. If economists do not conceive of their task thusly, it is doubtful whether there will be any practical opportunity in the future for the *scientific* pursuit of the implications of the principle of spontaneous order.

In order to pursue this goal, however, Austrian

economists in particular must settle among themselves certain theoretical and seemingly purely scientific issues. I have argued above that among the neo-classical economists, the Austrians have most consistently adhered to Adam Smith's conception of the economic problem. Ironically, recent debates indicate anything but agreement among living members of this school. The positions of some could be construed as an implicit attack on the idea that there is a spontaneous market order in the economy. It is thus that I am led into a final section, involving a discussion of the Austrian approach to the question of the operation of spontaneously-generated forces in a market economy.

THE AUSTRIAN SCHOOL AND SPONTANEOUS ORDERING FORCES

In a recent paper, Professor Kirzner speculates about the exact status of the proposition that profitable opportunities have a tendency to be exploited.[47] He concludes that the propensity to discover opportunities is "inseparable from our insight that human beings act purposefully".[48] In fact, he even suggests a sympathetic reinterpretation of the perfect knowledge assumption of neoclassical price theory. Though orthodox use of the assumption is "carefree",[49] it does reflect a real insight: our "instinct" is seen as assuring us that profitable opportunities will be discovered. He then concludes that: "The perfect knowledge assumption of neo-classical economics carried this instinctive assurance to altogether unjustified lengths. In rejecting this dangerous assumption, we must take care not to expunge the entirely healthy instinct on which it rested".[50]

Kirzner's approach to the issue of profit exploitation in a market economy differs markedly from Lachmann's. Nonetheless, this proposition is not easily demonstrated, for two, interrelated reasons. First, Lachmann nowhere to my knowledge *explicitly* asserts the contrary proposition, *viz.*, that we have no grounds for believing that market participants will discover and exploit profitable opportunities. Second, though the figure of Professor Lachmann lurks in the background throughout the second-half

of Kirzner's paper, the latter never brings this figure into the foreground.

The best way of elucidating this issue is to turn to Lachmann's own recent paper. Toward the end of his paper, Lachmann notes that:

...Skepticism about equilibrium need not deter us from appraising the relative strength and weakness of the equilibrating forces in various situations. In fact, it must encourage us to do so. To make confident use of the notion of equilibrium means to imply that the equilibrating forces will always be of sufficient strength to triumph over all obstacles. A skeptic might readily admit that such situations may exist, but he will probably doubt whether they occur with sufficient frequency to warrant our treating them as the norm. The more skeptical we are about general equilibrium as the central notion of economic analysis, the more encumbent on us it becomes to examine each situation individually with respect to the balance of strength of equilibrating and disequilibrating forces.[51]

It must be noted here that Kirzner's position is *not* that we should admire neoclassical price theory for its treatment of general equilibrium as "the central notion of economic analysis" or as "the norm". Rather, he suggests that we accept the proposition that equilibrating tendencies are strong. If the propensity to discover opportunities is "inseparable from our insight that human beings act purposefully", then we must likewise acknowledge a *tendency* toward equilibrium in all markets. *A fortiori,* there exist strong tendencies toward an overall, or general equilibrium *at each moment.* Individuals are, then, constantly revising their plans in a way that brings them into greater uniformity. This latter proposition, when thus phrased in dynamic terms, does seem to embody the principle of an undesigned order. It remains questionable, however, whether Lachmann wishes to embrace this principle. Thus he argues that:

Experience shows that in the real world of disequilibrium different persons will typically hold different expectations about the same future event. If so, at best one person's expectation can be confirmed and all other expectations will be disappointed. Hence the "assumption that all other expectations are confirmed" cannot possibly hold. Nobody can take his equilibrium bearings if he does not know how others will act. In such a situation, which we have every reason to regard as normal, his equilibrium, as Hayek admits, cannot serve as a source of a "feedback mechanism". *The beacon that had been designed to keep entrepreneurs from straying from the narrow path of convergent expectations turns out, on most nights, to be rather dim.*[52]

Lachmann makes much of "the autonomy of

the human mind'' (as must all Austrians):

> This source of...new knowledge may well be past
> experience, but the latter requires interpretation by a
> discerning mind, and optimists will interpret it
> differently from pessimists. The human mind is a filter
> of experience, but each individual's filter is different
> from every other filter. Divergent expectations are
> thus as ''natural'' a feature of the social landscape as
> are divergent tastes. Changes in the constellation of
> knowledge are an inevitable concomitant of the passing
> of time, and changes in the constellation of expectations
> are bound to follow them.[53]

There is no denying the autonomy of the human mind, but one is reluctant to follow Lachmann in his apparent conclusion that we can say nothing about the likelihood that individuals will make consistent and coordinated decisions in the face of new knowledge. If anything, he seems to be saying that they will not coordinate plans. Yet, one always supposed it was an Hayekian insight that prices facilitate the diffusion of information and the coordination of plans.[54]

We are faced here with an important question: Do different and disparate individuals have a common reaction to shared experience? We certainly would not want to say they always do, or there would be little sense in referring to ''individuals''. Yet, there are obvious cases in which people do react to shared experiences in the same or similar ways: the perception of a fire in an enclosed room will lead to virtually everyone's making for an exit. Each person could form a reasonable expectation about what the others will do.

Moreover, many events are implicit demonstrations of the degree to which expectations do coincide. Changes in clothing fashion might be cited as an example. The ''agreement'' among separate manufacturers of apparel can be amazing, though clearly retail customers do not register their preferences for new fashion in a clothing futures market. Apparently individual entrepreneurs, experiencing the same signals and trends, will often form similar expectations.

None of these considerations are decisive, of course, but they are suggestive. Lachmann has clearly done a great service in pointing out forcefully the absurdity of an approach in which expectations *always* prove consistent. It is an essential feature of markets that not everyone reacts equally quickly to the continual

changes in the data.[55] But it is true of at least some changes that they occur only because actors share a unanimous opinion about the future course of events.

Having eschewed the approach of assuming consistency among expectations at all times, one is not justified, without further argument, in arguing that we economists can make no assumptions about a tendency toward such uniformity, where this tendency is based on a universally recognized ''propensity to discover opportunities''. To do so would involve a nonsequitur. Again, to assume that all opportunities are at any moment fully exploited (and thus do not really exist as opportunities) would be, to paraphrase Kirzner a ''carefree'' use of concepts. But we must surely accept the existence of the propensity, or foresake the principle of spontaneous order. This point can be elaborated by recounting an event that happened at a recent (December, 1975) conference on Austrian economics.

Professor Lerner argued that without the concept of general equilibrium, defenders of the market system have no basis with which to carry on their defense. His criticism was in response to Lachmann's approach to the question of general equilibrium. I confess that I rose to the latter's defense at the time, by pointing out that we need only assume that there is market-day equilibrium. If prices clear existing supplies, then markets can operate successfully. ''That is all we need.'' I am now not sure that I did not err. Lerner may have been raising an important issue for Austrians.

We must distinguish two functions of markets. The first consists simply in a method of allocating existing supplies peacefully. Without prices and free markets, society requires guns and dictatorship. Examples of the latter type of social allocation of resources are numerous. But I am not sure that defenders of the market system can be satisfied with demonstrating that free trade is an alternative to the ''war of all against all'', however important this insight may be. For if supplies of goods are autonomous, if not gratuitous, it is dubious in what sense it can be said that prices coordinate activity. Indeed, I suspect that there is no coordination in the conventional sense in Lachmann's system.

For him apparently, *ex ante* plans bear no relation to *ex post* reality. Nor is there reason to believe that actors will move in the right direction in correcting past errors.

Lachmann does feel that the market "cannot make bulls and bears change their expectations, but it nevertheless can coordinate these". He continues:

> To coordinate bullish and bearish expectations is, as Keynes showed, the economic function of the Stock Exchange and of asset markets in general. This is achieved because in such markets the price will move until the whole market is divided into equal halves of bulls and bears. In this way divergent expectations are cast into a coherent pattern and a measure of coordination is accomplished.[56]

"Coordination" is being used here in a highly ambiguous sense. As Lachmann notes subsequently, he is talking not about *ex ante* consistency, but a Marshallian *ex post,* market day equilibrium.[57] This usage of coordination is in sharp contrast to the more conventional usage, and the usage that Austrians have traditionally employed.[58] "Coordination of plans" in traditional usage means there is *ex ante* consistency among transactors' plans. It is certainly scant comfort for one interested in this problem to be informed that there will be "coordination" *ex post.* Though related, *ex ante* and *ex post* "coordination" are conceptually distinct issues. To conflate the two issues is scarcely to contribute to the solution of either problem.[59]

It is certainly not the case that Austrian economists maintain that there ever exists *ex ante* consistency among all transactors' plans. But they have traditionally maintained, as Lachmann himself notes, that there is a tendency ("a strong tendency") toward diffusion of knowledge and increased consistency of plans. In other words, Austrian economists have always viewed the problem of economic coordination in dynamic terms. Do plans become more consistent over time? Lachmann apparently sloughs over the distinction between two very different propositions:

1. Economic activities are coordinated in the sense that all plans are successfully executed ("general equilibrium").
2. Economic activities are coordinated in the sense that a mechanism exists (i.e., the price system) that facilitates rational plan revision

and leads to greater consistency of plans over time.

Lachmann switches back and forth between discussions of "the relative strength and weakness of the equilibrating forces", and "general equilibrium as the central notion of economic analysis" as though he were talking about the same problem (see p. 20 above). Surely the statement that "the market produces strong equilibrating forces" is fundamentally different than the assertion that "the market is always in (general) equilibrium". Does Professor Lachmann acknowledge the difference? It is certainly not clear that his arguments against the second class of statements are telling against the first. It is true that elsewhere Lachmann apparently acknowledges the existence of a tendency toward equilibrium in some areas: "A tendency toward the integration of the [capital] structure does exist".[60] But even there, he seemingly takes back what he has just granted.[61] I am afraid his occasional concessions to the existence of a tendency to greater consistency of plans in markets only confuse matters.

What I find most disturbing about Lachmann's position is that he criticizes a *static* general equilibrium model, but concludes that the modern Austrian approach to coordination, in a *dynamic* sense, is thereby called into question. I am not at all clear what he thinks "the general equilibrium perspective" is. The reader is told that Hayek's "early work was clearly under the influence of the general equilibrium model".[62] Elsewhere the reader is reminded that as early as 1933 (in "Price Expectations, Monetary Disturbances and Malinvestments") Hayek dealt with expectations. It was in 1936 ("Economics and Knowledge") that Hayek launched his attack on the static, general equilibrium models of mathematical economics. From this one must conclude that Lachmann is critical even of theories espousing a tendency toward overall equilibrium (i.e., he denies the principle of spontaneous order). I can draw no other conclusion.

It also seems that what Kirzner treats as the "equilibrating market process", Lachmann treats as a "disequilibrating" process. At first, I thought there was a mere semantic confusion.

I now believe the apparent semantic confusion is masking real conceptual differences. Kirzner sees any disturbance as developing equilibrating market forces. Lachmann sees change as disequilibrating.[63] The only reason that I can adduce is that Lachmann does not see market forces as being equilibrating in nature. If this is his position for markets as a whole, then he is generalizing the position taken by Keynes about securities markets to markets as a whole, *viz.*, that we cannot rely on spontaneous market forces to bring us to an equilibrium position after a disturbance. And if this be the case, then Lachmann's views represent a radical challenge not only to his fellow Austrians, but to all those who accept the existence of an undesigned market order. For it certainly seems that the only effective answer to the challenges with which I have been concerned lies in Kirzner's characterization of the entrepreneurial role.

As a final note, if I have misread Lachmann, I hope this section will at least serve to clarify issues and develop implications of the principle of spontaneous order. If the paper succeeded in nothing else, it would have served its purpose.

CONCLUSIONS

I would like to remind the reader that my original task was to demonstrate that seemingly diverse and particular problems are really instances of a more general theoretical disagreement. For it is only be directly addressing this general theoretical disagreement — disagreement that I have identified as devolving around the existence of an undesigned market order — that a fruitful search toward solutions of these individual problems can be begun. It is in the nature of an endeavor to demonstrate the interconnections between such seemingly disparate (but really connected) issues that no one of them is adequately treated. If the reader feels that each section calls for a separate paper on its topic, the author can only agree, and express the hope that more papers on these subjects will be forthcoming, albeit papers informed by the realization of the overall problem being studied.

NOTES

1. Adam Smith, *The Wealth of Nations,* ed. by Edwin Cannan (New York: The Modern Library, 1937), p. 651.
   It is frequently forgotten that Smith's defense of a relatively unhampered market is partly based on considerations of justice. Cf. Smith, pp. 141, 308 and 497. The ethical basis of Smith's system is emphasized in a paper by Joseph Cropsey, "The Invisible Hand: The Moral and Political Background", delivered as part of the Harry Girvetz Memorial Lecture Series at the University of California, Santa Barbara. Also, cf. James M. Buchanan, "The Justice of Natural Liberty" (Blacksburg, Virginia; Xerox, 1976).
2. My colleague, Roy Adams, first suggested this very apt analogy to me. Also: "...You can find in Keynes, as in Marx, almost anything..." F. A. Hayek, "No Escape: Unemployment Must Follow Inflation", in *Full Employment at Any Price?* (London: Institute of Economic Affairs, 1975), p. 43.
3. New York: Oxford University Press, 1968. Leijon-hufvud's "Keynes and the Classics" (London: Institute of Economic Affairs, 1969) is also of importance here.
4. Leijonhufvud has argued that, contrary to contemporary practice, Keynes aggregated assets according to their term to maturity, and not according to whether they are real or financial. Cf. Leijonhufvud, *Keynesian Economics,* pp. 130–157.
5. Sir John Hicks has demonstrated the remarkable stability of the return on British consols in the nineteenth century. If the yield of consols can be taken as proxy for the long-rate, then his findings give some empirical basis to Keynes' hypothesis. See John R. Hicks, "The Yield on Consols", in *Critical Essays on Monetary Theory* (Oxford: The Clarendon Press, 1967), pp. 83–102.
6. It would be well to recall why speculators seek liquidity in this hypothetical situation; or, more precisely, why they attempt to shift their holdings from long-lived to short-lived assets. If long-rates are falling, but are expected to rise once again, then wealth-holders have a double incentive to sell long assets and purchase short assets. By selling at the long end of the yield spectrum, they can capture capital gains. By "going short" in the interim, they can purchase these assets back at lower prices and higher yields, once interest rates have risen again.
   All this assumes, of course, that in the aggregate, transactors seek to avoid capital uncertainty. On this point, cf. Leijonhufvud, *Keynesian Economics,* pp. 45–46; 282–314.
7. Cf. Leijonhufvud, *Keynesian Economics,* pp. 49–109.
8. See F. A. von Hayek, "Reflections on the Pure Theory of Money of Mr. J. M. Keynes, Part I", *Economica,* XI (August, 1931), 279.
9. Hayek, *Economica,* XI, 279.
10. J. M. Keynes, "The Pure Theory of Money. A Reply to Dr. Hayek", *Economica,* XI (November, 1931), 394–395. Of course, the question of whether the issues with which Keynes dealt could be treated without reference to capital theory was one of the points of dispute.
11. Joan Robinson, "What has become of the Keynesian Revolution?", in Milo Keynes (ed.), *Essays on John Maynard Keynes* (Cambridge: Cambridge University

SPONTANEOUS ORDER AND THE COORDINATION OF ECONOMIC ACTIVITIES 149

Press, 1975), p. 125; quoted in F. A. Hayek, "No Escape: Unemployment Must Follow Inflation", in *Full Employment at Any Price?* (London: Institute of Economic Affairs, 1975), p. 43.

12. Leijonhufvud, *Keynesian Economics*. p. 43.

13. Cf. "Hayek and Keynes: A Retrospective Assessment", Iowa State University Department of Economics Staff Paper No. 20 (Ames, Iowa: Xerox, 1975).

14. See Leland Yeager, "The Keynesian Diversion", *Western Economic Journal*, XI (June, 1973), 150-163.
    It should be noted that what Clower and Leijonhufvud have done is to present an interpretation of Keynes that rationalizes his doubts concerning the strength of the spontaneous forces operating to maintain or restore full employment. This in no way indicates that these two authors share these doubts. Nonetheless, it is frequently assumed, without any firm basis, that because Leijonhufvud and Clower have attempted to explicate Keynes' views that they agree with them in their entirety!

15. Axel Leijonhufvud, "Effective Demand Failures", *Swedish Journal of Economics*, 75 (1973), 28. Leijonhufvud continues, noting that this issue "lies at the heart of two of the most prominent controversies in the field over the last decade: the Fiscalist vs. Monetarist controversy...and the controversy over the long-run stability of the Phillips-curve. The.volume of writings on each of these continues to mount steadily with no clear-cut resolution in sight–in large measure because this central issue is not being effectively addressed".

16. Discussions about the energy problem are a prime example of this. They almost never even consider what spontaneous market forces might exist that would lead to the discovery of a new, coordinated solution to the allocation of energy resources. One very probable solution — perhaps the most probable if market forces were permitted to operate unfettered — would involve the destruction of the international oil cartel, whose existence makes a reallocation of energy resources appear necessary. And it is not merely noneconomists who are guilty of ignoring these market forces!
    On a more sophisticated level, modern welfare economics is virtually predicated on the absence of a spontaneous order in society, though part of the problem here is the static quality of welfare analysis.
    On the general, 20th century reaction against the principle of spontaneous order, cf. Leijonhufvud, "Effective Demand Failures", 31-32. Though the principle of spontaneous order continues as a cornerstone of economics — particularly of microeconomics — this only shows the inconsistency of current micro and macro economics — a point Leijonhufvud develops at length. Cf. Leijonhufvud, "Effective Demand Failures", 30-33.

17. The reader is referred to footnote 15 and the relevant portion of the text footnoted therein.

18. As but one example, see F. A. Hayek, *The Counter-Revolution of Science* (New York: The Free Press of Glencoe, 1955), pp. 25-35.

19. I adopt here James Buchanan's terminology to describe the Chicago School. Professor Lachmann has proposed the term "Neo-Ricardian" to refer to the distinct foibles of yet another school of theorists, the Cambridge (U.K.) School.

20. As one example of this Ricardian tendency, cf. the discussion of the general glut controversy in Thomas Sowell, *Classical Economics Reconsidered* (Princeton: Princeton University Press, 1974), pp. 46ff.

21. See Smith, pp. 35-36.

22. On this point, cf. James M. Buchanan, "Public Goods and Natural Liberty" (Blacksburg, Virginia: Xerox, 1976), especially 3-10.

23. Thus, theorists disagree over whether Smith held a labor cost theory of value, an entrepreneurial cost theory, or merely a labor measure theory. Smith may also have been unwittingly articulating a factor-exhaustion theorem for the long run. Nor could he seemingly distinguish between quasi-historical observations about the role of labor in production and theoretical statements of labor's contribution. This latter difficulty reflects Smith's "speculative" or "theoretical" approach to history. On this, cf. A. Skinner, "Economics and History — The Scottish Enlightenment", *Scottish Journal of Political Economy* (February, 1965), 1-22.

24. An example of Ricardo's approach is his treatment of the effects of an increase in the money supply. On this, see Gerald P. O'Driscoll, Jr., *Economics as a Coordination Problem: The Contributions of Friedrich A. Hayek* (Ames, Iowa: Xerox, 1975), chapter 3.2.
    Ricardo is also famous for his so-called "Equivalence Theorem" for taxation and public debt. But though this may be the most famous case of the Ricardian vice, it is the one case where Ricardo was *not* a Ricardian! See *The Works and Correspondence of David Ricardo*, Vol. I: *On the Principles of Political Economy and Taxation*, ed. by Piero Sraffa (Cambridge: Cambridge University Press, 1951), pp. 247-248; *The Works*, Vol. VI: *Pamphlets and Papers, 1815-1823*, pp. 185-188; Sowell, pp. 67-68; and Gerald P. O'Driscoll, Jr., *The Ricardian Nonequivalence Theorem, Journal of Political Economy*, (1977) pp. 207-210.

25. Ludwig M. Lachmann, "From Mises to Shackle: An Essay on Austrian Economics and the Kaleidic Society", *Journal of Economic Literature*, XIV (March, 1976), 55. Cf. Hayek, *The Counter-Revolution of Science*, pp. 29-30.

26. Cf. Hayek, "The Meaning of Competition", in *Individualism and Economic Order* (Chicago: University of Chicago Press, 1948), pp. 97-98.

27. An example of this dilemma is the role of money in a general equilibrium model. On this, see Hayek, *The Pure Theory of Capital* (Chicago: University of Chicago Press, 1941), p. 31.

28. Cf. Sowell, pp. 58-59.

29. Cf. Israel M. Kirzner, *Competition and Entrepreneurship* (Chicago: University of Chicago Press, 1973), 32-37.

30. Ignoring the factors that govern the emergence of a spontaneous order is in some sense more objectionable (from the viewpoint of one who accepts the principle) than denying its relevance. Failure to discuss the conditions under which a spontaneous order would emerge in an economic system prejudices the case against unhampered, decentralized decision-making. Thus, when obvious misallocations and "market failures" develop in an economy, suggestions that policy be directed toward *freer* markets will be met with incredulity.
    On Walras' assumption that markets will clear so as to produce an overall order, cf. O'Driscoll, *Economics*

as a Coordination Problem, Chapter 2.2.

31. The hostility of the Chicago School to the approach of the Austrian School is a fact. What calls for explanation is the reason, which involves far more than a "family" squabble. The divisions between the two schools antedate each in the history of economic thought.

    For a recent example of the Chicago attitude toward the Austrian conception of economics, see the *Review of Competition and Entrepreneurship* by Benjamin Klein, *Journal of Political Economy,* 83 (December, 1975), 1305–1309. For an earlier example of similar treatment, see the *Review of Capital and Its Structure* by Martin J. Bailey, *Journal of Political Economy,* LXV (June, 1957), 265–266.

32. For instance, see the discussion in Hayek, *Monetary Theory and the Trade Cycle,* translated by N. Kaldor and H. M. Croome (New York: Augustus M. Kelley, 1966), pp. 43–45.

    In what follows, I will draw on my paper, "Friedrich Hayek and the Science of Choice", Iowa State University Staff Paper in Economics No. 24 (Ames, Iowa: Xerox, 1975).

33. Cf. Friedrich A. Hayek, *The Pure Theory of Capital,* pp. 33–34.

34. "Of course, it is one thing to assert that monetary changes are the key to major movements in money income; it is quite a different thing to know in any detail what is the mechanism that links monetary change to economic change; how the influence of the one is transmitted to the other; what sectors of the economy will be affected first; what the time pattern of the impacts will be, and so on. We have great confidence in the first assertion. We have little confidence in our knowledge of the transmission mechanism, except in such broad and vague terms as to constitute little more than an impressionistic representation rather than an engineering blueprint". Milton Friedman and Anna J. Schwartz, "Money and Business Cycle", in Friedman, *The Optimum Quantity of Money* (Chicago: Aldine Publishing Co., 1969), p. 222.

    Commenting on Ricardo's inattention to transitional periods, Schumpeter has remarked: "...In matters of monetary as of general theory, Ricardian teaching is a detour and...it slowed up the advance of analysis, which would have been much quicker and smoother had [Henry] Thornton's lead been followed — had Ricardo's force not prevailed over Thornton's insight". Joseph A. Schumpeter, *History of Economic Analysis* (New York: Oxford University Press, 1954), p. 704n.

35. Cf. Gerald P. O'Driscoll, Jr. and Sudha R. Shenoy, "Inflation, Recession and Stagflation", in Edwin G. Dolan, ed., *The Foundations of Modern Austrian Economics* (Kansas City: Sheed & Ward, 1976), pp. 185–211.

    For recent statements of Friedman's position, see "A Theoretical Framework for Monetary Analysis", *Journal of Political Economy,* 78 (March/April, 1970), 193–238; and "A Monetary Theory of National Income", *Journal of Political Economy,* 79 (March/April, 1971), 323–337.

36. I am referring here to the problem of distributional, or Cantillon-effects, which have been so long ignored in monetary theory. This gap in monetary theory is not accidental, for most theories of money incorporate neutrality assumptions. If money is neutral, then indeed there are no distribution effects. It is not remarkable, then, that monetary economists generally ignore the problem of distribution effects. What is remarkable is that the almost fantastic assumption of neutrality of money generally does not give economists pause. While it would be beyond the scope of this paper to demonstrate this proposition, it does seem that an economy in which money could be neutral is one in which there would be no demand for money. For where else but in a world of correct expectations and perfect coordination would changes in the supply-demand relation of money be neutral in their effects?

    The issue of the neutrality of money and distribution effects is considered in Friedrich A. Lutz, "On Neutral Money", in Erich Streissler, Gottfried Haberler, Friedrich A. Lutz and Fritz Machlup, *Roads to Freedom* (New York: Augustus M. Kelley, 1969), pp. 105–116.

37. Cf. O'Driscoll, *Economics as a Coordination Problem,* chapter 5.4.

38. I am quite aware that to some extent Friedman has dealt with the general institutional framework necessary for economic stability. And, indeed, I find his earlier work of more interest in this regard. I would point out that even in that he focused on price *levels,* and did not develop the problem of *coordination* at length. Cf. Milton Friedman, *A Program for Monetary Stability* (New York: Fordham University Press, 1960).

39. From the editorial introduction by Sudha R. Shenoy, ed., *A Tiger by the Tail* (London: Institute of Economic Affairs, 1972), p. 8.

40. The argument appearing in the beginning of this section was strongly influenced by a talk, "Adam Smith in Theory and Practice", delivered by Thomas Sowell in the Harry Girvetz Memorial Lecture Series at the University of California, Santa Barbara.

41. Adam Smith, *Theory of Moral Sentiments* (London: Henry G. Bohn, 1853), pp. 342–343.

42. Hayek, *The Morgan Guaranty Survey* (January, 1976), 4.

43. For one reason that might attract economists to this movement, see Hayek, *The Morgan Guaranty Survey,* 11.

44. See Wassily Leontief, "For a National Economic Planning Board", *The New York Times* (March 14, 1974), 37.

45. The modern Austrians have specifically emphasized this point. The work of Mises, Hayek, Lachmann and Kirzner are notable in this respect. For a recent example of a work written in the Austrian tradition that emphasizes the role of decentralized planning in a market economy, see Kirzner's *Competition and Entrepreneurship.*

46. This quotation appears in Chapter III of Hayek, *The Road to Serfdom* (Chicago: University of Chicago Press, 1944), pp. 34f; it is cited in Hayek, *The Morgan Guaranty Survey* (January, 1976), 5–6.

    The word "liberal" refers here, of course, to classical English liberalism, and not to twentieth century American liberalism.

47. Israel M. Kirzner, "Hayek, Knowledge and Market Processes", Paper Delivered at the Allied Social Science Association Meetings in Dallas, Texas (New York: Xerox, 1975); especially 28–29.

48. Kirzner, "Hayek, Knowledge and Market Processes", p. 29.

49. Kirzner, "Hayek, Knowledge and Market Processes",

p. 32.
50. Kirzner, "Hayek, Knowledge and Market Processes",
    p. 33.
51. L. M. Lachmann, "Reflections on Hayekian Capital
    Theory", Paper Delivered at the Allied Social Science
    Association Meetings in Dallas, Texas (New York:
    Xerox, 1975), 13.
52. Lachmann, "Reflections...," 8–9. Emphasis added.
    Aslo, cf. Lachmann, "From Mises to Shackle", 59–61.
53. Lachmann, "Reflections...", 9. "The Future is
    unknowable, though not unimaginable. Future
    knowledge cannot be had now, but it can cast its
    shadow ahead. In each mind, however, the shadow
    assumes a different shape, hence the divergence of
    expectations. The formation of expectations is an act
    of our minds by means of which we try to catch a
    glimpse of the unknown. Each one of us catches a
    different glimpse". Lachmann, "From Mises to
    Shackle...", 59.
54. In his most recent work, Lachmann notes that Mises,
    Hayek and Kirzner have emphasized the diffusion of
    knowledge in the market process. But he denies that
    the market can diffuse expectations in the same way.
    Cf. Lachmann, "From Mises to Shackle", 59. I
    believe the distinction between knowledge and
    expectations is a spurious one.
55. Cf. Kirzner, "Hayek, Knowledge and Market
    Processes", 30–31.
56. Lachmann, "From Mises to Shackle", 59.
57. Lachmann, "From Mises to Shackle", 61.
58. Cf. Hayek, "Economics and Knowledge", in *Individual-
    ism and Economic Order*, pp. 39–45.
59. It is true that one can find recent instances in which
    prominent economists imply "coordination" in the
    ex post sense. For instance, cf. Leijonhufvud,
    "Effective Demand Failures", 29. But there Leijon-
    hufvud is dealing, *inter alia*, with the question of
    whether markets clear at all. But the general issue with
    which Lachmann is dealing is surely the problem of
    ex ante coordination. If not, one must ask "why all
    the fuss?" Generally it is not denied by non-Marxists
    that at least output markets clear.
60. Ludwig M. Lachmann, "On Austrian Capital Theory",
    in E. G. Dolan, *The Foundations of Modern Austrian
    Economics* (Kansas City: Sheed & Ward, 1976), p. 149.
61. "...Expectations of early change in the present situa-
    tion may impede the process of adjustment, and even
    when this does not happen, the forces of adjustment
    themselves may be overtaken by other forces". Lach-
    mann, "On Austrian Capital Theory", pp. 149–150.
62. Lachmann, "From Mises to Shackle", 60; also see
    58n of that article.
63. In any event, this is what I make of his public statements
    on the issue, made at various times. Also, note the last
    line of the first Lachmann quotation appearing above.
    Lachmann juxtaposes "the forces of equilibrium" and
    "the forces of change". Lachmann, "From Mises to
    Shackle", 61.

[9]

Professor Kirzner on Entrepreneurship
by G.L.S. Shackle

it seems to me astounding that political economy should ever have been thought of as a *calculus*. A calculus is a means of re-arranging data so that they throw a different light upon their subject-matter. This fresh illumination may excite, startle and inspire its beholders. But this is only one kind of new knowledge. It is a fuller, more penetrating insight into material already within reach. It is a re-handling of the same data. We cannot use a calculus for practical ends until we have some data. Without data we can only play logic-games or indulge in science-fiction. Even a calculus is a playground with a wall around it. There are surely other playgrounds, fresh alphabets and languages, new grammars and new symbolisms, into which data could be poured in freshly glittering streams, once these new receptacles had been imagined. And such imaginations and originations merge into the apprehension of new data of new kinds, data made conceivable by new systems of classification, new categories of thought. Is not all this the legitimate field of the political economist, and of the business man, if their intellectual and history-making ambition is truly assurgent?

The practical man with an influence and a burden in the world is the business man. There is a question about him that cuts right down to the foundations of our view of life. Will his duties and his doings soon be taken over by the silicon chips? If we say yes, we are determinists who think that, in the last analysis, history is not of our making but we are simply bits of its fore-ordained pattern. Professor Kirzner's business man is the bold repudiation of that view. The Kirznerian entrepreneur is not threatened by the silicon-chips. He is their designer, and their out-reacher. What, then, does the business man really, essentially, indispensably do? He dreams dreams. He has thoughts that do not arise from any accepted programme or paradigm. He conjures knowledge that, in Professor Kirzner's words, no one knew existed. Professor Kirzner has not, perhaps, fitted words to the full impact of this thought. Our language seems to lack a word to give the full strength of it. The nearest we can come, I think, is *originate*. But this sometimes means merely the bringing together of ingredients. When we are speaking of

Continued on next page

Professor Kirzner on Entrepreneurship

(Continued)

knowledge, what we may call ingredients, ideas known and even familiar, may be visible at the same time to the same man without the sudden flash of fusion into something new ever taking place. Professor Kirzner is suggesting in effect, I think, that the natural entrepreneur is the man in whose mind such fusions do take place. I am not sure, however, that what he calls alertness is the heart of the matter. Were Dante, Michaelangelo, Shakespeare, Newton, and Beethoven merely alert? No doubt, if we look at biological Nature herself, we see a boundless prodigality of experiment, the random heritable mutations most of which are disadvantageous. The few that confer special fitness for an available environment give the new species a powerful ascendancy. Does this theory, then, teach us that all is random? The entrepreneur's special gift, even if not comparable to the poet's or the composer's, seems to need a special word. This gift is not merely a wild prodigality of random trial and error.

It seems quite plain why the businessman who attains and exploits a true novelty does not usually do so by seeking answers to questions posed ready-made by existing technology. Solving arithmetical problems does not (except at rare conjunctures) establish new arithmetical ideas. The very word we use for the seeking of answers to *existing* questions seems a little restrictive and oppressive. *Research* envisages results whose outlines we can in some sense see in advance. Thus there may even be some sense in trying to compare the cost and the value of 'research' in this confined sense. But does it make sense to put a price on the time spent in ranging untrodden fields? If we knew in an exploitable degree what we should find, we should not need to find it. If we do not know what we shall find, how can we say what it will be worth? The true entrepreneur, Professor Kirzner is saying in effect, is the man whose thoughts can encounter knowledge that nobody knew existed. Pure speculative thought can have no price. Will economists ever loosen the stranglehold upon their minds of the idea that economics is a *calculus*?

■

The Center for Libertarian Studies
AUSTRIAN ECONOMICS NEWSLETTER
200 Park Avenue South
New York, N.Y. 10003

12 Uncertainty, Discovery, and Human Action: A Study of the Entrepreneurial Profile in the Misesian System

Israel M. Kirzner

A central element in the economics of Ludwig von Mises is the role played by the entrepreneur and the function fulfilled by entrepreneurship in the market process. The character of that process for Mises is decisively shaped by the leadership, the initiative, and the driving activity displayed and exercised by the entrepreneur. Moreover, in an intellectual edifice built systematically on the notion of individual *human action*—on the manner in which reasoning human beings interact while seeking to achieve their individual purposes—it is highly significant that Mises found it of relevance to emphasize that each human actor is always, in significant respects, an entrepreneur.[1] The present paper seeks to explore the character of Misesian entrepreneurship, with special reference to the influence exercised by the inescapable uncertainty that pervades economic life. Both at the level of isolated individual human action and at the level of entrepreneurial activity in market context, we shall be concerned to determine the extent to which the Misesian entrepreneur owes his very existence and his function to the unpredictability of his environment and to the ceaseless tides of change that undergird that unpredictability.

On the face of it, this question may not seem worthy of new research. Mises, it may be pointed out, expressed himself quite clearly on numerous occasions to the effect that the entrepreneurial function is inseparable from speculation with respect to an uncertain future. For example he wrote that "the entrepreneur is always a speculator."[2] Or, again, he wrote that "entrepreneur means acting man in regard to the changes occurring in the data of the market."[3] Moreover when Mises points out that every individual acting man is an entrepreneur, this is because "every action is embedded in the flux of time and thus involves a speculation."[4] In other words the entrepreneurial element cannot be abstracted from the notion of individual human action, because the "uncertainty of the future is already implied in the very notion of action. That man acts and that the future is uncertain are by no means two independent matters, they are only two different modes of establishing one thing."[5]

139

140   Method, Process, and Austrian Economics

Thus it might seem that the essentiality of uncertainty for the Misesian entrepreneur hardly needs to be established anew. Certainly any thought of questioning that essentiality must, it might appear, be quickly dismissed.

What I shall argue in this chapter is not that the role of uncertainty in the function of the Misesian entrepreneur may be any less definitive than these clear-cut statements imply but that this role is a more subtle one than may on the surface appear to be the case. It is this subtlety in the role played by uncertainty in the Misesian system, I believe, that sets that system apart in significant respects from the views of other economists (such as Knight or Shackle) who have emphasized the phenomenon of uncertainty in the context of the market.

The Background of the Present Exploration

In earlier forays into the field of the Misesian entrepreneur, I developed an interpretation of the entrepreneurial function in which the role of uncertainty, while recognized and certainly not denied, was not emphasized. This failure to emphasize uncertainty was quite deliberate and was indeed explicitly acknowledged.[6] Instead of emphasizing the uncertainty in which entrepreneurial activity is embedded, these earlier treatments stressed the element of *alertness to hitherto unperceived opportunities* that is, I argued, crucial for the Misesian concept of entrepreneurship.[7] Since my position explicitly recognized the element of change and uncertainty, while it claimed to be able to explicate the elusive quality of entrepreneurship without need to emphasize the uncertainty element, it is perhaps not surprising that my treatment has drawn fire from two different perspectives. A number of critics have felt rather strongly that failure to emphasize the role of uncertainty renders my understanding of entrepreneurship fundamentally defective. At least one critic, on the other hand, has been persuaded by my exposition of entrepreneurship to the point that even my frugal references to uncertainty as an inescapable characteristic of the entrepreneurial scene appear altogether unnecessary and are seen as productive of confusion. Since all these critics are basically in agreement with me, I believe, on the broad accuracy of the general entrepreneurial character of the market process that I ascribe to Mises, it has for some time been my hope to delve into these questions more thoroughly. Some further brief recapitulation of these earlier discussions seems in order as an introduction to our present exploration.

My emphasis on alertness to hitherto unperceived opportunities as the decisive element in the entrepreneurial function stemmed from my pursuit of a didactic purpose. This purpose was to distinguish the analysis of the market *process* (a process in which the entrepreneur plays the crucial role)

as sharply as possible from the analysis of equilibrium states (in which all scope for entrepreneurial activity has been assumed away). In equilibrium, it turns out, all market decisions have somehow come already into complete mutual coordination. Market participants have been assumed to be making their respective decisions with perfectly correct information concerning the decisions that all other participants are making at the same time.[8] So long as the underlying present consumer attitudes and production possibilities prevail, it is clear that we can rely on the very same set of decisions being made in each of an indefinite number of future periods. On the other hand, in the absence of such complete equilibrium coordination of decisions, a market process is set in motion in which market participants are motivated to learn more accurately to anticipate the decisions of others; in this process the entrepreneurial, profit-motivated discovery of the gaps in mutual coordination of decisions is a crucial element. Entrepreneurial activity drives this market process of mutual discovery by a continually displayed alertness to profit opportunities (into which the market automatically translates the existing gaps in coordination). Whereas entrepreneurial activity is indeed speculative, the pursuit of profit opportunities is a purposeful and deliberate one, the "emphasis on the element of alertness in action [was] intended to point out that, far from being numbed by the inescapable uncertainty of our world, men *act upon their judgments of* what opportunities have been left unexploited by others."[9]

In developing this aspect of entrepreneurship I was led to emphasize the capture of pure entrepreneurial profit as reducible essentially to the exploitation of arbitrage opportunities. Imperfect mutual awareness on the part of other market participants had generated the emergence of more than one price for the same bundle of economic goods; the entrepreneur's alertness to the profit opportunity presented by this price discrepancy permits him to win these profits (and, in so doing, tends to nudge the prices into closer adjustment with each other). In so emphasizing the arbitrage character of pure profit, emphasis was deliberately withdrawn from the speculative character of entrepreneurial activity that wins pure profit by correctly anticipating *future* price movements.[10]

A number of (otherwise friendly) critics expressed serious reservations concerning my deliberate lack of stress on the speculative character of entrepreneurial activity. Henry Hazlitt pointed out that my repeated references to the entrepreneur's perceiving of opportunities fail to make clear that at best the entrepreneur *thinks* that he perceives opportunities; that what an entrepreneur "acts on may not be a perception but a *guess.*"[11] Murray Rothbard has endorsed a discussion by Robert Hébert in which my definition of the entrepreneur is sharply distinguished from that of Mises: "Mises conceives of the entrepreneur as the uncertainty bearer. . . . To Kirzner, on the other hand, entrepreneurship becomes reduced to the quality of *alert-*

ness; and uncertainty seems to have little to do with the matter."[12] Although conceding that my treatment of the entrepreneur has "a certain amount of textual justification in Mises," Rothbard sees this not as providing genuine support for my reading of the Misesian entrepreneur but as being the result of a "certain uncharacteristic lack of clarity in Mises' discussion of entrepreneurship."[13]

In a most thoughtful paper by Lawrence H. White several years ago, he too deplored my deliberate failure to emphasize uncertainty in the analysis of entrepreneurship. This treatment White argues, fosters neglect of important features of entrepreneurial activity that arise precisely from the passage of time and from the uncertainty generated by the prospect of unanticipated changes bound to occur during the journey to the future. To compress entrepreneurial activity into an arbitrage box is, in particular, to fail to recognize the highly important part played by entrepreneurial *imagination.*[14]

On the other hand my treatment of entrepreneurship has been criticized by J. High from a diametrically opposite point of view. High accepts the definition of entrepreneurship in terms of alertness to opportunities for pure profit. He proceeds to point out that "[n]othing in this definition requires uncertainty. The definition requires ignorance, because the opportunity has not been discovered earlier; it requires error, because the opportunity could have been discovered earlier, but the definition does not require uncertainty."[15] High is therefore critical of passages in which uncertainty is linked specifically with entrepreneurship.[16]

Clearly the role of uncertainty in the entrepreneurial environment, and in particular its relationship to the entrepreneur's alertness to error, demands further explication. What follows may not satisfy my critics (from both wings). I trust, however, that my discussion of some of the perhaps less obvious links between uncertainty and alertness will, if it does not quite absolve me of the charge of intransigence, at least bear witness to my grateful acknowledgement of the very deep importance of the problems raised by my critics.

Our inquiry will be facilitated by a careful examination of the sense in which each individual engaging in human action is, as already cited from Mises, exercising entrepreneurship.[17] Or, to put the issue somewhat differently, it will be helpful to explore more precisely what it is that distinguishes human action from purely calculative, allocative, economizing activity.

I have argued in earlier work that the concept of human action emphasized by Mises includes an ineradicable entrepreneurial element that is absent from the notion of economizing, of the allocation of scarce resources among competing ends, that was articulated by Lord Robbins.[18] On the face of it there appear to be two distinct aspects of Misesian human action that might be considered to set it apart from Robbinsian economizing activity. We shall have to ask whether these are indeed two distinct aspects of human action and how they relate to the entrepreneurial element that human action contains (but which Robbinsian allocative activity does not). These two aspects of human action (not present in economizing activity) may be identified as (1) the element in action that is beyond the scope of "rationality" as an explanatory tool, and (2) the element in action that constitutes discovery of error. Let us consider these in turn.

The Limits of Rationality

Perhaps the central feature of purely economizing activity is that it enables us to explain behavior by reference to the postulate of rationality. With a given framework of ranked goals sought, and of scarce resources available to be deployed, rationality (in the narrow sense of consistency of behavior with the relevant given ranking of ends) assures a unique pattern of resource allocation; decision making can be fully understood in the light of the given ends-means framework. There is no part of the decision that cannot be accounted for; given the framework, the decision taken is fully determined (and therefore completely explained); any other decision would have been simply unthinkable.

On the other hand the notion of Misesian human action embraces the very adoption of the ends-means framework to be considered relevant. The adoption of any particular ends-means framework is a step which is logically (although not necessarily chronologically) prior to that of allocating means consistently with the given ranking of ends. If the human decision is to be perceived as including the selection of the ends-means framework, then we have an element in that decision that cannot, of course, be explained by reference to rationality. Consistency in action is not sufficient to account for that ranking of ends in terms of which consistency itself is to be defined. So that the totality of human action cannot, even in principle, be explained on the basis of rationality. A science of human action cannot fail to acknowledge—even after full recognition of the formidable explanatory power of the postulate of rationality—that human history, depending as it does on unexplained adoption of goals and awareness of means, contains a strong element of the unexplained and even the spontaneous. These are themes that have, of course, been extensively developed by G.L.S. Shackle. "Choice and reason are things different in nature and function, reason *serves* the chosen purposes, not performs the selection of them."[19] "A man can be supposed to act always in rational response to his 'circumstances': but those 'circumstances' can, *and must,* be in part the creation of his own mind. . . . In this loose-textured history, men's choices of action being choices among thoughts which spring indeterminately in their minds, we can deem them to *initiate* trains of events in some real sense."[20]

In an earlier era, much criticism of the role of the rationality postulate in economic theory focused on the place of apparently nonrational behavior, behavior arising out of impetuous impulse or out of unthinking habit.[21] It is simply unrealistic, these criticisms ran, to assume that economic activity represents the exclusive result of deliberation. Man acts all too often without careful deliberation; he does not weigh the costs and benefits of his actions. This is not the place to evaluate these criticisms or deal with the debates that they engendered three-quarters of a century ago and more. But it is perhaps important to point out that limits of rationality discussed in this section have little to do with the arguments based on impulsiveness and on habit bondage. It is not at all being argued here that human action involves the *thoughtless* selection of goals. Human decision making may of course involve the most agonizingly careful appraisal of alternative courses of action to choose that which seems likely to offer the most estimable of outcomes. In emphasizing that the rationality postulate is unable to explain the selection of the relevant ends-means framework, we are not suggesting that that selection occurs without deliberation, but merely that the results of that deliberation cannot be predicted on the basis of the postulate of consistency; that deliberation is essentially creative. One may predict the answer that a competent mathematician will arrive at when he tackles a given problem in computation (in the same way that one may know in advance the answer to that problem that will be yielded by an electronic computer); but one cannot, in the same way, predict which computational problem the mathematician will deliberately choose to tackle (as one may not be able to predict which problems will be selected to be fed into the electronic computer).

The matter may be presented in an alternative version. One may always distinguish, within each human decision an element into which thought enters in self-aware fashion from an element into which thought enters without self-awareness. A man desires a specific goal with great eagerness; but deliberation persuades him, let us imagine, that it is in his interest not to reveal that eagerness to others (say, because others might then spitefully wish to deny that goal to him). The studied nonchalance with which he masks his pursuit of the goal exhibits scope for both elements: (1) his apparent nonchalance is indeed deliberate and studied, he knows precisely the reason why it is important that he pretend disinterest; but (2) he may not be at all self-aware as to how he arrived at this judgment to act on the assumption that others may spitefully seek to frustrate his achievement. He simply decides so to act. His decision is to refrain from naively pursuing with evident eagerness that which he eagerly desires; but his decision is yet naive in the sense that he has not, for example, sought (as reasons having to do with long-term strategy might well suggest) to ostentatiously pretend unawareness of the spitefulness of the others. No matter how calculative a man's behavior may be, it seems impossible to avoid having accepted, without cal-

Uncertainty, Discovery, and Human Action 145

culation, some framework within which to self-consciously engage in cost-benefit comparisons. A man decides to display behavior *a*. We may call the mental activity of making that decision, activity *b*. Now the man *may* have decided (in the course of decision-making activity *c*) to engage in decision-making activity *b*, (or he may have simply and impulsively engaged in decision-making activity *b*). But even if engaging in decision-making activity *b* (as a result of which behavior *a* was chosen) was itself the outcome of "higher" decisions, at some level our decision maker's highest decision was made quite unselfconsciously.

This extra-Robbinsian aspect of human action, the aspect which involves the creative, unpredictable selection of the ends-means framework, can also be usefully stated in terms of *knowledge*. Given his knowledge of the relevant ends-means framework, man's decision can be predicted without doubt; it is simply a matter of computation. To the extent, however, that man must "decide" what it is, so to speak, that he knows, and that this determination is not, in general, based ineluctably on other knowledge unambiguously possessed, man's behavior is not at all predictable. What a man believes himself to know is not itself the result of a calculative decision.[22] This expression of the notion of the existence of limits to rationality will facilitate our insight into the important linkage that exists between these limits and the phenomenon of uncertainty.

In the absence of uncertainty it would be difficult to avoid the assumption that each individual does in fact already know the circumstances surrounding his decision. Without uncertainty, therefore, decision making would no longer call for any imaginative, creative determination of what the circumstances really are. Decision making would call merely for competent calculation. Its results could, in general, be predicted without doubt. Human judgment would have no scope. "With uncertainty absent, man's energies are devoted altogether to doing things; . . . in a world so built . . . it seems likely that . . . all organisms [would be] automata. . . ."[23] "If man knew the future, he would not have to choose and would not act. He would be like an automaton, reacting to stimuli without any will of its own."[24] Thus the extra-Robbinsian aspect of human action, the aspect responsible for rendering human action unpredictable and incompletely explainable in terms of rationality, arises from the inherent uncertainty of human predicament. If, then, one chooses to identify entrepreneurship with the function of making decisions in the face of an uncertain present or future environment, it certainly appears that Misesian human action does (while Robbinsian economizing does not) include an entrepreneurial element.

But before making up our minds on this point, we must consider that second element, mentioned at the end of the preceding section, that distinguishes Misesian human action from Robbinsian allocative decision making.

The Discovery of Error

To draw attention to this element in human action I shall draw on an earlier paper in which I attempted to identify that which might represent "entrepreneurial profit" in successful individual action in a Crusoe context.[25] Entrepreneurial profit in the Crusoe context, it turned out, can be identified only where Crusoe discovers that he has up until now attached an erroneously low valuation to resources over which he has command. Until today Crusoe has been spending his time catching fish with his bare hands. Today he has realized that he can use his time far more valuably by building a boat or making a net. "He has discovered that he had placed an incorrectly low value on his time. His reallocation of his labor time from fishing to boat-building is an entrepreneurial decision and, assuming his decision to be a correct one, yields pure profit in the form of additional value discovered to be forthcoming from the labor time applied."[26] This (Crusonian) pure profit arises from the circumstance that at the instant of entrepreneurial discovery Menger's law is violated. Menger's law teaches that men value goods according to the value of the satisfactions that depend on possession of those goods. This law arises from man's propensity to attach the value of ends to the means needed for their achievement. At the moment of entrepreneurial discovery Crusoe realizes that the ends achievable with his labor time have higher value than the ends he had previously sought to achieve:

> The value Crusoe has until now attached to his time is *less* than the value of the ends he now seeks. This discrepancy is, at the level of the individual, pure profit. . . . Once the old ends-means framework has been completely and unquestionably replaced by the new one, of course, it is the value of the new ends that Crusoe comes to attach to his means. . . . But, during the instant of an entrepreneurial leap of faith . . . there is scope for the discovery that, indeed, the ends achieved are more valuable than had hitherto been suspected. *This,* is the discovery of pure (Crusonian) entrepreneurial profit.[27]

Scope for entrepreneurship thus appears to be grounded in the possibility of discovering error. In the market context, the state of general equilibrium, providing as it does absolutely no scope for the discovery of profitable discrepancies between prices and costs, affords no opportunity for entrepreneurial discovery and turns out to be populated entirely by Robbinsian maximizers. In the same way, it now appears, the situation in which Crusoe is errorlessly allocating his resources—with the value of ends being fully and faultlessly attached to the relevant means in strict accordance with Menger's law—affords no scope for the entrepreneurial element in human action. Human action, without scope for the discovery of error, collapses into Robbinsian allocative activity.

Uncertainty, Discovery, and Human Action   147

Clearly this way of identifying the entrepreneurial element that is present in Misesian human action but absent in Robbinsian economizing activity fits in well with the approach that defines enterpreneurship as alertness to hitherto unperceived opportunities.[28] In the market context entrepreneurship is evoked by the presence of as yet unexploited opportunities for pure profit. These opportunities are evidence of the failure of market participants, up until now, to correctly assess the realities of the market situation. At the level of the individual too, it is then attractive to argue, an entrepreneurial element in action is evoked by the existence of as-yet-unexploited private opportunities. To act entrepreneurially is to identify situations overlooked until now because of error.

Uncertainty and/or Discovery

Our discussion has led us to identify two apparently distinct elements in human action, each of which possesses plausible claims as constituting that entrepreneurial element in action that sets it apart from purely calculative economizing activity: (1) On the one hand we saw that it appears plausible to associate entrepreneurship with the department within human action in which the very framework for calculative economizing activity is, in an open-ended, uncertain world, selected as being relevant. It is here that we would find scope for the unpredictable, the creative, the imaginative expressions of the human mind—expressions that cannot themselves be explained in terms of the postulate of consistency. Thus entrepreneurship, at the Crusoe level, arises uniquely and peculiarly from the circumstance that, as a result of the inescapable uncertainty of the human predicament, acting man cannot be assumed to be sure of the framework relevant for calculative activity. He must, using whatever entrepreneurial gifts he can display, *choose* a framework. (2) On the other hand, as we have seen, it appears perhaps equally plausible to associate entrepreneurship with that aspect of human action in which the alert individual realizes the existence of opportunities that he has up until now somehow failed to notice. Scope for entrepreneurship, at the Crusoe level, arises then not from the present uncertainty that must now be grappled with in decision making but from earlier error from which entrepreneurial discovery must now provide protection.

We must emphasize that these alternative identifications of the entrepreneurial element in action do appear, at least on a first scrutiny, to be genuinely different from one another. It is of course true that past error (from which, on the one view, we look to entrepreneurial discovery to provide a rescue) may be attributed to the pervasive uncertainty that characterizes our world (and to the inevitably kaleidic changes responsible for that uncertainty.) But to discover hitherto unnoticed opportunities (unnoticed because of past failure to pierce correctly the fog of uncertainty) does not at all seem to be the same task as that of selecting between alternative present scenarios for the future within which calculative activity is to be undertaken. Moreover, whatever the possible reasons for past error, error itself implies merely ignorance, not necessarily uncertainty.[29] To escape ignorance is one thing; to deal with uncertainty is another.

This tension that we have discovered at the level of human action in the Crusoe context, between present uncertainty and earlier error as sources of entrepreneurship, is clearly to be linked immediately with our more general exploration in this chapter. This chapter is concerned with determining the extent to which the Misesian entrepreneur is to be perceived as the creature of uncertainty. The tension we have now discovered between present uncertainty and earlier error corresponds exactly to the disagreement that we encountered between those who see the Misesian entrepreneur as essentially the bearer of market uncertainty and those who see him as the discoverer of earlier market errors. It is my contention that our awareness of this apparent tension can in fact shed light on certain subtleties in the concept of entrepreneurship likely otherwise to be overlooked. Our procedure to develop this claim will be as follows: We will seek to show that, on a deeper understanding of the meaning of uncertainty and of the discovery of error at the level of individual action, the tension between them dissolves in a way that will reveal the full significance of entrepreneurial alertness at the level of the individual. Thereafter we will pursue the analogy between the scope of entrepreneurship at the individual level and that of the entrepreneurship at the level of the market, drawing on this analogy to identify precisely the relative roles, in market entrepreneurship, of uncertainty and of alertness.

Action and Alertness

Man acts, in the light of the future as he envisages it, to enhance his position in that future. The realized consequences of man's actions, however, flow from the impact of those actions on the actual (as contrasted with the envisaged) course of future events. The extent to which man's plans for the enhancement of his future prospects are fulfilled depends on the extent to which the future as he has envisaged it corresponds to the future as it in fact occurs. There is no natural set of forces or constraints assuring correspondence between the envisaged future and the realized future. The two may, it seems at first glance, diverge from one another with complete freedom. The future course of events is in general certainly not constrained by past forecasts; nor, unfortunately, are forecasts constrained by the actual future events these forecasts seek to foretell. On the face of it, then, with nothing to guarantee correspondence between the actual future and the future as it is

Uncertainty, Discovery, and Human Action   149

envisaged, it might seem as if successful action were entirely a matter of good fortune. Indeed, if man is aware of this apparent lack of ability to envisage the future correctly except as a matter of sheer good fortune, it is not clear why (apart from the joys of gambling itself) man bothers to act at all. But of course the overwhelming fact of human history is that man does act, and his choices are made in terms of an envisaged future that, although by no means a photographic image of the future as it will actually unfold, is yet not entirely without moorings in regard to that realized future. "To be genuine, choice must be neither random nor predetermined. There must be some grounds for choosing, but they must be inadequate; there must be some possibility of predicting the consequences of choice, but none of perfect prediction."[30] "The essence of the situation is action according to *opinion*, . . . neither entire ignorance nor complete and perfect information, but partial knowledge."[31] The genuine choices that do, we are convinced, make up human history express man's conviction that the future as he envisages it does hold correspondence, in some degree, to the future as it will in fact unfold. The uncertainty of the future reflects man's awareness that this correspondence is far from complete; the fact that he acts and chooses at all reflects his conviction that this correspondence is far from negligible. Whence does this correspondence, incomplete though it may be, arise? If there are no constraints assuring correspondence, how is successful action anything but the sheerest good fortune?

The answer to this dilemma surely lies in the circumstance that man is *motivated* to formulate the future as he envisages it, as accurately as possible. It is not a matter of two unfolding tapestries, one the realized future, the second a fantasized series of pictures of what the first might look like. Rather, acting man really does try to construct his picture of the future to correspond to the truth as it will be realized. He really does try to glimpse the future, to peer through the fog. He is thus motivated *to bring about* correspondence between the envisaged and the realized futures. Man's purposeful efforts to better his condition are responsible not only for his choices as constructed against a given envisaged future; that purposefulness is, perhaps even more importantly, responsible for the remarkable circumstance that that envisaged future does overlap significantly with the future as it actually unfolds. (Of course, these forecasts need not be made, explicitly, prior to action; they are embedded, possibly without self-awareness, in action itself.) We call this motivated propensity of man to formulate an image of the future man's *alertness*. Were man totally lacking in alertness, he could not act at all: his blindness to the future would rob him of any framework for action. (In fact, were man totally lacking in potential for alertness, it would be difficult to identify a notion of error altogether: were unalert man to act, it would not be on the basis of an erroneously forecast future. It would be on the basis of no relevant forecast at all. Not recogniz-

150   Method, Process, and Austrian Economics

ing that he might—had he been more alert—have avoided the incorrect picture of the future, he could not in any meaningful sense blame himself for having erred.)

It will surely be acknowledged that this alertness—which provides the only pressure to constrain man's envisaged future toward some correspondence with the future to be realized—is what we are searching for under the phrase "the entrepreneurial element in human action." Robbinsian allocation activity contains no such element, because within the assigned scope of such defined activity no possible divergence between a future as envisaged and a future to be realized is considered. What is incomplete in the notion of purely allocative activity is surely to be found precisely in this abstraction from the desperately important element of entrepreneurship in human action.

It should be observed that the entrepreneurial alertness we have identified does not consist merely in "seeing" the unfolding of the tapestry of the future in the sense of seeing a preordained flow of events. Alertness must, importantly, embrace the awareness of the ways in which the human agent can, by imaginative, bold leaps of faith, and determination, in fact *create* the future for which his present acts are designed. As we shall argue in a subsequent section, this latter expression of entrepreneurial alertness does not affect its essential formal character—which remains that of assuring a tendency for the future context envisaged as following present action to bear some realistic resemblance to the future as it will be realized.

We must notice, in understanding this entrepreneurial element in human action, two aspects of it: (1) We note what provides the scope for entrepreneurship. This scope is provided by the complete freedom with which the future as envisaged might, without entrepreneurial alertness, diverge from the future as it will in fact be. Entrepreneurial alertness has a function to perform. (2) We note what provides the incentive that switches on entrepreneurial alertness. This incentive is provided by the lure of pure entrepreneurial profit to be grasped in stepping from a less accurately envisaged future to a more accurately envisaged one. Each step taken in moving toward a vision of the future that overlaps more significantly with the truth is not merely a step toward truth (that is, a positive entrepreneurial success); it is also a profitable step (that is, a step that enhances the value of the resources with which action is available to be taken).

Viewed from this perspective, the tension between the uncertainty-environment in which action occurs, on the one hand, and the discovery-of-error aspect of action, on the other, can be seen to dissolve at a glance. These two aspects of action can be seen immediately as merely two sides of the same entrepreneurial coin. If uncertainty were merely an unpleasant condition of life to which man must passively adjust, then it would be reasonable to distinguish between the quite separate activities of bearing uncertainty on the one hand and of discovering error on the other. Escaping from current errors is one thing; grappling with the uncertainty of the future is another. But, as we have noticed, to choose means to *endeavor,* under the incentive to grasp pure profit, to identify a more truthful picture of the future. Dealing with uncertainty is motivated by the profit to be won by avoiding error. In this way of viewing the matter the distinction between escaping current error and avoiding potential future error is unimportant. The discovery of error is an interesting feature of action because it offers incentive. It is this incentive that inspires the effort to pierce the fog of uncertainty that shrouds the future. To deal with uncertainty means to seek to overcome it by more accurate prescience; to discover error is merely that aspect of this endeavor that endows it with incentive attraction. The imagination and creativity with which man limns his envisaged future are inspired by the pure gains to be won in ensuring that that envisaged future is in fact no less bright than that which can be made the truth.

We shall find in the next section that these insights surrounding entrepreneurship at the level of individual action have their exact counterparts in entrepreneurship in the market context. It will be useful to summarize briefly the key points we have learned about individual entrepreneurship:

1. Entrepreneurship in individual action consists in the endeavor to secure greater correspondence between the individual's future as he envisages it and his future as it will in fact unfold. This endeavor consists in the individual's alertness to whatever can provide clues to the future. This alertness, broadly conceived, embraces those aspects of imagination and creativity through which the individual may himself *ensure* that his envisaged future will be realized.

2. Scope for entrepreneurship is provided by the uncertainty of the future. For our purposes uncertainty means that, in the absence of entrepreneurial alertness, an individual's view of the future may diverge with total freedom from the realized future. In the absence of entrepreneurial alertness it is only sheer chance that can be responsible for successful action.

3. Incentive for the "switching on" of entrepreneurial alertness is provided by the pure gain (or avoidance of loss) to be derived from replacing action based on less accurate prescience by action based on the more realistically envisaged future. The avoidance of entrepreneurial error is not merely a matter of being more truthful, it happens also to be profitable.

Entrepreneurship in the Market

Our examination of the entrepreneurial element in individual action permits us to see the role of entrepreneurship in the market in a fresh light. We shall

152   Method, Process, and Austrian Economics

discover, in the market context, elements that correspond precisely to their analogues in the individual context. Let us consider what happens in markets.

In a market exchanges occur between market participants.[32] In the absence of perfect mutual knowledge, many of the exchanges are inconsistent with one another. Some sales are made at low prices when some buyers are buying at high prices. Some market participants are not buying at all because they are unaware of the possibility of buying at prices low enough to be attractive; some are refraining from selling because they are unaware of the possibility of selling at prices high enough to be attractive. Clearly the actions of these buyers and sellers are, from the perspective of omniscience, uncoordinated and inconsistent. We notice that, although the assumption of perfect knowledge that is necessary for market equilibrium would constrain different transactions in the market to complete mutual consistency, the actuality of imperfect knowledge permits these different transactions in different parts of the market to diverge with apparently complete freedom. What alone tends to introduce a modicum of consistency and coordination into this picture, preventing a situation in which even the slightest degree of coordination could exist only as a matter of sheerest chance, is market entrepreneurship, inspired by the lure of pure market profit. We are now in a position to identify, in the market context, elements that correspond to key features already identified in the context of individual entrepreneurship.

Corresponding to uncertainty as it impinges on individual action we have market discoordination. The freedom with which an individual's envisaged future may diverge from the future to be realized, corresponds precisely to the freedom with which transactions made in one part of the market may diverge from transactions made elsewhere. In the absence of entrepreneurship it is only out of the purest chance that market transactions by different pairs of buyers and sellers are made on anything but the most wildly inconsistent terms. There is nothing that constrains the mutually satisfactory price bargain reached between one pair of traders to bear any specific relation to corresponding bargains reached between other pairs of traders.

Corresponding to error at the level of the individual, we have price divergence at the level of the market. Perfect knowledge (such as in Robbinsian individual allocative activity) precludes error. Market equilibrium (implied by universal perfect knowledge) precludes price divergences.

The individual entrepreneurial element permits the individual to escape from the distressing freedom with which divergences between envisaged futures and realized futures may occur; the entrepreneur fulfills the same function for the market. The function of the entrepreneur is to bring different parts of the market into coordination with each other. The market

Uncertainty, Discovery, and Human Action   153

entrepreneur bridges the gaps in mutual knowledge, gaps that would otherwise permit prices to diverge with complete freedom.

Corresponding to the incentive for individual entrepreneurship provided by more realistic views of the future, we have, at the market level, the
incentive provided by opportunities for pure entrepreneurial profit. Market
profit consists in the gap between prices generated by error and market
inconsistency—just as the source for private gain is to be discovered in a
present divergence between the imagined and the actual future.

The following are propositions, in the context of the market, that concern entrepreneurship; they correspond precisely to those stated at the conclusion of the preceding section:[33]

1.° Entrepreneurship in the market consists in the function of securing
greater consistency between different parts of the market. It expresses itself
in entrepreneurial alertness to what transactions are in fact available in different parts of the market. It is only such alertness that is responsible for
any tendency toward keeping these transactions in some kind of mutual
consistency.

2.° Scope for market entrepreneurship is provided by the imperfect
knowledge that permits market transactions to diverge from what would be
a mutually inconsistent pattern.

3.° Incentive for market entrepreneurial activity is provided by the pure
gain to be won by noticing existing divergences between the prices at which
market transactions are available in different parts of the market. It is the
lure of market profits that inspires entrepreneurial alertness.

Time, Uncertainty, and Entrepreneurship

Our analogy between entrepreneurship at the level of the individual and
entrepreneurship in the market emphasized only the most salient respects of
the analogy. Certain additional features of the entrepreneurial function in
the market need to be dealt with more extensively. In the individual context
the divergence (which it is the function of entrepreneurship to limit) was a
divergence between anticipated and realized future. Its source in uncertainty
was immediately apparent. In the market context the divergence (which it is
the function of entrepreneurship to limit) was a divergence between the
transactions in different parts of the market. Its source was stated in terms
of imperfect mutual knowledge among market participants. Its relationship
to uncertainty was not asserted. This requires both amplification and modification.

Our statements concerning market entrepreneurship were couched in
terms of the market for a single commodity within a single period. It should
be clear that nothing essential is lost when our picture of the market is

expanded to include many commodities and, in particular, the passage of time. This should of course not be understood to mean that the introduction of the passage of time does not open up scope for additional insights. We merely argue that the insights we have gained in the single-period context for entrepreneurship are not to be lost sight of in the far more complex multiperiod case.

When we introduce the passage of time, the dimensions along which mutual ignorance may develop are multiplied. Market participants in one part of today's market not only may be imperfectly aware of the transactions available in another part of that market; they also may be imperfectly aware of the transactions that will be available in next year's market. Absence of consistency between different parts of today's market is seen as a special case of a more general notion of inconsistency that includes also inconsistency between today's transactions and those to be transacted next year. A low price today may be in this sense inconsistent with the high prices that will prevail next year. Scope for market entrepreneurship, in the context of the passage of time, arises then from the need to coordinate markets also across time. Incentive for market entrepreneurship along the intertemporal dimension is provided not by arbitrage profits generated by imperfectly coordinated present markets but, more generally, by the speculative profits generated by the as yet imperfectly coordinated market situations in the sequence of time. And, of course, the introduction of entrepreneurial activity to coordinate markets through time introduces, for individual entrepreneurs engaged in market entrepreneurship, precisely the considerations concerning the uncertain future that we have, until now, considered only in the context of the isolated individual.

It is because of this last circumstance that we must acknowledge that the introduction of the passage of time, although leaving the overall formal function of market entrepreneurship unchanged, will of course introduce substantial modification into the way we must imagine entrepreneurship to be exercised concretely. It is still the case, as noted, that the entrepreneurial function is that of bringing about a tendency for transactions in different parts of the market (conceived broadly now as including transactions entered into at different times) to be made in greater mutual consistency. But whereas in the case of entrepreneurship in the single-period market (that is, the case of the entrepreneur as arbitrageur) entrepreneurial alertness meant alertness to present facts, in the case of multiperiod entrepreneurship alertness must mean alertness to the future. It follows that market entrepreneurship in the multiperiod case introduces uncertainty as facing the entrepreneur not only as in the analogy offered in the preceding section—where the market analogue for uncertainty turned out to be the freedom with which transactions in different parts of today's market may unconstrainedly diverge from being mutually consistent—but also as in the

Uncertainty, Discovery, and Human Action   155

simple sense of the entrepreneur's awareness of the freedom with which his own envisaged future (concerning future market transactions) may diverge from the realized future. In particular the futurity that entrepreneurship must confront introduces the possibility that the entrepreneur may, by his own creative actions, in fact *construct* the future as *he* wishes it to be. In the single-period case alertness can at best discover hitherto overlooked current facts. In the multiperiod case entrepreneurial alertness must include the entrepreneur's perception of the way in which creative and imaginative action may vitally shape the kind of transactions that will be entered into in future market periods.

Thus the exercise of entrepreneurial alertness in the multiperiod market context will indeed call for personal and psychological qualifications that were unneeded in the single-period case. To be a successful entrepreneur one must now possess those qualities of vision, boldness, determination, and creativity that we associated earlier with the entrepreneurial element in isolated individual action with respect to an uncertain future. There can be no doubt that in the concrete fulfillment of the entrepreneurial function these psychological and personal qualities are of paramount importance. It is in this sense that so many writers are undoubtedly correct in linking entrepreneurship with the courage and vision necessary to *create* the future in an uncertain world (rather than with merely seeing that which stares one in the face).

However, the function of market entrepreneurship in the multiperiod context is nonetheless still that spelled out in the preceding section. What market entrepreneurship accomplishes is a tendency for transactions in different parts of the market (including the market at different dates) to become coordinated. The incentive that inspires this entrepreneurial coordinaton is the lure of pure profit—the difference in market values resulting from hitherto less complete coordination. These insights remain true for the multiperiod case no less than for the arbitrage case. For some purposes it is no doubt important to draw attention to the concrete psychological requirements on which successful entrepreneurial decision making depends. But for other purposes such emphasis is not required; in fact such emphasis may divert attention from what is, from the perspective of the overall functioning of the market system, surely the essential feature of entrepreneurship: its market-coordinative properties.

Let us recall that at the level of the individual, entrepreneurship involved not merely the bearing of uncertainty but also the overcoming of uncertainty. Uncertainty is responsible for what would, in the absence of entrepreneurship, be a failure to perceive the future in a manner sufficiently realistic to permit action. Entrepreneurship, so to speak, pushes aside to some extent the swirling fogs of uncertainty, permitting meaningful action. It is this function of entrepreneurship that must be kept in view when we study the market process. The uncertainty that characterizes the environment within which market entrepreneurship plays its coordinative role must be fully recognized; without it there would be no need and no scope for entrepreneurship. But an understanding of what entrepreneurship accomplishes requires us to recognize not so much the extent to which uncertainty is the ineradicable feature of human existence but rather the extent to which both individual action and social coordination through the market can occur significantly despite the uncertainty of the future (and in spite also of the uncertainty-analogue that would, in the absence of the arbitrageur, fog up even the single-period market).

Further Reflections on Uncertainty and Alertness

Thus we can see how those writers who have denied that the pure entrepreneurial role involves the bearing of uncertainty were both correct and yet at least partly irrelevant. Both J.A. Schumpeter[34] and J.B. Clark insisted that only the capitalist bears the hazards of business; the pure entrepreneur has, by definition, nothing to lose.[35] No doubt all this is true, as far as it goes, But what is important about linking the entrepreneur with the phenomenon of uncertainty is not that it is the entrepreneur who accepts the disutilities associated with the assumption of the hazards of business in an uncertain world. What is important is that the entrepreneur, motivated by the lure of pure profits, attempts to pierce through these uncertainties and endeavors to see the truth that will permit profitable action on his part.

A number of economists may be altogether unwilling to accept the notion of alertness with respect to uncertain future. In fact many may wish to reject the very formulation we have employed to schematize the uncertainty of the future. For us uncertainty meant the essential freedom with which the envisaged future may diverge from the realized future. Entrepreneurial alertness means the ability to impose constraints on that freedom, so that the entrepreneur's vision of the future may indeed overlap, to some significant extent, with that future that he is attempting to see. But many will be unwilling to treat the future as something to be seen at all. "The present is uniquely determined. It can be seen by the eye-witness. . . . What is the future but the void? To call it the future is to concede the presumption that it is already 'existent' and merely waiting to appear. If that is so, if the world is determinist, then it seems idle to speak of choice."[36] Similarly many are unwilling to see the entrepreneur as "alert to opportunities" if this terminology implies that future opportunities already "exist" and are merely waiting to be grasped. "Entrepreneurial projects are not waiting to be sought out so much as to be thought up."[37]

What perhaps needs to be emphasized once again is that in using phrases

Uncertainty, Discovery, and Human Action   157

such as "grasping future opportunities," "seeing the future correctly or incorrectly," or the "divergence between the envisaged future and the realized future," we do not wish to imply any determinacy regarding the future. No doubt, to say that one sees the future (with greater or lesser accuracy) is to employ a metaphor. No doubt the future that one "sees" is a future that may in fact be constructed significantly by one's action, which is supposed to be informed by that very vision. But surely these metaphors are useful and instructive. To dream realistically in a way that inspires successful, creative action is to "see correctly" as compared to the fantasies that inspire absurd ventures or the cold water poured by the unduly timid pessimist that stunts all efforts at improvement. "The future," we have learned, "is unknowable, though not unimaginable."[5] To acknowledge the unknowability of the future is to acknowledge the essential indeterminacy and uncertainty surrounding human existence. But surely in doing so we need not consign human existence to wholly uncoordinated chaos. To speak of entrepreneurial vision is to draw attention, by use of metaphor, to the formidable and benign coordinative powers of the human imagination. Austrian economists have, in principled fashion, refused to see the world as wholly knowable, as suited to interpretation by models of equilibrium from which uncertainty has been exhausted. It would be most unfortunate if, in pursuing this refusal, economists were to fall into a no-less-serious kind of error. This error would be the failure to understand how entrepreneurial individual action, and the systematic market forces set in motion by freedom for entrepreneurial discovery and innovation, harness the human imagination to achieve no less a result than the liberation of mankind from the chaos of complete mutual ignorance. Mises's concept of human action and his analysis of the role of entrepreneurial market processes surely remain, in this regard, unique and as yet insufficiently appreciated contributions to the profound understanding of human society.

Notes

1. L. von Mises, *Human Action* (New Haven: Yale University, 1949), p. 253.

2. Ibid., p. 288.

3. Ibid., p. 255.

4. Ibid., p. 254.

5. Ibid., p. 105.

6. I.M. Kirzner, *Competition and Entrepreneurship* (Chicago: University of Chicago, 1973), pp. 86–87.

7. Ibid., chap. 2. See also I.M. Kirzner, *Perception, Opportunity, and Profit* (Chicago: University of Chicago, 1979), chap. 10.

158 Method, Process, and Austrian Economics

8. F.A. Hayek, *Individualism and Economic Order* (London: Routledege and Kegan Paul, 1949), p. 42.

9. Kirzner, *Competition and Entrepreneurship,* pp. 86-87. (Italics in original.)

10. Such activity was subsumed under arbitrage by pointing out the formal similarity between (1) buying and selling in different markets today and (2) buying and selling in different markets at different dates. (See Kirzner, *Competition and Entrepreneurship,* pp. 85-86.)

11. Henry Hazlitt, review of *Competition and Entrepreneurship,* in *Freeman* (December 1974):759. Similar concerns seem to be expressed in a review of *Competition and Entrepreneurship* by Percy L. Greaves, Jr. in *Wertfrei* (Spring 1974): especially pp. 18-19.

12. See unpublished paper by Murray N. Rothbard, "Professor Hébert on Entrepreneurship," pp. 1-2. Reprinted with permission.

13. Ibid., p. 7.

14. L.H. White, "Entrepreneurship, Imagination, and the Question of Equilibrium," unpublished paper (1976). See also L.H. White, "Entrepreneurial Price Adjustment" (Paper presented at Southern Economic Association meetings Washington, D.C., November, 1978), p. 36, n. 3.

15. J. High, review article on *Perception, Opportunity and Profit* in *Austrian Economics Newsletter* (Spring 1980):14.

16. High's criticisms of my references to uncertainty as a characteristic of the entrepreneurial environment focus most specifically on what he believes to be my use of uncertainty to "serve as the distinguishing characteristic between entrepreneurship and luck." (Ibid.) Here there seems to be a definite misunderstanding of my position. So far from the presence of the uncertainty surrounding entrepreneurship being what separates entrepreneurial profit from the lucky windfall, almost the exact reverse is the case. What marks entrepreneurial profit as different from the lucky windfall is that the former was, despite the (inevitable) uncertainty that might have discouraged the entrepreneur, in fact deliberately pursued. Where luck confers gain may well reflect the circumstance that the uncertainty of this gain deterred the actor from even dreaming of winning it. High's reading apparently resulted from his understanding a passage that he cites (from Kirzner, *Perception, Opportunity and Profit,* pp. 159-160) to represent the case of a purely lucky gain. In fact the passage cited does not refer to luck at all. If one knows that one's labor can convert low-valued leisure into high-valued apples, the apples one so gains through one's hard work does not constitute a lucky windfall. The point of the cited passages is that Menger's law shows how there is no value gain at all derived from that labor, since one would already have attached the higher value of the ends to the available means. Our discussion in this chapter, however, proceeds on the assumption that High's unhappiness at my treatment of uncertainty in entrepreneurship

does not rest solely on the validity of the way in which I distinguish entrepreneurial profits from windfall gains.

17. Mises, *Human Action,* p. 253.

18. See Kirzner, *Competition and Entrepreneurship,* pp. 32–35. See also Kirzner, *Perception, Opportunity and Profit,* pp. 166–168.

19. G.L.S. Shackle, *Epistemics and Economics* (Cambridge: Cambridge University, 1972), p. 136. (Italics in original.)

20. Ibid., p. 351.

21. See also Kirzner, *The Economic Point of View* (Princeton: Van Nostrand, 1960), p. 167.

22. See also Kirzner, *Perception, Opportunity and Profit,* chap. 9.

23. F.H. Knight, *Risk, Uncertainty and Profit* (New York: Houghton Mifflin, 1921), p. 268.

24. Mises, *Human Action,* p. 105.

25. See Kirzner, *Perception, Opportunity and Profit,* chap. 10, especially pp. 158–164.

26. Ibid., p. 162.

27. Idid., p. 163.

28. See, for example, Kirzner, *Competition and Entrepreneurship,* p. 39.

29. See note 15 of this chapter.

30. B.J. Loasby, *Choice, Complexity and Ignorance* (Cambridge: Cambridge University, 1976), p. 5.

31. Knight, *Risk, Uncertainty and Profit,* p. 199.

32. Our discussion proceeds in terms of the market for a single commodity. It could be couched, without altering the essentials in any respect, in more general terms. See also the subsequent section of this chapter.

33. The three pairs of statements may be viewed as additions to the two lists of twelve statements developing the analogy between the individual and the market, provided in Kirzner, *Perception, Opportunity and Profit,* chap. 10, pp. 170–172, 173–175.

34. J.A. Schumpeter, *The Theory of Economic Development* (Cambridge, Mass.: Harvard University, 1934), p. 137; J.A. Schumpeter, *History of Economic Analysis* (Oxford: Oxford University, 1954), p. 556. See also S.M. Kanbur, "A Note on Risk Taking, Entrepreneurship and Schumpeter," *History of Political Economy* 12 (Winter 1980):489–498.

35. J.B. Clark, "Insurance and Business Profit," *Quarterly Journal of Economics* 7 (October 1892):46 (cited in Knight, *Risk, Uncertainty and Profit,* p. 38.)

36. Shackle, *Epistemics and Economics,* p. 122.

37. White, "Entrepreneurship, Imagination," p. 7.

38. L.M. Lachmann, "From Mises to Shackle: An Essay," *Journal of Economic Literature* 14 (March 1976):59.

11

6 Spontaneous Order and the Subjectivity of Expectations: A Contribution to the Lachmann-O'Driscoll Problem

ULRICH FEHL

The first, and most prominent, feature of Austrian economics is a radical subjectivism, today no longer confined to human preferences but extended to expectations.

Ludwig M. Lachmann

I THE LACHMANN-O'DRISCOLL PROBLEM

Littlechild's article "Radical Subjectivism or Radical Subversion?" ends up with the following question:

> Shackle's subjectivism is clearly sympathetic to Austrians, and constitutes a subversion of neoclassical economics quite as radical as the work of Keynes. But is Shackle *too* subjectivist even for Austrians? If we have understood correctly his emphasis on the role of imagination, he calls into question not only their concept of the market process, but even their very definition of economics. Is Shackle's message to Austrians merely one of radical subjectivism, or is it one of radical subversion too?[1]

This alternative is but the radical version of the issue O'Driscoll raises in his article "Spontaneous Order and the Coordination of Economic Activities" with respect to Ludwig M. Lachmann's conception of the market process.[2] While emphasizing the idea of a "spontaneous order" to be common belief in the tradition of Austrian economics he seems to be uneasy about Lachmann who could possibly deny this position, being at least unclear in this respect.[3] The crucial point is whether or not the market process has to have a strong tendency towards an equilibrium if there should result a spontaneous order. Although the latter is not identified with equilibrium, both notions are brought into close connection, "spontaneous order" thus meaning a state of the economy "near" equilibrium:

> If the propensity to discover opportunities is "inseparable from our insight that human beings act purposefully', then we must likewise acknowledge a *tendency* toward equilibrium in all markets. *A fortiori* there exist strong tendencies toward an overall or general equilibrium *at each moment*. Individuals are, then, constantly revising their plans in a way that brings them, into *greater uniformity*. [Emphasis added.] This latter proposition, when thus phrased in dynamic terms, does embody the principle of an undesigned order.[4]

Although conceding that Lachmann "nowhere *explicitly* asserts the contrary position, viz., that we have no grounds for believing that market participants will discover and exploit profitable opportunities,"[5] O'Driscoll tries to make clear that Lachmann does not stick to the notion of the market as a spontaneous order in the just described sense.[6] This interpretation primarily rests on Lachmann's conception of the subjectivity and therefore, in principle, diversity of expectations:

> Experience shows in the real world of disequilibrium different persons will typically hold different expectations about the same future event. If so, at best one person's expectation can be confirmed and all other expectations will be disappointed. ... The beacon that had been designed to keep entrepreneurs from straying from the narrow path of convergent expectations turns out, on most nights, to be rather dim.[7]

Thus it is the very diversity of subjective expectations that excludes the "greater conformity" O'Driscoll has stressed as a prerequisite for the "spontaneous order" in his sense, i.e., the "near-equilibrium" sense.

In realizing this difficulty O'Driscoll draws the conclusion that Austrian economists, in advocating the doctrine of a "spontaneous order," are faced with a serious problem.[8] If it is impossible to reconcile divergent expectations with a strong tendency of market forces towards an equilibrium one has either to abandon the notion of spontaneous order or, alternatively, to belittle the importance of conflicting expectations. Indeed, O'Driscoll tends to interpret Lachmann as being at least implicitly an adherent of the first alternative while he himself argues in favor of the latter.

In assessing Lachmann's position, O'Driscoll states: "There is no denying the autonomy of the human mind, but one is reluctant to follow Lachmann in his apparent conclusion that we can say nothing about the likelihood that individuals will make consistent and coordinated decisions in the face of new knowledge. If anything, he seems to be saying that they will *not coordinate plans*. [Emphasis added.]"[9] Or, "Indeed, I suspect that there is no coordination in the conventional sense in Lachmann's system. For him apparently, *ex ante* plans bear no relation to *ex post* reality. There is not even reason to believe that actors will move in the right direction in correcting past errors."[10] In order to eschew these conclusions Lachmann has seemingly drawn, O'Driscoll tries to reassess and delimit the importance of divergent expectations:

> Do different and disparate individuals have a common reaction to shared experience? We certainly would not want to say they always do, or there would be little sense in referring to "individuals". Yet, there are obvious cases in which people do react to shared experiences in the same or similar ways: the perception of a fire in an enclosed room will lead to virtually everyone's making for an exit. Each person could form a reasonable expectation about what the others will do.[11]

According to O'Driscoll the same is true with respect to entrepreneurs: "Apparently individual entrepreneurs, experiencing the same signals and trends will often form similar expectations."[12] It is no surprise that O'Driscoll refuses to make, as Lachmann does, a fundamental distinction between knowledge and expectation: "In his most recent work, Lachmann notes that Mises, Hayek, and Kirzner have emphasized the diffusion of knowledge in the market process. But he denies that the market can diffuse expectations in the same way. I believe the distinction between knowledge and expectations is a spurious one."[13] On the whole it seems to be O'Driscoll's firm conviction that the problem of divergent expectations is overcome by equilibrating market forces strong enough to establish a spontaneous order near market equilibrium in the Hayekian sense.

II   THE MARKET PROCESS AND ITS ORDER

Both escapes from the dilemma—to abandon the notion of a spontaneous order or to deny that there is an essential distinction between knowledge and expectation—are rather inconclusive. But, fortunately, the relationship between a spontaneous order and the diversity of subjective expectations can be analyzed from a completely different point of view. In this view, "spontaneous order" means an order of the market *process* itself which does not rest upon the latter being near the *state of equilibrium*. Being created by the market forces just in distance from equilibrium this "disequilibrium order" has to be assessed an order sui generis. Now, in this context the subjectivity of expectations and their inherent diversity become a productive power, i.e., divergent expectations are no longer an obstacle to the modus operandi of engendering "order." To see this, at first the working of the market process has to be analyzed and the notion of an "order far from equilibrium" has to be established.

The market process can formally be viewed as being propelled by the simultaneous activity of *arbitrage, accumulation* (or decumulation respectively) and *innovation* as its *driving forces*. Although, as a rule, two or all three driving forces are engaged in human actions, it is convenient to keep them separate for analytical purposes. It can be shown that the driving forces of the market refer to and thus depend on each other: Arbitrage is called the activity of comparing and exchange. This activity would come to an end, if all opportunities were discovered and used. Arbitrage only will go on, if it is supplied with new opportunities to be compared; in short, arbitrage refers to innovation. But it refers to accumulation as a driving force, too, because many actions of "arbitrage" can only be executed if production and investment take place. Arbitrage would be without consequences, if accumulation were not set in motion. But accumulation refers to arbitrage, too, being "directionless" without it. Furthermore there has to be reflected a relationship between accumulation and innovation: Without the latter, accumulation would come to a standstill, because of satiation. Again, innovation as a driving force would have no consequences, were it not diffused by accumulation. Finally, innovation as a driving force refers to arbitrage, because only with the help of the latter (taken in a broad sense) one can make out whether something is "new" and it pays to produce and invest.

Already these few remarks should have made clear that the working of the market process cannot be fully understood without regarding the *simultaneous running* of arbitrage, accumulation, and innovation as driving forces. Nevertheless, economists have restricted their endeavour to the analysis of one or two of the driving forces. By focusing on equilibrium states of economic systems neoclassical economists are mainly concerned with the "logic of arbitrage" (within a framework of fully perceived opportunities). Accumulation and innovation only come into the field of vision by means of comparative statics, the simultaneity of driving forces' activities being thus ignored.

Although analyzing the market as a process Austrian economists, at least partly, exclude from consideration innovation as a driving force of the market. As a consequence they are concerned primarily with the equilibrating process being propelled by the driving forces arbitrage (including the perception of opportunities) and accumulation. This process of equilibration, nevertheless, does not come to a standstill, mainly because there is a continuous change in the "data" of the market. This analytical procedure implies that innovation in the last resort has to be treated as an *exogenous* variable, and is thus analyzed incompletely, i.e., only in its consequences.[14] The above-mentioned desideratum of regarding the simultaneous performance of all three driving forces seems to be a desideratum with respect to the Austrians, too.

Schumpeter's analysis, it is true, comprises all of the three driving forces, but in order to show how, as a consequence of an innovation, the existing state of equilibrium is destroyed and transformed into a new equilibrium, he is concerned with the *successive* performance of innovation, arbitrage and accumulation. At least in his early writings, Schumpeter is not engaged in studying a permanent stream of (new) innovations beyond the scope of a somewhat comparative statics.[15]

It is obvious that there must exist a close relationship between the driving forces of the market and entrepreneurship, the entrepreneur being, so to speak, the driving force of the driving forces arbitrage, accumulation, and innovation. Thus, the driving forces arbitrage and accumulation refer to the neoclassical Robbinsian-type of entrepreneurship or—if arbitrage and accumulation are conceived of, more appropriately in somewhat broader terms including the perception of opportunities—to the Mises-Kirzner type of entrepreneur.[16] Inno-

vation as a driving force of the market has to be identified with the
activities performed by the Schumpeterian entrepreneur. It suggests
itself that economists' refusal to analyze the simultaneous efficacy of *all*
driving forces is reflected in the respective selection of a special type of
entrepreneur. For the sake of a full understanding of the working of the
market process economists should instead take into consideration the
whole spectrum of different types of entrepreneurs. At least they should
recognize that market-processes are characterized by the simultaneous
activity of the Schumpeterian and the Misesian-Kirznerian entrepreneur.[17] Thus some shortcomings of received theory could be overcome.

The main reason for stressing the proposition that all driving forces
of the market (or to say it in other words: different types of entrepreneurs) have to be analyzed with regard to being simultaneously at work
is the insight that it is just this "concerted action", by which the market
process is kept at a (far) distance from the state of equilibrium in the
conventional sense: And it is exactly this distance from the state of
equilibrium that makes possible the emergence of a structure which
implies an order sui generis, to be clearly distinguished from the order
of equilibrium or near-equilibrium.[18]

The process and the structure it exhibits can be illustrated by the
model of a homogeneous market. By definition producers offer the
same product. Assuming the market process to have the properties just
described we can take for granted that the producers will apply
different production techniques implying different marginal costs (fixed
costs being ignored), the differences being attributed to the continuing
process (of innovations) itself. As the introduction of new techniques
takes place before the diffusion of the older ones has come to an end,
there will coexist by the very notion of the continuing process a whole
spectrum of production techniques with differential marginal cost.
Thus the marginal cost curves of the producers can be organized to
construct the supply curve of the market (see Figure 1). Now suppose
innovation as a driving force of the market comes to a standstill. After
some periods of time have elapsed the market process will come to a
standstill, too, because all competitors will have adopted the technique
with the lowest marginal cost, the corresponding market supply curve
being shown in Figure 2.

Now, it can be inferred from comparing the supply curves in Figure 1
and Figure 2 that the structure being generated by the ongoing process
is destroyed in the state of equilibrium. To say it in different words, the
structure under discussion is a property of the continuing process
keeping the market in a state far from "equilibrium." Or seen from

78   *Spontaneous Order and the Subjectivity of Expectations*

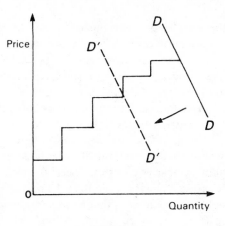

FIGURE 1

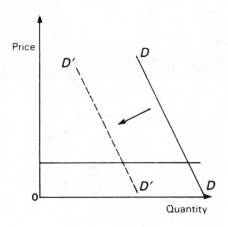

FIGURE 2

another point of view, it is the process which produces *heterogeneity*, while equilibrium is characterized by *homogeneity*.

It is precisely the heterogeneity characterizing the ongoing process which constitutes an order sui generis. To realize this suppose a shift of the market demand curve to the left. In Figure 1 it can easily be seen that some suppliers will become submarginal and will be eliminated.

This leads to the conclusion that the order of the process can be conceived of as a "selection order." The same is not true if the state of "equilibrium" has already been established before the shift of the market demand curve occurs, because in this situation no suppliers can be selected as submarginal, the market does not exhibit an order (of selection) in this case. One is tempted to conclude that the "equilibrium" state of the market in the explained sense reveals a form of "market failure" the market in process does not exhibit.[19] Thus, the latter may be adjudged a higher degree of order in comparison with the market equilibrium or near equilibrium. Seen from this point of view one should be cautious to infer a higher degree of order from the market's approaching the state of equilibrium, being accomplished by the equilibrating forces, a conclusion O'Driscoll obviously draws.[20] Identifying "spontaneous order" with the "order of process" or "selection order" one has to state just the opposite.

It has to be realized that the selection order associated with the market process places at the disposal of entrepreneurs (or market participants in general) a "schedule of orientation" transmitted to them by the working of the price system. The selection profile—together with a system of general rules and other institutions not to be discussed here—constitutes what Hayek has called *"Handelnsordnung."*[21] Thus self organization of individuals in a world of permanent change is rendered possible, without there being necessary any concern to the results of the process or the final state of affairs, i.e., equilibrium, not even in the sense of a vanishing point. This can be seen by the application of the model: If demand shifts—and such shifts have to be judged as regular in an evolving economy—the reallocation of the factors of production can be brought about without any concern to the state of equilibrium or even the approachment of such a state.

Furthermore it should be taken into account that the heterogeneity being generated by the permanent working of the market process is by no means confined to the case of production techniques but applies to the quality of goods and services as well. Permanent creation of new or better goods and their diffusion in the market system produces just another facet of the market's selection order. The same is true with respect to the creation of new markets, the emerging selection order now facilitating orientation for investment processes on a larger scale. These examples may be enough to show how the ongoing market process produces "heterogeneity" and thus the prerequisite for a selection order. But it is important to keep in mind that the selection-profile of the market system as a whole comprises many dimensions.

80   *Spontaneous Order and the Subjectivity of Expectations*

Finally the fact has to be stressed that the market process does not only generate heterogeneity and thus constitute a selection order and a schedule of orientation, but by its very nature *mobilizes* heterogeneous elements. As all individuals in a market system are allowed to make plans of their own and thus can utilize their skills, differences with regard to skill, creativity, experience, etc., will expand the scope of heterogeneity and thus lead to a refinement of the selection profile. One of these "natural" differences refers to the *expectation* of individuals.[22] The role divergent expectations exert in the context of a spontaneous order—the latter being interpreted after all as an order in a world of disequilibrium, i.e., as a selection order—now can be discussed.

III SPONTANEOUS ORDER AND THE ROLE OF DIVERGENT EXPECTATIONS

The significance of expectations can be derived from the fact that human actions are bound to refer to the future which is notoriously uncertain.[23] Human beings can only produce *imaginations* of future events.[24] Whether these are true or not, depends partially on chance or luck, but on experience and thus judgment, too.[25] As human beings differ in their faculty to judge, and because of their inherent element of subjectivity, imaginations of individuals will be different at least in principle. As a consequence, actions of people will differ, too. But different actions will produce different facts. In short, divergent imaginations and expectations will produce a heterogenous state of affairs. Therefore, a selection order generated by the very diversity of expectations will emerge when the future converts into present time. Clearly, because of the diversity of imaginations and actions not all individuals can have taken the right course. But in the light of the now present knowledge and needs, market participants can choose between the "results" being the outcomes of different actions of different people. Arbitrage as a driving force of the market can work! We can look at this phenomenon to be just a variant of the theorem presented in the market model above.

Subjectivity of expectations (or of imaginations) by no means does exclude learning processes and thus the diffusion of new knowledge. But in the context of an evolving market system the latter does not imply greater uniformity of imaginations. Instead, diversity is maintained, i.e., selection profiles are only shifted in the process.

The diversity of expectations does not lead to a situation in which the actions of the individuals are *coordinated* in the strict sense of the notion, because people will have made "false" plans basing on "wrong" imaginations or expectations, respectively. But this lack of coordination is only the price people have to pay for not being in the position to predict future events. Thus the case in which imaginations and expectations are diverse has to be compared with the case in which expectations are uniform. Then, all of the market participants could, by chance, have formed right imaginations, but the latter can be completely inadequate, too! The diversity of expectations thus serves as a provision that the market will at least be in the middle ground. At least in this sense the generating of a selection order emerging as a consequence of divergent expectations can be interpreted as a coordination process *ex ante*, if one regards the inherent uncertainty of the future. If O'Driscoll cannot make out coordination in the *ex ante* sense in the case of divergent expectations, this may be due to his equilibrium concept of spontaneous order.

Before discussing this point further, it should be regarded that the efficacy of the selection order as a rule does not always imply the elimination of firms. But it should be clear, too, that some firms will have to suffer from losses, while those firms that have formed adequate imaginations will make profits. Thus different impulses to act are transmitted by the market process because the latter exhibits a selection profile. Furthermore, there are cases in which the consequences of divergent expectations and subsequent actions will compensate each other. For example, the entrepreneur with too optimistic expectations will be in the position to utilize his enlarged capacity by the very fact that his pessimistic competitor has underestimated the rate of growth of market demand.

Whereas the existence of divergent expectations or at least a tendency to diversity can be taken for granted, there may be casually more uniformity or homogeneity with regard to both imagination and expectations.[26] As has already been stated, as a rule such a uniformity will prove to be counterproductive for the purposes of coordination, as long as the market process is propelled by the concerted action of arbitrage, accumulation and innovation, i.e., as long as a world of evolution and uncertainty is sustained. Only if innovation has come to a standstill one can conclude, as O'Driscoll does, that a "greater uniformity" of expectations will be a prerequisite for improving the coordination of plans. Outside such a near-equilibrium-situation a greater uniformity of expectations may just lead to discoordination. Imagine, for example, that all suppliers in a market react too optimistically, then errors will not compensate each other, but generate overca-

82   *Spontaneous Order and the Subjectivity of Expectations*

pacities. Similar consequences will arise in the case of too pessimistic and uniform expectations. The trade cycle at least can partly be explained by too uniform expectations, and can serve as a further example. Collusion in the market may be possible only, if expectations are sufficiently uniform.[27] Consequently, the full range of possible events is not accounted for and a selection order will not evolve. In this case, the market will reveal expectations to be wrong and at the same time reveal the counterproductivity of uniformity, too.[28]

IV CONCLUSION

Is the subjectivity and diversity of expectations (or better: imaginations) conducive or an obstacle to the emergence of a spontaneous order? This question raised by O'Driscoll obviously is central for economists, especially for Austrian economists stressing the role of subjectivity in general. According to O'Driscoll, Lachmann, by emphasizing the inherent subjectivity and diversity of expectations in the last resort, is bound to negate the idea of a spontaneous order. It can be shown that O'Driscoll's judgment depends on the very notion of spontaneous order. He is right, if the latter has to be interpreted as an "equilibrium"—or "near-equilibrium"—order. In this case, expectations (and imaginations!) by virtue of the equilibrating market forces are bound to become more uniform in the market process, thus favouring the emergence of a spontaneous order in the O'Driscoll sense. (But if the diversity of imagination prevails, spontaneity in this sense is challenged.)

It can be shown, however, that O'Driscoll is forced to treat innovations as exogenous to the market process. Instead, if innovation as a driving force is incorporated in the notion of the market process, the conception of a spontaneous order in the sense of an equilibrium—or near-equilibrium—state has to be replaced by a disequilibrium or selection order, the market process thus being conceived of generating what could be called a "dissipative structure." This structure is the result of the simultaneous working of arbitrage, accumulation, and innovation and can be thought of as being produced by the concerted action of the Schumpeterian and the Misesian-Kirznerian type of entrepreneur. It is exactly this type of the market process Lachmann has in mind:

What emerges from our reflections is an image of the market as a particular kind of process, a continuous process without beginning, or end, propelled by the interaction between the forces of equilibrium and the forces of change.[29]

Therefore it is adequate to apply the selection-order variant of the notion of a spontaneous order. Referring to this concept of "order," O'Driscoll's argument breaks down. Lachmann's as well as Shackle's radical subjectivism are not in conflict with the concept of economic and social order. It can be shown, on the contrary, that it is just the very diversity of individual imaginations which—together with general rules in the Hayekian sense and other institutional arrangements—constitutes economic order. Shackle's "kaleidic world" and Austrians' "spontaneous order" thus can be reconciled. There is no radical subversion of Austrian economics by Shackle's radical subjectivism.

NOTES

1. S. C. Littlechild, "Comment: Radical Subjectivism or Radical Subversion?" in *Time, Uncertainty and Disequilibrium* ed. M. J. Rizzo (Lexington, Mass.: Lexington Books, 1979), p. 47.
2. G. P. O'Driscoll, Jr., "Spontaneous Order and the Coordination of Economic Activities," in *New Directions in Austrian Economics* ed. L. M. Spadaro (Kansas City: Sheed Andrews & McMeel, 1976, p. 129.
3. "Those economists who view a system of free exchange—Adam Smith's 'obvious and simple system of natural liberty'—as the solution of the coordination problem in economics face intellectual challenges from at least four sources: first, the continuing challenge of the Keynesian legacy; second, the challenge from what James Buchanan has termed the 'modern Ricardians'; third, the challenge from the new movement for national planning; and finally, the challenge from certain economists in the Austrian school" (O'Driscoll, op. cit., pp. 111–12).
4. O'Driscoll, op. cit., p. 129.
5. O'Driscoll, op. cit., p. 128.
6. In quoting several passages of Lachmann's unpublished paper "Reflections on Hayekian Capital Theory," O'Driscoll demonstrates that Lachmann can indeed be interpreted in this way. For example: "To make confident use of the notion of equilibrium means to imply that the equilibrating forces will always be of sufficient strength to triumph over all obstacles. A skeptic might readily admit that such situations may exist, but he will probably doubt whether they occur with sufficient frequency to warrant our treating as the norm" (op. cit., pp. 128-9). Or: "The human mind is a filter of experience, but each individual's filter is different from every other filter. Divergent expectations are thus as 'natural', a feature of the social landscape, as are divergent tastes" (op. cit., p. 130). Or: "The

84   *Spontaneous Order and the Subjectivity of Expectations*

future is unknowable, though not unimaginable. Future knowledge cannot be had now, but it can cast its shadow ahead. In each mind, however, the shadow assumes a different shape, hence the divergence of expectations. The formation of expectations is an act of our minds by means of which we try to catch a glimpse of the unknown. Each one of us catches a different glimpse" (L. M. Lachmann, "From Mises to Shackle: An Essay on Austrian Economics and the Kaleidic Society," *Journal of Economic Literature*, XIV (1976), p. 59).

7. O'Driscoll, op. cit., p. 129.
8. O'Driscoll, op. cit., p. 130.
9. O'Driscoll, op. cit., p. 130.
10. O'Driscoll, op. cit., p. 132. In this context O'Driscoll confronts Lachmann's position with that of the "Austrians" in general: "It is certainly not the case that Austrian economists maintain that there ever exists *ex ante* consistency among all transactors' plans. But they have traditionally maintained, as Lachmann himself notes, that there is a *strong* tendency toward diffusion of knowledge and *increased consistency of plans.* (Emphasis added.)" (O'Driscoll, op. cit., p. 132). Furthermore O'Driscoll concludes: "I now believe the apparent semantic confusion is masking real conceptual differences. Kirzner sees any disturbance as developing equilibrating market forces. Lachmann sees change as disequilibrating. The only reason that I can adduce is that Lachmann does not see market forces as being equilibrating in nature" (O'Driscoll, op. cit., p. 134). Finally: "From this, one must conclude that Lachmann is critical even of theories espousing a tendency toward overall equilibrium (i.e., he denies the principle of spontaneous order). I can draw no other conclusion" (O'Driscoll, op. cit., p. 133).
11. O'Driscoll, op. cit., p. 130.
12. O'Driscoll, op. cit., p. 130.
13. O'Driscoll, op. cit., p. 141.
14. Regard for instance, that competitors lagging behind will not always try to overcome their difficulties by means of imitation but also by means of innovation as well. In other words, it seems inadequate to treat innovation as an exogenous variable separated from the process of competition.
15. The crucial point is that new innovations take place, *before* the market system has adapted itself to the preceding innovations, i.e., the process of diffusion has not yet come to an end.
16. With regard to the structuring of the ends–means framework by the entrepreneur see I. M. Kirzner, "Uncertainty, Discovery and Human Action: A Study of the Entrepreneurial Profile in the Misesian System," in *Method, Process and Austrian Economics: Essays in Honor of Ludwig von Mises* ed. I. M. Kirzner (Lexington, Mass.: Lexington Books, 1982), pp. 139–59.
17. That economic analysis can but profit by taking into account a broader range of different types of entrepreneurs is testified by E. Heuss, *Algemeine Markttheorie* (Tübingen-Zürich: J. C. B. Mohr (Paul Siebeck)—Polygraphischer Verlag, 1965).
18. Structures which emerge at some distance from equilibrium are called "dissipative structures." See G. Nicolis and I. Prigogine, *Self-organization*

in Non-Equilibrium Systems (New York, Wiley, 1977); I. Prigogine, *Vom Sein zum Werden: Zeit und Komplexität in den Naturwissenschaften* (München-Zürich: Piper, 1979); ed. E. Jantsch *The Evolutionary Vision, Toward a Unifying Paradigm of Physical, Biological and Sociocultural Evolution* (Boulder, Colorado: Westview Press, 1981); M. Zeleny, *Autopoiesis, Dissipative Structures, and Spontaneous Social Orders* (Boulder, Colorado: Westview Press, 1980). For an economic interpretation of dissipative structures see: K. E. Boulding, "Equilibrium, Entropy, Development and Autopoiesis: Towards a Disequilibrium Economics," *Eastern Journal*, VI (1980), pp. 179–88; U. Fehl, *Die Theorie disspativer Strukturen als Ansatzpunkt für die Analyse von Innovationsproblemen in alternativen Wirtschaftsordnungen*, in *Innovationsprobleme in Ost und West*, eds. A. Schüller, H. Leipold, H. Hamel (Stuttgart: Fischer, 1983), pp. 65–89.

19. Before generalizing the insights to be obtained from the model, its very character as a model should be emphasized, i.e., it should not be taken literally. Of course, the analysis has been carried out in a neoclassical equilibrium framework, and the process of selection, it is true, need not work in a textbook manner. But there will be a tendency in the direction it indicates, a tendency owing to the very existence of arbitrage as a driving force of the market, the latter being set in motion by entrepreneurs of the Mises-Kirzner type. Thus the model and its suggestions may be used for the sake of argument and illumination, so to speak as an ideal standard.

20. It should be clear that the spontaneous order understood as a selection order does not deny the existence of equilibrating forces in the sense of arbitrage activities but takes into account that these are, so to speak, balanced by the forces of innovation as another driving force of the market.

21. See Friedrich A. Hayek, "Rechtsordnung und Handelnsordnung," in *Freiburger Studien*, ed. A. Hayek (Tübingen: J. C. B. Mohr (Paul Siebeck), 1969), pp. 161–98.

22. The statement Garrison makes with respect to knowledge and expectations significantly applies to "natural" differences of individuals as well: "In effect Loasby criticizes the Austrians for not explaining why different people know different things and have different expectations. The issue of differential knowledge is symptomatic of a larger problem faced by any school of thought that does not follow every trend in the way of thinking of the mainstream. The repeated use of contrary-to-fact assumptions, such as perfect knowledge or homogenous products, can blunt our ability to deal with reality as it actually exists" (R. W. Garrison, "Austrian Economics as the Middle Ground: Comment on Loasby," in *Method, Process and Austrian Economics*, ed. I. M. Kirzner, op. cit., pp. 136–7).

23. As a consequence the driving forces of the market (arbitrage, accumulation, and innovation) have to be interpreted as being future oriented; the same is true for the respective activities of the entrepreneurs.

24. Shackle has deeply reflected on this question. See for example G. L. S. Shackle, "Imagination, Formalism and Choice," in *Time, Uncertainty and Disequilibrium*, ed. M. J. Rizzo, op. cit., pp. 19–31. Shackle point out that human action is basing on imaginations. So the driving forces of the market rest on imaginations, too.

86   *Spontaneous Order and the Subjectivity of Expectations*

25. Judgment as an element of imagination rightly is stressed by J. High, "Alertness and Judgment: Comment on Kirzner," in *Method, Process and Austrian Economics*, ed. I. M. Kirzner, op. cit., pp. 161–8.

26. It has already been stated that O'Driscoll favors the proposition that in certain circumstances even different and disparate individuals will have a common reaction to shared experience. But the example he chooses is not convincing because it refers to a simple situation. Situations that have to be mastered in the market process are far more complex than the actions to be taken for an exit, when a fire in an enclosed room has been conceived of. Thus, more interpretation, more judgment or more imagination is called for. But the simple story of O'Driscoll can demonstrate the advantage of divergent reactions: If all persons in the room will react in the same manner and immediately run to the door, it may well be that the exit will be blocked and no person can get out; divergent, i.e., successive reactions would do better!

27. This is especially the case when the "iterative" factors begin to dominate the "mutative" ones in the market. For a detailed analysis of the resulting consequences see E. Heuss, *Allgemeine Markttheorie*, op. cit., especially chaps 4–6.

28. "Like everyone else, entrepreneurs may seek to conceal the extent of their ignorance, by assuming a degree of continuity between past and future that cannot possibly be assured and that may well be greater than the continuity achieved in the past; alternatively they may place exaggerated reliance on the apparent plans of other entrepreneurs, who are credited with superior forsight. Entrepreneurial competition encourages a variety of opinions and of plans; but faced with the total inadequacy of any basis for rational expectation, we may sometimes find excessive conformity, both in undertaking particular kinds of business strategy and in abandoning such strategies. To rely on one's own imagination, and to await the eventual market test, requires greater resolution, perhaps greater arrogance, than most of us possess" (B. J. Loasby, "Economics of Dispersed and Incomplete Information," in *Method, Process and Austrian Economics*, ed. I. M. Kirzner, op. cit., p. 127). While the picture Loasby draws may be adequate in certain situations or certain phases of the market, on the whole Loasby rather seems to underestimate the vigor of subjectivity.

29. Lachmann, From Mises to Shackle, op. cit., p. 61.

Part III
The Competitive Market Process: Competition

[12]

CHAPTER VII

THE PROCESS OF CREATIVE DESTRUCTION

THE theories of monopolistic and oligopolistic competition and their popular variants may in two ways be made to serve the view that capitalist reality is unfavorable to maximum performance in production. One may hold that it always has been so and that all along output has been expanding in spite of the secular sabotage perpetrated by the managing bourgeoisie. Advocates of this proposition would have to produce evidence to the effect that the observed rate of increase can be accounted for by a sequence of favorable circumstances unconnected with the mechanism of private enterprise and strong enough to overcome the latter's resistance. This is precisely the question which we shall discuss in Chapter IX. However, those who espouse this variant at least avoid the trouble about historical fact that the advocates of the alternative proposition have to face. This avers that capitalist reality once tended to favor maximum productive performance, or at all events productive performance so considerable as to constitute a major element in any serious appraisal of the system; but that the later spread of monopolist structures, killing competition, has by now reversed that tendency.

First, this involves the creation of an entirely imaginary golden age of perfect competition that at some time somehow metamorphosed itself into the monopolistic age, whereas it is quite clear that perfect competition has at no time been more of a reality than it is at present. Secondly, it is necessary to point out that the rate of increase in output did not decrease from the nineties from which, I suppose, the prevalence of the largest-size concerns, at least in manufacturing industry, would have to be dated; that there is nothing in the behavior of the time series of total output to suggest a "break in trend"; and, most important of all, that the modern standard of life of the masses evolved during the period of relatively unfettered "big business." If we list the items that enter the modern workman's budget and from 1899 on observe the course of their prices not in terms of money but in terms of the hours of labor that will buy them—i.e., each year's money prices divided by each year's hourly wage rates—we cannot fail to be struck by the rate of the advance which, considering the spectacular improvement in qualities, seems to have been greater and not smaller than it ever was before. If we economists were given less to wishful thinking and more to the observation of facts, doubts would

82   Can Capitalism Survive?

immediately arise as to the realistic virtues of a theory that would
have led us to expect a very different result. Nor is this all. As soon
as we go into details and inquire into the individual items in which
progress was most conspicuous, the trail leads not to the doors of
those firms that work under conditions of comparatively free competition but precisely to the doors of the large concerns—which, as
in the case of agricultural machinery, also account for much of the
progress in the competitive sector—and a shocking suspicion dawns
upon us that big business may have had more to do with creating
that standard of life than with keeping it down.

The conclusions alluded to at the end of the preceding chapter are
in fact almost completely false. Yet they follow from observations and
theorems that are almost completely[1] true. Both economists and
popular writers have once more run away with some fragments of
reality they happened to grasp. These fragments themselves were
mostly seen correctly. Their formal properties were mostly developed
correctly. But no conclusions about capitalist reality as a whole follow
from such fragmentary analyses. If we draw them nevertheless, we
can be right only by accident. That has been done. And the lucky
accident did not happen.

The essential point to grasp is that in dealing with capitalism we
are dealing with an evolutionary process. It may seem strange that
anyone can fail to see so obvious a fact which moreover was long
ago emphasized by Karl Marx. Yet that fragmentary analysis which
yields the bulk of our propositions about the functioning of modern
capitalism persistently neglects it. Let us restate the point and see
how it bears upon our problem.

Capitalism, then, is by nature a form or method of economic change
and not only never is but never can be stationary. And this evolutionary character of the capitalist process is not merely due to the fact
that economic life goes on in a social and natural environment which
changes and by its change alters the data of economic action; this
fact is important and these changes (wars, revolutions and so on)
often condition industrial change, but they are not its prime movers.
Nor is this evolutionary character due to a quasi-automatic increase
in population and capital or to the vagaries of monetary systems of

[1] As a matter of fact, those observations and theorems are not completely satisfactory. The usual expositions of the doctrine of imperfect competition fail in
particular to give due attention to the many and important cases in which, even as
a matter of static theory, imperfect competition approximates the results of perfect
competition. There are other cases in which it does not do this, but offers com-
pensations which, while not entering any output index, yet contribute to what
the output index is in the last resort intended to measure—the cases in which a
firm defends its market by establishing a name for quality and service for instance.
However, in order to simplify matters, we will not take issue with that doctrine
on its own ground.

The Process of Creative Destruction   83

which exactly the same thing holds true. The fundamental impulse
that sets and keeps the capitalist engine in motion comes from the
new consumers' goods, the new methods of production or transportation, the new markets, the new forms of industrial organization that
capitalist enterprise creates.

As we have seen in the preceding chapter, the contents of the
laborer's budget, say from 1760 to 1940, did not simply grow on unchanging lines but they underwent a process of qualitative change.
Similarly, the history of the productive apparatus of a typical farm,
from the beginnings of the rationalization of crop rotation, plowing
and fattening to the mechanized thing of today—linking up with
elevators and railroads—is a history of revolutions. So is the history
of the productive apparatus of the iron and steel industry from the
charcoal furnace to our own type of furnace, or the history of the
apparatus of power production from the overshot water wheel to the
modern power plant, or the history of transportation from the mail-
coach to the airplane. The opening up of new markets, foreign or
domestic, and the organizational development from the craft shop
and factory to such concerns as U. S. Steel illustrate the same process
of industrial mutation—if I may use that biological term—that incessantly revolutionizes[2] the economic structure *from within*, incessantly
destroying the old one, incessantly creating a new one. This process
of Creative Destruction is the essential fact about capitalism. It is
what capitalism consists in and what every capitalist concern has got
to live in. This fact bears upon our problem in two ways.

First, since we are dealing with a process whose every element takes
considerable time in revealing its true features and ultimate effects,
there is no point in appraising the performance of that process *ex visu*
of a given point of time; we must judge its performance over time, as
it unfolds through decades or centuries. A system—any system, economic or other—that at *every* given point of time fully utilizes its
possibilities to the best advantage may yet in the long run be inferior
to a system that does so at *no* given point of time, because the latter's
failure to do so may be a condition for the level or speed of long-run
performance.

Second, since we are dealing with an organic process, analysis of
what happens in any particular part of it—say, in an individual concern or industry—may indeed clarify details of mechanism but is
inconclusive beyond that. Every piece of business strategy acquires its
true significance only against the background of that process and

---

[2] Those revolutions are not strictly incessant; they occur in discrete rushes which
are separated from each other by spans of comparative quiet. The process as a
whole works incessantly however, in the sense that there always is either revolution
or absorption of the results of revolution, both together forming what are known
as business cycles.

84   Can Capitalism Survive?

within the situation created by it. It must be seen in its role in the
perennial gale of creative destruction; it cannot be understood irrespective of it or, in fact, on the hypothesis that there is a perennial lull.

But economists who, *ex visu* of a point of time, look for example
at the behavior of an oligopolist industry—an industry which consists of a few big firms—and observe the well-known moves and
countermoves within it that seem to aim at nothing but high prices
and restrictions of output are making precisely that hypothesis. They
accept the data of the momentary situation as if there were no past or
future to it and think that they have understood what there is to
understand if they interpret the behavior of those firms by means of
the principle of maximizing profits with reference to those data. The
usual theorist's paper and the usual government commission's report
practically never try to see that behavior, on the one hand, as a result
of a piece of past history and, on the other hand, as an attempt to
deal with a situation that is sure to change presently—as an attempt
by those firms to keep on their feet, on ground that is slipping away
from under them. In other words, the problem that is usually being
visualized is how capitalism administers existing structures, whereas
the relevant problem is how it creates and destroys them. As long as
this is not recognized, the investigator does a meaningless job. As
soon as it is recognized, his outlook on capitalist practice and its
social results changes considerably.[3]

The first thing to go is the traditional conception of the *modus
operandi* of competition. Economists are at long last emerging from
the stage in which price competition was all they saw. As soon as
quality competition and sales effort are admitted into the sacred
precincts of theory, the price variable is ousted from its dominant
position. However, it is still competition within a rigid pattern of
invariant conditions, methods of production and forms of industrial
organization in particular, that practically monopolizes attention.
But in capitalist reality as distinguished from its textbook picture, it
is not that kind of competition which counts but the competition
from the new commodity, the new technology, the new source of
supply, the new type of organization (the largest-scale unit of control
for instance)—competition which commands a decisive cost or quality
advantage and which strikes not at the margins of the profits and the
outputs of the existing firms but at their foundations and their very
lives. This kind of competition is as much more effective than the
other as a bombardment is in comparison with forcing a door, and

[3] It should be understood that it is only our appraisal of economic performance
and not our moral judgment that can be so changed. Owing to its autonomy, moral
approval or disapproval is entirely independent of our appraisal of social (or any
other) results, unless we happen to adopt a moral system such as utilitarianism
which makes moral approval and disapproval turn on them *ex definitione*.

The Process of Creative Destruction 85

so much more important that it becomes a matter of comparative indifference whether competition in the ordinary sense functions more or less promptly; the powerful lever that in the long run expands output and brings down prices is in any case made of other stuff.

It is hardly necessary to point out that competition of the kind we now have in mind acts not only when in being but also when it is merely an ever-present threat. It disciplines before it attacks. The businessman feels himself to be in a competitive situation even if he is alone in his field or if, though not alone, he holds a position such that investigating government experts fail to see any effective competition between him and any other firms in the same or a neighboring field and in consequence conclude that his talk, under examination, about his competitive sorrows is all make-believe. In many cases, though not in all, this will in the long run enforce behavior very similar to the perfectly competitive pattern.

Many theorists take the opposite view which is best conveyed by an example. Let us assume that there is a certain number of retailers in a neighborhood who try to improve their relative position by service and "atmosphere" but avoid price competition and stick as to methods to the local tradition—a picture of stagnating routine. As others drift into the trade that quasi-equilibrium is indeed upset, but in a manner that does not benefit their customers. The economic space around each of the shops having been narrowed, their owners will no longer be able to make a living and they will try to mend the case by raising prices in tacit agreement. This will further reduce their sales and so, by successive pyramiding, a situation will evolve in which increasing potential supply will be attended by increasing instead of decreasing prices and by decreasing instead of increasing sales.

Such cases do occur, and it is right and proper to work them out. But as the practical instances usually given show, they are fringe-end cases to be found mainly in the sectors furthest removed from all that is most characteristic of capitalist activity.[4] Moreover, they are transient by nature. In the case of retail trade the competition that matters arises not from additional shops of the same type, but from the department store, the chain store, the mail-order house and the supermarket which are bound to destroy those pyramids sooner or later.[5]

[4] This is also shown by a theorem we frequently meet with in expositions of the theory of imperfect competition, viz., the theorem that, under conditions of imperfect competition, producing or trading businesses tend to be irrationally small. Since imperfect competition is at the same time held to be an outstanding characteristic of modern industry we are set to wondering what world these theorists live in, unless, as stated above, fringe-end cases are all they have in mind.

[5] The mere threat of their attack cannot, in the particular conditions, environmental and personal, of small-scale retail trade, have its usual disciplining influence. for the small man is too much hampered by his cost structure and, however

86   Can Capitalism Survive?

Now a theoretical construction which neglects this essential element
of the case neglects all that is most typically capitalist about it; even
if correct in logic as well as in fact, it is like *Hamlet* without the
Danish prince.

well he may manage within his inescapable limitations, he can never adapt him
self to the methods of competitors who can afford to sell at the price at which
he buys.

CHAPTER VIII

MONOPOLISTIC PRACTICES

W HAT has been said so far is really sufficient to enable the reader
to deal with the large majority of the practical cases he is likely
to meet and to realize the inadequacy of most of those criticisms of the
profit economy which, directly or indirectly, rely on the absence of
perfect competition. Since, however, the bearing of our argument on
some of those criticisms may not be obvious at a glance, it will be
worth our while to elaborate a little in order to make a few points
more explicit.

1. We have just seen that, both as a fact and as a threat, the impact
of new things—new technologies for instance—on the existing structure of an industry considerably reduces the long-run scope and importance of practices that aim, through restricting output, at conserv-
ing established positions and at maximizing the profits accruing from
them. We must now recognize the further fact that restrictive practices
of this kind, as far as they are effective, acquire a new significance in
the perennial gale of creative destruction, a significance which they
would not have in a stationary state or in a state of slow and balanced
growth. In either of these cases restrictive strategy would produce no
result other than an increase in profits at the expense of buyers except
that, in the case of balanced advance, it might still prove to be the
easiest and most effective way of collecting the means by which to
finance additional investment.[1] But in the process of creative destruction, restrictive practices may do much to steady the ship and to alle-
viate temporary difficulties. This is in fact a very familiar argument
which always turns up in times of depression and, as everyone knows,
has become very popular with governments and their economic advisers—witness the NRA. While it has been so much misused and
so faultily acted upon that most economists heartily despise it, those

---

[1] Theorists are apt to look upon anyone who admits this possibility as guilty
of gross error, and to prove immediately that financing by borrowing from banks
or from private savers or, in the case of public enterprise, financing from the
proceeds of an income tax is much more rational than is financing from surplus
profits collected through a restrictive policy. For some patterns of behavior they
are quite right. For others they are quite wrong. I believe that both capitalism
and communism of the Russian type belong in the latter category. But the point
is that theoretical considerations, especially theoretical considerations of the short-
run kind, cannot solve, although they contribute to the solution of, the problem
which we shall meet again in the next part.

88   Can Capitalism Survive?

same advisers who are responsible for this[2] invariably fail to see its
much more general rationale.

Practically any investment entails, as a necessary complement of
entrepreneurial action, certain safeguarding activities such as insuring
or hedging. Long-range investing under rapidly changing conditions,
especially under conditions that change or may change at any moment under the impact of new commodities and technologies, is like
shooting at a target that is not only indistinct but moving—and moving jerkily at that. Hence it becomes necessary to resort to such
protecting devices as patents or temporary secrecy of processes or, in
some cases, long-period contracts secured in advance. But these protecting devices which most economists accept as normal elements of
rational management[3] are only special cases of a larger class comprising many others which most economists condemn although they
do not differ fundamentally from the recognized ones.

If for instance a war risk is insurable, nobody objects to a firm's
collecting the cost of this insurance from the buyers of its products.
But that risk is no less an element in long-run costs, if there are no
facilities for insuring against it, in which case a price strategy aiming
at the same end will seem to involve unnecessary restriction and to be
productive of excess profits. Similarly, if a patent cannot be secured
or would not, if secured, effectively protect, other means may have to
be used in order to justify the investment. Among them are a price
policy that will make it possible to write off more quickly than would
otherwise be rational, or additional investment in order to provide
excess capacity to be used only for aggression or defense. Again, if
long-period contracts cannot be entered into in advance, other means
may have to be devised in order to tie prospective customers to the
investing firm.

In analyzing such business strategy *ex visu* of a given point of time,
the investigating economist or government agent sees price policies
that seem to him predatory and restrictions of output that seem to him
synonymous with loss of opportunities to produce. He does not see
that restrictions of this type are, in the conditions of the perennial
gale, incidents, often unavoidable incidents, of a long-run process of
expansion which they protect rather than impede. There is no more
of paradox in this than there is in saying that motorcars are travel-
ing faster than they otherwise would *because* they are provided with
brakes.

  [2] In particular, it is easy to show that there is no sense, and plenty of harm, in a
policy that aims at preserving "price parities."
  [3] Some economists, however, consider that even those devices are obstructions
to progress which, though perhaps necessary in capitalist society, would be absent
in a socialist one. There is some truth in this. But that does not affect the proposition that the protection afforded by patents and so on is, in the conditions of a
profit economy, on balance a propelling and not an inhibiting factor.

[13]

V. The Meaning of Competition

1

THERE are signs of increasing awareness among economists that what they have been discussing in recent years under the name of "competition" is not the same thing as what is thus called in ordinary language. But, although there have been some valiant attempts to bring discussion back to earth and to direct attention to the problems of real life, notably by J. M. Clark and F. Machlup,[1] the general view seems still to regard the conception of competition currently employed by economists as the significant one and to treat that of the businessman as an abuse. It appears to be generally held that the so-called theory of "perfect competition" provides the appropriate model for judging the effectiveness of competition in real life and that, to the extent that real competition differs from that model, it is undesirable and even harmful.

For this attitude there seems to me to exist very little justification. I shall attempt to show that what the theory of perfect competition discusses has little claim to be called "competition" at all and that its conclusions are of little use as guides to policy. The reason for this seems to me to be that this theory throughout assumes that state of affairs already to exist which, according to the truer view of the older theory, the process of competition tends to bring about (or to approximate) and that, if the state of affairs assumed by the theory of perfect competition ever existed, it would not only deprive of their scope all the activities which the verb "to compete" describes but would make them virtually impossible.

* This essay reproduces the substance of the Stafford Little Lecture delivered at Princeton University on May 20, 1946.

1. J. M. Clark, "Toward a Concept of Workable Competition," *American Economic Review*, Vol. XXX (June, 1940); F. Machlup, "Competition, Pliopoly, and Profit," *Economica*, Vol. IX (new ser.; February and May, 1942).

The Meaning of Competition

If all this affected only the use of the word "competition," it would not matter a great deal. But it seems almost as if economists by this peculiar use of language were deceiving themselves into the belief that, in discussing "competition," they are saying something about the nature and significance of the process by which the state of affairs is brought about, which they merely assume to exist. In fact, this moving force of economic life is left almost altogether undiscussed.

I do not wish to discuss here at any length the reasons which have led the theory of competition into this curious state. As I have suggested elsewhere in this volume,[2] the tautological method which is appropriate and indispensable for the analysis of individual action seems in this instance to have been illegitimately extended to problems in which we have to deal with a social process in which the decisions of many individuals influence one another and necessarily succeed one another in time. The economic calculus (or the Pure Logic of Choice) which deals with the first kind of problem consist of an apparatus of classification of possible human attitudes and provides us with a technique for describing the interrelations of the different parts of a single plan. Its conclusions are implicit in its assumptions: the desires and the knowledge of the facts, which are assumed to be simultaneously present to a single mind, determine a unique solution. The relations discussed in this type of analysis are logical relations, concerned solely with the conclusions which follow for the mind of the planning individual from the given premises.

When we deal, however, with a situation in which a number of persons are attempting to work out their separate plans, we can no longer assume that the data are the same for all the planning minds. The problem becomes one of how the "data" of the different individuals on which they base their plans are adjusted to the objective facts of their environment (which includes the actions of the other people). Although in the solution of this type of problem we still must make use of our technique for rapidly working out the implications of a given set of data, we have now to deal not only with several separate sets of

2. See the second and fourth chapters.

Individualism and Economic Order

data of the different persons but also—and this is even more important
—with a process which necessarily involves continuous changes in the
data for the different individuals. As I have suggested before, the
causal factor enters here in the form of the acquisition of new knowledge by the different individuals or of changes in their data brought
about by the contacts between them.

The relevance of this for my present problem will appear when it is
recalled that the modern theory of competition deals almost exclusively with a state of what is called "competitive equilibrium" in which it
is assumed that the data for the different individuals are fully adjusted
to each other, while the problem which requires explanation is the
nature of the process by which the data are thus adjusted. In other
words, the description of competitive equilibrium does not even attempt to say that, if we find such and such conditions, such and such
consequences will follow, but confines itself to defining conditions in
which its conclusions are already implicitly contained and which may
conceivably exist but of which it does not tell us how they can ever be
brought about. Or, to anticipate our main conclusion in a brief statement, competition is by its nature a dynamic process whose essential
characteristics are assumed away by the assumptions underlying
static analysis.

2

That the modern theory of competitive equilibrium *assumes* the
situation to exist which a true explanation ought to account for as the
effect of the competitive process is best shown by examining the familiar list of conditions found in any modern textbook. Most of these conditions, incidentally, not only underlie the analysis of "perfect" competition but are equally assumed in the discussion of the various
"imperfect" or "monopolistic" markets, which throughout assume
certain unrealistic "perfections."[3] For our immediate purpose, however, the theory of perfect competition will be the most instructive case
to examine.

3. Particularly the assumptions that *at all times* a uniform price must rule for a given
commodity throughout the market and that sellers know the shape of the demand curve.

The Meaning of Competition

While different authors may state the list of essential conditions of perfect competition differently, the following is probably more than sufficiently comprehensive for our purpose, because, as we shall see, those conditions are not really independent of each other. According to the generally accepted view, perfect competition presupposes:

1. A homogeneous commodity offered and demanded by a large number of relatively small sellers or buyers, none of whom expects to exercise by his action a perceptible influence on price.
2. Free entry into the market and absence of other restraints on the movement of prices and resources.
3. Complete knowledge of the relevant factors on the part of all participants in the market.

We shall not ask at this stage precisely for what these conditions are required or what is implied if they are assumed to be given. But we must inquire a little further about their meaning, and in this respect it is the third condition which is the critical and obscure one. The standard can evidently not be perfect knowledge of everything affecting the market on the part of every person taking part in it. I shall here not go into the familiar paradox of the paralyzing effect really perfect knowledge and foresight would have on all action.[4] It will be obvious also that nothing is solved when we assume everybody to know everything and that the real problem is rather how it can be brought about that as much of the available knowledge as possible is used. This raises for a competitive society the question, not how we can "find" the people who know best, but rather what institutional arrangements are necessary in order that the unknown persons who have knowledge specially suited to a particular task are most likely to be attracted to that task. But we must inquire a little further what sort of knowledge it is that is supposed to be in possession of the parties of the market.

If we consider the market for some kind of finished consumption goods and start with the position of its producers or sellers, we shall find, first, that they are assumed to know the lowest cost at which the commodity can be produced. Yet this knowledge which is assumed to

4. See O. Morgenstern, "Vollkommene Voraussicht und wirtschaftliches Gleichgewicht," *Zeitschrift für Nationalökonomie*, Vol. VI (1935).

Individualism and Economic Order

be given to begin with is one of the main points where it is only through the process of competition that the facts will be discovered. This appears to me one of the most important of the points where the starting-point of the theory of competitive equilibrium assumes away the main task which only the process of competition can solve. The position is somewhat similar with respect to the second point on which the producers are assumed to be fully informed: the wishes and desires of the consumers, including the kinds of goods and services which they demand and the prices they are willing to pay. These cannot properly be regarded as given facts but ought rather to be regarded as problems to be solved by the process of competition.

The same situation exists on the side of the consumers or buyers. Again the knowledge they are supposed to possess in a state of competitive equilibrium cannot be legitimately assumed to be at their command before the process of competition starts. Their knowledge of the alternatives before them is the result of what happens on the market, of such activities as advertising, etc.; and the whole organization of the market serves mainly the need of spreading the information on which the buyer is to act.

The peculiar nature of the assumptions from which the theory of competitive equilibrium starts stands out very clearly if we ask which of the activities that are commonly designated by the verb "to compete" would still be possible if those conditions were all satisfied. Perhaps it is worth recalling that, according to Dr. Johnson, competition is "the action of endeavouring to gain what another endeavours to gain at the same time." Now, how many of the devices adopted in ordinary life to that end would still be open to a seller in a market in which so-called "perfect competition" prevails? I believe that the answer is exactly none. Advertising, undercutting, and improving ("differentiating") the goods or services produced are all excluded by definition—"perfect" competition means indeed the absence of all competitive activities.

Especially remarkable in this connection is the explicit and complete exclusion from the theory of perfect competition of all personal rela-

96

The Meaning of Competition

tionships existing between the parties.[5] In actual life the fact that our inadequate knowledge of the available commodities or services is made up for by our experience with the persons or firms supplying them—that competition is in a large measure competition for reputation or good will—is one of the most important facts which enables us to solve our daily problems. The function of competition is here precisely to teach us *who* will serve us well: which grocer or travel agency, which department store or hotel, which doctor or solicitor, we can expect to provide the most satisfactory solution for whatever particular personal problem we may have to face. Evidently in all these fields competition may be very intense, just because the services of the different persons or firms will never be exactly alike, and it will be owing to this competition that we are in a position to be served as well as we are. The reasons competition in this field is described as imperfect have indeed nothing to do with the competitive character of the activities of these people; it lies in the nature of the commodities or services themselves. If no two doctors are perfectly alike, this does not mean that the competition between them is less intense but merely that any degree of competition between them will not produce exactly those results which it would if their services were exactly alike. This is not a purely verbal point. The talk about the defects or competition when we are in fact talking about the necessary difference between commodities and services conceals a very real confusion and leads on occasion to absurd conclusions.

While on a first glance the assumption concerning the perfect knowledge possessed by the parties may seem the most startling and artificial of all those on which the theory of perfect competition is based, it may in fact be no more than a consequence of, and in part even justified by, another of the presuppositions on which it is founded. If, indeed, we start by assuming that a large number of people are producing the same commodity and command the same objective facili-

5. Cf. G. J. Stigler, *The Theory of Price* (1946), p. 24: "Economic relationships are never perfectly competitive if they involve any personal relationships between economic units" (see also *ibid.*, p. 226).

Individualism and Economic Order

ties and opportunities for doing so, then indeed it might be made plausible (although this has, to my knowledge, never been attempted) that they will in time all be led to know most of the facts relevant for judging the market of that commodity. Not only will each producer by his experience learn the same facts as every other but also he will thus come to know what his fellows know and in consequence the elasticity of the demand for his own product. The condition where different manufacturers produce the identical product under identical conditions is in fact the most favorable for producing that state of knowledge among them which perfect competition requires. Perhaps this means no more than that the commodities can be identical in the sense in which it is alone relevant for our understanding human action only if people hold the same views about them, although it should also be possible to state a set of physical conditions which is favorable to all those who are concerned with a set of closely interrelated activities learning the facts relevant for their decisions.

However that be, it will be clear that the facts will not always be as favorable to this result as they are when many people are at least in a position to produce the same article. The conception of the economic system as divisible into distinct markets for separate commodities is after all very largely the product of the imagination of the economist and certainly is not the rule in the field of manufacture and of personal services, to which the discussion about competition so largely refers. In fact, it need hardly be said, no products of two producers are ever exactly alike, even if it were only because, as they leave his plant, they must be at different places. These differences are part of the facts which create our economic problem, and it is little help to answer it on the assumption that they are absent.

The belief in the advantages of perfect competition frequently leads enthusiasts even to argue that a more advantageous use of resources would be achieved if the existing variety of products were reduced by *compulsory* standardization. Now, there is undoubtedly much to be said in many fields for assisting standardization by agreed recommendations or standards which are to apply unless different requirements

The Meaning of Competition

are explicitly stipulated in contracts. But this is something very different from the demands of those who believe that the variety of people's tastes should be disregarded and the constant experimentation with improvements should be suppressed in order to obtain the advantages of perfect competition. It would clearly not be an improvement to build all houses exactly alike in order to create a perfect market for houses, and the same is true of most other fields where differences between the individual products prevent competition from ever being perfect.

3

We shall probably learn more about the nature and significance of the competitive process if for a while we forget about the artificial assumptions underlying the theory of perfect competition and ask whether competition would be any less important if, for example, no two commodities were ever exactly alike. If it were not for the difficulty of the analysis of such a situation, it would be well worth while to consider in some detail the case where the different commodities could not be readily classed into distinct groups, but where we had to deal with a continuous range of close substitutes, every unit somewhat different from the other but without any marked break in the continuous range. The result of the analysis of competition in such a situation might in many respects be more relevant to the conditions of real life than those of the analysis of competition in a single industry producing a homogeneous commodity sharply differentiated from all others. Or, if the case where no two commodities are exactly alike be thought to be too extreme, we might at least turn to the case where no two producers produce exactly the same commodity, as is the rule not only with all personal services but also in the markets of many manufactured commodities, such as the markets for books or musical instruments.

For our present purpose I need not attempt anything like a complete analysis of such kinds of markets but shall merely ask what would be the role of competition in them. Although the result would, of course, within fairly wide margins be indeterminate, the market would still

Individualism and Economic Order

bring about a set of prices at which each commodity sold just cheap enough to outbid its potential close substitutes—and this in itself is no small thing when we consider the unsurmountable difficulties of discovering even such a system of prices by any other method except that of trial and error in the market, with the individual participants gradually learning the relevant circumstances. It is true, of course, that in such a market correspondence between prices and marginal costs is to be expected only to the degree that elasticities of demand for the individual commodities approach the conditions assumed by the theory of perfect competition or that elasticities of substitution between the different commodities approach infinity. But the point is that in this case this standard of perfection as something desirable or to be aimed at is wholly irrelevant. The basis of comparison, on the grounds of which the achievement of competition ought to be judged, cannot be a situation which is different from the objective facts and which cannot be brought about by any known means. It ought to be the situation as it would exist if competition were prevented from operating. Not the approach to an unachievable and meaningless ideal but the improvement upon the conditions that would exist without competition should be the test.

In such a situation how would conditions differ, if competition were "free" in the traditional sense, from those which would exist if, for example, only people licensed by authority were allowed to produce particular things, or prices were fixed by authority, or both? Clearly there would be not only no likelihood that the different things would be produced by those who knew best how to do it and therefore could do it at lowest cost but also no likelihood that all those things would be produced at all which, if the consumers had the choice, they would like best. There would be little relationship between actual prices and the lowest cost at which somebody would be able to produce these commodities; indeed, the alternatives between which both producers and consumers would be in a position to choose, their data, would be altogether different from what they would be under competition.

The real problem in all this is not whether we will get *given* com-

100

The Meaning of Competition

modities or services at *given* marginal costs but mainly by what commodities and services the needs of the people can be most cheaply
satisfied. The solution of the economic problem of society is in this respect always a voyage of exploration into the unknown, an attempt to
discover new ways of doing things better than they have been done
before. This must always remain so as long as there are any economic
problems to be solved at all, because all economic problems are created
by unforeseen changes which require adaptation. Only what we have
not foreseen and provided for requires new decisions. If no such
adaptations were required, if at any moment we knew that all change
had stopped and things would forever go on exactly as they are now,
there would be no more questions of the use of resources to be solved.

A person who possesses the exclusive knowledge or skill which enables him to reduce the cost of production of a commodity by 50 per
cent still renders an enormous service to society if he enters its production and reduces its price by only 25 per cent—not only through that
price reduction but also through his additional saving of cost. But it is
only through competition that we can assume that these possible savings of cost will be achieved. Even if in each instance prices were only
just low enough to keep out producers which do not enjoy these or
other equivalent advantages, so that each commodity were produced
as cheaply as possible, though many may be sold at prices considerably
above costs, this would probably be a result which could not be
achieved by any other method than that of letting competition operate.

4

That in conditions of real life the position even of any two producers
is hardly ever the same is due to facts which the theory of perfect competition eliminates by its concentration on a long-term equilibrium
which in an ever changing world can never be reached. At any given
moment the equipment of a particular firm is always largely determined by historical accident, and the problem is that it should make
the best use of the given equipment (including the acquired capacities

Individualism and Economic Order

of the members of its staff) and not what it should do if it were given unlimited time to adjust itself to constant conditions. For the problem of the best use of the given durable but exhaustible resources the long-term equilibrium price with which a theory discussing "perfect" competition must be concerned is not only not relevant; the conclusions concerning policy to which preoccupation with this model leads are highly misleading and even dangerous. The idea that under "perfect" competition prices should be equal to long-run costs often leads to the approval of such antisocial practices as the demand for an "orderly competition" which will secure a fair return on capital and for the destruction of excess capacity. Enthusiasm for perfect competition in theory and the support of monopoly in practice are indeed surprisingly often found to live together.

This is, however, only one of the many points on which the neglect of the time element makes the theoretical picture of perfect competition so entirely remote from all that is relevant to an understanding of the process of competition. If we think of it, as we ought to, as a succession of events, it becomes even more obvious that in real life there will at any moment be as a rule only one producer who can manufacture a given article at the lowest cost and who may in fact sell below the cost of his next successful competitor, but who, while still trying to extend his market, will often be overtaken by somebody else, who in turn will be prevented from capturing the whole market by yet another, and so on. Such a market would clearly never be in a state of perfect competition, yet competition in it might not only be as intense as possible but would also be the essential factor in bringing about the fact that the article in question is supplied at any moment to the consumer as cheaply as this can be done by any known method.

When we compare an "imperfect" market like this with a relatively "perfect" market as that of, say, grain, we shall now be in a better position to bring out the distinction which has been underlying this whole discussion—the distinction between the underlying objective facts of a situation which cannot be altered by human activity and the nature of the competitive activities by which men adjust themselves to the

The Meaning of Competition

situation. Where, as in the latter case, we have a highly organized market of a fully standardized commodity produced by many producers, there is little need or scope for competitive activities because the situation is such that the conditions which these activities might bring about are already satisfied to begin with. The best ways of producing the commodity, its character and uses, are most of the time known to nearly the same degree to all members of the market. The knowledge of any important change spreads so rapidly and the adaptation to it is so soon effected that we usually simply disregard what happens during these short transition periods and confine ourselves to comparing the two states of near-equilibrium which exist before and after them. But it is during this short and neglected interval that the forces of competition operate and become visible, and it is the events during this interval which we must study if we are to "explain" the equilibrium which follows it.

It is only in a market where adaptation is slow compared with the rate of change that the process of competition is in continuous operation. And though the reason why adaptation is slow *may* be that competition is weak, e.g., because there are special obstacles to entry into the trade, or because of some other factors of the character of natural monopolies, slow adaptation does by no means necessarily mean weak competition. When the variety of near-substitutes is great and rapidly changing, where it takes a long time to find out about the relative merits of the available alternatives, or where the need for a whole class of goods or services occurs only discontinuously at irregular intervals, the adjustment must be slow even if competition is strong and active.

The confusion between the objective facts of the situation and the character of the human responses to it tends to conceal from us the important fact that competition is the more important the more complex or "imperfect" are the objective conditions in which it has to operate. Indeed, far from competition being beneficial only when it is "perfect," I am inclined to argue that the need for competition is nowhere greater than in fields in which the nature of the commodities or services makes it impossible that it ever should create a perfect market

103

Individualism and Economic Order

in the theoretical sense. The inevitable actual imperfections of competition are as little an argument against competition as the difficulties of achieving a perfect solution of any other task are an argument against attempting to solve it at all, or as little as imperfect health is an argument against health.

In conditions where we can never have many people offering the same homogeneous product or service, because of the ever changing character of our needs and our knowledge, or of the infinite variety of human skills and capacities, the ideal state cannot be one requiring an identical character of large numbers of such products and services. The economic problem is a problem of making the best use of what resources we have, and not one of what we should do if the situation were different from what it actually is. There is no sense in talking of a use of resources "as if" a perfect market existed, if this means that the resources would have to be different from what they are, or in discussing what somebody with perfect knowledge would do if our task must be to make the best use of the knowledge the existing people have.

5

The argument in favor of competition does not rest on the conditions that would exist if it were perfect. Although, where the objective facts would make it possible for competition to approach perfection, this would also secure the most effective use of resources, and, although there is therefore every case for removing human obstacles to competition, this does not mean that competition does not also bring about as effective a use of resources as can be brought about by any known means where in the nature of the case it must be imperfect. Even where free entry will secure no more than that at any one moment all the goods and services for which there would be an effective demand if they were available are in fact produced at the least current[6] expenditure of resources at which, in the given historical situation, they can be produced, even though the price the consumer is made to pay for them

6. "Current" cost in this connection excludes all true bygones but includes, of course, "user cost."

The Meaning of Competition

is considerably higher and only just below the cost of the next best way in which his need could be satisfied, this, I submit, is more than we can expect from any other known system. The decisive point is still the elementary one that it is most unlikely that, without artificial obstacles which government activity either creates or can remove, any commodity or service will for any length of time be available only at a price at which outsiders could expect a more than normal profit if they entered the field.

The practical lesson of all this, I think, is that we should worry much less about whether competition in a given case is perfect and worry much more whether there is competition at all. What our theoretical models of separate industries conceal is that in practice a much bigger gulf divides competition from no competition than perfect from imperfect competition. Yet the current tendency in discussion is to be intolerant about the imperfections and to be silent about the prevention of competition. We can probably still learn more about the real significance of competition by studying the results which regularly occur where competition is deliberately suppressed than by concentrating on the shortcomings of actual competition compared with an ideal which is irrelevant for the given facts. I say advisedly "where competition is deliberately suppressed" and not merely "where it is absent," because its main effects are usually operating, even if more slowly, so long as it is not outright suppressed with the assistance or the tolerance of the state. The evils which experience has shown to be the regular consequence of a suppression of competition are on a different plane from those which the imperfections of competition may cause. Much more serious than the fact that prices may not correspond to marginal cost is the fact that, with an intrenched monopoly, costs are likely to be much higher than is necessary. A monopoly based on superior efficiency, on the other hand, does comparatively little harm so long as it is assured that it will disappear as soon as anyone else becomes more efficient in providing satisfaction to the consumers.

In conclusion I want for a moment to go back to the point from which I started and restate the most important conclusion in a more

105

Individualism and Economic Order

general form. Competition is essentially a process of the formation of opinion: by spreading information, it creates that unity and coherence of the economic system which we presuppose when we think of it as one market. It creates the views people have about what is best and cheapest, and it is because of it that people know at least as much about possibilities and opportunities as they in fact do. It is thus a process which involves a continuous change in the data and whose significance must therefore be completely missed by any theory which treats these data as constant.

106

[14]

CHAPTER TWELVE

Competition as a Discovery Procedure*

I

It is difficult to defend economists against the charge that for some 40 to 50 years they have been discussing competition on assumptions that, *if* they were true of the real world, would make it wholly uninteresting and useless. If anyone really knew all about what economic theory calls the *data*, competition would indeed be a very wasteful method of securing adjustment to these facts. It is thus not surprising that some people have been led to the conclusion that we can either wholly dispense with the market, or that its results should be used only as a first step towards securing an output of goods and services which we can then manipulate, correct, or redistribute in any manner we wish. Others, who seem to derive their conception of competition solely from modern textbooks, have not unnaturally concluded that competition does not exist.

Against this, it is salutary to remember that, *wherever* the use of competition can be rationally justified, it is on the ground that we do *not* know in advance the facts that determine the actions of competitors. In sports or in examinations, no less than in the award of government contracts or of prizes for poetry, it would clearly be pointless to arrange for competition, if we were certain beforehand who would do best. As indicated in the title of this lecture, I propose to consider competition as a procedure for the discovery of such facts as, without resort to it, would not be known to anyone, or at least would not be utilised.[1]

* This lecture was originally delivered, without the present section 2, to a meeting of the Philadelphia Society at Chicago on 29 March 1968 and later, on 5 July 1968, in German, without the present final section, to the Institut für Weltwirtschaft of the University of Kiel. Only the German version has been published before, first in the series of 'Kieler Vorträge', N.S. 56, Kiel, 1968, and then reprinted in my collected essays entitled *Freiburger Studien*, Tübingen, 1969.

1 Since I wrote this my attention has been drawn to a paper by Leopold von Wiese on 'Die Konkurrenz, vorwiegend in soziologisch-systematischer Betrachtung', *Verhandlungen des 6. Deutschen Soziologentages*, 1929, where, on p. 27, he discusses the 'experimental' nature of competition.

Competition as a Discovery Procedure

This may at first appear so obvious and incontestable as hardly to deserve attention. Yet, some interesting consequences that are not so obvious immediately follow from the explicit formulation of the above apparent truism. One is that competition is valuable *only* because, and so far as, its results are unpredictable and on the whole different from those which anyone has, or could have, deliberately aimed at. Further, that the generally beneficial effects of competition must include disappointing or defeating some particular expectations or intentions.

Closely connected with this is an interesting methodological consequence. It goes far to account for the discredit into which the micro-economic approach to theory has fallen. Although this theory seems to me to be the only one capable of explaining the role of competition, it is no longer understood, even by some professed economists. It is therefore worthwhile to say at the outset a few words about the methodological peculiarity of any theory of competition, because it has made its conclusions suspect to many of those who habitually apply an over-simplified test to decide what they are willing to accept as scientific. The necessary consequence of the reason why we use competition is that, *in those cases in which it is interesting*, the validity of the theory can never be tested empirically. We can test it on conceptual models, and we might conceivably test it in artificially created real situations, where the facts which competition is intended to discover are already known to the observer. But in such cases it is of no practical value, so that to carry out the experiment would hardly be worth the expense. If we do not know the facts we hope to discover by means of competition, we can never ascertain how effective it has been in discovering those facts that might be discovered. All we can hope to find out is that, on the whole, societies which rely for this purpose on competition have achieved their aims more successfully than others. This is a conclusion which the history of civilisation seems eminently to have confirmed.

The peculiarity of competition – which it has in common with scientific method – is that its performance cannot be tested in particular instances where it is significant, but is shown only by the fact that the market will prevail in comparison with any alternative arrangements. The advantages of accepted scientific procedures can never be proved scientifically, but only demonstrated by the common experience that, on the whole, they are better

Competition as a Discovery Procedure

adapted to delivering the goods than alternative approaches.[2]

The difference between economic competition and the successful procedures of science consists in the fact that the former is a method of discovering particular facts relevant to the achievement of specific, temporary purposes, while science aims at the discovery of what are sometimes called 'general facts', which are regularities of events. Science concerns itself with unique, particular facts only to the extent that they help to confirm or refute theories. Because these refer to general, permanent features of the world, the discoveries of science have ample time to prove their value. In contrast, the benefits of particular facts, whose usefulness competition in the market discovers, are in a great measure transitory. So far as the theory of scientific method is concerned, it would be as easy to discredit it on the ground that it does not lead to testable predictions about what science will discover, as it is to discredit the theory of the market on the ground that it fails to predict particular results the market will achieve. This, in the nature of the case, the theory of competition cannot do in any situation in which it is sensible to employ it. As we shall see, its capacity to predict is necessarily limited to predicting the kind of pattern, or the abstract character of the order that will form itself, but does not extend to the prediction of particular facts.[3]

2

Having relieved myself of this pet concern, I shall return to the central subject of this lecture, by pointing out that economic theory sometimes appears at the outset to bar its way to a true appreciation of the character of the process of competition, because it starts from the assumption of a 'given' supply of scarce goods. But which goods are scarce goods, or which things are goods, and how scarce or valuable they are – these are precisely the things which competition has to discover. Provisional results from the market process at each stage alone tell individuals what to look for. Utilisation of knowledge widely dispersed in a society with extensive division

2 Cf. the interesting studies of the late Michael Polanyi in *The Logic of Liberty*, London, 1951, which show how he has been led from the study of scientific method to the study of competition in economic affairs; and see also K. R. Popper, *The Logic of Scientific Discovery*, London, 1959.

3 On the nature of 'pattern prediction' see my essay on 'The theory of complex phenomena' in *Studies in Philosophy, Politics and Economics*, London and Chicago, 1967.

Competition as a Discovery Procedure

of labour cannot rest on individuals knowing all the particular uses to which well-known things in their individual environment might be put. Prices direct their attention to what is worth finding out about market offers for various things and services. This means that the, in some respects always unique, combinations of individual knowledge and skills, which the market enables them to use, will not merely, or even in the first instance, be such knowledge of facts as they could list and communicate if some authority asked them to do so. The knowledge of which I speak consists rather of a capacity to find out particular circumstances, which becomes effective only if possessors of this knowledge are informed by the market which kinds of things or services are wanted, and how urgently they are wanted.[4]

This must suffice to indicate what kind of knowledge I am referring to when I call competition a discovery procedure. Much would have to be added to clothe the bare bones of this abstract statement with concrete flesh, so as to show its full practical importance. But I must be content with thus briefly indicating the absurdity of the usual procedure of starting the analysis with a situation in which all the facts are supposed to be known. This is a *state* of affairs which economic theory curiously calls 'perfect competition'. It leaves no room whatever for the *activity* called competition, which is presumed to have already done its task. However, I must hurry on to examine a question, on which there exists even more confusion – namely, the meaning of the contention that the market adjusts activities spontaneously to the facts it discovers – or the question of the purpose for which it uses this information.

The prevailing confusion here is largely due to mistakenly treating the order which the market produces as an 'economy' in the strict sense of the word, and judging results of the market process by criteria which are appropriate only to such a single organised community serving a given hierarchy of ends. But such a hierarchy of ends is not relevant to the complex structure composed of countless individual economic arrangements. The latter, unfortunately, we also describe by the same word 'economy', although it is something fundamentally different, and must be judged by different standards.

---

4 Cf. Samuel Johnson in J. Boswell, *Life of Samuel Johnson*, L. F. Powell's revision of G. B. Hill's edition, Oxford, 1934, vol. II, p. 365 (18 April 1775): 'Knowledge is of two kinds. We know a subject ourselves, or we know where we can find information about it.'

Competition as a Discovery Procedure

An economy, in the strict sense of the word, is an organisation or arrangement in which someone deliberately allocates resources to a unitary order of ends. Spontaneous order produced by the market is nothing of the kind; and in important respects it does not behave like an economy proper. In particular, such spontaneous order differs because it does *not* ensure that what general opinion regards as more important needs are always satisfied before the less important ones. This is the chief reason why people object to it. Indeed, the whole of socialism is nothing but a demand that the market order (or catallaxy, as I like to call it, to prevent confusion with an economy proper)[5] should be turned into an economy in the strict sense, in which a common scale of importance determines which of the various needs are to be satisfied, and which are not to be satisfied.

The trouble with this socialist aim is a double one. As is true of every deliberate organisation, only the knowledge of the organiser can enter into the design of the economy proper, and all the members of such an economy, conceived as a deliberate organisation, must be guided in their actions by the unitary hierarchy of ends which it serves. On the other hand, advantages of the spontaneous order of the market, or the catallaxy, are correspondingly two. Knowledge that is used in it is that of all its members. Ends that it serves are the separate ends of those individuals, in all their variety and contrariness.

Out of this fact arise certain intellectual difficulties which worry not only socialists, but all economists who want to assess the accomplishments of the market order; because, if the market order does not serve a definite order of ends, indeed if, like any spontaneously formed order, it cannot legitimately be said to *have* particular ends, it is also not possible to express the value of the results as a sum of its particular individual products. What, then, do we mean when we claim that the market order produces in some sense a maximum or optimum?

The fact is, that, though the existence of a spontaneous order not made for a particular purpose cannot be properly said to have a purpose, it may yet be highly conducive to the achievement of many different individual purposes not known as a whole to any single person, or relatively small group of persons. Indeed, rational action is

5 For a fuller discussion see now my *Law, Legislation and Liberty*, vol. II, *The Mirage of Social Justice*, London and Chicago, 1976, pp. 107–20.

[183]

Competition as a Discovery Procedure

possible only in a fairly orderly world. Therefore it clearly makes sense to try to produce conditions under which the chances for any individual taken at random to achieve his ends as effectively as possible will be very high – even if it cannot be predicted which particular aims will be favoured, and which not.

As we have seen, the results of a discovery procedure are in their nature unpredictable; and all we can expect from the adoption of an effective discovery procedure is to improve the chances for unknown people. The only common aim which we can pursue by the choice of this technique of ordering social affairs is the general kind of pattern, or the abstract character, of the order that will form itself.

3

Economists usually ascribe the order which competition produces as an equilibrium – a somewhat unfortunate term, because such an equilibrium presupposes that the facts have already all been discovered and competition therefore has ceased. The concept of an 'order' which, at least for the discussion of problems of economic policy, I prefer to that of equilibrium, has the advantage that we can meaningfully speak about an order being approached to various degrees, and that order can be preserved throughout a process of change. While an economic equilibrium never really exists, there is some justification for asserting that the kind of order of which our theory describes an ideal type, is approached in a high degree.

This order manifests itself in the first instance in the circumstance that the expectations of transactions to be effected with other members of society, on which the plans of all the several economic subjects are based, can be mostly realised. This mutual adjustment of individual plans is brought about by what, since the physical sciences have also begun to concern themselves with spontaneous orders, or 'self-organising systems', we have learnt to call 'negative feedback'. Indeed, as intelligent biologists acknowledge, 'long before Claude Bernard, Clerk Maxwell, Walter B. Cannon, or Norbert Wiener developed cybernetics, Adam Smith has just as clearly used the idea in *The Wealth of Nations*. The "invisible hand" that regulated prices to a nicety is clearly this idea. In a free market, says Smith in effect, prices are regulated by negative feedback.'[6]

6 G. Hardin, *Nature and Man's Fate* (1951), Mentor ed. 1961, p. 54.

Competition as a Discovery Procedure

We shall see that the fact that a high degree of coincidence of expectations is brought about by the systematic disappointment of some kind of expectations is of crucial importance for an understanding of the functioning of the market order. But to bring about a mutual adjustment of individual plans is not all that the market achieves. It also secures that whatever is being produced will be produced by people who can do so more cheaply than (or at least as cheaply as) anybody who does not produce it (and cannot devote his energies to produce something else comparatively even more cheaply), and that each product is sold at a price lower than that at which anybody who in fact does not produce it could supply it. This, of course, does not exclude that some may make considerable profits over their costs if these costs are much lower than those of the next efficient potential producer. But it does mean that of the combination of commodities that is in fact produced, as much will be produced as we know to bring about by any known method. It will of course not be as much as we might produce if all the knowledge anybody possessed or can acquire were commanded by some one agency, and fed into a computer (the cost of finding out would, however, be considerable). Yet we do injustice to the achievement of the market if we judge it, as it were, from above, by comparing it with an ideal standard which we have no known way of achieving. If we judge it, as we ought to, from below, that is, if the comparison in this case is made against what we could achieve by any other method – especially against what would be produced if competition were prevented, so that only those to whom some authority had conferred the right to produce or sell particular things were allowed to do so. All we need to consider is how difficult it is in a competitive system to discover ways of supplying to consumers better or cheaper goods than they already get. Where such unused opportunities seem to exist we usually find that they remain undeveloped because their use is either prevented by the power of authority (including the enforcement of patent privileges), or by some private misuse of power which the law ought to prohibit.

It must not be forgotten that in this respect the market only brings about an approach towards some point on that n-dimensional surface, by which pure economic theory represents the horizon of all possibilities to which the production of any one proportional combination of commodities and services could conceivably be carried. The market leaves the particular combination of goods, and

[185]

Competition as a Discovery Procedure

its distribution among individuals, largely to unforeseeable circumstances – and, in this sense, to accident. It is, as Adam Smith already
understood,[7] as if we had agreed to play a game, partly of skill and
partly of chance. This competitive game, at the price of leaving the
share of each individual in some measure to accident, ensures
that the real equivalent of whatever his share turns out to be, is as
large as we know how to make it. The game is, to use up-to-date
language, not a zero-sum game, but one through which, by playing
it according to the rules, the pool to be shared is enlarged, leaving
individual shares in the pool in a great measure to chance. A mind
knowing all the facts could select any point he liked on the surface
and distribute this product in the manner he thought right. But the
only point on, or tolerably near, the horizon of possibilities which we
know how to reach is the one at which we shall arrive if we leave its
determination to the market. The so-called 'maximum' which we
thus reach naturally cannot be defined as a sum of particular things,
but only in terms of the chances it offers to unknown people to get as
large a real equivalent as possible for their relative shares, which
will be determined partly by accident. Simply because its results
cannot be assessed in terms of a single scale of values, as is the case in
an economy proper, it is very misleading to assess the results of a
catallaxy as if it were an economy.

4

Misinterpretation of the market order as an economy that can and
ought to satisfy different needs in a certain order of priority, shows
itself particularly in the efforts of policy to correct prices and incomes
in the interest of what is called 'social justice'. Whatever meaning
social philosophers have attached to this concept, in the practice of
economic policy it has almost always meant one thing, and one
thing only: the protection of certain groups against the necessity to
descend from the absolute or relative material position which they
have for some time enjoyed. Yet this is not a principle on which it is
possible to act generally without destroying the foundations of the
market order. Not only continuous increase, but in certain circumstances even mere maintenance of the existing level of incomes,
depends on adaptation to unforeseen changes. This necessarily

7 Adam Smith, *The Theory of Moral Sentiments*, London, 1759, part VI, chapter 2, penul-
timate paragraph, and part VII, section II, chapter 1.

Competition as a Discovery Procedure

involves the relative, and perhaps even the absolute, share of some having to be reduced, although they are in no way responsible for the reduction.

The point to keep constantly in mind is that *all* economic adjustment is made necessary by unforeseen changes; and the whole reason for employing the price mechanism is to tell individuals that what they are doing, or can do, has for some reason for which they are not responsible become less or more demanded. Adaptation of the whole order of activities to changed circumstances rests on the remuneration derived from different activities being changed, without regard to the merits or faults of those affected.

The term 'incentives' is often used in this connection with somewhat misleading connotations, as if the main problem were to induce people to exert themselves sufficiently. However, the chief guidance which prices offer is not so much how to act, but *what to do*. In a continuously changing world even mere maintenance of a given level of wealth requires incessant changes in the direction of the efforts of some, which will be brought about only if the remuneration of some activities is increased and that of others decreased. With these adjustments, which under relatively stable conditions are needed merely to maintain the income stream, no 'surplus' is available which can be used to compensate those against whom prices turn. Only in a rapidly growing system can we hope to avoid absolute declines in the position of some groups.

Modern economists seem in this connection often to overlook that even the relative stability shown by many of those aggregates which macro-economics treats as data, is itself the result of a micro-economic process, of which changes in relative prices are an essential part. It is only thanks to the market mechanism that someone else is induced to step in and fill the gap caused by the failure of anyone to fulfil the expectations of his partners. Indeed, all those aggregate demand and supply curves with which we like to operate are not really objectively given facts, but results of the process of competition going on all the time. Nor can we hope to learn from statistical information what changes in prices or incomes are necessary in order to bring about adjustments to the inevitable changes.

The chief point, however, is that in a democratic society it would be wholly impossible by commands to bring about changes which are not felt to be just, and the necessity of which could never be clearly demonstrated. Deliberate regulation in such a political system must

[187]

Competition as a Discovery Procedure

always aim at securing prices which appear to be just. This means in practice preservation of the traditional structure of incomes and prices. An economic system in which each gets what others think he deserves would necessarily be a highly inefficient system – quite apart from its being also an intolerably oppressive system. Every 'incomes policy' is therefore more likely to prevent than to facilitate those changes in the price and income structures that are required to adapt the system to new circumstances.

It is one of the paradoxes of the present world that the communist countries are probably freer from the incubus of 'social justice', and more willing to let those bear the burden against whom developments turn, than are the 'capitalist' countries. For some Western countries at least the position seems hopeless, precisely because the ideology dominating their politics makes changes impossible that are necessary for the position of the working class to rise sufficiently fast to lead to the disappearance of this ideology.

5

If even in highly developed economic systems competition is important as a process of exploration in which prospectors search for unused opportunities that, when discovered, can also be used by others, this is to an even greater extent true of underdeveloped societies. My first attention has been deliberately given to problems of preserving an efficient order for conditions in which most resources and techniques are generally known, and constant adaptations of activities are made necessary only by inevitably minor changes, in order to maintain a given level of incomes. I will not consider here the undoubted role competition plays in the advance of technological knowledge. But I do want to point out how much more important it must be in countries where the chief task is to discover yet unknown opportunities of a society in which in the past competition has not been active. It may not be altogether absurd, although largely erroneous, to believe that we can foresee and control the structure of society which further technological advance will produce in already highly developed countries. But it is simply fantastic to believe that we can determine in advance the social structure in a country where the chief problem still is to discover what material and human resources are available, or that for such a country we can predict the particular consequences of any measures we may take.

Competition as a Discovery Procedure

Apart from the fact that there is in such countries so much more to be discovered, there is still another reason why the greatest freedom of competition seems to be even more important there than in more advanced countries. This is that required changes in habits and customs will be brought about only if the few willing and able to experiment with new methods can make it necessary for the many to follow them, and at the same time to show them the way. The required discovery process will be impeded or prevented, if the many are able to keep the few to the traditional ways. Of course, it is one of the chief reasons for the dislike of competition that it not only shows how things can be done more effectively, but also confronts those who depend for their incomes on the market with the alternative of imitating the more successful or losing some or all of their income. Competition produces in this way a kind of impersonal compulsion which makes it necessary for numerous individuals to adjust their way of life in a manner that no deliberate instructions or commands could bring about. Central direction in the service of so-called 'social justice' may be a luxury rich nations can afford, perhaps for a long time, without too great an impairment of their incomes. But it is certainly not a method by which poor countries can accelerate their adaptation to rapidly changing circumstances, on which their growth depends.

Perhaps it deserves mention in this connection that possibilities of growth are likely to be greater the more extensive are a country's yet unused opportunities. Strange though this may seem at first sight, a high rate of growth is more often than not evidence that opportunities have been neglected in the past. Thus, a high rate of growth can sometimes testify to bad policies of the past rather than good policies of the present. Consequently it is unreasonable to expect in already highly developed countries as high a rate of growth as can for some time be achieved in countries where effective utilisation of resources was previously long prevented by legal and institutional obstacles.

From all I have seen of the world the proportion of private persons who are prepared to try new possibilities, if they appear to them to promise better conditions, and if they are not prevented by the pressure of their fellows, is much the same everywhere. The much lamented absence of a spirit of enterprise in many of the new countries is not an unalterable characteristic of the individual inhabitants, but the consequence of restraints which existing customs

[189]

Competition as a Discovery Procedure

and institutions place upon them. This is why it would be fatal in such societies for the collective will to be allowed to direct the efforts of individuals, instead of governmental power being confined to protecting individuals against the pressures of society. Such protection for private initiatives and enterprise can only ever be achieved through the institution of private property and the whole aggregate of libertarian institutions of law.

[15]

Prices, the Communication of Knowledge, and the Discovery Process
Israel M. Kirzner

Among the fundamental contributions that Professor Hayek has made to economic science, certainly one of the most significant and far-reaching must be judged to be his path-breaking articulation of the nature of the "economic problem which society faces".[1] It was in this context that Hayek decisively drew the attention of the economics profession to the unique problems that arise from the *dispersal of knowledge*.

> The economic problem of society is ... not merely a problem of how to allocate 'given' resources – if 'given' is taken to mean given to a single mind which deliberately solves the problem set by these 'data'. It is rather a problem, of how to secure the best use of resources known to any of the members of society, for ends whose relative importance only these individuals know. Or, to put it briefly, it is a problem of the utilization of knowledge which is not given to anyone in its totality.[2]

Hayek's insight represented a breakthrough, of course, in the modern history of welfare economics, as well as providing a brilliant new way of stating the crucial arguments making up the "Austrian" side of the socialist-economic-calculation debate.[3] In addition, however, Hayek's emphasis on the role of knowledge constituted an important step forward in our understanding of the way in which markets work, and of how the price system in fact tends to solve the economic problem which society faces. Indeed it seems to be this aspect of Hayek's contribution that has attracted the most attention in the economics profession. While accounts of modern developments in welfare economics rarely refer to Hayek's dismissal of the allocative-efficiency criterion (in favor of the "coordination" perspective), and while accounts of the socialist-economic-calculation debate have, notoriously, thoroughly and unforgivably muddled it up,[4] Hayek's insights into the role of prices in solving the knowledge-dispersal problem have been widely cited, and often by the most orthodox of neo-classical economists. I shall argue in this paper that in spite of its citation of Hayek's work in this regard, the economic literature has regrettably failed to do justice to the full significance of that work. As a result professional concern with problems of knowledge dispersal has tended to remain, unfortunately, at a rather superficial level. In demonstrating the validity of this assertion it will be necessary to distinguish sharply between two quite different "communications" challenges arising out of knowledge-dispersal, and (consequently) two quite different functions that markets may possibly fulfil in the context of the "economic problem which society faces". It may perhaps be helpful to start with an analogy drawn from a rather different context, that of automobile traffic through a busy urban street intersection.

Automobiles and the Problem of Dispersed Knowledge

Consider cars approaching the intersection of two urban streets, the one north-south, the other east-west. The driver of a car approaching from (say) the north, must decide whether or not to stop before proceeding south across the east-west street. The driver's decision will depend on his knowledge or expectations concerning the decisions that the drivers of other cars (that may possibly be driving towards the intersection from the other directions) will make when *they* reach the cross-roads. In order for traffic to move smoothly and safely through the intersection it is clearly necessary that these various decisions be somehow *coordinated*. Absence of coordination may, rather obviously result in regrettable, costly (because perhaps quite unnecessary) delays at the intersection before proceeding through it, or in even more regrettable and costly automobile collisions. It is easy to see that such regrettable events are to be attributed at least in part to the dispersal of knowledge: the driver of one car knows, at the moment when he makes his decision, what he has decided to do, but the drivers of other cars do not know what the first driver has decided (or perhaps even that there *is* this first driver.) *Their* decisions are then likely to fail to be coordinated as well as is possible with that of the first driver, and so on. Were an omniscient single mind to make the decisions for *all* the drivers, that mind might arrange the drivers' actions in smooth and safe fashion. In the absence of such a central omniscient mind, a well-designed (and fully enforced) system of traffic signals, can achieve coordination by providing each driver of a vehicle with confident assurance as to what the other drivers will decide to do. The green light beckoning a southward-bound driver is in fact assuring him that cars proceeding in the east-west street will not cross the intersection in the immediate minute or minutes ahead. A red light directs him to stop, while at the same time it provides conviction (in a well-designed system) that the waiting is not wasted (since it implies that cars are being permitted to proceed east and west). By timing the light-changes appropriately, smoothly coordinated traffic conditions can be achieved. Let us analyze what we mean when we say that a signal system "achieves coordination". It will be convenient to focus on the manner in which the system eliminates *unnecessary delays*. (Rather similar considerations apply to the system's elimination of avoidable collisions.)

A successful traffic signalling system will not only succeed in avoiding collisions, it will avoid requiring cars to wait needlessly (such as at times when traffic along the other direction is extremely light.)
Superior coordination would permit the timing of light-changes to reflect the relative intensities of traffic along the two intersecting streets. "To achieve coordination" is thus a phrase which, in the context of the automobile example, can have two quite distinct meanings.

First, a traffic signal system may be said to be achieving coordination when its timing is, from the very installation of the system, such as in fact to control the flow of traffic in some optimal manner. No undesired collisions, no unjustified waiting, result from unanimous obedience of the traffic signals. This successful achievement of coordination has clearly involved the efficient communication of correct information. The information fed to the drivers of cars has been such as (a) correctly to inform each of them of the consequences of the decisions of other drivers, leading them, in turn, (b) in fact to make those decisions that permit this above property (a) to hold, with the resulting set of drivers' decisions being such as (c) to result in no unnecessary waiting. This is certainly a valid sense of the phrase "to achieve coordination". But a second possible meaning may be intended by use of this phrase.

For this second meaning consider a traffic signal system that is, when installed, timed sub-optimally. Southbound drivers find themselves waiting at red lights, let us say at 3:00 in the afternoon, for several minutes during which no traffic flows at all in the east-west directions. Clearly this waiting is unnecessary; it means that north-south drivers are compelled to act in a fashion that is not coordinated with the decisions of east-west drivers (since the latter have decided not to pass through the intersection at this time, yet the former have been prevented from taking advantage of those east-west decisions.) But imagine now that the signal system is programmed in a manner that, at the beginning of each day, alters the system's timing to reflect yesterday's actual time-profile of traffic experience (registering not only the dearth of traffic in the east-west direction at three in the afternoon, but also the heavy volume of traffic in the north-south direction). Then the very experience that results today from the as-yet-imperfectly coordinated system plays its part in bringing about a revision in the system's timing, in a way that substitutes a better-coordinated system in place of the less-coordinated one. This kind of signal system (including its property of improving itself by "learning" from the unfortunate results of its earlier imperfections) may also be described as one that "achieves coordination". However here the phrase refers to the property of the system that permits it to identify and begin to correct its earlier weaknesses. The system begins its coordinating task at the very time when its signals promote *un*coordinated activity on the part of drivers – since it is that very uncoordinated activity that provides the information necessary for improved timing. The system's ability to achieve coordination, in this sense, certainly does *not* mean that, at the outset, it achieved the sets of results (a), (b), and (c), described in the preceding paragraph. Drivers proceeding south who have been directed to wait needlessly at the red light have, in effect, been informed *incorrectly* concerning the rate of traffic flow in the east-west direction. Yet, as we have seen, the system has, from the very outset, possessed the property of "achieving coordination" in the sense of incorporating a feedback mechanism that deploys the results of its own inadequacies towards their systematic elimination. Here too the coordinating property of the system arises from the way that it provides information – but in a sense quite different from that relevant to the system that is *already* perfectly timed. In this second, initially faulty system, the coordinating properties arise from its ability *to communicate information concerning its own faulty information-communication properties.*

Let us return to the role of the price system in coping with the problems arising from dispersed knowledge – the "economic problem which society faces". We shall find (a) that prices tend to "achieve coordination" in *both* of the senses we have noticed in the traffic signal example, while (b) the literature has in fact recognized (and cited Hayek in regard to) only one of these two senses.

Equilibrium Prices and Market Coordination

Economists often speak, nowadays, of the competitive equilibrium price system as an effective way in which the individual decisions of many market participants can be coordinated. Prices are, indeed, often compared to signals. Without knowing the details concerning the preferences of other market participants, or concerning the conditions surrounding production processes, decision makers are, through the guidance of these price signals, led – economists explain – to that pattern of attempted activities that permits all of them to be carried out without disappointment and without regret.

In the Marshallian market for a single commodity, for example, the equilibrium market price for that commodity inspires the pattern of market clearing bids and offers. The price is such as to motivate potential buyers to ask for exactly that aggregate quantity of the commodity that potential suppliers have been motivated – by that same price – to produce. No buyer has been misled by the lowness of the price to seek to buy *more* than is in fact offered for sale. (And no buyer is discouraged from bidding for what is in fact available to him at a price he is prepared to pay.) No supplier has been misled by the height of this price to seek to produce more than is in fact being sought to be bought. (Nor is any supplier discouraged from offering that for which a price acceptable to him can be obtained.) No buyer need in fact know anything at all about the conditions of supply, the availabilities or the costs of inputs, and the like. Nor need any seller know anything about the preferences of consumers, the availability to them of substitute commodities, and the like. All that market participants need to know, for the Marshallian market to coordinate buying and selling conditions perfectly, is the prevailing equilibrium price of the commodity. By offering to buy all they wish to buy at this price, buyers find that their offers smoothly dovetail with the offers of sellers to sell (with the latter merely offering to sell all they wish to sell at this same prevailing equilibrium price.) The equilibrium price coordinates. All this is of course well understood, and is part of the basic equipment common to all economists.

Hayek's emphasis on knowledge is frequently cited in the context of this understanding of what equilibrium prices can achieve. Equilibrium prices are explained to be communicating to potential buyers and sellers, in highly economical fashion, the information necessary for coordinated decisions to emerge. It is because the detailed information concerning the preferences of individual potential buyers, and concerning the peculiar productive capabilities of individual sources of potential supply, is so scattered and dispersed, that the coordinative ability of the equilibrium price system is so valuable and impressive.

This kind of coordinative ability recognized as being possessed by equilibrium prices, is clearly analogous to the ability of an optimally-timed traffic signal system, smoothly and safely to coordinate traffic.[5] Equilibrium prices, like optimally-timed signal changes, correctly communicate the information that (by virtue of the very notion of "correctness" in this context) motivates and enables individual decision makers to generate a smoothly dovetailing set of decisions; a set that will entail neither disappointment nor regret. We must now show that, in addition to this possible sense in which prices may be said to achieve coordination (i. e. when the prices are already equilibrium prices – analogous to the already-optimally-timed signal system), there is also a much more important other possible sense in which prices may be said to achieve coordination. This sense refers to the possible ability of *dis*equilibrium prices to generate systematic changes in market decisions about price offers and bids, in a way that, by responding to the regrettable results of initially *un*coordinated sets of decisions, tends to replace them by less uncoordinated sets. (Here, of course, the analogy is to the non-optimally-timed traffic signal system that contains a feedback mechanism through which the regrettable results of initial poor timing generate a tendency towards improved timing.[6])

Disequilibrium Prices and Market Coordination

Consider the market for a single commodity (say, a given quality of tea) that has *not* attained equilibrium. Imagine, for example, that in different parts of this market there have occurred during the past "day", sales of tea at widely differing prices. Imagine, moreover, that by the end of the day the total quantity of tea that has changed hands is far less than that which the realities of supply and demand conditions in fact warrant. So that potential suppliers remain holding inventories of tea which could, in truth, have been reduced by sale to eager buyers at prices that these suppliers would have found attractive. These market conditions express the coordination failures that have occurred: prices have failed to clear the market. The signals offered by bids and offers have failed to generate completely dovetailing sets of decisions; market participants, because of inadequate information concerning each other's attitudes, preferences, and capabilities, have failed to take advantage of existing opportunities for mutually gainful exchange.

These unfortunate market conditions can be expected to result, sooner or later, in both disappointment and regret. Disappointment and regret may occur because sooner or later buyers will, perhaps, realize that, had they offered higher prices, they could have obtained more tea (and that they would have been happy to do so, even at the higher price, rather than go without tea because they foolishly believed it would be forthcoming at lower prices). Or sellers may realize that they might, had they only offered to sell at lower prices, have sold more tea (and that they would have preferred to do so rather than refusing to sell because of a mistaken belief that higher prices were available). In these cases disappointments arise as buyers (sellers) discover that their hopes to buy (sell) at low (high) prices were unrealistic. Regrets arise at not having realized that they would have been better advised to have offered to buy (sell) at higher (lower) prices. In addition, of course, since tea was sold at many different prices during the same day, many of those who sold (bought) at the low (high) prices will regret not having done so at the higher (lower) prices at which in fact tea exchanged elsewhere in the very same market.

These disappointments and regrets may generate sharp changes in the decisions made by potential buyers and sellers (even in the absence of change in the sets of "real" determinants of their preferences and productive capabilities). Buyers who paid the high prices and sellers who accepted the low prices, may revise their market attitudes, so that a tendency towards a uniform price may occur. Buyers (or sellers) who had overestimated the willingness of potential suppliers (or buyers) to sell (or buy) will realize their earlier errors and adjust their offers to the realities. In fact it is precisely because all these adjustments are likely to cause the initial sets of prices to give way to a different set (a set perhaps less divergent, and perhaps less likely to generate disappointments and regrets), that the initial market must be described as having been in disequilibrium. Without any outside forces whatever (such as changes in preferences or in supply conditions) the initial sets of buying and selling offers are likely to give way to different sets. Where the changes generated in this way are systematically in the direction of better-coordinated sets of decisions (than in the initial period), we may, surely, describe the market (even in its early, grossly discoordinated state) as possessing, to some degree, an ability to achieve coordination. The very disappointments and regrets that result from initial coordination-failures, systematically bring about improved sets of market decisions. Here the appropriate analogy, surely, is to the initially faulty traffic signal system.[7]

It should be noticed that here too the "coordinative properties" of the (disequilibrium) market derive from the ability of prices to communicate information, *but in a sense quite different from that in which equilibrium prices may be said to coordinate through the accurate communication of information.* Equilibrium prices coordinate because they are *already* so adjusted ("pre-reconciled") that decisions that take these prices into account turn out to be mutually reinforcing. Disequilibrium prices can, if at all, be described as "coordinating" only in the sense that they reveal, to alert market participants, how *altered* decisions on their part (from those that contributed to the emergence of these disequilibrium prices) may be wiser for the future. Thus disequilibrium prices that are "too low" (and which therefore generated excess demand) suggest to some disappointed buyers that they should offer to pay higher prices. Or again, to the extent that disequilibrium has manifested itself in the emergence of many prices in the same market for tea, this very spread between high and low prices, suggests to some alert entrepreneurs that arbitrage profits may be won through offering to buy at somewhat higher (than the lowest) prices and simultaneously offering to sell elsewhere at somewhat lower (than the highest) prices. The information that inspires these "coordinating" changes is indeed information that is supplied by the initial structure of prices, but is so supplied only through alert *realization of the failures* of those initial prices to achieve the kind of coordination that we found in the case of equilibrium prices.

Dispersed Knowledge, the Price System, and Economic Literature

We have thus seen that the Hayekian insights into the nature of the economic problem facing society permit us to recognize the coordinative role of prices in a sense far more important than that played by equilibrium prices. The circumstance that information is dispersed offers society a "communication" challenge not only because even the most fully coordinated set of decentralized decisions must *presuppose* and *contain* an effective signalling system. The circumstance that information is dispersed offers society a far more important "communications" challenge – that of generating flows of information or of signals that might somehow stimulate the *revision* of initially *un*coordinated decisions in the direction of greater mutual coordinatedness.

So long as economists saw the economic problem to be one of achieving an efficient allocation of social resources (in the same way as the individual economizer faces the problem of private resource allocation), there could, of course, hardly be appreciation for the "coordinative" contributions to social well-being that a price system can offer in helping overcome the problem of dispersed knowledge. As is by now fairly widely understood, as a consequence of what we have learned from Hayek, to talk of the problem of efficiently allocating society's resources is completely *to assume away and thus to overlook* the dispersed knowledge problem.

What is disappointing, in the way in which the profession has absorbed the Hayekian lesson, is that the literature appears to have failed to grasp the way in which the price system meets the "communications" challenge, offered by the circumstance of dispersed knowledge, that we have described as being by far the more important one. Instead it appears to have focussed entirely on the more superficial sense in which a price system may be said to communicate information, viz. on the signalling role fulfilled by equilibrium prices.

Now, for textbook purposes this limited exploitation of the Hayekian insights is arguably understandable and defensible. Thus a number of contemporary textbooks[8] cite Hayek's well-known example of the tin market.

Assume that somewhere in the world a new opportunity for the use of ... tin, has arisen, or that one of the sources of supply of tin has been eliminated. It does not matter for our purpose – and it is significant that it does not matter – which of these two causes has made tin more scarce. All that the users of tin need to know is that ... they must economize tin. There is no need for the great majority of them even to know ... in favor of what other needs they ought to husband the supply ... The mere fact that there is one price for any commodity ... brings about the solution which ... might have been arrived at by one single mind possessing all the information which is in fact dispersed among all the people involved in the process.[9]

201

It is certainly true that this particular example of Hayek's is concerned only with the communication-of-information function fulfilled by equilibrium prices. (This is quite clear, for example, from the concluding sentences referring to the single price and to the coincidence between the results of there being a single price for tin throughout the market, and the solution that might be arrived at by a single omniscient mind.) This example does not focus on the communication problem that confronts a price system in which, as yet, the bewildering arrays of market prices reflect only highly *un*coordinated decisions on the parts of potential buyers and sellers. Yet there is no need to criticize the textbooks for not going beyond the simplest communication function of prices. There can be no doubt that an understanding of this simpler Hayekian lesson at the beginning of one's study of economics can be profoundly beneficial.

What is more puzzling is that the deeper implications of the Hayekian lesson have somehow failed to be noticed, not only in the textbooks, but also in the more advanced literature that has referred to Hayek's contribution. Thus, a considerable mathematical literature has emerged exploring the extent to which market prices convey information in the face of stochastic supply and/or demand conditions.[10] The questions asked in this literature concern whether or not uninformed market participants can derive correct information from market prices themselves. Nowhere, in this literature, is there inquiry as to whether entrepreneurial alertness and motivation may perhaps be "switched on" by the configuration of market prices, to conjecture (and to try out!) hunches that may in fact be closer to the truth (than the information that the prices themselves reflect.) Similarly, in what must surely be regarded as the most extensive and wide-ranging development of the implications of the Hayekian insights, Thomas Sowell's monumental *Knowledge and Decisions,* one looks in vain for any discussion of the way in which prices and price differences may stimulate a deployment of existing information, that might be superior to that which these prices themselves express.

To emphasize, as Sowell does throughout his work, that prices *summarize* economic knowledge,[11] is of unquestioned value. But this insight into the relationship between prices and knowledge ignores the far more important truth that it is the very *inadequacies* that cloud the manner in which these price-summaries express existing knowledge, that create the market incentives for their modification. The profit opportunities embedded in existing prices are thus extraordinarily effective communicators of knowledge (in a sense quite different from that in which prices summarize knowledge). So that governmentally imposed obstacles to price flexibility not only (as Sowell so well, and in such rich detail, explains) prevent prices from telling the truth – they smother the emergence of those disequilibrium-price-generated incentives upon which the system depends for its very ability to discover and announce the truth.

Hayek and the Market Discovery Process

Hayek himself was, (especially in the earlier work in which he developed his seminal insights concerning the social significance of the circumstance of dispersed knowledge), not as explicit as one might have wished on the role of prices in the discovery process of the market. A reader mistakenly believing that the only sense in which prices may be said to carry information is that in which equilibrium prices correctly reflect ("summarize") the true supply and demand conditions, might be excused for coming away from a reading of Hayek's papers on knowledge of 1937 and of 1945 without sensing any challenge to that belief. Although a number of passages in these earlier papers of Hayek criticized the standard view among welfare economists and others (viz. the view that saw the economic problem as that of securing an efficient allocation by society of its given scarce resources) as reflecting undue emphasis on the equilibrium state,[12] these papers did not explicitly show how disequilibrium prices play their role in solving Hayek's problems of dispersed knowledge. Yet, as we have seen, there can be no doubt, once one has understood the coordination problems implied by dispersed knowledge, about the role of disequilibrium prices in this regard. That Hayek did in fact intend his formulation of the knowledge problem to include also the role of prices in providing the incentives for their own modification, appears clear from his discussions of competition-as a process, and particularly from his later work on competition as a discovery procedure.[13]

In Hayek's 1946 lecture "The Meaning of Competition", Hayek brilliantly distinguished the *state* of perfect competition from the dynamic competitive *process*. One of the conditions required for the former is perfect knowledge; the central achievement of the latter is that "it is

only through the process of competition that the facts will be discovered".
When Hayek in this paper talks of "spreading information" (pp. 96, 106),
he is not referring to the instantaneous transmission, through
equilibrium price signals, of already known information. He is referring,
instead, to the "process of the formation of opinion" (p. 106). This
process of opinion-formation is one built out of series of entrepreneurial
steps, made possible by competitive freedom of entrepreneurial entry,
and exemplified by the entry of one "who possesses the exclusive
knowledge ... to reduce the cost of production of a commodity by 50
percent" and thus "reduces its price by ... 25 percent" (p. 101).

These insights were deepened and made even more explicit in Hayek's
later "Competition as a Discovery Procedure". In this paper what is
emphasized is not that prices act as signals transmitting existing
information – but rather that it is the competitive process which *digs out*
what is in fact discovered. The competitive process relies upon market
data at any particular time only in the sense that "provisional results from
the market process at each stage ... tell individuals what to look for".[14]
The "high-degree of coincidence of expectations" that the market
achieves "is brought about by the systematic disappointment of some
kind of expectations".[15]   The "generally beneficial effects of competition must include disappointing or defeating some particular expectations or intentions".[16]   In fact, "competition is valuable *only* because,
and so far as, its results are unpredictable and on the whole different from
those which anyone has, or could have, deliberately aimed at".[17]

What emerges from these Hayekian insights into the *discovery*
properties inherent in the competitive process, is the recognition, surely,
that the incentives offered by market prices *during* this competitive
process, are the key elements in motivating competitive-entrepreneurial
entry and discovery. In this sense prices play a role in "spreading
information" quite different from their role as signals communicating
already discovered information under equilibrium conditions.

Communication and Discovery

Equilibrium prices permit market participants to "read" the relevant
information needed for their activities to be mutually adjusted in
coordinated fashion. Disequilibrium prices are far less helpful in this
regard; in fact a good deal of the "information" that trusting market

participants "learn" from disequilibrium prices is quite incorrect and may be responsible for waste and frustration. As communicators, as signals, disequilibrium prices are relatively poor performers (when compared, of course, with the questionably-relevant standard set in this regard by equilibrium prices). Indeed, markets and the market system have often been criticized for the coordination failures that disequilibrium prices both express and help generate. What Hayek's "Austrian" insights permit us to see is that the social function served by market prices is captured far more significantly by the concept of *discovery*, than by that of communication.

In regard to discovery, market prices (especially disequilibrium prices) should be seen not so much as known signals to be deliberately consulted *in order to find out* the right thing to do, but rather as spontaneously-generated flashing red lights *alerting* hitherto unwitting market participants to the possibility of pure entrepreneurial profit or the danger of loss. These discoveries, surely, constitute the crucial steps through which markets tend to achieve coordination, gradually replacing earlier states of widespread mutual ignorance by successively better-coordinated states of society.

No doubt the economics profession has much to learn about the subtle manner in which this market discovery procedure works. Surely the future historian of economic thought will trace back future development in this branch of social understanding, to those seminal and pathbreaking papers in which Hayek taught us the crucial importance of dispersed knowledge in creating *the* economic problem which society faces.

Notes

The author gratefully acknowledges the stimulation of and the ideas contained in a paper, presented at the Austrian Economics Colloquium at New York University, by S. Ikeda, "An Essay on Equilibrium Prices, Disequilibrium Prices, and Information".

[1] F. A. Hayek, "The Use of Knowledge in Society", *American Economic Review, 35*, September 1945, reprinted in F. A. Hayek, *Individualism and Economic Order* (London: Routledge and Kegan Paul, 1949), p. 77. (Page numbers in this note and in all subsequent notes referring to Hayek's work refer, unless otherwise specified, to this book.)
[2] *Op. cit.* pp. 77–78.
[3] On this see particularly D. Lavoie's forthcoming book on the history of the socialist-economic-calculation debate.
[4] D. Lavoie, *op. cit.*

5 An important limitation in this analogy is that, for a traffic signal system to be effective, it must depend on some *extraneous* circumstance (e. g. compulsion, or custom) to provide assurance that signals will in fact be obeyed by all drivers. No such extraneous circumstance is required in the case of the equilibrium price system. The very *meaning* of such a system is that the set of prices is such as spontaneously to motivate directly a completely coordinated set of activities.

6 Here, too, the analogy is incomplete. As will be seen in the next section of the paper, the errors expressed in disequilibrium prices generate disappointments and regrets that may motivate those responsible for the errors *themselves* to revise, for subsequent periods, their bids and offers. For the traffic signal system we had to assume that someone in control, (or some robot), responds to the consequences of imperfect timing: the signals which changed at the "wrong" time do not improve their timing as a result of their own determination to "learn" from past "errors" and "regrets", their timing is changed by someone, or some machine, from the "outside".

7 For a more detailed account of such a coordination process see the writer's *Market Theory and the Price System* (Princeton: Van Nostrand, 1963) chapter 7.

8 See, for example, H. Kohler, *Intermediate Microeconomics, Theory and Applications* (Scott, Foresman and Co., 1982) pp. 28f; E. Dolan, *Basic Economics*, 3rd Edition, (The Dryden Press, 1983), p. 62; J. D. Gwartney and R. Stroup, *Economics, Private and Public Choice*, 3rd Edition, (Academic Press, 1982), chapter 3, especially pp. 56f. (On pp. 57f. this book goes beyond the communication role of prices in equilibrium to draw attention to the coordination properties of entrepreneurial activity in the dynamic market process.)

9 Hayek, "Use of Knowledge in Society", pp. 85f.

10 See, e. g. S. Grossman, "On the Efficiency of Competitive Stock Markets Where Traders Have Diverse Information", *Journal of Finance*, May 1976, *31*, pp. 573–85; S. Grossman and J. E. Stiglitz, "Information and Competitive Price Systems", *American Economic Review Proceedings*, May 1976, *66*, pp. 246–53; S. Grossman and J. E. Stiglitz, "On the Impossibility of Informationally Efficient Markets", *American Economic Review*, June 1980, *70*, pp. 393–402; R. Frydman, "Towards an Understanding of Market Processes: Individual Expectations, Learning and Convergence to Rational Expectations Equilibrium", *American Economic Review*, September 1982, *72*, pp. 652–668.

11 See especially T. Sowell, *Knowledge and Decisions* (Basic Books, 1980), p. 38.

12 See e. g. Hayek, *Individualism and Economic Order*, p. 93 ftn. 2; p. 188.

13 See F. A. Hayek, "The Meaning of Competition", "Competition as a Discovery Procedure", first presented as a lecture in 1968, reprinted in F. A. Hayek, *New Studies in Philosophy, Politics, Economics and the History of Ideas*, (Chicago: University of Chicago Press, 1978).

14 "Competition as a Discovery Procedure", p. 181.

15 *Ibid.* p.185.

16 *Ibid.* p. 180.

17 *Ibid.*

[16]

Chapter Six

GOVERNMENT REGULATION AND THE MARKET DISCOVERY PROCESS

The perils associated with government regulation of the economy addressed here arise out of the *impact that regulation can be expected to have on the discovery process, which the unregulated market tends to generate.* Even if current market outcomes in some sense are judged unsatisfactory, intervention, and even intervention that can successfully achieve its immediate objectives, cannot be considered the obviously correct solution. After all, the very problems apparent in the market might generate processes of discovery and correction superior to those undertaken deliberately by government regulation; deliberate intervention by the state not only might serve as an imperfect substitute for the spontaneous market process of discovery; but also might impede desirable processes of discovery the need for which has *not* been perceived by the government. Again, government regulation itself may generate new (unintended and undesired) processes of market adjustments that produce a final outcome even less preferred than what might have emerged in the free market.

The Perils of Regulation: A Market-Process Approach   137

Here I discuss critically the impact of government
regulation on the discovery process of the unregulated
market at four distinct levels. First, I consider the likelihood that would-be regulators may not correctly assess
the course the market might itself take in the absence of
regulation. Second, I consider the likelihood that, because
of the presumed absence of entrepreneurial incentives operating on government decision makers, government regulatory decisions will fail to exploit opportunities for
social betterment waiting to be discovered. Third, I consider the likelihood that government regulation may stifle or inhibit desirable discovery processes which the
market might have generated. Finally, I consider the likelihood that government regulation may influence the
market by creating opportunities for new, and not necessarily desirable, market discovery processes which would
not be relevant in an unregulated market.

The Undiscovered Discovery Process

We assumed earlier that regulation is demanded because of undesirable conditions that emerge in the market
in the absence of regulation. But the urge to regulate, to
control, to alter these outcomes must presume not only
that these undesirable conditions are attributable to the
absence of regulation, but also that the speedy removal of
such conditions cannot be expected from the future course
of unregulated market events. To attribute undesirable
conditions to absence of regulation, moreover, also may
require the denial of the proposition that were a better
state of affairs indeed feasible, the market probably would
have already discovered how to achieve it.

More specifically, many demands for government
intervention into the market rest on one or both of two
possible misunderstandings concerning the market discovery process. Demand for government intervention, on
the one hand, might grow out of a failure to realize that
the market already may have discovered virtually everything worth discovering (so that what appears to be ob-

vious inefficiency might be able to be explained altogether satisfactorily if government officials had all the information the market has long since discovered and taken
advantage of). Demand for regulation, on the other hand,
may stem from the belief that unsatisfactory conditions
will never be corrected unless by deliberate intervention.
Such demands for regulation might be muted, that is,
were it understood that genuine inefficiencies can be relied upon in the *future* to generate market processes for
their own correction. (This second misunderstanding itself may rest on either of two bases. First, the tendency of
markets to discover and eliminate inefficiency simply is
not recognized. Second, by contrast, it is assumed, far too
sanguinely, that market processes are *so* rapid that our
awareness of an unmistakably unsatisfactory condition
proves that some kind of market "failure" has occurred
and that one cannot rely on future corrective processes.)

These misunderstandings, so often the foundation
for demands for intervention, surely derive from an unawareness of several basic principles of the theory of market process. These principles show that, first, were
knowledge perfect, it would be inconceivable that unexploited opportunities could yet remain for rearranging the
pattern of input utilization or output consumption in
such a way as to improve the well-being of all market
participants; second, the existence of such unexploited
opportunities, reflecting imperfect knowledge throughout the market, expresses itself in the unregulated market
in the form of opportunities for pure entrepreneurial profit; and third, the tendency for such pure profit opportunities to be discovered and exploited tends more or less
rapidly to eliminate unexploited opportunities for improving the allocation of resources.[27] These principles of
the theory of market process suggest that if genuine inefficiency exists, then (perhaps because of a recent sudden
change in conditions of resource supply, of technology, or
of consumer tastes) the market has not yet discovered *all
that it will surely soon tend to discover.*

These principles may be denied either by expressing a lack of confidence in the systematic tendency for imperfect knowledge to be spontaneously improved or by attributing to the market the ability to attain equilibrium instantaneously (that is, by assuming that ignorance is not merely a disequilibrium phenomenon, but that ignorance disappears the very instant it emerges). Both denials may lead to demands for government intervention. The denial based on a lack of confidence about improving knowledge leads to the belief that current inefficiencies will not tend to be corrected spontaneously (and also to the propensity to see inefficiency where the market *already* has made necessary corrections). The denial based on the belief in instantaneous correction of disequilibrium conditions leads to the view that existing inefficiencies somehow are consistent with market equilibrium and that therefore extramarket steps are called for to achieve correction.

THE UNSIMULATED DISCOVERY PROCESS

Government regulation takes the general form of imposed price ceilings and floors, of mandated quality specifications, and of other restraints or requirements imposed in interpersonal market transactions. The hope surrounding such government impositions, I continue to assume, is that they will constrain market activities to desired channels and at desired levels. But what is the likelihood that government officials, with the best of intentions, will *know* what imposed prices, say, might evoke the "correct," desired actions by market participants? This question parallels that raised by Mises and Hayek with respect to "market" socialism.[28] Government officials in the regulated economy do enjoy the advantage (*not* shared by socialist planning officials) of making their decisions within the framework of genuine market prices. But the question remains: How do government officials know what prices to set (or qualities to require, and so forth)? Or to press the point further: How will government officials know if their earlier decisions were in error and in what direction to make corrections? In other words, how will government officials *discover* ← those opportunities for improving the allocation of resources, which one cannot assume to be automatically known to them at the outset of a regulatory endeavor?

The compelling insight underlying these questions rests heavily on the circumstance that officials institutionally are precluded from capturing *pecuniary* profits in the market, in the course of their activities (even though they are as eager as anyone else for entrepreneurial "profit" in the broadest sense of the term). The regulators' estimates of the prices consumers are prepared to pay, or of the prices resource owners are prepared to accept, for example, *are not profit-motivated estimates.* The estimates are not profit motivated at the time of an initial government regulatory action, and they are not profit motivated at each subsequent date when modification of a regulation might be considered. But estimates of market demand conditions or market supply conditions that are not profit motivated cannot reflect the powerful, discovery-inspiring incentives of the entrepreneurial quest for profit.

Nothing in the course of the regulatory process suggests a tendency for as yet unperceived opportunities of resource allocation improvement to be discovered. Nothing ensures that government officials who might perceive market conditions more accurately than others will tend systematically to replace less competent regulators. There is no entrepreneurial process at work, and there is no proxy for entrepreneurial profit or loss that easily might indicate where errors have been made and how they should be corrected. What regulators know (or believe they know) at a given moment presumably remains only partly correct. No systematic process seems at work through which regulators might come to discover what they have not known, *especially since they have not known that they enjoy less than complete awareness of a particular situation.*

The Perils of Regulation: A Market-Process Approach   141

The problem raised here is not quite the same as the one identified in other literature critical of government intervention. It is often noted, for example, that government officials are not motivated to minimize costs, since they will not personally benefit from the resulting economies.[29] The problem raised here differs importantly from such questions of incentives for adopting known efficiencies. For even if one could imagine an official so dedicated to the citizenry that he would ensure the adoption of all known possible measures for cutting costs, one cannot yet imagine him somehow divining *as yet undiscovered* techniques for cutting costs. What the offical knows, he knows, and what he knows that he does *not* know, one may imagine him diligently undertaking to find out, through appropriate cost-benefit-calculated search. But one can hardly imagine him discovering, except by the sheerest accident, those opportunities for increasing efficiency of which he is completely unaware. The official is not subject to the entrepreneurial profit incentive, which somehow appears continually and successfully to inspire discovery of hitherto undreamed of possibilities for eliminating unnecessary expenditures. Nothing within the regulatory process seems able to simulate even remotely well the discovery process that is so integral to the unregulated market.

THE STIFLED DISCOVERY PROCESS

The most serious effect of government regulation on the market discovery process well might be the likelihood that regulation, in a variety of ways, may discourage, hamper, and even completely stifle the discovery process of the unregulated market. Indeed, that much regulation is introduced as a result of unawareness of the market's discovery process already has been noted.

Government regulation plainly might bar exploitation of opportunities for pure entrepreneurial profit. A price ceiling, a price floor, an impeded merger, or an imposed safety requirement might block possibly profitable entrepreneurial actions. Such restraints and requirements may be designed to block *particular* activities. If so, the likelihood is that since the possibility of such activities is so clearly seen and feared, the blocked activity may provide standard rates of return, but *not* particularly profitable ones in the entrepreneurial sense. Regulated restraints and requirements, though, are also likely to block activities that have *not* yet been foreseen by anyone, including the regulatory authorities. Regulatory constraints, that is, are likely *to bar the discovery* of pure profit opportunities.

That government regulation diminishes competition is common knowledge. Tariffs, licensing requirements, labor legislation, airline regulation, and bank regulation reduce the number of potential participants in particular markets. Government regulation, therefore, is responsible for imposing monopolylike inefficiencies ("deadweight" welfare losses) upon the economy. But such losses by no means constitute the full impact of the countercompetitive measures often embodied in regulatory constraints.

The beneficent aspect of competition in the sense of a rivalrous process, as noted earlier, arises out of *freedom of entry*. What government regulations so often erect are *regulatory barriers to entry*. Freedom of "entry," for the Austrian approach, refers to the freedom of potential competitors to discover and to move to exploit existing opportunities for pure profit. If entry is blocked, such opportunities simply may never be discovered, either by existing firms in the industry, or by regulatory authorities, or for that matter by outside entrepreneurs who *might* have discovered such opportunities were they allowed to be exploited when found.

From *this* perspective on regulation's anticompetitive impact, it follows that much regulation introduced explicitly to *create* or *maintain* competition is no less hazardous to the competitive-entrepreneurial process than are other forms of regulation that restrict competition. Entry of competitors, in the dynamic sense, need not mean entry of firms of about equal size. For example, entry might imply the *replacement*, by merger or other means, of a number of relatively high-cost producers by a *single* low-cost producer. Antitrust activity designed ostensibly to protect competition might *block* this kind of entry. Such regulatory activity thus blocks the capture of pure profit, obtainable in this case by the discovery and implementation of the possibility of lowering the price to consumers by taking advantage of hitherto unexploited, and perhaps unsuspected, economies of scale.

The literature critical of government regulation often draws attention to the undesirable effects of imposed prices. A price ceiling for a particular product or service (rent control, for example) tends to generate artificial shortages (of housing). A price floor for a particular product or service, (minimum wages, for example) tends to generate an artificial surplus (teenage unemployment). These important, well-recognized consequences of imposed prices flow from the efforts of the regulators to legislate prices at other than equilibrium levels.

Quite apart from the discoordination generated by such imposed prices in the markets for *existing* goods and services, price (and also quality) restraints also may well inhibit the discovery of wholly new opportunities. A price ceiling does not merely block the upper reaches of a given supply curve. Such a ceiling also may inhibit the discovery of as yet unsuspected sources of supply (which in the absence of the ceiling would have tended to shift the entire supply curve to the right) or of as yet wholly unknown new products (tending to create supply curves for wholly new graphs).[30] The lure of pure profit tends to uncover such as yet unknown opportunities.

Price and quality restraints and requirements and restrictions on organizational forms operate (in a generally understood but not precisely predictable way) to inhibit entrepreneurial discovery. Price ceilings, for example, not only restrict supply from known sources of natural gas (or from known prospects for search), but also inhibit the dis-

covery of wholly unknown sources. Drug testing regulations, as another example, not only reduce the flow of
new pharmaceutical drugs where successful research
might have been more or less predictable, but also discourage the entrepreneurial discovery of wholly unknown research procedures. Against whatever benefits
might be derived from government regulation and intervention, one is forced to weigh, as one of regulation's in-
trinsically immeasurable costs, the stifling of the market
discovery process.

THE WHOLLY SUPERFLUOUS DISCOVERY PROCESS

There is yet one more aspect of government regulation's complex impact on the discovery process. Whether
intended by the regulatory authorities or not and whether
suspected by them or not, the imposition of regulatory
restraints and requirements tends to create entirely new,
and not necessarily desirable opportunities for entrepreneurial discovery.

That such opportunities may be created follows
from the extreme unlikelihood that government-imposed
price, quality, or quantity constraints introduce anything
approaching an equilibrium configuration. These constraints, on the contrary, introduce pure profit opportunities that would otherwise have been absent, as they
simultaneously reduce or possibly eliminate other opportunities for pure profit that might otherwise have existed.
This rearrangement of opportunities for pure profits, of
course, is unlikely to be the explicit aim of regulation;
nor even, indeed, is such rearrangement ever likely to be
fully *known* to the authorities. Market ignorance is a fact
of economic life. It follows that the replacement of one
set of (unregulated) prices by another set of (partly regulated) prices, simply means that regulation has generated
a possibly major alteration in the pattern of the discovery
process. The now regulated market will tend to pursue
the altered discovery process.

This regulation-induced alteration in the pattern of
market discovery is closely related to the often noticed

The Perils of Regulation: A Market-Process Approach   145

circumstance that regulation may result in a different set
of *equilibrium* market consequences. Such consequences, moreover, may not have been correctly foretold
by the authorities and, indeed, may be wholly undesired
by them. Regulation often imposes costs not immediately
recognized.[31] Unless, quite fantastically, the regulatory
authorities (somehow all acting in completely coordinated fashion) are perfectly informed on all relevant data
about the market, they will *not* generally be able to perceive what new profit opportunities they create by their
own regulatory actions. Inevitably, therefore, the imposition of a set of regulatory constraints on a market must
set in motion a series of entrepreneurial actions that have
not been anticipated and, therefore, that may well lead to
wholly unexpected and even undesired final outcomes.[32]

The one kind of new "profit" opportunity created by
regulation that is by now well anticipated, though hardly
desired of course, involves bribery and corruption of the
regulators. There is widespread understanding of the un-
wholesome channels into which the entrepreneurial
quest for pure profit inevitably tends to be attracted if arbitrary restraints on otherwise profitable activities are
imposed.[33]

The basic insight underlying these conclusions, in
sum, is a simple one. The competitive-entrepreneurial
process, being a process of discovery of the as yet unknown, can hardly be predicted in any but the broadest
terms. The imposition of regulatory constraints necessarily results, therefore, in a pattern of consequences different from and, most plausibly, distinctly less desirable
than what would have occurred in the unregulated market. One might therefore refer to this unplanned, undesired pattern of consequences of regulation as the
wholly superfluous discovery process.

[17]

The Economic Journal, 91 (June 1981), 348–363
Printed in Great Britain

MISLEADING CALCULATIONS OF THE
SOCIAL COSTS OF MONOPOLY
POWER*

It has long been thought that monopoly is 'bad', but only comparatively recently have economists attempted to measure 'how bad'. The first and most influential of such studies (Harberger, 1954) found that the welfare losses attributable to monopoly were surprisingly small – of the order of one tenth of one percent of national income in the United States during the 1920s.

Harberger's work inspired a number of further studies, the latest of which is by Cowling and Mueller (1978)[1]. According to their calculations, 734 large firms in the United States generated welfare losses totalling $15 billion annually over the period 1963–6. This figure represents 13% of Gross Corporate Product (GCP).[2] General Motors and A T & T lead the list with annual welfare losses of over $1·7 and $1 billion respectively, which together represent over $1\frac{1}{2}$% of GCP during that period. In the United Kingdom, the top 103 firms generated welfare losses of £719m in the year 1968–9; this represents over 7% of GCP. More than a quarter of these losses are accounted for by three firms: BP (£83m), Shell (£54m) and BAT (£49m).

In the light of these results, Cowling and Mueller conclude that previous beliefs that the costs of monopoly are insignificant are no longer warranted. Indeed, they suggest that 'the tops of our lists of the largest welfare losses by firm are the logical starting points for intensified enforcement of anti-trust policy'. Elsewhere, Cowling (1978) advocates standing parliamentary committees to provide continuous surveillance of these 'major private centres of economic power'.

How reliable are these various calculations of the cost of monopoly? Previous studies have not lacked critics,[3] hence it is appropriate to begin by examining those modifications adopted by Cowling and Mueller which have not previously been discussed. However, the main purpose of this note is to examine the adequacy of the conceptual framework within which *all* the calculations have been made, and which has tacitly been accepted by all the critics. I shall argue (a) that even within the framework of their own model, Cowling and Mueller have overestimated the costs of monopoly in four major respects; (b) that the very framework of long-run equilibrium, used by all writers from Harberger onwards, precludes the recognition of profits due to uncertainty and innovation,

---

* I should like to acknowledge helpful comments from A. Charnes, M. E. Beesley, D. Friedman, I. M. Kirzner, D. S. Lees, A. J. McGuinness, J. McKie, W. D. Reekie, J. Wiseman, B. S. Yamey, two referees and numerous seminar participants.

[1] A reply by Cowling and Mueller to the present paper will be published in the September 1981 issue of the *Economic Journal*.

[2] Gross Corporate Product is a concept reportedly used by the US Department of Commerce in unpublished calculations. It is presumably less than national income, but it is not clear how Cowling and Mueller's results compare to those of previous authors. The calculated welfare losses for the firms they actually examine are of the order of 1% of national income.

[3] See papers by Bergson, Kamerschen, Schwartzman, Siegfield and Tiemann, Stigler, Wenders, Wisecarver and Worcester, as referred by Cowling and Mueller.

and wrongly interprets them as due to monopoly; (c) that in consequence all these studies are completely misleading as to the location, extent, duration and costs of monopoly power; and (d) that such studies are therefore quite inappropriate as a basis for public policy.

The ideas presented here are by no means original, and no fresh calculations of the costs of monopoly power are made. Nevertheless, the fact that academic and government economists appear to take the previous studies seriously suggests that the present brief critique may not be out of place, and the alternative approach which is suggested here may help to stimulate more reliable empirical studies.

I. THE STUDY BY HARBERGER

According to textbook economic theory, the main effects of monopoly are to misallocate resources, to reduce aggregate welfare and to redistribute income in favour of monopolists. Assuming that long run average costs are approximately constant, for both firm and industry, Harberger represents the situation as in Fig. 1. If price were set equal to unit cost C (which includes the cost of capital), then output equal to the competitive level Q^* would be demanded and produced. If, instead, a monopolist is able to raise price to P and restrict output to Q, he enjoys a monopoly profit π, given by the rectangle $ABCP$. However, this profit is merely a transfer of wealth from consumers to the monopolist producer. Assuming that we are interested only in the aggregate net value of output, regardless of who obtains it, the net loss to society as a whole is given by the 'welfare triangle' ABE, denoted Δ. This represents the net value (to consumers) of the lost output QQ^* over and above the value of the resources (BEQ^*Q) used to produce it.

To calculate the cost of monopoly in the economy as a whole it is necessary to estimate empirically the size of the welfare triangles Δ for each industry. This involves making assumptions about the magnitudes of profit rates PC (equal to AB) and output restrictions BE. These two magnitudes are related by the elasticity of demand. Harberger calculated average profit rates for 2,046 corporations in 73 industries in 1924–8, which accounted for some 45% of total manufacturing output in the United States, and assumed a unit elastic demand curve for each industry. Grossing up the resulting figures yielded an estimated annual welfare loss of $59m for the manufacturing sector of the United States economy. This represented less than one tenth of one percent of national income, or less than $1·50 for every man, woman and child in the United States at 1953 prices.

Harberger concluded that, although monopoly might be a serious problem in certain industries, the United States economy as a whole was emphatically not an example of 'monopoly capitalism', and for many purposes the entire manufacturing sector of the economy could be treated as competitive.

II. THE STUDY BY COWLING AND MUELLER

Cowling and Mueller (henceforth CM) retain Harberger's partial equilibrium approach, and also his welfare criterion of aggregate net benefits to whomever

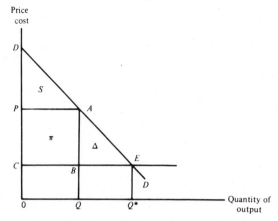

Fig. 1. The conventional welfare loss due to monopoly. *DD*, Demand function; *P*, monopoly price; *C*, unit cost (including cost of capital); π, profit (above normal return on capital); *S*, consumer surplus; Δ, welfare triangle.

they accrue. However, they make four criticisms and modifications of his procedure.

(i) *Pricing and elasticity of demand*

Prices and elasticities of demand are not independent, as Harberger assumed, since a monopolist will take elasticity into account in setting his price. In fact, the area of the welfare triangle will be approximately equal to half the (pre-tax) level of profit, so there is no need to make independent calculations of elasticities.[1]

(ii) *Cost of capital*

Harberger identified the normal competitive profit rate with the average profit rate earned, but the latter already includes an element of monopoly profit. CM therefore use an independent (and lower) estimate of the cost of capital as a yardstick by which to calculate monopoly profit rates. Furthermore, intangible assets such as goodwill and patents are subtracted from capital on the grounds that they largely represent capitalised monopoly rents.

(iii) *Aggregation*

The use of industry profit rates introduces an immediate aggregation bias into the calculation by allowing the high monopoly profits of those firms with the most market power to be offset by the losses of other firms in the industry. Calculations are therefore performed for individual firms rather than for industries.

[1] Briefly, the welfare triangle may be approximated by
$$\Delta \simeq \tfrac{1}{2}(P-C)^2 dQ/dP = (\pi/2)\ \eta(P-C)/P,$$
where η denotes absolute elasticity of demand. A profit-maxising monopolist will set price such that $\eta = P/(P-C)$, hence $\Delta \simeq \pi/2$.

(iv) *Cost of gaining and retaining monopoly power*

Tullock (1967) and Posner (1975) have pointed out that firms will find it worth-while to expend resources in order to receive or preserve an inflow of monopoly rents. If necessary, firms in competition for the monopoly will pay up to the whole amount of the prospective monopoly rent. Such expenses are considered social costs because they affect only the distribution of wealth, and not its magnitude. Moreover, to the extent that these expenses enter reported costs, estimates of welfare losses based on remaining profits will underestimate the monopolistic distortions in output.

CM assume that advertising expenditure is 'merely an instrument for securing market power', and make three adjustments to the calculation of welfare loss: advertising expenditure is added (back) to monopoly profit when calculating the welfare triangle, all of advertising expenditure is added to the welfare loss; all of after-tax profits above the competitive cost of capital are used as the estimate of the expenditures incurred by other (unsuccessful) firms to obtain control of monopoly rents.

As a result of these modifications, the social cost due to monopoly is defined for each firm by the computation

$$\frac{\pi}{2} + \frac{A}{2} + A + \pi - T \quad \text{or} \quad \tfrac{3}{2}(\pi + A) - T,$$

where A denotes advertising expenditure, T denotes the tax paid, and π denotes pre-tax book profit adjusted (upwards) by substituting a calculated competitive cost of capital (competitive rate of return times net assets less intangibles) for the firm's interest expenses. *The net effect is that the welfare loss imposed on society by any firm is defined as one and a half times its pre-tax profit (adjusted upwards) plus one and a half times its advertising expenditure less its tax payment.*

These assumptions provide the basis for the estimates reported in the introduction to this paper. Calculations are also provided for the separate components of welfare loss. These may be presented as illustrated in Table 1 to show the proportions of total welfare loss contributed by restrictions in output, advertising expenditure and expenses of rivals in rent-seeking activities. According to these calculations, advertising accounts for nearly two thirds of total welfare loss in the United States, and restrictions in output account for most of the remainder. In the United Kingdom restrictions in output account for over half of total welfare loss, while the other two components account about equally for the other half.[1]

III. THE NATURE OF PROFIT IN LONG RUN EQUILIBRIUM

All authors from Harberger to CM take as their reference point an economy in long-run equilibrium. If this economy were perfectly competitive, no profits or losses would be observed, i.e. rates of return would be precisely equal to the

[1] If our interpretation is correct, after-tax profits in the United States amount to only $992/(4{,}527 \times 2)$ $= 11\%$ of pre-tax profits; the corresponding figure for the United Kingdom is 23.5%. These figures seem to imply average tax rates which are implausibly high (89% and 76.5% respectively).

Table 1

Calculations of Monopoly Welfare Losses

	Restrictions in output $\frac{1}{2}\pi$	Advertising $A+\frac{1}{2}A$	Expenses of rivals $\pi-T$	Total welfare loss
U.S.A. ($m p.a.) 1963/6				
General Motors	1,061	287	433	1,780
AT & T	0	1,025	0	1,025
...	...	...	...	...
Total 734 firms	4,527	9,478	992	14,998
% of total welfare loss	30%	63%	7%	100%
U.K. (£m) 1968/9				
British Petroleum	74	1	8	83
Shell	49	4	0	54
British American Tobacco	27	1	22	49
...	...	...	...	...
Total 102 firms	386	152	182	719
% of total welfare loss	54%	21%	25%	100%

Source. Cowling and Mueller (1978), Table 4, cols. 1, 3–1, 4–3, 4 respectively.

cost of capital. If the economy were not perfectly competitive, positive profits would be observed which would be due to monopoly; strictly speaking, they would be monopoly rents.

In long-run equilibrium, there are essentially only two distinct sources of monopoly:

(1) a grant by the government protecting the recipient(s) from competition by others, e.g. via statutory monopoly, licensed entry, import duties, quotas, patents, etc.

(2) a permanent advantage enjoyed by the incumbent firm(s) over potential entrants, e.g. sole ownership of some necessary input, access to superior techniques of production, an ineradicable belief by customers in the superiority of established products (brand loyalty) etc. (Indivisibilities in capacity and economies of scale, which render new entry uneconomic given a competitive response, may be considered variants of this advantage to incumbents.)

Two other considerations are often mentioned in connection with monopoly profit. (i) The necessity of entering an industry on a large scale, with heavy investments in research and development or advertising, will limit the type of firm which can enter, and reduce the rate at which the entrant can put together the necessary resources. This consideration undoubtedly affects the rate at which (temporary) profits are computed away but the situation is not an equilibrium. (ii) As long as potential entrants expect incumbents to maintain or increase output in the face of entry, and to be better able to withstand the resulting price war, an incumbent firm (or firms) may enjoy positive profits by the use of 'limit pricing'. This situation is an equilibrium, but insofar as it relies on unjustified beliefs it is not a *long-run* equilibrium.

IV. AN EVALUATION OF THE CALCULATIONS BY COWLING AND MUELLER

Our first task is to evaluate CM's calculations within the framework of their model, i.e. assuming that the economy is in long-run equilibrium and that all profits are due to monopoly.

(1) *The welfare triangle*

CM assume that each firm maximises profit, leading to a welfare triangle approximately equal to half the level of profit. In practice, however, firms make extensive use of price discrimination, either directly or via multipart tariffs, tie-in sales, full-line forcing, retrospective discounts, etc. Price discrimination may well lead to increased output, a reduced welfare loss and a welfare triangle which is *less* than half of pre-tax profit.[1] Furthermore, firms may operate in competitive industries but obtain rents on superior assets or resources which they own. Even though reported profits are positive, there is no restriction of output, and consequently no welfare triangle.[2] Finally, for those companies with large export and/or overseas operations (such as BP, Shell and BAT), a restriction of output does not necessarily generate a welfare loss *in the United Kingdom*, and if higher prices generate more foreign exchange this is surely a welfare *gain* to the United Kingdom.

(2) *Advertising*

It is not entirely clear what role advertising plays in long-run equilibrium, but there appear to be two strands of thought in CM's model.

(i) Excess advertising, together with excess capacity and excess product differentiation, is assumed to be a means of dissuading potential entrants via limit pricing (Spence, 1977). We have already indicated that limit-pricing is incompatible with long-run equilibrium.

(ii) Firms are assumed to agree on prices, but advertising is one of the dimensions of non-price competition through which profits are dissipated (Baran and Sweezy, 1966). In this case, the monopoly must be conferred by the government, otherwise new rivals would enter the industry and compete on price alone. However, CM do not restrict their calculations to such monopolies.

CM admit that taking all of advertising expenditure to be a social loss 'takes the extreme view of advertising as merely an instrument for securing market power. To the extent that advertising provides useful information to consumers, this measure overstates the cost of monopoly'. If advertising affects market share, then it must provide information which consumers find relevant. To assume that most advertising is pure waste arguably implies a rather condescending view of ordinary consumers.[3]

---

[1] It is also possible to construct cases in which price discrimination reduces output and welfare (Yamey, 1974).

[2] It has also been argued that, in long-run equilibrium, sole owners of durable assets will not even be able to restrict output and command a monopoly rent (Coase, 1972).

[3] Dixit and Norman (1978) point out that a monopolist may reduce social welfare by advertising to exploit his monopoly power, but the advertising itself is neither the source of the monopoly nor a

(3) *Expenses of monopoly rent-seeking*

CM rightly take into account the notion that firms will spend resources to acquire monopoly rents. Not only the exercise of monopoly, but also the acquisition of it, may involve a welfare loss. But is it reasonable to assume that expenditures incurred by unsuccessful firms will *equal* the monopoly rents earned by successful firms? Posner (1975) argued that this would be so, provided that obtaining a monopoly is itself a perfectly competitive activity, and that the long-run supply of all inputs used to obtain monopolies is perfectly elastic. If the expected monopoly profit were positive, then the competing firms (or new entrants) would hire additional inputs in an effort to secure this profit. Even if the monopoly were obtained by bribery or any other transfer of income, which in itself would not generate a welfare loss, in the long-run resources would be drawn into the activity of becoming the official or supplier who receives such payments, and the use of these resources would constitute a social waste.

Posner does point out, however, that 'the production function of monopolies requires greater attention than I give it in this paper. The assumption of a perfectly elastic long-run supply may fail for an input as foreign to conventional economic analysis as political power' (p. 811). In the conventional neoclassical model, the extent and distribution of resources are assumed given, together with a set of property rights. Initial resource-owners will ultimately receive at least part of monopoly rents, and to this extent achieved post-tax profits are an overstatement of socially wasteful expenditures on acquiring monopoly.

(4) *Accounting conventions*

In calculating economic profit rates, both Harberger and CM adjust the reported profit rates *upwards* on the grounds that book-keeping assets such as patents and goodwill represent a capitalisation of monopoly profits, so that the accounting profit rate is an understatement of the actual profit rate on 'real capital'.

A quite opposite argument has been made. Advertising and research and development expenditures are generally 'expensed', i.e. written off as current expenses in the year in which they are incurred. However, to the extent that they generate income in future years, they should be treated as 'intangible assets', i.e. capitalised then depreciated against subsequent income. This approach will generally show different time-streams of asset values, net income and return on capital.

Several authors have shown that corrected rates of return on capital are significantly different from reported rates in those industries which engage in substantial advertising and R & D (Comanor and Wilson, 1967; Bloch, 1974; Ayanian, 1975; Clarkson, 1977). The balance of the empirical evidence suggests

---

measure of the welfare loss. Advertising may have other socially-useful by-products – e.g. in facilitating the supply of public goods such as newspapers and television programmes, which would otherwise be curtailed or require financial subsidy – but it could also lead to the over-supply of such products.

that corrected rates of return are in fact *lower* (Brozen, 1977*a*; Reekie and Bhoyrub, 1980). For example, the average corrected return in US pharmaceuticals over 1959–73 is 5·4 percentage points lower than the accounting return, leading Brozen to conclude that 'the higher profitability of the pharmaceutical industry turns out to be, in large part, an accounting illusion'.

To summarise this section, we have assumed with CM that the economy is in long-run equilibrium, and that all profits are due to monopoly. Nevertheless, we have argued that (1) the welfare triangle is probably less than half pre-tax profit; (2) advertising neither dissipates profit where monopoly is not conferred by government nor prevents long-run entry, and on the contrary provides relevant information to consumers; (3) the expenses of monopoly rent-seeking need to be taken into account, but are less than post-tax profits; (4) reported profit rates need to be corrected (downwards) to reflect the intangible assets generated by advertising and R & D. *In sum, even within the context of their own model, CM have overestimated the social cost of monopoly in four major respects.*

V. INADEQUACY OF THE EQUILIBRIUM FRAMEWORK

We now turn from the details of the calculations to the framework within which these calculations are made. The central notion is that of long-run equilibrium. Bergson (1973) has argued that a partial equilibrium approach is misleading, and shown that a general equilibrium approach can generate much higher estimates of the cost of monopoly.[1] In similar vein, a referee of the present paper argues that the welfare triangle cannot possibly be an appropriate measure of the cost of monopoly. For suppose each industry is a profit-maximising monopoly, and all industries face identical demand elasticities, then all industries will have the same markup of price over marginal cost. But this is precisely the competitive equilibrium which maximises welfare: there is no distortion and hence no social cost.[2]

But is an equilibrium approach, whether partial or general, justified at all? Following Harberger, all authors consciously choose data from a period 'reasonably close to a long-run equilibrium period' and then take an average of profits over these periods in order further to minimise transitory components. Yet embarrassing evidence of disequilibrium still remains. In Harberger's study, firms weaving woollens earned an average of only 2·6 % on capital over the five years 1924–8 (compared to an overall sample mean of 10·4 %). CM report that 421 of the 734 firms in their US sample enjoyed positive average pre-tax profits over the period 1963–6 (their Table 2), so that presumably 313 out of 734 – about 40 % of their sample – made losses.

Now as CM remark, 'the presence of firms earning profits less than the competitive norm creates a methodological problem' (p. 731). Presumably these firms did not intend to make losses. They found themselves with costs

---

[1] See, however, the argument by Pearce (1975) that the equilibrium model with monopoly is logically impossible, in that 'no point of general equilibrium with all firms maximising profits can exist'.
[2] It is not clear that this criticism applies to Harberger's calculation, which is based on divergences from mean profit rates.

above competitive levels through bad luck and/or inadequate foresight. By the same token, there were presumably other firms which found themselves with costs below competitive levels through good luck and/or superior foresight. That is, *some firms enjoyed profits above the competitive norm, because of luck and/or foresight, and not because of any monopoly power.*

The presence of loss-making firms compelled CM to the following frank admission.

> It is unreasonable to assume that the time periods investigated in Harberger's study, the others which followed, or our own, are long enough or stable enough so that all firms and industries are in equilibrium ... Some of the companies earning profits above competitive levels in our samples are in temporary disequilibrium, and the welfare losses associated with these firms can be expected to disappear over time. Thus, *our estimates of monopoly profits are a combination of both long-run monopoly profits and short-run disequilibrium profits* [p. 732, italics added].

Similarly, Harberger admits that

> We have actually included in the measurement *not only monopoly misallocations but also misallocations coming out of the dynamics of economic growth and development* and all other elements which would cause divergent profit rates to persist for some time even in an effectively competitive economy [p. 84, italics added].

In other words, the empirical calculations made by all these authors are unable to distinguish the *source and nature* of observed profit rates, nor are they able to estimate their *duration*. As for the long-run equilibrium model which is used as a framework, it can scarcely shed light on these questions because it does not even acknowledge the problem! Within this model, as remarked in section III, all profits are necessarily permanent monopoly profits: there is no such thing as a 'temporary profit'.

Furthermore, in the long-run equilibrium model, *all profits necessarily imply a welfare loss.* There is no scope for profits which might be harmless, let alone any scope for profits to play a socially beneficial role in the operation of the economy. Thus *the very choice of a long-run equilibrium framework within which to analyse monopoly misinterprets the nature of profits, overestimates the extent of monopoly power, and thereby overestimates the social cost of monopoly.* As a result of this inappropriate framework, retailers such as Great Universal Stores, Marks & Spencers and F. W. Woolworth, who have proved successful in one of the most actively competitive industries in the United Kingdom, are implausibly held responsible for welfare losses totalling £56m in 1968/9.

VI. THE INTRODUCTION OF UNCERTAINTY AND INNOVATION

In order adequately to analyse the nature and extent of monopoly power, it is necessary to employ a model of the economy which allows above-average rates of return to be derived from sources other than monopoly. These alternative sources are twofold:

(1) the occurrence of unexpected events, whether generated by 'nature' or the unanticipated actions of other market participants, which may augment intended profits or convert them into losses;

(2) differences between firms in the ability to create or notice profitable opportunities that are, in principle, available to anyone.

Thus, the rate of return obtained by any company actually comprises three elements: monopoly rent, 'windfall' gains and losses, and 'entrepreneurial' profit.[1]

In a risky environment, not all firms will succeed. Even if investment in an industry is carried forward to the point where the return expected ex ante is equal to the cost of capital (i.e. to the competitive level), the results achieved ex post will show that some firms obtained an above-average return and others a below-average return. But here, an above-average return does not imply any welfare loss. To select only the successful firms, and to assume that their above-average returns represent monopoly profit, with a corresponding welfare loss, would be a blatant error. Yet this is precisely what CM have done, by carrying out their calculations in terms of firms rather than industries (as Harberger did), and ignoring the losses made by unsuccessful firms.[2]

Furthermore, if certain industries are riskier than others, the companies operating therein will need to pay a 'risk premium' to attract capital. This premium is presumably reflected to some extent in the interest expenses reported in the company's books, but the company will also need to earn higher rates of return in order to pay higher dividends. Not only do CM not adjust rates of return for the risk premium, they in fact substitute a common cost of capital for a company's actual interest payments, and thereby misinterpret the costs of risk as monopoly profit.

VII. COMPETITION AS AN ENTREPRENEURIAL PROCESS

The notion of perfect competition as a static equilibrium state is a relatively recent development in economics. For Adam Smith and the classical writers, competition was a process of rivalry taking place over time (McNulty 1967). This latter view of competition was maintained and developed by members of the 'Austrian School'.[3] A similar approach has also been used by other authors in recent empirical work.[4]

As is well known, Schumpeter saw competition as 'a perennial gale of creative destruction'. Entrepreneurial profits can be earned by creativity and superior foresight, by being 'first in the field'. However, a profitable firm is always at the mercy of rivals attempting to develop new and better products. In the absence of artificial restrictions, there is always a tendency for entrepreneurial profits to be competed away.

[1] It might be argued that entrepreneurial profits could be attributed to monopoly if entrepreneurial ability were regarded as a factor of production in limited supply; for an argument against this, see Kirzner (1979, chapters 9, 10; 1980, pp. 10–2).

[2] For more extensive discussion and numerical examples, see Mancke (1974) and Brozen (1977b).

[3] Cf. Schumpeter (1950), von Mises (1949), Hayek (1948), Kirzner (1973, 1979).

[4] Cf. Alchian and Allen (1974), Brozen (1970), Demsetz (1973). For an exposition and integration of Austrian and other models of the competitive process see Littlechild (1978) or Reekie (1979).

With this idea of a competitive process in mind, we can reinterpret Fig. 1 to analyse the behaviour of an entrepreneur who discovers a new product before the rest of the market realises its potential. Assume he charges a monopoly price P, since for the moment he is the sole seller. It is true that he is restricting output compared to what he could produce, or compared to what would be produced if all his rivals shared his own insight. But they do *not* share his insight; this is not the relevant alternative. For the time being *the relevant alternative to his action is no product at all*. It would therefore be inappropriate to characterise his action as generating a social loss given by the welfare triangle Δ. On the contrary, *his action generates a social gain given by his own entrepreneurial profit π plus the consumer surplus S*.[1]

This social gain is enjoyed from the time at which the entrepreneur discovers and exploits the new product until the time at which the market would other-wise have done so. However, it is likely that the action of the first entrepreneur will stimulate the market to an earlier awareness of the situation, i.e. rivals will step in and compete the price down to cost. Insofar as entrepreneurial profit π is converted to consumer surplus, this is merely a transfer of income. However, there is a *further* social gain, namely, the *earlier* enjoyment of consumer surplus on output QQ^*, which of course is equal in value to the area of the welfare triangle Δ.

It may be argued, along Tullock–Posner lines, that the lure of entrepreneurial profits will stimulate other firms to spend resources in order to achieve such insights (e.g. via market research), and that such use of resources constitutes a social waste which will fully offset any social gains. There are at least four reasons (in addition to the property rights consideration of section IV. 3) why this argument is untenable here. (i) Firms typically differ in ability (there is not perfect competition) so the more efficient firms will not need to expend re-sources equal to prospective profits in order to match the efforts of rivals. (ii) If resources have to be spent in order to clarify the nature of profit opportunities, this merely pushes back the entrepreneurial element to an earlier stage (e.g. to the location of profitable opportunities for engaging in market research) (Kirzner, 1973, pp. 65–9). Differences in entrepreneurial ability at this earlier stage provide a further reason why successful firms can gain their prize without the expenditure of resources equal to the value of prospective profit – indeed, in the extreme case, an entrepreneur may achieve his innovation before his potential rivals realise that market research in that area would have been worth-while. (iii) Just as copying an existing innovation generates social benefits from the earlier enjoyment of lower prices, so too the very process of competing to make the innovation may bring forward the time of discovery and initial pro-duction, with corresponding welfare gains. (iv) Even if resources are expended to the value of private profit, the social benefits of innovation include, in addition, the consumer surplus which initially accompanies this profit and subsequently replaces it.

---

[1] For simplicity of exposition, we ignore the effects of introducing the new product on the demand for other products.

VIII. MONOPOLY AND THE COMPETITIVE PROCESS

Monopoly can still exist in the competitive process, deriving either from government protection or from ownership of superior resources. In the former case, rivals are legally prevented from providing specified products, while in the latter case they do not have access to equally effective techniques of production. As in the equilibrium model, the effect is to confer a monopoly rent. Two points of difference should be emphasised, however.

In the static equilibrium model, monopoly is permanent. There are no forces acting within the model to reduce the loss which it induces. In the dynamic process model, by contrast, there is both opportunity and incentive to discover new products or techniques which might *bypass* the monopoly, thereby reducing over time the extent of welfare loss. The market process thus continues *around* the monopoly, rather than being eliminated by it. (And of course the monopolist himself will simultaneously be searching for better ways to apply or extend his monopoly.) The loss imposed by a monopoly will thus depend crucially upon its scope, and will be reflected not merely by the restriction in current output, but by the restriction in access by others to potential but as yet undiscovered products and techniques. For this reason, a statutory monopoly which prohibits all potential rivals in some field is likely to be more onerous than a monopoly based on sole ownership of some input, since alternative techniques of production may render than input no longer crucial.[1]

Second, firms may use resources in order to acquire or retain a monopoly rent. But, just as with entrepreneurial profit, it does not follow that the total value of these expended resources is equal to monopoly rent, since potential monopolists differ in ability and alertness. Similarly, competition to acquire a monopoly may bring forward the date of producing the monopoly product; it may therefore be socially beneficial to *create* certain monopolies. (Indeed, this is the usual defence for patents.)

Finally, it is worth remarking that concepts such as limit pricing, predatory pricing and related phenomena, which are awkward to analyse in terms of long-run equilibrium, fit naturally into a framework of competitive process. If potential entrants are unsure about future demand and cost conditions, or apprehensive about the likely reactions of incumbents, they may delay entry (or use a safer alternative route such as merger). Incumbents may (in principle) be able to influence these decisions of entrants, at least temporarily. By the same token, however, the prospect of being able to delay subsequent entrants is an added incentive to be first in the field.

IX. EVIDENCE FOR THE COMPETITIVE PROCESS

If high rates of return can result from monopoly rent, windfall gains or entrepreneurial profit, how far, in practice, is it possible to ascertain the precise proportions of these three ingredients?

---

[1] An excellent example is the potential development of radio beams from satellites direct to homes and offices, which would make telephone exchanges obsolete, thereby removing the local monopoly currently enjoyed by the telephone company.

Detailed case-studies of particular firms could perhaps provide some insights e.g. by identifying areas where the firm enjoys some government protection from competition, by contrasting plans and achieved results, by comparing its costs of production with those of rivals, etc. (Thus, AT & T probably earned substantial monopoly rents from its position protected by the Federal Communications Commission, BP and Shell probably received larger windfall gains than companies in less risky industries, etc.)

Taking a broader view of the unregulated sector of the economy as a whole, there is accumulating evidence that monopoly rents are considerably less important than windfall gains and entrepreneurial profits.

It was once widely believed by economists that highly concentrated industries allowed explicit or implicit collusion, which in turn led to higher profit rates. The original evidence by Bain (1951), who himself was rather cautious, is now known to be in error (Brozen, 1971). Recent empirical work has shown that the effect of concentration on profits has at best been overstated, and may be negligible (Brozen, 1970, 1977*b*; Demsetz, 1973, 1974; Peltzman, 1977; Carter, 1978; and for the United Kingdom, Hart and Clarke, 1980). The evidence shows that industries with relatively high rates of return in one year tend to descend towards a middle rank in later years, whereas those with low returns tend to ascend (Brozen, 1970, 1977*b*). Additional resources are systematically attracted into high-return industries, causing capacity and supply to rise and prices and profits to fall. This would not be the case if high rates of return were based on monopoly power.

Secondly, the fact that, even within industries, firms exhibit 'higgledy-piggledy growth' (Little and Rayner, 1978; Prais, 1976) shows that success in the past, whether due to luck or foresight, does not guarantee success in the future. Mere size does not convey monopoly power.[1]

Finally, the empirical evidence suggests that advertising facilitates entry and leads to reductions in price i.e. it is primarily a means of competing rather than a means of preventing competition (Benham, 1972; Brozen, 1974).[2]

X. THE ANALYSIS OF POLICY

In the equilibrium framework the current situation is evaluated against the ideal benchmark of perfect competition. Profit is assumed due to monopoly, and as such is not only wasteful in itself but also the cause of waste in other firms. The task of public policy is therefore to eliminate profit (e.g. by controlling mergers or prices) – although, as CM rather belatedly acknowledged, 'any public policy has its own sets of costs and inefficiencies ... Thus it might be that any alternative for dealing with existing monopoly power would involve higher costs than the monopolies themselves create' (p. 746).

In the competitive process framework, there is no such ideal benchmark. One

[1] Larger firms tend to earn higher profit rates, but it is more plausible to interpret size as the *consequence*, rather than the *cause*, of profits. (Demsetz 1973).

[2] For contrary views on concentration and advertising, see papers by Weiss and Mann in Goldschmid (1974).

process is superior to another if, ceteris paribus, new products and techniques are discovered, exploited and diffused sooner. But in a world in which the number of potential discoveries is infinite, there is no 'soonest' time at which they can be made. The 'ideal benchmark' approach must therefore be abandoned in favour of a 'comparative institutions' approach (Demsetz, 1969), i.e. a comparison of the likely path of the market process as a result of alternative available government policies.

This point may be briefly illustrated. With respect to monopoly stemming from government-imposed barriers to entry (e.g. the statutory monopolies enjoyed by many nationalised industries, patent laws, import duties and quotas, 'self-regulation' based on government charters, etc.), the practical question is whether the benefits so obtained (e.g. as a result of diverted investment and output, reduced uncertainty, higher quality, income redistribution, etc.) are sufficient to offset the costs of intervention (e.g. higher prices, less initiative, slower response to change, expenses of intervention, etc.). With respect to monopoly stemming from sole ownership of necessary inputs, and 'barriers to entry' stemming from the conduct of firms (e.g. limit pricing, predatory pricing, 'tying' arrangements, restrictive practices, etc.), the relevant question is whether government action to remove such 'barriers' will in fact stimulate entry by previously thwarted firms, without at the same time reducing the ability of existing firms to cope with their uncertain and ever-changing environments, and without reducing the incentives to create, notice and exploit opportunities arising in future (Schumpeter, 1950; Richardson, 1960).[1]

XI. CONCLUSIONS

The recent work by Professors Cowling and Mueller is the latest in a series of papers designed to extend or reappraise the pioneering attempt by Harberger to measure the welfare loss due to monopoly. The principle innovation introduced by CM is a measurement of the waste of resources employed in trying to gain or retain a monopoly position. In principle, this element ought to be included. However, we have argued that, even within the context of the model employed by CM, there are serious deficiencies in the calculation of this and other components of welfare loss, so that the resulting figures are quite unreliable as an estimate of the social cost of monopoly (but surely a serious overestimate).

More importantly, we have further argued that the choice by all these authors of a long-run equilibrium framework in which to analyse monopoly is itself a source of bias and the cause of major difficulties. Within this framework, *all* profit is due to monopoly, and necessarily implies a serious welfare loss. The equilibrium model precludes any neutral or socially beneficial interpretation of profit.

An alternative model of competition as a continuing process of rivalry and

---

[1] Thus, the Petrol Report of the Monopolies and Mergers Commission (1979) found that selective price support did restrict and distort competition but that any attempts to control the practice would have even more adverse effects (due to administrative costs and delays and the facilitation of collusion).

adjustment in an uncertain environment was then sketched out. Within this framework, windfall gains and losses result from unanticipated shifts in demand and cost conditions, while creativity and alertness generate entrepreneurial profits which reflect innovation and increased co-ordination rather than monopoly. Empirical evidence concerning 'higgledy-piggledy growth' and the tendency of extreme profit rates to return over time to the mean suggests that these two sources of profit are more important than monopoly power. Finally, this model of competition as a process suggests that the attention of policy makers be directed away from the size of firms and concentration of industries to the conditions of entry into those industries. If one is concerned to promote competition, the obvious starting point is the wide variety of government restrictions which serve to protect vested interest groups. A policy of systematically attempting to eliminate profit, regardless of its source, is less likely to stimulate the competitive process than to destroy it.

University of Birmingham   S. C. LITTLECHILD

Date of receipt of final typescript: December 1980

REFERENCES

Alchian, A. A. and Allen, W. R. (1974). *University Economics*, 3rd ed. London: Prentice-Hall.
Ayanian, R. (1975). 'Advertising and rate of return.' *Journal of Law and Economics*, vol. 18, no. 2 (October), pp. 479–506.
Bain, J. S. (1951). 'Relation of profit rate to industry concentration: American manufacturing 1936–40.' *Quarterly Journal of Economics*, vol. 65, p. 293.
Baran, P. and Sweezy, P. (1966). *Monopoly Capital*. New York: Monthly Review Press.
Benham, L. (1972). 'The effect of advertising on the price of eyeglasses.' *Journal of Law and Economics*, vol. 15, no. 2 (October), pp. 337–52.
Bergson, A. (1973). 'On monopoly welfare losses.' *American Economic Review*, vol. 63 (December), pp. 853–70.
Bloch, H. (1974). 'Advertising and profitability: a reappraisal.' *Journal of Political Economy*, vol. 82, no. 2, part 1.
Brozen, Y. (1970). 'The antitrust-task force deconcentration recommendation', *Journal of Law and Economics*, vol. 13, no. 2 (October).
—— (1971). 'Bain's concentration and rates of return.' *Journal of Law and Economics*, vol. 14, no. 2 (October), pp. 351–70.
—— (1974). 'Entry barriers: advertising and product differentiation.' In Goldschmid (1974), pp. 115–37.
—— (1977a). *Foreword* to Clarkson (1977).
—— (1977b). 'The concentration–collusion doctrine.' *Antitrust Law Journal*, vol. 4, no. 3 (summer), pp. 826–62.
Carter, J. R. (1978). 'Collusion, efficiency, and antitrust.' *The Journal of Law and Economics*, vol. 21 (2) (October), pp. 435–44.
Clarkson, K. W. (1977). *Intangible Capital and Rates of Return*, American Enterprise Institute, Washington.
Comanor, W. S. and Wilson, T. S. (1967). 'Advertising, market structure and performance.' *Review of Economics and Statistics*, vol. 49, pp. 423–40.
Coase, R. H. (1972). 'Durability and monopoly'. *Journal of Law and Economics*, vol. 15, no. 1, (April), pp. 143–50.
Cowling, K. (1978). 'Monopolies and mergers policy: a view on the Green Paper.' University of Warwick (August).
—— and Mueller, D. C. (1978). 'The social costs of monopoly power,' ECONOMIC JOURNAL, vol. 88, (December), pp. 727–48.
Demsetz, H. (1969). 'Information and efficiency: another viewpoint'. *Journal of Law and Economics*, vol. 12, no. 1 (April), pp. 1–22.
—— (1973). 'Industry structure, market rivalry and public policy.' *Journal of Law and Economics*, vol. 16, no. 1 (April), pp. 1–10.
—— (1974). 'Two systems of belief about monopoly.' In Goldschmid (1974), pp. 164–84.

Dixit, A. and Norman, V. (1978). 'Advertising and welfare.' *Bell Journal of Economics*, vol. 9, no. 1 (spring), pp. 1–17.

Goldschmid, H. J. *et al.* (eds) (1974). *Industrial Concentration: The New Learning* Boston: Little, Brown.

Harberger, A. C. (1954). 'Monopoly and resource allocation.' *American Economic Review, Proceedings*, vol. 44 (May), pp. 73–87.

Hart, P. E. and Clarke, R. (1980). *Concentration in British Industry 1935–75*. Cambridge University Press (National Institute of Economic and Social Research, Occasional Papers, 32.)

Hayek, F. A. (1948) 'The meaning of competition.' In *Individualism and Economic Order*. Chicago: University of Chicago Press.

Kirzner, I. M. (1973). *Competition and Entrepreneurship*. Chicago: University of Chicago Press.

—— (1975). 'The social costs of monopoly: a comment.' Mimeo, New York University.

—— (1979) *Perception, Opportunity and Profit*. Chicago: University of Chicago Press.

—— (1980). 'The primacy of entrepreneurial discovery.' In *The Prime Mover of Progress* (ed. A. Seldon), pp. 3–28. London: Institute of Economic Affairs.

Little, I. M. D. and Rayner, A. C. (1978). *Higgledy Piggledy Growth Again: Investigation of the Predictability of Company Earnings in the U.K. 1951–1961*. Kelly.

Littlechild, S. C. (1978). *The Fallacy of the Mixed Economy*. Hobart Paper no. 80 (June). London: Institute of Economic Affairs.

Mancke, R. B. (1974). 'Interfirm profitability differences.' *The Quarterly Journal of Economics*. vol. 88, no. 2 (May), pp. 181–94.

McNulty, P. J. (1967). 'A note on the history of perfect competition.' *Journal of Political Economy*, vol. 75 (August).

Mises, L. von (1949). *Human Action*, 1st ed. Chicago: Henry Regnery. (3rd rev. ed. 1963).

Monopolies and Mergers Commission (1979). *Petroi* Cmnd. 7433. London: HMSO (January).

Pearce, I. F. (1975). 'Monopolistic competition and general equilibrium.' In *Current Economic Problems*. (ed. M. Parkin and A. R. Nobay) Cambridge University Press.

Peltzman, S. (1977). 'The gains and losses from industrial concentration.' *Journal of Law and Economics*, vol. 20, no. 2, (October), pp. 229–64.

Posner, R. A. (1975). 'The social costs of monopoly and regulation.' *Journal of Political Economy*, vol. 83 (August), pp. 807–27.

Prais, S. (1976). *The Evolution of Giant Firms in Britain: A Study of the Growth of Concentration in Manufacturing Industry in Britain, 1909–1970*. Cambridge University Press.

Reekie, W. Duncan (1979). *Industry, Prices and Markets*. Oxford: Philip Allan.

—— and Bhoyrub, P. (1980). 'Profitability and intangible assets – Another look at advertising and entry barriers.' Discussion Paper.

Richardson, G. B. (1960). *Information and Investment*. Oxford University Press.

Schumpeter, J. A. (1950). *Capitalism, Socialism and Democracy*, 3rd ed. New York: Harper & Row.

Spence, A. M. (1977). 'Entry, capacity, investment and oligopolistic pricing.' *Bell Journal of Economics*, vol. 8, no. 2 (Autumn), pp. 534–44.

Tullock, G. (1967). 'The welfare costs of tariffs, monopolies and theft.' *Western Economic Journal*, vol. 5 (June), pp. 224–32.

Yamey, B. (1974). 'Monopolistic price discrimination and economic welfare.' *Journal of Law and Economics*. vol. 17, no. 2 (1974), pp. 377–80.

[18]

BORK'S PARADOX: STATIC VS. DYNAMIC EFFICIENCY IN ANTITRUST ANALYSIS

JACK HIGH*

Judge Robert Bork holds two opposing attitudes towards perfect competition. It is a highly useful economic model for illustrating allocative efficiency, but it is a defective policy model because it deliberately omits productive efficiency. He reconciles these attitudes by combining perfectly competitive allocative efficiency with dynamically competitive productive efficiency in his analysis.

However, these two kinds of competition do not readily mix. One is a static equilibrium concept, the other a dynamic disequilibrium concept. One assumes perfect knowledge and the absence of change; the other assumes imperfect knowledge, learning, and continual flux. Each kind of competition is built on assumptions which, if true, would preclude the existence of the other.

Bork's policy conclusions require the simultaneous existence of both kinds of competition. If he drops dynamic competition from the analysis, a much more stringent antitrust policy is called for. If he drops static competition, economic theory does not justify even his strictures against mergers and cartels.

I. INTRODUCTION

" . . . [I]t is difficult to the point of impossibility to derive from Schumpeter's 'process of creative destruction' an analytical framework on which applicable and effective antitrust standards might be built . . ." (Edward S. Mason 1951).

"The confusion arises because many courts and many economists fail to realize that the 'competitive model' is silent on the subject of competition" (M. Bruce Johnson 1983).

Anyone who wishes to see economic sense brought to antitrust law should feel grateful to the "Chicago school" of law and economics.[1] Not only has this school, through a long series of scholarly articles, brought to light the usefulness of many business practices that have traditionally been considered harmful, but it has also begun to have an effect on antitrust practice.

---

*Professor High wrote this paper while he was a visiting lecturer at California State University, Long Beach, during the 1983-84 academic year. He was on leave from George Mason University, Fairfax, Virginia, where he currently is on the faculty.

1. For some interesting background on the development of this tradition, see Kitch (1983).

The virtual disappearance of cases involving "vertical restraints," and the recent emphasis at both the Justice Department and the Federal Trade Commission on promoting efficiency—rather than merely preventing bigness—is attributable to the influence of the Chicago school.[2]

Despite the accomplishments of this school, its analysis remains ambiguous about the meaning of one of the central terms of theory and policy—competition. Stigler (1965, 265-267), for example, has long been a champion of the superiority of the perfectly competitive model for both theory and policy, while Demsetz (1968, 1973, 1976) has typically given market rivalry center stage in his analysis and policy recommendations.

This ambiguity is evident in Robert Bork's *The Antitrust Paradox*. For purposes of interpreting the antitrust statutes, Bork rejects both perfect competition and market rivalry. Instead he takes competition to mean consumer welfare, which, he argues, antitrust laws are supposed to promote (Bork 1978, 58-61).

However, when we turn to Bork's analysis, we find that perfect competition and market rivalry both figure prominently. Perfect competition is used to derive a standard of allocational efficiency. This standard is then used to define output restrictions harmful to consumer welfare. Market rivalry is used to define productive efficiency, which is the method by which business activity enhances consumer welfare. Thus, competition as consumer welfare embodies *both* perfect competition and market rivalry.

There would be nothing worrisome in this, were it not that perfect competition and market rivalry rest on incompatible assumptions. They are two mutually exclusive ways of looking at market competition. As Hayek (1948, 96) pointed out more than 30 years ago, most of what we mean by the verb "to compete" is impossible under perfect competition. " 'Perfect competition' means indeed the absence of all competitive activities."

Given the incompatibility of perfect competition and rivalry (which we will say more about below), we should not be surprised if combining them leads to incongruity in our results. This has indeed happened in Bork's analysis; there is a fundamental inconsistency in Bork's interpretation of antitrust. This paper will draw attention to this inconsistency, examine its cause, and explore some of its implications for antitrust.

II. THE PARADOX

The task of antitrust, as Bork sees it, is to strike a proper balance between productive efficiency and allocative efficiency.

Productive efficiency is "any activity by a business firm that creates wealth" (Bork 1978, 105). With proper qualification, productive efficiency may be defined as "competitive effectiveness" (Bork 1978, 106). It is using resources more effectively than actual or potential rivals in an industry

---

2. On recent government attitudes toward antitrust, see Hiltzik (1984) and Grant (1984).

(Bork 1978, 178 and 192-194). Productive efficiency is not determined by some ideal standard, but rather by how well one business uses resources as compared with its competitors (Bork 1978, 121). Productive efficiency is obviously an outcome of market rivalry.

Allocative efficiency, on the other hand, is derived from the "perfect market" model.[3] A perfectly competitive economy equates the price of each good with the marginal cost of its production. The distribution of resources that equates price and marginal cost for each good is a welfare standard, because it insures that consumer welfare is maximized (Bork 1978, 97). Monopoly is bad because it creates a divergence between price and marginal cost. This implies resources could be rearranged to improve consumer welfare. "The evil of monopoly, then, is not higher prices or smaller production . . . but misallocated resources, or allocation inefficiency" (Bork 1978, 101).

These two kinds of efficiency—productive and allocative—can conflict with one another, and when they do, antitrust law bears the responsibility of adjudicating the conflict in favor of consumer welfare. "The whole task of antitrust can be summed up as the effort to improve allocative efficiency without impairing productive efficiency so greatly as to produce either no gain or a net loss in consumer welfare" (Bork 1978, 91). The foundation of Bork's antitrust edifice, then, consists of two different kinds of efficiency— the dynamic productive efficiency of market rivalry and the static allocational efficiency of perfect competition.

Combining these two leads to a paradox. From Bork's approval of the allocation of resources when price equals marginal cost, one might think that he would want antitrust laws to promote perfect competition. He does not. "A determined attempt to remake the American economy into a replica of the textbook model of competition would have roughly the same effect on national wealth as several dozen strategically placed nuclear explosions" (Bork 1978, 92). Perfect competition is fine for economic theory, "but it is utterly useless as a goal of law" (Bork 1978, 59).

Thus, we have the following set of propositions:

1) Maximum consumer welfare is achieved by equating price and marginal cost (Bork 1978, 97).

2) Price and marginal cost are equated when markets are perfectly competitive (Bork 1978, 94).

3) Perfect competition does *not* achieve maximum consumer welfare (Bork 1978, 92).

It is this set of propositions that we have labeled Bork's paradox. If we inquire into its cause, we see that it is not merely scale economies that are responsible for it (see section III). Perfect competition is unsuitable as a welfare ideal because it "leaves out too much" (Bork 1978, 92). "The model

---

3. The term is Stigler's (see Stigler 1965, 235 and 245).

deliberately leaves out considerations of technology (in the broadest sense) that prevent real markets from approximating the model . . . and it is a basic, though extremely common, error to suppose that markets do not work efficiently if they depart from the model" (Bork 1978, 59-60). The model will mislead if we forget that ". . . the (competitive) reality is one of shifting prices and costs, changing technologies and organizational structures, and attempts to alter and improve products" (Bork 1978, 95). Perfect competition is unsuitable as a welfare ideal because it does not adequately encompass the incomplete knowledge, change, and productive efficiency of market rivalry.

The paradox in Bork's system results from mixing static and dynamic theory. More specifically, it is the result of (a) deriving a welfare standard from static assumptions, (b) rejecting the assumptions because they are incompatible with dynamic market rivalry, yet (c) retaining the welfare standard based on the discarded premises.

Using one set of premises for a first welfare standard and another set of premises for a second welfare standard requires caution under any circumstances. But when both standards define consumer welfare, yet each rests on mutually exclusive assumptions, our analysis is built on a contradiction.

Bork's stepping outside the assumptions on which he bases his welfare standard partly was at issue in his controversy with Gould and Yamey. They pointed out (1968, 947-948) that if Bork wants to use the standard welfare criterion for allocational efficiency, then he is bound by the standard assumptions. Bork, to his credit, has refused to remain bound by the assumptions of static theory.[4] In fact, the prominent place he has given dynamic efficiency is singularly important to the modern antitrust debate, and Bork deserves far more credit for this than he has yet received. However, using dynamic efficiency requires us to jettison static welfare standards, a point that needs to be better understood (see Richardson 1956).

III. COMPETITION, MONOPOLY, EFFICIENCY: TWO TRADITIONS

There are two ways to resolve the paradox in Bork's system. Either we can substitute a static notion of productive efficiency for his dynamic one, or we can substitute a dynamic notion of allocative efficiency for his static one.

One of the assumptions of the perfectly competitive model is that the sellers have "perfect knowledge." Although the specific content of what firms know is somewhat vague, it must include a knowledge of market price (the demand side of the market), and of the marginal cost curve of the most efficient production method (the supply side of the market). Unless the producer knows the price and the marginal cost curve, he cannot equate the two. Unless he knows the most efficient production method, an equality

---

4. In his reply to Gould and Yamey, Bork (1968, 951-953) improperly mixes static and dynamic efficiency together. As should be evident, our criticism is not that Bork uses dynamic efficiency, but that he retains static efficiency in what is otherwise a dynamic analysis.

between price and marginal cost will not maximize consumer welfare. Thus, built into the assumptions of static equilibrium theory is a notion of productive efficiency, which is each firm's use of the least-cost method of production.

Under the assumptions of perfect markets, it may happen that large-scale production is less costly than small-scale production. If so, then perfect competition may not maximize consumer welfare. The welfare loss occasioned by monopolistic supply must be weighed against the welfare gains of increased efficiency. However, the lower cost curve of the monopolist does not merely "symbolize" efficiency gains. A lower cost curve resulting from scale economies is the only efficiency gain possible under static assumptions. A new product, better promotion, a new form of organization, or a new production method are ruled out by perfect knowledge. If they were not ruled out, then we could not conclude that equality between price and marginal cost represented a maximum for consumer welfare, even in the absence of scale economies.

The theory of market rivalry depends on knowledge being imperfect in the market. It is the uncertainty resulting from incomplete knowledge, especially of future market conditions, that makes profit opportunities possible (see Knight 1921, 20). Under these conditions, it is possible to introduce a new good, a new production technique, or a superior method of promotion, and earn profit. It is, of course, the prospect of earning profits that calls forth the attempts at increased productive efficiency. Market rivalry, in essence, is competition for profit.

However, incomplete knowledge alters the way we must look at monopoly and allocative efficiency. Under the perfect market assumptions, competitive firms are distinguished from monopolistic ones by the slope of the demand curve. Under market rivalry assumptions, virtually all firms will have downward sloping demand curves. The mere fact that consumers do not all know who the low-priced firms are implies that a firm will not lose all its customers if it charges a price higher than its competitors.[5]

Moreover, in disequilibrium, even small firms selling identical products will often have highly inelastic demand curves in the neighborhood of market price. If market price is below equilibrium, for example, so that there is excess demand in the market, the first firms to discover it will be able to raise their price without any perceptible loss of sales.

More importantly, competition occurs on many levels besides price. Improvements in marketing, distribution, and product quality do not result

---

5. See Salop (1976, 240) and Stiglitz (1977, 389). In all of the proofs for the existence of a search-theory equilibrium, the firms face downward sloping demand curves. See Axell (1977), Sutton (1980), and MacMinn (1981). Although search models are not much of an improvement over perfect market models for understanding the operation of market economies (see High 1983-84), they do illustrate (1) that market rivalry does not tend to converge to a perfectly competitive equilibrium, and (2) that even small firms selling identical products will have downward sloping demand curves when information is not perfect.

in horizontal demand curves, and do not necessarily increase elasticity of demand, but they are as much the result of competition as increased elasticities.[6]

If the downward slope of the demand curve facing firms does not signify lack of competition, then a downward-sloping demand curve is not a sign of monopoly. Some other criterion must be found for distinguishing competition from monopoly.

One method for distinguishing competition from monopoly is to define monopoly in its literal sense as a single seller of a good. However, this meaning of monopoly is not very satisfactory for either theory or policy; it is arbitrary, and it applies to firms that are highly competitive. If we define the good narrowly enough, every firm is a monopolist, if only because all goods are necessarily distinguished by their location (Pasour 1982, 217; Hayek 1948, 98). Also, brand names and the reputations of professional people confer monopoly status in this sense, even though they are productive, and even though their possessors may be in fierce competition with other brand names and reputations (cf. Knight 1921, 185-186).

Monopoly may also be defined as a legal privilege that restricts freedom of entry into a field. This is the early common law meaning and the one that Adam Smith predominantly used (see O'Driscoll 1982, 191-195; Thorelli 1955, 21). Rothbard (1962, 587-593) and Armentano (1982, 42) argue for this usage. This meaning is also implicit in Knight's characterization of monopoly as "violent interference with competition" (Knight 1921, 185), and in his statement that "[w]hat competition actually means is simply the freedom of the individual to 'deal' with any and all other individuals and to select the best terms as judged by himself, among those offered" (Knight 1941-1942, 103).

Monopoly as a government-granted privilege does not suffer from the analytical and policy drawbacks of the single-seller version. It draws a clear line of demarcation between market competition and monopoly, and in fact represents suppression of competition. It does not represent any production of utility that could not be achieved in its absence. It does not depend on output restrictions derived from static assumptions. Finally, it takes policy out of the realm of pure economics and places it partly in the realm of moral and legal theory. It is up to the law to decide which actions of the state protect right of property and contract, and which confer special privilege.[7] Since much of the animus against monopoly rests on the belief that it is unfair (e.g., Lande 1982, 94-96, 113-117, and 135-136), it seems desirable to define the term in such a way that morality and law can take their place alongside economics in policy discussions.

6. See J. Paul McNulty (1968, 645-648) on the importance of non-price competition, and its neglect by economists.

7. A recent article by Epstein (1982) shows that all of the practices presently condemned by antitrust are justifiable under a system of corrective justice, which explains why the early common law focused on monopoly as a special privilege.

If competition for profit depends on knowledge being imperfect, we must formulate notions of efficiency that recognize this. In particular, we cannot assume that consumers' value scales are complete and unchanging, and we cannot assume that businessmen know which goods consumers want most or which production methods are least-cost. Accordingly, we may define productive efficiency as discovering and implementing lower-cost methods of production, and allocative efficiency as channeling resources into more highly valued uses (i.e., uses that consumers are willing to pay more for).

Both productive and allocative efficiency are motivated by the desire for profit, and, unlike the static notions, there is no conflict between the two that the courts could resolve. To earn profits, businessmen in a particular industry will exercise their best judgment in discovering and implementing the production processes, organizations, and marketing techniques they think most efficient. In order to implement their plans, they must bid resources away from other businessmen, *not only in their own industry, but in other industries as well*. Thus, productive efficiency and allocative efficiency are simply different aspects of the same bidding process. Productive efficiency places an upper limit on how much a businessman will bid for resources. The higher bids secure the resources; resources flow to their more highly valued uses; allocational efficiency results.

Of course, this bidding process will not be perfect; anticipated profits will not always be realized, and some firms will suffer losses, indicating that resources had more highly valued uses elsewhere. Disappointed expectations and business losses are unavoidable in a system with uncertainty. Even here, though, there is an efficiency aspect at work. Businessmen whose decisions do not compare well with others will have a harder time attracting funds. Their control over deciding where to employ resources will be reduced as compared with the more successful. There is a selection process at work that fosters specialization in entrepreneurship, with the more successful rising to the top. Specialization in entrepreneurship is one of the main reasons the enterprise system is so efficient (see Knight 1921, 259-60; Richardson 1953, 146-148).

By substituting a dynamic allocative efficiency for the static one, we remove the conflict between productive and allocative efficiency, and, as a consequence, we remove the efficiency rationale for antitrust laws. Consistent use of dynamic theory does not support the contention that antitrust laws, as administered historically, or as Bork would have them administered, promote efficiency or consumer welfare. We will support this conclusion by considering what is meant by output restriction, and by discussing the efficiency effects of cartels.

IV. DYNAMIC EFFICIENCY AND OUTPUT RESTRICTION

By employing the price-equals-marginal-cost standard of allocative efficiency, Bork is able to derive a level of output that maximizes consumer welfare. By comparing that ideal output against the actual output of the market, he is able to identify an output restriction that harms consumers and represents allocational inefficiency. However, the ideal output of static theory has no claim to be set up as the ideal output of a market economy. This is a particularly important point. It removes the benchmark used to claim that large firms or cartels restrict output. It also implies that some hypothetical state towards which an economy supposedly tends cannot be set up as a welfare ideal nor used to derive standards against which the performance of an economy is judged.

Perhaps the best way to illustrate this point is to consider a company that successfully introduces a new product into the market and, by virtue of its success, obtains a "monopoly." As a policy matter, Bork would oppose the dissolution of this monopoly because it is efficient *on net*. Since it has achieved its monopoly position by internal growth, ". . . its [productive] efficiency must outweigh its output restriction, or entry would erode its position" (Bork 1978, 196).

In what sense can we say that this firm has restricted output? If innumerable other small firms could produce this new product as cheaply as the innovative firm, and if they were also producing this new product, then output would be greater and price lower; correspondingly, consumers would be better off.

If we are comparing two static states—one in which there is a single producer of the good, and one in which there are innumerable small producers—we can identify an output restriction and label it bad. But if we are looking at a competitive process in which the lure of profits stimulates innovation, this can hardly be called a restriction and cannot be judged as harmful to the consumer.

If, in deciding to produce a new product, a firm knows that many other firms will also enter the field and establish a competitive equilibrium, *then the firm is not facing a profit opportunity and has no incentive to innovate.* As G. B. Richardson (1959, 233-234) has emphasized:

> A profit opportunity which is known by and available to everybody is available to nobody in particular. A situation of general profit potential can be tapped by one entrepreneur only if similar action is not intended by too many others; otherwise, excess supply and general losses would result. In other words, a general opportunity of this kind will create a reliable profit expectation for a single entrepreneur only if there is some limitation on the competitive supply to be expected from other producers.

What is labeled an output restriction from a static point of view is a profit opportunity from a dynamic viewpoint. Far from being something that hurts consumers, these opportunties provide the incentive for productive and allocative efficiency. In the dynamic view, the successful introduction of a new product increases both productive and allocative efficiency. There is no conflict or trade-off.

Under static assumptions, there is no need to discover new or better production techniques; they are already known. But under dynamic assumptions, competition is the process by which these things are discovered and implemented. Not only is there "no point in appraising the performance of that process *ex visu* of a given point of time" (Schumpeter 1975, 83), but there is no reason to judge it by standards which, if true, would make the process itself impossible. Using a static welfare standard to measure output restrictions in a dynamic process involves both of these errors.

V. CARTELS AND DYNAMIC EFFICIENCY

Evaluating business practices using only dynamic efficiency has much in common with Bork's analysis. His recommendations that vertical and conglomerate mergers, resale price maintenance, requirements contracts, and tying arrangements be declared legal per se accord with the view that these are methods of competing, and if they survive in the market without government-granted privilege, they should be judged as efficient business practices.

Part of the reason for this accordance is the large measure of dynamic efficiency in Bork's analysis. But part of the reason, too, is the way in which Bork uses theory to arrive at his conclusions. Since productive efficiency presupposes incomplete knowledge and uncertainty, economists and lawyers cannot be expected to know the particular ways in which business practices serve consumers. However, economic theory can, in Bork's view, identify those practices that restrict output. Antitrust theory proceeds by a process of elimination. If a particular practice does not restrict output, we presume it serves efficiency. If a practice does restrict output, then we have to examine its potential also to serve productive efficiency (Bork 1978, 122).

Consequently, Bork's policy recommendations differ only in those areas where static output restrictions may be substantial. Those areas are (1) cartels, (2) large horizontal mergers, and (3) predatory practices. Of these, cartels seem the most clear-cut examples of practices that harm consumer welfare, so we will examine cartels from a dynamic efficiency viewpoint.

1. Firms will be more willing to develop and market new products if cartel arrangements are legal. One of the most difficult aspects of evaluating profit opportunities is the uncertainty surrounding the actions of other firms (see Richardson 1959). If a firm knows that it can enter into cartel arrangements with others which might be working along the same lines, the uncertainty of introducing new products will be reduced. The beneficial aspects of patents in this respect are well recognized. A cartel has similar effects in the introduction of new products, and can serve as a substitute for patents.

2. A new firm will be more likely to enter into competition with an already established firm in an industry if the newcomer knows that once it has made inroads, the established firm might enter into a cartel agreement. The output under the cartel will be larger than if the newcomer had not entered.

3. A cartel can mitigate the effects of a business downturn. Cartels enable firms which otherwise would go bankrupt to stay in business and expand industry output when demand again increases. This prevents price from falling too far during downturns and from rising too high during upswings. Even if average price over the period is higher than it would be in the absence of cartels, this can be looked upon as an insurance fee (Schumpeter 1975, 90-91).

A downturn in business conditions has been historically important in the formation of cartels (cf. Richardson 1953, 151). The Addyston Pipe cartel, for example, was motivated by a depression in the industry; after the cartel was dissolved, a merger by the firms in the cartel performed the same functions as the cartel. If these mergers had been prohibited, many of the firms would have gone bankrupt and the industry would have been more concentrated. Whether concentration is good or bad, "naked" price agreements are not necessarily harmful to consumers. Bork's praise of Taft in the Addyston Pipe case seems overstated (see Phillips 1962, 116-118; Bork 1978, 26-30).

4. Price fixing and market division can, by themselves, cut down on sales costs and promotion costs. Reduction of these costs are as much a part of productive and allocative efficiency as are any other cost reductions. Moreover, they can reduce the uncertainty of price fluctuations, which cuts down on the costs of planning production. Also, these agreements are often accompanied by joint sales agencies or other agreements. The price-fixing agreements of the railroads, for example, were an integral part of facilitating common standards, which greatly increased the speed of interregional shipping (see Chandler 1977, 124-133).

5. Setting price is both costly and risky when uncertainty is present. "Price leadership" or joint decisions on price may be the most efficient way of reducing costs and minimizing risk.

6. Finally, price-fixing agreements can be a first step in increased communication and cooperation that eventually lead to more efficient management in an industry (cf. Rothbard 1962, 579-580).

In general, in a world of uncertainty, cartels are an important means of securing profit opportunities by facilitating planning and reducing the risks of business enterprise (see Dewey 1979, esp. 593). They increase dynamic productive and allocative efficiency the same way that other business practices do. Cartels are not always efficient, of course, and when they are not, they will suffer losses or invite entry just as other inefficient businesses will. Competition for profit will check the inefficiency of cartels in the same way that it checks inefficiency in the internal growth of firms (see Dewey 1978, 519-521). If the cartel does not lose money or attract entry, then it is judged by entrepreneurs to be too efficient to compete with.[8] Where entry is not

---

8. In general, dynamic competition will determine efficient market structures (Johnson 1982, 4). This structure will include cartels if they are efficient.

blocked by legal privilege, dynamic theory presumes efficiency—a presumption that accords well with the history of cartels, trusts, and mergers around the turn of the century. Combinations that were efficient lasted; inefficient ones did not (see Chandler 1977, 122-144; Porter 1973, 78-82).

The argument that the law can prevent inefficiency more quickly than competition does not hold up in a dynamic context. Judges, economists, and legislators have less expertise in identifying inefficiency than do entrepreneurs. Besides, they do not bear financial responsibility for their decisions and, hence, have no monetary incentive to form correct judgments.

VI. SUMMARY AND CONCLUSIONS

There are two distinct meanings to competition in economic theory. One is a static notion that assumes given tastes, technology, and prices; the other is a dynamic notion based on changing tastes, technology, and prices. The static notion is predicated on perfect knowledge, the dynamic notion on incomplete knowledge and uncertainty. Static competition is an equilibrium state in which no firm earns profits; dynamic competition is a disequilibrium process in which successful entrepreneurs capture profits, and unsuccessful ones suffer losses.

Each of these meanings of competition has its own conception of monopoly and of efficiency. In static theory, monopoly means a downward sloping demand curve; in dynamic theory, monopoly means a state-granted privilege that prevents or hinders entry. In static theory, productive efficiency means using the least-cost method of production, and allocative efficiency means resources are distributed so that price equals marginal cost. In dynamic theory, productive efficiency means discovering and employing lower-cost methods of production, and allocative efficiency means channeling resources into more highly valued uses.

Bork's interpretation of antitrust laws rests on a conflict between dynamic productive efficiency and static allocative efficiency. By resolving this conflict in favor of the consumer, Bork argues that antitrust law can further consumer welfare. Although the courts have performed this task poorly in the past, at least there is the possibility that antitrust law, if properly administered, could work for the general welfare of consumers.

If we remove the standard of allocative efficiency derived from static equilibrium theory, we remove the conflict between productive and allocative efficiency. There is no trade-off between these two in the dynamic sense. Both efficiencies are brought about by the process of competition for profit. Dynamic allocative efficiency provides us with no theoretical benchmark for identifying harmful restrictions of output that result from the competitive process. Even cartels, which have no socially redeeming value in static theory, promote efficiency in a world of incomplete knowledge and uncertainty. Inefficient cartels, like other inefficient business practices, will be eliminated through losses or entry.

If our analysis is correct, antitrust laws find no support in economic efficiency. Laws that prevent voluntary cartels and large mergers obstruct the

competitive process and harm efficiency. Some grounds other than efficiency may be found for supporting antitrust, but those grounds are not
likely to be found in dynamically competitive theory. Neither Knight nor
Schumpeter nor Hayek has been sanguine about beneficial results from antitrust (although none has rejected it outright). Bork, despite having one foot
in the static camp, is very much a part of the dynamic tradition; yet he is also
highly critical of the bulk of antitrust. And recently, Armentano (1982) has
condemned the entire antitrust enterprise.

If dynamically competitive economic theory does not provide grounds for
antitrust laws, then we must look to political, legal, and moral theory. Here,
too, Bork has contributed. He is solidly pessimistic about the ability of the
American judiciary to formulate rational antitrust policy and moderately
pessimistic about the political trend of antitrust (Bork 1978, 408-425).

Epstein's views (1982) seem particularly important in this connection. He
argues that a strict application of property, contract, and tort law would
prohibit antitrust laws—which violate freedom of property and contract.
He concludes that antitrust must find justification outside the law of corrective justice, perhaps in wealth maximization or consumer welfare. But
these are the very things which from a dynamic viewpoint, antitrust laws do
not promote. It appears that a union of corrective justice and economic
theory of the dynamic sort may provide a strong case against antitrust law.

This does not mean that law and economics support monopoly. On the
contrary, many monopolistic practices—from tariffs through monopoly
franchises to state-granted licensing privileges—should be opposed. These
practices violate freedom of contract, and prevent the competitive process
from ferreting out and correcting inefficiencies. The emphasis given to
monopoly by the common law and Adam Smith—that it is a government-
granted privilege restricting entry—still seems the best way for economic
theory to approach the monopoly.

Part IV
Central Planning

[19]

III

ECONOMIC CALCULATION IN THE SOCIALIST COMMONWEALTH [1]

By LUDWIG von MISES

(Translated from the German by S. Adler)

INTRODUCTION.

1. THE DISTRIBUTION OF CONSUMPTION-GOODS IN THE SOCIALIST COMMONWEALTH.
2. THE NATURE OF ECONOMIC CALCULATION.
3. ECONOMIC CALCULATION IN THE SOCIALIST COMMONWEALTH.
4. RESPONSIBILITY AND INITIATIVE IN COMMUNAL CONCERNS.
5. THE MOST RECENT SOCIALIST DOCTRINES AND THE PROBLEM OF ECONOMIC CALCULATION.

CONCLUSION.

INTRODUCTION

THERE are many socialists who have never come to grips in any way with the problems of economics, and who have made no attempt at all to form for themselves any clear conception of the conditions which determine the character of human society. There are others, who have probed deeply into the economic history of the past and present, and striven, on this basis, to construct a theory of economics of the " bourgeois " society. They have criticized freely enough the economic structure of " free " society, but have consistently neglected to apply to the

[1] [This article appeared originally under the title " Die Wirtschafts-rechnung im sozialistischen Gemeinwesen " in the *Archiv für Sozialwissenschaften*, vol. 47, 1920.—*Ed.*]

COLLECTIVIST ECONOMIC PLANNING

economics of the disputed socialist state the same caustic acumen, which they have revealed elsewhere, not always with success. Economics, as such, figures all too sparsely in the glamorous pictures painted by the Utopians. They invariably explain how, in the cloud-cuckoo lands of their fancy, roast pigeons will in some way fly into the mouths of the comrades, but they omit to show how this miracle is to take place. Wherever they do in fact commence to be more explicit in the domain of economics, they soon find themselves at a loss—one remembers, for instance, Proudhon's fantastic dreams of an " exchange-bank "—so that it is not difficult to point out their logical fallacies. When Marxism solemnly forbids its adherents to concern themselves with economic problems beyond the expropriation of the expropriators, it adopts no new principle, since the Utopians throughout their descriptions have also neglected all economic consider-ations, and concentrated attention solely upon painting lurid pictures of existing conditions and glowing pictures of that golden age which is the natural consequence of the New Dispensation.

Whether one regards the coming of socialism as an unavoidable result of human evolution, or considers the socialization of the means of production as the greatest blessing or the worst disaster that can befall mankind, one must at least concede, that investigation into the conditions of society organized upon a socialist basis is of value as something more than " a good mental exercise, and a means of promoting political clearness and con-sistency of thought ".[1] In an age in which we are approaching nearer and nearer to socialism, and even,

[1] v. Kautsky, *The Social Revolution and on the Morrow of the Social Revolution*, London, 1907, Part II, p. 1.

ECONOMIC CALCULATION

in a certain sense, are dominated by it, research into the problems of the socialist state acquires added significance for the explanation of what is going on around us. Previous analyses of the exchange economy no longer suffice for a proper understanding of social phenomena in Germany and its eastern neighbours to-day. Our task in this connection is to embrace within a fairly wide range the elements of socialistic society. Attempts to achieve clarity on this subject need no further justification.

1. The Distribution of Consumption-goods in the Socialist Commonwealth.

Under socialism all the means of production are the property of the community. It is the community alone which can dispose of them and which determines their use in production. It goes without saying that the community will only be in a position to employ its powers of disposal through the setting up of a special body for the purpose. The structure of this body and the question of how it will articulate and represent the communal will is for us of subsidiary importance. One may assume that this last will depend upon the choice of personnel, and in cases where the power is not vested in a dictatorship, upon the majority vote of the members of the corporation.

The owner of production-goods, who has manufactured consumption-goods and thus becomes their owner, now has the choice of either consuming them himself or of having them consumed by others. But where the community becomes the owner of consumption-goods, which it has acquired in production, such a choice will no longer obtain. It cannot itself consume ; it has perforce to

89

COLLECTIVIST ECONOMIC PLANNING

allow others to do so.   Who is to do the consuming and
what is to be consumed by each is the crux of the problem
of socialist distribution.

It is characteristic of socialism that the distribution
of consumption-goods must be independent of the
question of production and of its economic conditions.
It is irreconcilable with the nature of the communal
ownership of production-goods that it should rely even
for a part of its distribution upon the economic imputation of the yield to the particular factors of production.
It is logically absurd to speak of the worker's enjoying
the " full yield " of his work, and then to subject to a
separate distribution the shares of the material factors
of production.   For, as we shall show, it lies in the very
nature of socialist production that the shares of the particular factors of production in the national dividend
cannot be ascertained, and that it is impossible in fact to
gauge the relationship between expenditure and income.

What basis will be chosen for the distribution of consumption-goods among the individual comrades is for us
a consideration of more or less secondary importance.
Whether they will be apportioned according to individual
needs, so that he gets most who needs most, or
whether the superior man is to receive more than the
inferior, or whether a strictly equal distribution is envisaged as the ideal, or whether service to the State is
to be the criterion, is immaterial to the fact that, in any
event, the portions will be meted out by the State.

Let us assume the simple proposition that distribution
will be determined upon the principle that the State
treats all its members alike ; it is not difficult to conceive
of a number of peculiarities such as age, sex, health,
occupation, etc., according to which what each receives

ECONOMIC CALCULATION

will be graded. Each comrade receives a bundle of coupons, redeemable within a certain period against a definite quantity of certain specified goods. And so he can eat several times a day, find permanent lodgings, occasional amusements and a new suit every now and again. Whether such provision for these needs is ample or not, will depend on the productivity of social labour.

Moreover, it is not necessary that every man should consume the whole of his portion. He may let some of it perish without consuming it ; he may give it away in presents ; he may even in so far as the nature of the goods permit, hoard it for future use. He can, however, also exchange some of them. The beer-tippler will gladly dispose of non-alcoholic drinks allotted to him, if he can get more beer in exchange, whilst the teetotaller will be ready to give up his portion of drink if he can get other goods for it. The art-lover will be willing to dispose of his cinema-tickets in order the more often to hear good music ; the Philistine will be quite prepared to give up the tickets which admit him to art exhibitions in return for opportunities for pleasure he more readily understands. They will all welcome exchanges. But the material of these exchanges will always be consumption-goods. Production-goods in a socialist commonwealth are exclusively communal ; they are an inalienable property of the community, and thus *res extra commercium*.

The principle of exchange can thus operate freely in a socialist state within the narrow limits permitted. It need not always develop in the form of direct exchanges. The same grounds which have always existed for the building-up of indirect exchange will continue in a socialist state, to place advantages in the way of those

91

who indulge in it. It follows that the socialist state will thus also afford room for the use of a universal medium of exchange—that is, of Money. Its rôle will be fundamentally the same in a socialist as in a competitive society ; in both it serves as the universal medium of exchange. Yet the significance of Money in a society where the means of production are State-controlled will be different from that which attaches to it in one where they are privately owned. It will be, in fact, incomparably narrower, since the material available for exchange will be narrower, inasmuch as it will be confined to consumption-goods. Moreover, just because no production-good will ever become the object of exchange, it will be impossible to determine its monetary value. Money could never fill in a socialist state the rôle it fills in a competitive society in determining the value of production-goods. Calculation in terms of money will here be impossible.

The relationships which result from this system of exchange between comrades cannot be disregarded by those responsible for the administration and distribution of products. They must take these relationships as their basis, when they seek to distribute goods per head in accordance with their exchange value. If, for instance 1 cigar becomes equal to 5 cigarettes, it will be impossible for the administration to fix the arbitrary value of 1 cigar = 3 cigarettes as a basis for the equal distribution of cigars and cigarettes respectively. If the tobacco coupons are not to be redeemed uniformly for each individual, partly against cigars, partly against cigarettes, and if some receive only cigars and others only cigarettes, either because that is their wish or because the coupon office cannot do anything else at the moment, the market

ECONOMIC CALCULATION

conditions of exchange would then have to be observed. Otherwise everybody getting cigarettes would suffer as against those getting cigars. For the man who gets one cigar can exchange it for five cigarettes, and he is only marked down with three cigarettes.

Variations in exchange relations in the dealings between comrades will therefore entail corresponding variations in the administrations' estimates of the representative character of the different consumption-goods. Every such variation shows that a gap has appeared between the particular needs of comrades and their satisfactions because in fact, some one commodity is more strongly desired than another.

The administration will indeed take pains to bear this point in mind also as regards production. Articles in greater demand will have to be produced in greater quantities while production of those which are less demanded will have to suffer a curtailment Such control may be possible, but one thing it will not be free to do ; it must not leave it to the individual comrade to ask the value of his tobacco ticket either in cigars or cigarettes at will. If the comrade were to have the right of choice, then it might well be that the demand for cigars and cigarettes would exceed the supply, or vice versa, that cigars or cigarettes pile up in the distributing offices because no one will take them.

If one adopts the standpoint of the labour theory of value, the problem freely admits of a simple solution. The comrade is then marked up for every hour's work put in, and this entitles him to receive the product of one hour's labour, less the amount deducted for meeting such obligations of the community as a whole as maintenance of the unfit, education, etc.

93

COLLECTIVIST ECONOMIC PLANNING

Taking the amount deducted for covering communal expenses as one half of the labour product, each worker who had worked a full hour would be entitled only to obtain such amount of the product as really answered to half an hour's work. Accordingly, anybody who is in a position to offer twice the labour-time taken in manufacturing an article, could take it from the market and transfer to his own use or consumption. For the clarification of our problem it will be better to assume that the State does not in fact deduct anything from the workers towards meeting its obligations, but instead imposes an income tax upon its working members. In that way every hour of work put in would carry with it the right of taking for oneself such amount of goods as entailed an hour's work.

Yet such a manner of regulating distribution would be unworkable, since labour is not a uniform and homogeneous quantity. Between various types of labour there is necessarily a qualitative difference, which leads to a different valuation according to the difference in the conditions of demand for and supply of their products. For instance, the supply of pictures cannot be increased, *ceteris paribus*, without damage to the quality of the product. Yet one cannot allow the labourer who had put in an hour of the most simple type of labour to be entitled to the product of an hour's higher type of labour. Hence, it becomes utterly impossible in any socialist community to posit a connection between the significance to the community of any type of labour and the apportionment of the yield of the communal process of production. The remuneration of labour cannot but proceed upon an arbitrary basis ; it cannot be based upon the economic valuation of the yield as in a competitive state

ECONOMIC CALCULATION

of society, where the means of production are in private hands, since—as we have seen—any such valuation is impossible in a socialist community. Economic realities impose clear limits to the community's power of fixing the remuneration of labour on an arbitrary basis : in no circumstances can the sum expended on wages exceed the income for any length of time.

Within these limits it can do as it will. It can rule forthwith that all labour is to be reckoned of equal worth, so that every hour of work, whatever its quality, entails the same reward ; it can equally well make a distinction in regard to the quality of work done. Yet in both cases it must reserve the power to control the particular distribution of the labour product. It will never be able to arrange that he who has put in an hour's labour shall also have the right to consume the product of an hour's labour, even leaving aside the question of differences in the quality of the labour and the products, and assuming moreover that it would be possible to gauge the amount of labour represented by any given article. For, over and above the actual labour, the production of all economic goods entails also the cost of materials. An article in which more raw material is used can never be reckoned of equal value with one in which less is used.

2. THE NATURE OF ECONOMIC CALCULATION

Every man who, in the course of economic life, takes a choice between the satisfaction of one need as against another, *eo ipso* makes a judgment of value. Such judgments of value at once include only the very satisfaction of the need itself ; and from this they reflect back upon the goods of a lower, and then further upon goods of

95

COLLECTIVIST ECONOMIC PLANNING

a higher order. As a rule, the man who knows his own mind is in a position to value goods of a lower order. Under simple conditions it is also possible for him without much ado to form some judgment of the significance to him of goods of a higher order. But where the state of affairs is more involved and their interconnections not so easily discernible, subtler means must be employed to accomplish a correct [1] valuation of the means of production. It would not be difficult for a farmer in economic isolation to come by a distinction between the expansion of pasture-farming and the development of activity in the hunting field. In such a case the processes of production involved are relatively short and the expense and income entailed can be easily gauged. But it is quite a different matter when the choice lies between the utilization of a water-course for the manufacture of electricity or the extension of a coal-mine or the drawing up of plans for the better employment of the energies latent in raw coal. Here the roundabout processes of production are many and each is very lengthy ; here the conditions necessary for the success of the enterprises which are to be initiated are diverse, so that one cannot apply merely vague valuations, but requires rather more exact estimates and some judgment of the economic issues actually involved.

Valuation can only take place in terms of units, yet it is impossible that there should ever be a unit of subjective use-value for goods. Marginal utility does not posit any unit of value, since it is obvious that the value of two units of a given stock is necessarily greater than, but less than double, the value of a single unit. Judgments

---

[1] Using that term, of course, in the sense only of the valuating subject, and not in an objective and universally applicable sense.

ECONOMIC CALCULATION

of value do not measure ; they merely establish grades and scales.[1] Even Robinson Crusoe, when he has to make a decision where no ready judgment of value appears and where he has to construct one upon the basis of a more or less exact estimate, cannot operate solely with subjective use-value, but must take into consideration the intersubstitutability of goods on the basis of which he can then form his estimates. In such circumstances it will be impossible for him to refer all things back to one unit. Rather will he, so far as he can, refer all the elements which have to be taken into account in forming his estimate to those economic goods which can be apprehended by an obvious judgment of value—that is to say, to goods of a lower order and to pain-cost. That this is only possible in very simple conditions is obvious. In the case of more complicated and more lengthy processes of production it will, plainly, not answer.

In an exchange economy the objective exchange-value of commodities enters as the unit of economic calculation. This entails a threefold advantage. In the first place, it renders it possible to base the calculation upon the valuations of all participants in trade. The subjective use-value of each is not immediately comparable as a purely individual phenomenon with the subjective use-value of other men. It only becomes so in exchange-value, which arises out of the interplay of the subjective valuations of all who take part in exchange. But in that case calculation by exchange-value furnishes a control over the appropriate employment of goods. Anyone who wishes to make calculations in regard to a complicated process of production will immediately notice whether he has worked more economically than others

[1] Čuhel, *Zur Lehre von den Bedürfnissen*, Innsbruck, 1907, pp. 198 ff.

COLLECTIVIST ECONOMIC PLANNING

or not ; if he finds, from reference to the exchange-relations obtaining in the market, that he will not be able to produce profitably, this shows that others understand how to make a better use of the goods of a higher order in question. Lastly, calculation by exchange-value makes it possible to refer values back to a unit. For this purpose, since goods are mutually substitutable in accordance with the exchange-relations obtaining in the market, any possible good can be chosen. In a monetary economy it is money that is so chosen.

Monetary calculation has its limits. Money is no yardstick of value, nor yet of price. Value is not indeed *measured* in money, nor is price. They merely consist in money. Money as an economic good is not of stable value as has been naïvely, but wrongly, assumed in using it as a " standard of deferred payments ". The exchange-relationship which obtains between money and goods is subjected to constant, if (as a rule) not too violent, fluctuations originating not only from the side of other economic goods, but also from the side of money. However, these fluctuations disturb value calculations only in the slightest degree, since usually, in view of the ceaseless alternations in other economic data—these calculations will refer only to comparatively short periods of time—periods in which " good " money, at least normally, undergoes comparatively trivial fluctuations in regard to its exchange-relations. The inadequacy of the monetary calculation of value does not have its mainspring in the fact that value is then calculated in terms of a universal medium of exchange, namely money, but rather in the fact that in this system it is exchange-value and not subjective use-value on which the calculation is based. It can never obtain as a measure for the calculation of those

ECONOMIC CALCULATION

value-determining elements which stand outside the domain of exchange transactions. If, for example, a man were to calculate the profitability of erecting a waterworks, he would not be able to include in his calculation the beauty of the waterfall which the scheme might impair, except that he may pay attention to the diminution of tourist traffic or similar changes, which may be valued in terms of money. Yet these considerations might well prove one of the factors in deciding whether or no the building is to go up at all.

It is customary to term such elements "extra-economic". This perhaps is appropriate ; we are not concerned with disputes over terminology ; yet the considerations themselves can scarcely be termed irrational. In any place where men regard as significant the beauty of a neighbourhood or of a building, the health, happiness and contentment of mankind, the honour of individuals or nations, they are just as much motive-forces of rational conduct as are economic factors in the proper sense of the word, even where they are not substitutable against each other on the market and therefore do not enter into exchange-relationships.

That monetary calculation cannot embrace these factors lies in its very nature ; but for the purposes of our every-day economic life this does not detract from the significance of monetary calculation. For all those ideal goods are goods of a lower order, and can hence be embraced straightway within the ambit of our judgment of values. There is therefore no difficulty in taking them into account, even though they must remain outside the sphere of monetary value. That they do not admit of such computation renders their consideration in the affairs of life easier and not harder. Once we see

COLLECTIVIST ECONOMIC PLANNING

clearly how highly we value beauty, health, honour and
pride, surely nothing can prevent us from paying a
corresponding regard to them.   It may seem painful to
any sensitive spirit to have to balance spiritual goods
against material.   But that is not the fault of monetary
calculation ; it lies in the very nature of things themselves.   Even where judgments of value can be established directly without computation in value or in money,
the necessity of choosing between material and spiritual
satisfaction cannot be evaded.   Robinson Crusoe and the
socialist state have an equal obligation to make the choice.

Anyone with a genuine sense of moral values experiences no hardship in deciding between honour and
livelihood.   He knows his plain duty.   If a man cannot
make honour his bread, yet can he renounce his bread
for honour's sake.   Only they who prefer to be relieved
of the agony of this decision, because they cannot bring
themselves to renounce material comfort for the sake of
spiritual advantage, see in the choice a profanation of true
values.

Monetary calculation only has meaning within the
sphere of economic organization.   It is a system whereby
the rules of economics may be applied in the disposition
of economic goods.   Economic goods only have part in
this system in proportion to the extent to which they
may be exchanged for money.   Any extension of the
sphere of monetary calculation causes misunderstanding.
It cannot be regarded as constituting a kind of yardstick for the valuation of goods, and cannot be so treated
in historical investigations into the development of social
relationships ; it cannot be used as a criterion of national
wealth and income, nor as a means of gauging the value
of goods which stand outside the sphere of exchange, as

100

ECONOMIC CALCULATION

who should seek to estimate the extent of human losses through emigrations or wars in terms of money?[1] This is mere sciolistic tomfoolery, however much it may be indulged in by otherwise perspicacious economists.

Nevertheless within these limits, which in economic life it never oversteps, monetary calculation fulfils all the requirements of economic calculation. It affords us a guide through the oppressive plenitude of economic potentialities. It enables us to extend to all goods of a higher order the judgment of value, which is bound up with and clearly evident in, the case of goods ready for consumption, or at best of production-goods of the lowest order. It renders their value capable of computation and thereby gives us the primary basis for all economic operations with goods of a higher order. Without it, all production involving processes stretching well back in time and all the longer roundabout processes of capitalistic production would be gropings in the dark.

There are two conditions governing the possibility of calculating value in terms of money. Firstly, not only must goods of a lower, but also those of a higher, order come within the ambit of exchange, if they are to be included. If they do not do so, exchange relationships would not arise. True enough, the considerations which must obtain in the case of Robinson Crusoe prepared, within the range of his own hearth, to exchange, by production, labour and flour for bread, are indistinguishable from those which obtain when he is prepared to exchange bread for clothes in the open market, and, therefore, it is to some extent true to say that every economic action, including Robinson Crusoe's own production, can be

[1] Cf. Wieser, *Über den Ursprung und die Hauptgesetze des wirtschaf - lichen Wertes*, Vienna, 1884, pp. 185 ff.

COLLECTIVIST ECONOMIC PLANNING

termed *exchange*.[1] Moreover, the mind of one man
alone—be it never so cunning, is too weak to grasp the
importance of any single one among the countlessly
many goods of a higher order. No single man can ever
master all the possibilities of production, innumerable as
they are, as to be in a position to make straightway
evident judgments of value without the aid of some
system of computation. The distribution among a
number of individuals of administrative control over
economic goods in a community of men who take part
in the labour of producing them, and who are economically
interested in them, entails a kind of intellectual division
of labour, which would not be possible without some
system of calculating production and without economy.

The second condition is that there exists in fact a
universally employed medium of exchange—namely,
money—which plays the same part as a medium, in the
exchange of production-goods also. If this were not the
case, it would not be possible to reduce all exchange-
relationships to a common denominator.

Only under simple conditions can economics dispense
with monetary calculation. Within the narrow confines
of household economy, for instance, where the father
can supervise the entire economic management, it is
possible to determine the significance of changes in the
processes of production, without such aids to the mind,
and yet with more or less of accuracy. In such a case
the process develops under a relatively limited use
of capital. Few of the capitalistic roundabout processes of production are here introduced : what is
manufactured is, as a rule, consumption-goods or at

[1] Cf. Mises, *Theorie des Geldes u. der Umlaufsmittel*, Munich and
Leipzig, 1912, p. 16, with the references there given.

ECONOMIC CALCULATION

least such goods of a higher order as stand very near to consumption-goods. The division of labour is in its rudimentary stages : one and the same labourer controls the labour of what is in effect, a complete process of production of goods ready for consumption, from beginning to end. All this is different, however, in developed communal production. The experiences of a remote and bygone period of simple production do not provide any sort of argument for establishing the possibility of an economic system without monetary calculation.

In the narrow confines of a closed household economy, it is possible throughout to review the process of production from beginning to end, and to judge all the time whether one or another mode of procedure yields more consumable goods. This, however, is no longer possible in the incomparably more involved circumstances of our own social economy. It will be evident, even in a socialist society, that 1,000 hectolitres of wine are better than 800, and it is not difficult to decide whether it desires 1,000 hectolitres of wine rather than 500 of oil. There is no need for any system of calculation to establish this fact : the deciding element is the will of the economic subjects involved. But once this decision has been taken, the real task of rational economic direction only commences, i.e. economically, to place the means at the service of the end. That can only be done with some kind of economic calculation. The human mind cannot orientate itself properly among the bewildering mass of intermediate products and potentialities of production without such aid. It would simply stand perplexed before the problems of management and location.[1]

[1] Gottl-Ottlilienfeld, *Wirtschaft u. Technik* (Grundriss d. Sozialökonomik, Section II, Tübingen, 1914), p. 216.

COLLECTIVIST ECONOMIC PLANNING

It is an illusion to imagine that in a socialist state calculation *in natura* can take the place of monetary calculation. Calculation *in natura*, in an economy without exchange, can embrace consumption-goods only ; it completely fails when it comes to deal with goods of a higher order. And as soon as one gives up the conception of a freely established monetary price for goods of a higher order, rational production becomes completely impossible. Every step that takes us away from private ownership of the means of production and from the use of money also takes us away from rational economics.

It is easy to overlook this fact, considering that the extent to which socialism is in evidence among us constitutes only a socialistic oasis in a society with monetary exchange, which is still a free society to a certain degree. In one sense we may agree with the socialists' assertion which is otherwise entirely untenable and advanced only as a demagogic point, to the effect that the nationalization and municipalization of enterprise is not really socialism, since these concerns in their business organizations are so much dependent upon the environing economic system with its free commerce that they cannot be said to partake to-day of the really essential nature of a socialist economy. In state and municipal undertakings technical improvements are introduced because their effect in similar private enterprises, domestic or foreign, can be noticed, and because those private industries which produce the materials for these improvements give the impulse for their introduction. In these concerns the advantages of reorganization can be established, because they operate within the sphere of a society based upon the private ownership of the means of production

ECONOMIC CALCULATION

and upon the system of monetary exchange, being thus capable of computation and account. This state of affairs, however, could not obtain in the case of socialist concerns operating in a purely socialistic environment.

Without economic calculation there can be no economy. Hence, in a socialist state wherein the pursuit of economic calculation is impossible, there can be—in our sense of the term—no economy whatsoever. In trivial and secondary matters rational conduct might still be possible, but in general it would be impossible to speak of rational production any more. There would be no means of determining what was rational, and hence it is obvious that production could never be directed by economic considerations. What this means is clear enough, apart from its effects on the supply of commodities. Rational conduct would be divorced from the very ground which is its proper domain. Would there, in fact, be any such thing as rational conduct at all, or, indeed, such a thing as rationality and logic in thought itself? Historically, human rationality is a development of economic life. Could it then obtain when divorced therefrom?

For a time the remembrance of the experiences gained in a competitive economy, which has obtained for some thousands of years, may provide a check to the complete collapse of the art of economy. The older methods of procedure might be retained not because of their rationality but because they appear to be hallowed by tradition. Actually, they would meanwhile have become irrational, as no longer comporting with the new conditions. Eventually, through the general reconstruction of economic thought, they will experience alterations which will render them in fact uneconomic. The supply

COLLECTIVIST ECONOMIC PLANNING

of goods will no longer proceed anarchically of its own accord ; that is true. All transactions which serve the purpose of meeting requirements will be subject to the control of a supreme authority. Yet in place of the economy of the " anarchic " method of production, recourse will be had to the senseless output of an absurd apparatus. The wheels will turn, but will run to no effect.

One may anticipate the nature of the future socialist society. There will be hundreds and thousands of factories in operation. Very few of these will be producing wares ready for use ; in the majority of cases what will be manufactured will be unfinished goods and production-goods. All these concerns will be interrelated. Every good will go through a whole series of stages before it is ready for use. In the ceaseless toil and moil of this process, however, the administration will be without any means of testing their bearings. It will never be able to determine whether a given good has not been kept for a superfluous length of time in the necessary processes of production, or whether work and material have not been wasted in its completion. How will it be able to decide whether this or that method of production is the more profitable ? At best it will only be able to compare the quality and quantity of the consumable end-product produced, but will in the rarest cases be in a position to compare the expenses entailed in production. It will know, or think it knows, the ends to be achieved by economic organization, and will have to regulate its activities accordingly, i.e. it will have to attain those ends with the least expense. It will have to make its computations with a view to finding the cheapest way. This computation will naturally have to

106

ECONOMIC CALCULATION

be a value-computation. It is eminently clear, and requires no further proof, that it cannot be of a technical character, and that it cannot be based upon the objective use-value of goods and services.

Now, in the economic system of private ownership of the means of production, the system of computation by value is necessarily employed by each independent member of society. Everybody participates in its emergence in a double way : on the one hand as a consumer and on the other as a producer. As a consumer he establishes a scale of valuation for goods ready for use and consumption. As a producer he puts goods of a higher order into such use as produces the greatest return. In this way all goods of a higher order receive a position in the scale of valuations in accordance with the immediate state of social conditions of production and of social needs. Through the interplay of these two processes of valuation, means will be afforded for governing both consumption and production by the economic principle throughout. Every graded system of pricing proceeds from the fact that men always and ever harmonize their own requirements with their estimation of economic facts.

All this is necessarily absent from a socialist state. The administration may know exactly what goods are most urgently needed. But in so doing, it has only found what is, in fact, but one of the two necessary prerequisites for economic calculation. In the nature of the case it must, however, dispense with the other—the valuation of the means of production. It may establish the value attained by the totality of the means of production ; this is obviously identical with that of all the needs thereby satisfied. It may also be able to calculate

107

COLLECTIVIST ECONOMIC PLANNING

the value of any means of production by calculating the consequence of its withdrawal in relation to the satisfaction of needs. Yet it cannot reduce this value to the uniform expression of a money price, as can a competitive economy, wherein all prices can be referred back to a common expression in terms of money. In a socialist commonwealth which, whilst it need not of necessity dispense with money altogether, yet finds it impossible to use money as an expression of the price of the factors of production (including labour), money can play no role in economic calculation.[1]

Picture the building of a new railroad. Should it be built at all, and if so, which out of a number of conceivable roads should be built ? In a competitive and monetary economy, this question would be answered by monetary calculation. The new road will render less expensive the transport of some goods, and it may be possible to calculate whether this reduction of expense transcends that involved in the building and upkeep of the next line. That can only be calculated in money. It is not possible to attain the desired end merely by counterbalancing the various physical expenses and physical savings. Where one cannot express hours of labour, iron, coal, all kinds of building material, machines and other things necessary for the construction and upkeep of the railroad in a common unit it is not possible to make calculations at all. The drawing up of bills

[1] This fact is also recognized by Neurath (*Durch die Kriegswirtschaft zur Naturalwirtschaft*, Munich, 1919, pp. 216 f.). He advances the view that every complete administrative economy is, in the final analysis, a natural economy. " Socialization ", he says, " is thus the pursuit of natural economy." Neurath merely overlooks the insuperable difficulties that would have to develop with economic calculation in the socialist commonwealth.

ECONOMIC CALCULATION

on an economic basis is only possible where all the goods concerned can be referred back to money. Admittedly, monetary calculation has its inconveniences and serious defects, but we have certainly nothing better to put in its place, and for the practical purposes of life monetary calculation as it exists under a sound monetary system always suffices. Were we to dispense with it, any economic system of calculation would become absolutely impossible.

The socialist society would know how to look after itself. It would issue an edict and decide for or against the projected building. Yet this decision would depend at best upon vague estimates ; it would never be based upon the foundation of an exact calculation of value.

The static state can dispense with economic calculation. For here the same events in economic life are ever recurring ; and if we assume that the first disposition of the static socialist economy follows on the basis of the final state of the competitive economy, we might at all events conceive of a socialist production system which is rationally controlled from an economic point of view. But this is only conceptually possible. For the moment, we leave aside the fact that a static state is impossible in real life, as our economic data are for ever changing, so that the static nature of economic activity is only a theoretical assumption corresponding to no real state of affairs, however necessary it may be for our thinking and for the perfection of our knowledge of economics. Even so, we must assume that the transition to socialism must, as a consequence of the levelling out of the differences in income and the resultant readjustments in consumption, and therefore production, change all economic data in such a way that a connecting

COLLECTIVIST ECONOMIC PLANNING

link with the final state of affairs in the previously existing competitive economy becomes impossible. But then
we have the spectacle of a socialist economic order
floundering in the ocean of possible and conceivable
economic combinations without the compass of economic
calculation.

Thus in the socialist commonwealth every economic
change becomes an undertaking whose success can be
neither appraised in advance nor later retrospectively
determined. There is only groping in the dark.
Socialism is the abolition of rational economy.

3. ECONOMIC CALCULATION IN THE SOCIALIST COMMONWEALTH

Are we really dealing with the necessary consequences
of common ownership of the means of production ? Is
there no way in which some kind of economic calculation might be tied up with a socialist system ?

In every great enterprise, each particular business or
branch of business is to some extent independent in its
accounting. It reckons the labour and material against
each other, and it is always possible for each individual
group to strike a particular balance and to approach the
economic results of its activities from an accounting
point of view. We can thus ascertain with what success each particular section has laboured, and accordingly draw conclusions about the reorganization, curtailment, abandonment, or expansion of existing groups and
about the institution of new ones. Admittedly, some
mistakes are inevitable in such a calculation. They arise
partly from the difficulties consequent upon an allocation
of general expenses. Yet other mistakes arise from the

ECONOMIC CALCULATION

necessity of calculating with what are not from many
points of view rigorously ascertainable data, e.g. when
in the ascertainment of the profitability of a certain
method of procedure we compute the amortization of
the machines used on the assumption of a given duration for their usefulness. Still, all such mistakes can
be confined within certain narrow limits, so that they
do not disturb the net result of the calculation. What
remains of uncertainty comes into the calculation of the
uncertainty of future conditions, which is an inevitable
concomitant of the dynamic nature of economic life.

It seems tempting to try to construct by analogy a
separate estimation of the particular production groups
in the socialist state also. But it is quite impossible.
For each separate calculation of the particular branches
of one and the same enterprise depends exclusively on
the fact that it is precisely in market dealings that market
prices to be taken as the bases of calculation are formed
for all kinds of goods and labour employed. Where
there is no free market, there is no pricing mechanism ;
without a pricing mechanism, there is no economic
calculation.

We might conceive of a situation, in which exchange
between particular branches of business is permitted, so
as to obtain the mechanism of exchange relations (prices)
and thus create a basis for economic calculation even
in the socialist commonwealth. Within the framework
of a uniform economy knowing not private ownership
of the means of production, individual labour groups
are constituted independent and authoritative disposers,
which have indeed to behave in accordance with the
directions of the supreme economic council, but which
nevertheless assign each other material goods and services

III

COLLECTIVIST ECONOMIC PLANNING

only against a payment, which would have to be made in the general medium of exchange. It is roughly in this way that we conceive of the organization of the socialist running of business when we nowadays talk of complete socialization and the like. But we have still not come to the crucial point. Exchange relations between production-goods can only be established on the basis of private ownership of the means of production. When the " coal syndicate " provides the " iron syndicate " with coal, no price can be formed, except when both syndicates are the owners of the means of production employed in their business. This would not be socialization but workers' capitalism and syndicalism.

The matter is indeed very simple for those socialist theorists who rely on the labour theory of value.

> As soon as society takes possession of the means of production and applies them to production in their directly socialised form, each individual's labour, however different its specific utility may be, becomes *a priori* and directly social labour. The amount of social labour invested in a product need not then be established indirectly ; daily experience immediately tells us how much is necessary on an average. Society can simply calculate how many hours of labour are invested in a steam engine, a quarter of last harvest's wheat, and a 100 yards of linen of given quality. . . . To be sure, society will also have to know how much labour is needed to produce any consumption-good. It will have to arrange its production plan according to its means of production, to which labour especially belongs. The utility yielded by the various consumption-goods, weighted against each other and against the amount of labour required to produce them, will ultimately determine the plan. People will make everything simple without the mediation of the notorious " value ".[1]

Here it is not our task once more to advance critical objections against the labour theory of value. In this

[1] Engels, *Dührings Umwälzung des Wissenschaft*, 7th ed., pp. 335 f.

connection they can only interest us in so far as they
are relevant to an assessment of the applicability of labour
in the value computations of a socialist community.

On a first impression calculation in terms of labour
also takes into consideration the natural non-human
conditions of production. The law of diminishing returns is already allowed for in the concept of socially
necessary average labour-time to the extent that its
operation is due to the variety of the natural conditions
of production. If the demand for a commodity increases
and worse natural resources must be exploited, then the
average socially necessary labour-time required for the
production of a unit increases too. If more favourable
natural resources are discovered, the amount of socially
necessary labour diminishes.[1] The consideration of the
natural condition of production suffices only in so far
as it is reflected in the amount of labour socially necessary. But it is in this respect that valuation in terms
of labour fails. It leaves the employment of material
factors of production out of account. Let the amount
of socially necessary labour-time required for the production of each of the commodities P and Q be 10 hours.
Further, in addition to labour the production of both
P and Q requires the raw material a, a unit of which
is produced by an hour's socially necessary labour;
2 units of a and 8 hours' labour are used in the production of P, and one unit of a and 9 hours' labour in
the production of Q. In terms of labour P and Q are
equivalent, but in value terms P is more valuable than Q.
The former is false, and only the latter corresponds
to the nature and purpose of calculation. True, this
surplus, by which according to value calculation P is

[1] Marx, *Capital*, translated by Eden and Cedar Paul, p. 9.

COLLECTIVIST ECONOMIC PLANNING

more valuable than Q, this material sub-stratum " is
given by nature without any addition from man ".[1]
Still, the fact that it is only present in such quantities
that it becomes an object of economizing, must be taken
into account in some form or other in value-calculation.

The second defect in calculation in terms of labour
is the ignoring of the different qualities of labour. To
Marx all human labour is economically of the same
kind, as it is always " the productive expenditure of
human brain, brawn, nerve and hand ".[2]

> Skilled labour counts only as intensified, or rather multiplied,
> simple labour, so that a smaller quantity of skilled labour is
> equal to a larger quantity of simple labour. Experience shows
> that skilled labour can always be reduced in this way to the
> terms of simple labour. No matter that a commodity be the
> product of the most highly skilled labour, its value can be
> equated with that of the product of simple labour, so that it
> represents merely a definite amount of simple labour."

Böhm-Bawerk is not far wrong when he calls this
argument " a theoretical juggle of almost stupefying
naïveté ".[3] To judge Marx's view we need not ask if it
is possible to discover a single uniform physiological
measure of all human labour, whether it be physical or
" mental ". For it is certain that there exist among men
varying degrees of capacity and dexterity, which cause
the products and services of labour to have varying
qualities. What must be conclusive in deciding the
question whether reckoning in terms of labour is applicable or not, is whether it is or is not possible to bring
different kinds of labour under a common denominator
without the mediation of the economic subject's valuation
of their products. The proof Marx attempts to give is

[1] Marx, ibid., p. 12.   [2] Marx, ibid., pp. 13 et seq.
[3] Cf. Böhm-Bawerk, *Capital and Interest*, p. 384.

ECONOMIC CALCULATION

not successful. Experience indeed shows that goods are consumed under exchange relations without regard of the fact of their being produced by simple or complex labour. But this would only be a proof that given amounts of simple labour are directly made equal to given amounts of complex labour, if it were shown that labour is the source of exchange value. This not only is not demonstrated, but is what Marx is trying to demonstrate by means of these very arguments.

No more is it a proof of this homogeneity that rates of substitution between simple and complex labour are manifested in the wage rate in an exchange economy—a fact to which Marx does not allude in this context. This equalizing process is a result of market transactions and not its antecedent. Calculation in terms of labour would have to set up an arbitrary proportion for the substitution of complex by simple labour, which excludes its employment for purposes of economic administration.

It was long supposed that the labour theory of value was indispensable to socialism, so that the demand for the nationalization of the means of production should have an ethical basis. To-day we know this for the error it is. Although the majority of socialist supporters have thus employed this misconception, and although Marx, however much he fundamentally took another point of view, was not altogether free from it, it is clear that the political call for the introduction of socialized production neither requires nor can obtain the support of the labour theory of value on the one hand, and that on the other those people holding different views on the nature and origin of economic value can be socialists according to their sentiments. Yet the labour theory of value is inherently necessary for the supporters of

COLLECTIVIST ECONOMIC PLANNING

socialist production in a sense other than that usually intended. In the main socialist production might only appear rationally realizable, if it provided an objectively recognizable unit of value, which would permit of economic calculation in an economy where neither money nor exchange were present. And only labour can conceivably be considered as such.

4. RESPONSIBILITY AND INITIATIVE IN COMMUNAL CONCERNS

The problem of responsibility and initiative in socialist enterprises is closely connected with that of economic calculation. It is now universally agreed that the exclusion of free initiative and individual responsibility, on which the successes of private enterprise depend, constitutes the most serious menace to socialist economic organization.[4]

The majority of socialists silently pass this problem by. Others believe they can answer it with an allusion to the directors of companies ; in spite of the fact that they are not the owners of the means of production, enterprises under their control have flourished. If society, instead of company shareholders, becomes the owner of the means of production, nothing will have altered. The directors would not work less satisfactorily for society than for shareholders.

We must distinguish between two groups of joint-stock companies and similar concerns. In the first group, consisting for the large part of smaller companies, a

[4] Cf. *Vorläufiger Bericht der Sozialisierungskommission über die Frage der Sozialisierung des Kohlenbergbaues*, concluded 15th February, 1919 (Berlin, 1919), p. 13.

116

ECONOMIC CALCULATION

few individuals unite in a common enterprise in the legal form of a company. They are often the heirs of the founders of the company, or often previous competitors who have amalgamated. Here the actual control and management of business is in the hands of the shareholders themselves or at least of some of the shareholders, who do business in their own interest; or in that of closely related shareholders such as wives, minors, etc. The directors in their capacity as members of the board of management or of the board of control, and sometimes also in an attenuated legal capacity, themselves exercise the decisive influence in the conduct of affairs. Nor is this affected by the circumstance that sometimes part of the share-capital is held by a financial consortium or bank. Here in fact the company is only differentiated from the public commercial company by its legal form.

The situation is quite different in the case of large-scale companies, where only a fraction of the shareholders, i.e. the big shareholders, participate in the actual control of the enterprise. And these usually have the same interest in the firm's prosperity as any property holder. Still, it may well be that they have interests other than those of the vast majority of small shareholders, who are excluded from the management even if they own the larger part of the share-capital. Severe collisions may occur, when the firm's business is so handled on behalf of the directors that the shareholders are injured. But be that as it may, it is clear that the real holders of power in companies run the business in their own interest, whether it coincides with that of the shareholders or not. In the long run it will generally be to the advantage of the solid company administrator,

COLLECTIVIST ECONOMIC PLANNING

who is not merely bent on making a transient profit, to represent the shareholders' interests only in every case and to avoid manipulations which might damage them. This holds good in the first instance for banks and financial groups, which should not trifle at the public's expense with the credit they enjoy. Thus it is not merely on the prescriptiveness of ethical motives that the success of companies depends.

The situation is completely transformed when an undertaking is nationalized. The motive force disappears with the exclusion of the material interests of private individuals, and if State and municipal enterprises thrive at all, they owe it to the taking over of "management" from private enterprise, or to the fact that they are ever driven to reforms and innovations by the business men from whom they purchase their instruments of production and raw material.

Since we are in a position to survey decades of State and socialist endeavour, it is now generally recognized that there is no internal pressure to reform and improvement of production in socialist undertakings, that they cannot be adjusted to the changing conditions of demand, and that in a word they are a dead limb in the economic organism. All attempts to breathe life into them have so far been in vain. It was supposed that a reform in the system of remuneration might achieve the desired end. If the managers of these enterprises were interested in the yield, it was thought they would be in a position comparable to that of the manager of large-scale companies. This is a fatal error. The managers of large-scale companies are bound up with the interests of the businesses they administer in an entirely different way from what could be the case in public concerns. They

ECONOMIC CALCULATION

are either already owners of a not inconsiderable fraction of the share capital, or hope to become so in due course. Further, they are in a position to obtain profits by stock-exchange speculation in the company's shares. They have the prospect of bequeathing their positions to, or at least securing part of their influence for, their heirs. The type to which the success of joint-stock companies is to be attributed, is not that of a complacently prosperous managing director resembling the civil servant in his outlook and experience ; rather it is precisely the manager, promoter, and man of affairs, who is himself interested as a shareholder, whom it is the aim of all nationalization and municipalization to exclude.

It is not generally legitimate to appeal in a socialist context to such arguments in order to ensure the success of an economic order built on socialist foundations. All socialist systems, including that of Karl Marx, and his orthodox supporters, proceed from the assumption that in a socialist society a conflict between the interests of the particular and general could not possibly arise. Everybody will act in his own interest in giving of his best because he participates in the product of all economic activity. The obvious objection that the individual is very little concerned whether he himself is diligent and enthusiastic, and that it is of greater moment to him that everybody else should be, is either completely ignored or is insufficiently dealt with by them. They believe they can construct a socialist commonwealth on the basis of the Categorical Imperative alone. How lightly it is their wont to proceed in this way is best shown by Kautsky when he says, " If socialism is a social necessity, then it would be human nature and not socialism which would have to readjust itself, if ever the

COLLECTIVIST ECONOMIC PLANNING

two clashed." [1] This is nothing but sheer Utopianism.

But even if we for the moment grant that these Utopian expectations can actually be realized, that each individual in a socialist society will exert himself with the same zeal as he does to-day in a society where he is subjected to the pressure of free competition, there still remains the problem of measuring the result of economic activity in a socialist commonwealth which does not permit of any economic calculation. We cannot act economically if we are not in a position to understand economizing.

A popular slogan affirms that if we think less bureaucratically and more commercially in communal enterprises, they will work just as well as private enterprises. The leading positions must be occupied by merchants, and then income will grow apace. Unfortunately " commercial-mindedness " is not something external, which can be arbitrarily transferred. A merchant's qualities are not the property of a person depending on inborn aptitude, nor are they acquired by studies in a commercial school or by working in a commercial house, or even by having been a business man oneself for some period of time. The entrepreneur's commercial attitude and activity arises from his position in the economic process and is lost with its disappearance. When a successful business man is appointed the manager of a public enterprise, he may still bring with him certain experiences from his previous occupation, and be able to turn them to good account in a routine fashion for some time. Still, with his entry into communal activity he ceases to be a merchant and becomes as much a bureaucrat as any other placeman in the public employ.

[1] Cf. Kautsky, Preface to Atlanticus (Ballod), *Produktion und Konsum im Sozialstaat*, Stuttgart, 1898, p. 14.

ECONOMIC CALCULATION

It is not a knowledge of bookkeeping, of business organization, or of the style of commercial correspondence, or even a dispensation from a commercial high-school, which makes the merchant, but his characteristic position in the production process, which allows of the identification of the firm's and his own interests.   It is no solution of the problem when Otto Bauer in his most recently published work proposes that the directors of the National Central Bank, on whom leadership in the economic process will be conferred, should be nominated by a Collegium, to which representatives of the teaching staff of the commercial high schools would also belong.[1] Like Plato's philosophers, the directors so appointed may well be the wisest and best of their kind, but they cannot be merchants in their posts as leaders of a socialist society, even if they should have been previously.

It is a general complaint that the administration of public undertakings lacks initiative.   It is believed that this might be remedied by changes in organization. This also is a grievous mistake.   The management of a socialist concern cannot entirely be placed in the hands of a single individual, because there must always be the suspicion that he will permit errors inflicting heavy damages on the community.   But if the important conclusions are made dependent on the votes of committees, or on the consent of the relevant government offices, then limitations are imposed on the individual's initiative. Committees are rarely inclined to introduce bold innovations.   The lack of free initiative in public business rests not on an absence of organization, it is inherent in the nature of the business itself.   One cannot transfer free disposal of the factors of production to an employee,

[1] Cf. Bauer, *Der Weg zum Sozialismus*, Vienna, 1919, p. 25.

COLLECTIVIST ECONOMIC PLANNING

however high his rank, and this becomes even less possible, the more strongly he is materially interested in the successful performance of his duties ; for in practice the propertyless manager can only be held morally responsible for losses incurred. And so ethical losses are juxtaposed with opportunities for material gain. The property owner on the other hand himself bears responsibility, as he himself must primarily feel the loss arising from unwisely conducted business. It is precisely in this that there is a characteristic difference between liberal and socialist production.

5. The Most Recent Socialist Doctrines and the Problem of Economic Calculation

Since recent events helped socialist parties to obtain power in Russia, Hungary, Germany and Austria, and have thus made the execution of a socialist nationalization programme a topical issue, Marxist writers have themselves begun to deal more closely with the problems of the regulation of the socialist commonwealth. But even now they still cautiously avoid the crucial question, leaving it to be tackled by the despised " Utopians ". They themselves prefer to confine their attention to what is to be done in the immediate future ; they are for ever drawing up programmes of the path to Socialism and not of Socialism itself. The only possible conclusion from all these writings is that they are not even conscious of the larger problem of economic calculation in a socialist society.

To Otto Bauer the nationalization of the banks appears the final and decisive step in the carrying through of the socialist nationalization programme. If all banks are

ECONOMIC CALCULATION

nationalized and amalgamated into a single central bank, then its administrative board becomes "the supreme economic authority, the chief administrative organ of the whole economy. Only by nationalization of the banks does society obtain the power to regulate its labour according to a plan, and to distribute its resources rationally among the various branches of production, so as to adapt them to the nation's needs."[1] Bauer is not discussing the monetary arrangements which will prevail in the socialist commonwealth after the completion of the nationalization of the banks. Like other Marxists he is trying to show how simply and obviously the future socialist order of society will evolve from the conditions prevailing in a developed capitalist economy. "It suffices to transfer to the nation's representatives the power now exercised by bank shareholders through the Administrative Boards they elect,"[2] in order to socialize the banks and thus to lay the last brick on the edifice of socialism. Bauer leaves his readers completely ignorant of the fact that the nature of the banks is entirely changed in the process of nationalization and amalgamation into one central bank. Once the banks merge into a single bank, their essence is wholly transformed ; they are then in a position to issue credit without any limitation.[3] In this fashion the monetary system as we know it to-day disappears of itself. When in addition the single central bank is nationalized in a society, which is otherwise already completely socialized, market dealings disappear and all exchange transactions are abolished. At the same time the Bank ceases to be a bank, its specific functions are extinguished, for there

[1] Bauer, op cit., pp. 26 f.   [2] Ibid., p. 25.
[3] Mises, op. cit., pp. 474 ff.

COLLECTIVIST ECONOMIC PLANNING

is no longer any place for it in such a society. It may be that the name " Bank " is retained, that the Supreme Economic Council of the socialist community is called the Board of Directors of the Bank, and that they hold their meetings in a building formerly occupied by a bank. But it is no longer a bank, it fulfils none of those functions which a bank fulfils in an economic system resting on the private ownership of the means of production and the use of a general medium of exchange-money. It no longer distributes any credit, for a socialist society makes credit of necessity impossible. Bauer himself does not tell us what a bank is, but he begins his chapter on the nationalization of the banks with the sentence : " All disposable capital flows into a common pool in the banks." [1] As a Marxist must he not raise the question of what the banks' activities will be after the abolition of capitalism ?

All other writers who have grappled with the problems of the organization of the socialist commonwealth are guilty of similar confusions. They do not realize that the bases of economic calculation are removed by the exclusion of exchange and the pricing mechanism, and that something must be substituted in its place, if all economy is not to be abolished and a hopeless chaos is not to result. People believe that socialist institutions might evolve without further ado from those of a capitalist economy. This is not at all the case. And it becomes all the more grotesque when we talk of banks, bank management, etc. in a socialist commonwealth.

Reference to the conditions that have developed in Russia and Hungary under Soviet rule proves nothing. What we have there is nothing but a picture of the

[1] Bauer, op. cit., p. 24.

ECONOMIC CALCULATION

destruction of an existing order of social production, for which a closed peasant household economy has been substituted. All branches of production depending on social division of labour are in a state of entire dissolution. What is happening under the rule of Lenin and Trotsky is merely destruction and annihilation. Whether, as the liberals hold, socialism must inevitably draw these consequences in its train, or whether, as the socialists retort, this is only a result of the fact that the Soviet Republic is attacked from without, is a question of no interest to us in this context. All that has to be established is the fact that the Soviet socialist commonwealth has not even begun to discuss the problem of economic calculation, nor has it any cause to do so. For where things are still produced for the market in Soviet Russia in spite of governmental prohibitions, they are valued in terms of money, for there exists to that extent private ownership of the means of production, and goods are sold against money. Even the Government cannot deny the necessity, which it confirms by increasing the amount of money in circulation, of retaining a monetary system for at least the transition period.

That the essence of the problem to be faced has not yet come to light in Soviet Russia, Lenin's statements in his essay on *Die nächsten Aufgaben der Sowjetmacht* best show. In the dictator's deliberations there ever recurs the thought that the immediate and most pressing task of Russian Communism is " the organization of bookkeeping and control of those concerns, in which the capitalists have already been expropriated, and of all other economic concerns ".[1] Even so Lenin is far

[1] Cf. Lenin, *Die nächsten Aufgaben der Sowjetmacht*, Berlin, 1918, pp. 12 f., 22 ff.

COLLECTIVIST ECONOMIC PLANNING

from realizing that an entirely new problem is here involved which it is impossible to solve with the conceptual instruments of " bourgeois " culture. Like a real politician, he does not bother with issues beyond his nose. He still finds himself surrounded by monetary transactions, and does not notice that with progressive socialization money also necessarily loses its function as the medium of exchange in general use, to the extent that private property and with it exchange disappear. The implication of Lenin's reflections is that he would like to re-introduce into Soviet business " bourgeois " bookkeeping carried on on a monetary basis. Therefore he also desires to restore " bourgeois experts " to a state of grace.[1] For the rest Lenin is as little aware as Bauer of the fact that in a socialist commonwealth the functions of the bank are unthinkable in their existing sense. He wishes to go farther with the " nationalization of the banks " and to proceed " to a transformation of the banks into the nodal point of social bookkeeping under socialism ".[2]

Lenin's ideas on the socialist economic system, to which he is striving to lead his people, are generally obscure.

> " The socialist state ", he says " can only arise as a net of producing and consuming communes, which conscientiously record their production and consumption, go about their labour economically, uninterruptedly raise their labour productivity and thus attain the possibility of lowering the working day to seven or six hours or even lower." [3] " Every factory, every village appears as a production and consumption commune having the right and obligation to apply the general Soviet legislation in its own way (' in its own way ' not in the

---

[1] Op. cit., p. 15.

[2] Ibid., pp. 21 and 26. Compare also Bucharin, *Das Programm der Kommunisten*, Zürich, 1918, pp. 27 ff.

[3] Cf. Lenin, op. cit., pp. 24 f.

ECONOMIC CALCULATION

sense of its violation but in the sense of the variety of its forms of realisation), and to solve in its own way the problem of calculating the production and distribution of products." [1]

" The chief communes must and will serve the most backward ones as educators, teachers, and stimulating leaders." The successes of the chief communes must be broadcast in all their details in order to provide a good example. The communes " showing good business results " should be immediately rewarded " by a curtailment of the working day and with an increase in wages, and by allowing more attention to be paid to cultural and aesthetic goods and values ".[2]

We can infer that Lenin's ideal is a state of society in which the means of production are not the property of a few districts, municipalities, or even of the workers in the concern, but of the whole community. His ideal is socialist and not syndicalist. This need not be specially stressed for a Marxist such as Lenin. It is not extraordinary of Lenin the theorist, but of Lenin the statesman, who is the leader of the syndicalist and small-holding peasant Russian revolution. However, at the moment we are engaged with the writer Lenin and may consider his ideals separately, without letting ourselves be disturbed by the picture of sober reality. According to Lenin the theorist, every large agricultural and industrial concern is a member of the great commonwealth of labour. Those who are active in this commonwealth have the right of self-government ; they exercise a profound influence on the direction of production and again on the distribution of the goods they are assigned for consumption. Still labour is the property of the whole society, and as its product belongs to society also,

[1] Ibid., p. 32.   [2] Ibid., p. 33.

127

COLLECTIVIST ECONOMIC PLANNING

it therefore disposes of its distribution. How, we must now ask, is calculation in the economy carried on in a socialist commonwealth which is so organized ? Lenin gives us a most inadequate answer by referring us back to statistics. We must

> bring statistics to the masses, make it popular, so that the active population will gradually learn by themselves to understand and realise how much and what kind of work must be done, how much and what kind of recreation should be taken, so that the comparison of the economy's industrial results in the case of individual communes becomes the object of general interest and education.[1]

From these scanty allusions it is impossible to infer what Lenin understands by statistics and whether he is thinking of monetary or *in natura* computation. In any case, we must refer back to what we have said about the impossibility of learning the money prices of production-goods in a socialist commonwealth and about the difficulties standing in the way of *in natura* valuation.[2] Statistics would only be applicable to economic calculation if it could go beyond the *in natura* calculation, whose ill-suitedness for this purpose we have demonstrated. It is naturally impossible where no exchange relations are formed between goods in the process of trade.

CONCLUSION

It must follow from what we have been able to establish in our previous arguments that the protagonists of a socialist system of production claim preference for it on the ground of greater rationality as against an economy so constituted as to depend on private ownership of the

[1] Op. cit., p. 33.

[2] Neurath, too (cf. op. cit., pp. 212 et seq.), imputes great importance to statistics for the setting up of the socialist economic plan.

ECONOMIC CALCULATION

means of production. We have no need to consider this opinion within the framework of the present essay, in so far as it falls back on the assertion that rational economic activity necessarily cannot be perfect, because certain forces are operative which hinder its pursuance. In this connection we may only pay attention to the economic and technical reason for this opinion. There hovers before the holders of this tenet a muddled conception of technical rationality, which stands in antithesis to economic rationality, on which also they are not very clear. They are wont to overlook the fact that " all technical rationality of production is identical with a low level of specific expenditure in the processes of production ".[1] They overlook the fact that technical calculation is not enough to realize the " degree of general and teleological expediency "[2] of an event ; that it can only grade individual events according to their significance ; but that it can never guide us in those judgments which are demanded by the economic complex as a whole. Only because of the fact that technical considerations can be based on profitability can we overcome the difficulty arising from the complexity of the relations between the mighty system of present-day production on the one hand and demand and the efficiency of enterprises and economic units on the other ; and can we gain the complete picture of the situation in its totality, which rational economic activity requires.[3]

These theories are dominated by a confused conception of the primacy of objective use-value. In fact, so far as economic administration is concerned, objective use-value can only acquire significance for the economy through the influence it derives from subjective use-value

[1] Cf. Gottl, op. cit., p. 220.   [2] Ibid., p. 219.   [3] Ibid., p. 225.

COLLECTIVIST ECONOMIC PLANNING

on the formation of the exchange-relations of economic goods. A second confused idea is inexplicably involved —the observer's personal judgment of the utility of goods as opposed to the judgments of the people participating in economic transactions. If anyone finds it " irrational " to spend as much as is expended in society on smoking, drinking, and similar enjoyments, then doubtless he is right from the point of view of his own personal scale of values. But in so judging, he is ignoring the fact that economy is a means, and that, without prejudice to the rational considerations influencing its pattern, the scale of ultimate ends is a matter for conation and not for cognition.

The knowledge of the fact that rational economic activity is impossible in a socialist commonwealth cannot, of course, be used as an argument either for or against socialism. Whoever is prepared himself to enter upon socialism on ethical grounds on the supposition that the provision of goods of a lower order for human beings under a system of a common ownership of the means of production is diminished, or whoever is guided by ascetic ideals in his desire for socialism, will not allow himself to be influenced in his endeavours by what we have said. Still less will those " culture " socialists be deterred who, like Muckle, expect from socialism primarily " the dissolution of the most frightful of all barbarisms—capitalist rationality ".[1] But he who expects a rational economic system from socialism will be forced to re-examine his views.

[1] Cf. Muckle, *Das Kulturideal des Sozialismus*, Munich and Leipzig, p. 213. On the other hand, Muckle demands the " highest degree of rationalisation of economic life in order to curtail hours of labour, and to permit man to withdraw to an island where he can listen to the melody of his being ".

[20]

Socialist Calculation : The Competitive 'Solution'[1]

By F. A. v. Hayek

I

Two chapters in the discussion of the economics of socialism may now be regarded as closed. The first deals with the belief that socialism will dispense entirely with calculation in terms of value and will replace it with some sort of calculation *in natura* based on units of energy or of some other physical magnitude. Although this view is not yet extinct and is still held by some scientists and engineers, it has been definitely abandoned by economists. The second closed chapter deals with the proposal that values, instead of being left to be determined by competition, should be found by a process of calculations carried out by the planning authority which would use the technique of mathematical economics. With regard to this suggestion, V. Pareto (who, curiously enough, is sometimes quoted as holding this view) has already said what probably will remain the final word. After showing how a system of simultaneous equations can be used to explain what determines prices on a market he adds :

"It may be mentioned here that this determination has by no means the purpose to arrive at a numerical calculation of prices. Let us make the most favourable assumption for such a calculation, let us assume that we have triumphed over all the difficulties of finding the data of the problem and that we know the *ophélimités* of all the different commodities for each individual, and all the conditions of production of all the commodities, etc. This is already an absurd hypothesis to make. Yet it is not sufficient to make the solution of the problem

---

[1] The two recent books with which this article is mainly concerned, Oskar Lange and Fred M. Taylor, *On the Economic Theory of Socialism*, edited by B. E. Lippincott, Minneapolis, 1938, and H. D. Dickinson, *Economics of Socialism*, Oxford, 1939, will be referred to throughout this article as LT (Lange-Taylor) and D (Dickinson) respectively.

possible. We have seen that in the case of 100 persons and 700 commodities there will be 70,699 conditions (actually a great number of circumstances which we have so far neglected will still increase that number); we shall therefore have to solve a system of 70,699 equations. This exceeds practically the power of algebraic analysis, and this is even more true if one contemplates the fabulous number of equations which one obtains for a population of forty millions and several thousand commodities. In this case the rôles would be changed: it would not be mathematics which would assist political economy, but political economy would assist mathematics. In other words, if one really could know all these equations, the only means to solve them which is available to human powers is to observe the practical solution given by the market."[1]

In the present article we shall be mainly concerned with a third stage in this discussion, for which the issue has now been clearly defined by the elaboration of proposals for a competitive socialism by Professor Lange and Dr. Dickinson. Since, however, the significance of the result of the past discussions is not infrequently represented in a way which comes very near to an inversion of the truth, and as at least one of the two books to be discussed is not quite free from this tendency, a few further remarks on the real significance of the past development seem not unnecessary.

The first point is connected with the nature of the original criticism directed against the more primitive conceptions of the working of a socialist economy which were current up to about 1920. The idea then current (and still advocated, e.g. by Dr. O. Neurath) is well expressed by F. Engels in his *Anti-Dühring*, when he says that the social plan of production " will be settled very simply, without the intervention of the famous ' value '." It was against this generally held belief that N. G. Pierson, L. v. Mises, and others pointed out that if the socialist community wanted to act rationally its calculation would have to be guided by the same *formal* laws which applied to a capitalist society. It seems necessary especially to underline the fact that this was a point made by the critics of the socialist plans, since Professor Lange and particularly his editor[2] now seem

---

[1] V. Pareto, *Manuel d'économie politique*, 2nd ed., 1927, pp. 233/4.
[2] See B. E. Lippincott in LT, p. 7.

inclined to suggest that the demonstration that the formal principles of economic theory apply to a socialist economy provides an answer to these critics. The fact is that it has never been denied by anybody, except socialists, that these formal principles *ought* to apply to a socialist society, and the question raised by Professor Mises and others was not whether they ought to apply but whether they could in practice be applied in the absence of a market. It is therefore entirely beside the point when Professor Lange and others quote Pareto and Barone as having shown that values in a socialist society would depend on essentially the same factors as in a competitive society. This of course had been shown long before, particularly by Wieser. But none of these authors has made an attempt to show how these values, which a socialist society ought to use if it wanted to act rationally, could be found, and Pareto, as we have seen, expressly denied that they could be determined by calculation.

It seems then that, on this point, the criticisms of the earlier socialist schemes have been so successful that the defenders, with few exceptions,[1] have felt compelled to appropriate the argument of their critics, and have been forced to construct entirely new schemes of which nobody thought before. While against the older ideas that it was possible to plan rationally without calculation in terms of value it could be justly argued that they were logically impossible, the newer proposals designed to determine values by some process other than competition based on private property raise a problem of a different sort. But it is surely unfair to say, as Professor Lange does, that the critics, because they deal in a new way with the new schemes evolved to meet the original criticism, " have given up the essential point " and " retreated to a second line of defence " (LT 63). Is this not rather a case of covering up the own retreat by creating confusion about the issue ?

There is a second point on which Professor Lange's presentation of the present state of the debate is seriously misleading. The reader of his study can hardly avoid the impression that the idea that values should and could be determined by using the technique of mathematical economics, i.e. by solving millions of equations, is a malicious

---

[1] The most notable exception is Dr. M. Dobb. See his *Political Economy and Capitalism*, 1937, chapter VIII, and his review of Professor Lange's book in the *Modern Quarterly*, 1939.

invention of the critics, intended to throw ridicule on the efforts of modern socialist writers. The fact, which cannot be unknown to Professor Lange, is of course that this procedure has more than once been seriously suggested by socialist writers as a solution of the difficulty—among others by Dr. Dickinson, who now, however, expressly withdraws this earlier suggestion.[1]

II

A third stage in the debate has now been reached with the proposal to solve the problems of determining values by the re-introduction of competition. When five years ago the present author tried to appraise the significance of these attempts[2] it was necessary to rely on what could be gathered from oral discussion among socialist economists, since no systematic exposition of the theoretical bases of competitive socialism was then available. This gap has now been filled by the two books here to be discussed. The first contains a reprint of an essay by Professor Lange, originally published in 1936 and 1937, together with an older article by the late Professor Taylor (dating from 1928) and an introduction by the editor, Professor B. E. Lippincott, which in addition to a quite unnecessary restatement of Professor Lange's argument in cruder terms, does much by the unmeasured praise he bestows on this argument and the extravagant claims he advances for it,[3] to prejudice the reader against the essentially scholarly piece of work that follows. Although written in a lively style and confining itself to the outlines of the subject, it does seriously grapple with some of the main difficulties in the field.

Dr. H. D. Dickinson's more recent book is a far more comprehensive survey of the field, proposing essentially the same solution.[4] It is unquestionably a book of great distinction, well organised, lucid and concise, and should rapidly establish itself as the standard work on its subject. To the economist, the reading of the book provides indeed the rare pleasure of feeling that recent advances of economic

---

[1] D, p. 104, and K. Tisch, *Wirtschaftsrechnung und Verteilung im zentralistisch organisierten sozialistischen Gemeinwesen*, 1932.

[2] In *Collectivist Economic Planning*, London, 1935, essay on "The Present State of the Debate."

[3] Dr. Lange's essay is described as the "first writing to mark an advance on Barone's contribution" and to show by "irrefutable" argument the "evident feasibility and superiority" of a socialist system (LT, pp. 13, 24, 37).

[4] It is a curious fact that Dr. Dickinson nowhere in his book (except in the bibliography) refers to Professor Lange's work.

theory have not been in vain and have even helped to reduce political differences to points which can be rationally discussed. Dr. Dickinson himself would probably agree that he shares all his economics with—and indeed has learnt most of it from—non-socialist economists, and that in his essential conclusions on the desirable economic policy of a socialist community he differs much more from most of his socialist colleagues than from " orthodox " economists. This, together with the open-mindedness with which the author takes up and considers the arguments advanced by his opponents, makes discussion of his views a real pleasure. If the socialists, like the economists, are ready to accept his book, as the most up-to-date general treatment of the economics of socialism from the socialist point of view, it should provide the basis for much fruitful further discussion.

As has already been mentioned, the main outlines of the solution offered by the two authors are essentially the same. They both rely to some extent on the competitive mechanism for the determination of relative prices. But they both refuse to let prices be determined directly in the market and propose instead a system of price-fixing by a central authority, where the state of the market of a particular commodity, i.e. the relation of demand to supply, merely serves as an indication to the authority whether the prescribed prices ought to be raised or lowered. Neither of the two authors explains why he refuses to go the whole hog and to restore the price mechanism in full. But as I happen to agree (although probably for different reasons) that this would be impracticable in a socialist community, we can leave this question aside for the moment and shall take it for granted that in such a society competition cannot play quite the same rôle as it does in a society based on private property, and that, in particular, the rates at which commodities will be exchanged by the parties in the market will have to be decreed by the authority.

We shall leave the details of the proposed organisation for later consideration and first consider the general significance of this solution under three aspects. We shall ask firstly how far this kind of socialist system still conforms to the hopes that were placed on the substitution of a planned socialist system for the chaos of competition ; secondly, how far the proposed procedure is an answer to the main difficulty, and, finally, how far it is applicable.

The first and most general point can be dealt with fairly briefly, although it is not unimportant if one wants to see these new proposals in their proper light. It is merely a reminder of how much of the original claim for the superiority of planning over competition is abandoned if the planned society is now to rely for the direction of its industries to a large extent on competition. Until quite recently, at least, planning and competition used to be regarded as opposites, and this is unquestionably still true of nearly all planners except a few economists among them. I fear that the schemes of Professor Lange and Dr. Dickinson will bitterly disappoint all those scientific planners who, in the recent words of Professor B. M. S. Blackett, believe that " the object of planning is largely to overcome the results of competition ".[1] This would be even more true if it were really possible to reduce the arbitrary elements in a competitive socialist system as much as is believed by Dr. Dickinson, who hopes that his " libertarian socialism " " may establish, for the first time in human history, an effective individualism " (D 26). Unfortunately, as we shall see, this is not likely to be the case.

III

The second general question we must consider is how far the proposed method of centralised price fixing, while leaving it to individual firms and consumers to adjust demand and supply to the given prices, is likely to solve the problem which admittedly cannot be solved by mathematical calculation. Here, I am afraid, I find it exceedingly difficult to understand the grounds on which such a claim is made. Professor Lange (LT 70, 86) as well as Dr. Dickinson (D 103 and 113) assert that even if the initial system of prices were chosen entirely at random, it would be possible by such a process of trial and error gradually to approach to the appropriate system. This seems to be much the same thing as if it were suggested that a system of equations which was too complex to be solved by calculation within reasonable time and whose values were constantly changing could be effectively tackled by arbitrarily inserting

[1] See Sir Daniel Hall and others, *The Frustration of Science*, London, 1935, p. 142.

tentative values and then trying about till the proper solution was found.   Or, to change the metaphor, the difference between such a system of regimented prices and a system of prices determined by the market seems to be about the same as that between an attacking army where every unit and every man could only move by special command and by the exact distance ordered by headquarters and an army where every unit and every man can take advantage of every opportunity offered to them.   There is of course no *logical impossibility* of conceiving a directing organ of the collective economy which is not only " omnipresent and omniscient " as Dr. Dickinson conceives it (D 191), but also omnipotent and which therefore would be in a position to change without delay every price by just the amount that is required.   When, however, one proceeds to consider the actual apparatus by which this sort of adjustment is to be brought about one begins to wonder whether anyone should really be prepared to suggest that, within the domain of practical possibility, such a system will ever even distantly approach the efficiency of a system where the required changes are brought about by the spontaneous action of the persons immediately concerned.

We shall later, when we consider the proposed institutional setting, come back to the question how this sort of mechanism is likely to function in practice.   In so far as the general question is concerned, however, it is difficult to suppress the suspicion that this particular proposal has been born out of an excessive pre-occupation with problems of the pure theory of stationary equilibrium.   If in the real world we had to deal with approximately constant data, that is, if the problem were, to find a price system which then could be left more or less unchanged for long periods, then the proposal under consideration would not be so entirely unreasonable.   With given and constant data such a state of equilibrium could indeed be approached by the method of trial and error.   But this is far from being the situation in the real world, where constant change is the rule.   Whether and how far anything approaching the desirable equilibrium is ever reached depends entirely on the speed with which the adjustments can be made.   The practical problem is not whether a particular method would eventually lead to a hypothetical equilibrium, but which method will secure the more rapid and complete adjustment to the daily changing conditions in different places and different industries. How great the difference in this respect would be between a method where prices are currently agreed upon by the parties of the market and a method where these prices are decreed from above is of course a matter of practical judgment. But I find it difficult to believe that anybody should doubt that in this respect the inferiority of the second method would be very great indeed.

The third general point is also one where I believe that preoccupation with concepts of pure economic theory has seriously misled both our authors. In this case it is the concept of perfect competition which apparently has made them overlook a very important field to which their method appears to be simply inapplicable. Wherever we have a market for a fairly standardised commodity it is at least conceivable that all prices should be decreed in advance from above for a certain period. The situation is however very different with respect to commodities which cannot be standardised, and particularly for those which to-day are produced on individual orders, perhaps after invitation for tenders. A large part of the product of the " heavy industries ", which of course would be the first to be socialised, belongs to this category. Much machinery, most buildings and ships and many parts of other products are hardly ever produced for a market, but only on special contract. This does not mean that there may not be intense competition in the market for the products of these industries, although it may not be " perfect competition " in the sense of pure theory ; the fact is simply that identical products are rarely produced twice in short intervals ; and the circle of producers who will compete as alternative suppliers in each instance will be different in almost every individual case, just as the circle of potential customers who will compete for the services of a particular plant will differ from week to week. What basis is there in all these cases for fixing prices of the product so as " to equalise demand and supply " ? If prices are here to be fixed by the central authority, they will have to be fixed in every individual case and on the basis of an examination by that authority of the calculations of all potential suppliers and all potential purchasers. It is hardly necessary to point out the various complications that will arise according as the prices are fixed before or after the prospective buyer has decided on the particular piece of machinery or building which he wants. Presumably it will be the estimates of the producer which, before they are submitted to the prospective customer, will have to be approved by the authority. Is it not clear that in all these cases, unless the authority in effect takes all the functions of the entrepreneur on itself (i.e. unless the proposed system is abandoned and one of complete central direction substituted), the process of price fixing would either become exceedingly cumbersome and the cause of infinite delay, or a pure formality ?

IV

All these considerations appear to be relevant whatever particular form of organisation is chosen. Before we go further, however, it becomes necessary to consider somewhat more in detail the concrete apparatus of industrial control which the two authors propose. The sketches they provide of the organisation are fairly similar, although in this respect Professor Lange gives us somewhat more information than Dr. Dickinson, who, for most of the problems of economic organisation, refers us to the works of Mr. and Mrs. Webb and Mr. G. D. H. Cole (D 30).

Both authors contemplate a socialist system in which the choice of occupation would be free and regulated mainly by the price mechanism (i.e. by the wage system) and in which the consumers also would be free to spend their incomes as they chose. Apparently both authors also want prices of consumers' goods to be fixed by the ordinary market processes (although Dr. Dickinson does not seem to be quite decided on this point) (LT 78, D 60), and also to leave the determination of wages to the bargaining between the parties concerned (LT 78, D 126). Both also agree that for various reasons not the whole of industry should be socialised, but that, besides the socialised there should also remain a private sector, consisting of small enterprises run on essentially capitalistic lines. I find it difficult to agree with their belief that the existence of such a private sector parallel with the socialised sector creates no special difficulties. But as it would be difficult within the space of this article to deal adequately with this problem, we shall, for the purposes of this discussion, disregard the existence of the private sector and assume that the whole of industry is socialised.

The determination of all prices, other than those of consumers' goods and of wages, is the main task of the central economic authority, Professor Lange's Central Planning Board or Dr. Dickinson's Supreme Economic Council. (We shall, following Dr. Dickinson, henceforth refer to this body as the S.E.C.) As regards the technique of how particular prices are announced and changed we get more information, although by no means enough, from Professor Lange, while Dr. Dickinson goes more fully into the question by what considerations the S.E.C. should be guided in the fixing of prices. Both questions have a special importance and they must be considered separately.

According to Professor Lange, the S.E.C. would from time to time issue what, following Professor Taylor, he calls " factor valuation tables ", that is, comprehensive lists of prices of all means of production (except labour) (LT 46, 52). These prices would have to serve as the sole basis for all transactions between different enterprises and the whole calculation of all the industries and plants during the period of their validity and the managers must treat these prices as constant (LT 81). What we are not told, however, either by Professor Lange or by Dr. Dickinson, is for what period these prices are to be fixed. This is one of the more serious obscurities in the exposition of both authors, a gap in their exposition which makes one almost doubt whether they have made a real effort to visualise their system at work. Are prices to be fixed for a definite period in advance, or are they to be changed whenever it seems desirable ? F.M. Taylor seemed to suggest the former alternative when he wrote that the appropriateness of particular prices would show itself at the end of the " productive period " (LT 53) ; and Professor Lange, on at least one occasion, gives the same impression when he says that " any price different from the equilibrium price would show at the end of the accounting period a surplus or shortage of the commodity in question " (LT 82). But on another occasion he says that "adjustments of those prices would be constantly made " (LT 86), while Dr. Dickinson confines himself to stating that after, " by a process of successive approximation," " a set of prices can ultimately be established in consonance with the principles of scarcity and substitution," " small adjustments will be sufficient to keep the system in equilibrium except in the case of major technical innovations or of big changes in consumers' tastes" (D 100, 102, 103). Could the failure to understand the true function of the price mechanism, caused by the modern preoccupation with stationary equilibrium, be better illustrated ?

While Dr. Dickinson is very uninformative on the mechanism of bringing price changes into effect, he goes much more fully than Professor Lange into the considerations on which the S.E.C. would have to base their decisions. Unlike Professor Lange, Dr. Dickinson is not satisfied with the S.E.C. merely watching the market and adjusting prices when an excess of demand or supply appears, and then trying to find by experimentation a new equilibrium level. He rather wants the S.E.C. to use statistically established demand and supply schedules as a guide to determine the equilibrium prices. This is evidently a residue of his earlier belief in the possibility of solving the whole problem by the method of simultaneous equations. But although he has now abandoned this idea (not because he regards it as impossible, since he still believes it could be done by solving merely " two or three thousand simultaneous equations " (D 104), but because he realises that " the data themselves, which would have to be fed into the equation-machine, are continually changing "), he still believes that the statistical determination of demand schedules would be useful as an aid to, if not as a substitute for, the method of trial and error, and that it would be well worth while to try and establish the numerical values of the constants (*sic*) in the Walrasian system of equilibrium.

V

Whatever the method by which the S.E.C. fixes prices, and particularly whatever the periods at which and for which prices are announced, there are two points about which there can be little question : the changes will occur later than they would if prices were determined by the market parties, and there will be less differentiation between prices of commodities according to differences of quality and the circumstances of time and place. While with real competition price changes occur when the parties immediately concerned know that conditions have changed, the S.E.C. will be able to act only after the parties have reported, the reports have been verified, contradictions cleared up, etc. ; and the new prices will become effective only after all the parties concerned have been notified, that is, either a date will have to be fixed in advance at which the new prices will become effective, or the accounting will have to include an elaborate system by which every manager of production is constantly notified of the new prices upon which he has to base his calculations. Since in fact every manager would have to be informed constantly on many more prices than those of the commodities which he is actually using (at least of those of all possible substitutes), some sort of periodic publication of complete lists of all prices would be necessary. It is clear that while economic efficiency demands that prices should be changed as promptly as possible, practicability would confine actual changes to intervals of fair length.

That the price fixing process will be confined to establishing uniform prices for classes of goods and that therefore distinctions based on the special circumstances of time, place and quality will find no expression in prices is probably obvious. Without some such simplification the number of different commodities for which separate prices would have to be fixed would be practically infinite. This means, however, that the managers of production will have no inducement and even no real possibility to make use of special opportunities, special bargains and all the little advantages offered by their special local conditions, since all these things could not enter into their calculations. It would also mean, to give only one other instance of the consequences, that it would never be practicable to incur extra costs to remedy a sudden scarcity quickly, since a local or temporary scarcity could not affect prices until the official machinery had acted.

For both these reasons, because prices would have to be fixed for periods and because they would have to be fixed generically for categories of goods, a great many prices would be at most times in such a system substantially different from what they would be in a free system. This is very important for the functioning of the system. Professor Lange makes great play with the fact that prices act merely as " indices of terms on which alternatives are offered " (LT 78) and that this " parametric function of prices " (LT 70, 86) by which prices are guiding the action of individual managers without being directly determined by them, will be fully preserved under such a system where prices are fixed. As he himself points out, " the determinateness of the accounting prices holds, however, only if all discrepancies between demand and supply of a commodity are met by an appropriate change of price ", and for this reason " rationing has to be excluded " and " the rule to produce at the minimum average cost has no significance unless prices represent the relative scarcity of the factors of production " (LT 93/4). In other words, prices will provide a basis for rational accounting only if they are such that at the ruling prices anyone can always sell as much or buy as much as he wishes, or that anyone should be free to buy as cheaply or to sell as dearly as is made possible by the existence of a willing partner. If I cannot buy more of a factor so long as it is worth more to me than the price, and if I cannot sell a thing as soon as it is worth less to me than the price which somebody else would be willing to pay for it, prices are no longer indices of alternative opportunities.

We shall see the significance of this more clearly when we consider the action of the managers of the socialist industries. But before we can consider their action we must see who these people are and with what functions they are invested.

VI

The nature of the industrial unit under separate management and the factors which determine its size and the selection of its management is another point on which both our authors are deplorably vague. Professor Lange seems to contemplate the organisation of the different industries in the form of national trusts, although this important point is only just touched upon once when the National Coal Trust is mentioned as an example (LT 78). The very important and relevant question of what is *one* industry is nowhere discussed, but he apparently assumes that the various " managers of production " will have monopolistic control of the particular commodities with which they are concerned. In general Professor Lange uses the term " managers of production " exceedingly vaguely (LT 75, 79, 86), leaving it obscure whether the directors of a whole " industry " or of a single unit are meant ; but at critical points (LT 76, 82 note) a distinction between the managers

of plant and the managers of a whole industry appears
without any clear limitation of their function. Dr. Dickinson
is even more vague when he speaks of economic activities
being " decentralised and carried on by a large number of
separate organs of collective economy " which will have
" their own nominal capital and their own profit and loss
account and will be managed very much as separate enterprises under capitalism " (D 213).

Whoever these managers of production are, their main
function would appear to be to decide how much and how
to produce on the basis of the prices fixed by the S.E.C.
(and the prices of consumers' goods and the wages determined by the market). They would be instructed by the
S.E.C. to produce at the lowest possible average costs (LT
75) and to expand production of the individual plants till
marginal costs are equal to price (LT 76, D 107). According
to Professor Lange the directors of the industries (as distinguished from the managers of individual plants) would
have also the further task of seeing that the amount of
equipment in the industry as a whole is so adjusted that
" the marginal cost incurred by the industry " in producing
an output which " can be sold or ' accounted for ' at a price
which equals marginal cost " is the lowest possible (LT 77).

In this connection a special problem arises which unfortunately cannot be discussed here as it raises questions
of such difficulty and complexity that a separate article
would be required. It concerns the case of decreasing
marginal costs where, according to both our authors, the
socialist industries would act differently from capitalist
industry by expanding production till prices are equal, not
to average, but to marginal costs. Although the argument
employed possesses a certain specious plausibility it can
hardly be said even that the problem is adequately stated in
either of the two books, still less that the conclusions drawn
are convincing. Within the space available on this occasion
however we can do no more than seriously question Dr.
Dickinson's assertion that " under modern technical conditions, diminishing costs are far commoner than increasing
costs "—a statement which in the context in which it
occurs clearly refers to marginal costs (D 108).

Here we shall confine ourselves to considering one question arising out of this part of the proposal, the question
how the S.E.C. will ensure that the principle that prices
are equalised to the lowest marginal cost at which the quantity

concerned can be produced, is actually put into force. The question which arises here is not "merely" one of the loyalty or capacity of the socialist managers. For the purpose of this argument it may be granted that they will be as capable and as anxious to produce as cheaply as the average capitalist entrepreneur. The problem arises because one of the most important forces which in a truly competitive economy brings about the reduction of costs to the minimum discoverable will be absent, namely, price competition. In the discussion of this sort of problem, as in the discussion of so much of economic theory at the present time, the question is frequently treated as if the cost curves were objectively given facts. What is forgotten here is that the method which under given condition is the cheapest is a thing which has to be discovered, and to be discovered anew sometimes almost from day to day, by the entrepreneur, and that, in spite of the strong inducement, it is by no means regularly the established entrepreneur, the man in charge of the existing plant, who will discover what is the best method. The force which in a competitive society brings about the reduction of price to the lowest cost at which the quantity saleable at that cost can be produced is the opportunity for anybody who knows a cheaper method to come in at his own risk and to attract customers by underbidding the other producers. But if prices are fixed by the authority this method is excluded. Any improvement, any adjustment of the technique of production to changed conditions will be dependent on convincing the S.E.C. that the commodity in question can be produced cheaper and that therefore the price ought to be lowered. Since the man with the new idea will have no possibility of establishing himself by undercutting, the new idea cannot be proved by experiment till he has convinced the S.E.C. that his way of producing the thing is cheaper. Or, in other words, every calculation by an outsider who believes that he can do better will have to be examined and approved by the authority, which in this connection will have to take over all the functions of the entrepreneur.

VII

Let us briefly consider a few of the problems arising out of the relations between the "socialist managers of production" (whether of a plant or an industry) and the S.E.C. The manager's task is, as we have seen, to order production in such a way that his marginal costs are as low as possible and equal to price. How is he to do this and how is the fact of his success to be verified ? He has to take prices as given. This turns him into what has recently been called a pure " quantity adjuster ", i.e. his decision is confined to the quantities of factors of production and the combination in which he uses them. But as he has no means of inducing his suppliers to offer more, or to induce his purchasers to buy more, than they want to at the prescribed price, he will frequently be simply unable to carry out his instructions ; or at least, if he cannot get more of a material required at the prescribed price, the only way for him, e.g., to expand production so as to make his cost equal to price, would be to use inferior substitutes or to employ other uneconomic methods ; and when he cannot sell at the prescribed price and until the price is lowered by decree, he will have to stop production where under true competition he would have lowered his prices.

Another great difficulty arising out of the periodic price changes by decree is the problem of anticipations of future price movements. Professor Lange, somewhat too bravely, cuts this Gordian knot by prescribing that " for purposes of accounting, prices must be treated as constant, as they are treated by entrepreneurs on a competitive market " (!). Does that mean that the managers, although they know for certain that a particular price will have to be raised or lowered, must act as if they did not know ? Clearly this won't do. But if they are free to meet expected price movements by anticipatory action, are they to be allowed to take advantage of the administrative delays in making price changes effective ? And who is to be responsible for losses caused by wrongly timed or wrongly directed price changes ?

Closely connected with this problem is another one, to which we also get no answer. Both our authors speak about " marginal costs " as if they were independent of the period for which the manager can plan. Clearly actual costs depend in many instances as much as on anything on buying at the right time. And in no sense can costs during any period be said to depend solely on prices during that period. They depend as much on whether these prices have been correctly foreseen as on the views that are held about future prices. Even in the very short run costs will depend on the effects which current decisions will have on future

productivity. Whether it is economical to run a machine hard
or to economise in lubricants, whether to make major adjustments to a given change in demand or to carry on as well
as possible with the existing organisation, in fact almost
every decision on how to produce now depends at least in
part on the views held about the future. But while the
manager clearly must hold some views on these questions,
he can hardly be held responsible for anticipating future
changes correctly if these changes depend entirely on the
decision of the authority.

Not only, however, will the success of the individual
manager depend to a large extent on the action of the planning
authority. He will also have to satisfy the same authority
that he has done as well as was possible. Either beforehand,
or more likely retrospectively, all his calculations will have
to be examined and approved by the authority. This will
not be a perfunctory auditing directed to find out whether
his costs have actually been what he says they have been.
It will have to establish whether they have been the lowest
possible ones. This means that the control will have to
consider not only what he actually did but also what he
might have done and ought to have done. And from the
point of view of the manager it will be much more important
that he should always be able to prove that in the light
of the knowledge which he possessed the decision actually
taken was the right one than that he should prove to be
right in the end. If this must not lead to the worst forms
of bureaucracy I do not know what would.

This brings us to the general question of the responsibility of the managers. Dr. Dickinson clearly sees that
" responsibility means in practice financial responsibility "
and that unless the manager " bears responsibility for losses
as well as for profits he will be tempted to embark upon
all sorts of risky experiments on the bare chance that one
of them will turn out successful " (D 214). This is a difficult
problem with managers who have no property of their own.
Dr. Dickinson hopes to solve it by a system of bonuses.
This may indeed be sufficient to prevent managers from
taking too great risks. But is not the real problem the
opposite one, that managers will be afraid of taking risks
if, when the venture does not come off, it will be somebody
else who will afterwards decide whether they have been
justified in embarking on it ? As Dr. Dickinson himself

points out, the principle would be that " although the making
of profits is not necessarily a sign of success, the making of
losses is a sign of failure " (D 219). Need one say more
about the effects of such a system on all activities involving
risk ? It is difficult to conceive that under these circumstances any of the necessary speculative activities involving risk-bearing could be left to managerial initiative. But
the alternative is to fall back for them on that system of
strict central planning to avoid which the whole system has
been evolved.

VIII

All this is even more true when we turn to the whole
problem of new investments, that is, to all the questions
which involve changes in the size (i.e. the capital) of the
managerial units, whether they involve net changes in the
total supply of capital or not. Up to a point it is possible
to divide this problem into two parts, the decisions about
the distribution of the available capital supply and the
decisions about the rate at which capital is to be accumulated, although it is dangerous to carry this division too
far, since the decision about how much is to be saved is
necessarily also a decision about which needs for capital
are to be satisfied and which are not. Both our authors
agree that, as regards the problem of the distribution of
capital between industries and plants, the interest mechanism
should as far as possible be retained, but that the decision
of how much to save and invest would necessarily have to
be arbitrary (LT 85, D 80, 205).

Now however strong the desire may be to rely on the
interest mechanism for the distribution of capital, it is
fairly obvious that the market for capital can in no sense
be a free market. And while for Professor Lange the rate
of interest is also " simply determined by the condition
that the demand for capital is equal to the amount available " (LT 84), Dr. Dickinson takes great pains to show
how the S.E.C. will, on the basis of the alternative plans of
activity drawn up by the different undertakings, construct
an aggregate demand schedule for capital which will enable
it to determine that rate of interest at which the demand
for capital will equal supply. The ingenuity and the
astounding trust in the practicability of even the most complicated constructions which he displays in this connection

may be illustrated by his statement that in a certain case " it will be necessary to establish a provisional rate of interest, then to allow the different organs of collective economy to re-contract with each other on the basis of this provisional rate, and so to draw up their final demand schedule for capital " (D 83n).

All this, however, does not meet the main difficulty. If indeed it were possible to accept at their face value the statements of all the individual managers and would-be managers about how much capital they could with advantage use at various rates of interest, some such scheme as such might appear feasible. It cannot be too often repeated, however, that the planning authority cannot be conceived " simply as a kind of super-bank which lends the available funds to the highest bidder. It would lend to persons who have no property of their own. It would therefore bear all the risk and would have no claim for a definite amount of money as a bank has. It would simply have rights of ownership over all real resources. Nor can its decisions be confined to the redistribution of free capital in the form of money, and perhaps of land. It would have to decide whether a particular plant or piece of machinery should be left further to the entrepreneur who has used it in the past, at his valuation, or whether it should be transferred to another who promises a higher return for it."

These sentences are taken from the essay where the present author discussed five years ago the " possibility of real competition under socialism ".[1] At that time such systems had only been vaguely discussed and one could hope to find an answer when systematic expositions of the new ideas should become available. But it is most disappointing to find no answer whatever to these problems in the two books now under discussion. While throughout the two works claims are made about how beneficial the control of investment activity would be in many respects, no indication is given of how this control is to be exercised and of how the responsibilities are to be divided between the planning authorities and the managers of the " competing " industrial units. Such statements as we find, as for instance that " because the managers of socialist industry will be governed in some choices by the direction laid down by the planning authority, it does not follow that they will

[1] *Collectivist Economic Planning*, 1935, pp. 232–237.

have no choice at all " (D 217), are singularly unhelpful.
All that seems to be fairly clear is that the planning authority
will be able to exercise its function of controlling and directing investment only if it is in a position to check and repeat
all the calculations of the entrepreneur.

It seems that here the two writers are unconsciously led
to fall back on the earlier beliefs in the superiority of a
centrally directed system over a competitive system and
to console themselves with the hope that the " omnipresent,
omniscient organ of the collective economy " (D 191) will
possess at least as much knowledge as the individual entrepreneurs and will therefore be in as good if not in a better
position to make the decisions as the entrepreneurs are. As
I have tried to show on another occasion, it is the main merit
of real competition that through it use is made of knowledge divided between many persons which, if it were to be
used in a centrally directed economy, would have all to
enter the single plan.[1] To assume that all this knowledge
would be automatically in the possession of the planning
authority seems to me to be to miss the main point. It is
not quite clear whether Professor Lange means to assert
that the planning authority will have all this information
when he says that " the administrators of a socialist economy
will have exactly the same knowledge, or lack of knowledge,
of the production functions as the capitalist entrepreneurs
have " (LT 61). If the " administrators of a socialist
economy " here means merely all the managers of the units
as well as of the central organisation taken together, the
statement can of course be readily accepted, but does in
no way solve the problem. But if it is intended to convey
that all this knowledge can be effectively used by the
planning authority in drawing up the plan, it is merely
begging the whole question and seems to be based on the
" fallacy of competition ".[2]

On this whole all-important question of the direction of
new investment and all that it involves, the two studies do
not really give any new information. The problem remains
where it was five years ago and I can confine myself on this

[1] See the article on " Economics and Knowledge," ECONOMICA, February, 1937.
[2] Another and even worse instance of this fallacy occurs in Professor Lippincott's introduction to the essays of Professors Lange and Taylor, when he argues that " there can be no doubt
that the Central Planning Board would exercise great power, but would it be any greater
than that exercised collectively by private boards of directors ? Because the decisions of
private boards are made here and there, this does not mean that the consumer does not feel
their collective impact, even though it may take a depression to make him aware of it."

point to repeating what I said then : " The decision about the amount of capital to be given to an individual entrepreneur and the decisions thereby involved concerning the size of the individual firm under a single control are in effect decisions about the most appropriate combination of resources. It will rest with the central authority to decide whether one plant located at one place should expand rather than another plant situated elsewhere. All this involves planning on the part of the central authority on much the same scale as if it were actually running the enterprise. And while the individual entrepreneur would in all probability be given some definite contractual tenure for managing the plant entrusted to him, all new investments will be necessarily centrally directed. This division in the disposition over the resources would then simply have the effect that neither the entrepreneur nor the central authority would be really in a position to plan, and that it would be impossible to assess the responsibility for mistakes. To assume that it is possible to create conditions of full competition without making those who are responsible for the decisions pay for their mistakes seems to be pure illusion. It will be at best a system of quasi-competition where the persons really responsible will not be the entrepreneur but the official who approves his decisions and where in consequence all the difficulties will arise in connection with freedom of initiative and the assessment of responsibility which are usually associated with bureaucracy."[1]

IX

The question how far a socialist system can avoid extensive central direction of economic activity is of great importance quite apart from its relation to economic efficiency : it is crucial for the question of how much personal and political freedom can be preserved in such a system. Both authors show a reassuring awareness of the dangers to personal freedom which a centrally planned system would involve and seem to have evolved their competitive socialism partly in order to meet this danger. Dr. Dickinson even goes so far as to say that " capitalist planning can exist only on the basis of fascism " and that in the hands of an irresponsible controller even socialist planning " *could* be

[1] *Collectivist Economic Planning*, p. 237.

made the greatest tyranny the world has ever seen " (D 22, 227). But he and Professor Lange believe that their competitive socialism will avoid this danger.

Now if competitive socialism could really rely for the direction of production largely on the effects of consumers' choice as reflected in the price system and if the cases where the authority will have to decide what is to be produced and how were made the exception rather than the rule, this claim would be to a large extent substantiated. How far is this really the case ? We have already seen that with the retention of the control over investment the central authority wields most extensive powers over the direction of production, much more extensive indeed than is easily possible to show without making this discussion unduly long. To this have yet to be added however a further number of arbitrary elements of which Dr. Dickinson himself gives a quite substantial although by no means complete list (D 205). There is in the first instance the " allocation of resources between present and future consumption" which, as we have already seen, always involves a decision about what particular needs will be satisfied and which needs will not be satisfied. There is, secondly, the need for arbitrary decision in respect to the " allocation of resources between communal and individual consumption " which, in view of the great extension of the " division of communal consumption " which he envisages means that another very large part of the resources of the society is put outside the control of the price mechanism and subject to purely authoritarian decision. Dr. Dickinson expressly adds to this only " the choice between work and leisure " and the " geographical planning and the pricing of land ", but at other points of his exposition further questions emerge on which he wants effective planning in order to correct the results of the market. But although he (and still more so Professor Lange) frequently hint at the possibilities of " correcting " the results of the price mechanism by judicious interference, this part of the programme is nowhere clearly worked out.

What our authors here have in mind perhaps comes out clearest in Dr. Dickinson's attitude towards the problem of wage changes : " If wages are too low in any one industry, it is the duty of the planning organ to adjust prices and quantities produced, so as to yield equal wages to work of

equal skill, responsibility, and difficulty in every industry "
(D 21). Apparently here the price mechanism and the free
choice of occupation is not to be relied upon. Later we
learn that although " unemployment in any particular job
affords a prima facie case for lowering the standard wage "
(D 127), a lowering of wages is objectionable " on social
grounds, because a lowering in wages . . . causes discontent ; on economic grounds, because it perpetuates an
uneconomic allocation of labour to different occupations ".
(How ?) Therefore, " as invention and improved organisation makes less labour necessary to satisfy human wants,
society should set itself to discover new wants to satisfy "
(D 131). " The powerful engine of propaganda and adver-
tisement, employed by public organs of education and
enlightenment instead of by the hucksters and panders of
private profit-making industry, could divert demand into
socially desirable directions while preserving the subjective
impression (*sic*) of free choice " (D 32).

When we add to this and many other similar points where
Dr. Dickinson wants his S.E.C. to exercise a paternalistic
control,[1] the fact that it will be necessary to co-ordinate
national production " with a general plan of exports and
imports " (D 169), since free trade " is inconsistent with
the principles of collectivism " (D 176), it becomes fairly
evident that there will be precious little economic activity
which will not be more or less immediately guided by
arbitrary decisions. In fact, Dr. Dickinson expressly contemplates a situation where " the state, through a definite
planning organ, makes itself responsible for the consideration of economic activity as a whole " and even adds that
this destroys the " illusion " maintained in a capitalist
society " that the division of the product is governed by
forces as impersonal and inevitable as those which govern
the weather " (D 21). This can only mean that, with most
other planners, he himself thinks of production in his
system as one which is largely directed by conscious and
arbitrary decisions. Yet in spite of this extensive rôle which
arbitrary decisions are to play in his system, he is confident
(and the same applies to Professor Lange) that his system
will not degenerate into an authoritarian despotism.

Dr. Dickinson just mentions the argument that " even

[1] Cf. for instance the passage (D 52) where Dr. Dickinson speaks about the " people who
will not pay voluntarily beforehand for what they are only too glad to have once they have
it."

if a socialist planner wished to realise freedom he could not do so and remain a planner ", yet the answer he gives makes one doubt whether he has quite seen on what considerations this argument is based. His answer is merely that " a plan can always be changed " (D 227/8). But this is not the point. The difficulty is that, in order to plan at all on an extensive scale, a much more extensive agreement among the members of the society about the relative importance of the various needs is required than will normally exist, and that in consequence this agreement will have to be brought about and a common scale of values will have to be imposed by force and propaganda. I have developed this argument at length elsewhere and I have not space here to restate it.[1] And the thesis I have developed there, that socialism is bound to become totalitarian, now seems to receive support from the most unexpected quarters. This at least appears to be the meaning when Mr. Max Eastman, in a recent book on Russia, states that " Stalinism *is* socialism, in the sense of being an inevitable, although unforeseen, political and cultural accompaniment." [2]

In fact, although he does not seem to see it, Dr. Dickinson himself, in the concluding passages of his book, makes a statement which comes very much to the same thing. " In a socialist society," he says, " the distinction, always artificial, between economics and politics will break down ; the economic and the political machinery of society will fuse into one " (D 235). This is of course precisely the authoritarian doctrine preached by Nazis and Fascists. The distinction breaks down because in a planned system all economic questions become political questions, because it is no longer a question of reconciling as far as possible individual views and desires, but one of imposing a single scale of values, the " social goal " of which socialists ever since the time of Saint-Simon have been dreaming. In this respect it seems that the schemes of an authoritarian socialist, from those of Professor Hogben and Mr. Lewis Mumford, whom Dr. Dickinson mentions as an example (D 25), to those of Stalin and Hitler, are much more realistic and consistent than the beautiful and idyllic picture of the " libertarian socialism " in which Dr. Dickinson believes.

[1] See *Freedom and the Economic System* (Public Policy Pamphlet, No. 29), University of Chicago Press, 1939.

[2] Max Eastman, *Stalin's Russia and the Crisis in Socialism*, New York, 1940. As the book is not yet available in this country, the quotation is taken from a review that appeared in the American press.

X

There can be no better testimony of the intellectual quality of the two books under discussion than that after having written about them at such length one is conscious of having only just scratched on the surface of the problems raised by them.   But an examination in greater detail would clearly exceed the scope of an article; and since many of the doubts which are left with the reader concern points which are not answered in the two books, an adequate treatment of the subject would require another book even longer than those discussed.   There are however also important problems which are discussed at some length, particularly in Dr. Dickinson's book, which we have scarcely been able to mention.   This applies not only to the difficult problem of the combination of a private sector with the socialised sector, which both authors propose, but also to such important problems as the international relations of a socialist community and to the problems of monetary policy, to which Dr. Dickinson devotes a very brief, and on the whole the least satisfactory, section.

A fuller discussion would also have to point out various passages in the argument of both authors where apparently residues of earlier beliefs or views which are purely matters of political creed creep in and strike one as curiously inconsistent with the plane of the rest of the discussion.   This applies for instance to Dr. Dickinson's repeated references to class-conflict and exploitation or his gibes at the wastes of competition (D 22, 94), and to much of Professor Lange's interesting section on the " economist's case for socialism ", where he seems to employ arguments of somewhat questionable validity.

These, however, are minor points.   On the whole the books are so thoroughly unorthodox from a socialist point of view that one rather wonders whether their authors have not retained too little of the traditional trappings of socialist argument to make their proposals acceptable to socialists who are not economists.   As courageous attempts to face the real difficulties and completely to remould socialist doctrine to meet them they deserve our gratitude and respect.   Whether the solution offered will appear particularly practicable, even to socialists, may perhaps be doubted.   To those who, with Dr. Dickinson, wish to create " for the first time in human history, an effective individualism " (D 26), a different path will probably appear more promising.

[21]

The American Economic Review

VOLUME XXXV   SEPTEMBER, 1945   NUMBER FOUR

THE USE OF KNOWLEDGE IN SOCIETY

By F. A. HAYEK*

I

What is the problem we wish to solve when we try to construct a rational economic order?

On certain familiar assumptions the answer is simple enough. *If* we possess all the relevant information, *if* we can start out from a given system of preferences and *if* we command complete knowledge of available means, the problem which remains is purely one of logic. That is, the answer to the question of what is the best use of the available means is implicit in our assumptions. The conditions which the solution of this optimum problem must satisfy have been fully worked out and can be stated best in mathematical form: put at their briefest, they are that the marginal rates of substitution between any two commodities or factors must be the same in all their different uses.

This, however, is emphatically *not* the economic problem which society faces. And the economic calculus which we have developed to solve this logical problem, though an important step toward the solution of the economic problem of society, does not yet provide an answer to it. The reason for this is that the "data" from which the economic calculus starts are never for the whole society "given" to a single mind which could work out the implications, and can never be so given.

The peculiar character of the problem of a rational economic order is determined precisely by the fact that the knowledge of the circumstances of which we must make use never exists in concentrated or integrated form, but solely as the dispersed bits of incomplete and frequently contradictory knowledge which all the separate individuals possess. The economic problem of society is thus not merely a problem

* The author is Tooke professor of political economy and statistics at the University of London (London School of Economics and Political Science).

of how to allocate "given" resources—if "given" is taken to mean given to a single mind which deliberately solves the problem set by these "data." It is rather a problem of how to secure the best use of resources known to any of the members of society, for ends whose relative importance only these individuals know. Or, to put it briefly, it is a problem of the utilization of knowledge not given to anyone in its totality.

This character of the fundamental problem has, I am afraid, been rather obscured than illuminated by many of the recent refinements of economic theory, particularly by many of the uses made of mathematics. Though the problem with which I want primarily to deal in this paper is the problem of a rational economic organization, I shall in its course be led again and again to point to its close connections with certain methodological questions. Many of the points I wish to make are indeed conclusions toward which diverse paths of reasoning have unexpectedly converged. But as I now see these problems, this is no accident. It seems to me that many of the current disputes with regard to both economic theory and economic policy have their common origin in a misconception about the nature of the economic problem of society. This misconception in turn is due to an erroneous transfer to social phenomena of the habits of thought we have developed in dealing with the phenomena of nature.

II

In ordinary language we describe by the word "planning" the complex of interrelated decisions about the allocation of our available resources. All economic activity is in this sense planning; and in any society in which many people collaborate, this planning, whoever does it, will in some measure have to be based on knowledge which, in the first instance, is not given to the planner but to somebody else, which somehow will have to be conveyed to the planner. The various ways in which the knowledge on which people base their plans is communicated to them is the crucial problem for any theory explaining the economic process. And the problem of what is the best way of utilizing knowledge initially dispersed among all the people is at least one of the main problems of economic policy—or of designing an efficient economic system.

The answer to this question is closely connected with that other question which arises here, that of *who* is to do the planning. It is about this question that all the dispute about "economic planning" centers. This is not a dispute about whether planning is to be done or not. It is a dispute as to whether planning is to be done centrally, by one authority for the whole economic system, or is to be divided among many individuals. Planning in the specific sense in which the term is used in contemporary controversy necessarily means central planning—direction of the whole economic system according to one unified plan. Competition, on the other hand, means decentralized planning by many separate persons. The half-way house between the two, about which many people talk but which few like when they see it, is the delegation of planning to organized industries, or, in other words, monopoly.

Which of these systems is likely to be more efficient depends mainly on the question under which of them we can expect that fuller use will be made of the existing knowledge. And this, in turn, depends on whether we are more likely to succeed in putting at the disposal of a single central authority all the knowledge which ought to be used but which is initially dispersed among many different individuals, or in conveying to the individuals such additional knowledge as they need in order to enable them to fit their plans in with those of others.

III

It will at once be evident that on this point the position will be different with respect to different kinds of knowledge; and the answer to our question will therefore largely turn on the relative importance of the different kinds of knowledge; those more likely to be at the disposal of particular individuals and those which we should with greater confidence expect to find in the possession of an authority made up of suitably chosen experts. If it is today so widely assumed that the latter will be in a better position, this is because one kind of knowledge, namely, scientific knowledge, occupies now so prominent a place in public imagination that we tend to forget that it is not the only kind that is relevant. It may be admitted that, so far as scientific knowledge is concerned, a body of suitably chosen experts may be in the best position to command all the best knowledge available—though this is of course merely shifting the difficulty to the problem of selecting the experts. What I wish to point out is that, even assuming that this problem can be readily solved, it is only a small part of the wider problem.

Today it is almost heresy to suggest that scientific knowledge is not the sum of all knowledge. But a little reflection will show that there is beyond question a body of very important but unorganized knowledge which cannot possibly be called scientific in the sense of knowledge of general rules: the knowledge of the particular circumstances of time and place. It is with respect to this that practically every individual has some advantage over all others in that he possesses unique information of which beneficial use might be made, but of which use can be made only if the decisions depending on it are left to him or are made with his active coöperation. We need to remember only how much we have to learn in any occupation after we have completed our theoretical training, how big a part of our working life we spend learning particular jobs, and how valuable an asset in all walks of life is knowledge of people, of local conditions, and special circumstances. To know of and put to use a machine not fully employed, or somebody's skill which could be better utilized, or to be aware of a surplus stock which can be drawn upon during an interruption of supplies, is socially quite as useful as the knowledge of better alternative techniques. And the shipper who earns his living from using otherwise empty or half-filled journeys of tramp-steamers, or the estate agent whose whole knowledge is almost exclusively one of temporary opportunities, or the *arbitrageur* who gains from local differences of commodity prices, are all performing eminently useful functions based on special knowledge of circumstances of the fleeting moment not known to others.

It is a curious fact that this sort of knowledge should today be generally regarded with a kind of contempt, and that anyone who by such knowledge gains an advantage over somebody better equipped with theoretical or technical knowledge is thought to have acted almost disreputably. To gain an advantage from better knowledge of facilities of communication or transport is sometimes regarded as almost dishonest, although it is quite as important that society make use of the best opportunities in this respect as in using the latest scientific discoveries. This prejudice has in a considerable measure affected the attitude toward commerce in general compared with that toward production. Even economists who regard themselves as definitely above the crude materialist fallacies of the past constantly commit the same mistake where activities directed toward the acquisition of such practical knowledge are concerned—apparently because in their scheme of things all such knowledge is supposed to be "given." The common idea now seems to be that all such knowledge should as a matter of course be readily at the command of everybody, and the reproach of irrationality leveled against the existing economic order is frequently based on the fact that it is not so available. This view disregards the fact that the method by which such knowledge can be made as widely available as possible is precisely the problem to which we have to find an answer.

IV

If it is fashionable today to minimize the importance of the knowledge of the particular circumstances of time and place, this is closely connected with the smaller importance which is now attached to change as such. Indeed, there are few points on which the assumptions made (usually only implicitly) by the "planners" differ from those of their opponents as much as with regard to the significance and frequency of changes which will make substantial alterations of production plans necessary. Of course, if detailed economic plans could be laid down for fairly long periods in advance and then closely adhered to, so that no further economic decisions of importance would be required, the task of drawing up a comprehensive plan governing all economic activity would appear much less formidable.

It is, perhaps, worth stressing that economic problems arise always and only in consequence of change. So long as things continue as before, or at least as they were expected to, there arise no new problems requiring a decision, no need to form a new plan. The belief that changes, or at least day-to-day adjustments, have become less important in modern times implies the contention that economic problems also have become less important. This belief in the decreasing importance of change is, for that reason, usually held by the same people who argue that the importance of economic considerations has been driven into the background by the growing importance of technological knowledge.

Is it true that, with the elaborate apparatus of modern production, economic decisions are required only at long intervals, as when a new factory is to be erected or a new process to be introduced? Is it true that, once a plant has been built, the rest is all more or less mechanical, determined by the character of the plant, and leaving little to be changed in adapting to the ever-changing circumstances of the moment?

The fairly widespread belief in the affirmative is not, so far as I can ascertain, borne out by the practical experience of the business man. In a competitive industry at any rate—and such an industry alone can serve as a test—the task of keeping cost from rising requires constant struggle, absorbing a great part of the energy of the manager. How easy it is for an inefficient manager to dissipate the differentials on which profitability rests, and that it is possible, with the same technical facilities, to produce with a great variety of costs, are among the commonplaces of business experience which do not seem to be equally familiar in the study of the economist. The very strength of the desire, constantly voiced by producers and engineers, to be able to proceed untrammeled by considerations of money costs, is eloquent testimony to the extent to which these factors enter into their daily work.

One reason why economists are increasingly apt to forget about the constant small changes which make up the whole economic picture is probably their growing preoccupation with statistical aggregates, which show a very much greater stability than the movements of the detail. The comparative stability of the aggregates cannot, however, be accounted for—as the statisticians seem occasionally to be inclined to do—by the "law of large numbers" or the mutual compensation of random changes. The number of elements with which we have to deal is not large enough for such accidental forces to produce stability. The continuous flow of goods and services is maintained by constant deliberate adjustments, by new dispositions made every day in the light of circumstances not known the day before, by *B* stepping in at once when *A* fails to deliver. Even the large and highly mechanized plant keeps going largely because of an environment upon which it can draw for all sorts of unexpected needs; tiles for its roof, stationery for its forms, and all the thousand and one kinds of equipment in which it cannot be self-contained and which the plans for the operation of the plant require to be readily available in the market.

This is, perhaps, also the point where I should briefly mention the fact that the sort of knowledge with which I have been concerned is knowledge of the kind which by its nature cannot enter into statistics and therefore cannot be conveyed to any central authority in statistical form. The statistics which such a central authority would have to use would have to be arrived at precisely by abstracting from minor differences between the things, by lumping together, as resources of one kind, items which differ as regards location, quality, and other particulars, in a way which may be very significant for the specific decision. It follows from this that central planning based on statistical information by its nature cannot take direct account of these circumstances of time and place, and that the central planner will have to find some way or other in which the decisions depending on them can be left to the "man on the spot."

V

If we can agree that the economic problem of society is mainly one of rapid adaptation to changes in the particular circumstances of time and place, it would seem to follow that the ultimate decisions must be left to the people who are familiar with these circumstances, who know directly of the relevant changes and of the resources immediately available to meet them. We cannot expect that this problem will be solved by first communicating all this knowledge to a central board which, after integrating *all* knowledge, issues its orders. We must solve it by some form of decentralization. But this answers only part of our problem. We need decentralization because only thus can we ensure that the knowledge of the particular circumstances of time and place will be promptly used. But the "man on the spot" cannot decide solely on the basis of his limited but intimate knowledge of the facts of his immediate surroundings. There still remains the problem of communicating to him such further information as he needs to fit his decisions into the whole pattern of changes of the larger economic system.

How much knowledge does he need to do so successfully? Which of the events which happen beyond the horizon of his immediate knowledge are of relevance to his immediate decision, and how much of them need he know?

There is hardly anything that happens anywhere in the world that *might* not have an effect on the decision he ought to make. But he need not know of these events as such, nor of *all* their effects. It does not matter for him *why* at the particular moment more screws of one size than of another are wanted, *why* paper bags are more readily available than canvas bags, or *why* skilled labor, or particular machine tools, have for the moment become more difficult to acquire. All that is significant for him is *how much more or less* difficult to procure they have become compared with other things with which he is also concerned, or how much more or less urgently wanted are the alternative things he produces or uses. It is always a question of the relative importance of the particular things with which he is concerned, and the causes which alter their relative importance are of no interest to him beyond the effect on those concrete things of his own environment.

It is in this connection that what I have called the economic calculus proper helps us, at least by analogy, to see how this problem can be solved, and in fact is being solved, by the price system. Even the single controlling mind, in possession of all the data for some small, self-contained economic system, would not—every time some small adjustment' in the allocation of resources had to be made—go explicitly through all the relations between ends and means which might possibly be affected. It is indeed the great contribution of the pure logic of choice that it has demonstrated conclusively that even such a single mind could solve this kind of problem only by constructing and constantly using rates of equivalence (or "values," or "marginal rates of substitution"), *i.e.*, by attaching to each kind of scarce resource a numerical index which cannot be derived from any property possessed by that particular thing, but which reflects, or in which is condensed, its significance in view of the whole means-end structure. In any small change he will have to consider only these quantitative indices (or "values") in which all the relevant information is concentrated; and by adjusting the quantities one by one, he can appropriately rearrange his dispositions without having to solve the whole puzzle *ab initio,* or without needing at any stage to survey it at once in all its ramifications.

Fundamentally, in a system where the knowledge of the relevant facts is dispersed among many people, prices can act to coördinate the separate actions of different people in the same way as subjective values help the individual to coördinate the parts of his plan. It is worth contemplating for a moment a very simple and commonplace instance of the action of the price system to see what precisely it accomplishes. Assume that somewhere in the world a new opportunity for the use of some raw material, say tin, has arisen, or that one of the sources of supply of tin has been eliminated. It does not matter for our purpose—and it is very significant that it does not matter—which of these two causes has made tin more scarce. All that the users of tin need to know is that some of the tin they used to consume is now more profitably employed elsewhere, and that in consequence they must economize tin. There is no need for the great majority of them even to know where the more urgent need has arisen, or in favor of what other needs they ought to husband the supply. If only some of them know directly of the new demand, and switch resources over to it, and if the people who are aware of the new gap thus created in turn fill it from still other sources, the effect will rapidly spread throughout the whole economic system and influence not only all the uses of tin, but also those of its substitutes and the substitutes of these substitutes, the supply of all the things made of tin, and their substitutes, and so on; and all this without the great majority of those instrumental in bringing about these substitutions knowing anything at all about the original cause of these changes. The whole acts as one market, not because any of its members survey the whole field, but because their limited individual fields of vision sufficiently overlap so that through many intermediaries the relevant information is communicated to all. The mere fact that there is one price for any commodity—or rather that local prices are connected in a manner determined by the cost of transport, etc.—brings about the solution which (it is just conceptually possible) might have been arrived at by one single mind possessing all the information which is in fact dispersed among all the people involved in the process.

VI

We must look at the price system as such a mechanism for communicating information if we want to understand its real function—a function which, of course, it fulfills less perfectly as prices grow more rigid. (Even when quoted prices have become quite rigid, however, the forces which would operate through changes in price still operate to a considerable extent through changes in the other terms of the contract.) The most significant fact about this system is the economy of knowledge with which it operates, or how little the individual participants need to know in order to be able to take the right action. In abbreviated form, by a kind of symbol, only the most essential information is passed on, and passed on only to those concerned. It is more than a metaphor to describe the price system as a kind of machinery for registering change, or a system of telecommunications which enables individual producers to watch merely the movement of a few pointers, as an engineer might watch the hands of a few dials, in order to adjust their activities to changes of which they may never know more than is reflected in the price movement.

Of course, these adjustments are probably never "perfect" in the sense in which the economist conceives of them in his equilibrium analysis. But I fear that our theoretical habits of approaching the problem with the assumption of more or less perfect knowledge on the part of almost everyone has made us somewhat blind to the true function of the price mechanism and led us to apply rather misleading standards in judging its efficiency. The marvel is that in a case like that of a scarcity of one raw material, without an order being issued, without more than perhaps a handful of people knowing the cause, tens of thousands of people whose identity could not be ascertained by months of investigation, are made to use the material or its products more sparingly; *i.e.*, they move in the right direction. This is enough of a marvel even if, in a constantly changing world, not all will hit it off so perfectly that their profit rates will always be maintained at the same constant or "normal" level.

I have deliberately used the word "marvel" to shock the reader out of the complacency with which we often take the working of this mechanism for granted. I am convinced that if it were the result of deliberate human design, and if the people guided by the price changes understood that their decisions have significance far beyond their immediate aim, this mechanism would have been acclaimed as one of the greatest triumphs of the human mind. Its misfortune is the double one that it is not the product of human design and that the people guided by it usually do not know why they are made to do what they do. But those who clamor for "conscious direction"—and who cannot believe that anything which has evolved without design (and even without our understanding it) should solve problems which we should not be able to solve consciously—should remember this: The problem is precisely how to extend the span of our utilization of resources beyond the span of the control of any one mind; and, therefore, how to dispense with the need of conscious control and how to provide inducements which will make the individuals do the desirable things without anyone having to tell them what to do.

The problem which we meet here is by no means peculiar to economics but arises in connection with nearly all truly social phenomena, with language and most of our cultural inheritance, and constitutes really the central theoretical problem of all social science. As Alfred Whitehead has said in another connection, "It is a profoundly erroneous truism, repeated by all copy-books and by eminent people when they are making speeches, that we should cultivate the habit of thinking what we are doing. The precise opposite is the case. Civilization advances by extending the number of important operations which we can perform without thinking about them." This is of profound significance in the social field. We make constant use of formulas, symbols and rules whose meaning we do not understand and through the use of which we avail ourselves of the assistance of knowledge which individually we do not possess. We have developed these practices and institutions by building upon habits and institutions which have proved successful in their own sphere and which have in turn become the foundation of the civilization we have built up.

The price system is just one of those formations which man has learned to use (though he is still very far from having learned to make the best use of it) after he had stumbled upon it without understanding it. Through it not only a division of labor but also a coördinated utilization of resources based on an equally divided knowledge has become possible. The people who like to deride any suggestion that this may be so usually distort the argument by insinuating that it asserts that by some miracle just that sort of system has spontaneously grown up which is best suited to modern civilization. It is the other way round: man has been able to develop that division of labor on which our civilization is based because he happened to stumble upon a method which made it possible. Had he not done so he might still have developed some other, altogether different, type of civilization, something like the "state" of the termite ants, or some other altogether unimaginable type. All that we can say is that nobody has yet succeeded in designing an alternative system in which certain features of the existing one can be preserved which are dear even to those who most violently assail it—such as particularly the extent to which the individual can choose his pursuits and consequently freely use his own knowledge and skill.

VII

It is in many ways fortunate that the dispute about the indispensability of the price system for any rational calculation in a complex society is now no longer conducted entirely between camps holding different political views. The thesis that without the price system we could not preserve a society based on such extensive division of labor as ours was greeted with a howl of derision when it was first advanced by von Mises twenty-five years ago. Today the difficulties which some still find in accepting it are no longer mainly political, and this makes for an atmosphere much more conducive to reasonable discussion. When we find Leon Trotsky arguing that "economic accounting is unthinkable without market relations"; when Professor Oscar Lange promises Professor von Mises a statue in the marble halls of the future Central Planning Board; and when Professor Abba P. Lerner re-discovers Adam Smith and emphasizes that the essential utility of the price system consists in inducing the individual, while seeking his own interest, to do what is in the general interest, the differences can indeed no longer be ascribed to political prejudice. The remaining dissent seems clearly to be due to purely intellectual, and more particularly methodological, differences.

A recent statement by Professor Joseph Schumpeter in his *Capitalism, Socialism and Democracy* provides a clear illustration of one of the methodological differences which I have in mind. Its author is pre-eminent among those economists who approach economic phenomena in the light of a certain branch of positivism. To him these phenomena accordingly appear as objectively given quantities of commodities impinging directly upon each other, almost, it would seem, without any intervention of human minds. Only against this background can I account for the following (to me startling) pronouncement. Professor Schumpeter argues that the possibility of a rational calculation in the absence of markets for the factors of production follows for the theorist "from the elementary proposition that consumers in evaluating ('de-manding') consumers' goods *ipso facto* also evaluate the means of production which enter into the production of these goods."[1]

Taken literally, this statement is simply untrue. The consumers do nothing of the kind. What Professor Schumpeter's *"ipso facto"* pre-sumably means is that the valuation of the factors of production is

[1] J. Schumpeter, *Capitalism, Socialism, and Democracy* (New York, Harper, 1942), p. 175. Professor Schumpeter is, I believe, also the original author of the myth that Pareto and Barone have "solved" the problem of socialist calculation. What they, and many others, did was merely to state the conditions which a rational allocation of resources would have to satisfy, and to point out that these were essentially the same as the condi-tions of equilibrium of a competitive market. This is something altogether different from showing how the allocation of resources satisfying these conditions can be found in prac-tice. Pareto himself (from whom Barone has taken practically everything he has to say), far from claiming to have solved the practical problem, in fact explicitly denies that it can be solved without the help of the market. See his *Manuel d'économie pure* (2nd ed., 1927), pp. 233-34. The relevant passage is quoted in an English translation at the begin-ning of my article on "Socialist Calculation: The Competitive 'Solution,' " in *Economica*, ¹ew Series, Vol. VIII, No. 26 (May, 1940), p. 125.

implied in, or follows necessarily from, the valuation of consumers' goods. But this, too, is not correct. Implication is a logical relationship which can be meaningfully asserted only of propositions simultaneously present to one and the same mind. It is evident, however, that the values of the factors of production do not depend solely on the valuation of the consumers' goods but also on the conditions of supply of the various factors of production. Only to a mind to which all these facts were simultaneously known would the answer necessarily follow from the facts given to it. The practical problem, however, arises precisely because these facts are never so given to a single mind, and because, in consequence, it is necessary that in the solution of the problem knowledge should be used that is dispersed among many people.

The problem is thus in no way solved if we can show that all the facts, *if* they were known to a single mind (as we hypothetically assume them to be given to the observing economist), would uniquely determine the solution; instead we must show how a solution is produced by the interactions of people each of whom possesses only partial knowledge. To assume all the knowledge to be given to a single mind in the same manner in which we assume it to be given to us as the explaining economists is to assume the problem away and to disregard everything that is important and significant in the real world.

That an economist of Professor Schumpeter's standing should thus have fallen into a trap which the ambiguity of the term "datum" sets to the unwary can hardly be explained as a simple error. It suggests rather than there is something fundamentally wrong with an approach which habitually disregards an essential part of the phenomena with which we have to deal: the unavoidable imperfection of man's knowledge and the consequent need for a process by which knowledge is constantly communicated and acquired. Any approach, such as that of much of mathematical economics with its simultaneous equations, which in effect starts from the assumption that people's *knowledge* corresponds with the objective *facts* of the situation, systematically leaves out what is our main task to explain. I am far from denying that in our system equilibrium analysis has a useful function to perform. But when it comes to the point where it misleads some of our leading thinkers into believing that the situation which it describes has direct relevance to the solution of practical problems, it is time that we remember that it does not deal with the social process at all and that it is no more than a useful preliminary to the study of the main problem.

[22]

ECONOMIC CALCULATION UNDER SOCIALISM: THE AUSTRIAN CONTRIBUTION

KAREN I. VAUGHN*

Economic theories of socialism during the 1930's were based on Walrasian general equilibrium models in which the central planning board was to function as the auctioneer. Socialists assumed that "market socialism" would achieve all the efficiencies characteristic of perfect competition while avoiding the serious market failures of real capitalist economies. The Austrians, Ludwig von Mises and Friedrich Hayek, argued that even market socialism would fail to achieve the efficiency of real market capitalism because Walrasian models used to construct the economic theory of socialism left out important features of real markets that generate efficient outcomes. Specifically, the entrepreneurial nature of the adjustment process, the importance of decentralized information and the role of incentives under vaying institutional settings.

Between 1920 and 1940, a body of economic literature developed which became known as the debate over economic calculation under socialism. It began with the publication of Ludwig won Mises' article, "Economic Calculation in the Socialist Commonwealth,"[1] it took form first primarily in the German literature and then reached full flower in English language journals and books during the 1930's. The ostensible subject of the debate was whether it was possible for a real economy to operate efficiently without free markets and without private ownership of capital and land, but at the core of the debate were issues that were far-reaching and profound in their implications for economic theory in general. That the issues involved are still some of the most difficult in contemporary economic theory and remain unresolved amost forty years after the conclusion of the debate makes the identification of the differences between the two sides of more than historical interest.

It is indicative of the nature of the controversy that those who argued most effectively in favor of socialism were not advocates of a labor economists operating within the dominant neo-classical paradigm.[2] A few

*George Mason University. This paper is a revised version of one I presented at The Southern Economic Association meetings 1977. I would like to thank the Institute for Humane Studies, for financial assistance in preparing the paper. I have profited from helpful comments by Axel Leijonhufvud, Laurence Moss, Janet Rives and an anonymous referee.

1. Mises, (1920).

2. The people most responsible for developing the economic theory of socialism and who are referred to here are Fred Taylor, H. D. Dickinson, Oskar Lange, Abba Lerner, E. M. F. Durbin and Maurice Dobb. While many other economists wrote on the economies of socialism, these were the most influential writers on the subject and the ones whose work was accepted as a refutation of Mises.

535

took their inspiration from Marshall, more from Walras, but all agreed that given some "just" initial wealth distribution, equilibrium in the perfectly competitive model represented the maximization of human welfare, and all their programs for socialism were designed to reproduce the conclusions of perfect competition in a centrally directed economy.[3] They preferred socialism to capitalism because they believed under socialism it would be possible to eliminate the imperfections that they found existing simultaneously with free markets: monopolies, externalities, business cycles, and unjust income and wealth distributions.[4] Thus, they believed that capitalism was undesirable because it did not measure up to the ideal or perfect competiton.

Those most closely associated with the theoretical defense of capitalism,[5] on the other hand, were Ludwig von Mises, Friedrich Hayek and Lionnel Robbins.[6] Of the three, Mises and Hayek were both Austrian economists, and Robbins, although English, was much influenced by Carl Menger and was, therefore, at least partly in the Austrian tradition. As Austrians, they worked with a perception of economic activity that differed markedly from that mainstream economists. Primarily, they questioned the relevance and applicability of static equilibrium models in which all information is given, and emphasized instead the process by which decentralized economic actors operating in a world of uncertainty

3. The exception was Maurice Dobb who was far more Marxist than the others and who challenged the "sacredness of consumer preferences"((1933), p. 591) and who argued that reproducing the conclusions of perfect competition under socialism missed the point. As he put it, "Either planning means overriding the autonomy of private decisions or it apparently means nothing at all." ((1937), p. 279).

4. A belief in the superiority of socialism over capitalism both as it exists and as it is described in ideal models is implicit in all the socialists writings, but the best specific statement is found in Lange, (1962) Part IV, p. 98-120, "The Economist's Case for Socialism." There he claims that "only a socialist economy can distribute incomes so as to attain the maximum social welfare," (p. 99). In regard to externalities, a socialist economy would be able to "take into the cost accounts all the alternatives sacrificed . . . by doing so it would avoid much of the social waste connected with private enterprise." (p. 104). He further asserts that "as a result of the possibility of taking into account all the alternatives a socialist economy would not be subject to the fluctuations of the business cycle," (p. 105). See also Dickinson ((1933), p. 247).

5. I will use the terms "socialism" and "capitalism" to designate the opposing economic systems under debate. Although the words have no clearly recognized scientific definition (and even to the participants in the debate, the meanings shifted frequently between theoretical and empirical states), I will try to be consistent with the following meanings. *Socialism* will refer to any theoretical model which provides for collective ownership of land and capital goods and which designates some kind of planning board to oversee resource allocation and set official policy for capital accumulation and growth. This is a loose enough definition to encompass all of the systems proposed by socialist economists during the debate. *Capitalism* will mean a theoretical model where all resources are privately owned and where resource allocation, consumption patterns and capital accumulation are all determined by the coordination of individual preferences in unregulated markets. This definition seems closest to what Mises and Hayek had in mind when they talked about capitalism and capitalist methods of production.

6. Although he has not received nearly the publicity the others have, we should also include Hawtry in this list. In *The Economic Problem* (1926) he described a socialist model which closely resembled that developed by Dickinson and Lange a decade later and criticized it along much the same lines as Hayek criticized the later ones in 1935 and 1940. See especially pp. 336-340.

and constant change bring about the coordination of production and consumption plans. Consequently, the debate was a contest of theoretical models in which a mutually satisfactory resolution was precluded from the outset.

Although it is conventional to treat the economic calculation controversy as a debate between those who favored socialism and those who opposed it, this is not descriptive of the actual course of events. During the 1920's there was a genuine debate between Mises and the German and Austrian socialists, but by the 1930's, Mises had finished with the issue and it was Friedrich Hayek who took upon himself the role of critic of socialism in England. However, by that time, the real debate, in so far as one took place in the journals, was among the socialists themselves[7] who were busy hammering out a complete economic theory of socialism based on neo-classical static equilibrium analysis. Occasionally, Hayek's criticisms were noted in scholarly articles, but rarely for any purpose other than refutation. Mostly, Mises was ridiculed, and Hayek, on this issue seen as little more than Mises' apologist, was ignored. The unhappy result of this failure to see more than warmed over Mises in Hayek's work was an almost total lack of recognition of the subtleties of the issues Hayek raised in criticism of market socialism. If I had to offer a crude synopsis of the economic calculation debate, it would be this: Mises wrote an article claiming that rational economic calculation was impossible under socialism. This prompted those who favored socialism to try to refute him and thus forced them to construct a model of rationally administered centrally directed economy. Meanwhile, Hayek wrote two sophisticated and penetrating critiques of the socialist schemes which were in the main ignored. Mises seemed easy to refute, and so for twenty years, socialists continued to refute the same arguments, thereby avoiding consideration of the more difficult issues raised by Hayek.

In order to understand the principal issues raised in the literature on socialist economic calculation, it will be convenient to divide my discussion into four parts. The first part of this paper examines Mises' 1920 article to identify the sources of controversy, the second part briefly outlines the major developments in the economic theory of socialism during the 1930's, the third part presents Hayek's criticisms of socialist economic programs, and the fourth and final part attempts to summarize the theoretical problems raised during the debate in order to appreciate the relevance of the Austrian contribution to current problems in economic theory.

---

7. For instance, Dickinson's 1933 article drew sharp criticism from Maurice Dobb (1935). Dobb's criticism of Dickinson brought a stinging rebuke from Abba Lerner (1935). Lange managed to get by pretty much unscathed by his fellow socialists, but Durbin and Lerner had a somewhat hostile interchange on the subject of Durbin's 1936 article (Lerner (1937), Durbin (1937) and Lerner (1938)).

I.

The literature on the economics of socialism before 1920 is sparse. While there was no lack of scholarly (and not so scholarly) discussion of socialism as a social theory, Marxists, following the lead of Marx himself, paid little attention to the actual workings of a socialist economy. It was assumed that after the revolution was time enough to worry about the economic problem, assuming that one still existed after the demise of capitalism.[8] A few attempts were made to describe a theory of a centrally directed economy, but these attempts were significantly made by non-Marxist economists interested in a purely theoretical problem. F. von Weiser often made use of the construct of a centrally directed economy in explicating his economic theories, as did Pareto in his exposition of general equilibrium theory. Enrico Barone developed the most complete exploration into the economics of socialism applying neo-classical tools to the problem of a centrally directed economy in an article written in 1908.[9] None of these writers, however, were socialists and none were attempting to prescribe a formula for running a real socialist economy. More significantly, none of these efforts had any influence on socialists and Marxists prior to 1920.

What all of these early attempts to construct a theoretical model of a centrally directed economy had in common was the realization that the same economic logic can be applied both to capitalism and socialism. Therefore, if socialist economic planners want to allocate resources efficiently, they must be able to calculate correct resource and product values, including those two much despised by Marxists, interest and profits. Hence, in 1920, in a manner which suggested growing impatience with economically naive Marxists (some of whom were advocating a moneyless economy without exchange and denying the existence of resource scarcity), Mises wrote his famous article, "Economic Calculation in the Socialist Commonwealth."

Mises article was concerned with establishing two principal propositions. The first was a restatement of the Weiser-Pareto-Barone argument that all the same economic variables that guide resource use in a capitalist economy must also necessarily be taken account of under socialism. He

---

8. For a description of early socialist and Marxist literature which makes this point, see Schumpeter ((1954), pp. 877-885). This is not to say that there was no socialist economics before 1920. Rather there was no attempt by socialists to deal with the problem of efficient resource use and growth within the context of a consistent model before 1920. In his excellent review article of W. O. Henderson's *Life of Friedrich Engels,* T. W. Hutchison points out that Engels in his later work showed that he understood very well the vital importance of a competitive pricing mechanism when criticizing other socialists as "utopian," but ignored it when describing his and Marx' view of the workings of the economy after the Revolution. Hutchison comments, "Surely no one in the whole of intellectual history can have looked a major, pressing intellectual and practical problem so clearly and piercingly in the face and then so blithely and confidently passed on without a word." Hutchison ((1978), p. 317).

9. Weiser (1893) especially pp. 60-64, Pareto (1906) especially pp. 267-271, and Barone (1908).

argued specifically that it was naive to expect money and prices to disappear for very long under socialism, that as long as people have differing preferences (and as long as socialist leaders strive to satisfy consumer preferences), the allocation of consumer goods would present problems which could only be solved by resorting to some system of money and prices. In fact, since consumer goods presumably would be owned by consumers themselves, the development of prices and markets in consumer goods was inevitable.[10] The real problem, according to Mises, was in the allocation of capital goods — the means of production. Since these would not be privately owned, markets could not be utilized to determine resource prices, and hence, there would be no way to evaluate relative resource scarcities.[11] He conceded that while socialism may be possible in a static state where knowledge of unchanging economic parameters is universal and where the imputation problem, once solved, would remain solved forever, he emphasized that such a static state itself is only a "theoretical assumption corresponding to no real state of affairs."[12] In any real socialist world, the impediments to rational economic calculation are legion: the inevitability of change, the uncertainties that this implies in all economic decision-making,[13] the problem of initiative without private property,[14] and the necessary elimination of the "promoter and man of affairs"[15] who makes the market work to establish relevant prices. Mises second proposition, then, was that without free markets based on private resource ownership, economic calculation would be totally impossible. It was this second proposition that infuriated socialists, challenged conventional economists and became the focus of attempts to refute Mises.[16]

10. Mises ((1920), pp. 90-93).

11. Mises ((1920), pp. 104-109).

12. Mises ((1920), p. 109).

13. Mises ((1920), p. 111).

14. Mises ((1920), p. 116).

15. Mises ((1920), p. 119).

16. One reason Mises infuriated socialists is that he deliberately chose to clothe his arguments in highly polemical garb. He claimed, for example, that "Every step that takes us away from private ownership of the means of production and from the use of money also takes us away from rational economy," (p. 104), and "Where there is no free market, there is no pricing mechanism; without a pricing mechanism, there is no economic calculation." (p. 111), He even went so far as to claim that the absence of free markets under socialism would lead to the end of "rationality and logic in thought itself." (p. 105), While it is true that in so stating his arguments, he was using polemic to answer polemic, the result of his emotionally charged style was that the style was better remembered than the cogency of the argument.

II.

Although there was much discussion of the problems Mises raised during the 1920's in the German literature,[17] the creation of an economic model of socialism along neoclassical lines was a product of English speaking economists in the 1930's. Three men especially stand out as originators of socialist economics: H. D. Dickinson, Oskar Lange and and Abba Lerner. Of the three, Dickinson was first in print with his preliminary model, Lange's work came to represent the "economic theory of socialism" (and incidentally was credited with offering the definitive refutation of Mises), and Lerner's marginal cost rule made a significant contribution to the work of the other two.[18]

Dickinson and Lange developed very similar models of socialist economy in which there would be private ownership of consumer goods and freedom of choice in occupation, but public ownership of all capital goods and non-human productive resources. Where their models differed most significantly, at least initially, was in the methods suggested for obtaining relative values to guide resource allocation. Dickinson's solution to the pricing problem was to set up selling agencies which would determine the prices of all goods by a combination of several methods: The prices for consumer goods would be set according to what the market would bear, the agencies "raising (prices) when stocks fell short, lowering when they accumulate."[19] In this way they would be able to determine statistically all the demand functions for all goods which, when combined with technologically determined production functions and a given supply of resources, would enable the central planning board to impute factor valuations.[20] Dickinson also seemed to propose that the planning agency, operating within the "glass walls" of socialism (where all demand functions, production functions and resource supplies are known to planners) would be able to construct a mathematical model of the economy which would be solved for resource prices using a system of simultaneous equations á la Barone.[21]

17. Accounts of some of these clearly socialist responses can be found in Hayek ((1935), pp. 1-40), and Hoff ((1949), Chapter IV, V).

18. Dickinson's model was first published as an article in the *Economic Journal* in 1933. He later expanded and refined it in his booklength *The Economics of Socialism* (1939). Lange's major contribution was his two part article, "On the Economic Theory of Socialism" published in the *Review of Economic Studies* (1936, 1937) and later reprinted together with Fred Taylor's "The Guidance of Production in a Socialist State." See Lange and Taylor (1938). Lerner contributed several articles to the development of socialist economics, but perhaps his most famous is "Statics and Dynamics in Socialist Economies" (1937). Lerner has charmingly recalled the genesis of the marginal cost rule he proposed in that article and his personal conversations on the subject with Lange in Lerner (1973).

19. Dickinson ((1933), p. 239).

20. Dickinson ((1933), p. 240).

21. Dickinson ((1933), p. 245).

Lange's solution to the pricing problem was simpler. He too, proposed setting up a central planning board to administer prices, but only resource prices. Consumer goods would be priced in free markets in order to provide accurate information for factor valuation.[22] Factor prices would then be determined by a system of "trial and error" exclusively, the process partially adopted by Dickinson but originally proposed by F. M. Taylor in 1928. Lange's use of trial and error was a conscious attempt to overcome the myriad difficulties inherent in an attempt to solve for prices using statistical demand curves and econometric models, difficulties stressed by both Robbins and Hayek.[23] In response to the critics, Lange argued forcefully that there was no need to set up systems of simultaneous equations to find factor prices as long as the planning board "fixes the prices so as to balance the quantity supplied and the quantity demanded of each commodity."[24] Lange believed that trial and error described the process by which prices are formed in real markets, and he patterned his method after a Walrasian tâtonnement with the central planning board acting the part of the auctioneer.[25]

After Lange's work appeared in print, the socialists, as well as many non-socialists, agreed that the problem of pricing under socialism had been solved by the trial and error process, and what remained to be explored was how these prices should be used in the actual production of goods and services. Hence, after the publication of Lange's article, the problem of what set of rules would induce managers of socialist firms to make decisions that would lead to appropriate resource allocation replaced the problem of pricing in the literature on socialist economics.

Lange's contribution to the question of managerial rules had been to point out that in pure competition, profit maximization and the freedom of entry and exit are the mechanisms which assure allocative efficiency. Thus, to duplicate the results of perfect competition, it was necessary to force socialist managers to behave like perfect competitors by imposing two rules of behavior on them: As an alternative to profit maximization, they would be instructed to minimize factor costs for the given set of resource prices, and to equate marginal cost to product price in the production of output. The first would guarantee efficient use of resources and the second, appropriate plant size. When applied to the industry as a whole, the second rule would also control the size of the industry.[26] As long as socialist managers observed the "parametric function of price," that is, as long as they, like perfect competitors in genuine markets, treated resource and product prices as parameters rather than dependent

22. Lange ((1938), pp. 72-73).

23. Hayek ((1935), p. 212); Robbins ((1933), p. 148).

24. Lange ((1938), p. 83).

25. Lange ((1938), p. 70 and pp. 82-83).

26. Lange ((1938), pp. 75-79).

variables, his rules would lead to the same resource allocation as perfect competition.[27]

By the end of the decade, the outline of a neoclassical economic theory of market socialism was complete. Consumer goods are priced in genuine markets, communally owned resource prices are determined by a central planning board through the trial and error process, and managers at both firms and industries are told to produce where the marginal cost of output equals the price of the product produced and the price of any resource employed equals the marginal contribution of that resource to output. Any change in parameters will manifest itself as a change in price which will cause managers to alter firm production and industry size accordingly. Clearly, these neo-classical socialists believed they had shown that economic calculation was just as possible under socialism as it was under capitalism. That in order to do so they had to create a socialism that bore no resemblance to any existing political states and which had nothing to do with Marxist economics was irrelevant. Their economic model was still within the spirit of socialism although it retained many important features of capitalism.[28] In addition, they believed their brand of socialism was both economically and morally superior to free market capitalism. With a system of market socialism, one could more rationally direct economic growth through appropriate manipulation of the rate of interest, and production in general would increase because of the elimination of monopoly power and the waste associated with business cycles and inappropriate coordination of private production plans. Furthermore, income distribution under socialism would be morally superior to capitalism because of the absence of income derived from property ownership, and because of the ability of the central authority to adjust wages to eliminate rents.[29] Certainly, they believed Mises had been decidedly refuted many times over by the end of the decade.[30]

27. Lange ((1938), p. 81). The problem of managerial rules was also addressed by E. M. F. Durbin in his 1936 article in the *Economic Journal* although his instructions for socialist managers were somewhat different from Lange's. Durbin would tell them (a) to produce the largest output possible in any existing plant that is consistent with making normal profits, and (b) where normal profits could not be earned, to equate price to marginal cost (p. 686). Hence he, even more than Lange, was attempting to reproduce the symptoms of static equilibrium in perfect competition in a socialist economy. Lerner effectively attacked this position in Lerner (1937). There he formulated his famous marginal cost rule in which he argued that in so far as the goal of socialism is the maximization of the value of production, one should assure that no resources be used to produce a commodity which can be used to produce a more highly valued commodity elsewhere. This can be accomplished by equating prices to marginal cost at every decision point. (p. 251).

28. Mises would not have agreed with this statement. To him, socialism and markets were mutually exclusive categories (as they were to many Marxists at the time when Mises was writing). Hence any move to restore markets in a collectivist economy was a step away from original socialist aspirations. See Mises ((1936), pp. 705-706).

29. Lerner ((1937), pp. 269-270).

30. An interesting illustration of the degree to which Mises was anathema to the socialists was Lerner's comment in "Statics and Dynamics in Socialist Economics," (Lerner (1937)). Although he thoroughly and very effectively criticizes the many flaws in Durbin's formulation of managerial rules, he nevertheless introduces his comments by saying Durbin "refutes anew the well-known thesis of Professors Mises, Hayek and Halm that a socialist economic calculus is impossible." (p. 251)

III.

So far, we have considered only the socialists' contribution to the debate over economic calculation. It has been possible to review the development of the economic theory of socialism without reference to Hayek's writings because despite the fact that the socialists apparently read his essay, there was very little notice taken of the criticisms he offered of the socialist schemes. Hence, it is more in keeping with the actual course of the controversy to treat Hayek's comments as a critique apart from the development of socialist economic theory.

What seemed to trouble Hayek the most about neoclassical socialist economics was what he regarded as an inappropriate application of static equilibrium models to the formation of a new economic order. He respected the usefulness of the concept of equilibrium for limited explanatory purposes, but believed that the socialists were overstepping those limits by venturing into the realm of planning on the basis of equilibrium models. While the high level of abstraction of the Walrasian general equilibrium model in particular might be an advantage in explaining precisely the end point of a market process, this level of abstraction which is an asset in simplifying explanation also precludes the model's usefulness as a blueprint for constructing a different, non-market economy.[31] What this model omits — considerations of the process by which equilibrium is approached, the effects of uncertainty on the conclusions of the model, consideration of what constitutes economic information and to whom it is available — are, each one, sufficient to guarantee that an economic order resulting from conscious planning according to that model will be far different from the one envisioned by the planners. Thus, Hayek argued specifically that while the models the socialists were using to arrive at their solution to the pricing problem were not logically contradictory and socialism was not therefore impossible in the sense of being theoretically inconceivable, it was nevertheless practically impossible since the socialist models bore no relationship to the manner in which prices were formed in the real world.[32] In general,

31. Hayek published only three articles dealing specifically with the problem of economic calculation under socialism. The first two were original contributions to his volume of essays, *Collectivist Economic Planning* (1935). The lead essay in this volume (pp. 1-40) was a review of the controversy until 1935, and the concluding summary was a critical article, "The Present State of the Debate" (pp. 201-243). The third and final article which Hayek published on the subject was his 1940 review of Dickinson's and Lange's books on socialist economics. (Hayek ((1948), pp. 181-208)). However, in order to understand Hayek's position more fully, one should also consult several other articles he published during the 30's and 40's, "Economics and Knowledge" ((1948), pp. 33-56), "The Use of Knowledge in Society" ((1948), pp. 77-91) and "The Meaning of Competition" ((1948), pp. 92-106). Although not strictly directed to the debate, they all dealt in a more abstract manner with exactly the kinds of criticisms Hayek made of the socialist programs.

32. This is, for example, the sense of his statement that "all the difficulties which have been raised are 'only' due to the imperfections of the human mind. But while this makes it illegitimate to say that these proposals are impossible in any absolute sense, it remains not the less true that these very serious obstacles to the achievement of the desired end exist and that there seems to be no way in which they can be overcome." Hayek ((1935), p. 238). Hayek further developed his concept of the nature of economic equilibrium and its relationship to knowledge in "Economics and Knowledge." ((1948), pp. 33-56).

the market socialists misunderstood the nature of the market economy and were misapplying the market models they were using.

It is true that Hayek never said this in so many words all in one place; it unfortunately is the fate of a critic to have his own vision revealed only piecemeal and in reaction to the work of others. Yet this was the heart of Hayek's argument against the socialists, and whether or not he was correct, his argument was a profound one that deserved careful attention. Instead, there apparently was some confusion over what Hayek meant by the possible versus the practical in economic model building because Lange took Hayek's work to represent a "second line of defense" of capitalism. Lange claimed that Hayek now admitted that Mises had been wrong, that socialism *was* possible "in theory," but that there were just practical objections to its implementation.[33]

At the center of the confusion was a failure to agree on what constituted a theoretical objection to socialism (or any model meant to tell us something about the real world) and what was "merely" a practical one. The socialists (and most of the economics profession at the time) seemed to believe that the demonstration that the same economic logic applies to both capitalism and socialism was sufficient proof that socialism was "theoretically possible," and hence they pointed to Pareto and Barone as having refuted Mises' claim that socialism is impossible.[34] Neither Mises nor Hayek ever argued that the socialist models were inconsistent given their assumptions, however. What they argued was that the ability to calculate rationally under socialism was "practically impossible" because the theory, while logically consistent, did not capture enough important features of the real world to make it applicable. This is hardly a "practical" objection in any useful sense of the word. Certainly, this kind of "practical" objection can not be shrugged off as trivial. Nevertheless, it was Lange's simplistic interpretation of Hayek's sophisticated insight that was accepted by the profession with the unhappy result that the really interesting and important question of what constitutes an appropriate model for a socialist economy was never formally discussed.[35]

The major source of Hayek's criticisms of the wholesale application of general equilibrium models to socialist economies was his perception of the role of information in economic decision making, a problem which has only recently been recognized in the theoretical literature.[36] Standard neoclassical models begin with the assumption of given utility and

---

33. Lange ((1938), p. 63)

34. Lange ((1938), p. 59).

35. This might not have been so serious an omission if the market socialists were doing no more than playing theoretical games of market simulation. Instead they were purporting to describe the potential design and operation of a real economy which made exploration of the differences between capitalism and socialism, and the implications of these differences for modeling the economic structure, vastly important.

36. See for example, Rothschild (1973).

production functions which, when ground through the maximization model, imply a set of relative product and resource prices. Lange pointed out that the same information which guided economic decisions in capitalism would also be available in a socialized economy.[37] To Hayek, saying that the information was "available" was just the beginning of the problem of demonstrating the possibility of a non-market economy. The real problem of any economic model is to show how the information necessary for rational decision making which exists in the minds of millions of separate individuals can be transmitted to appropriate decision makers in such a way as to permit an orderly economy to emerge.[38] The market is one highly successful means of encouraging the production, transmission and use of information because it takes advantage of decentralization of knowledge and of decision making.[39] Hayek referred to this as the division of knowledge.[40] The burden of proof therefore was on the socialists to show that centralization could improve upon the market's production and use of information.

Hayek's emphasis on the role of information in the economic process is well illustrated in his discussion of the Dickinson-style mathematical solution to the pricing problem. Hayek objected to the mathematical solution in part because of the practical difficulties involved in solving what would necessarily be a formidable set of equations once the data is given. This was the objection upon which the socialists concentrated their rebuttals. However, Hayek's more profound criticism was that given the way in which information is discovered and used in a market economy, it would be physically impossible for a planning board to acquire the information necessary to specify those equations.[41]

The information that individuals use to guide their economic activity is vast, detailed and necessarily incomplete.[42] It is not neatly summarized in objective demand and cost functions which need only be revealed to central planners in order for them to take over the task of economic decision making. Even if it were possible to arrive at useful demand functions for consumer goods, it would not be possible to obtain objective production functions and cost functions which represent those which describe a free market. The major reason Hayek gave was that such information is not given, but is the subject of continuous discovery. Neoclassical economics emphasizes "engineering knowledge" or knowledge of production techniques as if it were the only information relevant to business decisions. In fact, efficient resource use depends as much upon

37. See for instance, Lange ((1938), pp. 60-61).

38. Hayek ((1948), p. 210). Gerald O'Driscoll, in his recent (1977) study of Hayek's contributions to economics, has dubbed this "the coordination problem."

39. Hayek ((1948), pp. 83-87).

40. Hayek ((1948), p. 50).

41. Hayek ((1935), pp. 208-212).

42. Hayek ((1935), pp. 212-213).

knowledge of "time and place" — the ability to perceive opportunities others miss and to know when to take advantage of them.[43] Further, some information may be no more than a "technique of thought" which enables a producer to "find new solutions rapidly as soon as he is confronted with a new constellation of circumstances."[44] Market prices are the result of transactions among individuals with unique and fragmented knowledge and are a means by which this decentralized knowledge is coalesced into a coordinated whole. To try to summarize all this information into a set of simultaneous equations would be quixotic at best.

Hayek's perception of the role of information in economic analysis also provided the basis for his criticism of the Lange-Taylor trial and error method of pricing — the socialists' solution to the difficulties inherent in trying to operate an economy using econometric models. Hayek argued that trial and error pricing would not be able to duplicate free market pricing for two reasons: One had to do with the timing of price changes and the other, with the problem of specifying the product accurately. As for the first, neither Lange nor Dickinson (who also adopted the trial and error techniques in his 1939 book, *The Economics of Socialism*) made clear at what intervals the central planning board would change prices in response to surpluses and shortages. Hayek pointed out that only if the price of every good was to be changed immediately whenever some imbalance was perceived would a planning board come close to approximating the market. More likely, however, there would be some accounting period at the end of which prices would be adjusted. Since the data are always changing, in between these accounting periods, the official prices would be disequilibrium prices which would prolong excess demands and supplies and hence, also prolong resource misallocation. Of course, he was not implying that market determined prices are never in disequilibrium: Rather the implication was that market prices will be in disequilibrium less often than centrally controlled prices and will always be changing in the "right" direction thus giving correct market signals even if they are technically in disequilibrium. Markets enable buyers and sellers to react more quickly to changing data because the path by which information must travel in order for corrective price changes to be effected is shorter than it would be under socialism.[45]

43. Hayek ((1948), p. 80).

44. Hayek ((1935), p. 196).

45. Hayek ((1948), pp. 187-188, 192-194). His position is summarized in the following: "If in the real world we had to deal with approximately constant data, that is if the problem were to find a price system which then could be left more or less unchanged for long periods, then the proposal under consideration would not be so entirely unreasonable. With given and constant data, such a state of equilibrium could indeed be approached by the method of trial and error. But this is far from being the situation in the real world, where constant change is the rule . . . The practical problem is not whether a particular method would eventually lead to a hypothetical equilibrium, but which method will secure the more rapid and complete adjustment to the daily changing conditions in different places and different industries. How great the difference in this respect would be between a method where these prices are decreed from above, is of course, a matter of practical judgment. But I find it difficult to believe that anybody would doubt that in this respect the inferiority of the second method would be very great indeed." (p. 188).

In addition to the problem of slower reaction time, Hayek also pointed to the problems a planning board would have with trying to specify the products to be assigned prices, and again this was a problem that refers to the kind of data available to decision-makers. In effect, Hayek argued that there are more dimensions to the objects of exchange than price and quantity. In the real world, unlike the model of perfect competition, many products are not standardized with uniform, competitive prices. In capital markets especially products are often physically unique, and where they are physically similar, they vary according to location, time of availability, and concomitantly offered services. It would be unlikely that any planning board would be able to take account of all these character-istics in defining products for which to set prices. Hence, a central planning board would be setting prices for aggregates of goods that were not representative of all the different products subject to economic exchange. This would necessarily reduce the informational content of prices, the adaptiveness of resources to various production processes and the variety of production techniques employed.[46]

Of these three criticisms Hayek offered of socialist pricing schemes, the misunderstanding of the character of the information which guides economic activity, the difference in the speed of adjustment to changing data between socialism and capitalism, and the difficulty in defining what a "product" is for accounting purposes, the first was not dealt with by the socialists (and apparently was not acknowledged to be a genuine problem by those who later evaluated the controversy),[47] and the second two were considered to be minor empirical objections to socialism which could be worked out and which in any case would not lead to serious distortions in resource allocation.

Even if the pricing problem were solved, Hayek, taking his cue from Mises, still believed that there would be great difficulties in attempting to operate an economy without private ownership of the means of produc-tion. Hence, he believed that even Lange's "competitive socialism" would necessarily fall short of the level of economic well-being the market is capable of yielding. Lange had claimed that all that was necessary to show that socialism was capable of allocating resources as well as capitalism was to refer to the "parametric function of price."[48] That is, all that was necessary for socialism to work was to insure that managers of firms and industries behave like perfect competitors and treat resource

---

46. Hayek ((1935), p. 209). Hayek ((1948), pp. 188, 193).

47. Schumpeter (1942) believed that "In any normal situation, it (the socialist economy) would command information sufficient to enable it to come at first throw fairly close to correct quantities of output in the major lines of production, and the rest would be matter of adjustments by informed trial and error." (p. 185). In addition, he claimed that since uncertainties about competitors' reactions and general business climate would be eliminated, solving practical business problems under socialism would be easier (p. 186). See also Bergson (1948).

48. Lange ((1938), p. 80).

and product prices as if they were independent of the producers' production decisions. The problem, aside from the question of whether or not the "parametric function" actually describes the way prices operate in a competitive economy, is that socialist managers would not really be perfect competitors. While there might very well be many firms in an industry with firm managers making output decisions on the basis of given prices, Lange's plan also required the existence of industry managers who would make decisions regarding the growth or decline of the industry as a whole. The industry manager, then, would really be in a position of a monopolist who knows his output decisions will affect the price of his product. Only if he could be convinced to ignore his effect on the price of the product, could Lange's solution be consistent with his model. Lange's method of dealing with the problem was for the Central Planning Board to impose an "accounting rule" which would instruct industry managers that "All accounting has to be done as if prices were independent of decisions taken."[49] Both Mises and Hayek questioned the likelihood of managers actually following such a rule when it easily could work contrary to their own personal long run interests.

Mises especially had argued that the role of the manager in a socialist state was crucial to the success or failure of the system. One of the reasons Mises gave for the "impossibility" of socialism was that managers could never be substitutes for private businessmen: that one had to risk one's own income on the consequences of the decisions one makes if the market is going to yield the most efficient outcome.[50] One particular socialist argument that Mises took pains to contradict was that managers in socialist enterprises would be no different from managers of private corporations who are not themselves owners of stock in the company. Mises acknowledged that this might be partially true, but countered that the most successful corporations were those whose managers did have a direct stake in the success of the business either through bonuses or shareholding.[51] While this claim is open to empirical testing, Mises also hinted at a more sophisticated theoretical argument against identifying corporation managers with socialist managers: that it is the capital markets which keep private managers in line, that the owners of private capital can shift resources from unprofitable to more profitable ventures and thus put poor managers out of a job.[52] Where profit or loss no longer serves as an objective test of managerial success, as it likely would not under socialism, it becomes exceedingly difficult to weed out inefficient managers.

Hayek enlarged on this theme when he argued that under socialism, where a manager's decisions are not subject to the objective test of profit

49. Lange ((1938), p. 80).

50. Mises ((1920), pp. 116-122).

51. Mises ((1920), p. 119).

52. Mises ((1922), p. 139).

or loss to determine their correctness, one's success as a manager would therefore depend upon convincing the planning board that the decisions he made in the past were the best given the alternatives available. As a result, managers would be less likely to make risky decisions regardless of their potential profitability because the consequences of failure far outweighed the benefits of success to their careers.[53]

While the actual propensity to take risks depends upon the constraints facing individual socialist managers and an argument can be made that they will be either more or less prone to risk taking than private entrepreneurs (in fact, Mises had argued that managers would be more prone to risk taking than private entrepreneurs since they did not have potential loss of personal wealth to constrain their behavior),[54] the problem both Mises and Hayek were approaching was essentially one of the effects of different specifications of property rights on individual economic decision making. The issue of property rights, which has provided such a fruitful framework for modern analysis of socialist economies,[55] was only touched on in the early literature on socialism. It was generally contained under the rubric of "incentives" with the critics arguing that without private property, people would have no incentive to produce and the early socialists countering with descriptions of the change in human nature which would occur after the abolition of the evils of the capitalist system. The later socialists tended to dismiss the problem of the relationship between managerial incentives and managerial decision-making entirely as being more in the province of sociology than economics.[56] Instead they concentrated their energies on defining a set of managerial rules which would lead to efficient levels of output without considering how to induce people to follow the rules they devised.

Even granting that a planning board could devise appropriate managerial rules and induce managers to follow them, Hayek implied that determining whether or not the rules had been followed was not as easy a task as it might seem at first blush. The socialists' managerial rules, as we have seen, generally involved instructing the manager to equate the "parametric" price to some measure of cost to achieve optimal output. The most theoretically satisfying rule was Lerner's which instructed managers to expand output (or input use) to that point where price equals marginal cost at every decision point.[57] Hayek criticized the workability of even this rule, however, and in so doing implicitly criticized all rules that assumed that costs could be treated as objective data.[58] In fact, only

53. Hayek ((1940), p. 199); ((1935), pp. 234-237). See also Hayek ((1935), p. 219) and Hayek ((1948), p. 198).

54. Mises ((1922), p. 140).

55. For a summary treatment of the property rights approach to study of socialist economies, see Furubotn and Pejovich ((1972), pp. 1154-1157).

56. See for example Lerner ((1937), p. 267), Lange ((1938), p. 109), and Durbin ((1937), p. 687).

57. Lerner ((1937), p. 251).

58. Hayek ((1935), p. 226) and Hayek ((1948), p. 196).

current prices are objective data available to producers while costs are ultimately subjective evaluations of the utility of foregone alternatives, the value of what could have been produced with the resources now being used to produce one's product. Hayek argued that in full market equilibrium, the value of foregone alternatives were accurately measured by market prices of resources, but in the real world where static equilibrium conditions do not obtain, the value of foregone alternatives can only be individual estimates of the possible effects of different courses of action.[59]

The relevance of this thoroughly "Austrian" view of costs to socialist economy is most pronounced in the valuation and use of capital in a non-market setting. Capital creation and use necessarily depends upon an entrepreneur's subjective estimates of future values. Since a socialist manager's estimates of current capital value would be based only partly on current prices, but more on his estimates of possible market changes, conjectures about the planning board's response to these changes, his evaluation of the risks involved in his decisions, and his propensity to take risks, it would be impossible for costs perceived by the manager to be objectively measured by some outside observer. If marginal cost is a subjective estimate that has no "correct" value, then the planning board would have no way of discovering if the firm had followed its directive. Hence, Hayek argued that the planning board would have to engage in detailed audits of the firm's books to see if at every decision point the manager took the "best" course of action available to him. But "best" would now mean best according to the planner who would have to substitute his judgment for that of the socialist manager in the evaluation of costs.[60] There were no simple rules for judging managerial success in a non-market setting.

IV.

To the modern reader who is aware of the empirical record of the last thirty years of East European and Russian Communism, the early work of Lange and Dickinson (as well as the professional acclaim accorded them)[61] seems naive at best. For the greater part of the short history of communist states, price has not been used as the primary allocative

59. Hayek ((1935), p. 226). Buchanan (1969), in his sympathetic treatment of the Austrian role in the economic calculation controversy, criticizes Hayek for failure to see the full implications of his theory of subjective costs by concentrating too much on the conditions of equilibrium in markets. (p. 22).

60. Hayek ((1935), pp. 236-237), and Hayek ((1948), pp. 198-199).

61. Professional evaluation of the calculation controversy in the 1940's was overwhelmingly that the socialists had the best of the argument. See, for example, Bergson (1948). Perhaps Schumpeter (1942) best summed up the current consensus when he stated that "as a matter of blueprint logic, it is undeniable that the socialist blueprint is drawn at a higher level of rationality," (p. 185)) (which in effect meant that a Walrasian general equilibrium model was more descriptive of socialism than it was of capitalism). While he later warned that this might have nothing to do with the workability of either capitalism or socialism (Schumpeter (1954, p. 989)) he nevertheless believed that the theoretical case for socialism was stronger than the one for capitalism.

mechanism. Output quotas instead have been the rule rather than the exception with all of the concomitant problems of resource misuse and sheer waste that even the socialists of the 1930's predicted. It is only recently that attempts have been made in the more liberal of the communist countries to move closer to lange-type market socialism in a belated vindication of both the Austrians and the market socialists.[62] However, one feature which stands out in the modern literature of market socialism is the attention paid to incentive structures. Despite an almost contemptuous dismissal of the problem during the original debate, even Lange in his later work put incentives in the forefront of the problems of socialist economy still to be solved.[63] The major problem now seems to be whether or not rational incentive structures can be built into a socialist economy so that economic agents actually do what the planners want them to do: whether there can be a good substitute for profits to make the system function effectively. Gone are the blithe assertions of the superiority of socialism in reaching the "perfection" of perfect competition more easily than capitalism.

It is not only as a predictor of actual economic events that Lange's 1936 work suffers by comparison to Hayek's essays but also as a contribution to theoretical economics. Of course, it is unfair to criticize Lange for failure to perceive all of the probelms inherent in the wholesale application of Walrasian general equilibrium to a socialist economy since he was writing before the major work on such models was even begun. In fact, when one considers the state of the art in 1936, Lange's use of Walras in comprehending and describing an economic system is a formidable achievement indeed. Yet, recognition of the greatness of Lange's work can only increase one's respect for Hayek's. Today Hayek seems more modern than Lange precisely because he was able to pinpoint many of the most crucial defects in Lange's exposition long before the economics profession came to recognize these same criticisms in their attempt to refine and extend simpler Walrasian models. In fact, a listing of Hayek's major criticisms of market socialism — the failure to take account of adjustment processes, the misunderstanding of the problem of decentralized and incomplete information, the lack of appropriate incentive structure —

---

62. There has been a wealth of articles describing and analyzing "soviet-type" economies in light of the reforms which took place during the late sixties. Representatives of just a portion of this group are Belassa (1970, Bornstein (1974), Furubotn and Pejovich (1970) and Prybyla (1966). For a favorable reevaluation of Hayek's original criticisms in light of the historical experience of socialist economies, see Bergson (1967).

63. Lange ((1962), p. 19). ". . . it seems that the greatest obstacle to further progress results from the lack of proper economic incentives in . . . bureaucratic, centralist-type management." And "There are also other economic laws which must be observed by the plan. These are the laws which result from the operation of economic incentives under the circumstances created by the plan . . . By utilizing economic means planning makes use of the automatic character of people's responses to given incentives." (p. 24) It is interesting to note that at least one socialist economist has suggested a means by which some form of profits might be incorporated into socialist incentive structures. See Bajt (1968).

reads like a research program for general equilibrium theorists for the last three decades.[64]

To dwell for a moment on a single, far reaching example, one has only to consult the growing literature on the economics of information to see the contemporary relevance of Hayek's work. The modern literature asks "how individuals should and do behave when imperfectly informed"[65] and then goes on to construct models based on different assumptions about economic behavior and the amount of knowledge available to market participants. While it shows that it is possible to construct models with imperfect information which converge toward an equilibrium, the equilibria vary with the assumption about the knowledge and market behavior. These models are a far cry from Lange's "parametric function of price," and in them we see partly why Hayek's early work, in which the information problem was always central, is quoted and referred to today with increasing frequency in the theoretical literature.

I began this essay by claiming that the controversy between the advocates of socialism and their critics was at heart a contest of theoretical models based on differing perceptions of what a market economy really was. The socialists seemed to regard the market as a mechanism, the salient features of which were accurately captured in simple general equilibrium model. Human beings were assumed to react automatically to market signals and could be counted on to react just as automatically to commands from a central planning agency. The institutional structure and the system of incentives implicit in the structure were assumed to have no affect on economic behavior. Hayek, on the other hand, understood the market to be fundamentally entrepreneurial in nature. Equilibrium models, he argued, could be no more than a useful preliminary to the study of the main problem,[66] which was to show how the market enables profit seeking individuals to make choices in an environment of decentralized and incomplete information and uncertainty about the future, and in which they bear the consequences of their choices. To Hayek, the market economy is essentially a spontaneously evolved institutional response to the difficulties of coordinating economic activity in a complex and changing world. Because the real world is so complex and so changeable, it was clear to him that the simplistic models constructed by the market socialists, if used to operate a real socialist economy, were doomed to produce an economic environment far different from, and far inferior to the one they envisioned in their plans.

64. A good summary of modern attempts to take into account adjustment processes, information content of models, and incentive structures can be found in Hurwicz (1973).

65. Rothschild ((1973) p. 1286). This article suggests that current work in models with imperfect information is a direct outgrowth of Stigler's 1961 article, "The Economics of Information." One major difference between the modern approach and Hayek's view of information is that Hayek saw incomplete and decentralized information to be the distinguishing feature of markets and the reason for their existence while the modern literature, following the implications of earlier general equilibrium models, still sees imperfect information as a defect that needs to be explained away within the context of maximization models.

66. Hayek ((1948), pp. 44-45).

VAUGHN: AUSTRIAN CONTRIBUTION   553

REFERENCES

Bajt, A., "Property in Capital and the Means of Production in Socialist Economies," *Journal of Law and Economies, 11,* (April 1968), 1-4, Reprinted in Furubotn and Pejovich, (eds.), *The Economics of Property Rights,* (Cambridge, Mass.: Ballinger Publishing Co., 1974), 253-256.

Belassa, Bela, "The Economic Reforms in Hungary," *Economica* (February, 1970), 1-22.

Bergson, Abram, "Socialism" in Howard Ellis (ed.), *A Survey of Contemporary Economics, Vol. I,* (Homewood, Ill.: Richard D. Irwin, Inc., 1948), 412-488.

_____, "Market Socialism Revisited," *Journal of Political Economy, 75,* (October, 1967), 655-673.

Bornstein, Morris, "Soviet Price Theory and Policy" in Bornstein and Fusfeld (eds.), *The Soviet Economy,* (Homewood, Ill.: Richard D. Irwin, Inc., 1974), 85-115.

Buchanan, James, *Cost and Choice,* (Chicago: Markham Publishing Company, 1969.)

_____ and Thirlby, G.F., *L.S.E. Essays on Cost,* (London School of Economics and Political Science: Weidenfeld and Nicholson, 1973.)

Dickinson, H.D., "Price Formation in a Socialist Community," *Economic Journal, 43,* (June, 1933), 237-250.

_____, *The Economics of Socialism,* (Oxford: University Press, 1939.)

Dobb, Maurice, "Economic Theory and the Problems of a Socialist Economy," *Economic Journal, 43,* (December, 1933), 588-598.

_____, "Economic Theory and Social Economy; A Reply," in *Review of Economic Studies, 2,* (February, 1935), 144-154.

Durbin, E.M.F., "Economic Calculus in a Planned Economy," *Economic Journal, 46,* (December, 1936), 676-690.

Furubotn, Eric and Pejovich, Svetozar, "Property Rights and the Behavior of the Firm in a Socialist State: The Example of Yugoslavia," *Zeitschrift fur Nationalokonomie, 30,* (1970), 431-454.

_____, "Property Rights and Economic Theory: A Survey of Recent Literature," *Journal of Economic Literature, 10, (December, 1972), 1137-1162.*

Hawtry, R.G., *The Economic Problem,* (London: Longmans, Green and Co. Ltd., 1926.)

Hayek, Friedrich, *Collectivist Economic Planning,* (London: George Routledge and Sons, Ltd., 1935.)

_____, *Individualism and Economic Order,* (Chicago: The University of Chicago Press, 1948.)

Hirshleifer, J, "Where Are We in the Theory of Information?" *The American Economic Review, 63,* (May, 1973), 31-39.

Hoff, Trygve J.B., *Economic Calculation in the Socialist Society,* (London: William Hodge and Company, Ltd., 1949.)

Hurwicz, Leonid, "The Design of Mechanisms for Resource Allocation," *The American Economic Review, 63,* (May, 1973), 1-30.

Hutchison, T.W., "Friedrich Engels and Marxist Economy Theory," *Journal of Political Economy, 86,* (April, 1978), 303-320.

Lange, Oskar and Taylor, Fred M., *On the Economic Theory of Socialism,* (New York: McGraw-Hill Company, 1938.)

_____, *Problems of Political Economy of Socialism,* (New Delhi: People's Publishing House, 1962.)

Lerner, Abba, "Economic Theory and Socialist Economy," *Review of Economic Studies, 2,* (October, 1934), 51-61.

_____, "Statistics and Dynamics in Socialist Economics," *Economic Journal, 47,* (June, 1937), 251-270.

_____, "Theory and Practice in Socialist Economics," *Review of Economic Studies, 6,* (October, 1938), 71-75.

_____, "Marginal Cost Pricing in the 1930's," *The American Economic Review, 67,* (February, 1977), 235-239.

Mises, Ludwig von., "Economic Calculation in the Socialist Commonwealth" in F. Hayek (ed.) *Collectivist Economic Planning*, (London: George Routledge and Sons, 1935), 87-130, Originally published as "Die Wirtschaftsrechnung im Sozialistischen Gemeinwesen" (1920).

_____ , *Human Action: A Treatise on Economics*, (New Haven: Yale University Press, 1963), Originally published 1949.

O'Driscoll, Gerald P., *Economics as a Coordination Problem*, (Kansas City: Sheed, Andrews and McMeel, Inc., 1977.)

Prybyla, Jan, "Soviet Command: From Liberman to Liberalism?" *Bulletin Institute for the Study of the USSR, 13*, (July, 1966), 19-77.

Robbins, Lionnel, *The Great Depression*, (London: MacMillan and Company, 1933.)

Roberts, Paul Craig, *Alienation in the Soviet Economy*, (Albuquerque: University of New Mexico Press, 1971.)

Rothschild, Michael, "Models of Market Organization with Imperfect Information: A Survey," *Journal of Political Economy, 81*, (Nov./Dec., 1973), 1283-1308.

Rothbard, Murray N., "Ludwig von Mises and Economic Calculation under Socialism" in Laurence S. Moss, (ed.), *The Economics of Ludwig von Mises*, (Kansas City: Sheed and Ward, Inc., 1976), 67-68.

Samardzija, Milos, "The Market and Social Planning in the Yugoslav Economy," in Prybyla, J.S., (ed.), *Comparative Economic Systems*, (New York: Appleton-Century-Crofts, 1969), 340-349.

Schumpeter, Joseph, *Capitalism, Socialism and Democracy*, (New York: Harper and Row, 1963), Originally published 1942.

_____ , *History of Economic Analysis*, (New York: Oxford University Press, 1954.)

von Weiser, Friedrich, *Natural Value*, (New York: Augustus M. Kelley, 1971.)

[23]

The Journal of Libertarian Studies, Vol. V, No. 1 (Winter 1981)

A Critique of the Standard Account of the Socialist Calculation Debate

by Don Lavoie

Department of Economics, George Mason University

As the Marxian philosopher Louis Althusser used to put it, no reading is innocent. The meaning a reader derives from a particular piece of scholarly literature is unavoidably influenced by his premises and analytical framework. When the underlying theoretical framework of the reader differs sharply from that of the writers under examination the result is likely to be profound misunderstanding. Few instances of "non-innocent" reading can match the distortion that the standard account of the socialist calculation debate has imparted to that famous controversy. Many of the most influential early readers of the debate later corrected at least part of their initial errors of interpretation. However, the version of the history of thought of the debate that has come to dominate the profession still retains most of those initial errors. This essay will survey the origins and development of the standard view of the socialist controversy, offering suggestions along the way about how and why this interpretation seriously misreads some of the arguments of the debate.

The two sides of this controversy can be designated as the "Austrians" who issued the challenge to socialism — notably Ludwig Mises, Friedrich Hayek and Lionel Robbins[1] — and, on the opposite side, the "neoclassicals" who defended one form or another of socialism from this challenge — primarily the so-called "market socialists" Oskar Lange, H. D. Dickinson, Fred M. Taylor, Abba P. Lerner, and E. F. M. Durbin, and, from a somewhat different point of view, Maurice Dobb.[2]

The entire debate concentrated on attempts to answer the initial challenge by Mises that rational central planning of the vast and complex modern economy would be "impossible." Without private ownership of the means of production, he argued, there could be no competitive market for these capital goods, and without markets, there could be no prices for the various scarce means of production. Lacking the guide of market prices, the central planners would be "in the dark" as to the *relative* scarcity of different components of the capital structure and so would invariably fail to combine and use them efficiently.

The famous "market-socialist" response by Lange is generally understood to have effectively answered Mises by first admitting the indispensability of "markets" and "prices," and by then arguing that these could be reconciled with "public" or "common" ownership of the means of production. Lange considered the Walrasian simultaneous-equation formulation that had been advanced by Enrico Barone in 1908 to be a rigorous and conclusive answer to Mises' claim that socialism was "theoretically impossible." He invoked Fred Taylor's "trial and error" method[3] as a refutation of the Hayek-Robbins thesis that socialism, though theoretically possible, was impracticable.

However, this entire elaborate answer to the Austrian challenge is premised upon a particular neoclassical reading of that challenge. Clearly if, as this paper contends, the neoclassicals, including Lange himself, fundamentally misunderstood the Austrian challenge they are supposed to have refuted, the challenge ought to be considered anew. However, before we can confidently embark on such a reconsideration, we should attempt to offer a plausible explanation of how the economics profession came to misunderstand the calculation debate so thoroughly.

This misunderstanding, we will argue, is rooted in basic differences between the "Austrian" and "neoclassical" paradigms which were not yet evident to either side at the time of the debate, but which have since become clarified, especially in Professor Kirzner's Austrian critique of neoclassical choice theory.[4] These implicit differences made it easy for neoclassical participants and readers of the debate to attach inappropriate neoclassical meanings to the concepts the Austrians were employing. In particular the concepts "economic theory" (misunderstood to mean static equilibrium theory), "efficiency" (mistaken for "Pareto optimality"), "ownership" (taken to mean formal legal title, rather than *de facto* control, over resources), and "competition" (read as the state of perfect competition rather than as a process) were "lost in the translation" by the neoclassical historians of thought of the debate.

We begin by outlining (1) the major elements of the standard account of the debate, documenting in footnotes that this interpretation thoroughly permeates contemporary economics, and (2) contrasting elements of what we will call the "alternative" interpretation. We will then conduct a critique of this standard account, selecting seven representative interpreters of the debate (including some of the most respected scholars in economics) for analysis. It will be our contention that, despite the accumulated weight of scholarly authority associated with such names as Joseph Schumpeter, Abram Bergson, Benjamin Ward, and Frank Knight, this prevailing interpretation ought to be rejected in favor of an alternative, "revisionist" interpretation which carries the authority of a rather less famous name like that of Trygve Hoff.[5] It would seem that this is an ambitious enough task for one paper; thus it is hoped that we will be forgiven for not venturing to offer a thoroughgoing reexamination of the calculation debate from this alternative perspective. We only intend to demonstrate that the generally accepted view of the debate is riddled with errors and thus urgently requires such a thorough reexamination.

The Two Interpretations of the Debate in Outline

1) The Standard Account of the Debate

    a) pre-1920: Before the debate, it is generally agreed, very little attention had been paid to the economics of socialism.[6] Much of what did exist in such literature failed to realize that some form of market prices and some use of money were indispensable for rational planning. The failure of the War Communism period in the Soviet Union is often cited as evidence that many early socialists erred in underestimating the importance of prices for central planning.[7] The view is occasionally expressed that in actuality this conception of socialism without prices was a straw man fabricated by Mises and Hayek and that it was never seriously held by socialists.[8] The more common view, however, is that at least some early socialists had to be taught their economics by neoclassical economists. In any case, few modern socialists believe that prices, money, and markets (at least for consumer goods and labor) can be dispensed with until scarcity itself is eliminated.[9]

    b) Mises: Mises' calculation argument is generally credited with having shaken socialists out of their neglect of the economics of planning, but few commentators on the debate are willing to grant him much more than this stimulative accomplishment.[10] His argument is usually interpreted in neoclassical terms, as a denial of the "logical credentials" of socialism,[11] and thus as an assertion that rational economic calculation is not only "impracticable," but also "theoretically" impossible without private ownership of the means of production, even under static conditions.[12] Some discussants say that the practical experience of socialist planning in the USSR refutes Mises' claim,[13] many claim that either Lange's or Barone's argument conclusively counters Mises', but there is a remarkably wide consensus that he was wrong.[14]

    c) equation-solving: It is generally held that, before Mises issued his challenge, Barone's equilibrium argument had already established the "theoretical" possibility of socialism by showing that in principle the Central Planning Board (CPB) could solve a set of simultaneous equations, in much the same way as is done in practice by the market. The same general equilibrium logic of choice which Walras had developed to analyze capitalism could be applied to socialism.[15]

    d) impracticability: The view is common that Hayek's and Robbins' arguments were substantially different from Mises', constituting a retreat to the acceptance of the theoretical possibility, but a denial of the practicability of socialism. The essence of their argument is taken to be that solving Barone's equations is not feasible as a method of central planning.[16] Hayek is sometimes also credited with having raised some important issues concerning the centralization of knowledge, risk, and managerial incentives, though these are generally held as considerations to be taken into account by central planners rather than as arguments against central planning.

e) trial and error: It is widely held that the market-socialists, particularly Lange, met Mises on his own terms[17] and thoroughly proved that Mises and his school were wrong.[18] They demonstrated that a determinate equilibrium can be defined for socialism as Barone had shown, and that, contrary to Hayek and Robbins, the CPB could "find" this equilibrium set of prices by a process of trial and error. Thus it is claimed that socialism is practicable in principle.[19]

f) conclusion: The implication that is usually drawn from the debate is that economic theory *per se* cannot decide the great controversy between capitalism and socialism. Neither system is as praiseworthy in practice as the debaters depicted them in theory.[20] The efficiency criteria of the debate were developed under strictly static welfare assumptions,[21] while under more realistic, non-static assumptions neither system can boast the virtues of Pareto-optimality.[22] Most economists agree that there are strengths and weaknesses of each system. Some stress that market-socialism has the potential of improving upon capitalism;[23] others emphasize that, though socialism is theoretically unassailable, it nevertheless has other, major deficiencies deemed to be outside the province of economic theory, notably the danger of bureaucratization.[24] Most economists criticize both sides of the famous controversy for dealing on too abstract a level and for comparing the idealization of one system with the practical weaknesses of its opposite.[25] A related reaction to the debate is the argument that the participants focused too much on alternative "Isms," that the controversy was a stale quarrel over unworkable extremes — "plan *vs.* market" — while contemporary economists agree that both institutions are indispensable.[26] Modern dispute is only over the proper mix of the two.[27]

g) beyond the debate: The most significant element in the standard account of the calculation debate is the view that the debate was marred by its exclusive attention to "statics." Two of the major subsequent developments in socialist economic theory can be understood as differing attempts to advance central planning theory beyond this static equilibrium context. Thus one branch of modern socialist economics, "planometrics," seeks to produce mathematical procedures for getting prices to approach their equilibrium values, as against the debate's focus on formal conditions for static equilibrium.[28] Another branch, which we will call "macroplanning," seeks to examine ways to control and improve the overall growth rate of the economy and to influence the direction of new investment in broad macroeconomic categories of production toward this end, as against the debate's emphasis on static microeconomic efficiency.[29] The consensus seems to be that, with these "dynamic" developments, central planning theory has rid itself of its earlier static perspective.

2) *The Alternative Account of the Debate*

    a) *pre-1920:* The standard view is not sufficiently cognizant of the extent to which the Marxian model of socialism was dominant — if not particularly explicit — in socialist economics before 1920. It is true that most socialists avoided any direct discussion of the workings of proposed socialist institutions, but a very definite idea of their conception of central planning is nonetheless evident from their critique of capitalism. Both the dismal failure of the attempt to abolish markets and money during the War Communism period in the USSR, and the arguments of Mises and Hayek, make this early idea of socialism very difficult to defend today. However, this largely rejected early vision of central planning is the most consistent and important of any that have been developed, and therefore its abandonment marks a far more serious retreat by socialists than the standard view suggests.

    b) *Mises:* Mises was not denying the validity of the "pure logic of choice" for socialism; he was, on the contrary, insisting that central planners *must* find a way to apply this kind of logic to socialism or they will be doomed to calculational chaos and be unable to use resources efficiently. By our interpretation Mises was definitely *not* making an equilibrium argument and was aware that under static assumptions there is no problem for central planning. His discussion was primarily directed at proponents of Marxian socialism and was thus centered mainly on the argument that prices (and not some objective value measure such as labor hours) are necessary for rational calculation. However, contrary to the standard view, his argument is fully applicable to all forms of socialism which advocate common or state ownership of the means of production. Properly interpreted, this challenge has yet to be adequately answered by advocates of central planning.

    c) *equation-solving:* Barone's argument is fully consistent with, but much less complete than, Mises' challenge. It simply establishes the formal similarity between socialism and capitalism under static conditions: if the number of (independent) equations equals the number of unknowns the system is "determinate". Mises maintained that such equations were inapplicable to the real world of continuous change even if, given a powerful enough computer, they were solvable.

    d) *impracticability:* The central arguments advanced by Hayek and Robbins did not constitute a "retreat" from Mises, but rather a clarification directing the challenge to the later versions of central planning via "equation-solving" and "trial and error." Although comments by both Hayek and Robbins about computational difficulties of the equation-solving approach were responsible for misleading interpretations of their arguments, in fact their main contributions were fully consistent with Mises' challenge and were similarly unanswered.

e) *trial and error:* The "trial and error" response to the Austrians was based on a close analogy with the perfect competition model which itself does not explain dynamic price adjustment under realistic conditions of change. Thus, contrary to the standard view, Lange's model does not constitute an answer to the Misesian argument.

f) *conclusion:* The usual conclusion that economic theory cannot decide any important issues in comparative economics is valid only if "economic theory" is seen as strictly static equilibrium analysis. The broader Austrian conception of an economic theory that deals with change can shed considerable light on comparative economics issues and can help us to understand many of the practical problems of the mixed economies of both the East and the West. The Austrians did not limit discussion to the extreme "Isms," but explicitly contrasted mixed economy models with "pure" capitalism and socialism.

g) *beyond the debate:* The modern "planometric" and "macroplanning" attempts to advance central planning theory beyond the static framework of the early market-socialists have retained essentially static assumptions in their analyses.

Part V
Public Policy

[24]

XVII

Toward a Reconstruction of Utility and Welfare Economics

by MURRAY N. ROTHBARD

I. *Introduction*

INDIVIDUAL valuation is the keystone of economic theory. For, fundamentally, economics does not deal with things or material objects. Economics analyzes the logical attributes and consequences of the existence of individual valuations. "Things" enter into the picture, of course, since there can be no valuation without things to be valued. But the essence and the driving force of human action, and therefore of the human market economy, are the valuations of individuals. Action is the result of choice among alternatives, and choice reflects values, i.e., individual preferences among these alternatives.

Individual valuations are the direct subject matter of the theories of utility and of welfare. Utility theory analyzes the laws of the values and choices of an individual; welfare theory discusses the relationship between the values of many individuals, and the consequent possibilities of a scientific conclusion on the "social" desirability of various alternatives.

Both theories have lately been foundering in stormy seas. Utility theory is galloping off in many different directions at once; welfare theory, after reaching the heights of popularity among economic theorists, threatens to sink, sterile and abandoned, into oblivion.

The thesis of this paper is that both related branches of economic theory can be salvaged and reconstructed, using as a guiding principle of both fields the concept of "demonstrated preference."

THE ECONOMICS OF FREE ENTERPRISE   225

II. *Demonstrated Preference*

a. A Statement of the Concept. Human action is the use of means to arrive at preferred ends. Such action contrasts to the observed behavior of stones and planets, for it implies *purpose* on the part of the actor. Action implies choice among alternatives. Man has means, or resources, which he uses to arrive at various ends; these resources may be time, money, labor energy, land, capital goods, etc. He uses these resources to attain his most preferred ends. From his action, we can deduce that he has acted so as to satisfy his most highly valued desires or preferences.

The concept of *demonstrated preference* is simply this: that actual choice reveals, or demonstrates, a man's preferences; i.e., that his preferences are deducible from what he has chosen in action. Thus, if a man chooses to spend an hour at a concert rather than a movie, we deduce that the former was preferred, or ranked higher on his value scale. Similarly, if a man spends five dollars on a shirt we deduce that he preferred purchasing the shirt to any other uses he could have found for the money. This concept of preference, rooted in real choices, forms the keystone of the logical structure of economic analysis, and particularly of utility and welfare analysis.

While a similar concept played a role in the writings of the early utility economists, it had never received a name, and it therefore remained largely undeveloped and unrecognized as a distinct concept. It was generally discarded in the 1930's, before it had even achieved recognition. This view of preference as derived from choice was present in varying degree in the writings of the early Austrian economists, as well as in the works of Jevons, Fisher, and Fetter. Fetter was the only one who clearly employed the concept in his analysis. The clearest and most thorough formulation of the concept has been in the works of Professor Mises.[1]

b. Positivism and the Charge of Tautology. Before developing some of the applications of the demonstrated preference principle to utility and welfare theory, we must consider the methodological objections that have been levelled against it. Professor Alan Sweezy, for example, seizes on a sentence of Irving Fisher's which

---

[1] Cf. Alan R. Sweezy, "The Interpretation of Subjective Value Theory in the Writings of the Austrian Economists," *Review of Economic Studies*, June 1934, pp. 176-85, for an historical survey. Sweezy devotes a good part of the article to a criticism of Mises as the leading exponent of the demonstrated preference approach. For Mises' views, cf. *Human Action* (New Haven, 1949), pp. 94-96, 102-03; *Theory of Money and Credit* (3rd Ed. New Haven, 1951), pp. 46 ff. Also cf. Frank A. Fetter, *Economic Principles* (New York, 1915), pp. 14-21.

226 ON FREEDOM AND FREE ENTERPRISE

very succinctly expressed the concept of demonstrated preference: "Each individual acts as he desires." Sweezy is typical of the majority of present-day economists in not being able to understand how such a statement can be made with absolute validity. To Sweezy, insofar as it is not an empirically testable proposition in psychology, such a sentence must simply reduce to the meaningless tautology: "each individual acts as he acts."

This criticism is rooted in a fundamental epistemological error that pervades modern thought: the inability of modern methodologists to understand how economic science can yield substantive truths by means of logical deduction (i.e., the method of "praxeology"). For they have adopted the epistemology of positivism (now dubbed "logical empiricism" or "scientific empiricism" by its practitioners), which uncritically applies the procedures appropriate in physics to the sciences of human action.[2]

In physics, simple facts can be isolated in the laboratory. These isolated facts are known directly, but the laws to explain these facts are not. The laws may only be hypothecated. Their validity can only be determined by logically deducing consequents from them which can be verified by appeal to the laboratory facts. Even if the laws explain the facts, however, and their inferences are consistent with them, the laws of physics can never be *absolutely* established. For some other law may prove more elegant or capable of explaining a wider range of facts. In physics, therefore, postulated explanations have to be hypothecated in such a way that they or their consequents can be empirically tested. Even then, the laws are only tentatively rather than absolutely valid.

In human action, however, the situation is reversed. There is here no laboratory where "facts" can be isolated and broken down into their simple elements. Instead, there are only historical "facts" which are complex phenomena, resultants of many casual factors. These phenomena must be explained, but they cannot be isolated or used to verify or falsify any law. On the other hand, economics, or praxeology, has full and complete knowledge of its original and basic axioms. These are the axioms *implicit in the very existence of human action,* and they are absolutely valid so long as human beings exist. But if the axioms of praxeology are absolutely valid for human existence, then so are the consequents which can logically be deduced from them. Hence, economics, in contrast to physics, can derive absolutely valid substantive truths about the real world

[2] Cf. the methodological treatises of Kaufmann, Hutchison, Souter, Stonier, Myrdal, Morgenstern, etc.

THE ECONOMICS OF FREE ENTERPRISE   **227**

by deductive logic. The axioms of physics are only hypothecated and hence subject to revision; the axioms of economics are already known and hence absolutely true.[3] The irritation and bewilderment of positivists over the "dogmatic" pronouncements of praxeology stem, therefore, from their universal application of methods proper only to the physical sciences.[4]

The suggestion has been made that praxeology is not really scientific, because its logical procedures are verbal ("literary") rather than mathematical and symbolic.[5] But mathematical logic is uniquely appropriate to physics, where the various logical steps along the way are not in themselves meaningful, for the axioms and therefore the deductions of physics are in themselves meaningless, and only take on meaning "operationally," insofar as they can explain and predict given facts. In praxeology, on the contrary, the axioms themselves are known as true and are therefore meaningful. As a result, each step-by-step deduction is meaningful and true. Meanings are far better expressed verbally than in meaningless formal symbols. Moreover, simply to translate economic analysis from words into symbols, and then to retranslate them so as to explain the conclusions, makes little sense, and violates the great scientific principle of Occam's Razor that there should be no unnecessary multiplication of entities.

The crucial concept of the positivists, and the one that forms the basis for their attack on demonstrated preference, is that of "operational meaning." Indeed, their favorite critical epithet is that such and such a formulation or law is "operationally meaningless."[6] The

[3] On the methodology of praxeology and physics, cf. Mises, *Human Action*, *op. cit.*, and F. A. Hayek, *The Counter Revolution of Science* (Glencoe, Ill., 1952), Part I.

[4] It is even dubious that positivists accurately interpret the proper methodology of physics itself. On the widespread positivist misuse of the Heisenberg Uncertainty Principle in physics as well as in other disciplines, cf. A. H. Hobbs, *Social Problems and Scientism* (Harrisburg, Pa., 1953), pp. 220-32.

[5] For a typical suggestion, cf. George J. Schuller, "Rejoinder," *American Economic Review*, March 1951, p. 188. For a realization that mathematical logic is essentially subsidiary to basic verbal logic, cf. the remarks of André Lalande and René Poirier, on "Logique" and "Logistique," in (A. Lalande, ed.), *Vocabulaire Technique et Critique de la Philosophie* (6th Ed., Paris, 1951), pp. 574, 579.

[6] Paul Samuelson has added the weight of his authority to Sweezy's criticism of Mises and demonstrated preference, and has couched his endorsement in terms of "operational meaning." Samuelson explicitly rejects the idea of a *true* utility theory in favor of one that is merely hypothetical. Cf. Paul A. Samuelson, "The Empirical Implications of Utility Analysis," *Econometrica*, 1938, pp. 344 ff; and *id.*, *Foundations of Economic Analysis* (Cambridge, 1947), pp. 91-92.

The concept of operational meaning was originated by the physicist Percy W.

228 ON FREEDOM AND FREE ENTERPRISE

test of "operationally meaningful" is derived strictly from the procedures of physics as outlined above. An explanatory law must be framed so that it can be tested and found empirically false. Any law which claims to be absolutely true and not empirically capable of being falsified is therefore "dogmatic" and operationally meaningless—hence, the positivist's view that if a statement or law is not capable of being falsified empirically, it must simply be a tautologous definition. And consequently, Sweezy's attempted reduction of Fisher's sentence to a meaningless identity.[7]

Sweezy objects that Fisher's "each man acts as he desires" is circular reasoning, because action implies desire, and yet desires are not arrived at independently, but are only discoverable through the action itself. Yet this is not circular. For desires exist by virtue of the concept of human action, and of the existence of action. It is precisely the characteristic of human action that it is motivated by desires and ends, in contrast to the unmotivated bodies studied by physics. Hence, we can say validly that action is motivated by desires, and yet confine ourselves to deducing the *specific* desires from the real actions.

c. Professor Samuelson and "Revealed Preference." "Revealed preference"—preference revealed through choice—would have been an apt term for our concept. It has, however been pre-empted by Samuelson for a seemingly similar but actually quite different concept of his own. The critical difference is this: Samuelson assumes the existence of an underlying preference scale that forms the basis of a man's actions, and that remains *constant* in the course of his actions over time. Samuelson then uses complex mathematical procedures in an attempt to "map" the individual's preference scale on the basis of his numerous actions.

The prime error here is the assumption that the preference scale remains constant over time. There is no reason whatever for making any such assumption. All we can say is that an action, at a specific point of time, reveals part of a man's preference scale *at that time.*

Bridgman *explicitly* to explain the methodology of physics. Cf. Bridgman, *The Logic of Modern Physics* (New York, 1927). Many founders of modern positivism, such as Mach and Boltzmann, were also physicists.

[7] The heroes of positivism, Rudolf Carnap and Ludwig Wittgenstein, disparaged deductive inference as merely drawing out "tautologies" from the axioms. Yet all reasoning is deductive, and this process is peculiarly vital to arriving at truth. For a critique of Carnap and Wittgenstein, and a demonstration that inference is not merely identity or "tautology," cf. A. Lalande, "Tautologie," in *Vocabulaire, op. cit.,* pp. 1103-04.

THE ECONOMICS OF FREE ENTERPRISE   229

There is no warrant for assuming that it remains constant from one point of time to another.[8]

The "revealed preference" theorists do not recognize that they are assuming constancy; they believe that their assumption is simply that of *consistent* behavior, which they identify with "rationality." They will admit that people are not always "rational," but uphold their theory as being a good first approximation or even as having normative value. However, as Mises has pointed out, *constancy* and *consistency* are two entirely different things. Consistency means that a person maintains a transitive order of rank on his preference-scale (if A is preferred to B and B is preferred to C, then A is preferred to C). But the revealed preference procedure does not rest on this assumption so much as on an assumption of *constancy*—that an individual maintains the same value-scale over time. While the former might be called irrational, there is certainly nothing irrational about someone's value scales changing through time. Hence, no valid theory can be built on a constancy assumption.[9]

One of the most absurd procedures based on a constancy assumption has been the attempt to arrive at a consumer's preference scale not through observed real action, but through quizzing him by questionnaries. *In vacuo*, a few consumers are questioned at length on which abstract bundle of commodities they would prefer to another abstract bundle, etc. Not only does this suffer from the constancy error; no assurance can be attached to the mere questioning of people when they are not confronted with the choices in actual practice. Not only will a person's valuation differ when talking about them than when he is actually choosing, but there is also no guarantee that he is telling the truth.[10]

---

[8] Samuelson's analysis suffers from other errors as well, such as the use of invalid "index number" procedures. On the theoretical fallacies of index numbers, cf. Mises, *Theory of Money and Credit, op. cit.,* pp. 187-94.

[9] Cf. Mises, *Human Action, op. cit.,* pp. 102-03. Mises demonstrates that Wicksteed and Robbins committed a similar error.

[10] It is to Samuelson's credit that he rejects the questionnaire approach. Professors Kennedy and Keckskemeti, for different reasons, defend the questionnaire method. Kennedy simply says, rather illogically, that *in vacuo* procedures are being used anyway, when the theorist states that *more* of a good is preferred to *less*. But this is not *in vacuo;* it is a conclusion based on the praxeological knowledge that since a *good* is any object of action, more must be preferred to less while it remains a good. Kennedy is wrong, therefore, when he asserts that this is a circular argument, for the fact that action exists is not "circular."

Keckskemeti actually asserts that the questionnaire method is preferable to observing behavior in discovering preferences. The basis of his argument is a spurious dichotomy between utility and ethical valuations. Ethical valuations may be con-

230   ON FREEDOM AND FREE ENTERPRISE

The bankruptcy of the revealed-preference approach has never been better portrayed than by a prominent follower, Professor Charles Kennedy. Says Kennedy: "In what respectable science would the assumption of consistency (i.e., constancy) be accepted for one moment?" [11] But he asserts it must be retained anyway, else utility theory could not serve any useful purpose. The abandonment of truth for the sake of a spurious usefulness is a hallmark of the positivist-pragmatist tradition. Except for certain auxiliary constructions, it should be clear that the false cannot be useful in constructing a true theory. This is particularly the case in economics, which is explicitly built on *true* axioms.[12]

  d. *Psychologizing and Behaviorism: Twin Pitfalls.* The revealed-preference doctrine is one example of what we may call the fallacy of "psychologizing," the treatment of preference-scales as if they existed as separate entities apart from real action. Psychologizing is a common error in utility analysis. It is based on the common assumption that utility analysis is a kind of "psychology," and that, therefore, economics must enter into psychological analysis in laying the foundations of its theoretical structure.

  Praxeology, the basis of economic theory, differs from psychology, however. Psychology analyzes the *how* and the *why* of people forming values. It treats the concrete *content* of ends and values. Economics, on the other hand, rests simply on the assumption of the *existence* of ends and then deduces its valid theory from such a general assumption.[13] It therefore has nothing to do with the con-

_____

sidered either as identical with, or a subset of, utility judgments, but they cannot be separated.

  Cf. Charles Kennedy, "The Common Sense of Indifference Curves," *Oxford Economic Papers*, January 1950, pp. 123-31; Kenneth J. Arrow, "Review of Paul Keckskemeti's *Meaning, Communication, and Value,*" *Econometrica*, January 1955, p. 103.

  11 Kennedy, *loc. cit.* Kennedy's article furnishes the best brief explanation of the revealed-preference approach.

  12 This error again stems from physics, where such assumptions as absence of friction are useful as first approximations—to *known* facts from *unknown* explanatory laws! For a refreshing skepticism on the value of false axioms, cf. Martin Bronfenbrenner, "Contemporary Economics Resurveyed," *Journal of Political Economy*, April 1953.

  13 The axiom of the existence of ends may be considered a proposition in philosophical psychology. In that sense, praxeology is grounded in psychology, but its development then completely diverges from psychology proper. On the question of purpose, praxeology takes its stand squarely with the Leibnizian tradition of philosophical psychology as opposed to the Lockean tradition upheld by positivists, behaviorists, and associationists. For an illuminating discussion of this issue, cf. Gordon W. Allport, *Becoming* (New Haven, 1955), pp. 6-17.

THE ECONOMICS OF FREE ENTERPRISE   231

tent of ends or with the internal operations of the mind of the acting man.[14]

If psychologizing is to be avoided, so is the opposite error of
behaviorism. The behaviorist wishes to expunge "subjectivism," i.e.,
motivated action, completely from economics, since he believes that
any trace of subjectivisim is unscientific. His ideal is the method of
physics in treating observed movements of unmotivated, inorganic
matter. In adopting this method, he throws away the subjective
knowledge of *action* upon which economic science is founded; indeed, he is making any scientific investigation of human beings
impossible. The behaviorist approach in economics began with
Cassel, and its most prominent modern practitioner is Professor
Little. Little rejects the demonstrated preference theory because
it assumes the existence of preference. He glories in the fact that,
in his analysis, the maximizing individual "at last disappears" which
means, of course, that economics disappears as well.[15]

The errors of psychologizing and of behaviorism have in common
a desire by their practitioners to endow their concepts and procedures with "operational meaning," either in the areas of observed
behavior or in mental operations. Vilfredo Pareto, perhaps the
founder of an explicitly positivist approach in economics, championed both errors. Discarding a demonstrated preference approach
as "tautologous," Pareto, on the one hand, sought to eliminate subjective preferences from economics, and on the other, to investigate
and measure preference-scales apart from real action. Pareto was,
in more ways than one, the spiritual ancestor of most current utility
theorists.[16, 17]

[14] Thus, the law of diminishing marginal utility does *not* at all rest on some
postulated psychological law of satiety of wants, but on the *praxeological* truth that
the first units of a good will be allocated to the most valuable uses, the next units
to the next-most valuable uses, etc.

[15] I. M. D. Little, "A Reformation of the Theory of Consumers' Behavior," *Oxford
Economic Papers*, January 1949, pp. 90-99.

[16] Vilfredo Pareto, "On the Economic Phenomenon," *International Economic
Papers*, No. 3, (London, 1953), pp. 188-94. For an excellent rebuttal, cf. Benedetto
Croce, "On the Economic Principle, Parts I and II," *ibid.*, pp. 175-76, 201. The
famous Croce-Pareto debate is an illuminating example of early debate between
praxeologic and positivist views in economics.

[17] V. C. Walsh is an interesting current example of the combinations of both types
of error. On the one hand, he is an extreme behaviorist, who refuses to recognize
that any preferences are relevant to, or can be demonstrated by, action. On the
other hand, he also takes the extreme psychologizing view that psychological states
per se can be directly observed. For this, he falls back on "common sense." But
this position fails because Walsh's psychological "observations" are *ideal types* and
not analytic categories. Thus, Walsh says that: "saying that someone is a smoker
is different from saying that he is smoking now," upholding the former type of

e. A Note on Professor Armstrong's Criticism. Professor Armstrong has delivered a criticism of the revealed-preference approach which he would undoubtedly apply to demonstrated preference as well. He asserts that when more than one commodity is being ranked, individual preference-scales cannot be unitary, and we cannot postulate the ranking of the commodities on one scale.[18] On the contrary, it is precisely the characteristic of a deduced preference-scale that it is unitary. Only if a man ranks two alternatives as *more* and *less* valuable on one scale can he choose between them. Any of his means will be allocated to his more preferred use. Real choice therefore always demonstrates relevant preferences ranked on a unitary scale.

III. *Utility Theory*

Utility theory, over the last generation, has been split into two warring camps: (1) those who cling to the old concept of cardinal, measurable utility, and (2) those who have thrown over the cardinal concept, but have dispensed with the utility concept as well and have substituted an analysis based on indifference-curves.

In its pristine form, the cardinalist approach has been abandoned by all but a rearguard. On demonstrated preference grounds, cardinality must be eliminated. Psychological magnitudes cannot be measured since there is no objectively extensive unit—a necessary requisite of measurement. Further, actual choice obviously cannot demonstrate any form of *measurable* utility; it can only demonstrate one alternative being preferred to another.[19]

a. Ordinal Marginal Utility and "Total Utility." The ordinalist rebels, led by Hicks and Allen in the early 1930's, felt it necessary to overthrow the very concept of marginal utility along with measurability. In doing so, they threw out the Utility baby together with the Cardinal bathwater. They reasoned that marginal utility

---

statement for economics. But such statements are historical ideal types, relevant to history and psychology, but not to economic analysis. Cf. V. C. Walsh, "On Descriptions of Consumers' Behavior," *Economica*, August 1954, pp. 244-52. On ideal types and relation to praxeology, cf. Mises, *Human Action, op. cit.*, pp. 59-64.

[18] W. E. Armstrong, "A Note on the Theory of Consumers' Behavior," *Oxford Economic Papers*, January 1950, pp. 119 ff. On this point, cf. Little's rebuttal, in I. M. D. Little, "The Theory of Consumers' Behavior—A Comment" *ibid.*, pp. 132-35.

[19] Mises' priority in establishing this conclusion is acknowledged by Professor Robbins; cf. Lionel Robbins, "Robertson on Utility and Scope," *Economica*, May 1953, pp. 99-111; Mises, *Theory of Money and Credit, op. cit.*, pp. 38-47 and *passim*. Mises' role in forging an ordinal marginal utility theory has suffered almost total neglect.

THE ECONOMICS OF FREE ENTERPRISE   233

itself implies measurability. Why? Their notion rested on the implicit neo-classical assumption that the "marginal" in marginal
utility is equivalent to the "marginal" of the differential calculus.
Since, in mathematics, a total "something" is the integral of marginal "somethings," economists early assumed that "total utility" was
the mathematical integral of a series of "marginal utilities." [20] Perhaps, too, they realized that this assumption was essential to a
mathematical representation of utility. As a result, they assumed,
for example, that the marginal utility of a good with a supply of
six units is equal to the "total utility" of six units minus the "total
utility" of five units. If utilities can be subjected to the arithmetical operation of subtraction, and can be differentiated and integrated, then obviously the concept of marginal utility must imply
cardinally measurable utilities.[21]

The mathematical representation of the calculus rests on the
assumption of *continuity,* i.e., infinitely small steps. In human action, however, there can be no infinitely small steps. Human action
and the facts on which it is based must be in observable and discrete
steps and not infinitely small ones. Representation of utility in the
manner of the calculus is therefore illegitimate.[22]

There is, however, no reason why marginal utility must be conceived in calculus terms. In human action, "marginal" refers not
to an infinitely small unit, but to the *relevant* unit. Any unit relevant to a particular action is marginal. For example, if we are dealing in a specific situation with single eggs, then each egg is the
unit; if we are dealing in terms of six-egg cartons, then each six-egg
carton is the unit. In either case, we can speak of a marginal
utility. In the former case, we deal with the "marginal utility of
an egg" with various supplies of eggs; in the latter, with the "marginal utility of the cartons" whatever the supply of cartons of eggs.

[20] The error began perhaps with Jevons. Cf. W. Stanley Jevons, *Theory of Political
Economy* (London, 1888), pp. 49 ff.

[21] That this reasoning lay at the base of the ordinalists' rejection of marginal utility
may be seen in John R. Hicks, *Value and Capital* (2nd Ed., Oxford, 1946), p. 19.
That many ordinalists regret the loss of marginal utility may be seen in the statement
by Arrow that: "The older discussion of diminishing marginal utility as aiming for
the satisfaction of more intense wants first makes more sense" than the current
"indifference-curve" analysis, but that, unfortunately it is "bound up with the
untenable notion of measurable utility." Quoted in D. H. Robertson, "Utility and
All What?" *Economic Journal,* December 1954, p. 667.

[22] Hicks concedes the falsity of the continuity assumption but blindly pins his
faith on the hope that all will be well when individual actions are aggregated.
Hicks, *op. cit.,* p. 11.

Both utilities are marginal. In no sense is one utility a "total" of the other.

To clarify the relationship between marginal utility and what has been misnamed "total utility," but actually refers to a marginal utility of a larger-sized unit, let us hypothetically construct a typical value-scale for eggs:

> *Ranks in*
> *Value*
> —— 5 eggs
> —— 4 eggs
> —— 3 eggs
> —— 2 eggs
> —— 1 egg
> —— 2nd egg
> —— 3rd egg
> —— 4th egg
> —— 5th egg.

This is a man's ordinal value, or preference, scale for eggs. The higher the ranking, the higher the value. At the center is one egg, the first egg in his possession. By the Law of Diminishing Marginal Utility (ordinal), the second, third, fourth eggs, etc., rank below the first egg on his value-scale, and in that order. Now, since eggs are goods and therefore objects of desire, it follows that a man will value two eggs more than he will one, three more than he will two, etc. Instead of calling this "total utility," we will say that *the marginal utility of a unit of a good is always higher than the marginal utility of a unit of smaller size.* A bundle of 5 eggs will be ranked higher than a bundle of 4 eggs, etc. It should be clear that the only arithmetic or mathematical relationship between these marginal utilities is a simple ordinal one. On the one hand, given a certain sized unit, the marginal utility of that unit declines as the supply of units increases. This is the familiar Law of Diminishing Marginal Utility. On the other hand, the marginal utility of a larger-sized unit is greater than the marginal utility of a smaller-sized unit. This is the law just underlined. And there is no mathematical relationship between, say, the marginal utility of 4 eggs and the marginal utility of the 4th egg except that the former is greater than the latter.

We must conclude then that *there is no such thing as total utility;* all utilities are marginal. In those cases where the supply of a good totals only one unit, then the "total utility" of that whole supply is

THE ECONOMICS OF FREE ENTERPRISE   235

simply the marginal utility of a unit the size of which equals the whole supply. The key concept is the *variable size* of the marginal unit, depending on the situation.[23]

A typical error on the concept of marginal utility is a recent statement by Professor Kennedy that "the word 'marginal' presupposes increments of utility" and hence measurability. But the word "marginal" presupposes *not* increments of utility, *but the utility of increments of goods*, and this need have nothing to do with measurability.[24]

b. Professor Robbins' Problem. Professor Lionel Robbins, in the course of a recent defense of ordinalism, raised a problem which he left unanswered. Accepted doctrine, he declared, states that if *differences* between utility rankings can be judged by the individual, as well as the rankings themselves, then the utility scale can in some way be *measured*. Yet, Robbins says, he *can* judge differences. For example, among three paintings, he can say that he prefers a Rembrandt to a Holbein far less than he prefers a Holbein to a Munnings. How, then, can ordinalism be saved?[25] Is he not conceding measurability? Yet Robbins's dilemma had already been answered twenty years earlier in a famous article by Oskar Lange.[26] Lange pointed out that in terms of what we would call demonstrated preference, only pure rankings are revealed by acts of choice. "Differences" in rank are not so revealed, and are therefore mere psychologizing, which, however interesting, are irrelevant to economics. To this, we need only add that differences of rank *can* be

[23] This analysis of total utility was first put forward by Mises, in *Theory of Money and Credit, op. cit.*, pp. 38-47. It was continued by Harro F. Bernardelli, especially in his "The End of the Marginal Utility Theory?", *Economica*, May 1938, p. 206. Bernardelli's treatment, however, is marred by laborious attempts to find some form of legitimate mathematical representation. On the failure of mathematical economists to understand this treatment of marginal and total, cf. the criticism of Bernardelli by Paul A. Samuelson, "The End of Marginal Utility: A Note on Dr. Bernardelli's Article," *Economica*, February 1939, pp. 86-87; and Kelvin Lancaster, "A Refutation of Mr. Bernardelli," *ibid.*, August 1953, pp. 259-62. For rebuttals cf. Bernardelli, "A Reply to Mr. Samuelson's Note," *ibid.*, February 1939, pp. 88-89; and *id.*, "Comment on Mr. Lancaster's Refutation," *ibid.*, August 1954, pp. 240-42.

[24] Cf. Charles Kennedy, "Concerning Utility," *Economica*, February 1954, p. 13. Kennedy's article, incidentally, is an attempt to rehabilitate a type of cardinalism by making distinctions between "quantity" and "Magnitude," and using the Bertrand Russell concept of "relational addition." Surely, this sort of approach falls with one slash of Occam's Razor—the great scientific principle that entities not be multiplied unnecessarily. For a criticism, cf. D. H. Robertson, *loc. cit.* pp. 668-69.

[25] Robbins, *loc. cit.*, p. 104.

[26] Oskar Lange, "The Determinateness of the Utility Function," *Review of Economic Studies,* June 1934, pp. 224 ff. Unfortunately, Lange balked at the implications of his own analysis and adopted an assumption of cardinality, solely because of his anxious desire to reach certain cherished "welfare" conclusions.

236   ON FREEDOM AND FREE ENTERPRISE

revealed through real choice, whenever the goods can be obtained by money. We need only realize that *money* units (which are characteristically highly divisible) can be lumped in the same value-scale as commodities. For example, suppose someone is willing to pay $10,000 for a Rembrandt, $8000 for a Holbein and only $20 for a Munnings. Then, his value-scale will have the following descending order: Rembrandt, $10,000; Holbein, $9000, $8000, $7000, $6000 . . .; Munnings, $20. We may observe these ranks, and no question of the measurability of utilities need arise.

That money and units of various goods can be ranked on one value-scale is the consequence of Mises' money-regression theorem, which makes possible the application of marginal utility analysis to money.[27] It is characteristic of Professor Samuelson's approach that he scoffs at the whole problem of circularity which money-regression had solved. He falls back on Leon Walras, who developed the idea of "general equilibrium in which all magnitudes are simultaneously determined by efficacious interdependent relations," which he contrasts to the "fears of literary writers" about circular reasoning.[28] This is one example of the pernicious influence of the mathematical method in economics. The idea of mutual determination is appropriate in physics, which tries to explain the unmotivated motions of physical matter. But in praxeology, the *cause* is known: individual purpose. In economics, therefore, the proper method is to proceed from the causing action to its consequent effects.

c. The Fallacy of Indifference. The Hicksian Revolutionaries replaced the cardinal utility concept with the concept of indifference-classes, and for the last twenty years, the economic journals have

[27] Cf. Mises, *Theory of Money and Credit, op. cit.*, pp. 97-123. Mises replied to critics in *Human Action, op. cit.*, pp. 405 ff. The only further criticism has been that of Gilbert, who asserts that the theorem does not explain how a paper money can be introduced after the monetary system has broken down. Presumably he refers to such cases as the German *Rentenmark*. The answer, of course, is that such paper was *not* introduced *de novo;* gold and foreign exchange existed previously, and the *Rentenmark* could exchange in terms of these previously existing moneys. Cf. J. C. Gilbert, "The Demand for Money: the Development of an Economic Concept," *Journal of Political Economy,* April 1953, p. 149.

[28] Samuelson, *Foundations, op. cit.*, pp. 117-18. For similar attacks on earlier Austrian economists, cf. Frank H. Knight, "Introduction" in Carl Menger, *Principles of Economics* (Glencoe, Ill., 1950), p. 23; George J. Stigler, *Production and Distribution Theories* (New York, 1946), p. 181. Stigler criticizes Böhm-Bawerk for spurning "mutual determination" for "the older concept of cause and effect" and explains this by saying that Bohm was untrained in mathematics. For Menger's attack on the mutual determination concept, cf. T. W. Hutchison, *A Review of Economic Doctrines, 1870-1929* (Oxford, 1953), p. 147.

THE ECONOMICS OF FREE ENTERPRISE   237

been rife with a maze of two- and three-dimensional indifference curves, tangencies, "budget lines," etc. The consequence of an adoption of the demonstrated preference approach is that the entire indifference-class concept, along with the complicated superstructure erected upon it, must fall to the ground.

Indifference can never be demonstrated by action. Quite the contrary. Every action necessarily signifies a *choice*, and every choice signifies a definite preference. Action specifically implies the *contrary* of indifference. The indifference-concept is a particularly unfortunate example of the psychologizing error. Indifference-classes are assumed to exist somewhere underlying and apart from action. This assumption is particularly exhibited in those discussions that try to "map" indifference curves empirically by the use of elaborate questionnaires.

If a person is really indifferent between two alternatives, then he cannot and will not choose between them.[29] Indifference is therefore never relevant for action and cannot be demonstrated in action. If a man, for example, is indifferent between the use of 5.1 ounces and 5.2 ounces of butter because of the minuteness of the unit, then there will be no occasion for him to act on these alternatives. He will use butter in larger-sized units, where varying amounts are *not* indifferent to him.

The concept of "indifference" may be important for psychology, but not for economics. In psychology, we are interested in finding out intensities of value, possible indifference, etc. In economics, however, we are only interested in values revealed through choices. It is immaterial to economics whether a man chooses alternative A to alternative B because he strongly prefers A, or because he tossed a coin. The *fact of ranking* is what matters for economics, not the reasons for the individual's arriving at that rank.

In recent years, the indifference concept has been subjected to severe criticism. Professor Armstrong pointed out that under Hicks' curious formulation of "indifference," it is possible for an individual to be "indifferent" between two alternatives and yet choose one over the other.[30] Little has some good criticisms of the indifference concept, but his analysis is vitiated by his eagerness to use faulty theorems in order to arrive at welfare conclusions, and by his radi-

[29] The "indifference theorists" also err in assuming infinitely small steps, essential for their geometric representation, but erroneous for an analysis of human action.

[30] W. E. Armstrong, "The Determinateness of the Utility Function," *Economic Journal*, 1939, pp. 453-67. Armstrong's point that indifference is not a transitive relation, (as Hicks assumed), only applies to different-sized units of *one* commodity. Also cf. Armstrong, "A Note on the Theory of Consumers' Behavior," *loc. cit.*

238   ON FREEDOM AND FREE ENTERPRISE

cally behaviorist methodology.[31] A very interesting attack on the indifference concept from the point of view of psychology has been levelled by Professor Macfie.[32]

The indifference theorists have two basic defenses of the role of indifference in real action. One is to cite the famous fable of Buriden's Ass. This is the "perfectly rational" ass who demonstrates indifference by standing, hungry, equidistant from two equally attractive bales of hay.[33] Since the two bales are equally attractive in every way, the ass can choose neither one, and starves therefore. This example is supposed to indicate how indifference can be revealed in action. It is, of course, difficult to conceive of an ass, or a person, who could be *less* rational. Actually, he is not confronted with *two* choices but with *three*, the third being to starve where he is. Even on the indifference theorists' own grounds, this third choice will be ranked lower than the other two on the individual's value-scale. He will *not* choose starvation.

If both bundles of hay are equally attractive, then the ass or man, who must choose one or the other, will allow pure chance, such as the flip of a coin, to decide on either one. But then indifference is still not revealed by his choice, for the flip of a coin has enabled him to establish a preference! [34]

The other attempt to demonstrate indifference classes rests on the consistency-constancy fallacy, which we have analyzed above. Thus, Kennedy and Walsh claim that a man can reveal indifference if, when asked to repeat his choices between A and B *over time*, he chooses each alternative 50 per cent of the time.[35]

If the concept of the individual indifference-curve is completely fallacious, it is quite obvious that Baumol's concept of the "community indifference curve," which he purports to build up from individual curves, deserves the shortest possible shrift.[36]

d. The Neo-Cardinalists: the von Neumann-Morgenstern Approach. In recent years, the world of economics has been taken by

[31] Little, "Reformulation" and "Theory," *locs. cit.* It is another defect of Samuelson's revealed-preference approach that he attempts to "reveal" indifference-curves as well.

[32] Alec L. Macfie, "Choice in Psychology and as Economic Assumption," *Economic Journal*, June 1953, pp. 352-67.

[33] Thus, cf. Joseph A. Schumpeter, *History of Economic Analysis* (New York, 1954), pp. 94 *n.*, 1064.

[34] Also cf. Croce's warning about using animal illustrations in analyses of human action. Croce, "Economic Principle I," *loc. cit.*, p. 175.

[35] Kennedy, "Common Sense," and Walsh, *locs. cit.*

[36] Cf. William J. Baumol, *Welfare Economics and the Theory of the State* (Cambridge, 1952), pp. 47 ff.

THE ECONOMICS OF FREE ENTERPRISE   239

storm by a neo-cardinalist, quasi-measurement theory of utility. This approach, which has the psychological advantage of being garbed in a mathematical form more advanced than economics had yet known, was founded by von Neumann and Morgenstern in their celebrated work.[37] Their theory had the further advantage of being grounded on the most recent and fashionable (though incorrect) developments in the philosophy of measurement and the philosophy of probability. The Neumann-Morgenstern thesis was adopted by the leading mathematical economists and has gone almost unchallenged to this day. The chief consolation of the ordinalists has been the assurance by the neo-cardinalists that their doctrine applies only to utility under conditions of uncertainty, and therefore does not shake the ordinalist doctrine too drastically.[38] But this consolation is really quite limited, considering that some uncertainty enters into every action.

The Neumann-Morgenstern theory is briefly as follows: an individual can compare not only certain events, but also combinations of events with definite numerical probabilities for each event. Then, according to the authors, if an individual prefers alternative A to B, and B to C, he is able to decide whether he prefers B or a 50-50 probability combination of C and A. If he prefers B, then his preference of B over C is deduced as being greater than his preference of A over B. In a similar fashion, various combinations of probabilities are selected. A quasi-measurable numerical utility is assigned to his utility scale in accordance with the indifference of utilities of B as compared with various probability combinations of A or C. The result is a numerical scale given when arbitrary numbers are assigned to the utilities of two of the events.

The errors of this theory are numerous and grave:

(1) None of the axioms can be validated on demonstrated preference grounds, since admittedly all of the axioms can be violated by the individual actors.

[37] John von Neumann and Oskar Morgenstern, *Theory of Games and Economic Behavior* (2nd ed., 1947), pp. 8, 15-32, 617-32.

[38] Thus cf. the excellent expository article by Armen A. Alchian, "The Meaning of Utility Measurement," *American Economic Review*, March 1953, pp. 26-50. Also cf. Robert Strotz, "Cardinal Utility," *ibid.*, May 1953, pp. 384-97. The leading adherents of the Neumann-Morgenstern approach are Marschak, Friedman, Savage, and Samuelson.

Claims of the theory, even at its best, to measure utility in any way have been nicely exploded by Ellsberg, who also demolishes Marschak's attempt to make the theory normative. Ellsberg's critique suffers considerably, however, from being based on the "operational meaning" concept. Cf. D. Ellsberg, "Classic and Current Notions of Measurable Utility," *Economic Journal*, September 1954, pp. 528-56.

240   ON FREEDOM AND FREE ENTERPRISE

(2) The theory leans heavily on a constancy assumption so that utilities can be revealed by action over time.

(3) The theory relies heavily on the invalid concept of *indifference* of utilities in establishing the numerical scale.

(4) The theory rests fundamentally on the fallacious application of a theory of numerical probability to an area where it cannot apply. Richard von Mises has shown conclusively that numerical probability can be assigned only to situations where there is a class of entities, such that nothing is known about the members except they are members of this class, and where successive trials reveal an asymptotic tendency toward a stable proportion, or frequency of occurrence, of a certain event in that class. There can be no numerical probability applied to specific individual events.[39]

Yet, in human action, precisely the opposite is true. Here, there are no classes of homogeneous members. Each event is a unique event and is different from other unique events. These unique events are not repeatable. Therefore, there is no sense in applying numerical probability theory to such events.[40] It is no coincidence that, invariably, the application of the neo-cardinalists has always been to lotteries and gambling. It is precisely and *only* in lotteries that probability theory can be applied. The theorists beg the entire question of its applicability to general human action by confining their discussion to lottery cases. For the purchaser of a lottery ticket knows only that the individual lottery ticket is a member of a certain-sized class of tickets. The entrepreneur, in making his decisions, is on the contrary confronted with unique cases about which he has some knowledge and which have only limited parallelism to other cases.

[39] Richard von Mises, *Probability, Statistics, and Truth* (London, 1939). Also cf. Ludwig von Mises, *Human Action, op. cit.,* pp. 106-17. The currently fashionable probability theories of Rudolf Carnap and Hans Reichenbach have failed to shake the validity of R. von Mises' approach. Mises refutes them in the third German edition of his work, unfortunately unavailable in English. Cf. Richard von Mises, *Wahrscheinlichkeit, Statistik, und Wahrheit* (3rd ed. Vienna, 1951). The only plausible critique of R. Mises has been that of W. Kneale, who pointed out that the numerical assignment of probability depends on an *infinite* sequence, whereas in no human action can there be an infinite sequence. This, however, *weakens* the application of numerical probability even to cases such as lotteries, rather than enabling it to expand into other areas. Cf. Little, "Theory," *loc. cit.*

[40] Cf. Frank Knight's basic distinction between the narrow cases of actuarial "risk" and the more widespread, non-actuarial "uncertainty." Frank H. Knight, *Risk, Uncertainty, and Profit* (2nd ed. London, 1940). G. L. S. Schackle has also levelled excellent criticism at the probability approach to economics, especially that of Marschak. His own "surprise" theory, however, is open to similar objections; cf. C. F. Carter, "Expectations in Economics," *Economic Journal,* March 1950, pp. 92-105; G. L. S. Schackle, *Expectations in Economics* (Cambridge, 1949), pp. 109-23.

THE ECONOMICS OF FREE ENTERPRISE   241

(5) The neo-cardinalists admit that their theory is not even applicable to gambling if the individual has either a like or a dislike for gambling itself. Since the fact that a man gambles demonstrates that he likes to gamble, it is clear that the Neumann-Morgenstern utility doctrine fails even in this tailor-made case.[41]

(6) A curious new conception of measurement. The new philosophy of measurement discards concepts of "cardinal" and "ordinal" in favor of such labored constructions as "measurable up to a multiplicative constant" (cardinal); "measurable up to a monotonic transform" (ordinal); "measurable up to a linear transform" (the new quasi-measurement, of which the Neumann-Morgenstern proposed utility index is an example). This terminology, apart from its undue complexity (under the influence of mathematics), implies that everything, including ordinality, is somehow "measurable." The man who proposes a new definition for an important word must prove his case; the new definition of measurement has hardly done so. Measurement, on any sensible definition, implies the possibility of a unique assignment of numbers which can be meaningfully subjected to all the operations of arithmetic. To accomplish this, it is necessary to define a fixed unit. In order to define such a unit, the property to be measured must be *extensive* in space, so that the unit can be objectively agreed upon by all. Therefore, subjective states, being *intensive* rather than objectively extensive, cannot be measured and subjected to arithmetical operations. And utility refers to intensive states. Measurement becomes even more implausible when we realize that utility is a praxeologic, rather than a directly psychologic, concept.

A favorite rebuttal is that subjective states *have* been measured; thus, the old, unscientific subjective feeling of heat has given way to the objective science of thermometry.[42] But this rebuttal is erroneous; thermometry does *not* measure the intensive subjective feelings themselves. It assumes an approximate correlation between the intensive property and an objective extensive event—such as the physical expansion of gas or mercury. And thermometry can certainly lay no claim to precise measurement of subjective states: we all know that some people, for various reasons, feel warmer or colder at different times even if the external temperature

---

[41] It is curious how economists have been tempted to discuss gambling by first assuming that the participant doesn't like to gamble. It is on this assumption that Alfred Marshall based his famous "proof" that gambling (because of each individual's diminishing utility of money) is "irrational."

[42] Thus, cf. von Neumann and Morgenstern, *op. cit.*, pp. 16-17.

242   ON FREEDOM AND FREE ENTERPRISE

remains the same.[43] Certainly no correlation whatever can be found for demonstrated preference scales in relation to physical lengths. For preferences have no *direct* physical basis, as do feelings of heat.

No arithmetical operations whatever can be performed on ordinal numbers; therefore, to use the term "measurable" in any way for ordinal numbers is hopelessly to confuse the meaning of the term. Perhaps the best remedy for possible confusion is to avoid using *any* numbers for ordinal rank; the rank concept can just as well be expressed in letters (A,B,C . . .), using a convention that A, for example, expresses higher rank.

As to the new type of quasi-measurability, no one has yet proved it capable of existence. The burden of proof rests on the proponents. If an object is extensive, then it is at least theoretically capable of being measured, for an objective fixed unit can, in principle, be defined. If it is intensive, then no such fixed unit can apply, and any assignment of number would have to be ordinal. There is no room for an intermediate case. The favorite example of quasi-measurability that is always offered is, again, temperature. In thermometry, centigrade and Fahrenheit scales are supposed to be convertible into each other *not* at a multiplicative constant (cardinality) but by multiplying and then adding a constant (a "linear transform"). More careful analysis, however, reveals that both scales are simply derivations from one scale based on an absolute zero point. All we need to demonstrate the cardinality of temperature is to transform both centigrade and Fahrenheit scales into scales where "absolute zero" *is* zero, and then each will be convertible into the other by a multiplicative constant. Furthermore, the actual measurement in temperature is a measurement of *length* (say, of the mercury column) so that temperature is really a derived measure based on the cardinally measurable magnitude of length.[44]

Jacob Marschak, one of the leading members of the Neumann-Morgenstern school, has conceded that the temperature case is

---

[43] Cf. Morris R. Cohen, *A Preface to Logic* (New York, 1944), p. 151.

[44] On measurement, cf. Norman Campbell, *What Is Science?* (New York, 1952), pp. 109-34; *id., An Account of the Principles of Measurement and Calculation* (London, 1928). Although the above view of measurement is not currently fashionable, it is backed by the weighty authority of Mr. Campbell. A description of the controversy between Campbell and S. S. Stevens on the issue of measurement of intensive magnitudes was included in the unpublished draft of Carl G. Hempel's *Concept Formation,* but was unfortunately omitted from Hempel's published *Fundamentals of Concept Formation in Empirical Science* (Chicago, 1952). Campbell's critique can be found in A. Ferguson, *et. al. Interim Report* (British Association for the Advancement of Science, 1938), pp. 277-334; and in *id.* (Final Report, 1940), pp. 331-349.

THE ECONOMICS OF FREE ENTERPRISE   243

inappropriate for the establishment of quasi-measurability, because it is derived from the fundamental, cardinal, measurement of distance. Yet, astonishingly, he offers *altitude* in its place. But if "temperature readings are nothing but distance," what else is altitude, which is solely and purely distance and length? [45]

IV. *Welfare Economics: A Critique*

a. *Economics and Ethics.* It is now generally accepted among economists, at least *pro forma*, that economics *per se* cannot establish ethical judgments. It is not sufficiently recognized that to accept this need not imply acceptance of the Max Weber position that ethics can never be scientifically or rationally established. Whether we accept the Max Weber position, or we adhere to the older view of Plato and Aristotle that a rational ethics is possible, it should be clear that *economics* by itself cannot establish an ethical position. If an ethical science is possible, it must be built up out of data supplied by truths established by all of the other sciences.

Medicine can establish the fact that a certain drug can cure a certain disease, while leaving to other disciplines the problem whether the disease *should* be cured. Similarly, economics can establish that Policy A leads to the advancement of life, prosperity, and peace; while Policy B leads to death, poverty, and war. Both medicine and economics can establish these consequences scientifically, and without introducing ethical judgments into the analysis. It might be protested that doctors would not inquire into possible cures for a disease if they did not want a cure, or economists would not investigate causes of prosperity if they did not want the result. There are two answers to this point: (1) that this is undoubtedly true in almost all cases, but not *necessarily* so—some doctors or economists may care only about the discovery of truth, and (2) this only establishes the psychologic motivation of the scientists; it does not establish that the discipline itself arrives at values. On the contrary, it bolsters the thesis that ethics is arrived at apart from the specific sciences of medicine or economics.

Thus, whether we hold the view that ethics is a matter of nonrational emotions or taste, or whether we believe in a rational ethic, we must agree that economic science *per se* cannot establish ethical statements. As a political policy judgment is a branch of ethics, the same conclusion applies to politics. If prosperity vs. poverty, for

---

[45] Cf. Jacob Marschak, "Rational Behavior, Uncertain Prospects, and Measurability," *Econometrica*, April 1950, p. 131.

244   ON FREEDOM AND FREE ENTERPRISE

example, are political alternatives, economic science cannot decide between them; it simply presents the truth about the consequences of each alternative political decision. As citizens, we take these truths into account when we make our politico-ethical decisions.

b. The Problem of the New Welfare Economics: The Unanimity Rule. The problem of "welfare economics" has always been to find some way to circumvent this restriction on economics, and to make ethical, and particularly *political,* statements directly. Since economics discusses individuals' aiming to maximize their utility or happiness or welfare, the problem may be translated into the following terms: When can economics say that "society is better off" as a result of a certain change? Or alternatively, when can we say that "social utility" has been increased or "maximized"?

Neo-classical economists, led by Professor Pigou, found a simple answer. Economics can establish that a man's marginal utility of money diminishes as his money-income increases. Therefore, they concluded, the marginal utility of a dollar is less to a rich man than to a poor man. *Other things being equal,* social utility is maximized by a progressive income tax which takes from the rich and gives to the poor. This was the favorite demonstration of the "old welfare economics," grounded on Benthamite utilitarian ethics, and brought to fruition by Edgeworth and Pigou.

Economists continued blithely along this path until they were brought up short by Professor Robbins. Robbins showed that this demonstration rested on interpersonal comparisons of utility, and since utility is not a cardinal magnitude, such comparisons involve ethical judgments.[46] What Robbins actually accomplished was to reintroduce Pareto's Unanimity Rule into economics, and establish it as the iron gate where welfare economics must test its credentials.[47] This Rule runs as follows: We can only say that "social welfare" (or better, "social utility") has *increased* due to a change, if no individual is worse off because of the change (and at least one is better off). If one individual is worse off, the fact that interpersonal utilities cannot be added or subtracted prevents economics from saying anything about social utility. Any statement about social utility would, in the absence of unanimity, imply an ethical interpersonal comparison between the gainers and the losers from

[46] Cf. Lionel Robbins, "Interpersonal Comparisons of Utility," *Economic Journal,* December 1938, pp. 635-41; and *id., An Essay on the Nature and Significance of Economic Science* (2nd ed., London, 1935), pp. 138-41.

[47] Cf. Vilfredo Pareto, *Manuel d'Économie Politique* (2nd Ed., Paris, 1927), p. 617.

THE ECONOMICS OF FREE ENTERPRISE   245

a change. If X number of individuals gain, and Y number lose, from a change, any weighting to sum up in a "social" conclusion would necessarily imply an ethical judgment on the relative importance of the two groups.[48]

The Pareto-Robbins Unanimity Rule conquered economics and liquidated the old Pigovian welfare economics almost completely. Since then, an enormous literature known as the "new welfare economics" has flourished, devoting itself to a series of attempts to square the circle: to assert certain political judgments as scientific economics, while still retaining the unanimity rule.

c. Professor Robbins' Escape Route. Robbins' own formulation of the Unanimity Rule far undervalues the scope of its restrictive power over the assertions of economists. Robbins stated that only *one* ethical assertion would be necessary for economists to make interpersonal comparisons: namely, that every man has an "equal capacity for satisfaction" in similar circumstances. To be sure, Robbins grants that this ethical assumption cannot be established by economics; but he implies that since all good democrats are bound to make this egalitarian assumption, we can all pretty well act *as if* interpersonal comparisons of utility can be made, and go on to make ethical judgments.

In the first place, it is difficult, upon analysis, to make sense of the phrase "equal capacity for satisfaction." Robbins, as we have seen, admits that we cannot scientifically compare utilities or satisfactions between individuals. But since there is no unit of satisfactions by which we can make comparisons, there is no meaning to any assumption that different men's satisfactions will be "equal" in any circumstances. "Equal" in what way, and in what units? We are not at liberty to make any ethical assumption we please, because even an ethical assumption must be framed meaningfully, and its terms must be definable in a meaningful manner. Since there is no meaning to the term "equality" without some sort of definable unit, and since there is no unit of satisfaction or utility, it follows that there can be no ethical assumption of "equal capacity for satisfaction," and that this cannot provide a shortcut to permit the economist to make conclusions about public policy.

The Robbins' position, moreover, embodies a highly oversimplified

48 Kempt tries to alter the Unanimity Rule to read that social utility is only increased if *everyone* is better off, none being worse off *or* indifferent. But, as we have seen, indifference cannot be demonstrated in action, and therefore this alteration is invalid. Cf. Murray C. Kemp, "Welfare Economics: A Stocktaking," *Economic Record,* November 1954, p. 245.

ON FREEDOM AND FREE ENTERPRISE

view of ethics and its relation to politico-economic affairs. The problem of interpersonal comparisons of utility *is only one* of the very many ethical problems which must at least be discussed before any policy conclusions can rationally be framed. Suppose, for example, that two social changes take place, each of which causes 99% of the people to gain in utility and 1% to lose. Surely no assumption about the interpersonal comparison of utility can suffice to establish an ethical judgment, divorced from the *content* of the change itself. If, for example, one change was the enslavement of the 1% by the 99%, and the other was the removal of a governmental subsidy to the 1%, there is apt to be a great deal of difference in our ethical pronouncements on the two cases, even if the assumed "social utility" in the two cases is approximately the same.

d. The Compensation Principle. A particularly notable attempt to make policy conclusions within the framework of the Unanimity Rule was the Kaldor-Hicks "compensation principle," which stated that "social utility" may scientifically be said to increase, if the winners *may* be able to compensate the losers and still remain winners.[49] There are many fatal errors in this approach. In the first place, since the compensation principle is supposed to help economists form policy judgments, it is evident that we must be able to compare, at least in principle, *actual* social states. We are therefore always concerned with *actual*, and not *potential*, winners and losers from any change. Whether or not the winners *may* compensate the losers is therefore irrelevant; the important question is whether the compensation *does*, in fact, take place. Only if the compensation is actually carried out so that not a single person remains a loser, can we still assert a gain in social utility. But *can* this compensation ever be carried out? In order to do so, everybody's utility scale would have to be investigated by the compensators. But from the very nature of utility scales this is an impossibility. Who knows what has happened to anyone's utility scale? The compensation principle is necessarily divorced from demonstrated preference, and once this occurs, it is impossible to find out what has happened to

[49] On the compensation principle, cf. Nicholas Kaldor, "Welfare Propositions in Economics," *Economic Journal*, September 1939, p. 549; John R. Hicks, "The Foundations of Welfare Economics," *ibid.*, December 1939, p. 706. For a criticism, cf. William J. Baumol, "Community Indifference," *Review of Economic Studies*, 1946-47, pp. 44-48; Baumol, *Welfare Economics and the Theory of the State, op. cit.*, pp. 12 ff; Kemp, *loc. cit.*, pp. 246-50. For a summary of the discussion, cf. D. H. Robertson, *Utility and All That* (London, 1952), pp. 29-35. The weakness in Robbins' accession to the Unanimity Rule is demonstrated by his endorsement of the compensation principle. Cf. Robbins, "Robertson on Utility and Scope," *loc. cit.*

THE ECONOMICS OF FREE ENTERPRISE 247

anyone's utility. The reason for the divorce is that the act of compensation is, necessarily, a unilateral gift *to* a person rather than an act *of* that person, and therefore it is impossible to estimate how much his utility has increased as compared to its decrease in some other situation. Only if a person is actually confronted with a *choice* between two alternatives can we say that he prefers one to the other.

Certainly, the compensators could not rely on questionnaires in a situation where everyone need only *say* that he has lost utility in order to receive compensation. And suppose someone proclaims that his sensibilities are so hurt by a certain change that no monetary reward could ever compensate him? The existence of one such person would null any compensation attempt. But these problems necessarily occur when we leave the realm of demonstrated preference.

e. The Social Welfare Function. Under the impact of criticisms far less thoroughgoing than the above, the compensation principle has been abandoned by most economists. There have been recent attempts to substitute another device—the "Social Welfare Function." But after a flurry of activity, this concept, originated by Professors Bergson and Samuelson, quickly struck rocky waters, and virtually sank under the impact of various criticisms. It came to be regarded as an empty and therefore meaningless concept. Even its founders have given up the struggle and concede that economists must import ethical judgments from outside economics in order to make policy conclusions.[50] Professor Rothenberg has made a desperate attempt to salvage the social welfare function by radically changing its nature, i.e., by identifying it with an existing "social decision-making precess." To uphold this shift, Rothenberg must make the false assumption that "society" exists apart from individuals and makes "its" own valuation. Furthermore, as Bergson has pointed out, this procedure abolishes welfare economics, since the function of the economist would be to observe empirically the social decision-making process at work, and to pronounce its decisions as gains in "social utility."

[50] Cf. Abram Bergson, "On the Concept of Social Welfare," *Quarterly Journal of Economics*, May 1954, p. 249; Paul A. Samuelson, "Welfare Economics; Comment," in (B. F. Haley, ed.), *A Survey of Contemporary Economics, Vol. II* (Homewood, Ill., 1952), p. 37. Also cf. Jerome Rothenberg, "Conditions for a Social Welfare Function," *Journal of Political Economy*, October 1953, p. 397; Sidney Schoeffler, "Note on Modern Welfare Economics," *American Economic Review*, December 1952, p. 881; I. M. D. Little, "Social Choice and Individual Values," *Journal of Political Economy*, October 1952, pp. 422-32.

248 ON FREEDOM AND FREE ENTERPRISE

f. The Economist As Adviser. Failing the establishment of policy conclusions through the compensation principle or the social welfare function, there is another very popular route to enable the economist to participate in policy formation while still remaining an ethically neutral scientist. This view holds that someone else may set the ends, while the economist is justified in telling that person (and to be hired by that person) the correct means for attaining these desired ends. Since the economist takes *someone else's* hierarchy of ends as given, and only points out the means to attain them, he is alleged to remain ethically neutral and strictly scientific. This viewpoint, however, is a misleading and fallacious one. Let us take an example suggested by a passage in Professor Philbrook's seminal article; a monetary economist advising the Federal Reserve System.[51] Can this economist simply take the ends set by the heads of this System, and advise on the most efficient means to attain them? *Not unless the economist affirms these ends as being positively good,* i.e., not unless he makes an ethical judgment. For suppose that the economist is convinced that the entire Federal Reserve System is pernicious. In that case, his best course may well be to advise that policy which would make the System highly *inefficient* in the pursuit of its ends. The economist employed by the System cannot, therefore, give any advice whatever without abandoning ethical neutrality. If he advises the System on the best way to achieve its ends, it must be logically inferred that he supports these ends. His advice involves no less an ethical judgment on his part if he chooses to "tacitly accept the decisions of the community (*sic*) as expressed through the political machinery."[52]

g. The End of Welfare Economics? After twenty years of florid growth, welfare economics is once more confined to an even tighter Unanimity Rule. Its attempts to say anything about political affairs within the confines of this rule have been in vain.

The death of the New Welfare Economics has begun to be reluctantly recognized by all of its supporters, and each has taken turns in pronouncing its demise.[53] If the strictures advanced in this

[51] Clarence Philbrook, " 'Realism' in Policy Espousal," *American Economic Review*, December 1953, pp. 846-59. The entire article is of fundamental importance in the study of economics and its relation to public policy.

[52] E. J. Mishan, "The Principle of Compensation Reconsidered," *Journal of Political Economy*, August 1952, p. 312. Cf. especially the excellent note of I. M. D. Little, "The Scientist and the State," *Review of Economic Studies*, 1949-50, pp. 75-76.

[53] Thus, see the rather mournful discussion in the American Economic Association's second volume of the *Survey of Contemporary Economics, op. cit.*: Kenneth E. Boulding, "Welfare Economics," pp. 1-34; Melvin W. Reder, "Comment," pp. 34-36; and

paper are conceded, the burial rites will be accelerated, and the
corpse decently interred. Many New Welfare Economists under-
standably continue to grope for some way of salvaging something
out of the wreckage. Thus, Reder suggests that economics make
specific, piecemeal policy recommendations anyway. But surely this
is only a despairing refusal to take the fundamental problems into
account. Rothenberg tries to inaugurate a constancy assumption
based on psychologizing about underlying basic personalities.[54]
Aside from the fact that "basic" changes can take place at any time,
economics deals with *marginal* changes, and a change is no less a
change for being marginal. In fact, whether changes are marginal
or basic is a problem for psychology, not praxeology. Bergson tries
the mystical route of denying demonstrated preference, and claiming it to be possible that people's values "really differed" from
what they chose in action. He does this by adopting the "consistency"—constancy fallacy.

Does the Unanimity Rule then spell the end of *all* possible welfare economics, as well as the "old" and the "new" versions? Super-
ficially, it would seem so. For if all changes must injure nobody,
i.e., if no people must feel worse off as a result of a change, what
changes could pass muster as socially useful within the Unanimity
Rule? As Reder laments: "Consideration of the welfare implications
of envy, for example, make it impossible even to say that welfare
will be increased by everyone having more of every commodity."[55]

V. *Welfare Economics: A Reconstruction*

a. Demonstrated Preference and the Free Market. It is the contention of this paper that the wake for all welfare economics is
premature, and that welfare economics can be reconstructed with
the aid of the concept of demonstrated preference. This reconstruction, however, will have no resemblance to either of the "old" or
"new" edifices that preceded it. In fact, if Reder's thesis is correct,
our proposed resurrection of the patient may be considered by many
as more unfortunate than his demise.[56]

Samuelson, *loc. cit.* Also cf. the articles by Schoeffler, Bergson, and Kemp cited
above.

[54] Jerome Rothenberg, "Welfare Comparisons and Changes in Tastes," *American
Economic Review*, December 1953, pp. 885-90.

[55] Reder, *loc. cit.*, p. 35.

[56] "To a considerable extent, welfare (and related) theorizing of the 1930's and
'40's was an attempt to show the variety and importance of the circumstances under
which *laissez-faire* was inappropriate." *Ibid.*

250   ON FREEDOM AND FREE ENTERPRISE

Demonstrated preference, as we remember, eliminates hypothetical imaginings about individual value-scales. Welfare economics has until now always considered values as hypothetical valuations of hypothetical "social states." But demonstrated preference only treats values as revealed through chosen action.

Let us now consider exchanges on the free market. Such an exchange is voluntarily undertaken by both parties. Therefore, the very fact that an exchange takes place demonstrates that both parties benefit (or more strictly, *expect* to benefit) from the exchange. The fact that both parties chose the exchange demonstrates that they both benefit. The free market is the name for the array of all the voluntary exchanges that take place in the world. Since every exchange demonstrates a unanimity of benefit for both parties concerned, we must conclude that *the free market benefits all its participants*. In other words, welfare economics can make the statement that the free market increases social utility, while still keeping to the framework of the Unanimity Rule.[57]

But what about Reder's bogey: the envious man who hates the benefits of others? To the extent that he himself has participated in the market, to that extent he reveals that he likes and benefits from the market. And we are not interested in his opinions about the exchanges made by *others*, since his preferences are not demonstrated through action and are therefore irrelevant. How do we *know* that this hypothetical envious one loses in utility because of the exchanges of others? Consulting his verbal opinions does not suffice, for his proclaimed envy might be a joke or a literary game or a deliberate lie.

We are led inexorably, then, to the conclusion that the processes of the free market always lead to a gain in social utility. And we can say this with absolute validity as economists, without engaging in ethical judgments.

b. The Free Market and the "Problem of Distribution." Economics, in general, and welfare economics, in particular, have been plagued with the "problem of distribution." It has been maintained, for example, that assertions of increased social utility on the free market are all very well, but only within the confines of assuming

[57] Haavelmo criticizes the thesis that the free market maximizes social utility on the grounds that this "assumes" that the individuals "somehow get together" to make an optimal decision. But the free market is precisely the method by which the "get together" takes place! Cf. Trygve Haavelmo, "The Notion of Involuntary Economic Decision," *Econometrica*, January 1950, p. 8.

THE ECONOMICS OF FREE ENTERPRISE 251

a given distribution of income.[58] Since changes in the distribution of income seemingly injure one person and benefit another, no statements, it is alleged, can be made about social utility with respect to changes in distribution. And income distribution is always changing.

On the free market, however, there *is* no such thing as a separate "distribution." A man's monetary assets have been acquired precisely because his or his ancestors' services have been purchased by others on the free market. There is no distributional process apart from the production and exchange processes of the market; hence the very concept of "distribution" becomes meaningless on the free market. Since "distribution" is simply the result of the free exchange process, and since this process benefits all participants on the market and increases social utility, it follows directly that the "distributional" results of the free market also increase social utility.

The strictures of the critics do apply, however, to cases of State action. When the State takes from Peter and gives to Paul it is effecting a separate *distribution* process. Here, there does exist a process *separate* from production and exchange, and hence the concept becomes meaningful. Moreover, such State action obviously *and demonstrably* benefits one group and injures another, thus violating the Unanimity Rule.

c. The Role of the State. Until quite recently, welfare economics has never analyzed the role of the State. Indeed, economics in general has never devoted much attention to this fundamental problem. Specific problems, such as public finance, or price controls, have been investigated, but the State itself has been a shadowy figure in the economic literature. Usually, it has vaguely been considered as representing "society" or "the public" in some way. "Society," however, is not a real entity; it is only a convenient short-hand term for an array of all existing individuals.[59] The largely unexplored area of the State and State actions, however, can be analyzed with the powerful tools of Demonstrated Preference and the Unanimity Rule.

The State is distinguished from all other institutions in society in two ways: (1) it and it alone can interfere by the use of violence with actual or potential market exchanges of other people; and (2) it and it alone obtains its revenues by a compulsory levy, backed by violence. No other individual or group can legally act in these

---

[58] It would be more correct to say given distribution of money *assets.*

[59] On this fallacy of methodological collectivism, and the broader fallacy of conceptual realism, cf. the excellent discussion in Hayek, *Counter Revolution of Science, op. cit.,* pp. 53 ff.

ON FREEDOM AND FREE ENTERPRISE

ways.[60] Now what happens when the State, or a criminal, uses violence to interfere with exchanges on the market? Suppose that the government prohibits A and B from making an exchange they are willing to make. It is clear that the utilities of both A and B have been lowered, for they are prevented by threat of violence from making an exchange that they otherwise would have made. On the other hand, there has been a gain in utility (or at least an anticipated gain) for the government officials imposing this restriction, otherwise they would not have done so. As economists, we can therefore say nothing about social utility in this case, since some individuals have demonstrably gained, and some demonstrably lost in utility, from the governmental action.

The same conclusion follows in those cases where the government forces C and D to make an exchange which they otherwise would not have made. Once again, the utilities of the government officials gain. And *at least one* of the two participants (C or D) lose in utility, because at least one would not have wanted to make the exchange in the absence of governmental coercion. Again, economics can say nothing about social utility in this case.[61]

We conclude therefore that *no government interference with exchanges can ever increase social utility*. But we can say more than that. It is the essence of government that it alone obtains its revenue by the compulsory levy of taxation. All of its subsequent acts and expenditures, whatever their nature, rest on this taxing power. We have just seen that whenever government forces anyone to make an exchange which he would not have made, this person loses in utility as a result of the coercion. But taxation is just such a coerced exchange. If everyone would have paid just as much to the government under a system of voluntary payment, then there would be no need for the compulsion of taxes. The fact that coercion is used for taxes demonstrates that less would have been contributed under a completely voluntary arrangement. Since some lose by the existence of taxes, therefore, and since all government actions rest on its taxing power, we deduce that: *no act of government whatever can increase social utility*.

Economics, therefore, without engaging in any ethical judgment whatever, and following the scientific principles of the Unanimity Rule and Demonstrated Preference, concludes: (1) that the free

---

[60] *Criminals* also act in these ways, but they cannot do so legally. For the purpose of praxeologic rather than legal analysis, the same conclusions apply to both groups.

[61] We cannot discuss here the praxeological analysis of general economics which shows that, in the long run, for many acts of coercive interference, the coercer himself loses in utility.

THE ECONOMICS OF FREE ENTERPRISE   253

market always increases social utility; and (2) that no act of government can ever increase social utility. These two propositions are the pillars of the reconstructed welfare economics.

Exchanges between persons can take place either voluntarily or under the coercion of violence. There is no third way. If, therefore, free market exchanges always increase social utility, while no coerced exchange or interference can increase social utility, we may conclude that the maintenance of *a free and voluntary market "maximizes" social utility* (provided we do not interpret "maximize" in a cardinal sense).

Generally, even the most rigorously *Wertfrei* economists have been willing to allow themselves one ethical judgment: they feel free to recommend any change or process that increases social utility under the Unanimity Rule. Any economist who pursues this method would have to (a) uphold the free market as always beneficial, and (b) refrain from advocating any governmental action. In other words, he would have to become an advocate of *"ultra" laissez-faire*.

d. Laissez-faire Reconsidered. It has been quite common to scoff at the French "optimist" *laissez-faire* school of the nineteenth century. Usually, their "welfare economic" analysis has been dismissed as naïve prejudice. Actually, however, their writings reveal that their *laissez-faire* conclusions were *post-judices*—were judgments *based* on their analysis, rather than preconceptions of their analysis.[62] It was the discovery of the general social benefit from free exchange that led to the rhapsodies over the free exchange process in the works of such men as Frederic Bastiat, Edmond About, Gustave de Molinari, and the American, Arthur Latham Perry. Their analyses of State action were far more rudimentary (except in the case of Molinari), but their analyses generally needed only the ethical presumption in favor of social utility to lead them to a pure *laissez-faire* position.[63] Their treatment of exchange may be seen in this passage from the completely neglected Edmond About:

[62] Lionel Robbins' *The Theory of Political Economy* (London, 1952) is devoted to the thesis that the English classical economists were really "scientific" because they did *not* uphold *laissez-faire,* while the French optimists were dogmatic and "metaphysical" because they did. To uphold this, Robbins abandons his praxeological approach of twenty years before, and adopts positivism: "The final test whether a statement is metaphysical (*sic*) or scientific is . . . whether it argues dogmatically *a priori* or by way of appeal to experience." Naturally, Robbins cites examples from the physical sciences to bolster this fallacious dichotomy. *Ibid.*, pp. 23-24.

[63] Bastiat's writings are well known, but his "welfare" analysis was generally inferior to that of About or Molinari. For a brilliant analysis of State action, cf. Gustave de Molinari, *The Society of Tomorrow* (New York, 1904), pp. 19 ff., 65-96.

254   ON FREEDOM AND FREE ENTERPRISE

Now what is admirable in exchange is that it benefits the two contracting parties. . . . Each of the two, by giving what he has for that which he has not, makes a good bargain. . . . This occurs at every free and straightforward exchange. . . . In fact, whether you sell, whether you buy, you perform an act of preference. No one constrains you to give over any of your things for the things of another.[64]

The analysis of free exchange underlying the *laissez-faire* position has suffered general neglect in economics. When it is considered, it is usually dismissed as "simple." Thus, Hutchison calls the idea of exchange as mutual benefit "simple"; Samuelson calls it "unsophisticated." Simple it perhaps is, but simplicity *per se* is hardly a liability in science. The important consideration is whether the doctrine is correct; if it is correct, then Occam's Razor tells us that the simpler it is, the better.[65]

The rejection of the simple seems to have its root in the positivist methodology. In physics (the model of positivism), the task of science is to go beyond common-sense observation, building a complex structure of explanation of the common-sense facts. Praxeology, however, begins with common-sense truths as its *axioms*. The laws of physics need complicated empirical testing; the axioms of praxiology are known as obvious to all upon reflection. As a result, positivists are uncomfortable in the presence of universal truth. Instead of rejoicing in the ability to ground knowledge on universally accepted truth, the positivist rejects it as simple, vague, or "naïve." [66]

Samuelson's only attempt to refute the *laissez-faire* position was to refer briefly to the allegedly classic refutation by Wicksell.[67] Wicksell, however, also dismissed the approach of the French "harmony economists" without argument, and went on to criticize at length the far weaker formulation of Leon Walras. Walras tried to prove "maximum utility" from free trade in the sense of an interpersonally cardinal utility, and thus left himself wide open to refutation.

Furthermore, it should be stressed that the theorem of maximum

---

[64] Edmond About, *Handbook of Social Economy* (London, 1872), p. 104. Also cf. *ibid.*, pp. 101-12; and Arthur Latham Perry, *Political Economy* (21st Ed., New York, 1892), p. 180.

[65] Cf. T. W. Hutchison, *op. cit.*, p. 282; Samuelson, *Foundations, op. cit.*, p. 204.

[66] For an example of this attitude, cf. the critique of Hayek's *Counter-Revolution of Science* by May Brodbeck, in "On the Philosophy of the Social Sciences," *Philosophy of Science*, April 1954. Brodbeck complains that the praxeologic axioms are not "surprising"; if she pursued the analysis, however, she might find the *conclusions* surprising enough.

[67] Cf. Knut Wicksell, *Lectures on Political Economy, Vol. I* (London, 1934) pp. 72 ff.

THE ECONOMICS OF FREE ENTERPRISE   **255**

social utility applies not to any type of "perfect" or "pure" competition, or even to "competition" as against "monopoly." It applies simply to any voluntary exchange. It might be objected that a voluntary cartel's action in raising prices makes many consumers worse off, and therefore that assertion of the benefits of voluntary exchange would have to exclude cartels. It is not possible, however, for an observer scientifically to compare the social utilities of results on the free market from one period of time to the next. As we have seen above, we cannot determine a man's value-scales over a period of time. How much more impossible for all individuals! Since we cannot discover people's utilities over time, we must conclude that whatever the institutional conditions of exchange, however large or small the number of participants on the market, the free market at any time will maximize social utility. For all the exchanges are exchanges effected voluntarily by all parties. Thus, in Period 1 the free market will maximize social utility. Then, suppose some producers voluntarily form a cartel in an industry. This cartel makes its exchanges in Period 2. Social utility is again maximized, for again no one's exchanges are being altered by coercion. If, in Period 2, the government should intervene to prohibit the cartel, it could not increase social utility since the prohibition demonstrably injures the producers.[68]

   e. The State As a Voluntary Institution; A Critique. In the development of economic thought, far more attention has been paid to analysis of free exchange than to State action. Generally as we have indicated, the State has simply been assumed to be a voluntary institution. The most common assumption is that the State is voluntary because all government must rest on majority consent. If we adhere to the Unanimity Rule, however, it is obvious that a majority is not unanimity, and that therefore economics cannot consider the State as voluntary on this ground. The same comment applies to the majority voting procedures of democracy. The man who votes for the losing candidate, and even more the man who abstains from voting, can hardly be said voluntarily to approve of the action of the government.[69]

   [68] It is also possible to argue, on *general* economic, rather than welfare-economic, grounds, that a voluntary cartel action, *if profitable*, will benefit consumers. In that case, consumers as well as producers would be injured by governmental outlawry of the cartel. As we have indicated above, *welfare* economics demonstrates that no governmental action can increase social utility. *General* economics demonstrates that, in many instances of governmental action, even those who immediately benefit lose in the long run.

   [69] Schumpeter is properly scornful when he says: "The theory which construes taxes on the analogy of club dues or of purchase of services of, say, a doctor only

256   ON FREEDOM AND FREE ENTERPRISE

In the last few years, a few economists have begun to realize that the nature of the State needs careful analysis. In particular, they have realized that welfare economics must prove the State to be in some sense voluntary before it can advocate any State action whatever. The most ambitious attempt to designate the State as a "voluntary" institution is the work of Professor Baumol.[70] Baumol's "external economy" thesis may be put succinctly as follows: certain wants are by their nature "collective" rather than "individual." In these cases, every individual will rank the following alternatives on his value scale: (A) he would most prefer that *everyone but himself* be coerced to pay for the satisfaction of the group want (e.g., military protection, public parks, dams, etc.). But since this is not practicable, he must choose between alternatives B and C. In (B) *no one* is forced to pay for the service, in which case the service will probably not be provided since each man will tend to shirk his share; in (C) *everyone*, including the particular individual himself, is forced to pay for the service. Baumol concludes that people will pick C; hence the State's activities in providing these services are "really voluntary." Everyone cheerfully chooses that he be coerced.

This subtle argument can be considered on many levels. In the first place, it is absurd to hold that "voluntary coercion" can be a demonstrated preference. If the decision were truly voluntary, no tax coercion would be necessary—people would voluntarily and publicly agree to pay their share of contributions to the common project. Since they are all supposed to prefer getting the project to not paying for it and not getting it, they are then really *willing* to pay the tax-price to obtain the project. Therefore, the tax coercion apparatus is not necessary, and all people would bravely, if a bit reluctantly, pay what they are "supposed to" without any coercive tax system.

Secondly, Baumol's thesis undoubtedly is true for the *majority*, since the majority, passively or eagerly, must support a government if it is to survive any length of time. But even if the majority are willing to coerce themselves in order to coerce others (and perhaps tip the balance of coercion *against* the others), this proves nothing for welfare economics, which must rest its conclusions on *unanimity*, not majority, rule. Will Baumol contend that *everyone* has this

proves how far removed this part of the social sciences is from scientific habits of mind." Joseph A. Schumpeter, *Capitalism, Socialism, and Democracy* (New York. 1942), p. 198. For a realistic analysis cf. Molinari, *op. cit.*, pp. 87-95.

[70] Cf. William J. Baumol, "Economic Theory and the Political Scientist," *World Politics*, January 1954, pp. 275-77; and Baumol, *Welfare Economics and the Theory of the State, op. cit.*

THE ECONOMICS OF FREE ENTERPRISE   257

value ordering? Isn't there *one* person in the society who prefers
freedom for all to coercion over all? If one such person exists,
Baumol can no longer call the State a voluntary institution. On
what grounds, *a priori* or empirical, can anyone contend that no
such individual exists? [71]

But Baumol's thesis deserves more detailed consideration. For
even though he cannot establish the existence of a voluntary coercion, if it is really true that certain services simply cannot be obtained on the free market, then this would reveal a serious weakness
in the free-market "mechanism." Do cases exist where only coercion
can yield desired services? At first glance, Baumol's "external economy" grounds for an affirmative answer seem plausible. Such services as military protection, dams, highways, etc., are important.
People desire that they be supplied. Yet wouldn't each person tend
to slacken his payment, hoping that the others would pay? But to
employ this as a rationale for State provision of such services is a
question-begging example of circular reasoning. For this peculiar
condition holds only and precisely because the State, not the market,
provides these services! The fact that the State provides a service
means that, unlike the market, its *provision of the service is completely separated from its collection of payment.* Since the service
is generally provided free and more or less indiscriminately to the
citizens, it naturally follows that every individual—assured of the
service—will try to shirk his taxes. For, unlike the market, his individual tax payment brings him nothing directly. And this condition
cannot be a justification for the State action; for it is only the *consequence* of the existence of the State action itself.

But perhaps the State must satisfy some wants because these
wants are "collective" rather than "individual"? This is Baumol's
second line of attack. In the first place, Molinari has shown that
the existence of collective wants does not necessarily imply State
action. But, furthermore, the very concept of "collective" wants is
a dubious one. For this concept must imply the existence of some
existent collective entity who does the wanting! Baumol struggles
against conceding this, but he struggles in vain. The necessity for
assuming such an entity is made clear in Haavelmo's discussion of
"collective action," cited favorably by Baumol. Thus, Haavelmo
grants that deciding on collective action "requires a way of thinking

[71] Galbraith, in effect, does make such an assumption, but obviously without
adequate basis. Cf. John K. Galbraith, *Economics and the Art of Controversy* (Cambridge, 1954), pp. 77-78.

ON FREEDOM AND FREE ENTERPRISE

and a power to act which are outside the functional sphere of any individual group as such." [72]

Baumol attempts to deny the necessity for assuming a collective entity by stating that some services can be financed only "jointly," and will serve many people jointly. Therefore, he argues that individuals on the market cannot provide these services. This is a curious position indeed. For all large-scale businesses are "jointly" financed with huge aggregations of capital, and they also serve many consumers, often jointly. No one maintains that private enterprise cannot supply steel or automobiles or insurance because they are "jointly" financed. As for joint consumption, in one sense no consumption can be joint, for only individuals exist and can satisfy their wants, and therefore everyone must consume separately. In another sense, almost all consumption is "joint." Baumol, for example, asserts that parks are an example of "collective wants" jointly consumed, since many individuals must consume them. Therefore, the government must supply this service. But going to a theater is even more joint, for all must go at the same time. Must all theaters therefore be nationalized and run by the government? Furthermore, in a broad view, all modern consumption depends on mass production methods for a wide market. There are no grounds by which Baumol can separate certain services and dub them "examples of interdependence" or "external economies." What individuals could buy steel or automobiles or frozen foods, or almost anything else, if enough other individuals did not exist to demand them and make their mass-production methods worth while? Baumollian interdependencies are all around us, and there is no rational way to isolate a few services and call them "collective."

A common argument related to, though more plausible than, Baumol's thesis is that certain services are so vital to the very existence of the market that they must be supplied collectively outside the market. These services (protection, transportation, etc.) are so basic, it is alleged, that they permeate market affairs and are a prior necessary condition for its existence. But this argument proves far too much. It was the fallacy of the classical economists that they considered goods in terms of large *classes*, rather than in terms of *marginal units*. All actions on the market are marginal, and this is precisely the reason that valuation, and imputation of value-pro-

---

[72] Haavelmo, *loc. cit.* Yves Simon, cited favorably by Rothenberg, is even more explicit, postulating a "public reason" and a "public will," as contrasted to individual reasonings and wills. Cf. Yves Simon, *Philosophy of Democratic Government* (Chicago, 1951); Rothenberg, "Conditions," *loc. cit.*, pp. 402-03.

THE ECONOMICS OF FREE ENTERPRISE   259

ductivity to factors, can be effected. If we start dealing with whole
classes rather than marginal units, we can discover all sorts of activities which are necessary prerequisites of, and vital to, all market
activity; land room, food, clothing, shelter, power, etc.—and even
paper! Must all of these be supplied by the State and the State
only?

Stripped of its many fallacies, the whole "collective wants" thesis
boils down to this: certain people on the market will receive benefits
from the action of others without paying for them.[73] This is the
long and short of the criticism of the market, and this is the only
relevant "external economy" problem.[74] A and B decide to pay for
the building of a dam for their uses; C benefits though he did not
pay. A and B educate themselves at their expense and C benefits
by being able to deal with educated people, etc. This is the problem
of the Free Rider. Yet it is difficult to understand what the hulla-
baloo is all about. Am I to be specially taxed because I enjoy the
sight of my neighbor's garden without paying for it? A's and B's
purchase of a good reveals that *they* are willing to pay for it; if it
indirectly benefits C as well, no one is the loser. If C feels that he
would be deprived of the benefit if only A and B paid, then he is
free to contribute too. In any case, all the individuals consult their
own preferences in the matter.

In fact, we are *all* free riders on the investment, and the technological development, of our ancestors. Must we wear sackcloth and
ashes, or submit ourselves to State dictation, because of this happy
fact?

Baumol and others who agree with him are highly inconsistent.
On the one hand, action cannot be left up to voluntary individual
choice because the wicked free rider might shirk and obtain benefits
without payment. On the other hand, individuals are often de-
nounced because people will not *do enough* to benefit free riders.
Thus, Baumol criticizes investors for not violating their own time-
preferences and investing more generously. Surely, the sensible
course is neither to penalize the free rider nor to grant him special

---

[73] Cf. the critique of a similar position of Spencer's by "S.R.", "Spencer As His
Own Critic," *Liberty*, June 1904.

[74] The famous "external diseconomy" problems (noise, smoke nuisance, fishing,
etc.) are really in an entirely different category, as Mises has shown. These "problems" are due to insufficient defense of private property against invasion. Rather
than a defect of the free market, therefore, they are the results of invasions of
property, invasions which are ruled out of the free market by definition. Cf. Mises,
Human Action, op. cit., pp. 650-56.

ON FREEDOM AND FREE ENTERPRISE

privilege. This would also be the only solution consistent with the unanimity rule and demonstrated preference.[75]

Insofar as the "collective want" thesis is not the problem of the Free Rider, it is simply an ethical attack on individual valuations, and a desire by the economist (stepping into the role of an ethicist) to substitute his valuations for those of other individuals in deciding the *latter's* actions. This becomes clear in the assertion by Suranyi-Unger; "he (an individual) may be led by a niggardly or thoughtless or frivolous evaluation of utility and disutility and by a correspondingly low degree or complete absence of group responsibility."[76]

Tibor Scitovsky, while engaging in an analysis similar to Baumol's, also advances another objection to the free market based on what he calls "pecuniary external economies."[77] Briefly, this conception suffers from the common error of confusing the general (and unattainable!) equilibrium of the evenly rotating economy with an ethical "ideal," and therefore belaboring such ever-present phenomena as the existence of profits as departures from such an ideal.

Finally, we must mention the very recent attempts of Professor Buchanan to designate the State as a voluntary institution.[78] Buchanan's thesis is based on the curious dialectic that majority rule in a democracy is really unanimity because majorities can and do always shift! The resulting pulling and hauling of the political process, because obviously not irreversible, are therefore supposed to yield a social unanimity. The doctrine that endless political conflict and stalemate really amount to a mysterious social unanimity must be set down as a lapse into a type of Hegelian mysticism.[79]

[75] In a good, though limited, criticism of Baumol, Reder points out that Baumol completely neglects voluntary social organizations formed by individuals, for he assumes the State to be the only social organization. This error may stem partly from Baumol's peculiar definition of "individualistic" as meaning a situation where no one considers the effects of his actions on anyone else. Cf. Melvin W. Reder, "Review of Baumol's *Welfare Economics and the Theory of the State*," *Journal of Political Economy*, December 1953, p. 539.

[76] Theo Suranyi-Unger, "Individual and Collective Wants," *Journal of Political Economy*, February 1948, pp. 1-22. Suranyi-Unger also employs such meaningless concepts as the "aggregate utility" of the "collectivized want satisfaction."

[77] Tibor Scitovsky, "Two Concepts of External Economies," *Journal of Political Economy*, April 1954, pp. 144-51.

[78] Cf. James M. Buchanan, "Social Choice, Democracy, and Free Markets," *Journal of Political Economy*, April 1954, pp. 114-23; and *id.*, "Individual Choice in Voting and the Market," *ibid.*, August 1954, pp. 334-43. In many other respects, Buchanan's articles are quite good.

[79] How flimsy this "unanimity" is, even for Buchanan, is illustrated by the following very sensible passage: "a dollar vote is never overruled; the individual is never placed in the position of being a member of dissenting minority"—as he is in the voting process. Buchanan, "Individual Choice," *loc. cit.*, p. 339. Buchanan's ap-

THE ECONOMICS OF FREE ENTERPRISE   261

VI. *Conclusion*

In his brilliant survey of contemporary economics, Professor Bronfenbrenner described the present state of economic science in the
gloomiest possible terms.[80] "Wilderness" and "hash" were typical
epithets, and Bronfenbrenner ended his article in despair by quoting the famous poem *Ozymandias*. Applied to currently fashionable
theory, his attitude is justified. The 1930's was a period of eager
activity and seemingly pathbreaking advances in economic thought.
Yet one by one, reaction and attenuation have set in, and in the
mid-1950's the high hopes of twenty years ago are either dying or
fighting desperate rearguard action. None of the formerly new approaches any longer inspire fresh theoretical contributions. Bronfenbrenner specifically mentions in this connection the imperfect
competition and the Keynesian theories, and justly so. He could
also have mentioned utility and welfare theory. For the mid-1930's
saw the development of the Hicks-Allen indifference curve analysis,
and the New Welfare Economics. Both of these theoretical revolutions have been enormously popular in the upper reaches of economic theory; and both are now crumbling.

The contention of this paper is that while the formerly revolu-
tionary and latei orthodox theories of utility and welfare deserve
an even speedier burial then they have been receiving, they need
not be followed by a theoretical vacuum. The tool of Demonstrated
Preference, in which economics deals only with preference as demonstrated by real action, combined with a strict Unanimity Rule
for assertions of social utility, can serve to effect a thoroughgoing
reconstruction of utility and welfare economics. Utility theory
can finally be established as a theory of ordinal marginal utility.
And welfare economics can become a vital *corpus* again, even
though its new personality might not attract its previous creators.
It must not be thought that we have, in our discussion of welfare
economics, been attempting to set forth any ethical or political program. On the contrary, the proposed welfare economics has been
put forward without inserting ethical judgments. Economics by
itself and standing alone cannot establish an ethical system, and we
must grant this regardless of what philosophy of ethics we hold.
The fact that the free market maximizes social utility, or that State
action cannot be considered voluntary, or that the *laissez-faire*

---

proach leads him so far as to make a positive virtue out of inconsistency and indeci-
sion in political choices.

[80] Bronfenbrenner, *loc. cit.*

ON FREEDOM AND FREE ENTERPRISE

economists were better welfare analysts than they are given credit for, in itself implies no plea for *laissez-faire* or for any other social system. What welfare economics does is to present these conclusions to the framer of ethical judgments as part of the data for his ethical system. To the person who scorns social utility or admires coercion, our analysis might furnish powerful arguments for a policy of thoroughgoing Statism.

Austrian Economics Newsletter

Winter 1988 • The Ludwig von Mises Institute

The Justice of Economic Efficiency

by
Hans-Hermann Hoppe

Professor Hans-Hermann Hoppe

The central problem of political economy is how to organize society so as to promote the production of wealth. The central problem of political philosophy is how to arrange society so as to make it a just social order.

The first question is a question regarding matters of efficiency: what means are appropriate for achieving a specific result--in this case: wealth.

The second question falls outside the realm of the so-called positive sciences. It asks whether or not the goal which political economy assumes to be given can be justified as a goal, and whether or not, then, the means which political economy recommends can be regarded as efficient means for just ends.

In the following I will present an *a priori* justification for the thesis that those means recommended by political economy are indeed efficient means for just ends.

I will begin by describing the means recommended by political economy and explain systematically all the production of wealth attained by adopting them is greater than that produced by choosing any other means. Since my main task is to demonstrate the justice of these means of producing wealth, my description and explanation of economic efficiency will be extremely brief.

Political economy begins by recognizing scarcity. It is only because we do not live in the Garden of Eden that we are concerned about the problem of economic efficiency. According to political economy, the most efficient means of at least alleviating, if not overcoming, scarcity is the institution of private property. The rules underlying this institution have been correctly identified for the most part by John Locke. They are as follows: Every person owns his own body as well as all scarce goods which he puts to use with the help of his body before anyone else does. This ownership implies the right to employ these scarce goods however one sees fit so long as in so doing one does not aggress against anyone else's property, i.e., so long as one does not uninvitedly change the physical integrity of another's property or delimits another's control over it without his consent. In particular, once a good has first been appropriated or homesteaded by mixing one's labor with it--this being Locke's phrase--then ownership in it can only be acquired by means of a contractual transfer of property title from a previous to a later owner.

The reasons this institution leads to the greatest possible production of wealth is straightforward: Any deviation from this set of rules implies, by definition, a redistribution of property titles, and hence of income, away from user-producers and contractors of goods and onto non-user-producers and non-contractors. As a consequence, any such deviation implies that there will be relatively less original appropriation of resources whose scarcity is realized, there will be less production of new goods, less maintenance of existing goods, and less mutually beneficial contracting and trading. And this naturally implies a lower standard of living in terms of exchangeable goods and services. Further, the provision that only the first user (not a later one) of a good acquires ownership assures that productive efforts will be as high as possible *at all times*. And the provision that only the physical integrity of property (not property values) be protected guarantees that every owner will undertake the greatest possible *value*-productive efforts, i.e., efforts to promote favorable changes in property values and also to prevent or counter any

(Continued on page 2)

unfavorable changes in property values (as they might result from another person's actions regarding his property). Thus, any deviation from these rules also implies reduced levels of value productive efforts at all times.

Now on to my main task of demonstrating that the institution of private property as just characterized is just. In fact, that only this institution is just and that any deviation from it is not only economically inefficient but unethical as well.

First, however, let me clarify an essential similarity between the problem facing political economy and that facing political philosophy--a similarity that political philosophers in their widespread ignorance of economics generally overlook only to wind up in endless *ad hoceries*. The recognition of scarcity is not only the starting point for political economy; it is the starting point of political philosophy as well. Obviously, if there were a superabundance of goods, no economic problem whatsoever could exist. And with a superabundance of goods such that my present use of them would neither reduce my own future supply, nor the present or future supply of them for any other person, ethical problems of right or wrong, just or unjust, would not emerge either, since no conflict over the use of such goods could possibly arise. Only insofar as goods are scarce, then, are economics and ethics required. And in the same way, just as the answer to the problem of political economy must be formulated in terms of rules constraining the possible uses of resources qua scarce resources, political philosophy, too, must answer in terms of property rights. In order to avoid inescapable conflicts, it must formulate a set of rules assigning rights of exclusive control over scarce goods. (Note, by the way, that even in the Garden of Eden, a person's body, the space occupied by that body, and time would still be scarce and to that extent political economy and philosophy would still have some--however limited--task to fulfill.)

Now to the actual proof of the thesis that out of the infinitely conceivable ways of assigning rights of exclusive ownership to people, only the previously described rules of private property are actually justifiable. I will present my argument in a step-by-step fashion:

(1) First, while scarcity is a necessary condition for the emergence of the problem of political philosophy, it is not sufficient. For obviously, we could have conflicts regarding the use of scarce resources with, let us say, an elephant or a mosquito, and yet we would not consider it possible to resolve these conflicts by means of proposing property norms. The avoidance of possible conflicts, in such cases, is merely a technological, not an ethical problem. For it to turn into an ethical problem, it is also necessary that the conflicting actors be capable, in principle, of argumentation. In fact, this is undeniably so because we are also engaged in argumentation here. Denying that political philosophy presupposes argumentation is contradictory, as the very denial would itself be an argument. Only with argumentation does the idea of validity and truth--and by no means only the idea of truth in ethical matters but of truth in general--emerge. Only within argumentation are truth claims of any kind made; and it is only in the course of an argumentation that truth claims are decided upon. And this proposition, it turns out, is itself undeniably true: one cannot argue that one cannot argue; and

one cannot dispute knowing what it means to make a truth claim without implicitly claiming at least the very negation of this proposition to be true. My very first step in the following chain of reasoning, then, has been called "the *a priori* of argumentation" by such philosophers as Juergen Habermas and K.O. Apel.[1]

(2) In the same way as it is undeniably true that ethics requires argumentation, it is also undeniably true that any argument requires an arguing person. Arguing does not consist of free-floating propositions. It is an activity. But if aside from whatever is said in its course, argumentation is also a practical affair, and if argumentation is the presupposition of truth-claiming and possibly true propositions, then it follows that intersubjectively meaningful norms must exist--namely those which make an action an argumentation--which must have a special cognitive status in that they are the practical preconditions of truth. And once more, this is true *a priori*, so that anyone, like an empiricist-positivist-emotivist, who denied the possibility of a rational ethics and who declared the acceptance or rejection of norms an arbitrary affair, would invariably get caught in a practical contradiction. For, contrary to what he would say, he would in fact have to presuppose the norms which underlay any argumentation whatsoever as valid simply in order to say anything at all.

(3) With this step I lose, once and for all, the company of philosophers like Habermas and Apel.[2] And yet, as will become clear immediately, it is directly implied in the previous step. That Habermas and Apel are unable to take this step, I submit, is due to the fact that they, too, suffer, as do many other philosophers, from a complete ignorance of economics, and a corresponding blindness towards the fact of scarcity. The step is simply this: To recognize that argumentation is a form of action and does not consist of free-floating sounds, implies the recognition of the fact that any argumentation whatsoever requires that a person must have exclusive control over the scarce resource of his body. As long as there is argumentation, there is a mutual recognition of each other's property right in his own body. It is this recognition of each other's exclusive control over one's own body, presupposed by any argumentation, which explains the unique feature of verbal communication that, while one may disagree about what has been said, it is still possible to agree at least on the fact that there is such disagreement. And again, such a property right in one's own body must be said to be justified *a priori*: for anyone who would try to justify any norm whatsoever would already have to presuppose an exclusive right to control over his body as a valid norm simply in order to say "I propose such and such." And any person who would try to dispute the property right in his body would become caught up in a practical contradiction, since arguing in this way would already implicitly have to accept the very norm which he was disputing. He would not even open his mouth if he were right.

(4) The final argument extends the idea of private property as justified, and justified *a priori*, from the very prototype of a scarce good, i.e. a person's body, to other goods. It consists of two parts. I will first demonstrate that argumentation, and argumentative justification of anything, presupposes not only the right to exclusively control one's body but the right to control other scarce goods as well. For if no one had the

right to control anything except his own body, then we would all cease to exist and the problem of justifying norms--as well as all other human problems--simply would not exist. We do not live on air alone, and hence, simply by virtue of the fact of being alive, property rights to other things must be presupposed to be valid, too. No one who is alive could argue otherwise.

The second part of the argument demonstrates that only the Lockean idea of establishing property claims through homesteading is a just principle of property acquisition. The proof employs a simple *argumentum a contrario:* If a person did not acquire the right of exclusive control over other, nature-given goods by his own work, that is, if other people, who had not previously used such goods, had the right to dispute the homesteader's ownership claim, then this would only be possible if one would acquire property titles not through labor, i.e., by establishing some objective link between a particular person and a particular scarce resource, but simply by means of verbal declaration. Yet this solution--apart from the obvious fact that it would not even qualify as a solution in a purely technical sense in that it would not provide a basis for deciding between rivaling declarative claims--is incompatible with the already justified ownership of a person over his body. For if one could indeed appropriate property by decree, this would imply that it would also be possible for one to simply declare another person's body to be one's own. Yet, as we have already seen, to say that property is acquired not through homesteading action but through declaration involves a practical contradiction: nobody could say and declare anything, unless his right to use his body was already assumed to be valid simply because of the very fact that regardless of what he said, it was he, and nobody else, who had homesteaded it as his instrument of saying anything.

With this, my *a priori* justification of the institution of private property is essentially complete. Only two supplementary arguments may be needed in order to point out why and where all other ethical proposals, let me call them socialist, turn out to be argumentatively indefensible.

(1) According to the private property ethics, scarce resources that are under the exclusive control of their owners are defined in physical terms, and, *mutatis mutandis,* aggression is also defined as an invasion of the physical integrity of another person's property. As indicated, the economic effect of this provision is that of maximizing value productive efforts. A popular deviation from this is the idea of defining aggression as an invasion of the value or psychic integrity of another person's property instead. This idea underlies, for instance, John Rawls' "difference principle" that all inequalities have to be expected to be to everyone's advantage regardless of how such inequalities have come about;[3] and also Robert Nozick's claim that a "dominant protection agency" has the right to outlaw competitors regardless of their actual actions, and his related claim that "non-productive exchanges" in which one party would be better off if the other one did not exist may be outlawed, again regardless of whether or not such exchange involved any physical aggression.[4]

Such proposals are absurd as well as indefensible. While every person can have control over whether or not his actions cause the physical integrity of something to change, control over whether or not one's actions affect the value of someone's property to change rests with other people and their evaluations. One would have to interrogate and come to an agreement with the entire world population to make sure that one's planned actions would not change another person's evaluations regarding his property. Everyone would be long dead before this was even accomplished. Moreover, the idea that property value should be protected is argumentatively indefensible: For even in order to argue, it must be presupposed that actions must be allowed prior to any actual agreement, because if they were not, one could not even argue so. Yet if one can, then this is only possible because of objective borders of property, i.e., borders which every person can recognize as such on his own, without having to agree first with anyone else with respect to one's system of values and evaluations. Rawls and Nozick could not even open their mouths if it were otherwise. The very fact, then, that they do open them proves what they say is wrong.

(2) The second popular deviation, equally absurd and indefensible, is this: Instead of recognizing the vital importance of the prior-later distinction in deciding between conflicting property claims--as the private property ethics do, thereby, as indicated, assuring value productive efforts to be as high as possible at all times--the claim is made, in essence, that priority is irrelevant and that late-comers have rights to ownership just as first comers. Again, Rawls with his belief in the rights of future generations, just savings rates and such things, may be cited as an example. However, if late-comers indeed had legitimate ownership claims to things, then literally no one would be allowed to do anything with anything as one would have to have all of the later-comers' consent prior to ever doing what one wanted to do. Neither we, our forefathers, nor our progeny could, do or will survive if one were to follow this rule. Yet in order for any person--past, present, or future--to argue anything it must evidently be possible to survive then and now. And in order to do just this--and even people behind a Rawlsian "veil of ignorance" would have to be able to survive--property rights cannot be conceived of as being timeless and non-specific regarding the number of people concerned. Rather, they must necessarily be thought of as originating through acting at specific points in time for specific acting individuals. Otherwise, it would be impossible for anyone to first say anything at a definite point in time and for someone else to be able to reply. Simply saying, then, that the prior-later distinction can be ignored, implies a contradiction, as one's being able to say so must presuppose one's existence as an independent decision-making unit at a given point in time.

Hence, I conclude that any socialist ethic is a complete failure. Only the institution of private property, which also assures the greatest possible production of wealth, can be argumentatively justified, because it is the very precondition of argumentation.

Notes

1) K.O. Apel, "Das Apriori der Kommunikationsgemeinschaft und die Grundlagen der Ethik," in: the same, *Transformation der Philosophie,* Vol. II, Frankfurt/M. 1973; Juergen Habermas, *Moralbewusstsein und Kommunikatives Handeln,* Frankfurt/M. 1983.

3

2)Apel and Habermas are essentially silent on the all-decisive question of what ethical prescription actually follows from the recognition of the "*a priori* of argumentation." However, there are remarks indicating that they both seem to believe some sort of participatory social democracy to be implied in this *a priori*. The following explains why hardly anything could be farther from the truth.

3)John Rawls, *A Theory of Justice*, Cambridge 1971, p. 60, pp. 75f, p. 83.

4)Robert Nozick, *Anarchy, State and Utopia*, New York 1974, pp. 55f, pp. 83-86.

Hans-Hermann Hoppe is associate professor of economics at the University of Nevada, Las Vegas, and a senior fellow of the Mises Institute. ∎

[26]

LAW AMID FLUX: THE ECONOMICS OF NEGLIGENCE AND STRICT LIABILITY IN TORT

*MARIO J. RIZZO**

THE economic efficiency approach to the analysis of the common law, particularly the law of torts, has been growing rapidly in recent years and shows no sign of abatement. Nevertheless, some very fundamental analytic problems have not even been recognized in this literature, much less solved. It is the purpose of this essay to raise these problems in the context of the perennial conflict between negligence and strict liability. The first and major part of this paper will consist of a detailed study of the efficiency rationale for negligence law. Next, we shall analyze some of the economic aspects of a system of strict liability. The overall conclusion is that efficiency, as normally understood, is impossible as a goal for tort law. The law cannot and should not aim toward the impossible. Consequently, both the normative and positive justifications for the efficiency approach to tort law must be rejected. Our reasons for this conclusion can be divided into static and dynamic considerations. The most important by far, however, are the dynamic factors: Precisely because we live outside of general competitive equilibrium and in a world of unpredictable flux, the efficiency case for negligence must fail. In such a world, it is impossible to compare alternative liability systems in terms of judicial cost-benefit analysis or "fine tuning." Instead, they must be analyzed in terms of institutional efficiency—the certainty and stability that these rules impart to the social framework. A static world of general equilibrium would make an efficient tort law possible, and yet render it unnecessary; in such a world, markets would be universal. A dynamic world, however, demands the certainty and simplicity of static law.

* Assistant Professor of Economics, New York University. I am indebted to the Institute for Humane Studies and the Scaife Foundation for financial support of my research. I am also indebted to Michael Becker, Richard Epstein, William Landes, Richard Posner, and Paul Rubin for comments on previous versions. Responsibility for errors remains mine alone.

VI. Institutional Efficiency of Strict Liability

If we are correct in the central thesis of this paper that efficiency in the form of judicial cost-benefit analysis represents an impossible *raison d'être* for the law of torts, then it would seem that, *even on economic grounds,* a system of strict liability is to be preferred to one of negligence. In a dynamic world in which the uncertainties of technological change, the ambiguities of foreseeability, and the absence of a unique objective measure of social cost all conspire to make the efficiency paradigm a delusion, the importance of certainty in the legal order is clear. Strict liability obviates or minimizes the need for courts to grapple, if only implicitly, with such impossibly elusive problems as foreseeability, cheaper-cost avoider, social cost, and second best. It provides a series of basically simple, strict presumptions. The *prima facie* case is based on straightforward commonsense causal paradigms, whereas the defenses and later pleas minimize the number of issues which must be considered in a given case.

Having said farewell to the fleeting and sometimes superficial guesses about efficiency and having adopted the simple static framework of strict liability, we should find that there is considerably greater certainty about the locus of responsibility in accidents. This greater certainty promotes efficiency in the basic institutional sense because property rights, in effect, become more clearly or definitely defined.

It has been suggested, however, that the simplicity of strict liability may also be its undoing. While admitting that strict liability would simplify "the issues in a trial" and remove "an element of uncertainty," Richard Posner believes that it would increase "the scope of liability" and, hence, the absolute number of claims might rise.[83] It is a fundamental mistake to believe that strict liability would necessarily increase the scope of liability. The following example should make this clear. Consider:

1. A created a dangerous condition on his land that resulted in harm to B (*prima facie* case).
2. B entered on A's land (defense).

Unless B has a good reply (for example, A gave his permission or A compelled B to enter), the case is closed without any examination of the "reasonableness" of A's behavior: B cannot recover. The scope of liability is in these circumstances decreased, not increased. The primary effect of strict liability is to change both the instances and the rationale for liability. In addition, by simplifying the grounds on which cases are decided, the parties to a dispute are more likely to agree on the probabilities of the outcome. This

---

[83] Richard A. Posner, Strict Liability: A Comment, 2 J. Legal Stud. 205, 209 (1973).

will ensure less litigation and more out-of-court settlements.[84] Administrative costs will, therefore, be lower.

A more formal analysis of the certainty-enhancing aspects of strict liability would undoubtedly be worthwhile. Yet it already seems clear that since the "fine-tuning" paradigm is a mere delusion, the only basis on which the "efficiency" of systems can be compared is on a fundamental institutional level. The *central* question is then: which legal framework provides a more stable environment for individuals to pursue their own ends in harmony with each other? Ironically, it is precisely because we live in a dynamic world where the information needed by the "fine-tuners" is not available that the answer must be the antiquated and static system of strict liability.

[84] See Landes & Posner, *supra* note 6, at 272.

[27]

RULES VERSUS COST-BENEFIT ANALYSIS IN THE COMMON LAW

Mario J. Rizzo

> When they speak so resonantly of "public policy," do lawyers have the slightest idea what they're talking about?
>
> —B. A. Ackerman[1]

I. Introduction

The relation between economic liberty and the judiciary is far broader than that evident from those areas of law that are explicitly concerned with policy. Everyone recognizes this interrelation in antitrust, securities regulation, environmental policy, labor law, and countless other areas. In each of these it is universally accepted that as long as we have law it must be based on specific policy goals. The idea of economic legislation that is policy-neutral is a contradiction in terms. In the 20th century this emphasis on policy considerations has spread to all areas of the law including the classic common law fields (Prosser and Keeton 1984, pp. 15–20). Economic policy factors (as well as other forms of policy) are said to be relevant to the formulation of society's contract, property, and tort rules. The fundamental purpose of this paper is to demonstrate that this need not be the case. The common law, that is, judge-made private law, can be policy neutral in the sense that it need not impose a specific hierarchy of values on society. It can restrict itself to the provision of abstract rules that enhance the possibilities of an order in which individuals can pursue and attain their own goals. In other words, the purpose

---

Cato Journal, Vol. 4, No. 3 (Winter 1985). Copyright © Cato Institute. All rights reserved.

The author is Associate Professor of Economics at New York University. He wishes to thank the Earhart Foundation and the Sarah Scaife Foundation for financial support in preparing this paper. He also acknowledges the Civil Liability Program at the Yale Law School for providing him with a congenial atmosphere during the spring of 1984 in which to think about the issues discussed in this paper.

[1]Ackerman (1984, p. 22).

of this paper is to show that we can eliminate, or at least drastically reduce, consideration of specific public policy questions even in those areas where we must have law. The judiciary can promote economic and other forms of liberty by returning to the classic common law adherence to abstract rules and eschewing the now-fashionable balancing of economic or social interests.

The remainder of this paper is organized as follows. In Section II we argue that there is a lack of appreciation of the principle of spontaneous order among many economists and most legal theorists. This principle is central to understanding the nature of a policy-neutral legal system. In Section III we show that the function of the pure common law is to promote such a spontaneous order of individual actions. Section IV demonstrates that the common law is itself a spontaneous order that is not the result of conscious direction.[2] Section V elucidates the concept of an abstract or general rule by contrasting it with the idea of interest balancing. Section VI illustrates the tension between rules and balancing in the law of negligence, while Section VII demonstrates the superior rule-orientation of strict liability in tort. In Section VIII, we offer a brief discussion of a recent and important explanation for the decline in the common law's emphasis on rules, and in Section IX, we present some concluding remarks.

II. Decline of Spontaneous Order in Economics and Law

The concept of spontaneous order is a general principle of social organization that once commanded widespread recognition in economics and significant adherence in legal theory. In economics it has been best known in the form of Adam Smith's "invisible hand." The system of natural liberty—the free interaction of individual producers, merchants, and consumers—would tend to yield socially beneficial outcomes, as if by an invisible hand. During most of the 20th century, however, the principle of spontaneous order has been out of favor with the majority of the economics profession.

In recent years there has been a revival of interest in spontaneous ordering forces, but most economists still remain skeptical. Among general equilibrium theorists, especially, these forces have been given an interpretation that renders the principle entirely useless. Frank Hahn, for example, identifies the invisible hand with the

---

[2]Sections II and III draw heavily on, and in some respects expand, the seminal work of F. A. Hayek (1973, 1976, 1979).

The Common Law

formal model of general equilibrium developed by Kenneth Arrow and Gerard Debreu (Hahn 1973, p. 324):

> When the claim is made—and the claim is as old as Adam Smith—that a myriad of self-seeking agents left to themselves will lead to a coherent and efficient disposition of economic resources, Arrow and Debreu show what the world would have to look like if this claim is to be true. *In doing this they provide the most potent avenue of falsification of the claims* [emphasis added].

The Arrow-Debreu general equilibrium construct is based on extremely stringent assumptions: perfect information and foresight, complete futures markets, perfect divisibility, and a host of other technical requirements. When these assumptions are met, it can be shown that an unregulated system results in a Pareto-efficient allocation of resources. In the real world, however, the assumptions are not even remotely satisfied, and hence an "efficient" disposition of resources is not possible. Thus, argues Hahn, the claims of Adam Smith and other spontaneous order theorists must be false, because the necessary conditions for the realization of these claims are absent.[3] Hahn's argument is held together, though, by a weak logical link: the identification of the principle of spontaneous order with the Arrow-Debreu formal construct. On the contrary, the principle has little to do with and is far broader than its general equilibrium representation. The lesson to be drawn from Hahn's remarks is not the illusory character of the spontaneous order principle, but rather the intellectual aridity of the general equilibrium style of thought (Coddington 1975; Demsetz 1969).

The concept of spontaneous order has never dominated legal theorizing to the extent it once dominated economics. Even so staunch an advocate of economic liberty as Jeremy Bentham thought of law solely in terms of conscious design. Law, for Bentham, was "a command issuing from the requisite source" (Bentham 1973a, p. 155) or, more specifically, "the will of the sovereign in a state" (Bentham 1973b, p. 157). In modern times the Benthamite banner was held, although in far more sophisticated fashion, by the great legal realist Roscoe Pound. Pound thought of law as an instrument for the satisfaction of specific human desires and for the rational balancing of those desires when they conflict. He believed that the instrumental character of law could be more perfectly attained "if we have a clear picture before us of what we are seeking to do and to what end" and

---

[3]Hahn is guilty of a logical error. The assumptions of the Arrow-Debreu construction are merely sufficient conditions for an efficient allocation of resources (Hausman 1981, p. 152). The absence of these conditions does not imply inefficient resource allocation.

insofar "as we consciously build and shape the law" (Pound 1954, p. 45). Pound saw the entire history of law as a gradual unfolding of this vision (p. 47):

> For present purposes I am content to see in legal history the record of a continually wider recognizing and satisfying of human wants or claims or desires through social control: a more embracing and more effective securing of social interests; a continually more complete and effective elimination of waste and precluding of friction in human enjoyment of the goods of existence—in short, a continually more efficacious social engineering.

F. A. Hayek, on the other hand, has seen the development of the law as a manifestation of spontaneous ordering forces. For Hayek the idea of consciously building and shaping law completely misconstrues the nature of the common law process (however accurately it may describe administrative law). The common law is a system that is grown or evolved, not a system that is made. It is an order quite unlike the changeless equilibrium of Arrow and Debreu or the system of conscious compromises produced by Pound's realist judges. The common law is a dynamic order that allows for and even promotes change. It is also an abstract order that is unbound by the specific value hierarchies or compromises of its judges. The purpose of the law is to promote "that abstract order of the whole which does not aim at the achievement of known particular results but is preserved as a means for assisting in the pursuit of a great variety of individual purposes" (Hayek 1976, p. 5).

Hayek applies the principle of spontaneous order to the legal system in two different but interrelated ways. First, he uses it to explain the function of a pure common law system; second, he uses it to elucidate the process by which that system grows or adapts to change. There is thus both a functional and dynamic aspect to Hayek's theory, and each aspect is necessary for understanding his concept of a legal rule. These aspects of the spontaneous order approach are explored in the following two sections.

III. Function of the Common Law

Authority and Legitimacy of the Common Law

Hayek's fundamental model of the common law is one of purely private rule creation. The law and the courts are not creations of the sovereign but rather are evolved institutions within which all individuals, including the sovereign, must operate. The common law antedates legislation, and it draws on preexisting implicit societal rules or customs, as well as on previous judicial decisions (Hayek

THE COMMON LAW

1973, p. 72). It is by deference to this preexisting opinion that the common law judge can lay claim to authority and legitimacy. People respect his judgments because, in part, they see in those judgments the crystallization of commonly held moral views.

The legitimacy of the law is also enhanced by the abstract character of the rules that the judges draw upon and that is manifest in their opinions. A defendant is not subject to a particular judgment because of his personality or individual circumstances, but because his conduct belongs to a certain general class that is deemed legally relevant. Jones, for example, may be prima facie liable to Smith for the latter's injuries because Jones hit Smith, and thus his behavior is subsumed into a general class of causal relationships, *A* hit *B* (Epstein 1973, pp. 166–71). All who act in this way—not only Jones—are subject to liability. On the basis of their perception of the general rule, people grow to expect a certain outcome in a particular class of cases. These expectations are then reinforced by the continual application and reinforcement of the rule in future cases (Hayek 1973, p. 98).

Nature of the Order

Because the common law is abstract (that is, in all cases of a given type, independent of particulars, a certain consequence follows), it gives rise to expectations that are similarly abstract. Suppose we say that valid contracts require consideration. This rule does not assist us in predicting the specific content of future contractual relationships. It does, however, help us in forming reasonable expectations about the overall character of these relationships. By voluntarily complying or failing to comply with this and other contractual rules, an individual can widen or narrow the range of his protected domain. Inasmuch as he validly contracts, his claims on others become, as it were, an extended "property right" (just as their claims on him become part of their extended property rights).

The order thus engendered by common law rules is an abstract order, one in which only general features of individual interaction are constant through time. The abstract order of expectations consequently enhances, but does not guarantee, the coordination of individual plans. Or, to put matters another way, the order coordinates the *pattern* of plans and activities, rather than the particulars of those plans and activities (O'Driscoll and Rizzo 1985, chap. 5).

An abstract order ensures certain expectations, but permits others to be disappointed. Individuals may (forward) contract today for 1986 soybeans in the hope that the spot price at that future time will be higher than the contract price. The common law does not seek to ensure anyone's expectations about the future price of soybeans.

"The task of rules of just conduct can . . . only be to tell people which expectations they can count on and which not" (Hayek 1973, p. 102).

Even if it were in some sense desirable to ensure all expectations, it would be impossible to do so. The necessary condition for the fulfillment of some expectations is the disappointment of others (Hayek 1973, p. 103). For example, we could not be continually supplied with the products we want (and expect) if producers refused or could not change their behavior in the light of new circumstances. It might even be physically impossible for them to continue as before if resource constraints significantly change. Paradoxically, change of the particulars within an abstract order is vital to the maintenance of that order. "It will only be through unforeseeable changes in the particulars that a high degree of predictability of the overall results can be achieved" (Hayek 1973, p. 104). For Hayek, then, uncertainty with respect to certain features of our environment is necessary for certainty with respect to other features.

The most we can expect from a system of abstract rules is that, on balance, individuals will be able to pursue their own purposes more effectively within the system than outside of it. The role of the common law, therefore, is not to enshrine any particular hierarchy of specific ends, but rather to "maximize the fulfillment of expectations as a whole," and thus to promote the achievement of as many individual ends as possible (Hayek 1973, p. 103).[4] The pure common law system is "purposeless" and does not seek to achieve specific social goals or to balance them when they are in conflict.

IV. The Common Law Process

Hayek has both a micro and macro analysis of the common law process. The macro story, based on a Darwinian survival mechanism, is not extremely relevant to understanding those aspects of legal rules in which we are interested, and so we do not pursue it here.[5] The micro story, on the other hand, does shed considerable light on our subject by elucidating the judicial decision-making or reasoning process that gives rise to common law rules.

---

[4]In the second volume of *Law, Legislation and Liberty* Hayek clarifies somewhat this idea of maximizing the fulfillment of expectations. "A policy making use of spontaneously ordering forces . . . must aim at increasing, for any person picked out at random, the prospects that the effect of all changes required by that order will be to increase his chances of attaining his ends" (Hayek 1976, p. 114).

[5]Hayek argues that a society based on a system of abstract rules will prosper relative to those societies that do not rely on such ordering mechanisms (Hayek 1979, pp. 153–76).

THE COMMON LAW

The process or, perhaps more exactly, the method of arriving at decisions in a common law system does not rest on deduction from a closed and limited set of explicit premises. It is based instead on "trained intuition" that draws on the unarticulated rules of society and adapts the reasoning and results of previous cases (Hayek 1973, pp. 116–17). The common law judge makes decisions in new cases on the basis of analogies with earlier cases (Levi 1949) and with simpler hypothetical situations in which there is a clear right answer.

The process of common law reasoning has important implications for the nature and function of the rules it generates. To see this clearly, it is useful to trace the evolution of rules in a specific area of law. One important area that is currently undergoing significant change is that of negligent infliction of emotional distress.[6]

The doctrine that originally prevailed in the 19th century was the "impact rule." To recover for his emotional distress, the plaintiff also had to be physically injured by the defendant. Without such physical impact, no recovery was allowed. In time the courts began to interpret the impact requirement more and more liberally. Eventually, even the slightest physical contact could be construed as sufficient to allow recovery for emotional distress. This loosening of the impact requirement transformed it into what many felt was a meaningless formality. Still worse was the apparent injustice of permitting recovery for emotional distress to one who had been simply scratched and denying such recovery to one who had narrowly escaped being killed by a truck.

Consequently the impact rule gave way to the "zone of the physical danger" doctrine. Under this approach, if the plaintiff had been in danger of physical injury, he could recover for his emotional distress even if he escaped actual physical harm. The logic of the new rule, however, seemed to be that only emotional distress arising out of fear for one's *own* safety could be compensable. Suppose, for example, the plaintiff had been in a situation where he narrowly escaped physical injury and, at the same time, saw his children physically injured. Could he recover for fear of his *children's* safety? By the strict logic of the zone rule, he could not. The courts were then faced with the impossible task of apportioning the plaintiff's distress between the two sources: fear for his own safety and fear for that of his children. Most courts, of course, never even tried to do this. As a consequence it began to appear rather awkward for plaintiffs, who were themselves in the zone of danger, to recover for their distress over the safety of

[6]For a survey of the development of the law in this area see Epstein, Gregory, and Kalven (1984, pp. 1049–83).

others, while plaintiffs not in personal danger could not recover. The distress was, after all, the same in both cases. Accordingly, some states (for example, California, Hawaii, and Massachusetts) shifted to a broader "bystander rule." Mothers, fathers, and possibly other close relatives could now recover for the emotional distress suffered upon seeing their child or relative physically injured in an accident. In California the bystander rule requires that the plaintiff contemporaneously observe the accident, be physically close to it, and be a close relative of the person injured. As should be apparent, this rule also contains the seeds of its further development. How should the courts decide, under the bystander rule, a case in which the mother of a child happens on the scene of an auto accident three minutes after her child is killed? The image of a mother seeing her child in a pool of blood may provide ample "justification" for extending the rule to cases of "almost contemporaneous" observance.

Our story could go on, but doubtless the reader can now imagine possible extensions himself. The important point to appreciate is that analogous reasoning provides a dynamic whereby the law develops, changes, and adjusts. While the problem of recovery for emotional distress is extremely difficult and current developments may well be unfortunate, this brief doctrinal history is a vivid illustration of two important and related theoretical insights. The pure common law process is both incremental and purposeless. Observe that in none of the developments sketched above was there a sharp break with what had been the previous rule. The process of change is as close to a continuous development as one is likely to see in human affairs.

The purposelessness of the process, although somewhat more difficult to appreciate, is nonetheless the crucial element in our analysis. The current state of the law of emotional distress could not have been predicted or directed when the impact rule was the prevailing doctrine. There are two reasons for this (Hart 1977, p. 125). First, and primary, is the indeterminacy of judges' aims. Judges do not start out with a clear objective function to which they then fit the facts of each case. Instead, they reason by analogy or similarity with already decided cases. Second, due to our inability to predict future fact patterns, even if judges had tentative policy goals, they could not foresee the full consequences of any rule they might adopt. These consequences would obviously differ in different concrete situations and judges would be forced, at least in large part, to adhere to rules irrespective of their specific consequences in order to ensure the stability of the legal order. These two factors in effect guarantee that a common law system will tend to be dominated by what to outsiders must seem to be myopia. This "myopic" vision is really the working of the spontaneous order principle and a manifestation of the purposeless of the common law.

V. Rules versus Balancing

The abstract character of the common law is intimately related to the tension between rule-oriented methods and cost-benefit or balancing methods of resolving disputes. The more abstract a legal order is, the more heavily it depends on rules. Recall that the function of an abstract order is to maximize the fulfillment of individual expectations and plans rather than to impose upon society a particular hierarchy of ends. When the legal system engages in the balancing of interests or, equivalently, of social costs and benefits, it produces at best a particularistic order that supplants the ends sought by individuals with the ends desired by the courts. Rules, on the other hand, enable the legal system to adopt a more neutral position on the pursuit of private interests.

The need for rules is predicated on our ignorance (Hayek 1976, pp. 8–11). A utilitarian or balancing framework would require us to trace the full effects of each (tentative) judicial decision, and then evaluate it against the particular utilitarian standard adopted. It is, however, no mean feat to determine these effects in view of the substantial information problems and uncertainties likely to face a court (Hayek 1976, pp. 19–20; Rizzo 1980a, 1980b). There also are substantial interactive effects among decisions and rules that are often impossible to discern. Rules must therefore be applied in particular cases regardless of the hypothesized or "guessed-at" consequences. The very unpredictability of these consequences requires adherence to the given rule (Hayek 1976, pp. 16–17). If the law cannot systematically achieve specific social goals, then the best it can do is provide a stable order in which individuals are free to pursue their own goals. The unpredictability of a rule's effects in a concrete situation is the price we must pay so as to achieve predictability of the abstract order.

Much of the above discussion of rules versus balancing is couched in stark terms of contrast. This is because we are comparing, as it were, the ideal typical rule with ideal typical balancing. Admittedly, real-world legal systems simply tend to move in the one direction or the other. All legal doctrines are an admixture of rules and balancing. Both ideal types cannot be achieved in practice for what are surprisingly the same reasons. A thoroughgoing cost-benefit approach to law is impossible because, as we have seen, we are not always able to determine adequately the consequences of specific judgments.

Similarly, an unflinching rule-oriented approach will inevitably break down because unfamiliar factual situations will make the meaning of any previously announced rule unclear. At the same time, attempts to apply a rule rigidly to novel situations may appear patently unjust from the perspective of the more basic implicit (or unarticulated) rules that guide society. Thus the critical question concerns the direction in which the system tends—either toward more rules or more balancing.

VI. Negligence: Rules and Balancing

In this section and the following section, an analysis of two alternative theories of tort liability is used to illustrate the difference between a rule-oriented system and a system that rests on interest balancing. In the present section the tension between rules and balancing within a theory of negligence is explored; in the next section the analysis is extended to encompass the role of rules in a system based on strict liability. The purpose in both sections is to clarify the precise nature of an abstract legal order and the kind of rules it generates.

Negligence Congealed into Rules[7]

At its core the concept of negligence in tort is far more compatible with the balancing approach to dispute settlement than with the rule-oriented approach. Nevertheless, the late 19th century and early 20th century law and legal theory struggled to put reins on negligence liability. While notions of "due care" or "the care undertaken by the reasonable man" invite the weighing of costs and benefits according to some social calculus, many theorists were prone to interpret these generalities in ways that minimized discretion. As Oliver Wendell Holmes recognized, when "the elements are few and permanent, an inclination has been shown to lay down a definite rule" (1963, p. 102). Under static conditions it is possible to interpret the due care standard in terms of simple rules of thumb. Thus what was formerly a factual matter of jury determination becomes, in effect, a matter of law or a legal rule. Henry Terry made the point succinctly: "[A]lthough negligence is . . . always in its own nature a question of fact, a number of positive rules of considerable generality have been evolved, that certain conduct in certain circumstances is or is not negligent per se . . . When one of these rules applies, the question of negligence is really one of law" (1915–16, p. 50). Illustrative of these rules is the

---

[7]This subsection and the following two subsections are strongly influenced by the work of G. E. White (1980).

exhortation to "stop, look, and listen" at railroad crossings. Failure to do so could easily be construed as "negligence per se." The acknowledged function of these evolved rules of negligence was to promote certainty in the legal order by reducing the case-by-case discretion of juries. "[T]he tendency of the law must always be to narrow the field of uncertainty" (Holmes 1963, p. 101).

In addition to rules of thumb for negligence determination, the turn of the century saw efforts aimed at developing rules of proximate causation. Subsequent to a showing that the defendant's conduct fell below the due care standard, it still remained to demonstrate that his negligence was the legal cause of the plaintiff's injuries. If the method by which causation was established left room for a substantial amount of discretion, then most of the certainty that had been won at the initial stage through the use of rules would be lost at the subsequent stage. Joseph Beale and others tried to extract from the common law decisions certain rules or patterns of causal reasoning so as to constrain the use of discretion in later cases (Beale 1919–20). Among Beale's rules for determining the proximate consequences of an act were:

> [A] direct result of an active force is always proximate [p. 644].
>
> Though there is an active force intervening after defendant's act, the result will nevertheless be proximate if the defendant's act actively caused the intervening force [p. 646].
>
> [W]here defendant's active force has come to rest in a position of apparent safety, the court will follow it no longer; if some new force later combines with this condition to create harm, the result is remote from defendant's act [p. 651].

Rules such as these in the form of a judge's instructions to the jury, it was supposed, could reduce the range of their discretion. "The law does not place in the hands of the jurors power to decide that the causal relation may be inferred from any state of facts whatever. . . . It is for the judge to say whether the jury *can* reasonably so find" (Smith 1911–12, p. 306).

Assumption of Risk

The rule of assumption of risk functioned to narrow still further the scope for discretion generated by negligence liability. A plaintiff who had voluntarily assumed the risk of the type of injury he actually suffered could not recover even from a negligent defendant. Under 19th century evidence law, the burden of proof was on the plaintiff to show that he had not assumed the risk of his own injury (Warren 1894–95, p. 461). If he were not able to meet this burden, he would be barred from bringing a suit based on the negligence of the defendant. In fact, under such circumstances, there can be no negligence on the part of the defendant: There is no duty of care owed to those who assume the risk of injury (Warren 1894–95, pp. 458–59).

The plaintiff's assumption of risk effectively barred recovery whether it was "reasonable" or "unreasonable." Unlike the defense of contributory negligence where the reasonableness of the plaintiff's conduct is crucial, assumption of risk is a strict rule (Epstein 1974, pp. 185–201). It does not require any balancing of the social costs and benefits of the plaintiff's activity. All that matters is whether the risk was knowingly encountered and assumed.

The assumption of risk rule, taken in conjunction with the allocation of the burden of proof to the plaintiff, completely eliminated the need for any balancing whatsoever in a significant number of negligence cases. The plaintiff's case for recovery could be extinguished without any serious determination of the defendant's negligence simply by the plaintiff's failure to prove that he had not assumed the risk. Thus it is quite likely that a coal miner, who presumptively knows the risks of his occupation, would be barred from seeking compensation for a "typical" mining accident. Similarly, the plaintiff who sees defendant's automobile precariously wobbling at the edge of a cliff and yet decides to have a picnic on the grass below would be unsuccessful in an attempt to recover if the car hit him. In both of those cases the issue would be settled without worrying about the reasonableness of either party's behavior.

The general and abstract character of a strictly applied assumption of risk rule was clearly seen by many legal theorists at the turn of the century. Francis Bohlen, for example, summarized the dominant view: Assumption of risk "is a terse expression of the individualistic tendency of the common law, which . . . regards freedom of individual action as the keystone of the whole structure. Each individual is left free to work out his own destinies [sic]; . . . the common law does not assume to protect him from the effects of his own personality and from the consequences of his voluntary actions or of his careless misconduct" (Bohlen 1906–7, p. 14). The rule of assumption of risk thus makes any view of the social value of the plaintiff's actions or goals completely irrelevant to the resolution of the dispute.

Particularistic Negligence

Rule-oriented negligence was based on an abstract universal conception of duty (White 1980, pp. 16–18; Terry 1915–16, p. 52). The duty of care owed by the reasonable man was, with few exceptions, to everyone in the community. Thus, the utility of the defendant's general class of conduct was balanced against the general class of harms it might cause, and not merely the particular harm it did cause. From this perspective, certain types of conduct could be viewed as negligent in a broad category of circumstances; it would be unnecessary to reconsider the negligence of these types of conduct in each and every set of circumstances in which they recurred. The rules of thumb discussed above are consequently intimately related to the abstract universal conception of negligence.

In more recent times, however, a particularistic concept of negligence has emerged. This has been fundamental to the breakdown of a rule-oriented approach. In *Palsgraf v. Long Island Rail Road,*[8] Cardozo applied particularistic negligence to what was to become one of the most discussed set of facts in modern legal history. Two men were late for a train and ran to catch it as it was leaving the station. The first reached the train with no mishap; the second, who was carrying a package, seemed as if he was going to miss it. At that point one guard on the train pulled him aboard, while another guard on the platform pushed him onto the train. In the process the package he was carrying became dislodged. Unbeknownst to the guards it contained fireworks, and exploded upon hitting the ground. The force of the explosion tipped over some scales at the other end of the platform, injuring Mrs. Palsgraf.

Cardozo focused on the defendant's conduct relative to the particular harm that occurred, the injury to Mrs. Palsgraf. The conduct of the defendant had to be balanced against the likelihood of harm to the plaintiff. Since the ex ante likelihood of injury to Mrs. Palsgraf was undoubtedly miniscule, Cardozo found no negligence *relative to her.* The abstract view of negligence, on the other hand, would balance the defendant's conduct against the likelihood of harms to all members of society. Thus, possible harm to the man carrying the package, other trainmen, and those in the immediate area, as well as persons standing in Mrs. Palsgraf's position, would be considered. Consequently the conduct would be found either negligent or not relative to a large number of possible harms. Hence such a determination could be applicable to possible future cases with similar fact patterns. To single out, as Cardozo did, the particular harm that did occur fragments the entire process of negligence determination. Now the question becomes the utility of the defendant's conduct relative to each harm that occurs, *taken separately.* The rule orientation that Holmes and others had hoped to inculcate in the law of negligence was seriously compromised.

[b]248 N.Y. 339, 162 N.E. 99 (1928).

CATO JOURNAL

It is possible to preserve, at least formally, the abstract quality of negligence while undermining it through the doctrines of proximate causation. Consider the view, expounded by Arthur Goodhart, that liability for negligent acts should extend only to the foreseeable consequences of those acts (Goodhart 1931, p. 114). This idea accomplishes at the causation stage exactly what Cardozo's analysis accomplished at the duty stage. While the defendant might have violated a duty of care because of the general class of harms that could stem from his behavior, Goodhart's proximate cause doctrine would require a particularistic causal analysis. After establishing that the defendant had indeed been negligent (in the abstract universal sense), we would then proceed to determine whether the particular harm that occurred was foreseeable to the reasonable defendant. Since "foreseeability" generally refers not only to foresight but to a complete cost-benefit balancing, we are in effect balancing the utility of defendant's conduct against the prospect of a particular harm to a specific plaintiff (for example, Mrs. Palsgraf). Thus, by a circuitous route, we have returned to the particularistic concept of negligence.

The price of adopting this concept indirectly, however, is a loss of analytical coherence. What sense does it make to perform the cost-benefit balancing twice—once with respect to the general class of possible harms and then with respect to the specific harm alleged? (Hart and Honore 1959, pp. 234–48). Presumably the latter is contained in the former and is one of the reasons that the defendant's conduct was found negligent (if indeed it was). Nevertheless, the bifurcation of the balancing process clearly directs the analysis away from the overall potential consequences of an act to the specific, more nearly unique, consequences. The critical determination of liability turns on the foreseeability of those consequences.

Today, while many courts and tort theorists might refuse to go along with Cardozo's and Goodhart's formulations of particularistic negligence, they do accept their emphasis on the dominance of balancing considerations. Prosser and Keeton, for example, take a totally policy view of proximate causation, and hence, ultimately, of the entire law of negligence. "The real problem, and the one to which attention should be directed, would seem to be one of social policy: whether defendants in such cases should bear the heavy negligence losses of a complex civilization, rather than the individual plaintiff" (Prosser and Keeton 1984, p. 287). The solution to this problem, in their view, depends on such policy considerations as risk spreading, relative avoidance costs, and the desirability of promoting or retarding certain kinds of industrial development. The rules of proximate causation have all been tried and found wanting. "There is no substitute," we are told by Prosser (1953, p. 32), "for dealing with the *particular facts*" (emphasis added).

VII. Strict Liability as a System of Rules

While theorists and judges in the late 19th and early 20th centuries attempted to reduce the scope for discretion in negligence law, they were constrained in their efforts by the simple fact that negligence fundamentally involves the balancing of interests. Strict liability principles, on the other hand, fit far more naturally into a rule-oriented approach. These principles, long a fundamental part of the common law, have been developed into a general theory of tort liability by Richard Epstein (1973, 1974, 1975). His theory seeks to extract from the common law those traditions that are most consistent with rule-based protection of individual domains.

This brief discussion is not intended to constitute a comprehensive analysis of strict liability, but to merely demonstrate that, in its broad outlines, Epstein's system appears to be precisely the kind of rule-based abstract order about which Hayek has written.

Prima Facie Case

Under strict liability the plaintiff's prima facie case is established when he shows that the defendant has injured him in any of four patterns of causal relationship. These "causal paradigms" are (1) A hit B, (2) A frightened B, (3) A compelled C to hit B, and (4) A created a dangerous condition that resulted in harm to B (Epstein 1973). Unlike negligence, strict liability does not require implicit or explicit balancing in the prima facie case. The plaintiff is not claiming that, weighing the costs of avoidance against the likelihood of harm, the reasonable person would not have injured him. Instead he is merely asserting the fact of his injury at the "hands" of the defendant. The causal claims of the prima facie case function to protect, in a strict fashion, existing individual domains defined generally in terms of clear physical boundaries.

Causal Defenses

The causal paradigms that constitute plaintiff's case against the defendant can also be used as defenses against that case (Epstein 1974, pp. 174–85). The very strictness of the causal claims, prima facie, implies that these claims, when raised against the plaintiff, provide a sufficient answer. A causal defense means in effect that the plaintiff really injured himself.

Consider the following simple situation: (1) A hit B (prima facie case); (2) B compelled A to hit B (defense). The defense of compulsion, if proved, means simply that the plaintiff's own conduct compelled the blow. *A* was therefore merely an instrument of *B*'s injuring himself (Epstein 1974, pp. 174–75). Note that in both the prima facie case and defense no balancing of social costs and benefits takes place. There is simply a factual assertion of the defendant's invasion of the plaintiff's domain, answered by another factual assertion that the "invasion" was self-inflicted. The other causal paradigms also can be used in a similar way as defenses. Since the same underlying principle of strict defenses with no balancing is at work in these cases as well, the analysis is not pursued here.

Trespass as a Defense

There are also noncausal defenses under strict liability. One of them is assumption of risk in its strict form, unrelated to contributory negligence (discussed above in the analysis of a rule-oriented negligence system). The other noncausal defense is trespass (Epstein 1974, pp. 201–13). The ancient action of trespass functioned to protect the plaintiff's proprietary interests in his own body, his movable possessions, and his land. As such it was simply the corollary of individual autonomy. In a system of strict liability, trespass to land, for example, states a sufficient prima facie case. The plaintiff has a right to expect the defendant to keep off his land regardless of the costs of avoidance. Thus the trespass action is strict. Used as a defense it is an assertion of exclusive possession that shifts the risk of injury to the plaintiff.

Consider the following situation: (1) *A* created a dangerous condition that resulted in harm to *B* (prima facie case); (2) *B* trespassed on *A*'s land (defense). This defense is sufficient to overcome the prima facie allegation. Thus, if the crane on the defendant's land fell on the plaintiff as he trespassed, the latter's action for damages would fail. The plaintiff had no right, prima facie, to be on the defendant's land. Had he stayed off, there would have been no injury and hence no prima facie case at all. The trespass defense also is strict in the sense that the plaintiff's inability to stay off the land is an insufficient reply to the defense. An infant trespasser, for example, cannot successfully plead his diminished ability to avoid the defendant's land. In general the plaintiffs have no right to shift the burden of their problems or deficiencies to the defendant. While it may not be the "fault" of the infant that it trespassed, it is certainly not the "fault" of the defendant either.

The strict quality of the trespass defense means that there is no question of balancing the costs of trespass avoidance with those of greater safety precautions by the defendant. His property right does

THE COMMON LAW

not depend on whether he or the plaintiff were the "cheaper cost avoider" of the accident. Under strict liability principles, property rights are protected by rules and are not subject to the compromises of balancing considerations.

White (1980, p. 229) argues that Epstein's system implicitly introduces a form of balancing in the sense that, for example, the right to be free of trespass is accorded a higher status than the right to be free of the effects of the defendant's dangerous condition. Of course, all decision making involves the balancing or weighing of alternative courses of action; consequently, so long as there is any kind of dispute settlement, there will be weighing in this sense. This is not the sense, however, in which the term "balancing" is customarily used. Rather, the term is used to refer to two kinds of activity. First, there is the particularistic or case-by-case weighing of social costs and benefits, which is the essential thrust of the modern law of negligence. Second, even where there is an attempt to apply "rules," the balancing approach evaluates them by reference to specific (particularistic) social goals. Thus, the increasing tendency to impose liability on defendants in product cases has been interpreted as an attempt to achieve a greater degree of risk spreading (since manufacturers are assumed to pass liability costs on to all purchasers of the product). Rules in this area of law, such as defendant liability for "foreseeable misuse" of products, are therefore to be evaluated with respect to the risk-spreading goal. In other areas of law, however, there may be different goals and consequently different standards of evaluation. In all cases, then, balancing is a particularistic form of weighing because it often requires a case-by-case analysis of costs and benefits and because these costs and benefits are defined in terms of the pursuit of specific social goals.

The evolution of an order of priority among abstract rules is part of the overall process in which the rules themselves develop. In fact a rule is not fully defined unless its priority with respect to other rules is also determined. A rule is best viewed as a *complex* of pleadings and counterpleadings that ultimately establish a result. The system of law thus evolves as a whole in which the various parts interact with each other. Therefore, the order of priority among rules or pleadings, like the overall system itself, is not specific-goal directed; it is "purposeless." Judges do not know the particular outcomes produced by a given hierarchy of rules. All they know (and need to know) is that there is a *meta-rule* by which, for example, trespass is a sufficient defense to the allegation that the defendant created a dangerous condition that resulted in harm.

The function of a clearly defined priority of rules is identical to the function of the system itself. A complex of pleadings and counter-pleadings with no clear relationships in the form of an adequate prima facie case, sufficient defense, and sufficient reply to the defense, etc. would not produce an abstract order of expectations. Property owners, for example, would be unsure about whether trespassers could impose costs on them if something untoward were to happen on their land. The answer would all hinge on the outcome of a balancing endeavor. "The most frequent cause of uncertainty is probably that the order of rank of the different rules belonging to a system is only vaguely determined" (Hayek 1976, p. 24). In contrast, a system of strict liability implies a legal framework in which both the prima facie case and subsequent pleadings are all strict and accordingly largely free from the vagaries of cost-benefit balancing.

VIII. Common Law Process and Rules Revisited

Earlier in this paper it was argued that the pure common law process produces abstract rules that do not impose a particular hierarchy of ends on society, but simply facilitate the attainment of various individual ends. To some readers this may appear at odds with the recognition that contemporary doctrines in common law areas have been formulated increasingly in terms of interest balancing. The resolution of this paradox lies in understanding that we do not have a pure common law system. Indeed, as Hayek himself recognizes, it may be impossible to avoid certain legislative adjustments or "corrections" of evolved rules (Hayek 1973, pp. 88–89). Nevertheless, the degree to which the common law system is "contaminated" by outside influences is crucial to understanding the kinds of doctrines that have developed. While a detailed analysis of this issue is outside of the scope of this paper, it is important to at least mention a recent interesting, and probably correct, explanation of the change in the common law.

Ackerman (1984, pp. 9–18) argues that the rise of the administrative state in general and New Deal legislation in particular transformed a more nearly rule-based common law into one that became increasingly reliant on the balancing of social interests. Specific-goal-oriented legislation, passed in an ad hoc piecemeal fashion, destroyed the idea of law as a seamless web. Judges, lawyers, and litigants now had to be content with heterogeneous pockets of law with different, and frequently conflicting, policy goals. Indeed, many pieces of legislation were themselves each motivated by conflicting policies and so tradeoffs became a way of life. The growth of administrative agencies and of administrative law necessarily introduced a level of bureaucratic discretion that the law had not known before. This discretion is precisely in the form of balancing costs and benefits of one kind or another. That the legislature could delegate discretionary authority to various agencies means that, in a real sense, the agencies both interpret and "evolve" a type of law that is quite alien to the common law tradition. This tradition now found itself to be only one part of a triune legal system that also included heavy reliance on statutes and bureaucratic discretion.

Inevitably pressure mounted for a consistent mode of analysis in all three areas. Any legal system that continued to adhere to a rigidly dichotomized method of reasoning would, in the long run, incur the extremely heavy costs of increased complexity. There is little doubt that both the statutory/administrative and common law domains would have to interact because, while the law may not be a seamless web, society and the order of actions governed by law are so constituted. Consequently the balancing mode of reasoning and specific-goal orientation quickly rose to prominence in the "abstract common law."

IX. Concluding Remarks

In this paper it has been argued that it is possible to have a policy-neutral common law. This claim has been elucidated by contrasting rule-oriented and balancing approaches to law in the context of negligence and strict tort liability. Finally, it was suggested that the rise of the administrative state is at least partly responsible for the decline in legal rules.

References

Ackerman, B. A. *Reconstructing American Law*. Cambridge, Mass.: Harvard University Press, 1984.

Beale, J. H. "The Proximate Consequences of an Act." *Harvard Law Review* 33 (1919–20): 633–58.

Bentham, J. "What a Law Is." In *Bentham's Political Thought*. Edited by B. Parekh. New York: Barnes and Noble, 1973a.

Bentham, J. "Source of a Law." In *Bentham's Political Thought*. Edited by B. Parekh. New York: Barnes and Noble, 1973b.

Bohlen, F. "Voluntary Assumption of Risk I." *Harvard Law Review* 20 (1906–7): 14–34.

Coddington, A. "The Rationale of General Equilibrium Theory." *Economic Inquiry* 13 (December 1975): 539–58.

Demsetz, H. "Information and Efficiency: Another Viewpoint." *Journal of Law and Economics* 12 (April 1969): 1–22.

CATO JOURNAL

Epstein, R. A. "A Theory of Strict Liability." *Journal of Legal Studies* 2 (January 1973): 151–204.

Epstein, R. A. "Defenses and Subsequent Pleas in a System of Strict Liability." *Journal of Legal Studies* 3 (January 1974): 165–215.

Epstein, R. A. "Intentional Harms." *Journal of Legal Studies* 4 (June 1975): 391–442.

Epstein, R. A.; Gregory, C. O.; and Kalven, H. *Cases and Materials on Torts.* 4th ed. Boston, Mass.: Little, Brown and Company, 1984.

Goodhart, A. "The Palsgraf Case." In his *Essays in Jurisprudence and the Common Law,* pp. 129–50. Cambridge, England: Cambridge University Press, 1931.

Hahn, F. H. "The Winter of Our Discontent." *Economica* 40 (1973): 322–30.

Hart, H. L. A. *The Concept of Law.* 1961. Reprint. Oxford, England: Clarendon Press, 1977.

Hart, H. L. A., and Honore, A. M. *Causation in the Law.* Oxford, England: Clarendon Press, 1959.

Hausman, D. M. *Capital, Profits and Prices: An Essay in the Philosophy of Economics.* New York, N.Y.: Columbia University Press, 1981.

Hayek, F. A. *Law, Legislation and Liberty: Rules and Order.* Chicago, Ill.: University of Chicago Press, 1973.

Hayek, F. A. *Law, Legislation and Liberty: The Mirage of Social Justice.* Chicago, Ill.: University of Chicago Press, 1976.

Hayek, F. A. *Law, Legislation and Liberty: The Political Order of a Free People.* Chicago, Ill.: University of Chicago Press, 1979.

Holmes, O. W. *The Common Law.* 1881. Reprint. Edited by Mark DeWolfe Howe. Boston, Mass.: Little, Brown and Company, 1963.

Levi, E. H. *An Introduction to Legal Reasoning.* Chicago, Ill.: University of Chicago Press, 1949.

O'Driscoll, G. P., and Rizzo, M. J. *The Economics of Time and Ignorance.* Oxford, England: Basil Blackwell, 1985.

Pound, R. *An Introduction to the Philosophy of Law.* 1922. Reprint. New Haven, Conn.: Yale University Press, 1954.

Prosser, W. L. "Palsgraf Revisited." *Michigan Law Review* 52 (November 1953): 1–32.

Prosser, W. L. , and Keeton, W. P. *Prosser and Keeton on the Law of Torts.* St. Paul, Minn.: West Publishing Company, 1984.

Rizzo, M. J. "Law amid Flux: The Economics of Negligence and Strict Liability in Tort." *Journal of Legal Studies* 9 (March 1980a): 291–318.

Rizzo, M. J. "The Mirage of Efficiency." *Hofstra Law Review* 8 (Spring 1980b): 641–58.

Smith, J. "Legal Cause in Actions of Tort II." *Harvard Law Review* 25 (1911–12): 303–27.

Terry, H. "Negligence." *Harvard Law Review* 29 (1915–16): 40–54.

Warren, C. "Volenti Non Fit Injuria in Actions of Negligence." *Harvard Law Review* 8 (1894–95): 457–71.

White, G. E. *Tort Law in America: An Intellectual History.* New York: Oxford University Press, 1980.

[28]

6. The Limits of Property Rights and the Problems of External Costs and External Economies

Property rights as they are circumscribed by laws and protected by courts and the police, are the outgrowth of an age-long evolution. The history of these ages is the record of struggles aiming at the abolition of private property. Again and again despots and popular movements have tried to restrict the rights of private property or to abolish it altogether. These endeavors, it is true, failed. But they have left traces in the ideas determining the legal form and definition of property. The legal concepts of property do not fully take account of the social function of private property. There are certain inadequacies and incongruities which are reflected in the determination of the market phenomena.

Carried through consistently, the right of property would entitle

the proprietor to claim all the advantages which the good's employment may generate on the one hand and would burden him with all
the disadvantages resulting from its employment on the other hand.
Then the proprietor alone would be fully responsible for the outcome. In dealing with his property he would take into account all
the expected results of his action, those considered favorable as well
as those considered unfavorable. But if some of the consequences of
his action are outside of the sphere of the benefits he is entitled to
reap and of the drawbacks that are put to his debit, he will not bother
in his planning about *all* the effects of his action. He will disregard
those benefits which do not increase his own satisfaction and those
costs which do not burden him. His conduct will deviate from the line
which it would have followed if the laws were better adjusted to the
economic objectives of private ownership. He will embark upon
certain projects only because the laws release him from responsibility
for some of the costs incurred. He will abstain from other projects
merely because the laws prevent him from harvesting all the advantages derivable.

The laws concerning liability and indemnification for damages
caused were and still are in some respects deficient. By and large the
principle is accepted that everybody is liable to damages which his
actions have inflicted upon other people. But there were loopholes
left which the legislators were slow to fill. In some cases this tardiness
was intentional because the imperfections agreed with the plans of
the authorities. When in the past in many countries the owners of
factories and railroads were not held liable for the damages which
the conduct of their enterprises inflicted on the property and health
of neighbors, patrons, employees, and other people through smoke,
soot, noise, water pollution, and accidents caused by defective or
inappropriate equipment, the idea was that one should not undermine
the progress of industrialization and the development of transportation facilities. The same doctrines which prompted and still are
prompting many governments to encourage investment in factories
and railroads through subsidies, tax exemption, tariffs, and cheap credit
were at work in the emergence of a legal state of affairs in which the
liability of such enterprises was either formally or practically abated.
Later again the opposite tendency began to prevail in many countries
and the liability of manufacturers and railroads was increased as
against that of other citizens and firms. Here again definite political
objectives were operative. Legislators wished to protect the poor,
the wage earners, and the peasants against the wealthy entrepreneurs
and capitalists.

Whether the proprietor's relief from responsibility for some of the disadvantages resulting from his conduct of affairs is the outcome of a deliberate policy on the part of governments and legislators or whether it is an unintentional effect of the traditional wording of laws, it is at any rate a datum which the actors must take into account. They are faced with the problem of *external costs*. Then some people choose certain modes of want-satisfaction merely on account of the fact that a part of the costs incurred are debited not to them but to other people.

The extreme instance is provided by the case of no-man's property referred to above.[9] If land is not owned by anybody, although legal formalism may call it public property, it is utilized without any regard to the disadvantages resulting. Those who are in a position to appropriate to themselves the returns—lumber and game of the forests, fish of the water areas, and mineral deposits of the subsoil—do not bother about the later effects of their mode of exploitation. For them the erosion of the soil, the depletion of the exhaustible resources and other impairments of the future utilization are external costs not entering into their calculation of input and output. They cut down the trees without any regard for fresh shoots or reforestation. In hunting and fishing they do not shrink from methods preventing the re-population of the hunting and fishing grounds. In the early days of human civilization, when soil of a quality not inferior to that of the utilized pieces was still abundant, people did not find any fault with such predatory methods. When their effects appeared in a decrease in the net returns, the ploughman abandoned his farm and moved to another place. It was only when a country was more densely settled and unoccupied first class land was no longer available for appropriation, that people began to consider such predatory methods wasteful. At that time they consolidated the institution of private property in land. They started with arable land and then, step by step, included pastures, forests, and fisheries. The newly settled colonial countries overseas, especially the vast spaces of the United States, whose marvelous agricultural potentialities were almost untouched when the first colonists from Europe arrived, passed through the same stages. Until the last decades of the nineteenth century there was always a geographic zone open to newcomers—the frontier. Neither the existence of the frontier nor its passing was peculiar to America. What characterizes American conditions is the fact that at the time the frontier disappeared ideological and institutional factors

9. See above, p. 635.

impeded the adjustment of the methods of land utilization to the change in the data.

In the central and western areas of continental Europe, where the institution of private property had been rigidly established for many centuries, things were different. There was no question of soil erosion of formerly cultivated land. There was no problem of forest devastation in spite of the fact that the domestic forests had been for ages the only source of lumber for construction and mining and of fuel for heating and for the foundries and furnaces, the potteries and the glass factories. The owners of the forests were impelled to conservation by their own selfish interests. In the most densely inhabited and industrialized areas up to a few years ago between a fifth and a third of the surface was still covered by first-class forests managed according to the methods of scientific forestry.[10]

It is not the task of catallactic theory to elaborate an account of the complex factors that produced modern American land-ownership conditions. Whatever these factors were, they brought about a state of affairs under which a great many farmers and the majority of the lumbering enterprises had reason to consider the disadvantages resulting from the neglect of soil and forest conservation as external costs.[11]

It is true that where a considerable part of the costs incurred are external costs from the point of view of the acting individuals or firms, the economic calculation established by them is manifestly defective and their results deceptive. But this is not the outcome of alleged deficiencies inherent in the system of private ownership of the means of production. It is on the contrary a consequence of loopholes left in this system. It could be removed by a reform of the laws concerning liability for damages inflicted and by rescinding the institutional barriers preventing the full operation of private ownership.

10. Late in the eighteenth century European governments began to enact laws aiming at forest conservation. However, it would be a serious blunder to ascribe to these laws any role in the conservation of the forests. Before the middle of the nineteenth century there was no administrative apparatus available for their enforcement. Besides the governments of Austria and Prussia, to say nothing of those of the smaller German states, virtually lacked the power to enforce such laws against the aristocratic lords. No civil servant before 1914 would have been bold enough to rouse the anger of a Bohemian or Silesian magnate or a German mediatized *Standesherr*. These princes and counts were spontaneously committed to forest conservation because they felt perfectly safe in the possession of their property and were eager to preserve unabated the source of their revenues and the market price of their estates.

11. One could as well say that they considered the advantages to be derived from giving care to soil and forest conservation external economies.

The case of external economies is not simply the inversion of the case of external costs. It has its own domain and character.

If the results of an actor's action benefit not only himself, but also other people, two alternatives are possible:

1. The planning actor considers the advantages which he expects for himself so important that he is prepared to defray all the costs required. The fact that his project also benefits other people will not prevent him from accomplishing what promotes his own well-being. When a railroad company erects dikes to protect its tracks against snowslides and avalanches, it also protects the houses on adjacent grounds. But the benefits which its neighbors will derive will not hinder the company from embarking upon an expenditure that it deems expedient.

2. The costs incurred by a project are so great that none of those whom it will benefit is ready to expend them in full. The project can be realized only if a sufficient number of those interested in it share in the costs.

It would hardly be necessary to say more about external economies if it were not for the fact that this phenomenon is entirely misinterpreted in current pseudo-economic literature.

A project P is unprofitable when and because consumers prefer the satisfaction expected from the realization of some other projects to the satisfaction expected from the realization of P. The realization of P would withdraw capital and labor from the realization of some other projects for which the demand of the consumers is more urgent. The layman and the pseudo-economist fail to recognize this fact. They stubbornly refuse to notice the scarcity of the factors of production. As they see it, P could be realized without any cost at all, i.e., without foregoing any other satisfaction. It is merely the wantonness of the profit system that prevents the nation from enjoying gratuitously the pleasures expected from P.

Now, these short-sighted critics go on to say, the absurdity of the profit system becomes especially outrageous if the unprofitability of P is merely due to the fact that the entrepreneur's calculations neglect those advantages of P which for them are external economies. From the point of view of the whole of society such advantages are not external. They benefit at least some members of society and would increase "total welfare." The nonrealization of P is therefore a loss for society. As profit-seeking business, entirely committed to selfishness, declines to embark upon such unprofitable projects, it is the duty of government to fill the gap. Government should either run them as public enterprises or it should subsidize them in order to

The Data of the Market   655

make them attractive for the private entrepreneur and investor. The subsidies may be granted either directly by money grants from public funds or indirectly by means of tariffs the incidence of which falls upon the buyers of the products.

However, the means which a government needs in order to run a plant at a loss or to subsidize an unprofitable project must be withdrawn either from the taxpayers' spending and investing power or from the loan market. The government has no more ability than individuals to create something out of nothing. What the government spends more, the public spends less. Public works are not accomplished by the miraculous power of a magic wand. They are paid for by funds taken away from the citizens. If the government had not interfered, the citizens would have employed them for the realization of profit-promising projects the realization of which they must omit because their means have been curtailed by the government. For every unprofitable project that is realized by the aid of the government there is a corresponding project the realization of which is neglected merely on account of the government's intervention. Yet this nonrealized project would have been profitable, i.e., it would have employed the scarce means of production in accordance with the most urgent needs of the consumers. From the point of view of the consumers the employment of these means of production for the realization of an unprofitable project is wasteful. It deprives them of satisfactions which they prefer to those which the government-sponsored project can furnish them.

The gullible masses who cannot see beyond the immediate range of their physical eyes are enraptured by the marvelous accomplishments of their rulers. They fail to see that they themselves foot the bill and must consequently renounce many satisfactions which they would have enjoyed if the government had spent less for unprofitable projects. They have not the imagination to think of the possibilities that the government has not allowed to come into existence.[12]

These enthusiasts are still more bewildered if the government's interference enables submarginal producers to continue producing and to stand the competition of more efficient plants, shops, or farms. Here, they say, it is obvious that total production is increased and something is added to the wealth that would not have been produced without the assistance of the authorities. What happens in fact is just the opposite; the magnitude of total production and of total wealth is curtailed. Outfits producing at higher costs are brought into exist-

12. Cf. the brilliant analysis of public spending in Henry Hazlitt's book *Economics in One Lesson* (New York, 1946), pp. 19–29.

ence or preserved while other outfits producing at lower costs are forced to curtail or to discontinue their production. The consumers are not getting more, but less.

There is, for instance, the very popular idea that it is a good thing for the government to promote the agricultural development of those parts of the country which nature has poorly endowed. Costs of production are higher in these districts than in other areas; it is precisely this fact that qualifies a large part of their soil as submarginal. When unaided by public funds, the farmers tilling these submarginal lands could not stand the competition of the more fertile farms. Agriculture would shrink or fail to develop and the whole area would become a backward part of the country. In full cognizance of this state of affairs profit-seeking business avoids investing in the construction of railroads connecting such inauspicious areas with the centers of consumption. The plight of the farmers is not caused by the fact that they lack transportation facilities. The causation is the other way round; because business realizes that the prospects for these farmers are not propitious, it abstains from investing in railroads which are likely to become unprofitable for lack of a sufficient amount of goods to be shipped. If the government, yielding to the demands of the interested pressure groups, builds the railroad and runs it at a deficit, it certainly benefits the owners of farm land in those poor districts of the country. As a part of the costs that the shipping of their products requires is borne by the treasury, they find it easier to compete with those tilling more fertile land to whom such aid is denied. But the boon of these privileged farmers is paid for by the taxpayers who must provide the funds required to defray the deficit. It affects neither the market price nor the total available supply of agricultural products. It merely makes profitable the operation of farms which hitherto were submarginal and makes other farms, the operation of which was hitherto profitable, submarginal. It shifts production from land requiring lower costs to land requiring higher costs. It does not increase total supply and wealth, it curtails them, as the additional amounts of capital and labor required for the cultivation of high-cost fields instead of low-cost fields are withheld from employments in which they would have made possible the production of some other consumers' goods. The government attains its end of benefiting some parts of the country with what they would have missed, but it produces somewhere else costs which exceed these gains of a privileged group.

The External Economies of Intellectual Creation

The extreme case of external economies is shown in the "production" of the intellectual groundwork of every kind of processing and constructing. The characteristic mark of recipes, i.e., the mental devices directing the technological procedures, is the inexhaustibility of the services they render. These services are consequently not scarce, and there is no need to economize their employment. Those considerations that resulted in the establishment of the institution of private ownership of economic goods did not refer to them. They remained outside the sphere of private property not because they are immaterial, intangible, and impalpable, but because their serviceableness cannot be exhausted.

People began to realize only later that this state of affairs has its drawbacks too. It places the producers of such recipes—especially the inventors of technological procedures and authors and composers—in a peculiar position. They are burdened with the costs of production, while the services of the product they have created can be gratuitously enjoyed by everybody. What they produce is for them either entirely or almost entirely external economies.

If there are neither copyrights nor patents, the inventors and authors are in the position of an entrepreneur. They have a temporary advantage as against other people. As they start sooner in utilizing their invention or their manuscript themselves or in making it available for use to other people (manufacturers or publishers), they have the chance to earn profits in the time interval until everybody can likewise utilize it. As soon as the invention or the content of the book are publicly known, they become "free goods" and the inventor or author has only his glory.

The problem involved has nothing to do with the activities of the creative genius. These pioneers and originators of things unheard of do not produce and work in the sense in which these terms are employed in dealing with the affairs of other people. They do not let themselves be influenced by the response their work meets on the part of their contemporaries. They do not wait for encouragement.[13]

It is different with the broad class of professional intellectuals whose services society cannot do without. We may disregard the problem of second-rate authors of poems, fiction, and plays and second-rate composers and need not inquire whether it would be a serious disadvantage for mankind to lack the products of their efforts. But it is obvious that handing down knowledge to the rising generation and familiarizing the acting individuals with the amount of knowledge they need for the realization of their plans requires textbooks, manuals, handbooks, and other nonfiction works. It is unlikely that people would undertake the laborious task of writing such publications if everyone were free to reproduce them. This is still more manifest in the field of technological invention and discovery.

13. See above, pp. 138–140

The extensive experimentation necessary for such achievements is often very expensive. It is very probable that technological progress would be seriously retarded if, for the inventor and for those who defray the expenses incurred by his experimentation, the results obtained were nothing but external economies.

Patents and copyrights are results of the legal evolution of the last centuries. Their place in the traditional body of property rights is still controversial. People look askance at them and deem them irregular. They are considered privileges, a vestige of the rudimentary period of their evolution when legal protection was accorded to authors and inventors only by virtue of an exceptional privilege granted by the authorities. They are suspect, as they are lucrative only if they make it possible to sell at monopoly prices.[14] Moreover, the fairness of patent laws is contested on the ground that they reward only those who put the finishing touch leading to practical utilization of achievements of many predecessors. These precursors go empty-handed although their contribution to the final result was often much more weighty than that of the patentee.

It is beyond the scope of catallactics to enter into an examination of the arguments brought forward for and against the institution of copyrights and patents. It has merely to stress the point that this is a problem of the delimitation of property rights and that with the abolition of patents and copyrights authors and inventors would for the most part be producers of external economies.

Privileges and Quasi-privileges

The restrictions which laws and institutions impose upon the discretion to choose and to act are not always so insurmountable that they could not be overcome under certain conditions. To some favorites exemption from the obligation binding the rest of the people may be granted as an explicit privilege either by the laws themselves or by an administrative act of the authorities entrusted with the law's enforcement. Some may be ruthless enough to defy the laws in spite of the vigilance of the authorities; their daring insolence secures them a quasi-privilege.

A law that nobody observes is ineffectual. A law that is not valid for all or which not all obey, may grant to those who are exempt—whether by virtue of the law itself or by virtue of their own audacity—the opportunity to reap either differential rent or monopoly gains.

With regard to the determination of the market phenomena it does not matter whether the exemption is legally valid as a privilege or illegal as a quasi-privilege. Neither does it matter whether the costs, if any, incurred by the favored individual or firm for the acquisition of the privilege or quasi-privilege are legal (e.g., a tax levied on licensees) or illegal (e.g., bribes paid to corrupt officers). If an importation embargo is mitigated by the importation of a certain quantity, the prices are affected by the quantity

14. See above, pp. 360–361.

The Data of the Market

imported and the specific costs incurred by the acquisition and the utilization of the privilege or quasi-privilege. But whether the importation was legal (e.g., a license granted under the system of quantitative trade control to some privileged people), or illegal contraband does not affect the price structure.

Economics, Subjectivism And Public Choice

by Jack Wiseman

It is no cause for alarm that academics should be dissatisfied with the state of their chosen discipline: doubt is the yeast of intellectual progress.

But a group of scholars can lose its way, and new kinds of doubt then develop: doubt about the nature of the intellectual problem itself or about the "right" or "best" way to study it—what might be called, parodying the jargon of the relevant philosophers, "paradigm doubt". Economics today seems to me to have all the symptoms of this condition, with its concomitant factionalism. More, the problem is not a simple one of paradigm replacement, in that the disturbance is simply a reflection of the need for time in which a new paradigm, providing generally better "explanations", can replace an existing one. I have neither time nor space to embroil myself in such issues as the status of economics as an "innovative" science. I would assert simply that our problem is not of this kind, but is rather that we have no one developed system of thought that is adequately comprehensive (embracing), and hence none which as it stands is capable of displacing the others. I do not expect to remedy this defect in a couple of thousand words. I shall content myself with an attempt to identify the reasons for our malaise, in the hope of encouraging agreement about what is wrong and what sort of remedies are needed.

Also, in the space available I can deal only in generalizations. It is consequently inevitable that my descriptions of intellectual positions will have an element of parody. But I trust, and believe, that they are neither unrecognizable nor unfair.

At this general level, it is possible to make two useful distinctions, one more familiar than the other. The first concerns the approach to the "explanation" of economic phenomena, in respect of which what has come to be known as the "Austrian School" offers formulations and insights that stand in marked contrast to those of "mainstream" or "neo-classical" economics. The second concerns the appropriate subject matter. Both mainstream and Austrian economists concentrate attention on the logic of choice as expressed through markets. Non-market choice-situations are studied only incidentally, or as "offshoots" or addenda to this central concern with the market. The development of the study of public choice is a partial response to this restriction, but I shall argue is itself in danger of being treated as an addendum (an obligatory chapter in a textbook of economic analysis), rather than as the general and unifying construct that I believe to be needed.

Not everyone is agreed that there are significant intellectual differences between the Austrian School and what might be called the Chicago positivist school: distinguished members of the latter have been known to claim that there is little difference between their own intellectual position and, for example, that of Professor Hayek. My own perception is that there is one difference that is of fundamental importance, and abdications from (or misperceptions of) that difference that make the two views of the economic problem seem more similar than they in fact are, while in fact making them more difficult to integrate into a common intellectual

framework. The essential difference can be put in this way: while both schools are concerned with the characteristics of human behavior in response to scarcity, they specify the characteristics of the environment in which scarcity occurs in significantly different ways. For both, scarcity obligates choice, and choice implies sacrifice. Any chosen course of action implies a necessarily sacrificed alternative course, which both schools would identify as the opportunity-cost of the implemented decision. For the Austrian, opportunity-cost is a subjective concept: the value placed by an individual on the best course of action envisaged as feasible but rejected in favor of the chosen course. So conceived, opportunity-cost has no objective manifestation: it is a "non-event" (rejected plan), whose characteristics, insofar as they can be "known" at all, can be known only to the individual decision-maker. A Chicago positivist would not necessarily reject this description. But he would give the subjective plans objective content, by way of simplifying assumptions about the knowledge (information) available to the individual decision-maker. Readers will be familiar with the devices I have in mind. The simplest one is that entrepreneurs' plans are conceived in terms of known prices. When it is acknowledged that present plans concern the future, and future prices are not "known" now, the problem is emasculated by assuming that (objective) probabilities can be attached to possible outcomes and that individual risk-preferences are somehow "known". There are sophisticated models that allow for "mistakes": but "mistake-correction" follows pre-specified "rules" so that the models "run-down" to a stable world. The most sophisticated attempts to deal with the uncertainty problem within "mainstream" economics (such as those of Arrow and Debreu) continue to depend ultimately on the assumption that the future is "knowable" (indeed, known) in the sense that someone (Walras-with-Bayes?) is apprised of all the plans that are or could be considered by all decision-makers (since the models require that the number of possible plans be "finite"). Insofar as they treat historical data as a record of successfully-implemented plans (so that e.g. price series are never treated as a record of (at least partial) plan-failure) the econometric studies resting on such intellectual foundations can never permit trustworthy inferences about causal relations relevant to a decision-making world in which the future is not only unknown but unknowable, and in which the plans of individuals consequently not only produce unpredicted outcomes, but generate no particular surprise for the planners when they do so.

It is this "subjectivist insight": that the future is not only unknown but in a practical sense unknowable, that distinguishes the Austrian position. As a criticism of mainstream economics, it is difficult to answer. Indeed, I do not think it can be answered. The more usual defense is a counter-criticism: Destructive comment is one thing. But what alternative explanations can the Austrian/subjectivist school offer? Clearly, they cannot replicate the neat outcomes of the mainstream economic models, nor can they find a ready substitute for the (Paretian) efficiency concept that derives from such models. For the Austrian, the process of allocation of resources between uses is an individual decision-process continuously unfolding in time. The concept of "static" allocative outcome-efficiency is not particularly interesting, even if comprehensible. Thus, the Austrian response is to change the focus of interest, from the efficient *outcome* of the resource-allocation process to the efficiency of the process *per se*. This follows directly from the different assumptions of the two schools about knowledge and its distribution. It produces the paradoxical situation that the Austrian specification of the problem is clearly superior in terms of realism, but lends itself less readily to sophisticated analytical manipulation or formally precise conclusions. This in no way destroys the Austrian position, in that false precision deriving from a misleading specification of the relevant problem is not itself practically helpful. Nevertheless, the desire of Austrians to preserve the purity of their specification, and the simultaneous desire to make a positive as well as a critical contribution, together perhaps with a scholarly urge to impose intellectual order on a difficult problem, can and does confuse the issue by producing the misconceptions I referred to earlier. A few illustrations may help:

I have already drawn attention to the difficulty of interpreting causally a historical record which to an unknown extent is the record of the outcome of mistaken judgments: How are we to infer causality from such data? The reaction of some Austrians is simply to reject the use of statistics. But this is surely too extreme a position. The historical record is the only record we have got: we cannot ignore it, but clearly need to find ways to interpret it better—ways that must involve abandonment of some of the neo-classical simplifications. Again, it is a virtue of the Austrian approach that it places the entrepreneur/decision-maker/innovator at the center of the economic process. But in a truly subjectivist world, all individuals are decision-makers, and it is implausible to distinguish "the entrepreneur" as a special kind of decision-maker, as is sometimes done (though it may be useful to identify "entrepreneurial decisions" with particular kinds of choice-situation). Similar objections can be taken to the use of "orthodox" (neo-classical) supply-and-demand curves to "explain" the process of price change through time. The "orthodox" curves imply the existence of "objective" market demand and supply schedules: something that denies the Austrian postulate of an unknowable future. On the other hand, it is difficult to understand why an Austrian-subjectivist should find the idea of general equilibrium of interest either of itself or as an efficiency indicator, or why any kind of equilibrium state should ever emerge from the information-transmission which Austrians properly identify with competitive decision-making.

If the two schools are ultimately to be reconciled, it will have to be by way of the increasing willingness of mainstream economists to accept the superior behavioural insights of the Austrian formulation, and to direct their undoubted technical sophistication to the development of new insights within this new framework. The process would be helped rather than hindered by consistency among Austrians themselves in the interpretation of subjective cost in a truly uncertain world: a

consistency which is not always apparent at present.

Such a reconciliation will become more likely if and when both schools recognise the need to broaden their subject-matter. I have already pointed out that, for both schools, the study of economics is identified for practical purposes with the study of market or market-type phenomena. Mainstream economics generally treats other institutional arrangements as "inputs" to the behaviour of markets and, implicitly or explicitly, judges such arrangements, insofar as they are considered at all, in terms of their influence on the functioning of the market. The Austrian position is ambiguous: it emphasises the embracing nature of "human action" (and the consequent unrealism of e.g. the notion of an "economic" decision), but at the same time broadly identifies the subject-matter of economics with the study of the behaviour of markets.

The emergence of public choice as a sub-discipline of mainstream economics was undoubtedly influenced by a recognition of the inadequacy of this restriction, which e.g. has inhibited study of the behaviour of government and its institutions. Paradoxically, it matured as a critique/extension of mainstream economics, whose importance is now generally recognised e.g. by the incorporation of a public choice section in most standard texts. Yet the public choice insights have always fitted easily with the neo-classical "orthodoxy": the subjectivity of the decision-process, and of the nature of costs, becomes even more manifest when interest shifts from market-related to political or bureaucratic decision-making. Yet applied research in public choice still depends largely on the neo-classical model: it is surely incongruous to find the standard econometric techniques being used on public choice problems to which they are manifestly inappropriate.

The concept of subjective opportunity costs helps with an understanding of all human decision-problems—that is, all problems requiring a choice between mutually-excluding alternatives. Mainstream economics not only misspecifies the economic problem, but conceives the subject-matter too narrowly. It is now generally recognised that a policy-relevant economics must embrace public choice (I would personally prefer to say must be absorbed by it), and this requires embracing an "Austrian" methodology rather than persistence with the present Chicago-positivist model.

The practical problem is to develop an overarching public choice framework for the study of decision-making in society: it is the burden of my argument that such a framework can be evolved from the Austrian school insights, but that this will need a catholic interpretation of the subject-matter, and perhaps a less defensive attitude of mind from Austrians as well as from their critics. *MP*

[30]

Economic Freedom and Representative Government
F. A. HAYEK

I
THE SEEDS OF DESTRUCTION

THIRTY YEARS AGO I wrote a book[1] which, in a manner which many regarded as unduly alarmist, described the dangers that the then visible collectivist tendencies created for personal freedom. I am glad that these fears so far have not materialised, but I do not think this has proved me wrong. In the first instance I did not, as many misunderstood me, contend that if government interfered at all with economic affairs it was bound to go the whole way to a totalitarian system. I was trying to argue rather what in more homely terms is expressed by saying 'if you don't mend your principles you will go to the devil'.

Post-war revival: the 'Great Prosperity'
In the event developments since the war, in Britain as well as in the rest of the Western world, have gone much less in the direction which the prevalent collectivist doctrines seemed to suggest was likely. Indeed, the first 20 years after the war saw a revival of a free market economy much stronger than even its most enthusiastic supporters could have hoped. Although I like to think that those who worked for this consummation in the intellectual sphere, such as Harold Wincott, to whose memory this lecture is dedicated, have contributed to it, I do not overrate what intellectual debate can achieve. At least as important were probably the experiences of Germany, relying on a market economy, rapidly becoming the strongest economic power of Europe – and to some extent the practical efforts for a removal of the obstacles to international trade, such as GATT and perhaps in some measure the intentions if not the practice of the EEC.

[1] *The Road to Serfdom*, Routledge, 1944.

[7]

The result was the Great Prosperity of the last 20 to 25 years which, I fear, will in the future appear as an event as unique as the Great Depression of the 1930s now appears to us. To me at least it seems clear that, until six or eight years ago, this prosperity was due entirely to the freeing of the spontaneous forces of the economic system and not, as in the later years, to inflation. Since this is today often forgotten I may perhaps remind you that, in the most remarkable burst of prosperity of this period, that of the German Federal Republic, the average annual rise of prices remained below 2 per cent until 1966.

I believe that even this modest rate of inflation would not have been necessary to secure the prosperity, and indeed that we should all today have better prospects of continuing prosperity if we had been content with what was achieved without inflation and had not attempted to stimulate it further by an expansionist credit policy. Instead such a policy has created a situation in which it is thought necessary to impose controls which will destroy the main foundations of the prosperity, namely the functioning market. Indeed the measures supposedly necessary to combat inflation – as if inflation were something which attacks us and not something which we create – threaten to destroy the free economy in the near future.

Inflation: the threat to freedom

We find ourselves in the paradoxical situation that, after a period during which the market economy has been more successful than ever before in rapidly raising living standards in the Western world, the prospects of its continuance even for the next few years must appear slight. I have indeed never felt so pessimistic about the chances of preserving a functioning market economy as I do at this moment – and this means also of the prospects of preserving a free political order. Although the threat to free institutions now comes from a source different from that with which I was concerned 30 years ago, it has become even more acute than it was then.

That a systematically pursued incomes policy means the suspension of the price mechanism and before long the replacement of the market by a centrally-directed economy seems to me beyond doubt. I cannot here discuss the ways in which we may

still avoid this course, or the chances that we may still do so.
Although I regard it as at this time the chief duty of every economist to fight inflation – and to explain why a repressed inflation
is even worse than an open inflation – I devote this lecture to
another task. As I see it, inflation has merely speeded up the
process of the destruction of the market economy which has been
going on for other reasons, and brought much nearer the moment
when, seeing the economic, political and moral consequences of
a centrally-directed economy, we shall have to think how we can
re-establish a market economy on a firmer and more durable basis.

II

The Danger of Unlimited Government

FOR SOME TIME I have been convinced that it is not only the
deliberate attempts of the various kinds of collectivists to replace
the market economy by a planned system, nor the consequences of
the new monetary policies, which threaten to destroy the market
economy: the political institutions prevailing in the Western
world necessarily produce a drift in this direction which can be
halted or prevented only by changing these institutions. I have
belatedly come to agree with Joseph Schumpeter who 30 years
ago argued[1] that there was an irreconcilable conflict between
democracy and capitalism – except that it is not democracy as
such but the particular forms of democratic organisation, now
regarded as the only possible forms of democracy, which will
produce a progressive expansion of governmental control of
economic life even if the majority of the people wish to preserve
a market economy.

Majority rule and special interests
The reason is that it is now generally taken for granted that in a
democracy the powers of the majority must be unlimited, and that
a government with unlimited powers will be forced, to secure the
continued support of a majority, to use its unlimited powers in the

---

[1] *Capitalism, Socialism and Democracy*, Allen & Unwin, 1943 (Unwin
University Books, No. 28, 3rd edn., 1950).

[9]

service of special interests – such groups as particular traders, the inhabitants of particular regions, etc. We shall see this most clearly if we consider the situation in a community in which the mass of the people are in favour of a market order and against government direction, but, as will normally happen, most of the groups wish an exception to be made in their favour. In such conditions a political party hoping to achieve and maintain power will have little choice but to use its powers to buy the support of particular groups. They will do so not because the majority is interventionist, but because the ruling party would not retain a majority if it did not buy the support of particular groups by the promise of special advantages. This means in practice that even a statesman wholly devoted to the common interest of all the citizens will be under the constant necessity of satisfying special interests, because only thus will he be able to retain the support of a majority which he needs to achieve what is really important to him.

The root of the evil is thus the unlimited power of the legislature in modern democracies, a power which the majority will be constantly forced to use in a manner that most of its members may not desire. What we call the will of the majority is thus really an artefact of the existing institutions, and particularly of the omnipotence of the sovereign legislature, which by the mechanics of the political process will be driven to do things that most of its members do not really want, simply because there are no formal limits to its powers.

It is widely believed that this omnipotence of the representative legislature is a necessary attribute of democracy because the will of the representative assembly could be limited only by placing another will above it. Legal positivism, the most influential current theory of jurisprudence, particularly represents this sovereignty of the legislature as logically necessary. This, however, was by no means the view of the classical theorists of representative government. John Locke made it very clear that in a free state even the power of the legislative body should be limited in a definite manner, namely to the passing of laws in the specific sense of general rules of just conduct equally applicable to all citizens. That all coercion would be legitimate only if it meant the application of general rules of law in this sense became the basic principle of liberalism. For Locke, and for the later theorists of Whiggism and the separation of powers, it was not so much the source from which the laws originated as their character of general rules of just conduct equally applicable to all which justified their coercive application.

What is law ?

This older liberal conception of the necessary limitation of all power by requiring the legislature to commit itself to general rules has, in the course of the last century, been replaced gradually and almost imperceptibly by the altogether different though not incompatible conception that it was the approval of the majority which was the only and sufficient restraint on legislation. And the older conception was not only forgotten but no longer even understood. It was thought that any substantive limitation of the legislative power was unnecessary once this power was placed in the hands of the majority, because approval by it was regarded as an adequate test of justice. In practice this majority opinion usually represents no more than the result of bargaining rather than a genuine agreement on principles. Even the concept of the arbitrariness which democratic government was supposed to prevent changed its content: its opposite was no longer the general rules equally applicable to all but the approval of a command by the majority – as if a majority might not treat a minority arbitrarily.

III

THE FUNDAMENTAL PRINCIPLE

TODAY IT IS rarely understood that the limitation of all coercion to the enforcement of general rules of just conduct was the fundamental principle of classical liberalism, or, I would almost say, its definition of liberty. This is largely a consequence of the fact that the substantive (or 'material') conception of law (as distinguished from a purely formal one) which underlies it, and which alone gives a clear meaning to such ideas as that of the sep-

[11]

aration of powers, of the rule of law or of a government under the
law, had been rarely stated explicitly but merely tacitly presupposed by most of the classical writers. There are few passages
in their 17th- and 18th-century writings in which they explicitly
say what they mean by 'law'. Many uses of the term, however,
make sense only if it is interpreted to mean exclusively general
rules of just conduct and not every expression of the will of the
duly authorised representative body.

Tyranny of majorities

Though the older conception of law survives in limited connections, it is certainly no longer generally understood, and in
consequence has ceased to be an effective limit on legislation.
While in the theoretical concept of the separation of powers the
legislature derived its authority from the circumstance that it
committed itself to general rules and was supposed to impose only
general rules, there are now no limits on what a legislature may
command and so claim to be 'law'. While its power was thus once
supposed to be limited not by a superior will but by a generally
recognised principle, there are now no limits whatever. There is
therefore also no reason why the coalitions of organised interests
on which the governing majorities rest should not discriminate
against any widely-disliked group. Differences in wealth, education, tradition, religion, language or race may today become the
cause of differential treatment on the pretext of a pretended
principle of social justice or of public necessity. Once such
discrimination is recognised as legitimate, all the safeguards of
individual freedom of the liberal tradition are gone. If it is assumed
that whatever the majority decides is just, even if what it lays
down is not a general rule, but aims at affecting particular people,
it would be expecting too much to believe that a sense of justice
will restrain the caprice of the majority: in any group it is soon
believed that what is desired by the group is just. And since the
theoreticians of democracy have for over a hundred years taught
the majorities that whatever they desire is just, we must not be
surprised if the majorities no longer even ask whether what they
decide is just. Legal positivism has powerfully contributed to this
development by its contention that law is not dependent on
justice but determines what is just.

[12]

Mirage of 'social justice'

Unfortunately, we have not only failed to impose upon legislatures the limitations inherent in the necessity of committing themselves to general rules. We have also charged them with tasks which they can perform only if they are not thus limited but are free to use coercion in the discriminatory manner that is required to assure benefits to particular people or groups. This they are constantly asked to do in the name of what is called social or distributive justice, a conception which has largely taken the place of the justice of individual action. It requires that not the individuals but 'society' be just in determining the share of individuals in the social product; and in order to realise any particular distribution of the social product regarded as just it is necessary that government directs individuals in what they must do.

Indeed, in a market economy in which no single person or group determines who gets what, and the shares of individuals always depend on many circumstances which nobody could have foreseen, the whole conception of social or distributive justice is empty and meaningless; and there will therefore never exist agreement on what is just in this sense. I am not sure that the concept has a definite meaning even in a centrally-directed economy, or that in such a system people would ever agree on what distribution is just. I am certain, however, that nothing has done so much to destroy the juridical safeguards of individual freedom as the striving after this mirage of social justice. An adequate treatment of the topic of this lecture would indeed presuppose a careful dissection of this ideal which almost everybody seems to believe to have a definite meaning but which proves more completely devoid of such meaning the more one thinks about it. But the main subject of this lecture is what we have to do, if we ever again get a chance, to stop those tendencies inherent in the existing political systems which drive us towards a totalitarian order.

Compatibility of collective wants

Before I turn to this main problem, I should correct a widespread misunderstanding. The basic principle of the liberal tradition, that all the coercive action of government must be limited to the

enforcement of general rules of just conduct, does not preclude
government from rendering many other services for which, except
for raising the necessary finance, it need not rely on coercion. It
is true that in the 19th century a deep and not wholly unjustified
distrust of government often made liberals wish to restrain
government much more narrowly. But even then, of course, certain
collective wants were recognised which only an agency possessing
the power of taxation could satisfy. I am the last person to deny
that increased wealth and the increased density of population have
enlarged the number of collective needs which government can
and should satisfy. Such government services are entirely compatible with liberal principles so long as,

> *firstly*, government does not claim a monopoly and new methods
> of rendering services through the market (e.g. in some now
> covered by social insurance) are not prevented;
> *secondly*, the means are raised by taxation on uniform principles
> and taxation is not used as an instrument for the redistribution
> of income; and,
> *thirdly*, the wants satisfied are collective wants of the community
> as a whole and not merely collective wants of particular groups.

Not every collective want deserves to be satisfied: the desire of the
small bootmakers to be protected against the competition of the
factories is also a collective need of the bootmakers, but clearly
not one which in a liberal economic system could be satisfied.

Nineteenth-century liberalism in general attempted to keep the
growth of these service activities of government in check by
entrusting them to local rather than central government in the
hope that competition between the local authorities would control
their extent. I cannot consider here how far this principle had to
be abandoned and mention it only as another part of the traditional liberal doctrine whose rationale is no longer understood.

I had to consider these points to make it clear that those checks
on government activity with which for the rest of this lecture I
shall be exclusively concerned refer only to its powers of coercion
but not to the necessary services we today expect government to
render to the citizens.

I hope that what I have said so far has made it clear that the
task we shall have to perform if we are to re-establish and preserve

a free society is in the first instance an intellectual task: it pre-supposes that we not only recover conceptions which we have largely lost and which must once again become generally under-stood, but also that we design new institutional safeguards which will prevent a repetition of the process of gradual erosion of the safeguards which the theory of liberal constitutionalism had meant to provide.

IV

THE SEPARATION OF POWERS

The device to which the theorists of liberal constitutionalism had looked to guarantee individual liberty and the prevention of all arbitrariness was the separation of powers. If the legislature laid down only general rules equally applicable to all and the executive could use coercion only to enforce obedience to these general rules, personal liberty would indeed be secure. This presupposes, however, that the legislature is confined to laying down such general rules. But, instead of confining parliament to making laws in this sense, we have given it unlimited power simply by calling 'law' everything which it proclaims: a legislature is now not a body that makes laws; a law is whatever is resolved by a legislature.

This state of affairs was brought about by the loss of the old meaning of 'law' and by the desire to make government demo-cratic by placing the direction and control of government in the hands of the legislatures, which are in consequence constantly called upon to order all sorts of specific actions – to issue com-mands which are called laws, although in character they are wholly different from those laws to the production of which the theory of the separation of powers had intended to confine the legislatures.

The concept of 'lawyer's law'
Although the task of designing and establishing new institutions must appear difficult and almost hopeless, the task of reviving and making once more generally understood a lost concept for which we no longer have even an unambiguous name is perhaps even more difficult. It is a task which in this case has to be achieved in the face of the contrary teaching of the dominant school of jurisprudence. I will try briefly to state the essential character-

[15]

istics of laws in this specific narrow sense of the term before I turn
to the institutional arrangements which would secure that the
task of making such laws be really separated from the tasks of
governing.

A good way is to consider the peculiar properties which
judge-made law possesses of necessity, while they belong to the
products of legislatures in general only in so far as these have
endeavoured to emulate judge-made law. It is no accident that
this concept of law has been preserved much longer in the common
law countries whereas it was rarely understood in countries
which relied wholly on statute law.

This law consists essentially of what used to be known as
'lawyer's law' – which is and can be applied by courts of justice
and to which the agencies of government are as much subject as
are private persons. Since this judge-made law arises out of the
settlement of disputes, it relates solely to the relations of acting
persons towards one another and does not control an individual's
actions which do not affect others. It defines the protected
domains of each person with which others are prohibited from
interfering. The aim is to prevent conflicts between people who
do not act under central direction but on their own initiative,
pursuing their own ends on the basis of their own knowledge.

These rules must thus apply in circumstances which nobody
can foresee and must therefore be designed to cover a maximum
number of future instances. This determines what is commonly
but not very helpfully described as their 'abstract' character, by
which is meant that they are intended to apply in the same manner
to all situations in which certain generic factors are present and
not only to particular designated persons, groups, places, times,
etc. They do not prescribe to the individuals specific tasks or ends
of their actions, but aim at making it possible for them so mutually
to adjust their plans that each will have a good chance of achieving
his aims. The delimitation of the personal domains which achieve
this purpose is of course determined chiefly by the law of property,
contract, and torts, and the penal laws which protect 'life, liberty
and property'.

Limits to coercion

An individual who is bound to obey only such rules of just

[16]

conduct as I have called these rules of law in this narrow sense is free in the sense that he is not legally subject to anybody's commands, that within known limits he can choose the means and ends of his activities. But where everybody is free in this sense each is thrown into a process which nobody controls and the outcome of which for each is in large measure unpredictable. Freedom and risk are thus inseparable. Nor can it be claimed that the magnitude of each individual's share of the national income, dependent on so many circumstances which nobody knows, will be just. But nor can these shares meaningfully be described as unjust. We must be content if we can prevent them from being affected by unjust actions. We can of course in a free society provide a floor below which nobody need fall, by providing outside the market for all some insurance against misfortune. There is indeed much we can do to improve the framework within which the market will operate beneficially. But we cannot in such a society make the distribution of incomes correspond to some standard of social or distributive justice, and attempts to do so are likely to destroy the market order.

But if, to preserve individual freedom, we must confine coercion to the enforcement of general rules of just conduct, how can we prevent legislatures from authorising coercion to secure particular benefits for particular groups – especially a legislature organised on party lines where the governing majority frequently will be a majority only because it promises such special benefits to some groups? The truth is of course that the so-called legislatures have *never* been confined to making laws in this narrow sense, although the theory of the separation of powers tacitly assumed that they were. And since it has come to be accepted that not only legislation but also the direction of current government activities should be in the hands of the representatives of the majority, the direction of government has become the chief task of the legislatures. This has had the effect not only of entirely obliterating the distinction between laws in the sense of general rules of just conduct and laws in the sense of specific commands, but also of organising the legislatures not in the manner most suitable for making laws in the classical sense but in the manner required for efficient government, that is above all on party lines.

[17]

Representative government driven to serve sectional interests

Now, I believe we are right in wanting both legislation in the old
sense and current government to be conducted democratically.
But it seems to me it was a fatal error, though historically probably
inevitable, to entrust these two distinct tasks to the same representative assembly. This makes the distinction between legislation and government, and thereby also the observance of the
principles of the rule of law and of a government under the law,
practically impossible. Though it may secure that every act of
government has the approval of the representative assembly, it
does not protect the citizens against discretionary coercion.
Indeed, a representative assembly organised in the manner
necessary for efficient government, and not restrained by some
general laws it cannot alter, is bound to be driven to use its powers
to satisfy the demands of sectional interests.

It is no accident that most of the classical theorists of representative government and of the separation of powers disliked
the party system and hoped that a division of the legislature on
party lines could be avoided. They did so because they conceived
of the legislatures as concerned with the making of laws in the
narrow sense, and believed that there could exist on the rules of
just conduct a prevalent common opinion independent of particular
interests. But it cannot be denied that democratic *government*
requires the support of an organised body of representatives,
which we call parties, committed to a programme of action, and a
similarly organised opposition which offers an alternative government.

Separate legislative assembly

It would seem the obvious solution of this difficulty to have two
distinct representative assemblies with different tasks, one a true
legislative body and the other concerned with government proper,
i.e., everything except the making of laws in the narrow sense.
And it is at least not inconceivable that such a system might have
developed in Britain if at the time when the House of Commons
with the exclusive power over money bills achieved in effect sole
control of government, the House of Lords, as the supreme court
of justice, had obtained the sole right to develop the law in the
narrow sense. But such a development was of course not possible

so long as the House of Lords represented not the people at large but a class.

On reflection, however, one realises that little would be gained by merely having two representative assemblies instead of one if they were elected and organised on the same principles and therefore also had the same composition. They would be driven by the same circumstances which govern the decisions of modern parliaments and acting in collusion would probably produce the same sort of authorisation for whatever the government of the day wished to do. Even if we assume that the legislative chamber (as distinguished from the governmental one) were restricted by the constitution to passing laws in the narrow sense of general rules of just conduct, and this restriction were made effective through the control by a constitutional court, little would probably be achieved so long as the legislative assembly were under the same necessity of satisfying the demands of particular groups which force the hands of the governing majorities in today's parliaments.

Specific interests and permanent principles
While for the governmental assemblies we should want something more or less of the same kind as the existing parliaments, whose organisation and manner of proceeding have indeed been shaped by the needs of governing rather than the making of laws, something very different would be needed for the legislative assembly. We should want an assembly not concerned with the particular needs of particular groups but rather with the general permanent principles on which the activities of the community were to be ordered. Its members and its resolutions should represent not specific groups and their particular desires but the prevailing opinion on what kind of conduct was just and what kind was not. In laying down rules to be valid for long periods ahead this assembly should be 'representative of', or reproduce a sort of cross-section of, the prevailing opinions on right and wrong; its members should not be the spokesmen of particular interests, or express the 'will' of any particular section of the population on any specific measure of government. They should be men and women trusted and respected for the traits of character they had shown in the ordinary business of life, and not dependent on the

[19]

approval by particular groups of electors. And they should be wholly exempt from the party discipline necessary to keep a governing team together, but evidently undesirable in the body which lays down the rules that limit the powers of government.

Membership of legislative assembly

Such a legislative assembly could be achieved if, *first*, its members were elected for long periods, *secondly*, they were not eligible for re-election after the end of the period, and, *thirdly*, to secure a continuous renewal of the body in accord with gradually changing opinions among the electorate, its members were not all elected at the same time but a constant fraction of their number replaced every year as their mandate expired; or, in other words, if they were elected, for instance, for fifteen years and one-fifteenth of their number replaced every year. It would further seem to me expedient to provide that at each election the representatives should be chosen by and from only one age-group so that every citizen would vote only once in his life, say in his fortieth year, for a representative chosen from his age-group.

The result would be an assembly composed of persons between their fortieth and their fifty-fifth year, elected after they had opportunity to prove their ability in ordinary life (and, incidentally, of an average age somewhat below that of contemporary parliaments). It would probably be desirable to disqualify those who had occupied positions in the governmental assembly or other political or party organisations and it would also be necessary to assure to those elected for the period after their retirement some dignified, paid and pensionable position, such as lay-judge or the like.

The advantage of an election by age-groups, and at an age at which the individuals could have proved themselves in ordinary life, would be that in general a person's contemporaries are the best judges of his character and ability; and that among the relatively small numbers participating in each election the candidates would be more likely to be personally known to the voters and chosen according to the personal esteem in which they were held by the voters – especially if, as would seem likely and deserve encouragement, the anticipation of this common task led to the formation of clubs of the age-groups for the discussion of public affairs.

[20]

V

ADVANTAGES OF LEGISLATIVE SEPARATION

THE PURPOSE of all this would of course be to create a legislature which was not subservient to government and did not produce whatever laws government wanted for the achievement of its momentary purposes, but rather which with the law laid down the permanent limits to the coercive powers of government – limits within which government had to move and which even the democratically-elected governmental assembly could not overstep. While the latter assembly would be entirely free in determining the organisation of government, the use to be made of the means placed at the disposal of government and the character of the services to be rendered by government, it would itself possess no coercive powers over the individual citizens. Such powers, including the power to raise by taxation the means for financing the services rendered by government, would extend only to the enforcement of the rules of just conduct laid down by the legislative assembly. Against any overstepping of these limits by government (or the governmental assembly) there would be open an appeal to a constitutional court which would be competent in the case of conflict between the legislature proper and the governmental bodies.

A further desirable effect of such an arrangement would be that the legislature would for once have enough time for its proper task. This is important because in modern times legislatures frequently have left the regulation of matters which might have been effected by general rules of law to administrative orders and even administrative discretion simply because they were so busy with their governmental tasks that they had neither time for nor interest in making law proper. It is also a task which requires expert knowledge which a long-serving representative might acquire but is not likely to be possessed by a busy politician anxious for results which he can show his constituents before the next election. It is a curious consequence of giving the representative assembly unlimited power that it has largely ceased to be the chief determining agent in shaping the law proper, but has left this task more and more to the bureaucracy.

[21]

I must however not make you impatient by pursuing further the details of this utopia – though I must confess that I have found fascinating and instructive the exploration of the new opportunities offered by contemplating the possibility of separating the truly legislative assembly from the governmental body. You will rightly ask what the purpose of such a utopian construction can be if by calling it thus I admit that I do not believe it can be realised in the foreseeable future. I can answer in the words of David Hume in his essay on 'The Idea of a Perfect Commonwealth', that

'in all cases, it must be advantageous to know what is the most perfect in the kind, that we may be able to bring any real constitution or form of government as near it as possible, by such gentle alterations and innovations as may not give too great a disturbance to society'.

Name Index